Chapter Correlation Guide for Feenstra/Taylor, *International Economics*, Second Edition, and Three Versions

International Economics		*International Trade*	*International Macro-economics*	*Essentials of International Economics*	*Online*
Chapter number	Chapter title	Chapter number	Chapter number	Chapter number	Chapter number
1	Trade in the Global Economy	1			
1	The Global Economy *(Essentials)*			1	
2	Trade and Technology: The Ricardian Model	2		2	
3	Gains and Losses from Trade in the Specific-Factors Model	3		3	
4	Trade and Resources: The Heckscher-Ohlin Model	4		4	
5	Movement of Labor and Capital between Countries	5		5	
6	Increasing Returns to Scale and Monopolistic Competition	6		6	
7	Offshoring of Goods and Services	7			ONLINE
8	Import Tariffs and Quotas under Perfect Competition	8		7	
9	Import Tariffs and Quotas under Imperfect Competition	9		8	
10	Export Subsidies in Agriculture and High-Technology Industries	10			
11	International Agreements: Trade, Labor and the Environment	11		9	
12	The Global Macroeconomy		1		
13	Introduction to Exchange Rates and the Foreign Exchange Market		2	10	
14	Exchange Rates I: The Monetary Approach in the Long Run		3	11	
15	Exchange Rates II: The Asset Approach in the Short Run		4	12	
16	National and International Accounts: Income, Wealth, and the Balance of Payments		5	13	
17	Balance of Payments I: The Gains from Financial Globalization		6		
18	Balance of Payments II: Output, Exchange Rates, and Macroeconomic Policies in the Short Run		7	14	
19	Fixed Versus Floating: International Monetary Experience		8	15	
20	Exchange Rate Crises: How Pegs Work and How They Break		9		
21	The Euro		10		ONLINE
22	Topics in International Macroeconomics		11		

second edition

international macroeconomics

second edition

international macroeconomics

ROBERT C. FEENSTRA
University of California, Davis

ALAN M. TAYLOR
University of California, Davis

WORTH PUBLISHERS

Senior Publisher: Catherine Woods
Executive Editor: Charles Linsmeier
Senior Acquisitions Editor: Sarah Dorger
Development Editors: Jane Tufts and Bruce Kaplan
Media and Supplements Editor: Jaclyn Castaldo Ferry
Executive Marketing Manager: Scott Guile
Associate Managing Editor: Tracey Kuehn
Project Editor: Anthony Calcara
Art Director: Babs Reingold
Senior Designer: Kevin Kall
Photo Editor: Cecilia Varas
Photo Researcher: Dena Betz
Production Manager: Barbara Anne Seixas
Composition: TSI Graphics
Printing and Binding: RR Donnelley

Cover Photo Credits: *Globes:* Fusion/Getty Images; *ECB tower and Euro symbol:* © vario images GmbH & Co. KG/Alamy; *Mayumi Torii:* Ko Sasaki/*The New York Times; Protestors (Euro vs. Pound):* Stefan Rousseau/PA Archive/PA Photos; *Zimbabwean boy with money:* Reuters/Howard Burditt/Newscom; *Man and pilot shaking hands:* AP Photo/Andy Eames

Library of Congress Cataloging in Publication Data: 2010935913

ISBN-13: 978-1-4292-4103-8
ISBN-10: 1-4292-4103-9

© 2008, 2012 by Worth Publishers

All rights reserved.

Printed in the United States of America

Second printing

Worth Publishers
41 Madison Avenue
New York, NY 10010
www.worthpublishers.com
www.wortheconomics.com

About the Authors

Robert C. Feenstra and **Alan M. Taylor** are Professors of Economics at the University of California, Davis. They each began their studies abroad: Feenstra received his B.A. in 1977 from the University of British Columbia, Canada, and Taylor received his B.A. in 1987 from King's College, Cambridge, U.K. They trained as professional economists in the United States, where Feenstra earned his Ph.D. in economics from MIT in 1981 and Taylor earned his Ph.D. in economics from Harvard University in 1992. Feenstra has been teaching international trade at the undergraduate and graduate levels at UC Davis since 1986, where he holds the C. Bryan Cameron Distinguished Chair in International Economics. Taylor has been teaching international macroeconomics, growth, and economic history at UC Davis since 1999, where he directs the Center for the Evolution of the Global Economy.

Both Feenstra and Taylor are active in research and policy discussions in international economics. They are research associates of the National Bureau of Economic Research, where Feenstra directs the International Trade and Investment research program. They have both published graduate-level books in international economics: *Offshoring in the Global Economy* and *Product Variety and the Gains from Trade* (MIT Press, 2010), by Robert C. Feenstra, and *Global Capital Markets: Integration, Crisis and Growth* (Cambridge University Press, 2004), by Maurice Obstfeld and Alan M. Taylor. Feenstra received the Bernhard Harms Prize from the Institute for World Economics, Kiel, Germany, in 2006, and delivered the Ohlin Lectures at the Stockholm School of Economics in 2008. Taylor was awarded a Guggenheim Fellowship in 2004 and was a visiting professor at the American University in Paris and London Business School in 2005–06.

Feenstra lives in Davis, California, with his wife, Gail, and has two grown children: Heather, who is a genetics counselor, and Evan, who recently graduated from Pitzer College. Taylor also lives in Davis, with his wife, Claire, and has two young children, Olivia and Sebastian.

To our parents

Brief Contents

Preface xxv

PART 1 Introduction to International Macroeconomics

Chapter 1 The Global Macroeconomy 1

PART 2 Exchange Rates

Chapter 2 Introduction to Exchange Rates and the Foreign Exchange Market 25

Chapter 3 Exchange Rates I: The Monetary Approach in the Long Run 63

Chapter 4 Exchange Rates II: The Asset Approach in the Short Run 111

PART 3 The Balance of Payments

Chapter 5 National and International Accounts: Income, Wealth, and the Balance of Payments 157

Chapter 6 Balance of Payments I: The Gains from Financial Globalization 199

Chapter 7 Balance of Payments II: Output, Exchange Rates, and Macroeconomic Policies in the Short Run 253

PART 4 Applications and Policy Issues

Chapter 8 Fixed versus Floating: International Monetary Experience 303

Chapter 9 Exchange Rate Crises: How Pegs Work and How They Break 345

Chapter 10 The Euro 399

Chapter 11 Topics in International Macroeconomics 441

Index I-1

Contents

Preface xxv

PART 1 Introduction to International Macroeconomics

CHAPTER 1 The Global Macroeconomy 1

1 Foreign Exchange: Currencies and Crises 2
How Exchange Rates Behave 3
Why Exchange Rates Matter 4
When Exchange Rates Misbehave 5
Summary and Plan of Study 6
　　HEADLINES Economic Crisis in Argentina 7

2 Globalization of Finance: Debts and Deficits 8
Deficits and Surpluses: The Balance of Payments 8
Debtors and Creditors: External Wealth 11
Darlings and Deadbeats: Defaults and Other Risks 12
Summary and Plan of Study 13

3 Government and Institutions: Policies and Performance 14
Integration and Capital Controls: The Regulation of International Finance 14
Independence and Monetary Policy: The Choice of Exchange Rate Regimes 16
Institutions and Economic Performance: The Quality of Governance 17
　　HEADLINES The Wealth of Nations 18
Summary and Plan of Study 20

4 Conclusions 21
Key Points, Key Terms, and Problems

PART 2 Exchange Rates

CHAPTER 2 Introduction to Exchange Rates and the Foreign Exchange Market 25

1 Exchange Rate Essentials 26
Defining the Exchange Rate 26
Appreciations and Depreciations 28
Multilateral Exchange Rates 30
Example: Using Exchange Rates to Compare Prices in a Common Currency 31

2 Exchange Rates in Practice 33
Exchange Rate Regimes: Fixed Versus Floating 33
APPLICATION Recent Exchange Rate Experiences 34

3 The Market for Foreign Exchange 39
The Spot Contract 39
Transaction Costs 40
Derivatives 40
APPLICATION Foreign Exchange Derivatives 41
Private Actors 42
Government Actions 42

4 Arbitrage and Spot Exchange Rates 43
Arbitrage with Two Currencies 44
Arbitrage with Three Currencies 45
Cross Rates and Vehicle Currencies 46

5 Arbitrage and Interest Rates 47
Riskless Arbitrage: Covered Interest Parity 47
APPLICATION Evidence on Covered Interest Parity 49
Risky Arbitrage: Uncovered Interest Parity 51
SIDE BAR Assets and Their Attributes 51
APPLICATION Evidence on Uncovered Interest Parity 54
Uncovered Interest Parity: A Useful Approximation 55
Summary 56

6 Conclusions 57
Key Points, Key Terms, and Problems

CHAPTER 3 Exchange Rates I: The Monetary Approach in the Long Run 63

1 Exchange Rates and Prices in the Long Run: Purchasing Power Parity and Goods Market Equilibrium 64
The Law of One Price 65
Purchasing Power Parity 66
The Real Exchange Rate 67
Absolute PPP and the Real Exchange Rate 67
Absolute PPP, Prices, and the Nominal Exchange Rate 68
Relative PPP, Inflation, and Exchange Rate Depreciation 68
Summary 70
APPLICATION Evidence for PPP in the Long Run and Short Run 70

How Slow Is Convergence to PPP? 71
What Explains Deviations from PPP? 72
> SIDE BAR Forecasting When the Real Exchange Rate Is Undervalued or Overvalued 73
>
> HEADLINES The Big Mac Index 74

2 Money, Prices, and Exchange Rates in the Long Run: Money Market Equilibrium in a Simple Model 76
What Is Money 76
The Measurement of Money 76
The Supply of Money 77
The Demand for Money: A Simple Model 78
Equilibrium in the Money Market 79
A Simple Monetary Model of Prices 79
A Simple Monetary Model of the Exchange Rate 80
Money Growth, Inflation, and Depreciation 81

3 The Monetary Approach: Implications and Evidence 82
Exchange Rate Forecasts Using the Simple Model 82
> APPLICATION Evidence for the Monetary Approach 85
>
> APPLICATION Hyperinflations of the Twentieth Century 86
>
>> HEADLINES The First Hyperinflation of the Twenty-First Century 89
>>
>> SIDE BAR Currency Reform 90

4 Money, Interest Rates, and Prices in the Long Run: A General Model 90
The Demand for Money: The General Model 91
Long-Run Equilibrium in the Money Market 92
Inflation and Interest Rates in the Long Run 92
The Fisher Effect 93
Real Interest Parity 94
> APPLICATION Evidence on the Fisher Effect 95

The Fundamental Equation under the General Model 96
Exchange Rate Forecasts Using the General Model 97

5 Monetary Regimes and Exchange Rate Regimes 99
The Long Run: The Nominal Anchor 100
> APPLICATION Nominal Anchors in Theory and Practice 102

6 Conclusions 104
Key Points, Key Terms, and Problems

CHAPTER 4 Exchange Rates II: The Asset Approach in the Short Run 111

1 Exchange Rates and Interest Rates in the Short Run: UIP and FX Market Equilibrium 112
Risky Arbitrage 112
Equilibrium in the FX Market: An Example 114
Adjustment to FX Market Equilibrium 115
Changes in Domestic and Foreign Returns and FX Market Equilibrium 116
Summary 118

2 Interest Rates in the Short Run: Money Market Equilibrium 118
Money Market Equilibrium in the Short Run: How Nominal Interest Rates Are Determined 118
Money Market Equilibrium in the Short Run: Graphical Solution 120
Adjustment to Money Market Equilibrium in the Short Run 120
Another Building Block: Short-Run Money Market Equilibrium 121
Changes in Money Supply and the Nominal Interest Rate 121
APPLICATION Can Central Banks Always Control the Interest Rate? A Lesson from the Crisis of 2008–2009 123
Changes in Real Income and the Nominal Interest Rate 124
The Monetary Model: The Short Run versus the Long Run 124

3 The Asset Approach: Applications and Evidence 125
The Asset Approach to Exchange Rates: Graphical Solution 125
Short-Run Policy Analysis 127
APPLICATION The Rise and Fall of the Dollar, 1999–2004 130

4 A Complete Theory: Unifying the Monetary and Asset Approaches 131
Long-Run Policy Analysis 132
SIDE BAR Confessions of a Forex Trader 134
Overshooting 138
SIDE BAR Overshooting in Practice 140

5 Fixed Exchange Rates and the Trilemma 141
What Is a Fixed Exchange Rate Regime? 141
Pegging Sacrifices Monetary Policy Autonomy in the Short Run: Example 141
Pegging Sacrifices Monetary Policy Autonomy in the Long Run: Example 143
The Trilemma 144
SIDE BAR Intermediate Regimes 146
APPLICATION The Trilemma in Europe 147

6 Conclusions 148
    APPLICATION News and the Foreign Exchange Market in Wartime 148
    Key Points, Key Terms, and Problems

PART 3
The Balance of Payments

CHAPTER 5 National and International Accounts: Income, Wealth, and the Balance of Payments 157

1 Measuring Macroeconomic Activity: An Overview 158
    The Flow of Payments in a Closed Economy: Introducing the National Income and Product Accounts 158
    The Flow of Payments in an Open Economy: Incorporating the Balance of Payments Accounts 160

2 Income, Product, and Expenditure 162
    Three Approaches to Measuring Economic Activity 163
    From GNE to GDP: Accounting for Trade in Goods and Services 163
    From GDP to GNI: Accounting for Trade in Factor Services 164
    APPLICATION Celtic Tiger or Tortoise? 165
    From GNI to GNDI: Accounting for Transfers of Income 167
    What the National Economic Aggregates Tell Us 168
        HEADLINES Are Rich Countries "Stingy" with Foreign Aid? 169
    Understanding the Data for the National Economic Aggregates 170
    What the Current Account Tells Us 172
    APPLICATION Global Imbalances 173

3 The Balance of Payments 178
    Accounting for Asset Transactions: the Financial Account 178
    Accounting for Asset Transactions: the Capital Account 178
    Accounting for Home and Foreign Assets 179
    How the Balance of Payments Accounts Work: A Macroeconomic View 180
    How the Balance of Payments Accounts Work: A Microeconomic View 180
        SIDE BAR The Double-Entry Principle in the Balance of Payments 182
    Understanding the Data for the Balance of Payments Account 182
    What the Balance of Payments Account Tells Us 186

4 External Wealth 186
    The Level of External Wealth 187
    Changes in External Wealth 187
    Understanding the Data on External Wealth 188
    What External Wealth Tells Us 190

5 Conclusions 191
SIDE BAR Beware of Greeks Bearing Statistics 191
Key Points, Key Terms, and Problems

Appendix to Chapter 5 197

CHAPTER 6 Balance of Payments I: The Gains from Financial Globalization 199

1 The Limits on How Much a Country Can Borrow: The Long-Run Budget Constraint 201
How The Long-Run Budget Constraint Is Determined 202
The Budget Constraint in a Two-Period Example 203
A Long-Run Example: The Perpetual Loan 205
Implications of the LRBC for Gross National Expenditure and Gross Domestic Product 206
Summary 207
APPLICATION The Favorable Situation of the United States 207
APPLICATION The Difficult Situation of the Emerging Markets 210

2 Gains from Consumption Smoothing 212
The Basic Model 212
Consumption Smoothing: A Numerical Example and Generalization 213
Summary: Save for a Rainy Day 217
SIDE BAR Wars and the Current Account 217
APPLICATION Consumption Volatility and Financial Openness 218
APPLICATION Precautionary Saving, Reserves, and Sovereign Wealth Funds 219

3 Gains from Efficient Investment 220
HEADLINES Copper-Bottomed Insurance 221
The Basic Model 222
Efficient Investment: A Numerical Example and Generalization 222
Summary: Make Hay While the Sun Shines 225
APPLICATION Delinking Saving from Investment 225
Can Poor Countries Gain from Financial Globalization? 227
APPLICATION A versus k 231
SIDE BAR What Does the World Bank Do? 235
HEADLINES A Brief History of Foreign Aid 235

4 Gains from Diversification of Risk 237
Diversification: A Numerical Example and Generalization 237
APPLICATION The Home Bias Puzzle 242
Summary: Don't Put All Your Eggs in One Basket 244

5 Conclusions 245
Key Points, Key Terms, and Problems

Appendix to Chapter 6 251

CHAPTER 7 Balance of Payments II: Output, Exchange Rates, and Macroeconomic Policies in the Short Run 253

1 Demand in the Open Economy 254
Preliminaries and Assumptions 254
Consumption 255
Investment 256
The Government 256
The Trade Balance 257
  HEADLINES Expenditure Switching and the Dollar Devaluation 259
  HEADLINES The Curry Trade 260
  APPLICATION The Trade Balance and the Real Exchange Rate 261
Exogenous Changes in Demand 262
  SIDE BAR Barriers to Expenditure Switching: Pass-Through and the J Curve 263

2 Goods Market Equilibrium: The Keynesian Cross 266
Supply and Demand 266
Determinants of Demand 266
Factors That Shift the Demand Curve 268
Summary 269

3 Goods and Forex Market Equilibria: Deriving the IS Curve 269
Equilibrium in Two Markets 270
Forex Market Recap 270
Deriving the IS Curve 272
Factors That Shift the IS Curve 273
Summing Up the IS Curve 275

4 Money Market Equilibrium: Deriving the LM Curve 275
Money Market Recap 276
Deriving the LM Curve 277
Factors That Shift the LM Curve 277
Summing Up the LM Curve 278

5 The Short-Run IS-LM-FX Model of an Open Economy 279
Macroeconomic Policies in the Short Run 280
Monetary Policy under Floating Exchange Rates 281
Monetary Policy under Fixed Exchange Rates 282

Fiscal Policy under Floating Exchange Rates 283
Fiscal Policy under Fixed Exchange Rates 284
Summary 286

6 Stabilization Policy 287

APPLICATION Australia, New Zealand, and the Asian Crisis of 1997 287
Problems in Policy Design and Implementation 290
APPLICATION Macroeconomic Policies in the Liquidity Trap 291

7 Conclusions 295

Key Points, Key Terms, and Problems

Appendix 1 to Chapter 7 300

Appendix 2 to Chapter 7 302

PART 4
Applications and Policy Issues

CHAPTER 8 Fixed versus Floating: International Monetary Experience 303

1 Exchange Rate Regime Choice: Key Issues 305

APPLICATION Britain and Europe: The Big Issues 305
Key Factors in Exchange Rate Regime Choice: Integration and Similarity 310
Economic Integration and the Gains in Efficiency 310
Economic Similarity and the Costs of Asymmetric Shocks 311
Simple Criteria for a Fixed Exchange Rate 312
APPLICATION Do Fixed Exchange Rates Promote Trade? 313
APPLICATION Do Fixed Exchange Rates Diminish Monetary Autonomy and Stability? 315

2 Other Benefits of Fixing 318

Fiscal Discipline, Seigniorage, and Inflation 318
SIDE BAR The Inflation Tax 319
Liability Dollarization, National Wealth, and Contractionary Depreciations 321
Summary 327

3 Fixed Exchange Rate Systems 328

Cooperative and Noncooperative Adjustments to Interest Rates 328
Cooperative and Noncooperative Adjustments to Exchange Rates 331
APPLICATION The Gold Standard 333

4 International Monetary Experience 335

The Rise and Fall of the Gold Standard 335
Bretton Woods to the Present 338

5 Conclusions 341

Key Points, Key Terms, and Problems

CHAPTER 9 Exchange Rate Crises: How Pegs Work and How They Break 345

1 Facts about Exchange Rate Crises 346
What Is an Exchange Rate Crises? 346
How Costly Are Exchange Rate Crises? 346
   SIDE BAR The Political Costs of Crises 349
Summary 350

2 How Pegs Work: The Mechanics of a Fixed Exchange Rate 351
Preliminaries and Assumptions 351
The Central Bank Balance Sheet 352
Fixing, Floating, and the Role of Reserves 354
How Reserves Adjust to Maintain the Peg 354
Graphical Analysis of the Central Bank Balance Sheet 355
Defending the Peg I: Changes in the Level of Money Demand 356
   APPLICATION Risk Premiums in Advanced and Emerging Markets 359
   APPLICATION The Argentine Convertibility Plan Before the Tequila Crisis 362
Defending the Peg II: Changes in the Composition of Money Supply 364
   APPLICATION The Argentine Convertibility Plan After the Tequila Crisis 370
The Central Bank Balance Sheet and the Financial System 371
Summary 373
   SIDE BAR The Great Reserve Accumulation in Emerging Markets 374

3 How Pegs Break I: Inconsistent Fiscal Policies 376
The Basic Problem: Fiscal Dominance 377
A Simple Model 377
   APPLICATION The Peruvian Crisis of 1986 381
Summary 384

4 How Pegs Break II: Contingent Monetary Policies 384
The Basic Problem: Contingent Commitment 385
A Simple Model 386
   APPLICATION The Man Who Broke the Bank of England 391
Summary 392

5 Conclusions 392
Can We Prevent Crises? 392
Key Points, Key Terms, and Problems

CHAPTER 10 The Euro 399

1 The Economics of the Euro 402
The Theory of Optimum Currency Areas 402
Simple Optimum Currency Area Criteria 403
What's the Difference between a Fix and a Currency Union? 404
Other Optimum Currency Area Criteria 405
APPLICATION Optimum Currency Areas: Europe versus the United States 407
Are the OCA Criteria Self-Fulfilling? 410
Summary 412
HEADLINES Currency Unions and Trade 413

2 The History and Politics of the Euro 414
A Brief History of Europe 414
Summary 421

3 Eurozone Tensions in Tranquil Times, 1999–2007 421
The European Central Bank 422
The Rules of the Club 425
Sticking to the Rules 429

4 The Eurozone in Crisis, 2008–2010 431
HEADLINES Can the Euro Survive? 434

5 Conclusions: Assessing the Euro 435
Key Points, Key Terms, and Problems

CHAPTER 11 Topics in International Macroeconomics 441

1 Exchange Rates in the Long Run: Deviations from Purchasing Power Parity 442
Limits to Arbitrage 442
APPLICATION It's Not Just the Burgers That Are Cheap 445
Nontraded Goods and the Balassa-Samuelson Model 447
Overvaluations, Undervaluations, and the Productivity Growth: Forecasting Implications for Real and Nominal Exchange Rates 449
APPLICATION Real Exchange Rates in Emerging Markets 451
Conclusion 453

2 Exchange Rates in the Short Run: Deviations from Uncovered Interest Parity 453
HEADLINES Eastern Europe and the Euro 454
APPLICATION The Carry Trade 454
HEADLINES Mrs. Watanabe's Hedge Fund 458

APPLICATION Peso Problems 459
The Efficient Markets Hypothesis 461
Limits to Arbitrage 464
Conclusion 467

3 Debt and Default 467
A Few Peculiar Facts about Sovereign Debt 469
A Model of Default, Part One: The Probability of Default 470
APPLICATION Is There Profit in Lending to Developing Countries? 475
A Model of Default, Part Two: Loan Supply and Demand 476
APPLICATION The Costs of Default 479
Conclusion 482
APPLICATION The Argentina Crisis of 2001–2002 483

4 The Global Macroeconomy and the 2007–2009 Crisis 486
HEADLINES Is the IMF "Pathetic"? 487
Backdrop to the Crisis 487
Panic and the Great Recession 494
Conclusion: Lessons for Macroeconomics 504
Key Points, Key Terms, and Problems

Index I-1

Preface

The twenty-first century is an age of unprecedented globalization. In looking at existing texts, we saw that the dramatic economic developments of recent years had not been incorporated into a newly written undergraduate text, and felt the time was ripe to incorporate fresh perspectives, current topics, and up-to-date approaches into the study of international economics. With this book, we have expanded the vision of international economics to encompass the latest theory and events in the world today.

In decades past, international economics was taught differently. There was a much greater emphasis on theory and a strong focus on the advanced countries. Policy analysis reflected the concerns of the time, whether strategic trade policy or the Bretton Woods system. Today, the concerns are not the same. In addition to new theoretical developments, there is a much greater emphasis on empirical studies. A wave of applied research in recent years has proved (or refuted) existing theories and taught us important new lessons about the determinants of trade, factor flows, exchange rates, and crises. Trade and capital flows have been liberalized and allowed to grow, and more attention is now devoted to emerging markets and developing countries, regions that now carry substantial weight in the global economy.

Covering new and expanding ground is part of the challenge and excitement of teaching and learning the international economics of the twenty-first century. Our goal is to provide new material that is rigorous enough to meet the challenge yet approachable enough to nurture the excitement. Many of the new topics stand apart from conventional textbook treatments and in the past have been bypassed in lectures or taught through supplementary readings. In our view they deserve a more prominent place in today's curriculum.

We have taught the chapters of this book ourselves a number of times, and have benefited from the feedback of professors at colleges and universities in the United States and throughout the world. Like us, they have been enthusiastic about the response from students to our fresh, accessible, and up-to-the-minute approach, and we hope that you also will enjoy the book.

Features

Each chapter includes several features that bring the material alive for the students:

- **Applications,** which are integrated into the main text and use material that has been covered to illuminate real-world policies, events, and evidence
- **Headlines,** which show how topics in the main text relate directly to media coverage of the global economy
- **Side Bars,** which include topics that, while not essential, are nonetheless of interest
- **Net Works,** provided at the ends of the chapters with homework problems, which provide an opportunity for the students to explore chapter concepts on the Internet

The book is issued in a combined edition *(International Economics)* and in two split editions *(International Trade* and *International Macroeconomics)*, allowing greater flexibility for instructors to assign their preferred text and keep costs down for students.

In addition, in response to the needs and feedback of those instructors who teach a one-semester course that combines international trade and macroeconomics, our text now comes in a one-semester version called **Essentials of International Economics.** We include fifteen chapters most relevant to that setting. There is more information on this one-semester version later in the Preface.

New in the Second Edition

In this second edition we have updated the text (including most of the Headline features) to reflect the rapid changes in international economic news during the last three years culminating in extensive coverage of the global financial crisis of 2008–2009 in Chapter 11. The financial crisis is also covered in many other chapters: how central banks can face difficulties with interest rate policies in the presence of market risk premiums or at the zero bound (Chapters 3 and 7); how countries have used creative accounting to disguise their economic problems (Chapter 5); and how some countries have used foreign reserves to cushion the effects of shocks (Chapter 10). In addition to updating the text to cover these new topics, we have benefited from the comments of faculty using the book and from our own experiences in teaching from it. From this feedback, we have rearranged some material to make a more natural flow in teaching. For example, the presentation of the national and international accounts in Chapter 5 has been streamlined, as has the treatment of the gains from financial globalization in Chapter 6.

Topics and Approaches

Reviewers and class testers have been enthusiastically supportive of the topics we have included in our presentation. Topics covered in *International Economics* or *International Trade* include the offshoring of goods and services (Chapter 6); tariffs and quotas under imperfect competition (Chapter 9); and international agreements on trade, labor, and the environment (Chapter 11). These topics are in addition to core chapters on the Ricardian model (Chapter 2), the specific-factors model (Chapter 3), the Heckscher-Ohlin model (Chapter 4), trade with increasing returns to scale and imperfect competition (Chapter 6), import tariffs and quotas under perfect competition (Chapter 8), and export subsidies (Chapter 10).

Chapters in *International Economics* or *International Macroeconomics* include the gains from financial globalization (Chapter 17 in the combined edition, or Chapter 6 in the *International Macroeconomics* split edition), fixed versus floating regimes (Chapter 19/Chapter 8), exchange-rate crises (Chapter 20/Chapter 9), and the euro (Chapter 21 or Chapter 10). These topics are in addition to core chapters on foreign exchange markets and exchange rates in the short run and the long run (Chapters 13–15/Chapters 2–4), the national and international accounts (Chapter 16/Chapter 5), the open economy IS-LM model (Chapter 18/Chapter 7), and a chapter on current important issues (Chapter 22/Chapter 11).

In writing our chapters we have made every effort to link them analytically. For example, although immigration and foreign direct investment are sometimes treated as an afterthought in international economics books, we integrate these topics into the discussion of the trade models by covering the movement of labor and capital between countries in Chapter 5. Specifically, we analyze the movement of labor and capital between countries in the short run using the specific-factors model, and explore the long-run implications using the Heckscher-Ohlin model. Chapter 5 therefore builds on the models that the student has learned in Chapters 3 and 4, and applies them to issues at the forefront of policy discussion.

In the macroeconomics section from *International Economics* or *International Macroeconomics* this analytical linking is seen in the parallel development of fixed and floating exchange rate regimes from the opening introductory tour in Chapter 12 (Chapter 1 in the split edition), through the workings of exchange rates in Chapters 13–15 (Chapters 2–4), the discussion of policy in the IS-LM model of Chapter 18 (Chapter 7), to the discussion of regime choice in Chapter 19 (Chapter 8). Many textbooks discuss fixed and floating regimes separately, with fixed regimes often treated as an afterthought. But given the widespread use of fixed rates in many countries, the rising macro weight of fixed regimes, and the collapse of fixed rates during crises, we think it is more helpful for the student to grapple with the different workings and cost-benefit tradeoffs of the two regimes by studying them side by side. This approach also allows us to address numerous policy issues such as the implications of the trilemma and the optimal choice of exchange rate regime.

In addition to expanding our coverage to include up-to-date theory and policy applications, our other major goal is to present all the material—both new and old—in the most teachable way. To do this, we ensure that all of the material presented rests on firm and up-to-the-minute empirical evidence. We believe this approach is the right way to study economics, and it is our experience, shared with many instructors, that teaching is more effective and more enlivened when students can see not just an elegant derivation in theory but, right next to it, some persuasive evidence of the economic mechanisms under investigation.

The Arrangement of Topics: International Trade (from *International Economics* and *International Trade*)

Part 1: Introduction to International Trade

The opening chapter sets the stage by discussing global flows of goods and services through international trade, of people through migration, and of capital through foreign direct investment. The chapter includes maps depicting these flows, so the student can get a feel for which countries have the greatest flows in each case. Historical examples of trade and barriers to trade are also provided. This chapter can serve as a full introductory lecture.

Part 2: Patterns of International Trade

The core models of international trade are presented here: the Ricardian model (Chapter 2), the specific-factors model (Chapter 3), and the Heckscher-Ohlin model (Chapter 4). Some of the topics conventionally included in the specific-factors and

Heckscher-Ohlin model, like the effects of changing the endowments of labor or capital, are not covered in those chapters but are instead examined in Chapter 5, which deals with the movement of labor and capital between countries. For example, the "factor price insensitivity" result is deferred to Chapter 5, as is the Rybczynski theorem. By discussing those two results in Chapter 5, we keep the discussion of the Heckscher-Ohlin model more manageable in Chapter 4, which focuses on the Heckscher-Ohlin theorem, the Stolper-Samuelson theorem, and empirical testing of the model. In summary, the ordering of topics among Chapters 3, 4, and 5, as well as many of the applications, is new, and these chapters are linked together tightly in their pedagogical approach.

Part 3: New Explanations for International Trade

In this section we cover two new explanations for international trade: increasing returns to scale (Chapter 6), and offshoring (Chapter 7).

Formal models of trade with increasing returns to scale and monopolistic competition have been popular since the early 1980s, but there is no standardized method for presenting this topic in undergraduate textbooks. In Chapter 6, we use the original, graphical discussion from Edward Chamberlin, who introduced the DD and dd curves (which we label in Chapter 6 as simply D and d). The D curve represents the share of the market going to each firm and traces out demand if all firms charge the same prices. In contrast, the d curve is the demand facing a firm when other firms keep their prices constant. The distinction between these two demands is crucial when analyzing the impact of trade liberalization: the d curve clearly shows the incentive for each individual firm to lower its price after trade liberalization, but the steeper D curve shows that when all firms lower prices, then losses occur and some firms must exit.

Chapter 7 is devoted to offshoring, and we have found that students enjoy learning and readily understand this new material. The model used illustrates a piece of intuition that students grasp easily: the movement of one student from, say, a physics class to an economics class can raise the average grade in *both* classes. Likewise, offshoring can raise the relative wage of skilled workers in both countries. The chapter deals with Paul Samuelson's 2004 critique that offshoring to China or India might be harmful to the United States. That argument is shown to depend on how offshoring affects the U.S. terms of trade: if the terms of trade fall, the United States is worse off, though it still gains overall from international trade. In fact, we argue that the U.S. terms of trade have been rising in recent years, not falling, so Samuelson's argument is hypothetical so far.

Part 4: International Trade Policies

The concluding part of the trade portion of the book deals is devoted to trade policy: tariffs and quotas under perfect competition (Chapter 8), under imperfect competition (Chapter 9), export subsidies (Chapter 10), and a discussion of international agreements on trade, labor, and the environment (Chapter 11). Our goal is to present this material in a more systematic fashion than found elsewhere, using both very recent and historical applications.

Chapter 8, dealing with tariffs and quotas under perfect competition, is the "bread and butter" of trade policy. We adopt the partial-equilibrium approach, using import demand and export supply curves, along with consumer and producer surplus. Our experience is that students feel very comfortable with this approach from their microeconomics training (so they can usually label the consumer surplus region, for example, in each diagram before the labels are shown). The chapter uses the tariffs applied by President George W. Bush on U.S. steel imports and by President Barack Obama on imported tires from China as motivating cases, which we analyze from both a "small country" and a "large country" perspective.

Chapters 9 and 10 bring in some of the insights from the literature on the strategic role of trade policy, which was developed in the later 1980s and 1990s. Whereas that literature focused on oligopoly interactions between firms, we simplify the analysis in Chapter 9 by focusing on home or foreign monopoly cases. Chapter 10 then presents the duopoly case in the analysis of export subsidies. Most of the theory in these chapters is familiar, but the organization is new, as are many of the applications, including infant industry protection in Chapter 9 and a detailed discussion of agricultural subsidies in Chapter 10.

Chapter 11 begins by drawing upon tariffs under perfect competition (from Chapter 8), and showing that large countries have a natural incentive to apply tariffs to move the terms of trade to their advantage. That creates a prisoner's dilemma situation that is overcome by rules in the WTO. The chapter then moves on to discuss international rules governing labor issues and the environment. Students are especially interested in the environmental applications.

The Arrangement of Topics: International Macroeconomics (from this book and *International Economics*)

Part 1 (Part 5 in *International Economics*): Introduction to International Macroeconomics

This part consists only of Chapter 1 (Chapter 12 in the combined edition), which sets the stage by explaining the field and major items of interest, with an elementary survey of the three main parts of the book: money and exchange rates, the balance of payments, and the role of policy.

Part 2 (Part 6): Exchange Rates

We depart from the traditional presentation by presenting exchange rates before balance of payments, an approach that we and our students find more logical and appealing. We begin the core macro material with exchange rates because (for macroeconomics) the exchange rate is the key difference between a closed economy and a world of open economies. Our approach, supported by our own experience and that of our reviewers and class testers, first treats all price topics together in one part, and then moves on to quantity topics.

Chapter 2 (Chapter 13 in the combined edition) introduces the basics of exchange rates and the foreign exchange (forex) market (including the principles of arbitrage) and exposes students to real-world data on exchange rate behavior. It describes how the forex market is structured and explains the principles of arbitrage in forex markets. It ends with interest parity conditions, which are then covered in more detail in Chapter 4 (Chapter 15).

Chapter 3 (Chapter 14) presents the monetary approach to the determination of exchange rates in the long run. We cover the long run before the short run because long-run expectations are assumed to be known in the short-run model. Topics include goods market arbitrage, the law of one price, and purchasing power parity. We first develop a simple monetary model (the quantity theory) and then look at the standard monetary model, the Fisher effect, and real interest parity. The chapter ends with discussion of nominal anchors and their relationship to monetary and exchange rate regimes.

Chapter 4 (Chapter 15) presents the asset approach to the determination of exchange rates in the short run. Uncovered interest parity, first introduced in Chapter 2 (Chapter 13), is the centerpiece of the asset approach, and the expected future exchange rate is assumed to be given by the long-run model. Short-run interest rates are explained using a money market model. We show how all the building blocks from the monetary and asset approaches fit together for a complete theory of exchange rate determination. Finally, we explain how the complete theory works for fixed as well as floating regimes, and demonstrate the trilemma.

Part 3 (Part 7): The Balance of Payments

Chapter 5 (Chapter 16 in the combined edition) introduces the key macroeconomic quantities: the national and international accounts and the balance of payments (BOP). The BOP is explained as the need for balancing trade on goods, services, and assets (with allowances for transfers). We also introduce external wealth and valuation effects, which are of increasing importance in the world economy.

Chapter 6 (Chapter 17) links the balance of payments to the key question of the costs and benefits of financial globalization, an increasingly important topic. The chapter begins by explaining the significance of the long-run budget constraint and then examines the three key potential benefits of financial globalization: consumptions smoothing, efficient investment, and risk sharing.

Chapter 7 (Chapter 18) presents the short-run open economy Keynesian model, which links the balance of payments to output, exchange rates, and macroeconomic policies. We use IS-LM and forex market diagrams, with the interest rate on a common axis. With this presentation, we use tools (IS-LM) that many students have already seen, and avoid inventing new ways to present the same model with new and challenging notation. In this chapter we also discuss fixed and floating rate regimes side by side, not in different chapters. We think it helpful throughout the book to study these regimes in parallel and at this point this presentation leads naturally to the next chapter.

The ordering of Part 3 (Part 7) echoes that of Part 2 (Part 6): we start with definitions, then cover long-run topics (the gains from financial globalization), then move to short-run topics (IS-LM). This ordering of topics allows a smooth transition from some key definitions in Chapter 5 (Chapter 16) to their application at the start of Chapter 6 (Chapter 17), a link that would be impossible if the balance of payments chapter were placed before the coverage of exchange rates.

Part 4 (Part 8) Applications and Policy Issues

Chapter 8 (Chapter 19 in the combined edition) confronts one of the major policy issues in international macroeconomics, the choice of fixed versus floating exchange rates. The analysis begins with the two classic criteria for two regions to adopt a fixed exchange rate—high levels of integration and symmetry of economic shocks. The chapter then goes on to consider other factors that could make a fixed exchange rate desirable, especially in developing countries—a need for a credible nominal anchor and the "fear of floating" that results from significant liability dollarization. Empirical evidence is provided for all of these influences. A brief section summarizes the debate over the desirability and possibility of coordination in larger exchange rate systems. Finally, a historical survey uses the uses the tools at hand to understand the evolution of international monetary arrangements since the nineteenth century.

Chapter 9 (Chapter 20) studies exchange rate crises. Before explaining how pegs break, we spend some time studying how pegs work. We begin by focusing on reserve management and the central bank balance sheet, when an economy faces shocks to output, interest rates, and risk premiums. We then extend the framework to consider lender of last resort actions, a structure that allows for more realism. This presentation allows us to discuss recent controversies over reserve accumulation in China and other emerging markets, and also suggests how pegs can fail. The chapter concludes by looking at two models of crises: a first-generation model with ongoing monetized deficits with fixed output and flexible prices, applying the logic of the flexible-price model of Chapter 3 (Chapter 14); and a second-generation model featuring an adverse shock with flexible output and fixed prices, applying the IS-LM-FX model of Chapter 7 (Chapter 18).

Chapter 10 (Chapter 21) discusses common currencies, with particular focus on the euro. We develop the basic Optimal Currency Area (OCA) criteria as an extension of the fixed versus floating analysis of Chapter 8 (Chapter 19). This framework allows us to consider additional economic and political reasons why countries might join a common currency area. We then present empirical evidence to show the differences between the United States and the Eurozone with respect to the OCA criteria and to explain why so many economists believe that the Eurozone currently is not an OCA. A complete explanation of the euro project requires an examination of other forces, which are considered in the remainder of the chapter: the possible endogeneity of the OCA criteria and the role of noneconomic factors. Thus, we examine the essential history, politics, and institutional details of the euro.

Chapter 11 (Chapter 22) is a collection of four "minichapters" that tackle important topics in macroeconomics. In this edition, these topics are the failure of UIP and exchange rate puzzles in the short run (including the carry trade and limits to arbitrage); the failure of PPP and exchange rates in the long run (including transaction costs and the Balassa-Samuelson effect); the debate over global imbalances (including the savings glut hypothesis and the role of exchange rate adjustments); the problem of default (including a simple model of default as insurance and a discussion of triple crises). Each of these topics is presented in a self-contained block that can be taught as is or in conjunction with earlier material. The UIP material could be added to Chapter 2 or 4 (Chapter 13 or 15). The PPP material would nicely augment Chapter 3 (Chapter 14). The global imbalances material could be presented with Chapter 5, 6, or 7 (Chapter 16, 17, or 18). The default topic could be paired with the discussion of currency crises in Chapter 9 (Chapter 20).

Alternative Routes through the Text

Because this book is available as a combined edition and as split volumes, it can be used for several types of courses, as summarized below and in the table on the next page.

A semester-length course in international trade (say, 15 weeks) would start at Chapter 1, but for a shorter, quarter-length course (say, 10 weeks), we suggest skipping Chapter 1 and going straight to the Ricardian model (Chapter 2). Chapters 2, 3 (the specific-factors model), and 4 (the Heckscher-Ohlin model) form the core of trade theory. The movement of labor and capital between countries (Chapter 5) builds on these chapters theoretically, and summarizes the empirical evidence on immigration and foreign direct investment.

The new approaches to international trade covered in Chapters 6 (economies of scale and imperfect competition) and 7 (offshoring) can be taught independently of each other. (A quarter course in international trade may not have time for both chapters.) The final four chapters in international trade deal with trade policy. Chapter 8 (tariffs and quotas under perfect competition) should be discussed in any course regardless of its length. Tariffs and quotas under imperfect competition (Chapter 9) digs more deeply into the effects of trade policy, and is followed by a discussion of export subsidies (Chapter 10). Some or all topics in the final chapter on international agreements can be covered as time permits.

A semester course in international macroeconomics (say, 15 weeks) would start at Chapter 12 in the combined edition (Chapter 1 in the *International Macroeconomics* split edition), but for a shorter quarter-length course (say, 10 weeks), we recommend skipping Chapter 12 (Chapter 1) and going straight to the foreign exchange market presented in Chapter 13 (Chapter 2). Core material on exchange rate theory then follows, with the long run in Chapter 14 (Chapter 3) followed by the short run in Chapter 15 (Chapter 4). Next come the core definitions of the national and international accounts and the balance of payments, presented in Chapter 16 (Chapter 5). After this point a course with a macro emphasis would cover the costs and benefits of globalization in Chapter 17 (Chapter 6) and IS-LM in Chapter 18 (Chapter 7). To allow time to cover crises in Chapter 20 (Chapter 9), treatment of regime choice in Chapter 19 (Chapter 8) might be combined with a discussion of the euro in Chapter 21 (Chapter 10). Topics from Chapter 22 (Chapter 11) can be selected as time permits: a more finance-oriented course might focus on the first two exchange rate topics; a more macro-oriented course might focus on global imbalances and default. In a semester-length course, there should be time for almost all the topics to be covered.

We recognize that many schools also offer a combined one-semester course in international trade and macroeconomics, sometimes to students outside the economics major. Because of the wealth of applications, we have found that our chapters on trade or macroeconomics serve those students very well. The one-semester version of our textbook, **Essentials of International Economics,** available for the first time with the second edition, brings together the chapters that are the most important for such a course. The one-semester *Essentials* edition has an introduction in Chapter 1 that incorporates both international trade and macroeconomic issues. It then moves to Chapters 2–6, the basic trade chapters, followed by two chapters on tariffs and quotas under perfect competition and under imperfect competition. The international trade section concludes with the chapter on trade agreements and the environment. An extra chapter on offshoring is available online. These chapters offer students a solid perspective on international trade and trade policy. These chapters are followed in the one-semester *Essentials* edition by six chapters dealing with the core concepts and models in international macroeconomics: the foreign exchange market, the monetary

SUGGESTED COURSE OUTLINES

Chapter Titles	Course Type and Length			
	Trade or Macroeconomics in one term		International Economics in two terms	International Economics in one term
	Chapter numbers from *International Trade* version		Chapter numbers from *International Economics*	Chapter numbers from *Essentials of International Economics*
	10 week quarter	13–15 week semester		
Trade in the Global Economy (*Essentials:* The Global Economy)	—	1	1	1 (introduces trade and macroeconomics)
Trade and Technology: The Ricardian Model	2	2	2	2
Gains and Losses from Trade in the Specific-Factors Model	3	3	3	3
Trade and Resources: The Heckscher-Ohlin Model	4	4	4	4
Movement of Labor and Capital between Countries	Choose two from 5, 6, 7	5	5	5
Increasing Returns to Scale and Monopolistic Competition		6	6	6
Offshoring of Goods and Services		7	7	Available online
Import Tariffs and Quotas under Perfect Competition	8	8	8	7
Import Tariffs and Quotas under Imperfect Competition	9	9	9	8
Export Subsidies in Agriculture and High-Technology Industries	10	10	10	—
International Agreements: Trade, Labor, and the Environment	As time permits	11	11	9
	Chapter numbers from *International Macroeconomics* version			
	10 week quarter	13–15 week semester		
The Global Macroeconomy	—	1	12	—
Introduction to Exchange Rates and the Foreign Exchange Market	2	2	13	10
Exchange Rates I: The Monetary Approach in the Long Run	3	3	14	11
Exchange Rates II: The Asset Approach in the Short Run	4	4	15	12
National and International Accounts: Income, Wealth, and the Balance of Payments	5	5	16	13
The Balance of Payments I: The Gains from Financial Globalization	6	6	17	—
The Balance of Payments II: Output, Exchange Rates, and Macroeconomic Policies in the Short Run	7	7	18	14
Fixed Versus Floating: International Monetary Experience	Combine with Chapter 8	8	19	15
Exchange Rate Crises: How Pegs Work and How They Break	9	9	20	—
The Euro	Combine with Chapter 10	10	21	Available online
Topics in International Macroeconomics	1 or 2 topics (as time permits)	3 or 4 topics (as time permits)	22	—

and asset approaches to exchange rates, national income and the balance of payments, short-run macroeconomic policy, and fixed-versus-floating exchange rates. An extra chapter on the euro is available online. This coverage will give students a basic grounding in international macroeconomics.

Supplements and Media Package

In addition to all its pedagogical innovations, our book brings to the market an innovative supplement and media package. These supplements were given the same careful thought, time, and preparation as the text. We are happy to provide a full suite of teaching materials for instructors along with a complete set of resources to aid students in reviewing the key concepts presented in the text.

The Aplia/Worth course for Feenstra/Taylor is the only fully integrated Aplia solution in International Economics. It enhances students' experiences through Aplia's interactive problem sets, news analyses, and tutorials—all in a format that saves time for professors while encouraging students in their learning.

The Feenstra/Taylor Aplia course includes a full eBook as well as offering:

- **Homework sets correlated to the text.** Online homework is easy to assign, and it grades automatically. The course gradebook quickly puts results at your fingertips.
- **Algorithmic problem sets.** All homework problem sets offer Grade It Now. Students can attempt any problem set up to three times with variables that randomize on each attempt..
- **Multiple purchase options.** Aplia access can be packaged with any version of the text, or purchased separately online as a less expensive alternative to the book because it includes an eBook. Students who purchase online access can also buy a physical textbook directly from Aplia at a significant discount.

Instructor Supplements

Instructor's Manual with Solutions Manual

Instructor's Manuals for each portion of the book, prepared by Anthony Lima (California State University, East Bay) and Alyson Ma (University of San Diego) are available. The Instructor's Manual is available on the Book Companion Site, and provides the following for each chapter in the textbook:

- *Notes to the instructor:* notes that include a chapter summary with additional comments
- *Lecture notes:* a complete set of notes, including a detailed outline of the chapter for aid in preparing class lectures
- *Teaching tips:* 4 or 5 activities per chapter that instructors can utilize in lectures, for in-class group work, or as take-home assignments
- *In-class problems:* 10 to 15 problems per chapter, including in-depth suggested answers.
- *Solutions to textbook problems:* detailed solutions to all end-of-chapter problems.

Printed Test Bank

The test bank provides a wide range of creative and versatile questions ranging in levels of difficulty and format to assess students' comprehension, interpretation, analysis, and synthesis skills. Averaging over 170 questions per chapter, the test bank offers a variety of multiple-choice, true/false, and short-answer questions. All questions have been checked for continuity with the text content and reviewed extensively for accuracy. The test bank was coordinated by Ron Davies (University College, Dublin) with the help of contributing author Millicent Taylor (Carson-Newman College).

Computerized Test Bank

The test bank is also available in CD-ROM format, powered by Brownstone, for both Windows and Macintosh users. With this Diploma software, instructors can easily create and print tests as well as write and edit questions.

Student and Instructor Supplements

Study Guide with Worked Examples

Students' economic thinking will be challenged and extended by a creative new Study Guide with Worked Examples prepared by Stephen Yeaple of Pennsylvania State University. This study guide complements the textbook by providing students with additional opportunities to develop their knowledge of international economics through active learning. This innovative resource reinforces the topics and key concepts covered in the text. For each key section of each chapter, the Study Guide with Worked Examples provides:

- *Key themes:* detailed discussions of key concepts
- *Key terms:* a summary of important vocabulary within the chapter, with space for students to make their own notes
- *Review questions with tips:* detailed, thorough problems for students to test their comprehension, along with tips to help students work through the problems. To identify common mistakes and to demonstrate common features of different types of economic problems, tips are provided immediately following questions that delve into particularly important or difficult topics.
- *Worked-out solutions:* including solutions to all Study Guide review questions.

Companion Website for Students and Instructors

The companion site www.worthpublishers.com/feenstrataylor2_intlmacro is a virtual study guide for students and an excellent resource for instructors. For each chapter in the textbook, the tools on the site include:

Student Tools
- *Practice quizzes:* A set of questions with feedback and page references to the textbook. Student answers are saved in an online database that can be accessed by instructors.
- *Key-term flashcards:* Students can test themselves on key vocabulary with these pop-up electronic flashcards.
- *Web exercises*

- *Web links* to relevant research and demonstrations with related questions for applied practive

Instructor Resources

- *Quiz gradebook:* The site gives instructors the ability to track students' interaction with the practice quizzes via an online gradebook. Instructors may choose to have student results emailed directly to them.
- *PowerPoint lecture presentations:* These customizable PowerPoint slides, prepared by Fernando Quijano (Dickinson State University) are designed to assist instructors with lecture preparation and presentation by providing original animations, graphs from the textbook, data tables, key concepts, and bulleted lecture outlines.
- *Image gallery:* A complete set of figures and tables from the textbook in JPEG and PowerPoint formats
- *Instructor's Manual*
- *Solutions Manual*
- *Answers to Web Link Questions*

CourseSmart eBooks

All four versions (*International Economics, International Trade, International Macroeconomics,* and *Essentials of International Economics*) are available as CourseSmart eBooks. Students who purchase the Feenstra/Taylor CourseSmart eBooks have instant access to their textbooks on any computer or handheld device with an Internet connection. CourseSmart eBooks offer an earth-friendly and wallet-friendly option for students.

CourseSmart eBook features include:

- Copy and paste text:

  Easy integration with word processing programs
- Textbook Search:

  Find words or topics fast within your online eTextbook
- Print what you need:

  From any printer connected to the computer
- Highlighting and Note-Taking:

  Highlight relevant sections or take notes on important topics
- Same "Evcrything Else":

  Online eTextbooks share the same page layout and numbering as the print version
- No Connection Necessary:

Once you download the eBook and save it to your computer, you don't need the Internet. Just start reading

Course Management System

The Feenstra Course Cartridge allows you to combine your Course Management System's most popular tools and easy-to-use interface with text-specific, rich Web content, including preprogrammed quizzes, links, activities, and a whole array of other materials. The result: an interactive, comprehensive online course that allows for effortless implementation, management, and use. The Worth electronic files are organized and prebuilt to work within your CMS software and can be easily downloaded from the CMS content showcases directly onto your department server. You can also obtain a CMS formatted version of the book's test bank.

Acknowledgments

A book like this would not be possible without the assistance of many people, which we gratefully acknowledge.

First, the renowned team at Worth has spared no effort to help us; their experience and skill in publishing economics textbooks were invaluable. Numerous individuals have been involved with this project, but we must give special mention to four: the project has been continually and imaginatively guided by acquisitions editor Sarah Dorger, now joined by executive editor Chuck Linsmeier and development editor Bruce Kaplan, and by marketing manager Scott Guile, who successfully brought the book to market. Through it all, the manuscript was improved endlessly by our primary development editor, Jane Tufts. We are greatly in their debt.

We have also relied on the assistance of a number of graduate students in collecting data for applications, preparing problems, and proofreading material. We would like to thank Leticia Arroyo Abad, Chang Hong, David Jacks, Alyson Ma, Ahmed Rahman, Seema Sangita, Radek Szulga, and Yingying Xu for their assistance. We are especially grateful to Benjamin Mandel, who has worked on many of the international trade chapters in the first edition, and to Philip Luck, who worked on all the chapters in this second edition. Thanks also to Christian Broda, Colin Carter, Michele Cavallo, Menzie Chinn, Sebastian Edwards, Ann Harrison, Mervyn King, Philip Lane, Karen Lewis, Christopher Meissner, Gian Maria Milesi-Ferretti, Michael Pakko, Ugo Panizza, Giovanni Peri, Eswar Prasad, Andrés Rodríguez-Clare, Jay Shambaugh, and Martin Wolf for providing data used in the applications.

We have taught the chapters of this book ourselves a number of times, and have benefited from the feedback of colleagues. The book has also been class-tested by a number of individuals.

For the second edition, we benefited from the suggestions of the following reviewers:

- Bradley Andrew, *Juniata College*
- Damyana Bakardzhieva, *George Washington University*
- Mina Baliamoune, *University of North Florida*
- Valerie Bencivenga, *University of Texas at Austin*
- Emily Blanchard, *University of Virginia*
- Nicola Borri, *Boston University*
- Drusilla Brown, *Tufts University*
- Vera Brusentsev, *University of Delaware*
- Colleen Callahan, *American University*
- Geoffrey Carliner, *Boston University*
- Ron Cronovich, *Carthage College*
- Firat Demir, *University of Oklahoma*
- Asim Erdilek, *Case Western Reserve University*
- John Gilbert, *Utah State University*
- William Hauk, *University of South Carolina*
- David Hummels, *Purdue University*
- Hakan Inal, *Virginia Commonwealth University*
- Alan Isaac, *American University*
- Robert Jerome, *James Madison University*
- Grace Johnson, *Oklahoma State University—Tulsa*
- Kathy Kelly, *University of Texas at Arlington*
- Bill Kosteas, *Cleveland State University*
- Ricardo Lopez, *Indiana University*
- Volodymyr Lugovskyy, *Georgia Tech*
- Nicolas Magud, *University of Oregon*
- Keith Malone, *University of North Alabama*
- Maria Muniagurria, *University of Wisconsin—Madison*
- Catherine Mann, *Brandeis University*
- Steven J. Matusz, *Michigan State University*
- Fabio Mendez, *University of Arkansas*
- William Mertens, *University of Colorado at Boulder*
- Rebecca Neumann, *University of Wisconsin—Milwaukee*
- Emanuel Ornelas, *London School of Economics*
- Perry Patterson, *Wake Forest University*
- Masha Rahnama, *Texas Tech University*
- Michael Rinkus, *Walsh College*
- Sheikh Shahnawaz, *University of Southern California*
- David Sobiechowski, *University of Michigan—Dearborn*
- Steve Steib, *University of Tulsa*
- Nicholas Stratis, *Florida State University*
- Edward Tower, *Duke University*
- Elizabeth Wheaton, *Southern Methodist University*
- Peter Wylie, *University of British Columbia—Okanagan*

We would like to thank the following instructors for sharing their ideas with us in the development of the first edition. These colleagues have been enthusiastic about the reception of their students to our fresh approach.

- Joshua Aizenman, *University of California, Santa Cruz*
- Scott Baier, *Clemson University*
- Paul Bergin, *University of California, Davis*
- Matilde Bombardini, *University of British Columbia—Vancouver*
- Drusilla Brown, *Tufts University*
- Avik Chakraborty, *University of Tennessee—Knoxville*
- Gordon Hanson, *University of California, San Diego*
- James Harrigan, *University of Virginia*
- Takeo Hoshi, *University of California, San Diego*
- David Hummels, *Purdue University*
- Samuel Kortum, *University of Chicago*
- John McLaren, *University of Virginia*
- Marc-Andreas Muendler, *University of California, San Diego*
- Robert Murphy, *Boston College*
- Constantin Ogloblin, *Georgia Southern University*
- Kevin O'Rourke, *Trinity College, Dublin*
- Sanjay Paul, *Elizabethtown College*
- Priya Ranjan, *University of California, Irvine*
- Andrés Rodriguez-Clare, *Pennsylvania State University*
- Katheryn Russ, *University of California, Davis*
- Stephen Stageberg, *University of Mary Washington*
- Bruce Wydick, *University of San Francisco*
- Stephen Yeaple, *Pennsylvania State University*

A huge number of colleagues were very helpful in reviewing the first-edition manuscript. We wish to thank the following reviewers:

Joshua Aizenman, *University of California, Santa Cruz*
Mohsen Bahmani-Oskooee, *University of Wisconsin—Milwaukee*
Scott Baier, *Clemson University*
Richard Baillie, *Michigan State University*
Joe Bell, *Missouri State University*
Paul Bergin, *University of California, Davis*
Robert Blecker, *American University*
Roger Butters, *University of Nebraska—Lincoln*
Francisco Carrada-Bravo, *Arizona State University*
Menzie Chinn, *University of Wisconsin—Madison*
Richard Chisik, *Florida International University*
Ann Davis, *Marist College*
Robert Driskill, *Vanderbilt University*
James Fain, *Oklahoma State University*
David H. Feldman, *The College of William & Mary*
Diane Flaherty, *University of Massachusetts, Amherst*
Jean-Ellen Giblin, *Fashion Institute of Technology*
Bill Gibson, *University of Vermont*
Thomas Grennes, *North Carolina State University*
Gordon Hanson, *University of California, San Diego*
Mehdi Haririan, *Bloomsburg University*
James Harrigan, *University of Virginia*
Takeo Hoshi, *University of California, San Diego*
Douglas Irwin, *Dartmouth College*
Michael Klein, *Tufts University*
Kala Krishna, *Pennsylvania State University*
Maria Kula, *Roger Williams University*
Ricardo Lopez, *Indiana University*
Mary Lovely, *Syracuse University*
Barbara Lowrey, *University of Maryland*
Steven J. Matusz, *Michigan State University*

Jose Mendez, *Arizona State University*
Shannon Mitchell, *Virginia Commonwealth University*
Farshid Mojaver Hosseini, *University of California, Davis*
Marc-Andreas Muendler, *University of California, San Diego*
Maria Muniagurria, *University of Wisconsin—Madison*
Robert Murphy, *Boston College*
Ranganath Murthy, *Bucknell University*
Kanda Naknoi, *Purdue University*
Constantin Ogloblin, *Georgia Southern University*
Kevin O'Rourke, *Trinity College, Dublin*
Kerry Pannell, *DePauw University*
Jaishankar Raman, *Valparaiso University*
Raymond Robertson, *Macalester College*
Andrés Rodriguez-Clare, *Pennsylvania State University*
Hadi Salehi-Esfahani, *University of Illinois at Urbana-Champaign*
Andreas Savvides, *Oklahoma State University*
Till Schreiber, *The College of William & Mary*
Gunjan Sharma, *University of Missouri, Columbia*
John Subrick, *James Madison University*
Mark P. Taylor, *University of Warwick*
Linda Tesar, *University of Michigan, Ann Arbor*
Geetha Vaidyanathan, *University of North Carolina at Greensboro*
Kristin Van Gaasbeck, *California State University, Sacramento*
Gary Wells, *Clemson University*
Mark Wohar, *University of Nebraska, Omaha*
Susan Wolcott, *SUNY Binghamton*
Bin Xu, *China Europe International Business School*
Stephen Yeaple, *Pennsylvania State University*

We received useful feedback from focus group participants. We would like to thank the following individuals:

Mohsen Bahmani-Oskooee, *University of Wisconsin—Milwaukee*
Roger Butters, *University of Nebraska—Lincoln*
Francisco Carrada-Bravo, *Arizona State University*
Mitchell Charkiewicz, *Central Connecticut State University*
Menzie Chinn, *University of Wisconsin—Madison*
Carl Davidson, *Michigan State University*
Ann Davis, *Marist College*
Robert Driskill, *Vanderbilt University*
Eric Fisher, *California Polytechnic State University, San Luis Obispo*
Diane Flaherty, *University of Massachusetts, Amherst*
Bill Gibson, *University of Vermont*
Thomas Grennes, *North Carolina State University*
Mehdi Haririan, *Bloomsburg University*
Andreas Hauskrecht, *Indiana University*
Andrew Hughes-Hallett, *George Mason University*
Eckhard Janeba, *University of Mannheim*
Mary Lovely, *Syracuse University*
Marc Melitz, *Harvard University*
Norman Miller, *Miami University of Ohio*
Shannon Mitchell, *Virginia Commonwealth University*
Ranganath Murthy, *Bucknell University*
Rebecca Neumann, *University of Wisconsin—Milwaukee*
Constantin Ogloblin, *Georgia Southern University*
Lucjan Orlowski, *Sacred Heart University*
Jeff Pliskin, *Hamilton College*
Francisca Richter, *Cleveland State University*
Hadi Salehi-Esfahani, *University of Illinois at Urbana-Champaign*
Bin Xu, *China Europe International Business School*

We would like to thank the following instructors who have provided feedback on the initial preliminary version of the first edition of our text:

Scott Baier, *Clemson University*
Paul Bergin, *University of California, Davis*
Luisa Blanco Raynal, *Pepperdine University*
James Cassing, *University of Pittsburgh*
Ted Fu, *Stanford University*
James Harrigan, *University of Virginia*
David Hummels, *Purdue University*
Farshid Mojaver Hosseini, *University of California, Davis*
Maria Muniagurria, *University of Wisconsin—Madison*
Kanda Naknoi, *Purdue University*
Raymond Robertson, *Macalester College*
Andrés Rodriguez-Clare, *Pennsylvania State University*
Jeffrey Rosensweig, *Emory University*
Jennifer Steele, *University of Texas at Austin*
Asha Sundaram, *Syracuse University*
Kristin Van Gaasbeck, *California State University, Sacramento*
Wolfgang Keller, *University of Colorado at Boulder*

We would like to thank the following individuals who have aided us in the preparation and extensive review of the ancillary package.

Francis Ahking, *University of Connecticut*
Ron Davies, *University College, Dublin*
Philip Luck, *University of California, Davis*
Alyson Ma, *University of San Diego*
Terry Monson, *Michigan Technological University*
Robert Murphy, *Boston College*
Sanjay Paul, *Elizabethtown College*
Jaishankar Raman, *Valparaiso University*
Millicent Sites, *Carson-Newman College*
Marie Truesdell, *Marian College*
Kristin Van Gaasbeck, *California State University, Sacramento*
Stephen Yeaple, *Pennsylvania State University*

We would also like to thank our families, especially Claire and Gail, for their sustained support during the time we have devoted to writing this book.

Finally, you will see an accompanying picture of children in Ciudad Dario, Nicaragua, with their teacher, in the classroom of a small schoolhouse that was built for them by Seeds of Learning (www.seedsoflearning.org), a nonprofit organization dedicated to improving educational opportunities in rural Latin America. A portion of the royalties from this book go toward supporting the work of Seeds of Learning.

Robert C. Feenstra

Alan M. Taylor
Davis, California
January 2011

Sixth-grade class with their teacher in La Carreta #2 school in Ciudad Darío, Nicaragua.

second edition

international
macroeconomics

The Global Macroeconomy

1 Foreign Exchange: Currencies and Crises

2 Globalization of Finance: Debts and Deficits

3 Government and Institutions: Policies and Performance

4 Conclusions

So much of barbarism, however, still remains in the transactions of most civilized nations, that almost all independent countries choose to assert their nationality by having, to their inconvenience and that of their neighbors, a peculiar currency of their own.

John Stuart Mill

Neither a borrower nor a lender be; / For loan oft loseth both itself and friend. / And borrowing dulls the edge of husbandry.

Polonius, in William Shakespeare's *Hamlet*

History, in general, only informs us of what bad government is.

Thomas Jefferson

International macroeconomics is devoted to the study of large-scale economic problems in interdependent economies. It is macroeconomic because it focuses on key economy-wide variables such as exchange rates, prices, interest rates, income, wealth, and the current account. It is international because a deeper understanding of the global economy emerges only when the interconnections among nations are fully considered. In the chapters that follow, we build on familiar macroeconomic ideas while examining the main features of the global macroeconomy that define and distinguish the field of international macroeconomics.

Drawing on the wisdom encapsulated in the preceding epigraphs, the essential and unique features of international macroeconomics can be reduced to three key elements: the world has many monies (not one), countries are financially integrated (not isolated), and in this context economic policy choices are made (but not always very well).

- **Money** John Stuart Mill echoes the complaints of many exasperated travelers and traders when he bemoans the profusion of different monies around the world. Mill's vision of a world with a single currency is even more distant today: in his day, the number of currencies was far smaller than the more than

150 currencies in use today. Why do all these monies exist, and what purposes do they serve? What are their implications for the working of our global economy? What are the causes and consequences of the changing value of one currency against another? Aside from national pride, does a country enjoy benefits from having its own money? Or does it suffer costs?

- **Finance** William Shakespeare's Polonius would surely be distressed by the sight of today's mounting debts owed by the United States and other borrower countries to the rest of world. For him, happiness meant financial isolation, with income exactly equal to expenditure. But over the centuries this has been a minority view among individuals and among nations, and today the scale of international financial transactions has risen to record levels as capital has become ever more mobile internationally. Why do all these transactions occur, and what purposes do they serve? Who lends to whom, and why? Why are some debts paid but not others? Is the free flow of finance a source of economic benefits? Are there potential economic costs?

- **Policy** Thomas Jefferson's assessment of government may be extreme, but looking at economic outcomes around the world today, it surely contains a germ of truth. If government policies were always optimal, recessions never happened, currencies never crashed, and debts were never in default . . . well, that would be a nice world to inhabit. The reality—all too apparent after the global financial crisis of 2008—is that policy making is frequently not optimal, even at the best of times in the best-run countries. And in the worst-run countries, poverty, underinvestment, hyperinflation, crises, and debt problems are common events. How can bad economic outcomes be avoided and better policy decisions be formulated? How should monetary and fiscal policies be conducted and how do exchange rates and international capital flows affect the economy? What are the trade-offs for each decision? Is there even a single "right" answer?

Many fundamental questions like the ones we have posed above must be answered if we are to understand the economic world around us. To that end, the chapters that follow combine relevant economic theory with compelling empirical evidence to explain the workings of today's global macroeconomy. This introductory chapter briefly explains the road ahead.

1 Foreign Exchange: Currencies and Crises

In most branches of economics, and even in studying international trade, it is common to assume that all goods are priced in a common currency. Despite this unrealistic assumption, these analyses deliver important insights into the workings of the global economy.

In the real world, however, countries have different currencies, and a complete understanding of how a country's economy works requires that we study the *exchange rate*, the price of foreign currency. Because products and investments move across borders, fluctuations in exchange rates have significant effects on the relative prices of home and foreign goods (such as autos and clothing), services (such as insurance and tourism), and assets (such as equities and bonds). By starting our analysis of the global economy with the theory of exchange rates, we see how and why they fluctuate. In later chapters, we see why exchange rates matter for economic outcomes and why they are an important focus of economic policy making.

How Exchange Rates Behave

In studying exchange rates, it is important to understand the types of behavior that any theory of exchange rate determination must explain. Figure 1-1, which displays two of the most noteworthy exchange rates in recent years, illustrates some basic facts about exchange rates. Panel (a) shows the exchange rate of China with the United States, in yuan per U.S. dollar ($).[1] Panel (b) shows the exchange rate of the United States with the Eurozone, in U.S. dollars per euro.

The behavior of the two exchange rates is very different. The yuan-dollar rate is almost flat. In fact, for many years it was literally unchanged, day after day, at 8.28 yuan/$. Finally, on July 23, 2005, it dropped exactly 2%. Then it followed a fairly smooth trend for a while: by September 2008 (when the global financial crisis began), it had fallen a further 15%. After the crisis, it reverted to a flat line once again at 6.83 yuan/$. During the period shown, the daily average absolute change in the exchange rate was only three-hundredths of one percent (0.03%).

FIGURE 1-1

Major Exchange Rates The chart shows two key exchange rates from 2003 to 2010. The China-U.S. exchange rate varies little and would be considered a fixed exchange rate, despite a period when it followed a gradual trend. The U.S.-Eurozone exchange rate varies a lot and would be considered a floating exchange rate.

Note: For comparative purposes, the two vertical scales have the same proportions: the maximum is twice the minimum.

Source: www.oanda.com.

---

[1] The Chinese yuan is also known as the *renminbi* ("people's currency").

100 Chinese yuan, U.S. dollars, Eurozone euros.

In contrast, the euro-dollar exchange rate experienced wide fluctuations over the same period. On a *daily* basis, the daily average absolute change in this exchange rate was one-third of one percent (0.33%), more than 10 times as large as the average change in the yuan-dollar rate.

Based on such observable differences in exchange rate behavior, economists divide the world into two groups of countries: those with **fixed** (or *pegged*) **exchange rates** and those with **floating** (or *flexible*) **exchange rates**. In Figure 1-1, China's exchange rate with the United States would be considered fixed. It was officially set at a fixed exchange rate with the dollar until July 2005, but even after that its very limited range of movement was so controlled that it was effectively "fixed."[2] In contrast, the euro-dollar exchange rate is a floating exchange rate, one that moves up and down over a much wider range.

Key Topics How are exchange rates determined? Why do some exchange rates fluctuate sharply in the short run, while others are almost constant? What explains why exchange rates rise, fall, or stay flat in the long run?

Why Exchange Rates Matter

Changes in exchange rates affect an economy in two ways:

- Changes in exchange rates cause a change in the international relative prices of goods. That is, one country's goods and services become more or less expensive relative to another's when expressed in a common unit of currency. In late 2002, for example, the dollar-euro exchange rate was 0.9 $/€, so something worth €10 in Europe had a U.S. dollar value of $9. By 2007, when the exchange rate had risen to 1.3$/€, a similar €10 item had a U.S. dollar value of $13. In the mid-2000s, the German automaker Volkswagen blamed this rise in the dollar-euro exchange rate for a decline in sales to U.S. car dealers. This decline in sales occurred because a VW that cost, say, €30,000 or $27,000 at the exchange rate of 0.9 $/€, would have cost $39,000 at the exchange rate of $1.3/€. By making costs higher in dollar terms, this increase in the exchange rate in the 2000s squeezed the profits of this trade and discouraged VW and all other European firms from trying to export to the United States. U.S. firms exporting goods to Europe faced the opposite situation: when the $/€ exchange rate rose, their goods were cheaper relative to those of their European rivals and so U.S. exporters saw shipments and profits rise.[3]

- Changes in exchange rates can cause a change in the international relative prices of assets. These fluctuations in wealth can then affect firms, governments, and individuals. For example, the Eurozone countries held about $200 billion in U.S. dollar assets at the end of 2002. These assets were worth approximately €200 billion, since €1 was then worth about $1. A year later, at the end of 2003, those same assets were worth the equivalent of only €160 billion.

---

[2] On June 21, 2010, China switched its policy again, and started to allow the yuan to appreciate gradually once again.

[3] Peter Gumbel, "Don't Blame It on the Euro," Time.com, May 11, 2003. Jack Ewing and Laura Cohn, "Beware the Brawny Euro: As It Strengthens, Europe's Currency Threatens to Snuff Out a Tenuous Recovery," BusinessWeek.com, November 29, 2004.

Why? The dollar was then worth only €0.80, and 0.8 times 200 equals 160. Hence, *simply as a result of a change in the exchange rate*, the inhabitants of the Eurozone suffered a €40 billion loss in their total wealth.[4]

Key Topics How do exchange rates affect the real economy? How do changes in exchange rates affect international prices, the demand for goods from different countries, and hence the levels of national output? How do changes in exchange rates affect the values of foreign assets, and hence change national wealth?

When Exchange Rates Misbehave

Even after studying how exchange rates behave and why they matter, we still face the challenge of explaining one type of event that is almost guaranteed to put exchange rates front and center in the news: an **exchange rate crisis.** In such a crisis, a currency experiences a sudden and pronounced loss of value against another currency, following a period in which the exchange rate had been fixed or relatively stable.

One of the most dramatic currency crises in recent history occurred in Argentina from December 2001 to January 2002. For a decade, the Argentine peso had been fixed to the U.S. dollar at a one-to-one rate of exchange. But in January 2002, the fixed exchange rate became a floating exchange rate. A few months later, one Argentine peso, which had been worth one U.S. dollar, had fallen in value to just $0.25 (equivalently, the price of a U.S. dollar rose from one peso to almost four pesos).

The drama was not confined to the foreign exchange market. The Argentine government declared a world-record **default** (i.e., a suspension of payments) on its $155 billion of debt; the financial system was in a state of near closure for months; inflation climbed; output collapsed and unemployment soared; and more than 50% of Argentine households fell below the poverty line. At the height of the crisis, violence flared and the country had five presidents in the space of two weeks (see **Headlines: Economic Crisis in Argentina**).

Argentina's experience was extreme but hardly unique. Exchange rate crises are fairly common. Figure 1-2 lists 24 exchange rate crises in the six-year period from 1997 to 2009. In almost all cases, a fairly stable exchange rate experienced a large and sudden change. The year 1997 was especially eventful, with 7 crises, 5 of them in East Asia. The Indonesian rupiah lost 49% of its U.S. dollar value, but severe collapses also occurred in Thailand, Korea, Malaysia, and the Philippines. Other notable crises during this period included Liberia in 1998, Russia in 1998, Brazil in 1999, as well as Argentina in 2002. More recently, Iceland experienced an exchange rate crisis during the global financial crisis of 2008.

Crisis episodes display some regular patterns. Output typically falls, banking and debt problems emerge, households and firms suffer. In addition, political turmoil often ensues. Government finances worsen and embarrassed authorities may appeal for external help from international development organizations, such as the **International Monetary Fund (IMF)** or **World Bank,** or other countries. The economic setbacks are often more pronounced in poorer countries. Although we could confine our study of exchange rates to normal times, the frequent and damaging occurrence of crises obliges us to pay attention to these abnormal episodes, too.

---

[4] Data for this example are based on U.S. Treasury reports.

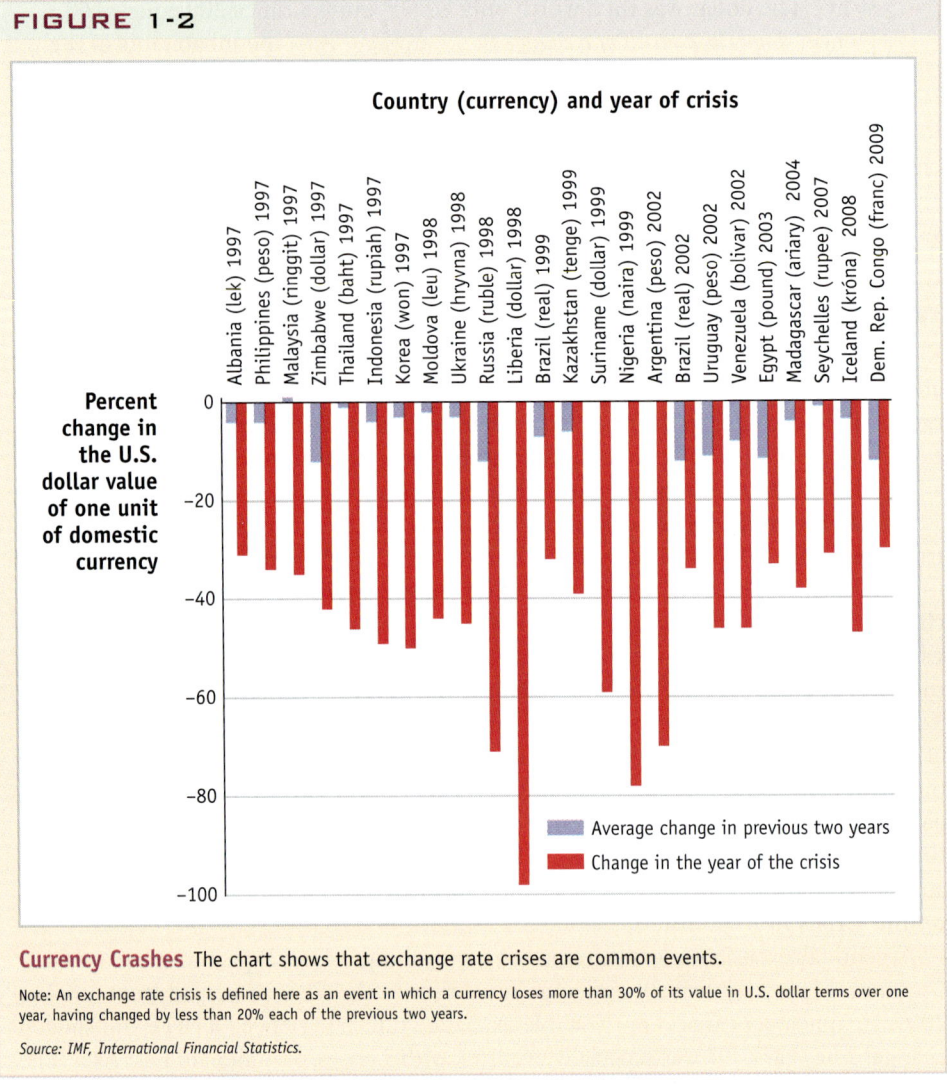

FIGURE 1-2

Currency Crashes The chart shows that exchange rate crises are common events.

Note: An exchange rate crisis is defined here as an event in which a currency loses more than 30% of its value in U.S. dollar terms over one year, having changed by less than 20% each of the previous two years.

Source: IMF, International Financial Statistics.

Key Topics Why do exchange rate crises occur? Are they an inevitable consequence of deeper fundamental problems in an economy or are they an avoidable result of "animal spirits"—irrational forces in financial markets? Why are these crises so economically and politically costly? What steps might be taken to prevent crises, and at what cost?

Summary and Plan of Study

International macroeconomists frequently refer to the exchange rate as "the single most important price in an open economy." If we treat this statement as more than self-promotion, we should learn why it might be true. In our course of study, we will explore what determines the exchange rate, how the exchange rate affects the economy, and how crises occur.

Our study of exchange rates proceeds as follows: in Chapter 2, we learn about the structure and operation of the markets in which foreign currencies are traded. Chapters 3 and 4 present the theory of exchange rates. Chapter 5 discusses how

HEADLINES

Economic Crisis in Argentina

International macroeconomics can often seem like a dry and abstract subject, but it must be remembered that societies and individuals can be profoundly shaken by the issues we will study. This article was written just after the start of the severe economic crisis that engulfed Argentina in 2002, following the collapse of its fixed exchange rate, a financial crisis, and a government default. Real output shrank by 15% and took years to regain its previous peak, as poverty and unemployment rates remained at high levels. The country sank into an economic depression worse even than those in the 1930s, 1910s, and 1890s.

ROSARIO, Argentina—Word spread fast through the vast urban slums ringing Rosario. There was food on the freeway—and it was still alive.

A cattle truck had overturned near this rusting industrial city, spilling 22 head of prime Angus beef across the wind-swept highway. Some were dead. Most were injured. A few were fine.

A mob moved out from Las Flores, a shantytown of trash heaps and metal shacks boiling over with refugees from the financial collapse of what was once Latin America's wealthiest nation. Within minutes, 600 hungry residents arrived on the scene, wielding machetes and carving knives. Suddenly, according to accounts from some of those present on that March day, a cry went up.

"Kill the cows!" someone yelled. "Take what you can!"

Cattle company workers attempting a salvage operation backed off. And the slaughter began. The scent of blood, death and fresh meat filled the highway. Cows bellowed as they were sloppily diced by groups of men, women and children. Fights broke out for pieces of flesh in bloody tugs of war.

"I looked around at people dragging off cow legs, heads and organs, and I couldn't believe my eyes," said Alberto Banrel, 43, who worked on construction jobs until last January, when the bottom fell out of the economy after Argentina suffered the world's largest debt default ever and a massive currency devaluation.

"And yet there I was, with my own bloody knife and piece of meat," Banrel said. "I felt like we had become a pack of wild animals . . . like piranhas on the Discovery Channel. Our situation has turned us into this."

The desolation of that day, neighbor vs. neighbor over hunks of meat, suggested how profoundly the collapse has altered Argentina. Traditionally proud, Argentines have begun to despair. Talk today is of vanished dignity, of a nation diminished in ways not previously imaginable. . . .

Until last year, Argentines were part of the richest, best-educated and most cultured nation in Latin America. . . . The poor here lived with more dignity than their equals anywhere else in the region. Argentina was, as the Argentines liked to say, very civilized.

Not anymore. . . .

With government statistics showing 11,200 people a day falling into poverty—earning less than $3 daily—Buenos Aires, a city once compared to Paris, has become the dominion of scavengers and thieves at night. Newly impoverished homeless people emerge from abandoned buildings and rail cars, rummaging through trash in declining middle- and upper-class neighborhoods. People from the disappearing middle class, such as Vicente Pitasi, 60 and jobless, have turned to pawn shops to sell their wedding rings.

"I have seen a lot happen in Argentina in my day, but I never lost hope until now," Pitasi said. "There is nothing left here, not even our pride.". . .

Severe hunger and malnutrition have emerged in the rural interior—something almost never seen in a country famous for

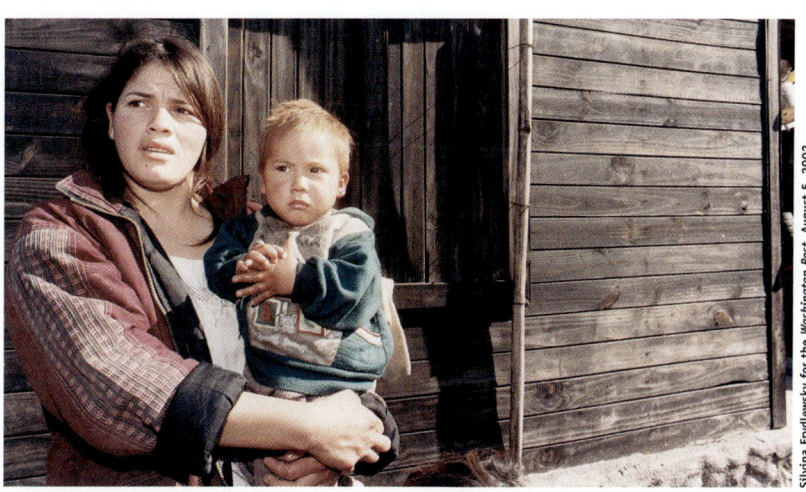

Beatriz Orresta, 20, holds her malnourished son in Rio Chico. She had been feeding her children soup made with the dried bones of a dead cow her husband had found.

Continued on next page

great slabs of beef and undulating fields of wheat. In search of someone to blame, Argentines have attacked the homes of local politicians and foreign banks. . . .

Economists and politicians differ on the causes of the brutal crisis. Some experts blame globalization and faulty policies imposed by the International Monetary Fund. But just as many blame the Argentine government for runaway spending and systematic corruption. The one thing everyone agrees on, however, is that there is no easy fix. . . .

What had been a snowball of poverty and unemployment has turned into an avalanche since January's default and devaluation. A record number of Argentines, more than half, live below the official poverty line. More than one in five no longer have jobs. . . .

For some rural families, the crisis has gone further. It has generated something rarely seen in Argentina: hunger. In the province of Tucuman, an agricultural zone of 1.3 million people, health workers say cases of malnutrition have risen 20 percent to 30 percent over the previous year.

"I wish they would cry," whispered Beatriz Orresta, 20, looking at her two young sons in a depressed Tucuman sugar cane town in the shadow of the Andes. "I would feel much better if they cried." Jonatan, 2, resting on the dirt floor behind the family's wooden shack, and Santiago, the 7-month-old she cradled in her arms, lay listlessly.

"They don't act it, but they're hungry. I know they are," she said.

Source: Excerpted from Anthony Faiola, "Despair in Once-Proud Argentina: After Economic Collapse, Deep Poverty Makes Dignity a Casualty," Washington Post, *August 6, 2002.*

exchange rates affect international transactions in assets. We examine the short-run impact of exchange rates on the demand for goods in Chapter 7, and with this understanding Chapter 8 examines the trade-offs governments face as they choose between fixed and floating exchange rates. Chapter 9 covers exchange rate crises in detail and Chapter 10 covers the euro, a common currency used in many countries. Chapter 11 presents further exploration of some exchange rate topics.

2 Globalization of Finance: Debts and Deficits

Financial development is a defining characteristic of modern economies. Households' use of financial instruments such as credit cards, savings accounts, and mortgages is taken for granted, as is the ability of firms and governments to use the products and services offered in financial markets. A few years ago, very little of this financial activity spilled across international borders; countries were very nearly closed from a financial standpoint. Today many countries are more open: financial globalization has taken hold around the world, starting in the economically advanced countries and spreading to many emerging market countries.

Although you might expect that you need many complex and difficult theories to understand the financial transactions between countries, such analysis requires only the application of familiar household accounting concepts such as income, expenditure, and wealth. We develop these concepts at the national level to understand how flows of goods, services, income, and capital make the global macroeconomy work. We can then see how the smooth functioning of international finance can make countries better off by allowing them to lend and borrow. Along the way, we also find that financial interactions are not always so smooth. Defaults and other disruptions in financial markets can mean that the potential gains from globalization are not so easily realized in practice.

Deficits and Surpluses: The Balance of Payments

Do you keep track of your finances? If so, you probably follow two important figures: your income and expenditure. The difference between the two is an important number: if it is positive, you have a surplus; if it is negative, you have a deficit. The number tells you if you are living within or beyond your means. What would you do with a surplus? The extra money could be added to savings or used to pay down debt. How would you handle a deficit? You could run down your savings or borrow and go into deeper debt. Thus, imbalances between income and expenditure require you to engage in financial transactions with the world outside your household.

At the national level, we can make exactly the same kinds of economic measurements of **income, expenditure, deficit,** and **surplus,** many of which are important barometers of economic performance and the subject of heated policy debate. For example, Table 1-1 shows measures of U.S. national income and expenditure since 1991 in billions of U.S. dollars. At the national level, the income measure is called *gross national disposable income*; the expenditure measure is called *gross national expenditure*. The difference between the two is a key macroeconomic aggregate called the *current account*.

Since posting a small surplus in 1991, the U.S. deficit on the current account (a negative number) has grown much larger and at times has approached $1 trillion per year, although it fell markedly in the latest recession. That is, U.S. income has not been high enough to cover U.S. expenditure in these years. How did the United States bridge this deficit? It engaged in financial transactions with the outside world and borrowed the difference, just as households do.

TABLE 1-1

Income, Expenditure, and the Current Account The table shows data for the United States from 1990 to 2009 in billions of U.S. dollars. During this period, in all but one year U.S. expenditure exceeded income, with the U.S. current account in deficit. The last (small) surplus was in 1991.

	Income Gross National Disposable Income	Expenditure Gross National Expenditure	Difference Current Account
1990	$5,801	$5,875	−$75
1991	5,992	5,984	+8
1992	6,342	6,388	−46
1993	6,667	6,746	−79
1994	7,085	7,200	−115
1995	7,415	7,520	−105
1996	7,839	7,953	−114
1997	8,332	8,462	−129
1998	8,794	8,998	−205
1999	9,354	9,645	−292
2000	9,952	10,362	−410
2001	10,286	10,678	−392
2002	10,642	11,094	−452
2003	11,142	11,658	−516
2004	11,868	12,492	−625
2005	12,638	13,379	−741
2006	13,399	14,197	−798
2007	14,078	14,802	−725
2008	14,441	15,149	−707
2009	14,256	14,686	−430

Source: U.S. National Income and Product Accounts, Tables 1.1.5 and 4.1, May 2010, bea.gov.

Because the world *as a whole* is a closed economy (we can't borrow from outer space, as yet), it is impossible for the world to run a deficit. If the United States is a net borrower, running a current account deficit with income less than expenditure, then the rest of the world must be a net lender to the United States, running surpluses with expenditure less than income. Globally, the world's finances must balance in this way, even if individual countries and regions have surpluses or deficits. Figure 1-3 shows the massive scale of some of these recent imbalances, dramatically illustrating the impact of financial globalization.

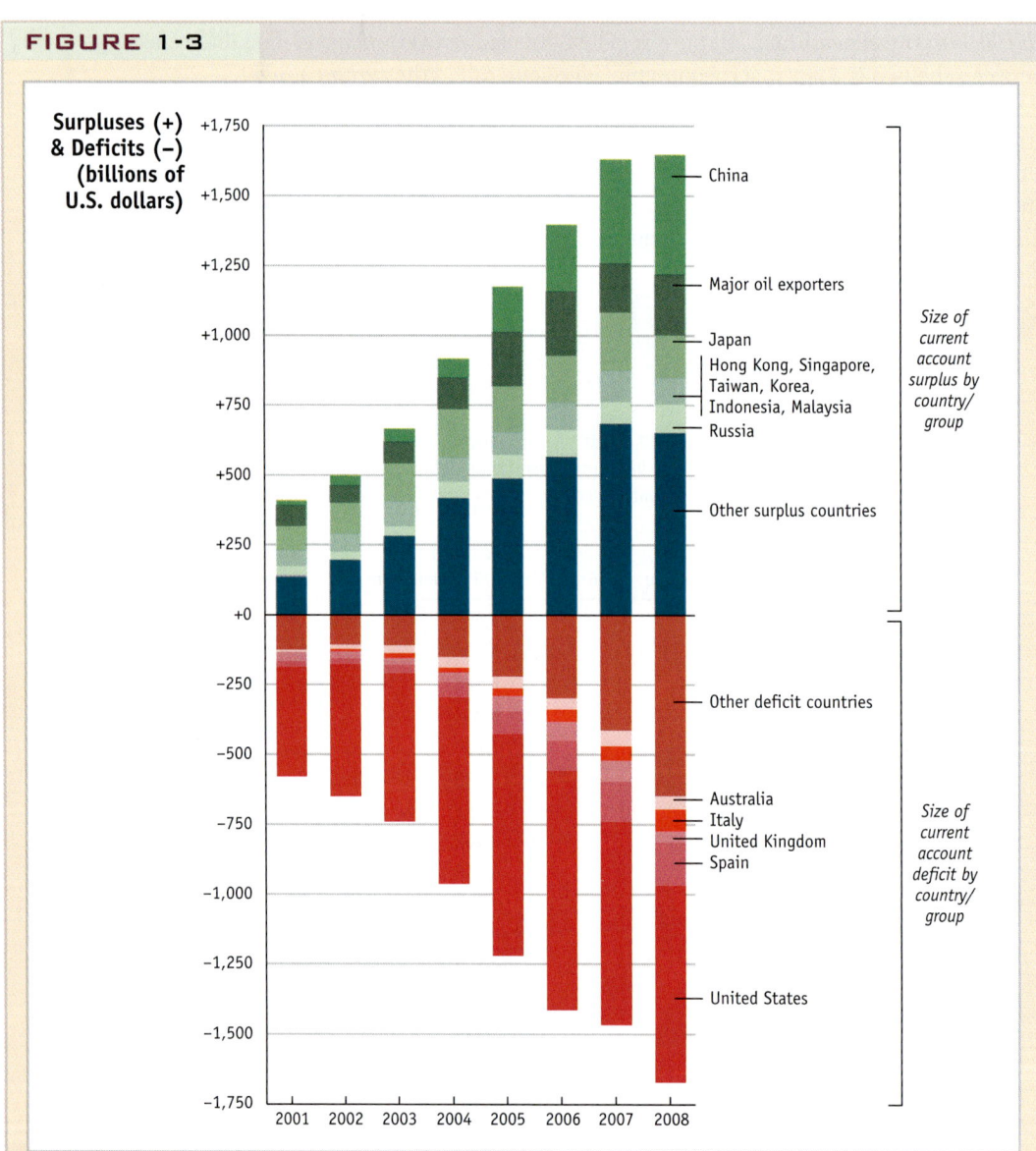

FIGURE 1-3

Global Imbalances Recently, the United States's current account deficit has accounted for over half of all deficits globally. Major offsetting surpluses have been seen in Asia (e.g., China and Japan) and in oil-exporting countries.

Source: IMF, International Financial Statistics.

Key Topics How do different international economic transactions contribute to current account imbalances? How are these imbalances financed? How long can they persist? Why are some countries in surplus and others in deficit? What role do current account imbalances perform in a well-functioning economy? Why are these imbalances the focus of so much policy debate?

Debtors and Creditors: External Wealth

To understand the role of wealth in international financial transactions, we revisit our household analogy. Your total **wealth** or net worth is equal to your assets (what others owe you) minus your liabilities (what you owe others). When you run a surplus, and save money (buying assets or paying down debt), your total wealth, or net worth, tends to rise. Similarly, when you have a deficit and borrow (taking on debt or running down savings), your wealth tends to fall. We can use this analysis to understand the behavior of nations. From an international perspective, a country's net worth is called its *external wealth* and it equals the difference between its foreign assets (what it is owed by the rest of the world) and its foreign liabilities (what it owes to the rest of the world). Positive external wealth makes a country a creditor nation (other nations owe it money); negative external wealth makes it a debtor nation (it owes other nations money).

Changes in a nation's external wealth can result from imbalances in its current account: external wealth rises when a nation has a surplus, and falls when it has a deficit, all else equal. For example, a string of U.S. current account deficits, going back to the 1980s, has been a major factor in the steady decline in U.S. external wealth, as shown in Figure 1-4, panel (a). The United States was generally a creditor nation until the mid-1980s when it became a debtor nation. By the end of 2009, the United States was the world's largest debtor, with external wealth equal to −$2,738 billion.[5] Argentina, another country with persistent current account deficits in the 1990s, also saw its external wealth decline, as panel (b) shows.

A closer look at these figures shows that there must be other factors that affect external wealth besides expenditure and income. For example, in years in which the United States ran deficits, its external wealth sometimes went up, not down. How can this be? Let us return to the household analogy. If you have ever invested in the stock market, you may know that even in a year when your expenditure exceeds your income, you may still end up wealthier because the value of your stocks has risen. For example, if you run a deficit of $1,000, but the value of your stocks rises by $10,000, then, on net, you are $9,000 wealthier. If the stocks' value falls by $10,000, your wealth will fall by $11,000. Again, what is true for households is true for countries: their external wealth can be affected **capital gains** (or, if negative, losses) on investments, so we need to think carefully about the complex causes and consequences of external wealth.

We also have to remember that a country can gain not only by having the value of its assets rise but also by having the value of its liabilities fall. Sometimes, liabilities fall because of market fluctuations; at other times they fall as a result of a deliberate action such as a nation deciding to default on its debts. For example, in 2002 Argentina announced a record default on its government debt by offering to pay about 30¢ for each dollar of debt in private hands. The foreigners who held most of this debt lost about $55 billion. At the same time, Argentina gained about $55 billion in external wealth, as

---

[5] Based on preliminary data released by bea.gov on June 25, 2010.

FIGURE 1-4

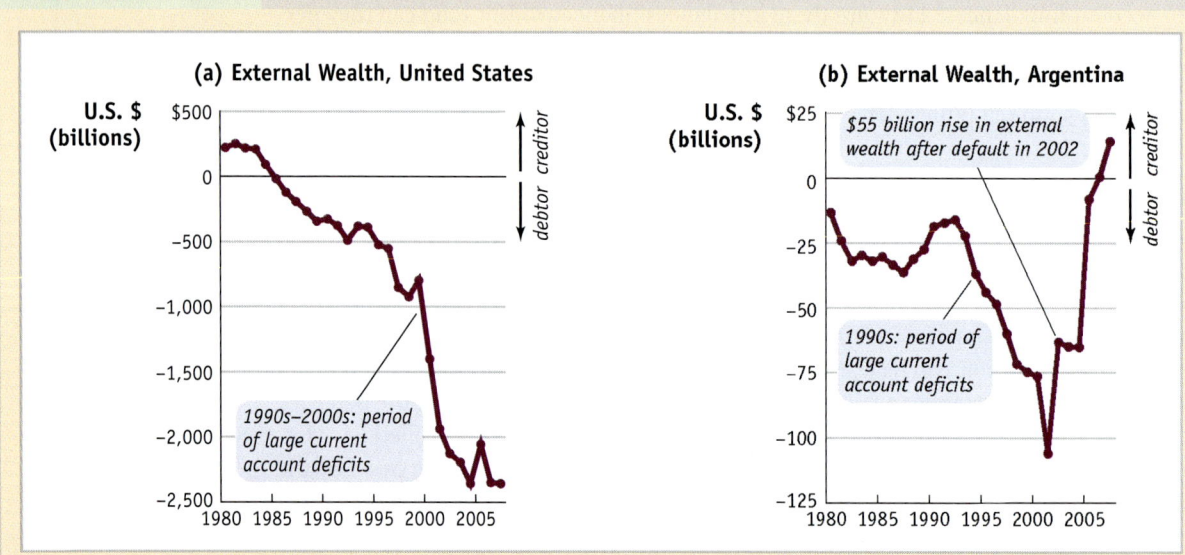

External Wealth A country's net credit position with the rest of the world is called external wealth. The time series charts show levels of external wealth from 1980 to 2007 for the United States in panel (a) and Argentina in panel (b). All else equal, deficits cause external wealth to fall; surpluses (and defaults) cause it to rise.

Source: Philip R. Lane and Gian Maria Milesi-Ferretti, 2007, "The External Wealth of Nations Mark II: Revised and Extended Estimates of Foreign Assets and Liabilities, 1970–2004," Journal of International Economics, 73(2), 223–250 (and updates).

shown by the sudden jump in Figure 1-4, panel (b). Thus, you don't have to run a surplus to increase external wealth—external wealth rises not only when creditors are paid off but also when they are blown off.

Key Topics What forms can a nation's external wealth take and does the composition of wealth matter? What explains the level of a nation's external wealth and how does it change over time? How important is the current account as a determinant of external wealth? How does it relate to the country's present and future economic welfare?

Darlings and Deadbeats: Defaults and Other Risks

The 2002 Argentine government's debt default was by no means unusual. The following countries (among many others) have defaulted (sometimes more than once) on private creditors since 1980: Argentina (twice), Chile, Dominican Republic (twice), Ecuador, Indonesia, Mexico, Nigeria, Pakistan, Peru (twice), Philippines, Russia (twice), South Africa (twice), Ukraine, and Uruguay (twice).[6] Dozens more countries could be added to the list if we expanded the definition of default to include the inability to make payments on loans from international financial institutions like the World Bank. (These debts may be continually rolled over, thus avoiding default by a technicality. In some cases, such loans are eventually forgiven, so they do not fall into the "default" category.)

---

[6] The list is limited to privately issued bond and bank debts since 1980. Data from Eduardo Levy-Yeyati and Ugo G. Panizza, "The Elusive Costs of Sovereign Defaults," CIF Working Paper No. 11/2006.

Defaults highlight a peculiar risk of international finance: creditors may be poorly protected in foreign jurisdictions. Sovereign governments can repudiate debt without legal penalty or hurt creditors in other ways such as by taking away their assets or changing laws or regulations after investments have already been made.

International investors try to avoid these risks as much as possible by careful assessment and monitoring of debtors. For example, any financial misbehavior by a nation or firm usually ends up on a credit report: a "grade-A" credit score means easy access to low interest loans; a "grade-C" score means more limited credit and very high interest rates. Advanced countries usually have good credit ratings, but emerging markets often find themselves subject to lower ratings.

In one important type of credit rating, countries are also rated on the quality of the bonds they issue to raise funds. Such bonds are rated by agencies such as Standard and Poor (S&P): bonds rated BBB– or higher are considered high-grade or *investment-grade* bonds and bonds rated BB+ and lower are called *junk bonds*. Poorer ratings tend to go hand in hand with higher interest rates. The difference between the interest paid on a safe "benchmark" U.S. Treasury bond and the interest paid by on a bond issued by a nation associated with greater risk is called **country risk.** Thus, if U.S. bonds pay 3% and another country pays 5% per annum on its bonds, the country risk is +2%.

For example, on June 21, 2010, the *Financial Times* reported that relatively good investment-grade governments such as Poland (grade A–) and Mexico (BBB) carried a country risk of +1.88% and +1.36% respectively, relative to U.S. Treasuries. Governments with junk-bond grades such as Colombia (grade BB+) and Turkey (BB+) had to pay higher interest rates, with a country risk of 2.16% and 2.64%, respectively. Finally, a country still considered to be technically in default, Argentina (grade D) had bonds trading so cheaply they carried a massive +33% of country risk.

Key Topics   Why do countries default? And what happens when they do? What are the determinants of risk premiums? How do risk premiums affect macroeconomic outcomes such as output and exchange rates?

Summary and Plan of Study

International flows of goods, services, income, and capital allow the global macroeconomy to operate. In our course of study, we build up our understanding gradually, starting with basic accounting and measurement, then moving on to the causes and consequences of imbalances in the flows and the accumulations of debts and credits. Along the way, we learn about the gains from financial globalization, as well as some of its potential risks.

In Chapter 5, we learn how international transactions enter into a country's national income accounts. Chapter 6 considers the helpful functions that imbalances can play in a well-functioning economy in the long run, and shows us the potential long-run benefits of financial globalization. Chapter 7 then explores how imbalances play a role in short-run macroeconomic adjustment and in the workings of monetary and fiscal policies that are used to manage a nation's aggregate demand. In Chapter 8, we learn that assets traded internationally are often denominated in different currencies, then see how wealth can be sensitive to exchange rate changes and what macroeconomic effects this might have. Chapter 9 examines the implications of risk premiums for exchange rates, and shows that exchange rate crises and default crises are linked. Chapter 11 explores in more detail topics such as global imbalances and default.

3 Government and Institutions: Policies and Performance

In theory, one could devise a course of study in international economics without reference to government, but the result might not shed much light on reality. As we know from other courses in economics, and as we have already started to see in this chapter, government actions influence economic outcomes in many ways by making decisions about exchange rates, macroeconomic policies, whether to pay (or not pay) their debts, and so on.

To gain a deeper understanding of the global macroeconomy, we can look at government activity on several distinct levels. In the traditional way we will study **policies,** which refers to direct government actions, including familiar textbook topics like monetary and fiscal policy. However, economists also consider the broader context of rules and norms, or **regimes** in which policy choices are made. At the broadest level, research also focuses on **institutions,** a term that refers to the overall legal, political, cultural, and social structures that influence economic and political actions.

To conclude this brief introduction to international macroeconomics, we highlight three important features of the broad macroeconomic environment that will play an important role in the remainder of this book: the rules that a government decides to apply to restrict or allow capital mobility; the decision that a government makes between a fixed and a floating exchange rate regime; and the institutional foundations of economic performance, such as the quality of governance that prevails in a country.

Integration and Capital Controls: The Regulation of International Finance

The United States is seen as one of the most financially open countries in the world, fully integrated into the global capital market. This is mostly true, but in recent years the U.S. government has blocked some foreign investment in ports, oil, and airlines. These are exceptional cases in the United States, but in many countries there are numerous, severe restrictions on cross-border financial transactions.

It is important to remember that globalization does not occur in a political vacuum. Globalization is often viewed as a technological phenomenon, a process driven by innovations in transport and communications such as container shipping and the Internet. But international economic integration has also occurred because some governments have allowed it to happen. In the past 60 years, international trade has grown as trade barriers have been slowly dismantled. More recently, many nations have encouraged international capital movement by lifting restrictions on financial transactions.

Figure 1-5 documents some of the important features of the trend toward financial globalization since 1970. Panel (a) employs an index of financial openness, where 0% means fully closed with tight capital controls and 100% means fully open with no controls. The index is compiled from measures of restriction on cross-border financial transactions. The average value of the index is shown for three groups of countries that will figure often in our analysis:

- **Advanced countries**—countries with high levels of income per person that are well integrated into the global economy
- **Emerging markets**—mainly middle-income countries that are growing and becoming more integrated into the global economy
- **Developing countries**—mainly low-income countries that are not yet well integrated into the global economy

FIGURE 1-5

(a) Increase in Financial Openness

(b) Increase in Financial Transaction

Financial Globalization Since the 1970s, many restrictions on international financial transactions have been lifted, as shown by the time series chart in panel (a). The volume of transactions has also increased dramatically, as shown in panel (b). These trends have been strongest in the advanced countries, followed by the emerging markets and the developing countries.

Sources: Philip R. Lane and Gian Maria Milesi-Ferretti, 2007, "The External Wealth of Nations Mark II: Revised and Extended Estimates of Foreign Assets and Liabilities, 1970–2004," Journal of International Economics 73(2), 223–250 (and updates); Menzie D. Chinn and Hiro Ito, 2006, "What Matters for Financial Development? Capital Controls, Institutions, and Interactions," Journal of Development Economics, 81(1), 163–192 (and updates). Country classifications are an extended version of those developed by M. Ayhan Kose, Eswar Prasad, Kenneth S. Rogoff, and Shang-Jin Wei, 2006, "Financial Globalization: A Reappraisal," NBER Working Paper No. 12484.

Using these data to gauge policy changes over the past three decades, we can see that the trend toward financial openness started first, and went the furthest, in the advanced countries, with a rapid shift toward openness evident in the 1980s, when many countries abolished capital controls that had been in place since World War II. We can also see that in the 1990s, emerging markets also started to liberalize financially and, to a lesser degree, so did some developing countries.

What were the consequences of these policy changes? Panel (b) looks at some economic outcomes and measures the extent of cross-border financial transactions by adding up total foreign assets and liabilities (expressed as a fraction of output) for the three country groups. As the world became more financially open, the extent of cross-border financial transactions increased by a factor of 10 or more. As one might expect, this trend has gone the furthest in the more financially open advanced countries, but the emerging markets and developing countries follow a similar path.

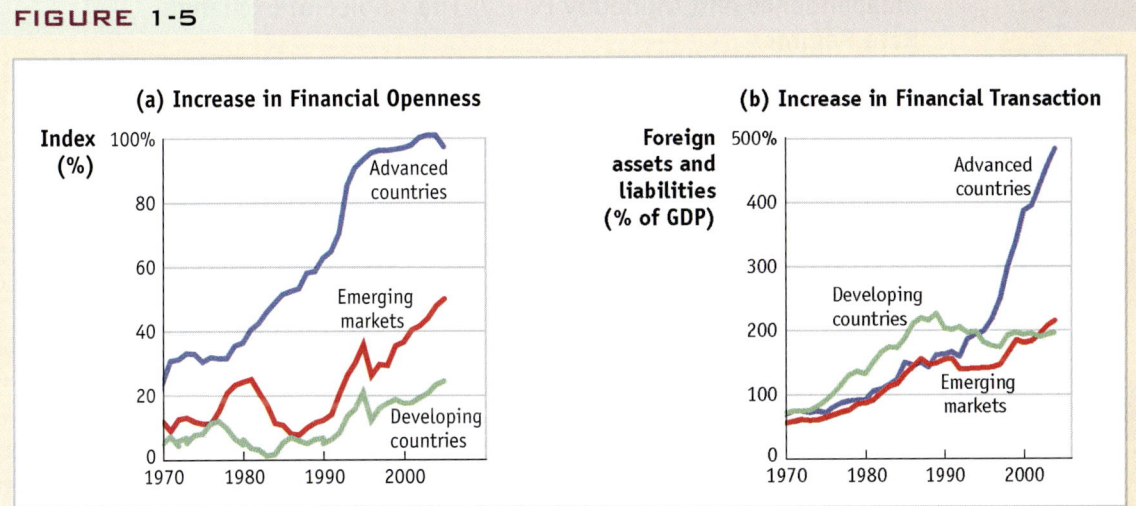

Evading control: For years, Zimbabwe imposed capital controls. In theory, U.S. dollars could be traded for Zimbabwe dollars only through official channels at an official rate. On the street, the reality was different.

Key Topics Why have so many countries made the choice to pursue policies of financial openness? What are the potential economic benefits of removing capital controls and adopting such liberalization policies? If there are benefits, why has this policy change been so slow to occur since the 1970s? Are there any potential costs that offset the benefits? If so, can capital controls benefit the country that imposes them?

Lithuanians and Letts do it . . . and others are falling in love with the euro, too. These are designs of euro coins for six current or future members (top to bottom): Cyprus, Estonia, Latvia, Lithuania, Malta, and Slovakia.

Independence and Monetary Policy: The Choice of Exchange Rate Regimes

There are two broad categories of exchange rate behavior: fixed regimes and floating regimes. How common is each type? Figure 1-6 shows that there are many countries operating under each kind of regime. Because fixed and floating are both common regime choices, we have to understand both.

The choice of exchange rate regime is a major policy problem. If you have noticed the attention given by journalists and policy makers in recent years to the exchange rate movements of the dollar, euro, yen, pound, yuan, and other currencies, you know that these are major important issues in debates on the global economy.

Exploring the evidence on exchange rate fluctuations, their origins, and their impact is a major goal of this book. On an intuitive level, whether we are confused travelers fumbling to change money at the bank or importers and exporters trying to conduct business in a predictable way, we have a sense that exchange rate fluctuations, especially if drastic, can impose real economic costs. If every country fixed its exchange rates, we could avoid those costs. Or, taking the argument to an extreme, if we had a single world currency, we might think that all currency-related transaction costs could be avoided. With more than 150 different currencies in existence today, however, we are very far from such a monetary utopia!

The existence of multiple currencies in the world dates back centuries, and for a state to possess its own currency has long been viewed as an almost essential aspect of sovereignty. Without control of its own national currency, a government's freedom to pursue its own monetary policy is sacrificed automatically. However, even with your own currency, it still remains to be seen how beneficial monetary independence is.

Despite the profusion of currencies, we also see newly emerging forms of monetary organization. Some groups of countries have sought to simplify their transactions through the adoption of a **common currency** with shared policy responsibility. The most notable example is the Eurozone, a subset of the European Union that in 2009 comprised 16 countries, but with more members expected to join soon. Still other countries have chosen to use currencies over which they have no policy control, as with the recent cases of **dollarization** in El Salvador and Ecuador.

FIGURE 1-6

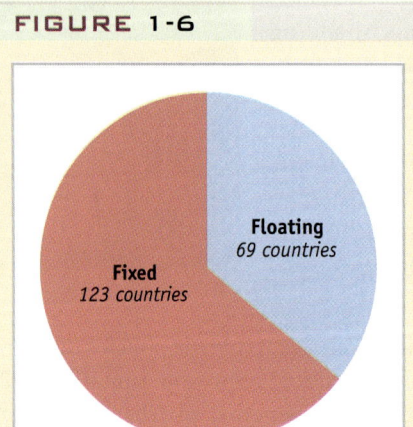

Exchange Rate Regimes The pie chart shows a classification of exchange rate regimes around the world using the most recent data for the year 2008.

Notes: The fixed category includes countries with no separate legal tender (46 countries), currency boards (7), other fixed pegs (58), pegs within horizontal bands (2), crawling pegs (8), and crawling bands (2). The floating category includes managed floating with no predetermined path for the exchange rate (25) and independently floating (44).

Source: IMF and author's classification. See Figure 5-4 for details.

Key Topics Why do so many countries insist on the "barbarism" of having their own currency (as John Stuart Mill put it)? Why do some countries create a common currency or adopt another nation's currency as their own? Why do some of the countries that have kept their own currencies maintain a fixed exchange rate with another currency? And why do others permit their exchange rate to fluctuate over time, making a floating exchange rate their regime choice?

Institutions and Economic Performance: The Quality of Governance

Going beyond specific policy choices, economists also consider the broader institutional context in which such choices are made. The legal, political, social, cultural, ethical, and religious structures of a society set the environment for economic prosperity and stability, or poverty and instability.

Figure 1-7 shows evidence on the importance of the quality of institutions or "governance" using national measures on five dimensions: voice and accountability,

FIGURE 1-7

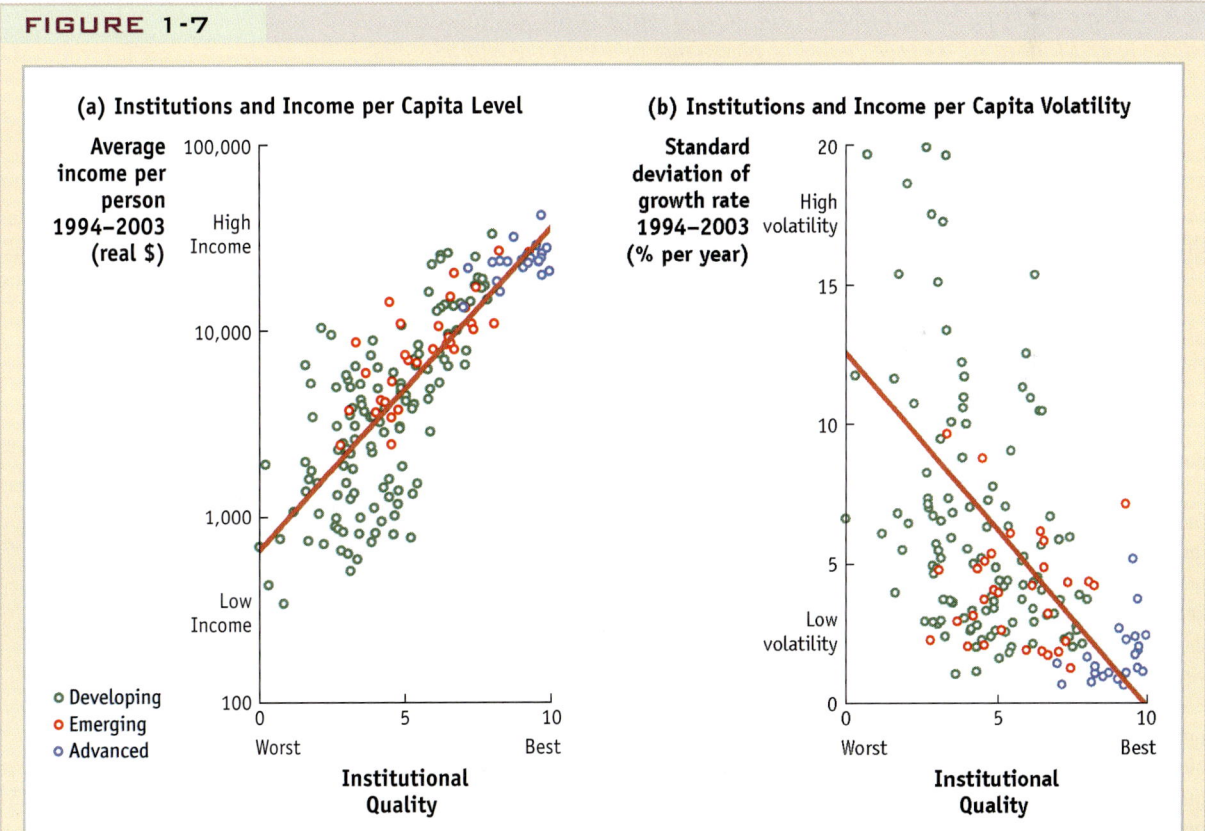

Institutions and Economic Performance The scatterplots show how an index measuring the quality of a country's institutions is positively correlated with the level of income per capita as shown in panel (a), and is inversely correlated with the volatility of income per capita as shown in panel (b). In each case, the line of best fit is shown.

Source: Real GDP per capita from Penn World Tables. Institutional quality from Daniel Kaufmann, Aart Kraay, and Massimo Mastruzzi, September 2006, "Governance Matters V: Governance Indicators for 1996–2005," World Bank Policy Research.

political stability, government effectiveness, regulatory quality, rule of law, and control of corruption. The figure shows that, across countries, an average or composite measure of all these dimensions is strongly correlated with economic outcomes (see **Headlines: The Wealth of Nations**).

HEADLINES

The Wealth of Nations

Social scientists have sought for centuries to understand the essential conditions that enable a nation to achieve prosperity. In The Wealth of Nations, *Adam Smith said: "Little else is requisite to carry a state to the highest degree of opulence from the lowest barbarism, but peace, easy taxes, and a tolerable administration of justice; all the rest being brought about by the natural course of things." The following article discusses the poor quality of governance in developing countries and the obstacle this poses to economic development.*

It takes 200 days to register a new business in Haiti and just two in Australia. This contrast perfectly encapsulates the gulf between one of the world's poorest countries and one of the richest. A sophisticated market economy is a uniquely powerful engine of prosperity. Yet, in far too many poor countries, the law's delays and the insolence of office prevent desperately needed improvements in economic performance.

That makes [the 2005] "World Development Report" among the most important the World Bank has ever produced.* It is about how to make market economies work. . . . The report is based on two big research projects: surveys of the investment climate . . . in 53 countries; and the "doing business" project, which identifies obstacles to business in 130 countries. . . . The argument starts with growth. As the report rightly notes: "With rising populations, economic growth is the only sustainable mechanism for increasing a society's standard of living."

Happily, "investment climate improvements in China and India have driven the greatest reductions in poverty the world has ever seen." . . . Governmental failure is the most important obstacle business faces. Inadequate enforcement of contracts, inappropriate regulations, corruption, rampant crime and unreliable infrastructure can cost 25 per cent of sales. This is more than three times what businesses typically pay in taxes. Similarly, when asked to enumerate the

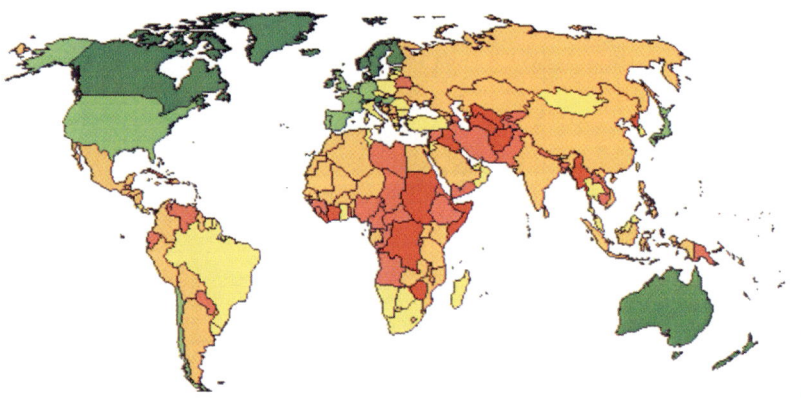

Green means grow: The map above shows the World Bank's composite Worldwide Governance Indicator in 2005. The index measures voice and accountability, political stability, government effectiveness, regulatory quality, rule of law, and control of corruption. Green indicates a country that is in the top 25% based on this measure, yellow next 25%, orange next 25%, and red bottom 25%. Dark green and dark red are the top and bottom 10%, respectively. The prosperity in Europe, North America, Australasia, and Japan coincides with the best institutions of governance; the poverty in so much of Africa and parts of Asia with the poorest ones.

Continued on next page

obstacles they face, businesses list policy uncertainty, macroeconomic instability, taxes and corruption at the head of the list. What do these have in common? Incompetence and malfeasance by governments is again the answer. . . .

In many developing countries, the requirement is not less government but more and better directed government. What does this involve? Four requirements are listed: a reduction in the "rent-seeking" that affects all countries but mars developing countries to an extreme extent; credibility in the making and execution of policy; the fostering of public trust and legitimacy; and the tailoring of policy responses to what works in local conditions.

One of the conclusions the report rightly draws from this list is that reform is not a one-off event but a process. What is involved is not just discrete and well-known policy changes (such as lower tariffs) but the fine-tuning of policy and the evolution of institutions. This is why, it suggests, the credibility of the government's journey, as in China, may be more important than the details of policy at each stage along the way.

Turning these broad objectives into specific policy is a tricky business. The Bank describes its core recommendation as "delivering the basics." These are: stability and security, which includes protection of property. . . , facilitating contract enforcement, curbing crime and compensating for expropriation; better regulation and taxation, which means focusing intervention where it is needed, broadening the tax base and lowering tax rates, and reducing barriers to trade; better finance and infrastructure, which requires both more competition and better regulation; and transforming labour market regulation, to foster skills, while avoiding the counterproductive interventions that so often destroy employment in the formal sector. . . .

The world's wealthy countries can also help by lifting their many barriers to imports from developing countries and by targeting aid on improving the investment climate.

Governments then are both the disease and the cure. This is why development is so hard and so slow. The big advance is in the richness of our understanding of what makes an economy thrive. But that understanding also demonstrates the difficulties. The Bank's recognition of the nature of the disease is at least a first step towards the cure.

---

*A Better Investment Climate for Everyone, World Development Report 2005. *Oxford University Press and the World Bank.*

Source: Martin Wolf, "Sweep Away the Barriers to Growth," Financial Times, *October 5, 2004.*

First, we see that better institutions are correlated with more **income per capita** in panel (a). A government that is unaccountable, unstable, ineffective, capricious, corrupt, and not based on laws is unlikely to encourage commerce, business, investment, or innovation. The effects of institutions on economic prosperity are very large. In the advanced countries at the top right of the figure, income per person is more than 50 times larger than in the poorest developing countries at the bottom left, probably the largest gap between rich and poor nations we have ever seen in history. Economists refer to this unequal outcome as "The Great Divergence."

We also see that better institutions are correlated with less **income volatility** (i.e., smaller fluctuations in the growth of income per capita, measured by the standard deviation). This result is shown in panel (b) and may also reflect the unpredictability of economic activity in poorly governed economies. There may be periodic shifts in political power, leading to big changes in economic policies. Or there may be internal conflict between groups that sporadically breaks out and leads to conflict over valuable economic resources. Or the state may be too weak to ensure that essential policies to stabilize the economy (such as bank regulation) are carried out.

Recent research has documented these patterns and has sought to show that causality runs from institutions to outcomes and to explore the possible sources of institutional variation. Institutional change is typically very slow, taking decades or even centuries, because vested interests may seek to block efficiency-enhancing reforms. Thus, as the institutional economist Thorstein Veblen famously pointed out, "Institutions are products of the past process, are adapted to past circumstances, and are therefore never in full accord with the requirements of the present." Consequently, influential recent research seeks to find deep historical origins for the divergence of institutions (and hence incomes), including factors such as the following:

- Actions of colonizing powers (helpful in setting up good institutions in areas settled by Europeans but harmful in tropical areas where Europeans did not transplant their own institutions, but instead supported elites with a strong interest in extracting revenue or resources);
- Types of legal codes that different countries developed (the British common law generally resulting in better outcomes than codes based on continental civil law);
- Resource endowments (tropical regions being more suitable for slave-based economies, elite rule, and high inequality; temperate regions being more suited to small-scale farming, decentralized democracy, and better governance).[7]

Key Topics Governance matters: it explains large differences between countries in their economic outcomes. Poor governance generally means that a country is poorer and is subject to more macroeconomic shocks. It may also be subject to more political shocks and a general inability to conduct policy in a reliable and consistent way. These characteristics force us to think carefully about the formulation of optimal policies and policy regimes in rich and poor countries. One size may not fit all, and policies that work well in a stable well-governed country may be less successful in an unstable developing country with poor governance.

Summary and Plan of Study

The functioning of the global macroeconomy is affected in many ways by the actions of governments. Throughout the book, we must pay attention to the possible actions that governments might take and try to understand their possible causes and consequences.

Chapter 4 explores the finding that if a country is financially open, then a fixed exchange rate is incompatible with monetary policy autonomy. Because both goals may be desirable, policy makers are often reluctant to face up to the difficult trade-offs implied by financial globalization. Chapter 6 explores the economic rationales for financial liberalization: if financial openness has clear economic benefits, why are countries slow to liberalize? We explore exchange rate regime choice in detail in

---

[7] Daron Acemoglu, Simon Johnson, and James A. Robinson, December 2001, "The Colonial Origins of Comparative Development: An Empirical Investigation," *American Economic Review*, 91(5), 1369–1401. Stanley L. Engerman and Kenneth L. Sokoloff, 1997, "Factor Endowments, Institutions, and Differential Paths of Growth among New World Economies: A View from Economic Historians of the United States," in Stephen Haber, ed., *How Latin America Fell Behind* (Stanford, CA: Stanford University Press). Rafael La Porta, Florencio Lopez-de-Silanes, Andrei Shleifer and Robert Vishny, April 1999, "The Quality of Government," *Journal of Law, Economics and Organization*, 15(1), 222–279.

Chapter 8 and study the trade-offs involved. Then, in Chapter 9, we study crises, and find that if a country's policy makers cling to fixed exchange rates, there is a risk of suffering costly crises. The remarkable Euro project, discussed in Chapter 10, throws these issues into sharper perspective in the one region of the world where economic integration has arguably progressed the furthest in recent decades. The main lessons of our study are that policy makers need to acknowledge trade-offs, formulate sensible goals, and exercise careful judgment when deciding when and how to financially open their economies. Sadly, history shows that, all too often, they don't.

4 Conclusions

Today's global macroeconomy is an economic system characterized by increasingly integrated markets for goods, services, and capital. To effectively study macroeconomic outcomes in this context, we must understand the economic linkages between different countries—their currencies, their trade, their capital flows, and so on. Only then can we begin to understand some of the most important economic phenomena in the world today, such as the fluctuations in currencies, the causes of crises, the determinants of global imbalances, the problems of economic policy making, and the origins of the growing gap between rich and poor countries.

KEY POINTS

1. Countries have different currencies, and the price at which these currencies trade is known as the exchange rate. In learning what determines this exchange rate and how the exchange rate is linked to the rest of the economy, we confront various questions: Why do some countries have fixed exchange rates and others floating? Why do some go from one to the other, often in response to a crisis? Why do some countries have no currency of their own?

2. When countries are financially integrated, it allows them to decouple their level of income from their level of expenditure; the difference between the two is the current account. An important goal is to understand what determines the current account and how the current account is linked to the rest of a nation's economy. Along the way, we learn how a country's current account affects its wealth, how its credits and debts are settled, and how the current account changes.

3. Countries differ in the quality of their policy choices and in the quality of the deeper institutional context in which policies are made. In studying international macroeconomic interactions and events, it is essential to understand how policy regimes and institutions affect policy choices and economic outcomes. How does quality of governance affect economic outcomes? Why might some policies, such as a fixed exchange rate, work better in some contexts than others? Do country characteristics affect the costs and benefits of financial globalization?

KEY TERMS

fixed exchange rate, p. 4
floating exchange rate, p. 4
exchange rate crisis, p. 5
default, p. 5
International Monetary Fund (IMF), p. 5
World Bank, p. 5
income, p. 9
expenditure, p. 9
deficit, p. 9
surplus, p. 9
wealth, p. 11
capital gains, p. 11
country risk, p. 13
policies, p. 14
regimes, p. 14
institutions, p. 14
advanced countries, p. 14
emerging markets, p. 14
developing countries, p. 14
common currency, p. 16
dollarization, p. 16
income per capita, p. 19
income volatility, p. 19

PROBLEMS

1. The data in Table 1-1 end in 2009. Visit the U.S. Bureau of Economic Analysis at www.bea.gov to find information for the latest full calendar year (or for the last four quarters). What is the latest estimate of the size of the annual U.S. current account deficit in billions of dollars?

2. The data in Figure 1-1 end in 2010. Visit www.oanda.com and download data on the same exchange rates (yuan per dollar and dollar per euro) for the past 12 months. What are the rates today? What were they a year ago? By what percentage amount did the rates change? At the OANDA website, click on "Currency Tools" and then "FXGraph" and use the tool to plot the last year of data for each exchange rate. Do you think the rates are floating or fixed? Why?

3. The data in Figure 1-3 end in the year 2008. Find the IMF's World Economic Outlook Databases. (*Hint:* Google "World Economic Outlook Databases.") Use this interactive tool to obtain the latest data on current accounts in U.S. dollars for all countries (actual data or IMF estimates). Which countries had the 10 largest deficits last year? Which countries had the 10 largest surpluses last year?

4. Visit the *Financial Times* website (at www.ft.com click on "Market data") to download data for country risk today. (*Hint:* Google "FT High yield emerging markets.") Which three emerging market countries have the highest spreads on their U.S. dollar debt? Which three have the lowest?

5. The map at the end of the chapter shows the World Bank's composite governance indicator. The World Bank has prepared other indicators to measure institutional differences among countries. Use the Internet to find the World Bank's "Ease of Doing Business Map." (*Hint:* Again, use Google.) Do you notice a correlation between the ease of doing business and the overall governance indicator? Can you find countries that rank high on the Ease of Doing Business indicator but low on the governance indicator? Are these countries rich or poor? (*Hint:* Look up their GNI per person at the World Bank by Googling "world bank gni per capita.")

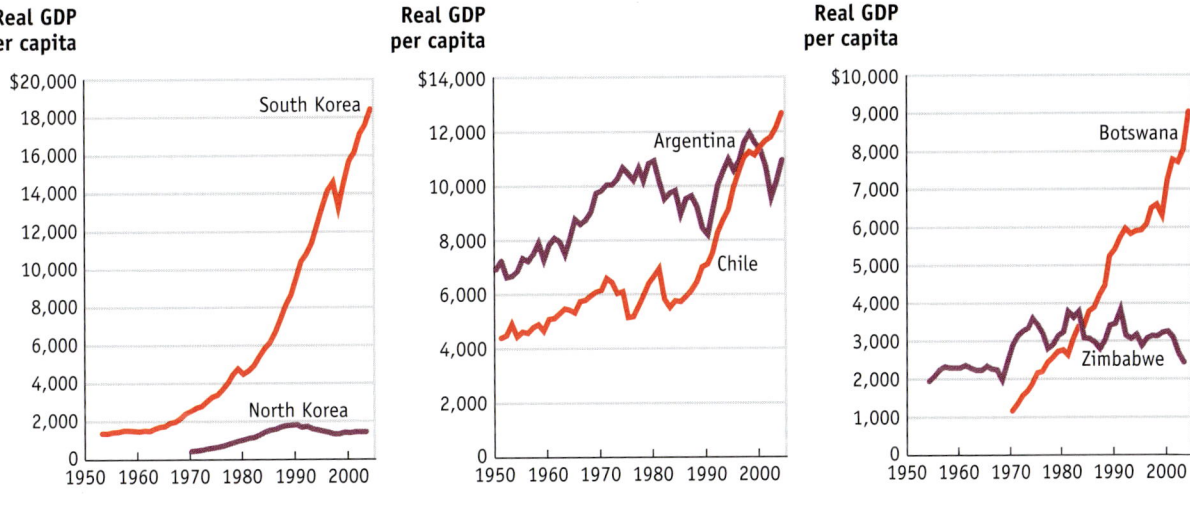

	Control of Corruption	Government Effectiveness	Political Stability and Absence of Violence	Rule of Law	Regulatory Quality	Voice and Accountability
South Korea	0.37	0.63	0.49	0.64	0.47	0.76
North Korea	−0.93	−1.10	0.66	1.08	−1.70	−2.02
Chile	1.56	1.34	0.85	1.31	1.38	0.56
Argentina	−0.34	0.28	0.48	0.17	0.45	0.44
Botswana	1.02	0.98	0.90	0.67	0.79	0.78
Zimbabwe	−0.87	−1.13	1.21	0.74	−1.61	−0.97

6. The charts above show the growth of real GDP per capita in three pairs of geographically adjacent countries: North and South Korea, Argentina and Chile, Zimbabwe and Botswana (using data from the Penn World Table).

   (a) Which country in each pair experienced faster growth in GDP per capita? Which one is now richest?

   (b) The World Bank's World Governance Indicators for each country in 2000 were as follows (higher is better):

   Based on these data, do you think institutions can explain the divergent outcomes in these countries? Explain. Why do you think it helps to compare countries that are physically contiguous?

7. Visit one of the many websites that lists all of the current exchange rates between different currencies around the world. Try a financial newspaper site such as www.ft.com (follow the links to "Market Data," and then "Currencies"), or try websites devoted to foreign exchange market data such as www.oanda.com or www.xe.com (dig down; don't just look at the major currency tables). According to these lists, how many distinct currencies exist around the world today? Are some currencies used in more than one country?

Introduction to Exchange Rates and the Foreign Exchange Market

The chapter on the Fall of the Rupee you may omit. It is somewhat too sensational.
  Miss Prism, in Oscar Wilde's *The Importance of Being Earnest*, 1895

The people who benefit from roiling the world currency market are speculators and as far as I am concerned they provide not much useful value.
  Paul O'Neill, U.S. Secretary of the Treasury, 2002

1. Exchange Rate Essentials
2. Exchange Rates in Practice
3. The Market for Foreign Exchange
4. Arbitrage and Spot Exchange Rates
5. Arbitrage and Interest Rates
6. Conclusions

Every few years, George, an American, takes a vacation in Paris. To make purchases in Paris, he buys foreign currency, or *foreign exchange*. He can purchase euros, the currency used in France, by trading his U.S. dollars for them in the *market for foreign exchange* at the prevailing market *exchange rate*. In 2003, 1 euro could be purchased for $1.10, so the €100 he spent on a night at the hotel cost him $110 in U.S. currency. In 2007, 1 euro cost $1.32, so each night at the same hotel (where the room price hadn't changed) made a $132 dent in his vacation budget. In 2010, 1 euro cost $1.24, not as much as in 2007, but still expensive enough in dollar terms to make George think about vacationing in northern California, where he reckoned he might find equally good hotels, restaurants, fine food, and wine at prices that were more affordable.

Tourists like George are not the only people affected by exchange rates. Exchange rates affect large flows of international trade by influencing the prices in different currencies of the imported goods and services we buy and the exported goods and services we sell. Foreign exchange also facilitates massive flows of international investment, which include the direct investments made by multinationals in overseas firms as well as the stock and bond trades made by individual investors and fund managers seeking to diversify their portfolios.

Individual foreign exchange transactions are far removed from deep macroeconomic and political consequences. In the aggregate, however, activity in the foreign exchange market can be responsible for "sensational" events (and we are not being ironic, unlike Oscar Wilde in the chapter opening quote) and can arouse strong passions (Paul O'Neill is only one of many to criticize the activities of foreign exchange traders). In the foreign exchange market, trillions of dollars are traded each day and the economic implications of shifts in the market can be dramatic. In times of crisis, the fates of nations and their leaders seem to hang, in part, on the state of the currency market. Why is that so?

In this chapter, we begin to study the nature and impact of activity in the foreign exchange market. We first survey exchange rate basics: the key definitions of exchange rates and related concepts. We then examine the evidence to see how exchange rates behave in the real world and establish some basic facts about exchange rate behavior that require explanation. We next look at the workings of the foreign exchange market, including the role of private participants as well as interventions by governments. Finally, we look in detail at how foreign exchange markets work, and we emphasize two key market mechanisms: *arbitrage* and *expectations*.

1 Exchange Rate Essentials

An **exchange rate** (E) is the price of some foreign currency expressed in terms of a home (or domestic) currency. Because an exchange rate is the relative price of two currencies, it may be quoted in either of two ways:

1. The number of home currency units that can be exchanged for one unit of foreign currency. For example, if the United States is considered home, the dollar/euro exchange rate might be $1.15 per euro (or 1.15 $/€). To buy one euro, you would have to pay $1.15.

2. The number of foreign currency units that can be exchanged for one unit of home currency. For example, the 1.15$/€ exchange rate can also be expressed as €0.87 per U.S. dollar (or 0.87 €/$). To buy one dollar, you would have to pay €0.87.

Knowing the format in which exchange rates are quoted is essential to avoid confusion, so we now establish a systematic rule, even if it is arbitrary.

Defining the Exchange Rate

It is common practice to quote the prices of items traded, whether goods or assets, as units of home currency per unit purchased. In the United States, coffee might be sold at 10 dollars per pound ($/lb); in France, at 20 euros per kilogram (€/kg).[1]

The usual way to quote the price of foreign currency is no different: units of home currency per unit of foreign currency. Confusion may arise because the price then depends on the perspective of the observer. Consider the dollar-euro exchange rate. For the U.S. citizen, who is accustomed to prices expressed as $/unit, the price of a foreign currency (say, the euro) is in terms of $/€. For someone in the Eurozone, however, the convention is to quote prices as €/unit, so €/$ would be the natural choice.

To avoid confusion, we must specify which country is the home country and which is foreign. Throughout the remaining chapters of this book, when we refer to a particular

---

[1] Coffee prices could also be quoted as 0.1 lb/$ or 0.05 kg/€, but this format is not the norm.

country's exchange rate, we will quote it in terms of units of home currency per units of foreign currency. For example, Denmark's exchange rate with the Eurozone is quoted as Danish krone per euro (or kr/€).

From now on, $E_{1/2}$ will denote the exchange rate in units of country 1 currency per unit of country 2 currency; it is the rate at which country 1's currency can be exchanged for one unit of country 2's currency. For example, $E_{\$/€}$ is the U.S. exchange rate (against the euro) in U.S. dollars per euro. In our previous example, $E_{\$/€}$ was 1.15 $/€.

We see different expressions of the same exchange rate all the time—even on the same page in the same publication! So it is important to keep things straight. Table 2-1 presents a typical display of exchange rate information as one might see it in the financial press.[2] Column (1) shows the reported price of U.S. dollars in various currencies (e.g., €/$); columns (2) and (3) show, respectively, the most recent price of British pounds sterling (e.g., $/£) and euros (e.g., $/€) on June 30, 2010.[3] Thus, the first three entries show the Canadian dollar's exchange rate against the U.S. dollar, the pound, and the euro. For comparison, columns (4) to (6) show the same rates one year earlier.

TABLE 2-1

Exchange Rate Quotations This table shows major exchange rates as they might appear in the financial media. Columns (1) to (3) show rates on June 30, 2010. For comparison, columns (4) to (6) show rates on June 30, 2009. For example, column (1) shows that on June 30, 2010, one U.S. dollar was worth 1.063 Canadian dollars, 6.081 Danish krone, 0.816 euros, and so on. The euro-dollar rates appear in bold type.

		EXCHANGE RATES ON JUNE 30, 2010			EXCHANGE RATES ON JUNE 30, 2009 ONE YEAR PREVIOUSLY		
		(1)	(2)	(3)	(4)	(5)	(6)
Country (currency)	Currency Symbol	Per $	Per £	Per €	Per $	Per £	Per €
Canada (dollar)	C$	1.063	1.590	1.302	1.161	1.913	1.629
Denmark (krone)	DKr	6.081	9.098	7.449	5.309	8.743	7.447
Euro (euro)	€	**0.816**	1.221	—	**0.713**	1.174	—
Japan (yen)	¥	88.49	132.39	108.39	96.49	158.90	135.34
Norway (krone)	NKr	6.503	9.729	7.966	6.437	10.600	9.028
Sweden (krona)	SKr	7.782	11.643	9.532	7.748	12.760	10.868
Switzerland (franc)	SFr	1.078	1.613	1.321	1.088	1.791	1.526
United Kingdom (pound)	£	0.668	—	0.819	0.607	—	0.852
United States (dollar)	$	—	1.496	**1.225**	—	1.647	**1.403**

Source: ft.com

---

[2] These are typically *midrange* or *central* rates—an end-of-day average of buying and selling rates from the market. As we discuss later in the chapter, such rates do not allow for the differences or *spreads*, between the prices at which currencies are bought and sold. In any market in which intermediaries are present, commissions and fees push buying prices above selling prices.
[3] The currency's price in terms of itself equals 1 and is omitted.

The four bold entries in this table correspond to the dollar-euro exchange rate. On June 30, 2010, for example, the euro was quoted at $1.225 per euro. According to our definition, this is the price from the U.S. perspective and it is sometimes called the *American terms*. Conversely, the dollar is quoted at €0.816 per dollar, the *European terms*.

We write these exchange rates using mathematical symbols as follows, with care given to the explicit expression of the relevant units:

$$E_{\$/€} = 1.225 = \text{U.S. exchange rate (American terms)}$$

$$E_{€/\$} = 0.816 = \text{Eurozone exchange rate (European terms)}$$

Just as there is complete equivalence when we express the relative price of coffee and dollars at 10 $/lb or 0.1 lb/$, the price of the euro in terms of dollars always equals the reciprocal (or inverse) of the price of dollars in terms of euros. Hence,

$$E_{\$/€} = \frac{1}{E_{€/\$}}$$

In our example,

$$1.225 = \frac{1}{0.816}$$

Similar calculations and notations apply to any pair of currencies.

Appreciations and Depreciations

Like many financial tables, Table 2-1 includes information on how prices have changed over time. Over the previous 12 months, the Eurozone exchange rate *increased* from $E_{€/\$} = 0.713$ a year ago to $E_{€/\$} = 0.816$ on June 30, 2010. The value of the euro relative to the dollar went down—more euros were needed to buy one dollar. This change is often described by saying that the euro got "weaker" or "weakened" against the dollar.

Symmetrically, the value of the dollar in euro terms also changed. We see this by computing the reciprocal American terms. Over the same year, the U.S exchange rate *decreased* from $E_{\$/€} = 1/0.713 = 1.403$ a year ago to $E_{\$/€} = 1/0.816 = 1.225$ on June 30, 2010. The value of the dollar relative to the euro went up—fewer dollars were needed to buy one euro. This change is often described by saying that the dollar got "stronger" or "strengthened" against the euro.

If one currency buys more of another currency, we say it has experienced an **appreciation**—its value has *risen*, *appreciated*, or *strengthened*. If a currency buys less of another currency, we say it has experienced a **depreciation**—its value has *fallen*, *depreciated*, or *weakened*.

In our example, we can understand appreciation and depreciation from both the U.S. and European perspective; this lesson generalizes to all other currency pairs.

In U.S. terms, the following holds true:

- When the U.S. exchange rate $E_{\$/€}$ *rises*, more dollars are needed to buy one euro. The price of one euro goes up in dollar terms, and the U.S. dollar experiences a depreciation.
- When the U.S. exchange rate $E_{\$/€}$ *falls*, fewer dollars are needed to buy one euro. The price of one euro goes down in dollar terms, and the U.S. dollar experiences an appreciation.

Similarly, in European terms, the following holds true:

- When the Eurozone exchange rate $E_{€/\$}$ *rises*, the price of one dollar goes up in euro terms and the euro experiences a depreciation.
- When the Eurozone exchange rate $E_{€/\$}$ *falls*, the price of one dollar goes down in euro terms and the euro experiences an appreciation.

If the dollar is appreciating against the euro, the euro must simultaneously be depreciating against the dollar. Because they are the reciprocal of each other, changes in $E_{\$/€}$ and $E_{€/\$}$ must always move in opposite directions.

It may seem confusing or counterintuitive that a fall in the U.S. exchange rate means the dollar is appreciating. Yet it is reasonable because we express the price of foreign currency in dollars, just as we express the prices of other goods. When the price of coffee falls from $10 to $9 per pound, it seems sensible to say that coffee is depreciating or falling in value—but relative to what? The dollars—the currency in which the price is denominated. Conversely, dollars are *appreciating* against coffee because it takes fewer dollars to buy the same amount of coffee! If we keep this analogy in mind, it makes sense that when the dollar price of a euro falls, the dollar has appreciated against the euro.

Exchange rate humor.

In addition to knowing whether a currency has appreciated or depreciated, we are often interested in the knowing the size of an appreciation or depreciation. To do this, we can calculate the proportional or fractional change in the foreign-currency value of the home currency. This proportional change is usually expressed in percentage terms.

In the previous example, we would describe these changes as follows:

- In 2009, at time t, the dollar value of the euro was $E_{\$/€,t} = \$1.403$.
- In 2010, at time $t + 1$, the dollar value of the euro was $E_{\$/€,t+1} = \$1.225$.
- The change in the dollar value of the euro was $\Delta E_{\$/€,t} = 1.225 - 1.403 = \$-0.178$.
- The percentage change was $\Delta E_{\$/€,t}/E_{\$/€,t} = -0.178/1.403 = -12.7\%$.
- Thus, the euro *depreciated* against the dollar by 12.7%.

Similarly, over the same year:

- In 2009, at time t, the euro value of the dollar was $E_{€/\$,t} = €0.713$.
- In 2010, at time $t + 1$, the euro value of the dollar was $E_{€/\$,t+1} = €0.816$.
- The change in the euro value of the dollar was $\Delta E_{€/\$,t} = 0.816 - 0.713 = €+0.103$.
- The percentage change was $\Delta E_{€/\$,t}/E_{€/\$,t} = +0.103/0.713 = +14.4\%$.
- Thus, the dollar *appreciated* against the euro by 14.4%.

Note that the size of one country's appreciation (here 14.4%) does not exactly equal the size of the other country's depreciation (here 12.7%). For small changes, however, the opposing movements are *approximately* equal. For example, if the

U.S. terms move slightly from $1.00 to $1.01 per euro, the European terms move from €1.00 to €0.99099; a 1% euro appreciation is approximately a 1% dollar depreciation.[4]

Multilateral Exchange Rates

Our discussion of exchange rates has focused on the simplest type of exchange rate between two countries or currencies, what economists refer to as a *bilateral* exchange rate. In reality, we live in a world of many countries and many currencies, and it is of great practical importance to ask whether a particular currency has strengthened or weakened not just against one other currency, but against other currencies in general.

The answer is not always obvious. For example, the U.S. dollar may be depreciating against some currencies, while remaining fixed or appreciating against others. To aggregate these different trends in bilateral exchange rates into one measure, economists calculate *multilateral* exchange rate changes for baskets of currencies using *trade weights* to construct an average of all the bilateral changes for each currency in the basket. The resulting measure is called the change in the **effective exchange rate**.

For example, suppose 40% of Home trade is with country 1 and 60% is with country 2; Home's currency appreciates 10% against 1 but depreciates 30% against 2. To calculate the change in Home's effective exchange rate, we multiply each exchange rate change by the corresponding trade share and then add up: (−10% · 40%) + (30% · 60%) = (−0.1 · 0.4) + (0.3 · 0.6) = −0.04 + 0.18 = 0.14 = +14%. In this example, Home's effective exchange rate has depreciated by 14%.

In general, suppose there are N currencies in the basket, and Home's trade with the N partners is Trade = Trade$_1$ + Trade$_2$ + . . . + Trade$_N$. Applying trade weights to each bilateral exchange rate change, the home country's effective exchange rate ($E_{\text{effective}}$) will change according to the following weighted average:

$$\frac{\Delta E_{\text{effective}}}{E_{\text{effective}}} = \underbrace{\frac{\Delta E_1}{E_1}\frac{\text{Trade}_1}{\text{Trade}} + \frac{\Delta E_2}{E_2}\frac{\text{Trade}_2}{\text{Trade}} + \ldots + \frac{\Delta E_N}{E_N}\frac{\text{Trade}_N}{\text{Trade}}}_{\text{Trade-weighted average of bilateral nominal exchange rate changes}}$$

Many discussions among policy makers and in the financial press focus on the effective exchange rate. An especially contentious topic in the last decade has been the path of the United States' effective exchange rate, shown in Figure 2-1. It is clear that, since

---

[4] In general, suppose that the home exchange rate is a, so one unit of home currency buys $1/a$ units of foreign currency. Now the home exchange rate depreciates to $b > a$, and one unit of home currency buys $1/b$ units of foreign currency, with $1/b < 1/a$. The size of the depreciation D of the home currency is

$$D = \left(\frac{1}{a} - \frac{1}{b}\right) \Big/ \left(\frac{1}{a}\right) = \left(1 - \frac{a}{b}\right) = \left(\frac{b-a}{b}\right)$$

Symmetrically, the foreign currency was initially worth a units of home currency but is now worth b. Thus, the size of the appreciation A of the foreign currency is

$$A = \frac{(b-a)}{a} = \frac{b}{a}D$$

Thus, the percentage appreciation A will be approximately equal to the percentage depreciation D when b/a is close to 1, or when b is approximately equal to a, that is, when the change in the exchange rate is small.

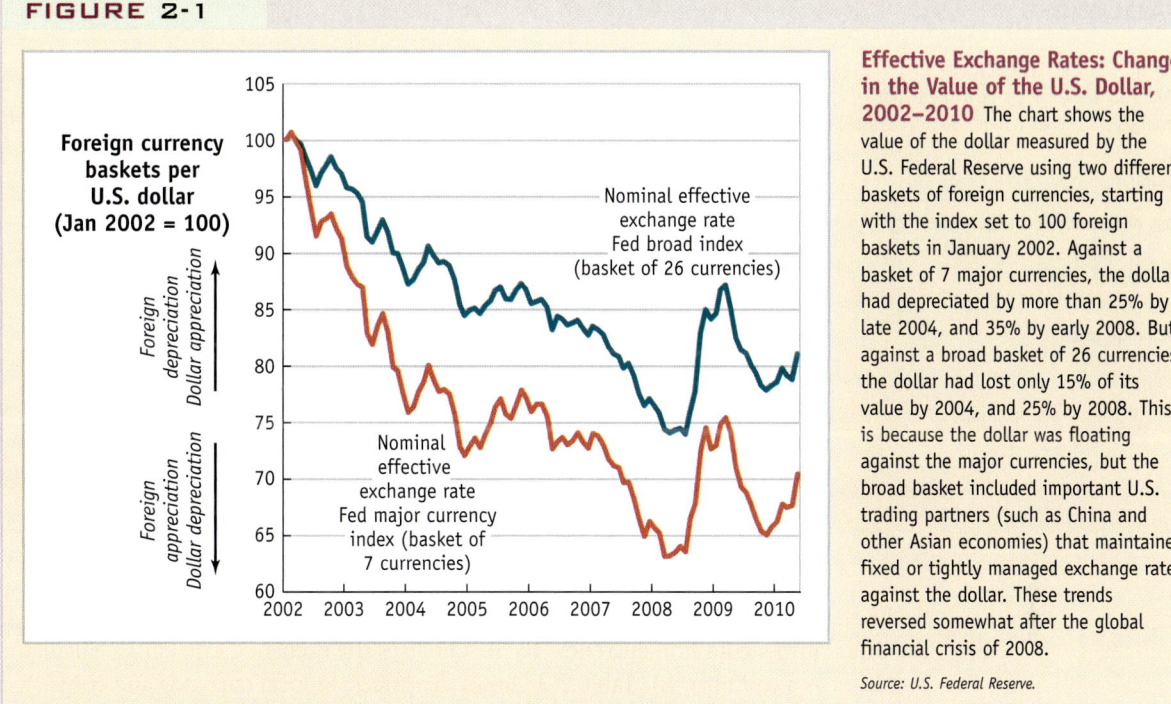

FIGURE 2-1

Effective Exchange Rates: Change in the Value of the U.S. Dollar, 2002–2010 The chart shows the value of the dollar measured by the U.S. Federal Reserve using two different baskets of foreign currencies, starting with the index set to 100 foreign baskets in January 2002. Against a basket of 7 major currencies, the dollar had depreciated by more than 25% by late 2004, and 35% by early 2008. But against a broad basket of 26 currencies, the dollar had lost only 15% of its value by 2004, and 25% by 2008. This is because the dollar was floating against the major currencies, but the broad basket included important U.S. trading partners (such as China and other Asian economies) that maintained fixed or tightly managed exchange rates against the dollar. These trends reversed somewhat after the global financial crisis of 2008.

Source: U.S. Federal Reserve.

2002, the U.S. dollar steadily has fallen in value against a basket of other currencies. It lost quite a lot of value against many well-known major currencies, such as the euro, the pound sterling, the Canadian dollar, and the Swiss franc. But on average, the weakening of the dollar was not as pronounced when measured against *all* U.S. trading partners. The simple reason for this was the fact that Japan and China, along with several other developing countries in Asia, sought to peg or control their exchange rates to limit their appreciation against the dollar. Thus in the figure, the downward trend for the broad basket of currencies is not as steep as that for the basket of seven major currencies.

Example: Using Exchange Rates to Compare Prices in a Common Currency

To make comparisons of prices across nations, we must convert prices to a common currency. The following examples show how we use exchange rates to accomplish this task.

James Bond is back from another mission and, what with all the explosions and shootouts, his wardrobe is looking ragged. He needs a new tuxedo. Bond will be in numerous cities On Her Majesty's Secret Service in the next few days, so he can shop around the globe. Although style is important, price is a key factor in Bond's choice, given the paltry MI6 clothing allowance. Should he visit a new tailor in Manhattan? Go back to his favorite cutter in Hong Kong? Or simply nip around the corner to Savile Row in London?

The London tailor sells a tux for £2,000; the Hong Kong shop is asking HK$30,000; and in New York, the going rate is $4,000. In the near future, when the decision must be made, these prices are fixed in their respective home currencies. Which tux will 007 choose?

TABLE 2-2

Using the Exchange Rate to Compare Prices in a Common Currency Now pay attention, 007! This table shows how the hypothetical cost of James Bond's next tuxedo in different locations depends on the exchange rates that prevail.

Scenario		1	2	3	4
Cost of the tuxedo in local currency	London	£2,000	£2,000	£2,000	£2,000
	Hong Kong	HK$30,000	HK$30,000	HK$30,000	HK$30,000
	New York	$4,000	$4,000	$4,000	$4,000
Exchange rates	HK$/£	15	16	14	14
	$/£	2.0	1.9	2.1	1.9
Cost of the tuxedo in pounds	London	£2,000	£2,000	£2,000	£2,000
	Hong Kong	£2,000	£1,875	£2,143	£2,143
	New York	£2,000	£2,105	£1,905	£2,105

To choose among goods priced in different currencies, Bond must first convert all the prices into a common currency; for this he uses the exchange rate (and a calculator disguised as a toothbrush). Table 2-2 shows the prices, in local currency and converted into pounds, under different hypothetical exchange rates.

Scenario 1 In the first column, the Hong Kong suit costs HK$30,000 and the exchange rate is HK$15 per £. Dividing HK$30,000 by 15, we find that this suit costs £2,000 in British currency. The U.S. suit has a price of $4,000, and at an exchange rate of $2 per pound we obtain a British currency price of £2,000. Here the exchange rates are such that all prices are the same when measured in a common currency (pounds). Bond has a difficult choice.

Scenario 2 Moving to the next column, the Hong Kong dollar has depreciated against the pound compared with scenario 1: it takes more HK$ (16 instead of 15) to buy £1. In contrast, the U.S. dollar has appreciated against the pound: it takes fewer dollars (1.9 instead of 2.0) to buy £1. At the new exchange rates, the cost of the New York tux has gone up to £2,105 (4,000/1.9), and the Hong Kong tux has fallen to £1,875 (30,000/16). Hong Kong now has the lowest price.

Scenario 3 Compared with scenario 1, the Hong Kong dollar has appreciated: it takes fewer $HK to buy £1 (14 instead of 15), and the price of the Hong Kong tux has risen to £2,143 (30,000/14). The U.S. dollar, on the other hand, has depreciated: it takes more dollars (2.1 instead of 2) to buy £1. With the dollar's depreciation, New York now has the best price of £1,905 (4,000/2.1).

Scenario 4 In this case, compared with scenario 1, the pound has depreciated against both of the other currencies, and they have each appreciated against the pound. It takes fewer Hong Kong dollars (14 instead of 15) and fewer U.S. dollars (1.9 instead of 2.0) to buy £1. Now London has the bargain price of £2,000 and the other cities have higher prices.

This example illustrates a key point. We assumed that while exchange rates may change, the prices of goods in each country are fixed in the short run (in domestic-currency terms). An economist would say the prices are *sticky* in the short run, and, as we see later, this is not an unreasonable assumption. Given that assumption, changes in exchange rates will cause changes in the common-currency prices of goods from different countries.

Generalizing The same logic applies to any exchange rate. All else equal, when the prices of goods are constant in each country, the following conclusions will apply:

- *Changes in the exchange rate cause changes in prices of foreign goods expressed in the home currency.*
- *Changes in the exchange rate cause changes in the relative prices of goods produced in the home and foreign countries.*
- *When the home country's exchange rate depreciates, home exports become less expensive as imports to foreigners, and foreign exports become more expensive as imports to home residents.*
- *When the home country's exchange rate appreciates, home exports become more expensive as imports to foreigners, and foreign exports become less expensive as imports to home residents.*

2 Exchange Rates in Practice

Having seen Table 2-1, it might be tempting to use the same figures as a guide to today's exchange rates between countries, but this would be a big mistake. Exchange rates fluctuate. They depreciate and appreciate. A lot. On a single day, in a matter of hours or even minutes, they can change substantially. Over a year, they move up and down, and may drift considerably in one direction or another. Any complete theory of exchange rate determination must account for observed behavior, so we should familiarize ourselves with the various patterns we seek to explain.

Exchange Rate Regimes: Fixed Versus Floating

Economists group different patterns of exchange rate behavior into categories known as **exchange rate regimes.** These regimes reflect choices made by governments, and the causes and consequences of exchange rate regimes are a major focus of our study.

There are two major regime types:

- **Fixed** (or **pegged**) exchange rate regimes are those in which a country's exchange rate fluctuates in a narrow range (or not at all) against some *base currency* over a sustained period, usually a year or longer. A country's exchange rate can remain rigidly fixed for long periods only if the government intervenes in the foreign exchange market in one or both countries.
- **Floating** (or **flexible**) exchange rate regimes are those in which a country's exchange rate fluctuates in a wider range, and the government makes no attempt to fix it against any base currency. Appreciations and depreciations may occur from year to year, each month, by the day, or every minute.

For example, earlier in the book we saw data for two of the most talked about exchange rates in the world today: the U.S. dollar–euro and the Chinese yuan–U.S. dollar rates. The dollar–euro rate fluctuated considerably and was said to be floating; the yuan–dollar rate held steady or changed very slowly and was said to be fixed.

However, the "fixed versus floating" classification is not without its problems. First, in practice, to judge whether a regime is fixed or floating, we have to decide where we draw the line between "narrow" and "wide" fluctuations. One rule of thumb is to use the size of annual variations (say, within ±2% or ±1%) as the sign of a fixed regime. Second, "fixed versus floating" is only a very broad description of exchange rate regimes. In reality, the distinctions are not so cut and dried. Fixed and floating provide important benchmarks throughout this book and deliver great insights, but we sometimes need more precise ways of describing *intermediate regimes*, as the following application illustrates.

APPLICATION

Recent Exchange Rate Experiences

If we spend a moment looking at recent exchange rate experiences in a variety of countries, we see not only some helpful illustrations of the differences between floating and fixed rate regimes but also some of the different varieties of fixed and floating behavior. We also encounter the phenomenon of regime change, in which one type of regime gives way to another, either smoothly or catastrophically.

Evidence from Developed Countries Figure 2-2 shows the daily exchange rates from 1996 to 2010 for various currency pairs. The top row shows the U.S. dollar exchange rate against two major currencies (the Japanese yen, the British pound) and against the currency of a neighboring country (the Canadian dollar, also called the *loonie* because it has a loon on it). The bottom row shows the exchange rate of the euro against the yen, the pound, and the Danish krone. In all six charts, the vertical scale varies by a factor of 2 from maximum to minimum, so all of these charts are comparable in terms of their representation of these exchange rates' volatility.

We can clearly see that the U.S. dollar is in a floating relationship with all three foreign currencies shown in the top row—the yen, pound, and loonie. How volatile are the exchange rates? The range of variation in each case is about the same, with the maximum being about one and a half times the minimum: the yen ranges from about $0.0065 to $0.0110, the pound from $1.3 to almost $2, the loonie from $0.6 to about $1. The movements between these peaks and troughs may take many months or years to occur, but the exchange rate also shows a great deal of short-run volatility, with lots of up-and-down movement from day to day. A floating regime of this sort is called a **free float**.

Similarly, the bottom row of Figure 2-2 shows that the euro floats against the yen and the pound. In the sixth and final chart, the Danish krone provides a contrast—an example of a fixed exchange rate in a developed country. Denmark is part of the European Union, but like Britain, it has kept its own national currency, at least for now, and does not use the euro as its currency. Unlike Britain, however, Denmark has fixed its exchange rate against the euro, keeping it very close to 7.44 krone per euro (0.134 euro per krone). There is only a tiny variation around this rate, no more than plus or minus 2%. This type of fixed regime is known as a **band**.

Evidence from Developing Countries Figure 2-3 shows the daily exchange rates against the U.S. dollar from 1996 to 2010 for some developing countries. Exchange rates in developing countries can be much more volatile than those in developed countries. The charts in the top row illustrate exchange rate behavior in three Asian

Exchange Rate Behavior: Selected Developed Countries, 1996–2010 This figure shows exchange rates of three currencies against the U.S. dollar and three against the euro. The euro rates begin in 1999 when the currency was introduced. The yen, pound, and Canadian dollar all float against the U.S. dollar. The pound and yen float against the euro. The Danish krone is fixed against the euro. The vertical scale ranges by a factor of 2 on all charts.

Source: oanda.com.

countries (India, Thailand, and South Korea); the maximum on the vertical axis is three times the minimum.

India had what looked like a fixed rate of about 35 rupees per dollar until a depreciation in 1997; there was then a period of pronounced movement more like a float. However, the government still acted to prevent abrupt currency movements even after 1997. This middle ground, somewhere between a fixed rate and a free float, is called a **managed float** (also known as a *dirty float*, or a policy of *limited flexibility*).

Thailand and South Korea show more extreme versions of the same pattern, except that in these cases the depreciation in 1997 was large and sudden, with the baht and the won exchange rates more than doubling in a matter of weeks. Such dramatic depreciations are called **exchange rate crises** and they are more common in developing countries than in developed countries. Indeed, South Korea had another mini-crisis in 2008.

FIGURE 2-3

Exchange Rate Behavior: Selected Developing Countries, 1996–2010 Exchange rates in developing countries show a wide variety of experiences and greater volatility. Pegging is common but is punctuated by periodic crises (you can see the effects of these crises in graphs for Thailand, South Korea, and Argentina). Rates that are unpegged may show some flexibility (India). Some rates crawl gradually (Colombia). Dollarization can occur (Ecuador). The vertical scale ranges by a factor of 3 on the upper charts and by a factor of 10 on the lower charts.

Source: oanda.com.

The bottom row of Figure 2-3 shows some Latin American countries and more varieties of exchange rate experience. The maximum on the vertical scale is now ten times the minimum, a change made necessary by the even more volatile exchange rates in this region.

Argentina initially had a fixed rate (of one peso per dollar), followed in 2001 by an exchange rate crisis. After a period of limited flexibility, Argentina returned to an almost fixed rate with a band that appeared to be centered at about three pesos per dollar, before drifting higher after 2008.

Colombia presents an example of a different kind of fixed exchange rate. Here the authorities did not target the level of the Colombian peso but allowed it to steadily depreciate at an almost constant rate for several years from 1996 to 2002. This type of fixed arrangement is called a **crawl** (if the exchange rate follows a simple trend, it is a *crawling peg*; if some variation about the trend is allowed, it is termed a *crawling band*).

In the final figure, Ecuador displays a different crisis pattern. Here a period of floating was followed by a fixed rate rather than the other way around. Episodes of very rapid depreciation like this represent a distinct form of exchange rate behavior; some economists have suggested, not jokingly, that these regimes be identified separately as *freely falling* exchange rate regimes.[5] The Ecuadorean currency stabilized at a fixed rate of 25,000 sucres per dollar, but then the sucre ceased to be. Ecuador took the remarkable step of dollarizing: abolishing its own national currency and adopting the U.S. dollar as its legal tender.

Currency Unions and Dollarization Almost every economy issues its own currency and jealously guards this sovereign right. There are only two exceptions: groups of economies that agree to form a currency or monetary union and adopt a common currency and individual economies that dollarize by adopting the currency of another country as their own.

Under a **currency union** (or **monetary** union), there is some form of transnational structure such as a single central bank or monetary authority that is accountable to the member nations. The most prominent example of a currency union is the Eurozone. Other currency unions include the CFA and CFP Franc zones (among some former French colonies in Africa and the Pacific) and the Eastern Caribbean Currency Union of nine member states.

Under **dollarization** one country unilaterally adopts the currency of another country. The reasons for this choice can vary. The adopting country may be very small, so the costs of running its own central bank and issuing its own currency may be prohibitive. Such is the case, for example, for the 50 or so Pitcairn Islanders (who use New Zealand as their standard currency). Other countries may have a poor record of managing their own monetary affairs and may end up "importing" a better policy from abroad. The currency changeover could be a de jure policy choice; or it may happen de facto if people are so fed up that they stop using the national currency and switch en masse to an alternative. Many of these economies use the U.S. dollar, but other popular choices include the euro, and the Australian and New Zealand dollars.

Exchange Rate Regimes of the World To move beyond specific examples, Figure 2-4 shows an IMF classification of exchange rate regimes around the world, which allows us to see the prevalence of different regime types across the whole spectrum from fixed to floating.[6]

The classification covers 192 economies for the year 2008, and regimes are ordered from the most rigidly fixed to the most freely floating. The first 46 countries are those

---

[5] Carmen M. Reinhart and Kenneth S. Rogoff, February 2004, "The Modern History of Exchange Rate Arrangements: A Reinterpretation," *Quarterly Journal of Economics*, 119(1), 1–48.

[6] The IMF now uses an unofficial classification based on observed exchange rate behavior. Most economists prefer this type of classification to the often misleading official classifications that were based on countries' official policy announcements. For example, as we saw in Figure 2-3, Thailand pegged to the dollar before the 1997 crisis, even though official statements denied this and the Thai authorities claimed the baht was floating. On unofficial or de facto classifications, see Carmen M. Reinhart and Kenneth S. Rogoff, February 2004, "The Modern History of Exchange Rate Arrangements: A Reinterpretation," *Quarterly Journal of Economics*, 119(1), 1–48. Jay C. Shambaugh, February 2004, "The Effect of Fixed Exchange Rates on Monetary Policy," *Quarterly Journal of Economics*, 119(1), 301–352. Eduardo Levy Yeyati and Federico Sturzenegger, August 2005, "Classifying Exchange Rate Regimes: Deeds vs. Words," *European Economic Review*, 49(6), 1603–1635.

A Spectrum of Exchange Rate Regimes The chart shows a recent classification of exchange rate regimes around the world.

Source: With the exception of Slovakia (which joined the Eurozone on January 1, 2009, and is classified as such) all classifications are for April 2008 and based on the IMF's "De Facto Classification of Exchange Rate Regimes and Monetary Policy Frameworks." Note that Estonia is expected to join the Eurozone on January 1, 2011.

that have no currency of their own—they are either dollarized or in a currency union. Next are 7 countries using an ultrahard peg called a **currency board,** a type of fixed regime that has special legal and procedural rules designed to make the peg "harder"—that is, more durable. Then come 58 conventional pegs, with variations of less than ±1%, some fixed to a single currency and a few pegging against a basket of currencies. These are followed by the less rigidly fixed arrangements such as the 2 bands, 8 crawling pegs, and 2 crawling bands. We then encounter two kinds of flexible regimes: the 44 regimes of managed floating rates, in which the authorities seem to restrict exchange rate movements to a noticeable degree, and lastly the 25 independently floating regimes.

Looking Ahead This brief look at the evidence supplies important motivation for the analysis in the remainder of this book. First, the world is divided into fixed and floating rate regimes, so we need to understand how *both* types of regime work. Studying fixed and floating regimes side by side will occupy much of our attention for the next few chapters. Second, when we look at who is fixed and who is floating, we start to notice patterns. Most of the floaters are advanced countries and most of the fixers are developing countries (the major exception is the euro area). The important question of why some countries fix while others float is covered in more detail in later chapters. ■

3 The Market for Foreign Exchange

Day by day, and minute by minute, exchange rates the world over are set in the **foreign exchange market** (or **forex** or **FX** market), which, like any market, is a collection of private individuals, corporations, and some public institutions that buy and sell. When two currencies are traded for each other in a market, the exchange rate is the price at which the trade was done, a price that is determined by market forces.

The forex market is not an organized exchange: trade is conducted "over the counter" between parties at numerous interlinked locations around the world. The forex market is massive and has grown dramatically in recent years. According to the Bank for International Settlements, in April 2007 the global forex market traded $3,210 billion per day in currency, 70% more than in 2004 and 290% more than in 1992. The three major foreign exchange centers—the United Kingdom ($1,359 billion per day, almost all in London), the United States ($664 billion, mostly in New York), and Japan ($238 billion, principally in Tokyo)—played home to more than half of the trade.[7] Other important centers for forex trade include Hong Kong, Paris, Singapore, Sydney, and Zurich. Thanks to time-zone differences, when smaller trading centers are included, there is not a moment in the day when foreign exchange is not being traded somewhere in the world. This section briefly examines the basic workings of this market.

The Spot Contract

The simplest forex transaction is a contract for the immediate exchange of one currency for another between two parties. This is known as a **spot contract** because it happens "on the spot." Accordingly, the exchange rate for this transaction is often called the **spot exchange rate.** In this book, the use of the term "exchange rate" always refers to the spot rate. Spot trades are now essentially riskless: technology permits settlement for most trades in real time, so that the risk of one party failing to deliver on its side of the transaction (*default risk* or *settlement risk*) is essentially zero.[8]

Most of our personal transactions in the forex market are small spot transactions via retail channels, but this represents just a tiny fraction of the activity in the foreign

---

[7] Data from BIS, *Triennial Central Bank Survey: Foreign Exchange and Derivatives Market Activity in 2007* (Basle, Switzerland: Bank for International Settlements, December 2007).
[8] Spot trades formerly took two days for settlement. If a bank failed in that period, spot trades could suffer occasional settlement failure. However, since 1997 a *continuously linked settlement* (CLS) system has been used by the major trading banks and now covers a substantial majority of cross-currency transactions all over the world.

exchange market each day. The vast majority of trading involves commercial banks in major financial centers around the world. But even there the spot contract is the most common type of trade and appears in almost 90% of all forex transactions, either on its own as a single contract or in trades where it is combined with other forex contracts.

Transaction Costs

When individuals buy a little foreign currency through a retail channel (such as a bank), they pay a higher price than the midrange quote typically seen in the press; and when they sell, they are paid a lower price. The difference or **spread** between the "buy at" and "sell for" prices may be large, perhaps 2% to 5%. These fees and commissions go to the many middlemen that stand between the person on the street and the forex market. But when a big firm or a bank needs to exchange millions of dollars, the spreads and commissions are very small. Spreads are usually less than 0.1%, and for actively traded major currencies, they are approximately 0.01% to 0.03%.

Spreads are an important example of **market frictions** or **transaction costs**. These frictions create a wedge between the price paid by the buyer and the price received by the seller. Although spreads are potentially important for any microeconomic analysis of the forex market, macroeconomic analysis usually proceeds on the assumption that, in today's world of low-cost trading, the transaction-cost spreads in markets are so low for the key investors that they can be ignored for all purposes.

FIGURE 2-5

Spot and Forward Rates The chart shows the U.S. spot and three-month forward exchange rates for the euro in dollars per euro in the year 2008. The spot and forward rates closely track each other.

Source: Federal Reserve Bank of New York.

Derivatives

The spot contract is undoubtedly the most important contract in the forex market, but there are many other related forex contracts. These contracts include *forwards*, *swaps*, *futures*, and *options*. Collectively, all these related forex contracts are termed **derivatives** because the contracts and their pricing are derived from the spot rate.

With the exception of forwards, the forex derivatives market is small relative to the entire global forex market. According to April 2007 data from the Bank for International Settlements, the trade in spot contracts amounted to $1,005 billion per day, while the trade in forward contracts (including swaps) was $2,076 billion per day. All other derivative trades amounted to just $291 billion per day, or less than 10% of all forex trades.

For the rest of this chapter, we focus on the two most important contracts—the spot and the forward. Figure 2-5 shows recent trends in the spot and forward rates in the dollar-euro market. The forward rate tends to track the spot rate fairly closely, and we will explore this relationship further in a moment.

The full study of derivative markets requires an in-depth analysis of risk that is beyond the scope of a course in international macroeconomics. Such topics are reserved for advanced courses in finance that explore derivative contracts in great detail. The following application supplies a basic guide to derivatives.

APPLICATION
Foreign Exchange Derivatives

There are many derivative contracts in the foreign exchange market, of which the following are the most common.

Forwards A **forward** contract differs from a spot contract in that the two parties make the contract today, but the *settlement date* for the delivery of the currencies is in the future, or forward. The time to delivery, or *maturity*, varies—30 days, 90 days, six months, a year, or even longer—depending on the contract. However, because the price is fixed as of today, the contract carries no risk.

Swaps A **swap** contract combines a spot sale of foreign currency with a forward repurchase of the same currency. This is a common contract for counterparties dealing in the same currency pair over and over again. Combining two transactions reduces transactions costs because the broker's fees and commissions are lower than on a spot and forward purchased separately.

Futures A **futures** contract is a promise that the two parties holding the contract will deliver currencies to each other at some future date at a prespecified exchange rate, just like a forward contract. Unlike the forward contract, however, futures contracts are standardized, mature at certain regular dates, and can be traded on an organized futures exchange. Hence, the futures contract does not require that the parties involved at the delivery date be the same two parties that originally made the deal.

Options An **option** provides one party, the buyer, with the right to buy (*call*) or sell (*put*) a currency in exchange for another at a prespecified exchange rate at a future date. The other party, the seller, must perform the trade if asked to do so by the buyer, but a buyer is under no obligation to trade and, in particular, will not exercise the option if the spot price on the expiration date turns out to be more favorable.

All of these products exist to allow investors to trade foreign currency for delivery at different times or with different contingencies. Thus, derivatives allow investors to engage in *hedging* (risk avoidance) and *speculation* (risk taking).

- Example 1: Hedging. As chief financial officer of a U.S. firm, you expect to receive payment of €1 million in 90 days for exports to France. The current spot rate is $1.20 per euro. Your firm will incur losses on the deal if the euro weakens to less than $1.10 per euro. You advise that the firm buy €1 million in call options on dollars at a rate of $1.15 per euro, ensuring that the firm's euro receipts will sell for at least this rate. This locks in a minimal profit even if the spot rate falls below $1.15. This is hedging.
- Example 2: Speculation. The market currently prices one-year euro futures at $1.30, but you think the dollar will weaken to $1.43 in the next 12 months. If you wish to make a bet, you would buy these futures, and if you are proved right, you will realize a 10% profit. Any level above $1.30 will generate a profit. If the dollar is at or below $1.30 a year from now, however, your investment in futures will be a total loss. This is speculation. ∎

Private Actors

The key actors in the forex market are the traders. Most forex traders work for **commercial banks.** These banks trade for themselves and also serve clients who want to import or export goods, services, or assets. Such transactions usually involve a change of currency, and commercial banks are the principal financial intermediaries that provide this service.

For example, suppose Apple Computer Inc. has sold €1 million worth of computers to a German distributor and wishes to receive payment for them in U.S. dollars. The German distributor informs its commercial bank, Deutsche Bank, which then debits €1 million from the distributor's bank account. Deutsche Bank then sells the €1 million bank deposit in the forex market in exchange for a $1.3 million deposit and credits that $1.3 million to Apple's bank in California, which, in turn, deposits $1.3 million into Apple's account. (In this example, we assume a euro is worth $1.3.)

This is an example of **interbank trading.** This business is highly concentrated: about three-quarters of all forex market transactions globally are handled by just ten banks, led by names such as Deutsche Bank, UBS, Citigroup, HSBC, and Barclays. They trade currencies not just for their clients but also on their own account in search of profit. The vast majority of forex transactions are profit-driven interbank trades, and it is the exchange rates for these trades that underlie quoted market exchange rates. Consequently, we focus on profit-driven trading as the key force in the forex market that affects the determination of the spot exchange rate.

Other actors are increasingly participating directly in the forex market. Some **corporations** may trade in the market if they are engaged in extensive transactions either to buy inputs or sell products in foreign markets. It may be costly for them to do this, but by doing so, they can bypass the fees and commissions charged by commercial banks. Similarly, some **nonbank financial institutions** such as mutual fund companies may invest so much overseas that they can justify setting up their own foreign exchange trading operations.

Government Actions

We have so far described the forex market in terms of the private actors. Our discussion of the forex market is incomplete, however, without mention of actions taken by government authorities. Such activities are by no means present in every market at all times, but they are sufficiently frequent that we need to fully understand them. In essence, there are two primary types of actions taken by governments in the forex market.

At one extreme, it is possible for a government to try to completely control the market by preventing its free operation, by restricting trading or movement of forex, or by allowing the trading of forex only through government channels. Policies of this kind are a form of **capital control,** a restriction on cross-border financial transactions. In the wake of the 1997 Asian exchange rate crisis, the Malaysian government temporarily imposed capital controls, an event that prompted Prime Minister Mahathir Mohamad to declare that "currency trading is unnecessary, unproductive and totally immoral. It should be stopped, it should be made illegal."[9]

---

[9] From a speech at the World Bank meeting in Hong Kong, September 20, 1997, in which Mr. Mohamad also referred to the legendary currency trader George Soros as a "moron." See Edward A. Gargan, "Premier of Malaysia Spars with Currency Dealer; Mahathir Says Soros and His Ilk Are 'Impoverishing Others' for Profit," *New York Times*, September 22, 1997, p. A1.

Capital controls are never 100% successful, however. Illegal trades will inevitably occur and are almost impossible to stop. The government may set up an **official market** for foreign exchange and issue a law requiring people to buy and sell in that market at officially set rates. But illicit dealings can persist "on the street" in **black markets** or *parallel markets* where individuals may trade at exchange rates determined by market forces and not set by the government. For example, in Italy in the 1930s, the Mussolini regime set harsh punishments for trading in foreign currency that gradually rose to include the death penalty, but trading still continued on the black market.

A less drastic action taken by the authorities is to let the private market for foreign exchange function but to fix or control forex prices in the market through **intervention**, a job typically given to a nation's central bank.

How do central banks intervene in the forex market? Indeed, how can a government control a price in any market? This is an age-old problem. Consider the issue of food supply in medieval and premodern Europe, one of the earliest examples of government intervention in markets. Rulers faced the problem that droughts or harvest failures lead to famines—and political unrest. Governments reacted by establishing state-run granaries, where wheat would be stored up in years of plenty and then released to the market in years of scarcity. The price could even be fixed if the government stood ready to buy or sell grain at a preset price—*and always had enough grain in reserve to do so.* Some authorities successfully followed this strategy for many years. Others failed when they ran out of grain reserves. Once a reserve is gone, market forces take over. If there is a heavy demand that is no longer being met by the state, a rapid price increase will inevitably follow.

Government intervention in the foreign exchange market works similarly. To maintain a fixed exchange rate, the central bank must stand ready to buy or sell its own currency, in exchange for the base foreign currency, at a fixed price. In practice, this means keeping some foreign currency reserves as a buffer, but having this buffer raises many problems. For one thing, it is costly—resources are tied up in foreign currency when they could be invested in more profitable activities. Second, these reserves are not an unlimited buffer, and if they run out, the game is up. In later chapters, we will explore why countries peg, how a peg is maintained, and under what circumstances pegs fail, leading to an exchange rate crisis.

To conclude, the extent of government intervention can vary. However, even with complete and watertight capital controls, including the suppression of the black market, private actors are always present in the market. Our first task is to understand how private economic motives and actions affect the forex market.

4 Arbitrage and Spot Exchange Rates

The most basic of activities pursued by private actors in any market is **arbitrage**, a trading strategy that exploits any profit opportunities arising from price differences. Understanding arbitrage is one of the keys to thinking like an economist in any situation and is essential in studying exchange rates.

In the simplest terms, arbitrage means to buy low and sell high. If such profit opportunities exist in a market, then it is considered to be out of equilibrium. If no such profit opportunities exist, there will be no arbitrage; the market is in **equilibrium** and satisfies a **no-arbitrage condition**.

Arbitrage with Two Currencies

Suppose you trade dollars and pounds for a bank with branches in New York and London. You can electronically transfer the funds cost free between the two branch locations. Forex trading commissions are the same in each city and so small as to be negligible. Suppose the exchange rate in New York is $E_{£/\$}^{\text{N.Y.}} = £0.50$ per dollar, in London $E_{£/\$}^{\text{London}} = £0.55$ per dollar. Can you make a profit for the bank?

Yes. You can buy \$1 for £0.50 in New York and sell it for £0.55 in London for an instant, riskless profit. Indeed, everyone would buy in New York and sell in London.

In general, one of the three outcomes can occur in the forex market. The spot rate can be higher in London: $E_{£/\$}^{\text{N.Y.}} < E_{£/\$}^{\text{London}}$; the spot rate can be higher in New York: $E_{£/\$}^{\text{N.Y.}} > E_{£/\$}^{\text{London}}$; or the spot rate can be the same in both locations: $E_{£/\$}^{\text{N.Y.}} = E_{£/\$}^{\text{London}}$. Arbitrage will occur in the first two cases. Only in the last case, in which spot rates are equal, does no arbitrage occur. Hence, the no-arbitrage condition for spot rates is

$$E_{£/\$}^{\text{N.Y.}} = E_{£/\$}^{\text{London}}$$

The no-arbitrage condition is shown diagrammatically in Figure 2-6. Following both sets of arrows, we see that on each path we start with a dollar and end up with pounds, but we are indifferent between these paths only when the end result is identical. That would be an equilibrium, where no arbitrage is possible.

If the market were out of equilibrium, arbitrage would drive up the price in the low-price market and drive down the price in the high-price market. In our example,

FIGURE 2-6

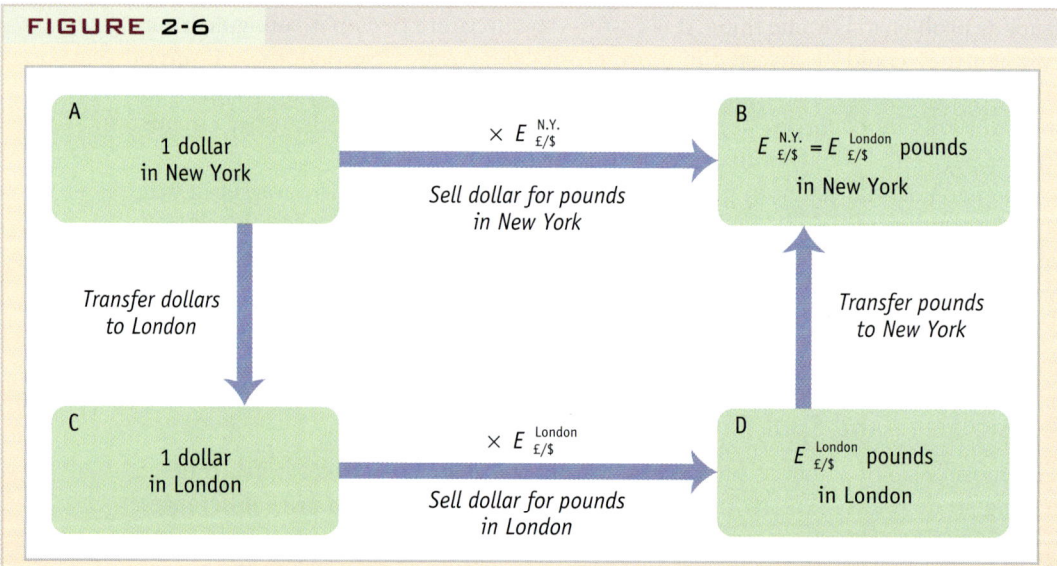

Arbitrage and Spot Rates Arbitrage ensures that the trade of currencies in New York along the path AB occurs at the same exchange rate as via London along path ACDB. At B the pounds received must be the same. Regardless of the route taken to get to B, $E_{£/\$}^{\text{N.Y.}} = E_{£/\$}^{\text{London}}$.

everyone buying dollars in New York and selling them in London would bid up the spot rate in New York from £0.50 and would bid down the spot rate in London from £0.55. This process would continue until the prices converged, arbitrage ceased, and equilibrium was attained. In forex markets, these adjustments happen nearly instantaneously, whether in the high-tech electronic markets of world financial centers or in the markets on street corners in the developing world.

Arbitrage with Three Currencies

The same logic that we just applied to transactions between two currencies can also be applied to transactions involving three currencies. Again, as the trader in New York, you are considering trading dollars and pounds, but you also consider indirect or "triangular" trade via a third currency, say, the euro. Triangular arbitrage works as follows: you sell dollars in exchange for euros, then immediately sell the same euros in exchange for pounds. This roundabout way to acquire pounds is feasible, but is it sensible? Perhaps.

For example, suppose euros can be obtained at $E_{€/\$} = €0.8$ per dollar, and pounds can be obtained at $E_{£/€} = £0.7$ per euro. Starting with \$1, you can obtain 0.8 euros, and with those 0.8 euros, you can obtain 0.7×0.8 pounds. Thus, setting aside the negligibly small commissions, the resulting pound-dollar exchange rate on the combined trade is $E_{£/€} \times E_{€/\$} = 0.7 \times 0.8 = 0.56$ pounds per dollar. If, say, the exchange rate on the direct trade from dollars to pounds is a less favorable $E_{£/\$} = 0.5$, we can trade \$1 for £0.56 via the euro, and then trade the £0.56 for \$1.12 by way of a direct trade (because $1.12 = 0.56/0.5$), a riskless profit of 12 cents.

In general, three outcomes are again possible. The direct trade from dollars to pounds has a better rate: $E_{£/\$} > E_{£/€}E_{€/\$}$; the indirect trade has a better rate: $E_{£/\$} < E_{£/€}E_{€/\$}$; or the two trades have the same rate and yield the same result: $E_{£/\$} = E_{£/€}E_{€/\$}$. Only in the last case are there no profit opportunities. This no-arbitrage condition can be written in two ways:

$$\underbrace{E_{£/\$}}_{\text{Direct exchange rate}} = E_{£/€}E_{€/\$} = \underbrace{\frac{E_{£/€}}{E_{\$/€}}}_{\text{Cross rate}}$$

Forex traders at their desks in London and money changers on the street in Kabul.

The right-hand expression, a ratio of two exchange rates, is called a **cross rate.** Examine the units carefully and notice how the two € cancel out. This no-arbitrage condition applies to all currency combinations. It is shown diagrammatically in Figure 2-7, and you can see why it is called *triangular arbitrage*.

The cross rate formula is very convenient. It means that we do not need to keep track of the exchange rate of every currency at all times. For example, if we know the exchange rates against, say, the dollar, for every currency, then for *any* pair of currencies A and B we can use the dollar rates of each currency and the cross rate formula to work out the rate at which the two currencies will trade: $E_{A/B} = E_{A/\$}/E_{B/\$}$. In practice, this is how most exchange rates are calculated.

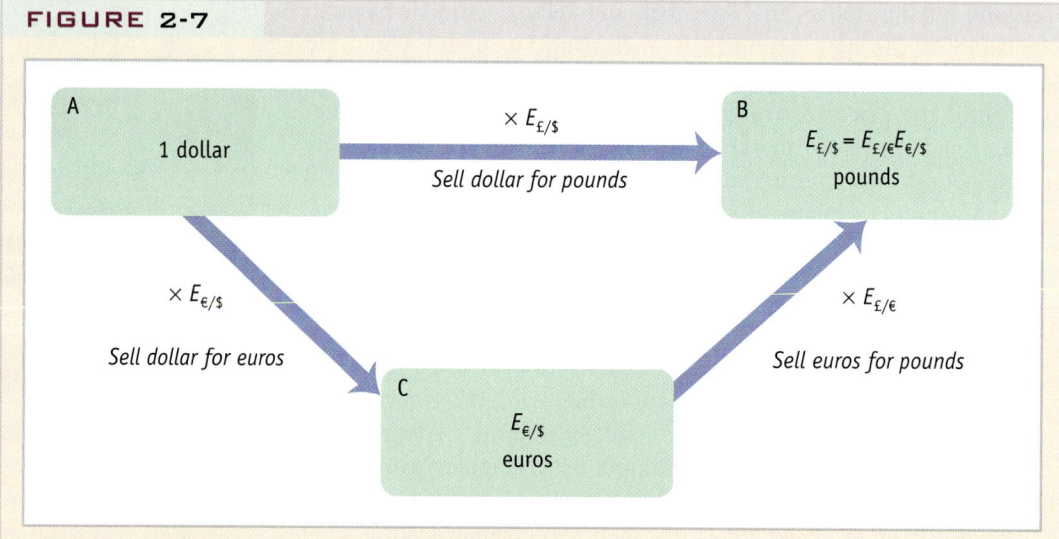

Arbitrage and Cross Rates Triangular arbitrage ensures that the direct trade of currencies along the path AB occurs at the same exchange rate as via a third currency along path ACB. The pounds received at B must be the same on both paths, and $E_{£/\$} = E_{£/€}E_{€/\$}$.

Cross Rates and Vehicle Currencies

The study of cross rates is not just an academic exercise because the vast majority of currency pairs are exchanged for one another through a third currency. There are 160 distinct currencies in the world at the time of this writing. If you write down every possible currency pair, then count them up, you would be expecting to see 12,720 forex markets in operation. You would be disappointed, however, and find only a fraction of this number. Why?

The vast majority of the world's currencies trade directly with only one or two of the major currencies, such as the dollar, euro, yen, or pound, and perhaps a few other currencies from neighboring countries. This is not too surprising. After all, to take some obscure examples, how often does somebody want to trade a Kenyan shilling for a Paraguayan guaraní? Or Mauritanian ouguiya for a Tongan pa'anga? These are small, far-apart countries between which there is very little international trade or investment. It is hard to find counterparties for forex trade in these currencies—so hard that the costs of trading become prohibitive. And there is no need to bear these costs because, to continue our example, Kenya, Paraguay, Mauritania, and Tonga do conduct a lot of business in major currencies such as the U.S. dollar, so individuals always have the option to engage in a triangular trade at the cross rate to convert shillings to dollars to guaranís (or ouguiyas to dollars to pa'angas), all for a reasonable commission.

When a third currency, such as the U.S. dollar, is used in these transactions, it is called a **vehicle currency** because it is not the home currency of either of the parties involved in the trade and is just used for intermediation. Market data illustrate the importance of vehicle currencies. According to year 2007 data from the Bank for International Settlements, the most common vehicle currency is the U.S. dollar, which appears on one side of more than 86% of all global trades. The euro is next, playing a role in 37% of all trades (many of them with the U.S. dollar). The yen appears in 17% of all trades and the British pound in 15% (many with the U.S. dollar and the euro).

5 Arbitrage and Interest Rates

So far, our discussion of arbitrage has shown how actors in the forex market—for example, the banks—exploit profit opportunities if currencies trade at different prices. But this is not the only type of arbitrage activity affecting the forex market.

An important question for investors is in which currency they should hold their liquid cash balances. Their cash can be placed in bank deposit accounts denominated in various currencies where it will earn a modest interest rate. For example, a trader working for a major bank in New York could leave the bank's cash in a euro deposit for one year earning a 2% euro interest rate or she could put the money in a U.S. dollar deposit for one year earning a 4% dollar interest rate. How can she decide which asset, the euro or the dollar deposit, is the best investment?

This is the final problem that we address in this chapter, and this analysis provides the tools we need to understand the forex market in the rest of this book. The analysis again centers on arbitrage. Would selling euro deposits and buying dollar deposits make a profit for the banker? Decisions like these drive the demand for dollars versus euros and the exchange rate between the two currencies.

The Problem of Risk A key issue for the trader is the exchange rate risk. The trader is in New York, and her bank cares about returns in U.S. dollars. The dollar deposit pays a known return, in dollars. But the euro deposit pays a return in euros, and one year from now we cannot know for sure what the dollar-euro exchange rate will be. Thus, how we analyze arbitrage in the sections that follow depends on how exchange rate risk is handled by the investor.

As we know from our discussion of derivatives, an investor may elect to cover or hedge their exposure to exchange rate risk by using a forward contract, and their decision then simplifies to a case of *riskless arbitrage*. On the other hand, an investor may choose not to use a forward, and instead wait to use a spot contract when their investment matures, whereupon their decision is a case of *risky arbitrage*. These two ways of doing arbitrage lead to two important implications, called *parity conditions*, which describe equilibria in the forward and spot markets. We now examine each one in turn.

Riskless Arbitrage: Covered Interest Parity

Suppose that contracts to exchange euros for dollars in one year's time carry an exchange rate of $F_{\$/€}$ dollars per euro. This is known as the **forward exchange rate** and it allows investors to be absolutely sure of the price at which they can trade forex in the future.

Assume you are trading for the bank in New York, and you have to decide whether to invest $1 for one year in either a dollar or euro bank deposit that pays interest. The interest rate offered in New York on dollar deposits is $i_\$$ and in Europe the interest rate offered on euro deposits is $i_€$. Which investment offers the higher return?

If you invest in a dollar deposit, your $1 placed in a U.S. bank account will be worth $(1 + i_\$)$ dollars in one year's time. The dollar value of principal and interest for the U.S. dollar bank deposit is called the *dollar return*. Note that we explicitly specify in what currency the return is measured, so that we may compare returns.

If you invest in a euro deposit, you first need to convert the dollar to euros. Using the spot exchange rate, $1 buys $1/E_{\$/€}$ euros today. These $1/E_{\$/€}$ euros would be placed in a euro account earning $i_€$, so in a year's time they would be worth $(1 + i_€)/E_{\$/€}$ euros. You would then convert the euros back into dollars, but you cannot know for sure what the future spot rate will be. To avoid that risk, you engage in a forward contract today to make the future transaction at a forward rate $F_{\$/€}$. The $(1 + i_€)/E_{\$/€}$ euros you will have in one year's time can then be exchanged for $(1 + i_€)F_{\$/€}/E_{\$/€}$ dollars, the dollar value of principal and interest, or the dollar return on the euro bank deposit.[10]

Three outcomes are possible when you compare the dollar returns from the two deposits. The U.S. deposit has a higher dollar return, the euro deposit has a higher dollar return, or both deposits have the same dollar return. In the first case, you would advise your bank to sell its euro deposits and buy dollar deposits; in the second case, you would advise the bank to sell its dollar deposits and buy euro deposits. Only in the third case is there no expected profit from arbitrage, so the corresponding no-arbitrage condition can be written as follows:

$$\text{Covered interest parity (CIP): } \underbrace{(1 + i_\$)}_{\substack{\text{Dollar return on} \\ \text{dollar deposits}}} = \underbrace{(1 + i_€)\frac{F_{\$/€}}{E_{\$/€}}}_{\substack{\text{Dollar return on} \\ \text{euro deposits}}} \quad (2\text{-}1)$$

This expression is called **covered interest parity (CIP)** because all exchange rate risk on the euro side has been "covered" by use of the forward contract. We say that such a trade employs *forward cover*. The condition is illustrated in Figure 2-8.

What Determines the Forward Rate?
Covered interest parity is a no-arbitrage condition that describes an equilibrium in which investors are indifferent between the returns on interest-bearing bank deposits in two currencies and exchange risk has been eliminated by the use of a forward contract. Because one of the returns depends on the forward rate, covered interest parity can be seen as providing us with a theory of what determines the forward exchange rate. We can rearrange the above equation and solve for the forward rate:

$$F_{\$/€} = E_{\$/€}\frac{1 + i_\$}{1 + i_€}$$

Thus, if covered interest parity holds, we can calculate the forward rate if we know all three right-hand side variables: the spot rate $E_{\$/€}$, the dollar interest rate $i_\$$, and the euro interest rate $i_€$. For example, suppose the euro interest rate is 3%, the dollar interest rate is 5%, and the spot rate is $1.30 per euro. Then the preceding equation says the forward rate would be $1.30 \times (1.05)/(1.03) = \$1.3252$ per euro.

---

[10] Note that this arbitrage strategy requires a spot and a forward contract. The two can be combined in a swap contract, and this helps explain the prevalence of swaps in the forex market.

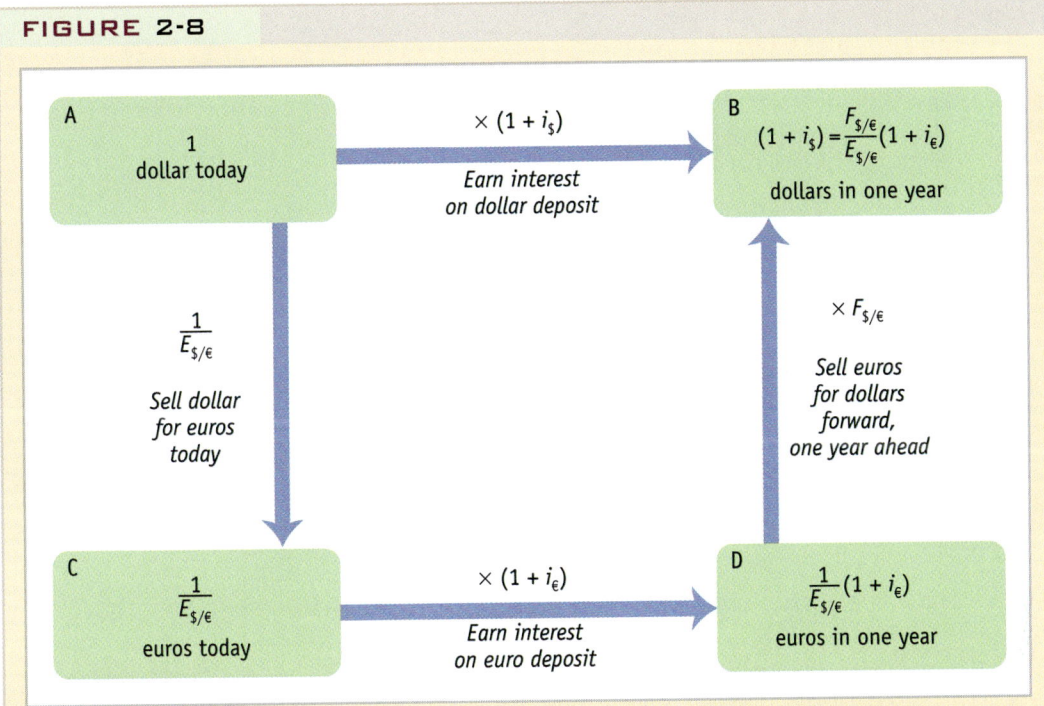

Arbitrage and Covered Interest Parity Under CIP, returns to holding dollar deposits accruing interest going along the path AB must equal the returns from investing in euros going along the path ACDB with risk removed by use of a forward contract. Hence, at B, the riskless payoff must be the same on both paths, and $(1 + i_\$) = \frac{F_{\$/€}}{E_{\$/€}}(1 + i_€)$.

In practice, this is exactly how the forex market works and how the price of a forward contract is set. Traders at their computers all around the world can see the interest rates on bank deposits in each currency, and the spot exchange rate. We can now also see why the forward contract is called a "derivative" contract: to establish the price of the forward contract (the forward rate F), we first need to know the price of the spot contract (the spot rate E). That is, the pricing of the forward contract is derived from the pricing of the underlying spot contract, using additional information on interest rates.

This result raises a new question: How are the interest rates and the spot rate determined? We return to that question in a moment, after looking at some evidence to verify that covered interest parity does indeed hold.

APPLICATION

Evidence on Covered Interest Parity

Does covered interest parity hold? We expect returns to be equalized only if arbitrage is possible. But if governments impose capital controls, there is no way for traders to exploit profit opportunities and no reason for the returns on different currencies to equalize.

For example, Figure 2-9 shows that covered interest parity held for the United Kingdom and Germany after the two countries abolished their capital controls in

Financial Liberalization and Covered Interest Parity: Arbitrage between the United Kingdom and Germany The chart shows the difference in monthly pound returns on deposits in British pounds and German marks using forward cover from 1970 to 1995. In the 1970s, the difference was positive and often large: traders would have profited from arbitrage by moving money from pound deposits to mark deposits, but capital controls prevented them from freely doing so. After financial liberalization, these profits essentially vanished, and no arbitrage opportunities remained. The CIP condition held, aside from small deviations resulting from transactions costs and measurement errors.

Source: Maurice Obstfeld and Alan M. Taylor, 2004, Global Capital Markets: Integration, Crisis, and Growth, Japan-U.S. Center Sanwa Monographs on International Financial Markets (Cambridge, UK: Cambridge University Press).

the period from 1979 to 1981. (The German deposits shown here were denominated in marks prior to 1999; after 1999, the euro replaced the mark as the German currency.)

The chart shows the profit that could have been made (measured in percent per annum in British currency, before transaction costs) if the investor had been able to move funds from the United Kingdom to Germany with forward cover (or, when the line is in negative territory, the profit from moving funds from Germany to the United Kingdom). From Equation (2-1), we know that the profit from this riskless arbitrage would be

$$\text{Profit} = \underbrace{(1 + i_{GER})\frac{F_{UK/GER}}{E_{UK/GER}}}_{\text{Pound return on German deposits}} - \underbrace{(1 + i_{UK})}_{\text{Pound return on U.K. deposits}}$$

This profit would be zero only if covered interest parity held. In the 1960s and 1970s, the *hypothetical* profits implied by this expression were large—or would have been had arbitrage been allowed. Instead, capital controls in both countries prevented arbitrage. Covered interest parity therefore failed to hold. Following the financial liberalization from 1979 to 1981, arbitrage became possible. From that time until the present, profits have been essentially zero. Computed profits are not exactly zero because of regulations, fees, other transaction costs, and measurement error. Once we allow for these factors, there are no profit opportunities left. Covered interest parity holds when capital markets are open, and, using similar calculations, this can be confirmed for all freely traded currencies today. ∎

Risky Arbitrage: Uncovered Interest Parity

As we noted above, the second way to engage in arbitrage is to use spot contracts, and accept that the future exchange rate is then subject to risk. We now examine this case, and by doing so, we will arrive at an understanding of how the exchange rate is determined in the spot market.

To keep things simple, let us suppose, for now, that investors focus *exclusively* on the expected dollar return of the two bank deposits and not on any other characteristics of the investment. (See **Side Bar: Assets and Their Attributes.**) Imagine you are

SIDE BAR

Assets and Their Attributes

The bank deposits traded in the forex market pay interest and are part of the wider portfolio of assets held by banks and other private actors. As we have argued, the forex market is heavily influenced by the demand for these deposits as assets.

An investor's entire portfolio of assets may include stocks, bonds, real estate, art, bank deposits in various currencies, and so on. What influences the demand for all these different kinds of assets? Viewed from a financial viewpoint (i.e., setting aside the beauty of a painting or sea-side mansion), all assets have three key attributes that influence demand: return, risk, and liquidity.

An asset's **rate of return** is the total net increase in wealth (measured in a given currency) resulting from holding the asset for a specified period of time, typically one year. For example, you start the year by buying one share of DotBomb Inc., a hot Internet stock, for $100. At year's end, the share is worth $150 and has paid you a dividend of $5. Your total return is $55: a $50 capital gain from the change in the stock price plus a $5 dividend. Your total annual rate of return is 55/100, or 55%. The next year, the stock falls from $150 to $75 and pays no dividend. You lose half of your money in the second year: your rate of return for that year equals –75/150, or –50%. All else equal, investors prefer investments with high returns.

The **risk** of an asset refers to the volatility of its rate of return. The **liquidity** of an asset refers to the ease and speed with which it can be liquidated, or sold. A stock may seem to have high risk because its rate of return bounces up and down quite a lot, but its risk must be considered in relation to the riskiness of other investments. Its degree of risk could be contrasted with the rate of interest your bank offers on a money market deposit, a return that is usually very stable over time. You will lose your bank deposit only if your bank fails, which is unlikely. Your bank deposit is also very liquid. You can go to a cash machine or write a check to instantly access that form of wealth. In contrast, a work of art, say, is much less liquid. To sell the art for the greatest amount, you usually need the services of an auctioneer. Art is also risky. Works by different artists go in and out of fashion. All else equal, investors prefer assets with low risk and high liquidity.

This discussion of an asset's attributes allows us to make two observations. First, because all else is never equal, investors are willing to trade off among these attributes. You may be willing to hold a relatively risky and illiquid asset if you expect it will pay a relatively high return. Second, what you expect matters. Most investments, like stocks or art, do not have a fixed, predictable, guaranteed rate of return. As a result, all investors have to forecast. We refer to the forecast of the rate of return as the **expected rate of return**.

once again trading for a bank in New York, and you must decide whether to invest $1 for one year in a dollar or euro bank deposit that pays interest. This time, however, you use spot contracts only and make no use of the forward contract to hedge against the riskiness of the future exchange rate.

The $1 invested in a dollar deposit will be worth $(1 + i_\$)$ in one year's time; this is the dollar return, as before.

If you invest in a euro deposit, a dollar buys $1/E_{\$/€}$ euros today. With interest, these will be worth $(1 + i_€)/E_{\$/€}$ euros in one year. At that time, you will convert the euros back into dollars using a spot contract at the exchange rate that will prevail in one year's time. In this case, traders like you face exchange rate risk and must make a *forecast* of the future spot rate. We refer to the forecast as $E^e_{\$/€}$, which we call the **expected exchange rate**. Based on the forecast, you expect that the $(1 + i_€)/E_{\$/€}$ euros you will have in one year's time will be worth $(1 + i_€)E^e_{\$/€}/E_{\$/€}$ when converted into dollars; this is the *expected dollar return* on euro deposits; that is, the expected dollar value of principal and interest for euro deposits.

Again, three outcomes are possible: the U.S. deposit has a higher expected dollar return, the euro deposit has a higher expected dollar return, or both deposits have the same expected dollar return.

We have assumed that traders like you are indifferent to risk and care only about expected returns. Thus, in the first two cases, you have expected profit opportunities and risky arbitrage is possible: you would sell the deposit with the low expected return and buy the deposit with the higher expected return. Only in the third case is there no expected profit from arbitrage. This no-arbitrage condition can be written as follows:

$$\text{Uncovered interest parity (UIP):} \quad \underbrace{(1 + i_\$)}_{\text{Dollar return on dollar deposits}} = \underbrace{(1 + i_€)\frac{E^e_{\$/€}}{E_{\$/€}}}_{\text{Expected dollar return on euro deposits}} \quad (2\text{-}2)$$

This expression is called **uncovered interest parity (UIP)** because exchange rate risk has been left "uncovered" by the decision not to hedge against exchange rate risk by using a forward contract and instead simply wait to use a spot contract in a year's time. The condition is illustrated in Figure 2-10.

What Determines the Spot Rate? Uncovered interest parity is a no-arbitrage condition that describes an equilibrium in which investors are indifferent between the returns on unhedged interest-bearing bank deposits in two currencies (where forward contracts are not employed). Because one of the returns depends on the spot rate, uncovered interest parity can be seen as providing us with a theory of what determines the spot exchange rate. We can rearrange the above equation and solve for the spot rate:

$$E_{\$/€} = E^e_{\$/€}\frac{1 + i_€}{1 + i_\$}$$

Thus, if uncovered interest parity holds, we can calculate today's spot rate if we know all three right-hand-side variables: the expected future exchange rate $E^e_{\$/€}$; the

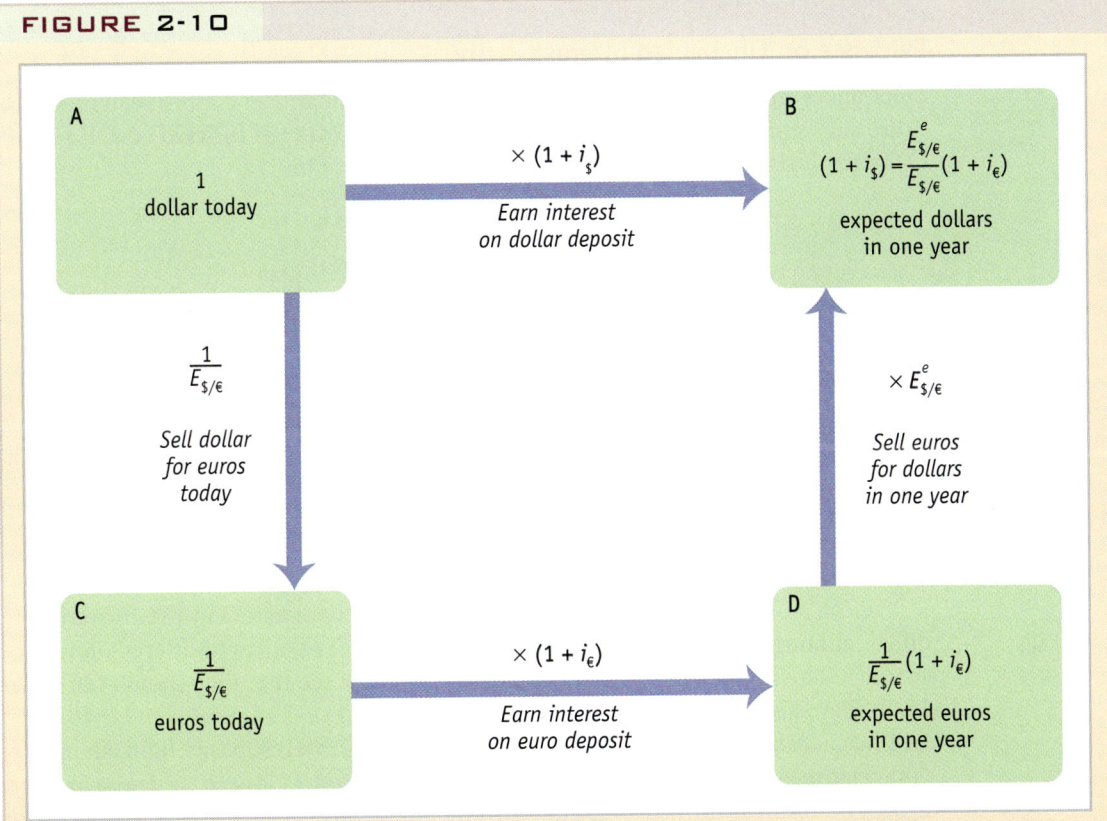

Arbitrage and Uncovered Interest Parity Under UIP, returns to holding dollar deposits accruing interest going along the path AB must equal the *expected* returns from investing in euros going along the risky path ACDB. Hence, at B, the expected payoff must be the same on both paths, and $(1 + i_\$) = \frac{E^e_{\$/€}}{E_{\$/€}}(1 + i_€)$.

dollar interest rate $i_\$$; and the euro interest rate $i_€$. For example, suppose the euro interest rate is 2%, the dollar interest rate is 4%, and the expected future spot rate is $1.40 per euro. Then the preceding equation says today's spot rate would be 1.40 × (1.02)/(1.04) = $1.3731 per euro.

However, this result raises more questions: How can the expected future exchange rate $E^e_{\$/€}$ be forecast? And, as we asked in the case of covered interest parity, how are the two interest rates determined?

In the next two chapters, we will address these unanswered questions, as we continue to develop the building blocks needed for a complete theory of exchange rate determination. We start by looking at the determinants of the expected future exchange rate $E^e_{\$/€}$, and developing a model of exchange rates in the long run, and then by looking at the determinants of the interest rates $i_\$$ and $i_€$. We will soon appreciate that future expectations make the solution of forward-looking economic problems tricky: we have to solve backward from the future to the present, and this motivates the order of the material in this textbook—we must understand exchange rates in the long run before we can understand them in the short run.

APPLICATION

Evidence on Uncovered Interest Parity

Does uncovered interest parity hold? The two interest parity equations seen previously are very similar. Equation (2-1), the CIP equation, uses the forward rate; Equation (2-2), the UIP equation, uses the expected future spot rate:

$$\text{CIP: } (1 + i_\$) = (1 + i_€)\frac{F_{\$/€}}{E_{\$/€}}$$

$$\text{UIP: } (1 + i_\$) = (1 + i_€)\frac{E^e_{\$/€}}{E_{\$/€}}$$

To allow us to see what this implies about the relationship between the expected future spot rate and the forward rate, we divide the second equation by the first, to obtain

$$1 = E^e_{\$/€}/F_{\$/€}, \text{ or}$$

$$F_{\$/€} = E^e_{\$/€}$$

We can now clearly see how the expected future spot rate and the forward rate differ: although they may be the instruments employed in two different forms of arbitrage—risky and riskless—in equilibrium, we now see that they should not differ at all; they should be exactly the same!

Thus, if *both* covered interest parity *and* uncovered interest parity hold, an important relationship emerges: *the forward rate $F_{\$/€}$ must equal the expected future spot rate $E^e_{\$/€}$*. The result is intuitive. In equilibrium, and *if investors do not care about risk* (as we have assumed in our presentation of UIP), then they have no reason to prefer to avoid risk by using the forward rate, or to embrace risk by awaiting the future spot rate; for them to be indifferent, as market equilibrium requires, the two rates must be equal.

With this result we can find an approach to testing UIP that is fairly easy to describe and implement. Because the evidence in favor of CIP is strong, as we have seen, we may assume that it holds. In that case, the previous equation then provides a test for whether UIP holds. But if the forward rate equals the expected spot rate, then we can also express this equivalence relative to today's spot rate, to show that the **expected rate of depreciation** (between today and the future period) equals the **forward premium** (the proportional difference between the forward and spot rates):

$$\underbrace{\frac{F_{\$/€}}{E_{\$/€}} - 1}_{\text{Forward premium}} = \underbrace{\frac{E^e_{\$/€}}{E_{\$/€}} - 1}_{\text{Expected rate of depreciation}}$$

For example, if the spot rate is $1.00 per euro, and the forward rate is $1.05, the forward premium is 5%. But if $F_{\$/€} = E^e_{\$/€}$, the expected future spot rate is also $1.05, and there is a 5% expected rate of depreciation.

The left-hand side of the preceding equation, the forward premium, is easily observed, since both the current spot and forward rates are data we can collect in the market. The difficulty is on the right-hand side: expectations are typically unobserved.

FIGURE 2-11

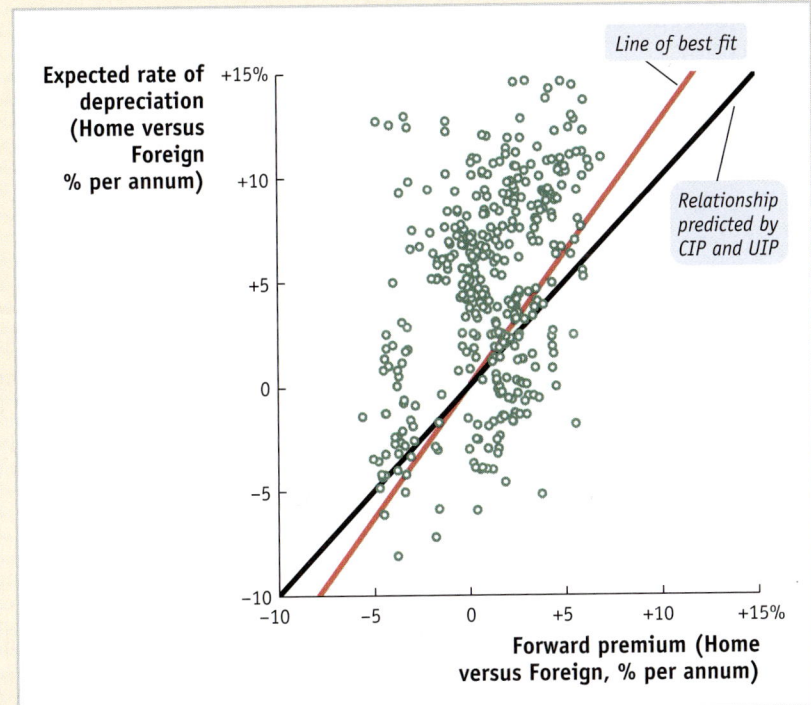

Evidence on Interest Parity When UIP and CIP hold, the 12-month forward premium should equal the 12-month expected rate of depreciation. A scatterplot showing these two variables should be close to the diagonal 45-degree line. Using evidence from surveys of individual forex traders' expectations over the period 1988 to 1993, UIP finds some support, as the line of best fit is close to the diagonal.

Notes: Line of best fit is through the origin. Data are monthly for the German mark, Swiss franc, Japanese yen, British pound, and Canadian dollar against the U.S. dollar from February 1988 to October 1993.

Source: Menzie Chinn and Jeffrey A. Frankel, 2002, "Survey Data on Exchange Rate Expectations: More Currencies, More Horizons, More Tests." In W. Allen and D. Dickinson, eds., Monetary Policy, Capital Flows and Financial Market Developments in the Era of Financial Globalisation: Essays in Honour of Max Fry (London: Routledge), pp. 145–167.

Still, the test can be attempted using surveys in which traders are asked to report their expectations. Using data from one such test, Figure 2-11 shows a strong correlation between expected rates of depreciation and the forward premium, with a slope close to 1. Still, the points do not lie exactly on the 45-degree line, so sometimes expected depreciation does not equal the interest differential. Does this profit opportunity mean that arbitrage is not working? Not necessarily. The deviations may be caused by sampling errors or noise (differences in opinion of individual traders). In addition, there may be limits to risky arbitrage in reality because of various factors such as transactions costs (market frictions) and aversion to risk, which we have so far neglected, but which we discuss in more detail in later chapters. That the slope "on average" is close to 1 provides some support for UIP. ∎

Uncovered Interest Parity: A Useful Approximation

Because it provides a theory of how the spot exchange rate is determined, the uncovered interest parity equation (2-2) is one of the most important conditions in international macroeconomics. Yet for most purposes, a simpler and more convenient concept can be used.

The intuition behind the approximation is as follows. Holding dollar deposits rewards the investor with dollar interest. Holding euro deposits rewards investors in two ways: they receive euro interest, but they also receive a gain (or loss) on euros equal to the rate of euro appreciation that approximately equals the rate of dollar depreciation. Thus, for UIP to hold, and for an investor to be indifferent between dollar deposits and euro deposits, any interest shortfall (excess) on the euro side must be offset by an expected gain (loss) in the form of euro appreciation or dollar depreciation.

We can write the approximation formally as follows:

$$\text{UIP approximation:} \quad \underbrace{i_\$}_{\substack{\text{Interest rate} \\ \text{on dollar} \\ \text{deposits =} \\ \text{Dollar rate of} \\ \text{return on} \\ \text{dollar deposits}}} = \underbrace{\underbrace{i_\euro}_{\substack{\text{Interest rate on} \\ \text{euro deposits}}} + \underbrace{\frac{\Delta E^e_{\$/\euro}}{E_{\$/\euro}}}_{\substack{\text{Expected rate of} \\ \text{depreciation of the} \\ \text{dollar}}}}_{\text{Expected dollar rate of return on euro deposits}} \quad (2\text{-}3)$$

There are three terms in this equation. The left-hand side is the interest rate on dollar deposits. The first term on the right is the interest rate on euro deposits. The second term on the right can be expanded as $\Delta E^e_{\$/\euro}/E_{\$/\euro} = (E^e_{\$/\euro} - E_{\$/\euro})/E_{\$/\euro}$ and is the expected fractional change in the euro's value, or the expected rate of appreciation of the euro. As we have seen, this expression equals the appreciation of the euro exactly, but for small changes it approximately equals the expected rate of depreciation of the dollar.[11]

The UIP approximation equation, Equation (2-3), says that the home interest rate equals the foreign interest rate plus the expected rate of depreciation of the home currency.

A numerical example illustrates the UIP approximation formula. Suppose the dollar interest rate is 4% per year and the euro interest rate 3% per year. If UIP is to hold, then the expected rate of dollar depreciation over a year must be 1%. In that case, a dollar investment put into euros for a year will grow by 3% due to euro interest and in dollar terms will grow by an extra 1% due to euro appreciation, so the total dollar return on the euro deposit is approximately equal to the 4% that is offered by dollar deposits.[12]

To sum up, the uncovered interest parity condition, whether in its exact form (2-2) or its approximate form (2-3), states that there must be parity between expected returns, *expressed in a common currency*, in the two markets.

Summary

All economic models produce an output (some unknown or *endogenous* variable to be explained) and require a set of inputs (some known or *exogenous* variables that are treated as given). The two interest parity conditions provide us with models that

---

[11] To derive Equation (2-3), we can write $E^e_{\$/\euro}/E_{\$/\euro} = (1 + \Delta E^e_{\$/\euro}/E_{\$/\euro})$, and so Equation (2-2) becomes

$$1 + i_\$ = (1 + i_\euro)\left(1 + \frac{\Delta E^e_{\$/\euro}}{E_{\$/\euro}}\right) = 1 + i_\euro + \frac{\Delta E^e_{\$/\euro}}{E_{\$/\euro}} + \left[i_\euro \frac{\Delta E^e_{\$/\euro}}{E_{\$/\euro}}\right]$$

When the euro interest rate and the expected rate of depreciation are small, the last term in brackets is very small and may be neglected in an approximation. We can then cancel out the 1 that appears in the first and third terms of the above equation to obtain Equation (2-3).

[12] Note that the $1 investment in euros will be worth $(1.03) \times (1.01) = \$1.0403$ after one year, which is very close to $1.04, the value of the dollar deposit after one year. The difference is just the approximation error. See the previous footnote.

FIGURE 2-12

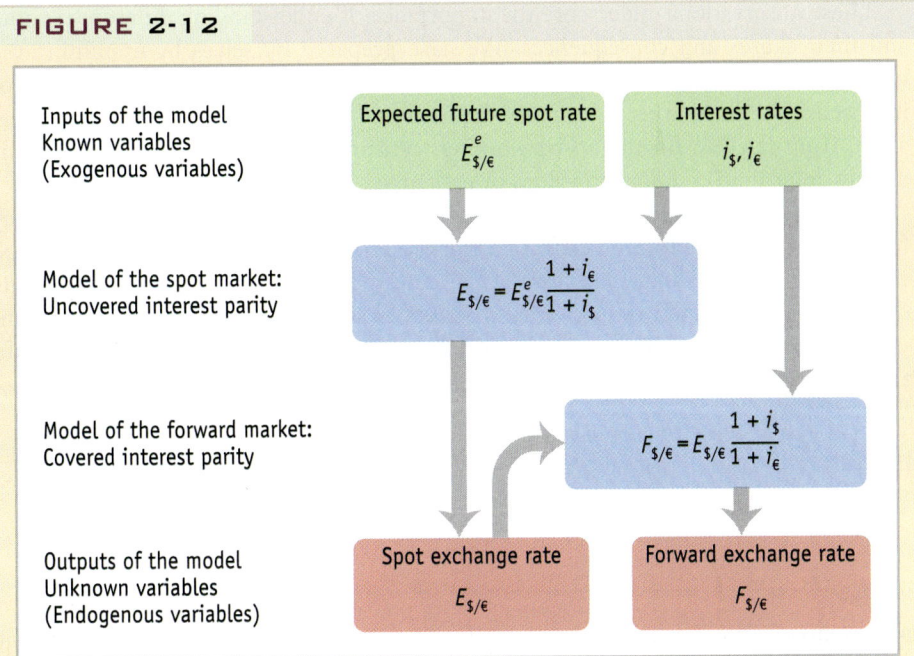

How Interest Parity Relationships Explain Spot and Forward Rates In the spot market, UIP provides a model of how the spot exchange rate is determined. To use UIP to find the spot rate, we need to know the expected future spot rate and the prevailing interest rates for the two currencies. In the forward market, CIP provides a model of how the forward exchange rate is determined. When we use CIP, we derive the forward rate from the current spot rate (from UIP) and the interest rates for the two currencies.

explain how the prices of the two most important forex contracts are determined in market equilibrium with no arbitrage possibilities. Uncovered interest parity applies to the spot market and determines the spot rate, based on interest rates and exchange rate expectations. Covered interest parity applies to the forward market and determines the forward rate based on interest rates and the spot rate. Figure 2-12 sums up what we have learned.

6 Conclusions

The foreign exchange market has a long and often tumultuous record and, in today's globalized world, exchange rates matter more than ever. They affect the prices of international transactions, can be a focus of government policy, and often play a major role in economic and political crises.

This chapter has set the stage for our study of exchange rates. We learned what exchange rates are and how they are used. We have also seen how they have behaved in reality under different exchange rate regimes. History shows a vast range of past experiences, and this experimentation continues.

These observations underscore the importance of understanding different regimes and their causes and consequences. We have prepared ourselves by examining the workings of the foreign exchange market in some detail. Government intervention (or its absence) in this market determines the nature of the exchange rate regime in operation, from fixed to floating. The workings of actors in the forex market then ultimately determine equilibrium values of exchange rates.

How is forex market equilibrium determined? We can now see that two key forces operate in the foreign exchange market: arbitrage and expectations. Through expectations, news about the future can affect expected returns. Through arbitrage, differences in expected returns are equalized, as summed up by the two important interest parity conditions, covered interest parity and uncovered interest parity. In the next two chapters, we build on these ideas to develop a complete theory of exchange rates.

KEY POINTS

1. The exchange rate in a country is the price of a unit of foreign currency expressed in terms of the home currency. This price is determined in the spot market for foreign exchange.

2. When the home exchange rate rises, less foreign currency is bought/sold per unit of home currency; the home currency has depreciated. If home currency buys $x\%$ less foreign currency, the home currency is said to have depreciated by $x\%$.

3. When the home exchange rate falls, more foreign currency is bought/sold per unit of home currency; the home currency has appreciated. If home currency buys $x\%$ more foreign currency, the home currency is said to have appreciated by $x\%$.

4. The exchange rate is used to convert the prices of goods and assets into a common currency to allow meaningful price comparisons.

5. Exchange rates may be stable over time or they may fluctuate. History supplies examples of the former (fixed exchange rate regimes) and the latter (floating exchange rate regimes) as well as a number of intermediate regime types.

6. An exchange rate crisis occurs when the exchange rate experiences a sudden and large depreciation. These events are often associated with broader economic and political turmoil, especially in developing countries.

7. Some countries may forgo a national currency to form a currency union with other nations (e.g., the Eurozone), or they may unilaterally adopt the currency of another country ("dollarization").

8. Looking across all countries today, numerous fixed and floating rate regimes are observed, so we must understand both types of regime.

9. The forex market is dominated by spot transactions, but many derivative contracts exist, such as forwards, swaps, futures, and options.

10. The main actors in the market are private investors and (frequently) the government authorities, represented usually by the central bank.

11. Arbitrage on currencies means that spot exchange rates are approximately equal in different forex markets. Cross rates (for indirect trades) and spot rates (for direct trades) are also approximately equal.

12. Riskless interest arbitrage leads to the covered interest parity (CIP) condition. CIP says that the dollar return on dollar deposits must equal the dollar return on euro deposits, where forward contracts are used to cover exchange rate risk.

13. Covered interest parity says that the forward rate is determined by home and foreign interest rates and the spot exchange rate.

14. Risky interest arbitrage leads to the uncovered interest parity (UIP) condition. UIP says that when spot contracts are used and exchange rate risk is not covered, the dollar return on dollar deposits must equal the expected dollar returns on euro deposits.

15. Uncovered interest parity explains how the spot rate is determined by the home and foreign interest rates and the expected future spot exchange rate.

KEY TERMS

exchange rate, p. 26
appreciation, p. 28
depreciation, p. 28
effective exchange rate, p. 30
exchange rate regimes, p. 33
fixed (or pegged) exchange rate regime, p. 33
floating (or flexible) exchange rate regime, p. 33
free float, p. 34
band, p. 34
managed float, p. 35
exchange rate crises, p. 35
crawl, p. 36
currency (or monetary) union, p. 37
dollarization, p. 37
currency board, p. 38
foreign exchange (forex or FX) market, p. 39
spot contract, p. 39
spot exchange rate, p. 39
spread, p. 40
market friction, p. 40
transaction costs, p. 40
derivatives, p. 40
forward, p. 41
swap, p. 41
futures, p. 41
option, p. 41
commercial banks, p. 42
interbank trading, p. 42
corporations, p. 42
nonbank financial institutions, p. 42
capital control, p. 42
official market, p. 43
black market, p. 43
intervention, p. 43
arbitrage, p. 43
equilibrium, p. 43
no-arbitrage condition, p. 43
cross rate, p. 45
vehicle currency, p. 46
forward exchange rate, p. 47
covered interest parity (CIP), p. 48
rate of return, p. 51
risk, p. 51
liquidity, p. 51
expected rate of return, p. 51
expected exchange rate, p. 52
uncovered interest parity (UIP), p. 52
expected rate of depreciation, p. 54
forward premium, p. 54

PROBLEMS

1. Refer to the exchange rates given in the following table:

Country	Today June 25, 2010 Per $	Today June 25, 2010 Per £	Today June 25, 2010 Per €	One Year Ago June 25, 2009 Per $
Australia	1.152	1.721	1.417	1.225
Canada	1.037	1.559	1.283	1.084
Denmark	6.036	9.045	7.443	5.238
Euro	0.811	1.215	1.000	0.703
Hong Kong	7.779	11.643	9.583	7.750
India	46.36	69.476	57.179	48.16
Japan	89.35	134.048	110.308	94.86
Mexico	12.697	18.993	15.631	13.22
Sweden	7.74	11.632	9.577	7.460
United Kingdom	0.667	1.000	0.822	0.609
United States	1.000	1.496	1.232	1.000

Source: U.S. Federal Reserve Board of Governors, H.10 release: Foreign Exchange Rates.

Based on the table provided, answer the following questions:

a. Compute the U.S. dollar-yen exchange rate $E_{\$/¥}$ and the U.S. dollar-Canadian dollar exchange rate $E_{\$/C\$}$ on June 25, 2010, and June 25, 2009.

b. What happened to the value of the U.S. dollar relative to the Japanese yen and Canadian dollar between June 25, 2009, and June 25, 2010? Compute the percentage change in the value of the U.S. dollar relative to each currency using the U.S. dollar-foreign currency exchange rates you computed in (a).

c. Using the information in the table for June 25, 2010, compute the Danish krone–Canadian dollar exchange rate $E_{krone/C\$}$.

d. Visit the website of the Board of Governors of the Federal Reserve System at http://www.federalreserve.gov/. Click on "Economic Research and Data" and then "Statistics: Releases and Historical Data." Download the H.10 release Foreign Exchange Rates (weekly data available). What has happened to the value of the U.S. dollar relative to the Canadian dollar, Japanese yen, and Danish krone since June 25, 2010?

e. Using the information from (d), what has happened to the value of the U.S. dollar relative to the British pound and the euro? *Note:* The H.10 release quotes these exchange rates as U.S. dollars per unit of foreign currency in line with long-standing market conventions.

2. Consider the United States and the countries it trades with the most (measured in trade volume): Canada, Mexico, China, and Japan. For simplicity, assume these are the only four countries with which the United States trades. Trade shares and exchange rates for these four countries are as follows:

Country (currency)	Share of Trade	$ per FX in 2009	$ per FX in 2010
Canada (dollar)	36%	0.9225	0.9643
Mexico (peso)	28%	0.0756	0.0788
China (yuan)	20%	0.1464	0.1473
Japan (yen)	16%	0.0105	0.0112

a. Compute the percentage change from 2009 to 2010 in the four U.S. bilateral exchange rates (defined as U.S. dollars per units of foreign exchange, or FX) in the table provided.

b. Use the trade shares as weights to compute the percentage change in the nominal effective exchange rate for the United States between 2009 and 2010 (in U.S. dollars per foreign currency basket).

c. Based on your answer to (b), what happened to the value of the U.S. dollar against this basket between 2009 and 2010? How does this compare with the change in the value of the U.S. dollar relative to the Mexican peso? Explain your answer.

3. Go to the website for Federal Reserve Economic Data (FRED): http://research.stlouisfed.org/fred2/. Locate the monthly exchange rate data for the following:

a. Canada (dollar), 1980–2009
b. China (yuan), 1999–2005 and 2005–2009

c. Mexico (peso), 1993–1995 and 1995—2009
d. Thailand (baht), 1986–1997 and 1997—2009
e. Venezuela (bolivar), 2003–2009

Look at the graphs and make a judgment as to whether each currency was fixed (peg or band), crawling (peg or band), or floating relative to the U.S. dollar during each time frame given.

4. Describe the different ways in which the government may intervene in the foreign exchange market. Why does the government have the ability to intervene in this way, while private actors do not?

5. Suppose quotes for the dollar-euro exchange rate $E_{\$/€}$ are as follows: in New York $1.50 per euro, and in Tokyo $1.55 per euro. Describe how investors use arbitrage to take advantage of the difference in exchange rates. Explain how this process will affect the dollar price of the euro in New York and Tokyo.

6. Consider a Dutch investor with 1,000 euros to place in a bank deposit in either the Netherlands or Great Britain. The (one-year) interest rate on bank deposits is 2% in Britain and 4.04% in the Netherlands. The (one-year) forward euro-pound exchange rate is 1.575 euros per pound and the spot rate is 1.5 euros per pound. Answer the following questions, using the *exact* equations for UIP and CIP as necessary.

    a. What is the euro-denominated return on Dutch deposits for this investor?
    b. What is the (riskless) euro-denominated return on British deposits for this investor using forward cover?
    c. Is there an arbitrage opportunity here? Explain why or why not. Is this an equilibrium in the forward exchange rate market?
    d. If the spot rate is 1.5 euros per pound, and interest rates are as stated previously, what is the equilibrium forward rate, according to covered interest parity (CIP)?
    e. Suppose the forward rate takes the value given by your answer to (d). Compute the forward premium on the British pound for the Dutch investor (where exchange rates are in euros per pound). Is it positive or negative? Why do investors require this premium/discount in equilibrium?
    f. If uncovered interest parity (UIP) holds, what is the expected depreciation of the euro (against the pound) over one year?
    g. Based on your answer to (f), what is the expected euro-pound exchange rate one year ahead?

7. You are a financial adviser to a U.S. corporation that expects to receive a payment of 40 million Japanese yen in 180 days for goods exported to Japan. The current spot rate is 100 yen per U.S. dollar ($E_{\$/¥}$ = 0.01000). You are concerned that the U.S. dollar is going to appreciate against the yen over the next six months.

    a. Assuming the exchange rate remains unchanged, how much does your firm expect to receive in U.S. dollars?
    b. How much would your firm receive (in U.S. dollars) if the dollar appreciated to 110 yen per U.S. dollar ($E_{\$/¥}$ = 0.00909)?
    c. Describe how you could use an options contract to hedge against the risk of losses associated with the potential appreciation in the U.S. dollar.

8. Consider how transactions costs affect foreign currency exchange. Rank each of the following foreign exchanges according to their probable spread (between the "buy at" and "sell for" bilateral exchange rates) and justify your ranking.

    a. An American returning from a trip to Turkey wants to exchange his Turkish lira for U.S. dollars at the airport.
    b. Citigroup and HSBC, both large commercial banks located in the United States and United Kingdom, respectively, need to clear several large checks drawn on accounts held by each bank.
    c. Honda Motor Company needs to exchange yen for U.S. dollars to pay American workers at its Ohio manufacturing plant.
    d. A Canadian tourist in Germany pays for her hotel room using a credit card.

N E T W O R K

Visit the ft.com website (or another financial website such as oanda.com or xe.com), and download the same exchange rates shown in Table 2-1 for today's date. For all currencies (other than the dollar), compute the one-year percentage appreciation or depreciation against the dollar. For the dollar, compute the one-year percentage appreciation or depreciation against each currency. (*Hint:* Google "ft.com cross rates.")

Visit the OANDA website (oanda.com) to explore recent exchange rate trends for any pair of countries in the world. Download some series to a spreadsheet for manipulation, or use the FXGraph on-line graphing tools to plot trends. Try to plot examples of some fixed and floating rates. See whether you can locate data for an exchange rate crisis during recent years. Can you tell from the data which countries are fixed and which are floating?

Next visit the IMF's website (imf.org) and locate the latest classification of the de facto exchange rate regimes in all countries around the world, the same source used in Figure 2-4. Do your regime classifications agree with the IMF's?

Exchange Rates I: The Monetary Approach in the Long Run

1. Exchange Rates and Prices in the Long Run
2. Money, Prices, and Exchange Rates in the Long Run
3. The Monetary Approach
4. Money, Interest, and Prices in the Long Run
5. Monetary Regimes and Exchange Rate Regimes
6. Conclusions

Our willingness to pay a certain price for foreign money must ultimately and essentially be due to the fact that this money possesses a purchasing power as against commodities and services in that foreign country.
  Gustav Cassel, of the Swedish school of economics, 1922

The fundamental things apply / As time goes by.
  Herman Hupfeld, songwriter, 1931 (featured in the film *Casablanca*, 1942)

The cost of living is usually rising, but it rises in some places more than others. From 1970 to 1990, for example, a standardized Canadian basket of consumer goods rose in price considerably. In 1970 a Canadian would have spent C$100 (100 Canadian dollars) to purchase this basket; by 1990 the same basket cost C$392. Thus, Canadian prices rose by 292%. Over the same period, in the United States, a basket of goods that initially cost $100 in 1970 had risen in cost to $336 by 1990. Thus, U.S. prices rose by only 236%. Both countries witnessed serious inflation, but Canadian prices rose more.

Did these price changes cause U.S. goods to appear relatively cheaper? Would they have caused Canadians to start spending more on U.S. goods, or Americans to spend less on Canadian goods?

The answer to all three questions is no. In 1970 C$1 was worth almost exactly $1 (1 U.S. dollar). So in 1970 both baskets cost the same *when their cost was expressed in a common currency*, about C$100 = $100. By 1990, however, the Canadian dollar (also called the loonie) had depreciated relative to its 1970 value and C$1.16 was needed to buy $1.00. Thus, the $336 U.S. basket in 1990 actually cost $336 × 1.16 = C$390 when expressed in Canadian currency—almost the same price as the C$392 Canadian basket! (Conversely, expressed in U.S. currency, the Canadian basket cost about 392/1.16 = $338, almost the same as the $336 U.S. basket.)

In this example, although Canadian prices rose about 16% more than U.S. prices, U.S. residents also found that each of their U.S. dollars could buy about 16% more loonies. From the U.S. point of view, the cost of the baskets in each country *expressed in U.S. dollars* rose by about the same amount. The same was true from the Canadian perspective with all prices expressed in loonies. Economists (such as Gustav Cassel, quoted previously) would say that the relative *purchasing power* of each currency (in terms of U.S. versus Canadian goods) had remained the same.

Is it a coincidence that the changes in prices and exchange rates turned out that way? A fundamental economic hypothesis, which we explore in this chapter, asserts that this outcome is *not* a coincidence at all—and that *in the long run*, prices and exchange rates will always adjust so that the purchasing power of each currency remains comparable over baskets of goods in different countries (as here, where $100 and C$100 could purchase comparable amounts of goods in 1970, and also in 1990). This hypothesis provides another key building block in the theory of how exchange rates are determined. How?

In the last chapter, uncovered interest parity provided us with a theory of how the spot exchange rate is determined, given knowledge of three variables: the expected future exchange rate, the home interest rate, and the foreign interest rate. In this chapter we look at the long run to see how the expected future exchange rate is determined; then, in the next chapter, we turn to the short run and discuss how interest rates are determined in each country. When all the pieces are put together, we will have a complete theory of how exchange rates are determined in the short run and the long run.

If investors are to make forecasts of future exchange rates, they need a plausible theory of how exchange rates are determined in the long run. The theory we develop in this chapter has two parts. The first part involves the theory of purchasing power, which links the exchange rate to price levels in each country in the long run. This theory provides a partial explanation of the determinants of long-run exchange rates, but it raises another question: How are price levels determined? In the second part of the chapter, we explore how price levels are related to monetary conditions in each country. Combining the monetary theory of price level determination with the purchasing power theory of exchange rate determination, we emerge with a *long-run* theory known as the **monetary approach to exchange rates.** The goal of this chapter is to set out the long-run relationships between money, prices, and exchange rates.

1 Exchange Rates and Prices in the Long Run: Purchasing Power Parity and Goods Market Equilibrium

Just as arbitrage occurs in the international market for financial assets, it also occurs in the international markets for goods. The result of goods market arbitrage is that the prices of goods in different countries expressed in a common currency must tend to be equalized. Applied to a single good, this idea is referred to as the *law of one price*; applied to an entire basket of goods, it is called the theory of *purchasing power parity*.

Why should these "laws" hold? If the price of a good were not the same in two locations, buyers would rush to buy at the cheap location (forcing prices up there) and would shy away from the expensive location (forcing prices down there). Some factors, such as the costs of transporting goods between locations, may hinder the process of arbitrage, and more refined models take such frictions into account. For now, however, our goal is to develop a simple yet useful theory based on an idealized world of *frictionless trade* where transaction costs can be neglected. We start at the microeconomic level with single goods and the law of one price. We then move to the macroeconomic level to consider baskets of goods and purchasing power parity.

The Law of One Price

The **law of one price (LOOP)** states that in the absence of trade frictions (such as transport costs and tariffs), and under conditions of free competition and price flexibility (where no individual sellers or buyers have power to manipulate prices and prices can freely adjust), identical goods sold in different locations must sell for the same price when prices are expressed in a common currency.

To see how the law of one price operates, consider the trade in diamonds that takes place between the United States and the Netherlands. Suppose that a diamond of a given quality is priced at €5,000 in the Amsterdam market, and the exchange rate is $1.20 per euro. If the law of one price holds, the same-quality diamond should sell in New York for (€5,000 per diamond) × (1.20 $/€) = $6,000 per diamond.

Why will the prices be the same? Under competitive conditions and frictionless trade, arbitrage will ensure this outcome. If diamonds were more expensive in New York, arbitragers would buy at a low price in Holland and sell at a high price in Manhattan. If Dutch prices were higher, arbitragers would profit from the reverse trade. *By definition*, in a market equilibrium there are no arbitrage opportunities. If diamonds can be freely moved between New York and Amsterdam, both markets must offer the same price. Economists refer to this situation in the two locations as an *integrated market*.

We can mathematically state the law of one price as follows, for the case of any good g sold in two locations, say, Europe (EUR, meaning the Eurozone) and the United States (US). The *relative price* of good g (denoted $q^g_{US/EUR}$) is the ratio of the good's price in Europe relative to the good's price in the United States where both prices are expressed in a common currency.

Using subscripts to indicate locations and currencies, the relative price can be written

$$\underbrace{q^g_{US/EUR}}_{\text{Relative price of good } g \text{ in Europe versus U.S.}} = \underbrace{(E_{\$/€} P^g_{EUR})}_{\text{European price of good } g \text{ in \$}} / \underbrace{P^g_{US}}_{\text{U.S. price of good } g \text{ in \$}}$$

where P^g_{US} is the good's price in the United States, P^g_{EUR} is the good's price in Europe, and $E_{\$/€}$ is the dollar-euro exchange rate used to convert euro prices into dollar prices.

Notice that $q^g_{US/EUR}$ expresses the rate at which goods can be exchanged: it tells us how many units of the U.S. good are needed to purchase one unit of the same good in Europe (hence, the subscript uses the notation US/EUR). This contrasts with the nominal exchange rate $E_{\$/€}$ which expresses the rate at which currencies can be exchanged ($/€).

The law of one price may or may not hold. Recall from Chapter 2 that there are three possibilities in an arbitrage situation of this kind: the ratio exceeds 1 and the good is costlier in Europe; the ratio is less than 1 and the good is cheaper in Europe; or $E_{\$/€} P^g_{EUR} = P^g_{US}$, the ratio is $q^g_{US/EUR} = 1$, and the good is the same price in both locations. Only in the final case is there no arbitrage, the condition that defines market equilibrium. In equilibrium, European and U.S. prices, expressed in the same currency, are equal; the relative price q equals 1, and the law of one price holds.

How does the law of one price further our understanding of exchange rates? We can rearrange the equation for price equality, $E_{\$/\euro} P^g_{EUR} = P^g_{US}$, to show that if the law of one price holds, then the exchange rate must equal the ratio of the goods' prices expressed in the two currencies:

$$\underbrace{E_{\$/\euro}}_{\text{Exchange rate}} = \underbrace{P^g_{US}/P^g_{EUR}}_{\text{Ratio of goods' prices}}$$

One final word of caution: given our concerns in the previous chapter about the right way to define the exchange rate, we must take care when using expressions that are ratios to ensure that the units on each side of the equation correspond. In the last equation, we know we have it right because the left-hand side is expressed in dollars per euro and the right-hand side is also a ratio of dollars to euros ($ per unit of goods divided by € per unit of goods).

Purchasing Power Parity

The principle of **purchasing power parity (PPP)** is the macroeconomic counterpart to the microeconomic law of one price (LOOP). The law of one price relates exchange rates to the relative prices of an individual good, while purchasing power parity relates exchange rates to the relative prices of a basket of goods. In studying international macroeconomics, purchasing power parity is the more relevant concept.

We can define a *price level* (denoted P) in each location as a weighted average of the prices of all goods g in a basket, using the same goods and weights in both locations. Let P_{US} be the basket's price in the United States and P_{EUR} the basket's price in Europe. *If the law of one price holds for each good in the basket, it will also hold for the price of the basket as a whole.*[1]

To express PPP algebraically, we can compute the relative price of the two baskets of goods in each location, denoted $q_{US/EUR}$:

$$\underbrace{q_{US/EUR}}_{\substack{\text{Relative price of} \\ \text{basket in Europe} \\ \text{versus U.S.}}} = \underbrace{(E_{\$/\euro} P_{EUR})}_{\substack{\text{European} \\ \text{price of basket} \\ \text{expressed in \$}}} / \underbrace{P_{US}}_{\substack{\text{U.S. price} \\ \text{of basket} \\ \text{expressed in \$}}}$$

Just as there were three possible outcomes for the law of one price, there are three possibilities for PPP: the basket is cheaper in United States; the basket is cheaper in Europe; or $E_{\$/\euro} P_{EUR} = P_{US}$; or the basket is the same price in both locations $q_{US/EUR} = 1$. In the first two cases, the basket is cheaper in one location and profitable arbitrage on the baskets is possible. Only in the third case is there no arbitrage. PPP holds *when price levels in two countries are equal when expressed in a common currency*. This statement about equality of price levels is also called **absolute PPP**.

---

[1] For example, if the law of one price holds and $P^g_{US} = (E_{\$/\euro}) \times (P^g_{EUR})$ for all goods g, this implies that for N goods, the *arithmetic* weighted average satisfies $\sum_{g=1}^{N} \omega^g P^g_{US} = (E_{\$/\euro}) \times \sum_{g=1}^{N} \omega^g P^g_{EUR}$ for any set of weights ω^g that sum to 1, so PPP holds. The same is also true for *geometric* averages. Technically speaking, this follows for *any* price index definition that satisfies the usually required property that the index be homogeneous of degree 1 in the individual goods' prices.

For example, suppose the European basket costs €100, and the exchange rate is $1.20 per euro. For PPP to hold, the U.S. basket would have to cost $1.20 \times 100 = \$120$.

The Real Exchange Rate

The relative price of the two countries' baskets (denoted q) is the macroeconomic counterpart to the microeconomic relative price of individual goods (q^g). The relative price of the baskets is one of the most important variables in international macroeconomics, and it has a special name: it is known as the **real exchange rate.** The real exchange rate $q_{US/EUR} = E_{\$/€}P_{EUR}/P_{US}$ tells us how many U.S. baskets are needed to purchase one European basket.

As with the nominal exchange rate, we need to be careful about what is in the numerator of the real exchange rate and what is in the denominator. According to our definition (based on the case we just examined), we will refer to $q_{US/EUR} = E_{\$/€}P_{EUR}/P_{US}$ as the home country, or U.S. real exchange rate: it is the price of the European basket in terms of the U.S. basket (or, if we had a Home–Foreign example, the price of a Foreign basket in terms of a Home basket).

To avoid confusion, it is essential to understand the difference between nominal exchange rates (which we have studied so far) and real exchange rates. The exchange rate for currencies is a *nominal* concept; it says how many dollars can be exchanged for one euro. The real exchange rate is a *real* concept; it says how many U.S. baskets of goods can be exchanged for one European basket.

The real exchange rate has some terminology similar to that used with the nominal exchange rate:

- If the real exchange rate rises (more Home goods are needed in exchange for Foreign goods), we say Home has experienced a **real depreciation.**
- If the real exchange rate falls (fewer Home goods are needed in exchange for Foreign goods), we say Home has experienced a **real appreciation.**

Absolute PPP and the Real Exchange Rate

We can restate absolute PPP in terms of real exchange rates: *purchasing power parity states that the real exchange rate is equal to 1*. Under absolute PPP, all baskets have the same price when expressed in a common currency, so their relative price is 1.

It is common practice to use the absolute PPP-implied level of 1 as a benchmark or reference level for the real exchange rate. This leads naturally to some new terminology:

- If the real exchange rate $q_{US/EUR}$ is below 1 by $x\%$, then Foreign goods are relatively cheap, $x\%$ cheaper than Home goods. In this case, the Home currency (the dollar) is said to be *strong*, the euro is *weak*, and we say the euro is **undervalued** by $x\%$.
- If the real exchange rate $q_{US/EUR}$ is above 1 by $x\%$, then Foreign goods are relatively expensive, $x\%$ more expensive than Home goods. In this case, the Home currency (the dollar) is said to be *weak*, the euro is *strong*, and we say the euro is **overvalued** by $x\%$.

For example, if a European basket costs $E_{\$/€}P_{EUR} = \$550$ in dollar terms, and a U.S. basket costs only $P_{US} = \$500$, then $q_{US/EUR} = E_{\$/€}P_{EUR}/P_{US} = \$550/\$500 = 1.10$, the euro is strong, and the euro is 10% overvalued against the dollar.

Absolute PPP, Prices, and the Nominal Exchange Rate

Finally, just as we did with the law of one price, we can rearrange the no-arbitrage equation for the equality of price levels, $E_{\$/€}P_{EUR} = P_{US}$, to allow us to solve for the exchange rate that would be implied by absolute PPP:

$$\text{Absolute PPP:} \quad \underbrace{E_{\$/€}}_{\text{Exchange rate}} = \underbrace{P_{US}/P_{EUR}}_{\text{Ratio of price levels}} \tag{3-1}$$

This is one of the most important equations in our course of study because it shows how PPP (or absolute PPP) makes a clear prediction about exchange rates:

Purchasing power parity implies that the exchange rate at which two currencies trade equals the relative price levels of the two countries.

For example, if a basket of goods costs $460 in the United States and the same basket costs €400 in Europe, the theory of PPP predicts an exchange rate of $460/€400 = $1.15 per euro.

Thus, if we know the price levels in different locations, we can use PPP to determine an implied exchange rate, subject to all of our earlier assumptions about frictionless trade, flexible prices, free competition, and identical goods. The PPP relationship between the price levels in two countries and the exchange rate is therefore a key building block in our theory of how exchange rates are determined, as shown in Figure 3-1. Moreover, the theory is not tied to any point in time: if we can forecast future price levels, then we can also use PPP to forecast the expected future exchange rate implied by those forecasted future price levels, which is the main goal of this chapter.

Relative PPP, Inflation, and Exchange Rate Depreciation

PPP in its absolute PPP form involves price levels, but in macroeconomics we are often more interested in the rate at which price levels change than we are in the price levels themselves. The rate of change of the price level is known as the *rate of inflation*, or simply **inflation.** For example, if the price level today is 100, and one year from now it is 103.5, then the rate of inflation is 3.5% (per year). Because inflation is such an important variable in macroeconomics, we examine the implications of PPP for the study of inflation.

To consider changes over time, we introduce a subscript t to denote the time period, and calculate the rate of change of both sides of Equation (3-1) from period t to

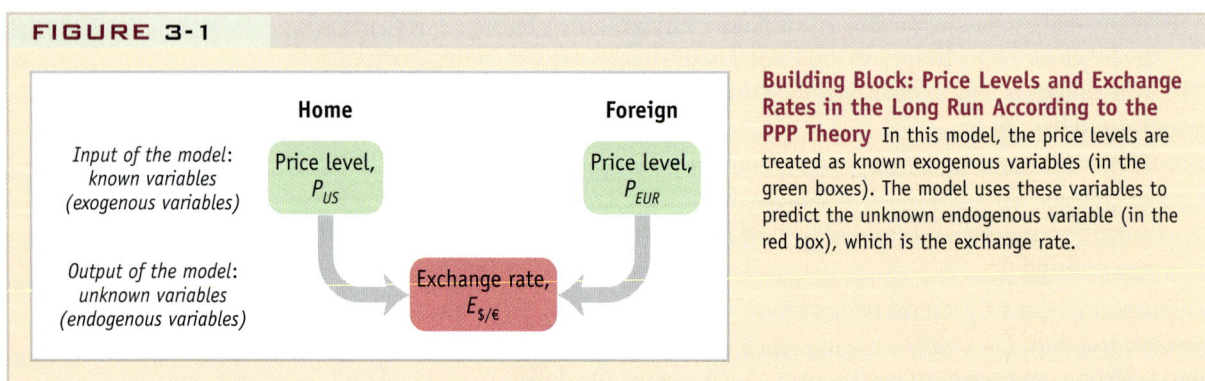

FIGURE 3-1

Building Block: Price Levels and Exchange Rates in the Long Run According to the PPP Theory In this model, the price levels are treated as known exogenous variables (in the green boxes). The model uses these variables to predict the unknown endogenous variable (in the red box), which is the exchange rate.

period $t + 1$. On the left-hand side, the rate of change of the exchange rate in Home is the rate of exchange rate depreciation in Home given by[2]

$$\frac{\Delta E_{\$/€,t}}{E_{\$/€,t}} = \underbrace{\frac{E_{\$/€,t+1} - E_{\$/€,t}}{E_{\$/€,t}}}_{\text{Rate of depreciation of the nominal exchange rate}}$$

On the right of Equation (3-1), the rate of change of the ratio of two price levels equals the rate of change of the numerator minus the rate of change of the denominator:[3]

$$\frac{\Delta(P_{US}/P_{EUR})}{(P_{US}/P_{EUR})} = \frac{\Delta P_{US,t}}{P_{US,t}} - \frac{\Delta P_{EUR,t}}{P_{EUR,t}}$$

$$= \underbrace{\left(\frac{P_{US,t+1} - P_{US,t}}{P_{US,t}}\right)}_{\text{Rate of inflation in U.S. }\pi_{US,t}} - \underbrace{\left(\frac{P_{EUR,t+1} - P_{EUR,t}}{P_{EUR,t}}\right)}_{\text{Rate of inflation in Europe }\pi_{EUR,t}} = \pi_{US} - \pi_{EUR}$$

where the terms in brackets are the inflation rates in each location, denoted π_{US} and π_{EUR}, respectively.

If Equation (3-1) holds for levels of exchange rates and prices, then it must also hold for rates of change in these variables. By combining the last two expressions, we obtain

$$\text{Relative PPP:} \quad \underbrace{\frac{\Delta E_{\$/€,t}}{E_{\$/€,t}}}_{\text{Rate of depreciation of the nominal exchange rate}} = \underbrace{\pi_{US,t} - \pi_{EUR,t}}_{\text{Inflation differential}} \quad (3\text{-}2)$$

This way of expressing PPP is called **relative PPP,** and it *implies that the rate of depreciation of the nominal exchange rate equals the difference between the inflation rates of two countries (the inflation differential).*

We saw relative PPP in action in the example at the start of this chapter. Over 20 years, Canadian prices rose 16% more than U.S. prices, and the Canadian dollar depreciated 16% against the U.S. dollar. Converting these to annual rates, Canadian prices rose by 0.75% per year more than U.S. prices (the inflation differential), and the loonie depreciated by 0.75% per year against the dollar. Relative PPP held in this case.[4]

Two points should be kept in mind about relative PPP. First, unlike absolute PPP, relative PPP predicts a relationship between *changes* in prices and *changes* in exchange rates, rather than a relationship between their levels. Second, remember that relative PPP is *derived from* absolute PPP. Hence, the latter always implies the former: *if absolute PPP holds, this implies that relative PPP must hold also.* But the converse need not be true: *relative PPP does not necessarily imply absolute PPP* (if relative PPP holds, absolute PPP can hold or fail). For example, imagine that all goods consistently cost 20% more in country A than in country B, so absolute PPP fails; however, it still can be the case that the inflation differential between A and B (say, 5%) is always equal to the rate of depreciation (say, 5%), so relative PPP will still hold.

---

[2] The rate of depreciation at Home and the rate of appreciation in Foreign are approximately equal, as we saw in the previous chapter.
[3] This expression is exact for small changes and otherwise holds true as an approximation.
[4] Note that the rates of change are approximate, with $1.0075^{20} = 1.16$.

Summary

The purchasing power parity theory, whether in the absolute PPP or relative PPP form, suggests that price levels in different countries and exchange rates are tightly linked, either in their absolute levels or in the rates at which they change. To assess how useful this theory is, let's look at some empirical evidence to see how well the theory matches reality. We can then reexamine the workings of PPP and reassess its underlying assumptions.

APPLICATION

Evidence for PPP in the Long Run and Short Run

Is there evidence for PPP? The data offer some support for relative PPP most clearly over the long run, when even moderate inflation mounts and leads to large cumulative changes in price levels and, hence, substantial cumulative inflation differentials.

The scatterplot in Figure 3-2 shows average rates of depreciation and inflation differentials for a sample of countries compared with the United States over three decades from 1975 to 2005. If relative PPP were true, then the depreciation of each country's currency would exactly equal the inflation differential, and the data would line up on the 45-degree line. We see that this is not literally true in the data, but the correlation

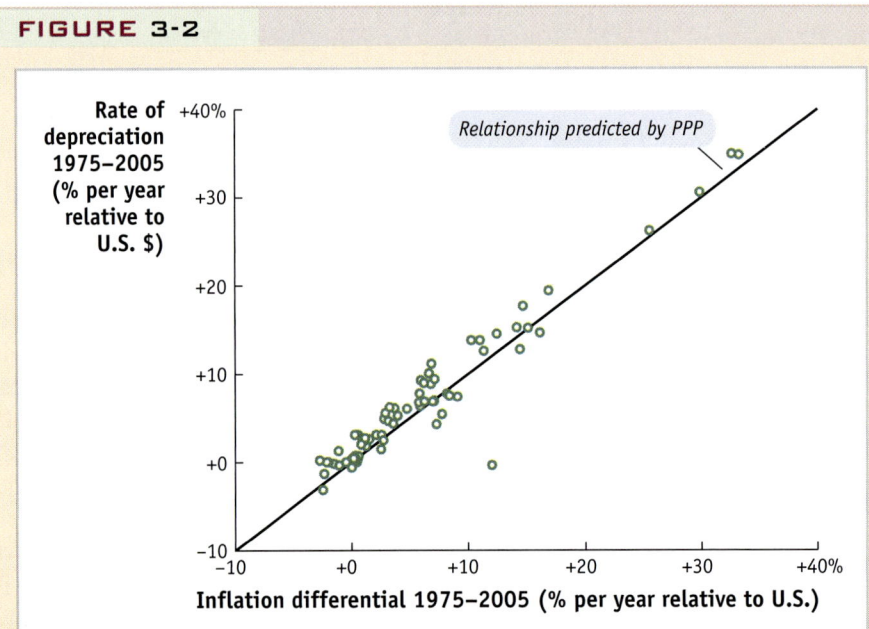

FIGURE 3-2

Inflation Differentials and the Exchange Rate, 1975–2005 This scatterplot shows the relationship between the rate of exchange rate depreciation against the U.S. dollar (the vertical axis) and the inflation differential against the United States (horizontal axis) over the long run, based on data for a sample of 82 countries. The correlation between the two variables is strong and bears a close resemblance to the theoretical prediction of PPP that all data points would appear on the 45-degree line.

Source: IMF, International Financial Statistics.

is close. Relative PPP is an approximate, useful guide to the relationship between prices and exchange rates in the long run, over horizons of many years or decades.

But the purchasing power theory turns out to be a fairly useless theory in the short run, over horizons of just a few years. This is easily seen by examining the time series of relative price ratio and exchange rates for any pair of countries, and looking at the behavior of these variables from year to year and not just over a long period. If absolute PPP held at all times, then the exchange rate would always be equal to the relative price ratio. Figure 3-3 shows 35 years of data for the United States and United Kingdom from 1975 to 2009. This figure confirms the relevance of absolute and relative PPP in the long run because the price-level ratio and the exchange rate have similar levels and drift together along a common trend. In the short run, however, the two series show substantial and persistent differences. In any given year the differences can be 10%, 20%, or more. These year-to-year differences in levels and changes show that absolute and relative PPP fail in the short run. For example, from 1980 to 1985, the pound depreciated by 45% (from $2.32 to $1.28), but the cumulative inflation differential over these five years was only 9%. ∎

How Slow Is Convergence to PPP?

If PPP were taken as a strict proposition for the short run, it would require price adjustment via arbitrage to happen fully and instantaneously, rapidly closing the gap between common-currency prices in different countries for all goods in the basket. This doesn't happen. The evidence suggests that PPP works better in the long run. But how long is the long run?

Research shows that price differences—the deviations from PPP—can be quite persistent. Estimates suggest that these deviations may die out at a rate of about 15% per year. This kind of measure is often called a *speed of convergence*: in this case, it implies that after one year, 85% (0.85) of an initial price difference persists; compounding, after two years, 72% of the gap persists ($0.72 = 0.85^2$); and after four years, 52%

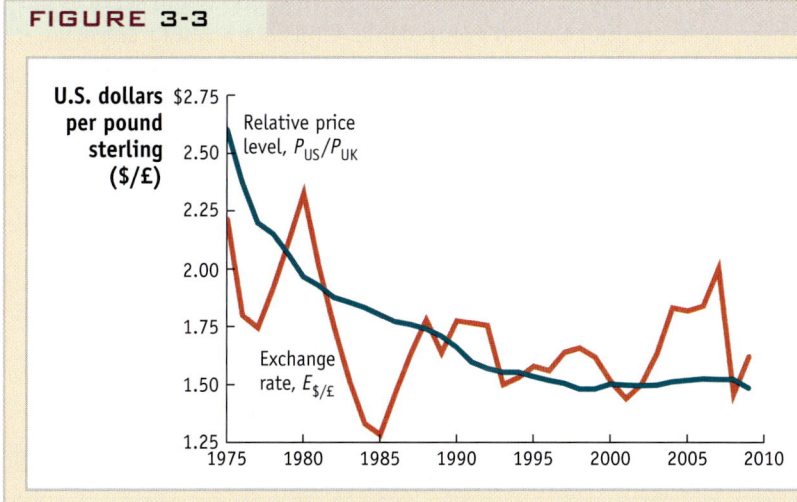

FIGURE 3-3

Exchange Rates and Relative Price Levels Data for the United States and United Kingdom for 1975 to 2009 show that the exchange rate and relative price levels do not always move together in the short run. Relative price levels tend to change slowly and have a small range of movement; exchange rates move more abruptly and experience large fluctuations. Therefore, relative PPP does *not* hold in the short run. However, it is a better guide to the long run, and we can see that the two series do tend to drift together over the decades.

Source: Penn World Tables, version 6.3, updated using IMF data for 2008–2009.

($0.52 = 0.85^4$). Thus, approximately half of any PPP deviation still remains after four years: economists would refer to this as a four-year *half-life*.

Such estimates provide a rule of thumb that is useful as a guide to forecasting real exchange rates. For example, suppose the home basket costs $100 and the foreign basket $90, in home currency. Home's real exchange rate is 0.900, and the home currency is overvalued, with foreign goods less expensive than home goods. The deviation of the real exchange rate from the PPP-implied level of 1 is −10% (or −0.1). Our rule of thumb tells us that next year 15% of this deviation will have disappeared (i.e., 0.015), so the new deviation will be only −0.085, meaning that Home's real exchange rate would be forecast to be 0.915 after one year and thus end up a little bit closer to 1, after a small depreciation. Similarly, after four years, all else being equal, 52% of the deviation (or 0.052) would have been erased, and the real exchange rate would by then be 0.952, only −5% from PPP. (See **Side Bar: Forecasting When the Real Exchange Rate Is Undervalued or Overvalued.**)

What Explains Deviations from PPP?

If it takes four years for even half of any given price difference to dissipate, as research has indicated, it is no surprise that PPP does not hold in the short run. But how can arbitrage take so long to eliminate price differences? Economists have found a variety of reasons why PPP fails in the short run:

- *Transaction costs.* Trade is not frictionless as we have assumed thus far because the costs of international transportation are significant for most goods and because some goods also bear additional costs, such as tariffs and duties, when they cross borders. By some recent estimates, transportation costs may add about 20% on average to the price of goods moving internationally, while tariffs (and other policy barriers) may add another 10%.[5] Other costs arise due to the time it takes to ship goods, and the costs and time delays associated with developing distribution networks and satisfying legal and regulatory requirements in foreign markets.

- *Nontraded goods.* Some goods are inherently nontradable; one can think of them as having infinitely high transaction costs. Most goods and services fall somewhere between tradable and nontradable. Consider a restaurant meal; it includes traded goods such as some raw foods and nontraded goods such as the work of the chef. As a result, PPP may not hold. (See **Headlines: The Big Mac Index.**)

- *Imperfect competition and legal obstacles.* Many goods are not simple undifferentiated commodities, as LOOP and PPP assume, but are differentiated products with brand names, copyrights, and legal protection. For example, consumers have the choice of cheaper generic acetaminophen or a pricier brand-name product such as Tylenol, but these are not seen as perfect substitutes. Such differentiated goods create conditions of *imperfect competition* because firms have some power to set the price of their good. With this kind of *market power*, firms can charge different prices not just across brands but also across countries

---

[5] There is also evidence of other significant border-related barriers to trade. See James Anderson and Eric van Wincoop, September 2004, "Trade Costs," *Journal of Economic Literature*, 42, 691–751.

SIDE BAR

Forecasting When the Real Exchange Rate Is Undervalued or Overvalued

When relative PPP holds, forecasting exchange rate changes is simple: just compute the inflation differential. But how do we forecast when PPP doesn't hold, as is often the case? Even if the real exchange rate is not equal to 1, knowing the real exchange rate and the convergence speed may still allow us to construct a forecast of real and nominal exchange rates.

To see how, let's take an example. Start with the definition of the real exchange rate, $q_{US/EUR} = E_{\$/€} P_{EUR}/P_{US}$. Rearranging, we find $E_{\$/€} = q_{US/EUR} \times (P_{US}/P_{EUR})$. By taking the rate of change of that expression, we find that the rate of change of the nominal exchange rate equals the rate of change of the real exchange rate plus home inflation minus foreign inflation:

$$\underbrace{\frac{\Delta E_{\$/€,t}}{E_{\$/€,t}}}_{\substack{\text{Rate of depreciation} \\ \text{of the nominal} \\ \text{exchange rate}}} = \underbrace{\frac{\Delta q_{US/EUR,t}}{q_{US/EUR,t}}}_{\substack{\text{Rate of depreciation} \\ \text{of the real exchange} \\ \text{rate}}} + \underbrace{\pi_{US,t} - \pi_{EUR,t}}_{\text{Inflation differential}}$$

When the real exchange rate q is constant, the first term on the right is zero and we are back to the simple world of relative PPP and Equation (3-2). For forecasting purposes, the predicted nominal depreciation is then just the second term on the right, the inflation differential. For example, if the forecast is for U.S. inflation to be 3% next year and for European inflation to be 1%, then the inflation differential is +2% and we would forecast a U.S. dollar depreciation, or rise in $E_{\$/€}$, of +2% next year.

What if q isn't constant and PPP fails? If there is currently a deviation from absolute PPP, but we still think that there will be convergence to absolute PPP in the long run, the first term on the right of the formula is not zero and we can estimate it given the right information.

To continue the example, suppose you are told that a U.S. basket of goods currently costs $100, but the European basket of the same goods costs $130. You would compute a U.S. real exchange rate $q_{US/EUR}$ of 1.30 today. But what will it be next year? If you expect absolute PPP to hold in the long run, then you expect that the U.S. real exchange rate will move toward 1. How fast? At this point, you need to know the convergence speed. Using the 15% rule of thumb, you estimate that 15% of the 0.3 gap between 1 and 1.3 (i.e., 0.045) will dissipate over the coming year. Hence, you forecast that the U.S. real exchange will fall from 1.3 to 1.255, implying a change of −3.46% in the coming year. In this case, adding the two terms on the right of the expression given previously, you forecast that the approximate change in E next year will be the change in $q_{US/EUR}$ of −3.46% plus the inflation differential of +2%, for a total of −1.46%; that is, a dollar appreciation of 1.46% against the euro.

The intuition for the result is as follows: the U.S. dollar is undervalued against the euro. If convergence to PPP is to happen, then some of that undervaluation will dissipate over the course of the year through a real appreciation of the dollar (predicted to be 3.46%). That real appreciation can be broken down into two components:

1. U.S. goods will experience higher inflation than European goods (we have predicted that the inflation differential will be +2%).
2. The remainder of the real appreciation will be accomplished via a 1.46% nominal dollar appreciation (predicted based on a convergence speed of 15% per year).

(pharmaceutical companies, e.g., charge different prices for drugs in different countries). This practice is possible because arbitrage can be shut down by legal threats or regulations. If you try to import large quantities of a firm's pharmaceutical and resell them, then, as an unauthorized distributor, you will probably hear very quickly from the firm's lawyers and/or from the government regulators. The same would apply to many other goods such as automobiles and consumer electronics.

- *Price stickiness.* One of the most common assumptions of macroeconomics is that prices are "sticky" in the short run—that is, they do not or cannot adjust quickly and flexibly to changes in market conditions. PPP assumes that arbitrage can force prices to adjust, but adjustment will be slowed down by price stickiness. Empirical evidence shows that many goods' prices do not adjust quickly in the short run. For example, in Figure 3-3, we saw that the nominal exchange rate moves up and down in a very dramatic fashion but that price levels are much more sluggish in their movements and do not fully match exchange rate changes.

Despite these problems, the evidence suggests that as a long-run theory of exchange rates, PPP is still a useful approach.[6] And PPP may become even more relevant in the future as arbitrage becomes more efficient and more goods and services are traded. Years ago we might have taken it for granted that certain goods and services (such as pharmaceuticals, customer support, health-care services) were strictly nontraded and thus not subject to arbitrage, at the international level. Today, many consumers shop for pharmaceuticals overseas to save money. If you dial a U.S. software support call center, you may find yourself being assisted by an operator in India. In some countries, citizens motivated by cost considerations may travel overseas for dental treatment, eye care, hip replacements, and other health services (so-called medical tourism or health tourism). These globalization trends may well continue.

HEADLINES

The Big Mac Index

For more than 20 years, The Economist *newspaper has engaged in a whimsical attempt to judge PPP theory based on a well-known, globally uniform consumer good: the McDonald's Big Mac. The over- or undervaluation of a currency against the U.S. dollar is gauged by comparing the relative prices of a burger in a common currency, and expressing the difference as a percentage deviation from one:*

$$\text{Big Mac Index} = q^{\text{Big Mac}} - 1 = \left(\frac{E_{\$/\text{local currency}} P_{\text{local}}^{\text{Big Mac}}}{P_{\text{US}}^{\text{Big Mac}}} \right) - 1.$$

Home of the undervalued burger?

Table 3-1 shows the July 2009 survey results, and some examples will illustrate how the calculations work. Row 1 shows the average U.S. dollar price of the Big Mac of $3.57. An example of undervaluation appears in Row 2, where we see that the Buenos Aires correspondent found the same burger cost 11.5 pesos, which, at an actual exchange rate of 3.81 pesos per dollar, worked out to be $3.02 in U.S. currency, or 15% less than the U.S. price. So the peso was 15% undervalued against the U.S. dollar according to this measure, and Argentina's exchange rate would have had to appreciate to 3.22 pesos per dollar to attain the level implied by a burger-based PPP theory. An example of overevaluation appears in Row 4, in the case of neighboring Brazil. There a Big Mac cost 8.03 reais, or $4.02 in U.S. currency at the prevailing exchange rate of 2.00 reais per dollar, making the Brazilian burgers 13% more expensive than their U.S. counterparts. To get to its PPP-implied level, and put the burgers at parity, Brazil's currency would have needed to depreciate to 2.25 reais per dollar. Looking through the table, burger disparity is typical, with only Britain, Costa Rica, Czech Republic, Hungary, Japan, and Turkey coming within ±5% of PPP.

---

[6] Alan M. Taylor and Mark P. Taylor, Fall 2004, "The Purchasing Power Parity Debate," *Journal of Economic Perspectives,* 8, 135–158.

TABLE 3-1

The Big Mac Index The table shows the price of a Big Mac in July 2009 in local currency (column 1) and converted to U.S. dollars (column 2) using the actual exchange rate (column 4). The dollar price can then be compared with the average price of a Big Mac in the United States ($3.57 in column 1, row 1). The difference (column 5) is a measure of the overvaluation (+) or undervaluation (−) of the local currency against the U.S. dollar. The exchange rate against the dollar implied by PPP (column 3) is the hypothetical price of dollars in local currency that would have equalized burger prices, which may be compared with the actual observed exchange rate (column 4).

	Big Mac Prices		Exchange rate (local currency per U.S. dollar)		Over (+)/ under (−) valuation against dollar, % (5)
	In local currency (1)	In U.S. dollars (2)	Implied by PPP (3)	Actual, July 13th (4)	
United States	$ 3.57	3.57			
Argentina	Peso 11.5	3.02	3.22	3.81	−15
Australia	A$ 4.34	3.37	1.22	1.29	−6
Brazil	Real 8.03	4.02	2.25	2.00	+13
Britain	£ 2.29	3.69	0.64	0.62	+3
Canada	C$ 3.89	3.35	1.09	1.16	−6
Chile	Peso 1750	3.19	490	549	−11
China	Yuan 12.5	1.83	3.50	6.83	−49
Colombia	Peso 7000	3.34	1,961	2,096	−6
Costa Rica	Colones 2000	3.43	560	583	−4
Czech Rep.	Koruna 67.92	3.64	19.0	18.7	+2
Denmark	DK 29.5	5.53	8.26	5.34	+55
Estonia	Kroon 32	2.85	8.96	11.2	−20
Egypt	Pound 13	2.33	3.64	5.58	−35
Euro area	€ 3.31	4.62	0.93	0.72	+29
Hong Kong	HK$ 13.3	1.72	3.73	7.75	−52
Hungary	Forint 720	3.62	202	199	+1
Iceland	Kronur 640	4.99	179	128	+40
Indonesia	Rupiah 20900	2.05	5,854	10,200	−43
Israel	Shekel 15	3.77	4.20	3.97	+6
Japan	Yen 320	3.46	89.6	92.6	−3
Latvia	Lats 1.55	3.09	0.43	0.50	−13
Lithuania	Litas 7.1	2.87	1.99	2.48	−20
Malaysia	Ringgit 6.77	1.88	1.90	3.60	−47
Mexico	Peso 33	2.39	9.24	13.8	−33
New Zealand	NZ$ 4.9	3.08	1.37	1.59	−14
Norway	Kroner 40	6.15	11.2	6.51	+72
Pakistan	Rupee 190	2.30	53.2	82.6	−36
Peru	New Sol 8.056	2.66	2.26	3.03	−25
Philippines	Peso 99.39	2.05	27.8	48.4	−42
Poland	Zloty 7.6	2.41	2.13	3.16	−33
Russia	Rouble 67	2.04	18.8	32.8	−43
Saudi Arabia	Riyal 11	2.93	3.08	3.75	−18
Singapore	S$ 4.22	2.88	1.18	1.46	−19
South Africa	Rand 17.95	2.17	5.03	8.28	−39
South Korea	Won 3400	2.59	952	1,315	−28
Sri Lanka	Rupee 210	1.83	58.8	115	−49
Sweden	SKr 39	4.93	10.9	7.90	+38
Switzerland	SFr 6.50	5.98	1.82	1.09	+68
Taiwan	Taiwan$ 75	2.26	21.0	33.2	−37
Thailand	Baht 64.49	1.89	18.1	34.2	−47
Turkey	Lire 5.65	3.65	1.58	1.55	+2
UAE	Dirhams 10	2.72	2.80	3.67	−24
Ukraine	Hryvnia 14	1.83	3.92	7.66	−49
Uruguay	Peso 61	2.63	17.1	23.2	−26

Source: "Cheesed Off," *The Economist*, July 16, 2009, and author's calculations.

2 Money, Prices, and Exchange Rates in the Long Run: Money Market Equilibrium in a Simple Model

It is time to take stock of the theory developed so far in this chapter. Up to now, we have concentrated on PPP, which says that in the long run the exchange rate is determined by the ratio of the price levels in two countries. But this prompts a question: What determines those price levels?

Monetary theory supplies an answer: according to this theory, in the long run, price levels are determined in each country by the relative demand and supply of money. You may recall this theory from previous macroeconomics courses in the context of a closed economy. This section recaps the essential elements of monetary theory and shows how they fit into our theory of exchange rates in the long run.

What Is Money?

We recall the distinguishing features of this peculiar asset that is so central to our everyday economic life. Economists think of **money** as performing three key functions in an economy:

1. Money is a *store of value* because, as with any asset, money held from today until tomorrow can still be used to buy goods and services in the future. Money's rate of return is low compared with many other assets. Because we earn no interest on it, there is an opportunity cost to holding money. If this cost is low, we will hold money more willingly than we hold other assets (stocks, bonds, etc.).

2. Money also gives us a *unit of account* in which all prices in the economy are quoted. When we enter a store in France, we expect to see the prices of goods to read something like "100 euros"—not "10,000 Japanese yen" or "500 bananas," even though, in principle, the yen or the banana could also function as a unit of account in France (bananas would, however, be a poor store of value).

3. Money is a *medium of exchange* that allows us to buy and sell goods and services without the need to engage in inefficient barter (direct swaps of goods). The ease with which we can convert money into goods and services is a measure of how *liquid* money is compared with the many illiquid assets in our portfolios (such as real estate). Money is the most liquid asset of all.

The Measurement of Money

What counts as money? Clearly, the currency in circulation is money. But do checking accounts count as money? What about savings accounts, mutual funds, and other securities? Figure 3-4 depicts the most widely used measures of the money supply and illustrates their relative magnitudes with recent data from the United States. The most basic concept of money is currency in circulation (i.e., in the hands of the nonbank public). After that, M0 is typically the narrowest definition of money (also called "base money"), and it includes both currency in circulation and the reserves of commercial banks (liquid cash held in their vaults or on deposit at the Fed). Normally, in recent years, banks' reserves have been very small indeed (they have been permitted, and preferred, to rely on other securities to provide liquidity *and* some interest income) and so M0 has been virtually identical to currency in circulation. This changed dramatically after the financial crisis of 2008 gave rise to liquidity problems, and banks began to

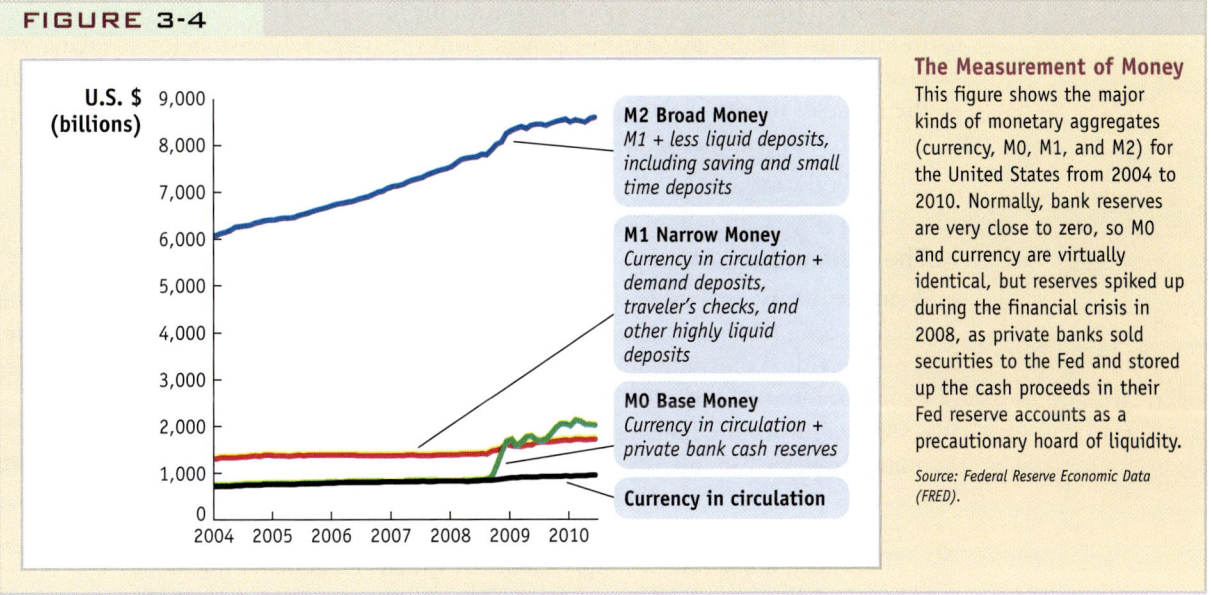

FIGURE 3-4

The Measurement of Money This figure shows the major kinds of monetary aggregates (currency, M0, M1, and M2) for the United States from 2004 to 2010. Normally, bank reserves are very close to zero, so M0 and currency are virtually identical, but reserves spiked up during the financial crisis in 2008, as private banks sold securities to the Fed and stored up the cash proceeds in their Fed reserve accounts as a precautionary hoard of liquidity.

Source: Federal Reserve Economic Data (FRED).

maintain huge reserves at the Fed as a precaution. (When and how this unprecedented hoard of cash will be unwound remains to be seen, and this is a matter of some concern to economists and policy makers.)

A different narrow measure of money, M1, includes currency in circulation plus highly liquid instruments such as demand deposits in checking accounts and traveler's checks, but it *excludes* bank's reserves, and thus may be a better gauge of money available for transactions purposes. A much broader measure of money, M2, includes slightly less liquid assets such as savings and small time deposits.[7]

For our purposes, money is defined as the *stock of liquid assets that are routinely used to finance transactions*, in the sense implied by the "medium of exchange" function of money. So when we speak of money (denoted M), we will generally mean M1, currency in circulation plus demand deposits. Many important assets are excluded from M1, including longer-term assets held by individuals and the voluminous interbank deposits used in the foreign exchange market discussed in the previous chapter. These assets do not count as money in the sense used here because they are relatively illiquid and not used routinely for transactions.

The Supply of Money

How is the supply of money determined? In practice, a country's **central bank** controls the **money supply.** Strictly speaking, by issuing notes and coins, the central bank controls directly only the level of M0, or base money, the amount of currency in the

---

[7] There is little consensus on the right broad measure of money. Until 2006 the U.S. Federal Reserve collected data on M3, which included large time deposits, repurchase agreements, and money market funds. This was discontinued because the data were costly to collect and thought to be of limited use to policy makers. In the United Kingdom, a slightly different broad measure, M4, is still used. Some economists now prefer a money aggregate called MZM, or "money of zero maturity," as the right broad measure, but its use is not widespread.

economy. However, it can *indirectly* control the level of M1 by using monetary policy to influence the behavior of the private banks that are responsible for checking deposits. The intricate mechanisms by which monetary policy affects M1 are beyond the scope of this book. In our analysis, we make the simplifying assumption that the central bank's policy tools are sufficient to allow it to control indirectly, but accurately, the level of M1.[8]

The Demand for Money: A Simple Model

A simple theory of household money demand is motivated by the assumption that the need to conduct transactions is in proportion to an individual's income. For example, if an individual's income doubles from $20,000 to $40,000, we expect his or her demand for money (expressed in dollars) to double also.

Moving from the individual or household level up to the aggregate or macroeconomic level, we can infer that the aggregate **money demand** will behave similarly. *All else equal, a rise in national dollar income (nominal income) will cause a proportional increase in transactions and, hence, in aggregate money demand.*

This insight suggests a simple model in which the demand for money is proportional to dollar income. This model is known as the **quantity theory of money**:

$$\underbrace{M^d}_{\text{Demand for money (\$)}} = \underbrace{\overline{L}}_{\text{A constant}} \times \underbrace{PY}_{\text{Nominal income (\$)}}$$

Here, PY measures the total nominal dollar value of income in the economy, equal to the price level P times real income Y. The term $\overline{L}$ is a constant that measures how much demand for liquidity is generated for each dollar of nominal income. To emphasize this point, we assume for now that every $1 of nominal income requires $\overline{L}$ of money for transactions purposes and that this relationship is constant. (Later, we relax this assumption.)

The intuition behind the equation is clear. If the price level rises by 10% and real income is fixed, we are paying a 10% higher price for all goods, so the dollar cost of transactions rises by 10%. Similarly, if real income rises by 10% but prices stay fixed, the dollar amount of transactions will rise by 10%. Hence, the *demand for nominal money balances*, M^d, is proportional to the *nominal* income PY.

Another way to look at the quantity theory is to convert all quantities into real quantities by dividing the previous equation by P, the price level (the price of a basket of goods). Quantities are then converted from nominal dollars to real units (specifically, into units of baskets of goods). These conversions allow us to derive the *demand for real money balances*:

$$\underbrace{\frac{M^d}{P}}_{\text{Demand for real money}} = \underbrace{\overline{L}}_{\text{A constant}} \times \underbrace{Y}_{\text{Real income}}$$

Real money balances are simply a measure of the purchasing power of the stock of money in terms of goods and services. The expression just given says that the

---

[8] A full treatment of this topic can be found in a textbook on money and banking. See Laurence M. Ball, *Money, Banking, and Financial Markets* 2nd edition (New York: Worth, 2010 forthcoming).

demand for real money balances is strictly proportional to real income. The more real income we have, the more real transactions we have to perform, so the more real money we need.

Equilibrium in the Money Market

The condition for equilibrium in the money market is simple to state: the demand for money M^d must equal the supply of money M, which we assume to be under the control of the central bank. Imposing this condition on the last two equations, we find that nominal money supply equals nominal money demand:

$$M = \overline{L}PY$$

and, equivalently, that real money supply equals real money demand:

$$\frac{M}{P} = \overline{L}Y$$

A Simple Monetary Model of Prices

We are now in a position to put together a simple model of the exchange rate, using two building blocks. The first building block, the quantity theory, is a model that links prices to monetary conditions. The second building block, PPP is a model that links exchange rates to prices.

We consider two countries, as before, and for simplicity we will consider the United States as the home country and Europe as the foreign country. (The model generalizes to any pair of countries.)

Let's consider the last equation given and apply it to the United States, adding U.S. subscripts for clarity. We can rearrange this formula to obtain an expression for the U.S. price level:

$$P_{US} = \frac{M_{US}}{\overline{L}_{US}Y_{US}}$$

Note that the price level is determined by how much nominal money is issued relative to the demand for real money balances: the numerator on the right-hand side is the total supply of *nominal* money; the denominator is the total demand for *real* money balances.

We can do the same rearrangement for Europe to obtain the analogous expression for the European price level:

$$P_{EUR} = \frac{M_{EUR}}{\overline{L}_{EUR}Y_{EUR}}$$

The last two equations are examples of the **fundamental equation of the monetary model of the price level.** Two such equations, one for each country, give us another important building block for our theory of prices and exchange rates as shown in Figure 3-5.

In the long run, we assume prices are flexible and will adjust to put the money market in equilibrium. For example, if the amount of money in circulation (the nominal money supply) rises, say, by a factor of 100, and real income stays the same, then there will be "more money chasing the same quantity of goods." This leads to inflation, and

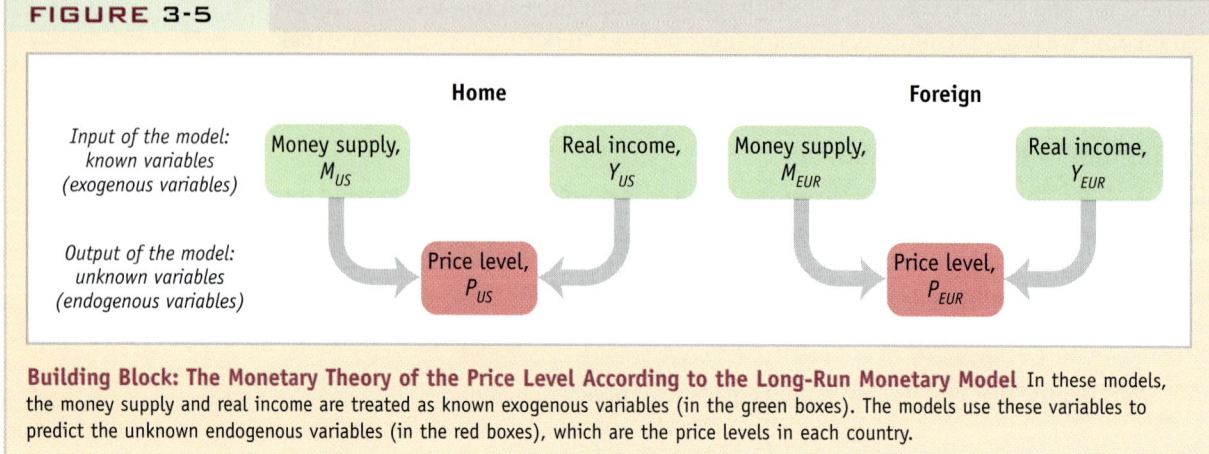

Building Block: The Monetary Theory of the Price Level According to the Long-Run Monetary Model In these models, the money supply and real income are treated as known exogenous variables (in the green boxes). The models use these variables to predict the unknown endogenous variables (in the red boxes), which are the price levels in each country.

in the long run, the price level will rise by a factor of 100. In other words, we will be in the same economy as before except that all prices will have two zeros tacked on to them.

A Simple Monetary Model of the Exchange Rate

A long-run model of the exchange rate is close at hand. If we take the last two equations, which use the monetary model to find the price level in each country, and plug them into Equation (3-1), we can use absolute PPP to solve for the exchange rate:

$$\underbrace{E_{\$/€}}_{\text{Exchange rate}} = \underbrace{\frac{P_{US}}{P_{EUR}}}_{\substack{\text{Ratio of} \\ \text{price levels}}} = \frac{\left(\frac{M_{US}}{\overline{L}_{US}Y_{US}}\right)}{\left(\frac{M_{EUR}}{\overline{L}_{EUR}Y_{EUR}}\right)} = \underbrace{\frac{(M_{US}/M_{EUR})}{(\overline{L}_{US}Y_{US}/\overline{L}_{EUR}Y_{EUR})}}_{\substack{\text{Relative nominal money} \\ \text{supplies divided by relative} \\ \text{real money demands}}} \quad (3\text{-}3)$$

This is the **fundamental equation of the monetary approach to exchange rates.** By substituting the price levels from the monetary model into PPP, we have put together the two building blocks from Figures 3-1 and 3-5. The implications of this equation are intuitive.

- Suppose the U.S. money supply increases, all else equal. The right-hand side increases (the U.S. nominal money supply increases relative to Europe), causing the exchange rate to increase (the U.S. dollar depreciates against the euro). For example, if the U.S. money supply doubles, then all else equal, the U.S. price level doubles. That is, a bigger U.S. supply of money leads to a weaker dollar. That makes sense—there are more dollars around, so you expect each dollar to be worth less.
- Now suppose the U.S. real income level increases, all else equal. Then the right-hand side decreases (the U.S. real money demand increases relative to Europe), causing the exchange rate to decrease (the U.S. dollar appreciates against the euro). For example, if the U.S. real income doubles, then all else

equal, the U.S. price level falls by a factor of one-half. That is, a stronger U.S. economy leads to a stronger dollar. That makes sense—there is more demand for the same quantity of dollars, so you expect each dollar to be worth more.

Money Growth, Inflation, and Depreciation

The model just presented uses absolute PPP to link the level of the exchange rate to the level of prices and uses the quantity theory to link prices to monetary conditions in each country. But as we have said before, macroeconomists are often more interested in rates of change of variables (e.g., inflation) rather than levels.

Can our theory be extended for this purpose? Yes, but this task takes a little work. We convert Equation (3-3) into growth rates by taking the rate of change of each term.

The first term of Equation (3-3) is the exchange rate $E_{\$/€}$. Its rate of change is the rate of depreciation $\Delta E_{\$/€}/E_{\$/€}$. When this term is positive, say, 1%, the dollar is depreciating at 1% per year; if negative, say, −2%, the dollar is appreciating at 2% per year.

The second term of Equation (3-3) is the ratio of the price levels P_{US}/P_{EUR}, and as we saw when we derived relative PPP at Equation (3-2), its rate of change is the rate of change of the numerator (U.S. inflation) minus the rate of change of the denominator (European inflation), which equals the inflation differential $\pi_{US,t} - \pi_{EUR,t}$.

What is the rate of change of the third term in Equation (3-3)? The numerator represents the U.S. price level, $P_{US} = M_{US}/\overline{L}_{US}Y_{US}$. Again, the growth rate of a fraction equals the growth rate of the numerator minus the growth rate of the denominator. In this case, the numerator is the money supply M_{US}, and its growth rate is μ_{US}:

$$\mu_{US,t} = \underbrace{\frac{M_{US,t+1} - M_{US,t}}{M_{US,t}}}_{\text{Rate of money supply growth in U.S.}}$$

The denominator is $\overline{L}_{US}Y_{US}$, which is a constant $\overline{L}_{US}$ times real income Y_{US}. Thus, $\overline{L}_{US}Y_{US}$ grows at a rate equal to the growth rate of real income g_{US}:

$$g_{US,t} = \underbrace{\frac{Y_{US,t+1} - Y_{US,t}}{Y_{US,t}}}_{\text{Rate of real income growth in U.S.}}$$

Putting all the pieces together, the growth rate of $P_{US} = M_{US}/\overline{L}_{US}Y_{US}$ equals the money supply growth rate μ_{US} minus the real income growth rate g_{US}. We have already seen that the growth rate of P_{US} on the left-hand side is the inflation rate π_{US}. Thus, we know that

$$\pi_{US,t} = \mu_{US,t} - g_{US,t} \tag{3-4}$$

The denominator of the third term of Equation (3-3) represents the European price level, $P_{EUR} = M_{EUR}/\overline{L}_{EUR}Y_{EUR}$, and its rate of change is calculated similarly:

$$\pi_{EUR,t} = \mu_{EUR,t} - g_{EUR,t} \tag{3-5}$$

The intuition for these last two expressions echoes what we said previously. When money growth is higher than real income growth, we have "more money chasing fewer goods" and this leads to inflation.

Combining Equation (3-4) and Equation (3-5), we can now solve for the inflation differential in terms of monetary fundamentals and finish our task of computing the rate of depreciation of the exchange rate:

$$\underbrace{\frac{\Delta E_{\$/€,t}}{E_{\$/€,t}}}_{\text{Rate of depreciation of the nominal exchange rate}} = \underbrace{\pi_{US,t} - \pi_{EUR,t}}_{\text{Inflation differential}} = (\mu_{US,t} - g_{US,t}) - (\mu_{EUR,t} - g_{EUR,t}) \quad (3\text{-}6)$$

$$= \underbrace{(\mu_{US,t} - \mu_{EUR,t})}_{\substack{\text{Differential in} \\ \text{nominal money supply} \\ \text{growth rates}}} - \underbrace{(g_{US,t} - g_{EUR,t})}_{\substack{\text{Differential in real} \\ \text{output growth rates}}}$$

The last term here is the rate of change of the fourth term in Equation (3-3).

Equation (3-6) is the fundamental equation of the monetary approach to exchange rates expressed in rates of change, and much of the same intuition we applied in explaining Equation (3-3) carries over here.

- If the United States runs a looser monetary policy in the long run measured by a faster money growth rate, the dollar will depreciate more rapidly, all else equal. For example, suppose Europe has a 5% annual rate of change of money and a 2% rate of change of real income; then its inflation would be the difference, 5% minus 2% equals 3%. Now suppose the United States has a 6% rate of change of money and a 2% rate of change of real income; then its inflation would be the difference, 6% minus 2% equals 4%. And the rate of depreciation of the dollar would be U.S. inflation minus European inflation, 4% minus 3%, or 1% per year.

- If the U.S. economy grows faster in the long run, the dollar will appreciate more rapidly, all else equal. In the last numerical example, suppose the U.S. growth rate of real income in the long run increases from 2% to 5%, all else equal. U.S. inflation equals the money growth rate of 6% minus the new real income growth rate of 5%, so inflation is just 1% per year. Now the rate of dollar depreciation is U.S. inflation minus European inflation, that is, 1% minus 3%, or −2% per year (meaning the U.S. dollar would now appreciate at 2% per year).

With a change of notation to make the United States the foreign country, the same lessons could be derived for Europe and the euro.

3 The Monetary Approach: Implications and Evidence

The monetary approach is the workhorse model in the study of long-run exchange rate movements. In this section, we look at some applications and empirical evidence.

Exchange Rate Forecasts Using the Simple Model

An important application of the monetary approach to exchange rate determination is to provide a forecast of the future exchange rate. Remember from the previous chapter that forex market arbitragers need such a forecast to be able to make arbitrage calculations using uncovered interest parity. Using Equation (3-3), we can see that a forecast of future exchange rates (the left-hand side) can be constructed as long as we know how to forecast future money supplies and real income (the right-hand side).

In practice, this is why expectations about money and real income in the future attract so much attention in the financial media, and especially in the forex market. The discussion returns with obsessive regularity to two questions. The first question, "What are central banks going to do?" leads to all manner of attempts to decode the statements of central bank officials. The second question, "How is the economy expected to grow in real terms?" leads to a keen interest in any economic indicators, such as productivity or investment, that might hint at changes in the rate of income growth.

Any such forecasts come with at least two major caveats. First, there is great uncertainty in trying to answer these questions, and forecasts of economic variables years in the future are inevitably subject to large errors. Nonetheless, this is one of the key tasks of financial markets. Second, whenever one uses the monetary model for forecasting, one is answering a hypothetical question: What path would exchange rates follow from now on *if prices were flexible and PPP held*? As forecasters know, in the short run there might be deviations from this prediction about exchange rate changes, but in the longer run, we expect the prediction will supply a more reasonable guide.

Forecasting Exchange Rates: An Example To see how forecasting might work, let's look at a simple scenario and focus on what would happen under flexible prices. Assume that U.S. and European real income growth rates are identical and equal to zero (0%) so that real income levels are constant. Assume also that the European money supply is constant. If the money supply and real income in Europe are constant, then the European price level is constant, and European inflation is zero, as we can see from Equation (3-5). These assumptions allow us to perform a controlled thought-experiment, and focus on changes on the U.S. side of the model, all else equal. Let's look at two cases.

Case 1: A one-time unanticipated increase in the money supply. In the first, and simpler, case, suppose at some time T that the U.S. money supply rises by a fixed proportion, say, 10%, all else equal. Assuming that prices are flexible, what does our model predict will happen to the level of the exchange rate after time T? To spell out the argument in detail, we look at the implications of our model for some key variables.

a. There is a 10% increase in the money supply M.

b. Real money balances M/P remain constant, because real income is constant.

c. These last two statements imply that price level P and money supply M must move in the same proportion, so there is a 10% increase in the price level P.

d. PPP implies that the exchange rate E and price level P must move in the same proportion, so there is a 10% increase in the exchange rate E; that is, the dollar depreciates by 10%.

A quicker solution uses the fundamental equation of the monetary approach at Equation (3-3): the price level and exchange rate are proportional to the money supply, all else equal.

Case 2: An unanticipated increase in the rate of money growth. The model also applies to more complex scenarios. Consider a second case in which the U.S. money supply is not constant, but grows at a steady fixed rate μ. Then suppose we learn at time T that the United States will raise the rate of money supply growth from some previously fixed rate μ to a slightly higher rate $\mu + \Delta\mu$. How would people expect the exchange rate to behave, assuming price flexibility? Let's work through this case step by step:

a. Money supply M is growing at a constant rate.
b. Real money balances M/P remain constant, as before.
c. These last two statements imply that price level P and money supply M must move in the same proportion, so P is always a constant multiple of M.
d. PPP implies that the exchange rate E and price level P must move in the same proportion, so E is always a constant multiple of P (and hence of M).

Corresponding to these four steps, the four panels of Figure 3-6 illustrate the path of the key variables in this example. This figure shows that if we can forecast the

FIGURE 3-6

An Increase in the Growth Rate of the Money Supply in the Simple Model Before time T, money, prices, and the exchange rate all grow at rate μ. Foreign prices are constant. In panel (a), we suppose at time T there is an increase $\Delta\mu$ in the rate of growth of home money supply M. In panel (b), the quantity theory assumes that the level of real money balances remains unchanged. After time T, if real money balances (M/P) are constant, then money M and prices P still grow at the same rate, which is now $\mu + \Delta\mu$, so the rate of inflation rises by $\Delta\mu$, as shown in panel (c). PPP and an assumed stable foreign price level imply that the exchange rate will follow a path similar to that of the domestic price level, so E also grows at the new rate $\mu + \Delta\mu$, and the rate of depreciation rises by $\Delta\mu$, as shown in panel (d).

money supply at any future period as in (a), and if we know real money balances remain constant as in (b), then we can forecast prices as in (c) and exchange rates as in (d). These forecasts are good in any future period, under the assumptions of the monetary approach. Again, Equation (3-3) supplies the answer more quickly; under the assumptions we have made, money, prices, and exchange rates all move in proportion to one another.

APPLICATION

Evidence for the Monetary Approach

The monetary approach to prices and exchange rates suggests that, all else equal, increases in the rate of money supply growth should be the same size as increases in the rate of inflation and the rate of exchange rate depreciation. Looking for evidence of this relationship in real-world data is one way to put this theory to the test.

The scatterplots in Figure 3-7 and Figure 3-8 show data from the 1975 to 2005 period for a large sample of countries. The results offer fairly strong support for the monetary theory. All else equal, Equation (3-6) predicts that an $x\%$ difference in money growth rates (relative to the United States) should be associated with an $x\%$ difference in inflation rates (relative to the United States) and an $x\%$ depreciation of the home exchange rate (against the U.S. dollar). If this association were literally true in the data, then each country in the scatterplot would be on the 45-degree line. This is not exactly true, but the actual relationship is very close and offers some support for the monetary approach.

One reason the data do not sit on the 45-degree line is that all else is *not* equal in this sample of countries. In Equation (3-6), countries differ not only in their relative

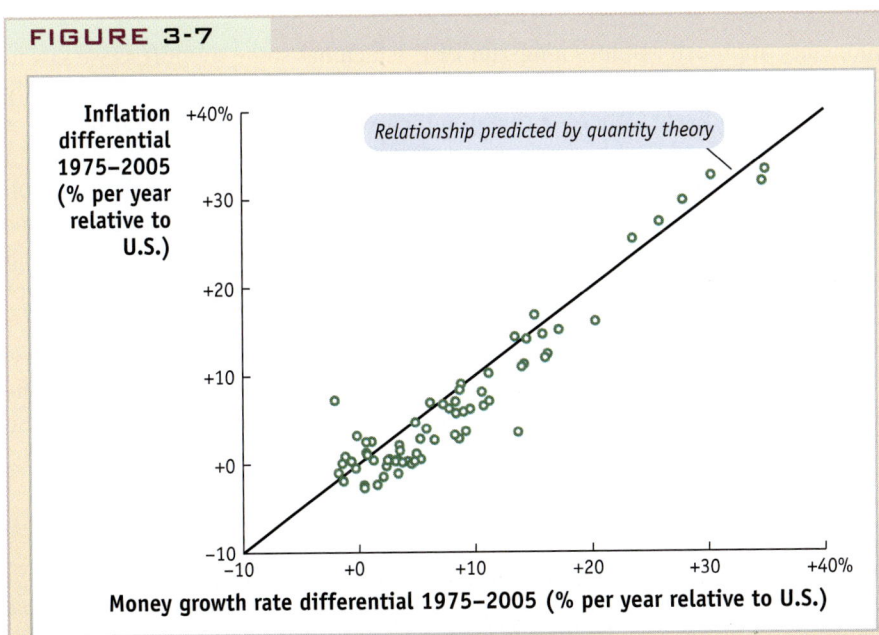

FIGURE 3-7

Inflation Rates and Money Growth Rates, 1975–2005
This scatterplot shows the relationship between the rate of inflation and the money supply growth rate over the long run, based on data for a sample of 76 countries. The correlation between the two variables is strong and bears a close resemblance to the theoretical prediction of the monetary model that all data points would appear on the 45-degree line.

Source: IMF, International Financial Statistics.

FIGURE 3-8

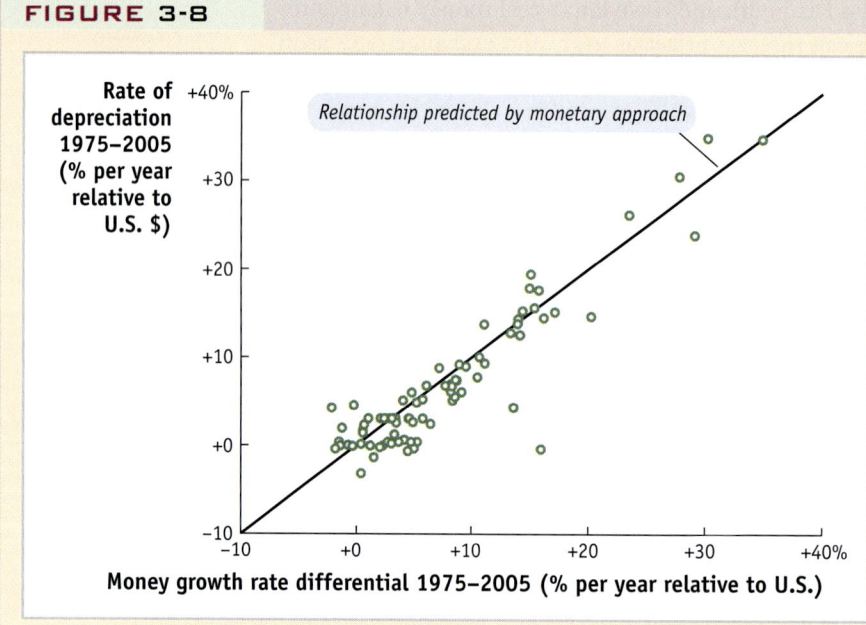

Money Growth Rates and the Exchange Rate, 1975–2005
This scatterplot shows the relationship between the rate of exchange rate depreciation against the U.S. dollar and the money growth rate differential versus the United States over the long run, based on data for a sample of 82 countries. The data show a strong correlation between the two variables and a close resemblance to the theoretical prediction of the monetary approach to exchange rates, which would predict that all data points would appear on the 45-degree line.

Source: IMF, International Financial Statistics.

money supply growth rates but also in their real income growth rates. Another explanation is that we have been assuming the money demand parameter L is constant, and this may not be true in reality. This is an issue we must now confront.[9] ■

APPLICATION

Hyperinflations of the Twentieth Century

The monetary approach assumes long-run PPP, which has some support as we saw in Figure 3-2. But we have been careful to note, again, that PPP generally works poorly in the short run. However, there is one notable exception to this general failure of PPP in the short run: hyperinflations.

Economists traditionally define a **hyperinflation** as occurring when the inflation rises to a sustained rate of more than 50% *per month* (which means that prices are doubling every 51 days). In common usage, some lower-inflation episodes are also called hyperinflations; for example, an inflation rate of 1,000% *per year* is a common rule of thumb (when inflation is "only" 22% per month).

There have been many hyperinflations worldwide since the early twentieth century. They usually occur when governments face a budget crisis, are unable to borrow to finance a deficit, and instead choose to print money to cover their financing needs. The situation is not sustainable and usually leads to economic, social, or political crisis,

---

[9] Economists can use sophisticated statistical techniques to address these issues and still find results favorable to the monetary approach in the long run. See David E. Rapach and Mark E. Wohar, 2002, "Testing the Monetary Model of Exchange Rate Determination: New Evidence from a Century of Data," *Journal of International Economics*, 58(2), 359–385.

which is eventually resolved with a return to price stability. (For more discussion of hyperinflations and their consequences, see **Headlines: The First Hyperinflation of the Twenty-First Century** and **Side Bar: Currency Reform**.)

PPP in Hyperinflations Each of these crises provides a unique laboratory for testing the predictions of the PPP theory. The scatterplot in Figure 3-9 looks at the data using changes in levels (from start to finish, expressed as multiples). The change in the exchange rate (with the United States) is on the vertical axis and the change in the price level (compared with the United States) is on the horizontal axis. Because of the huge changes involved, both axes use log scales in powers of 10. For example, 10^{12} on the vertical axis means the exchange rate rose (the currency depreciated) by a factor of a trillion against the U.S. dollar during the hyperinflation.

If PPP holds, changes in prices and exchange rates should be equal and all observations would be on the 45-degree line. The changes follow this pattern very closely, providing support for PPP. What the hyperinflations have in common is that a very large depreciation was about equal to a very large inflation differential. In an economy with fairly stable prices and exchange rates, large changes in exchange rates and prices only develop over the very long run of years and decades; in a hyperinflation, large inflations and large depreciations are compressed into the short run of years or months, so this is one case where PPP holds quite well even in the short run.

FIGURE 3-9

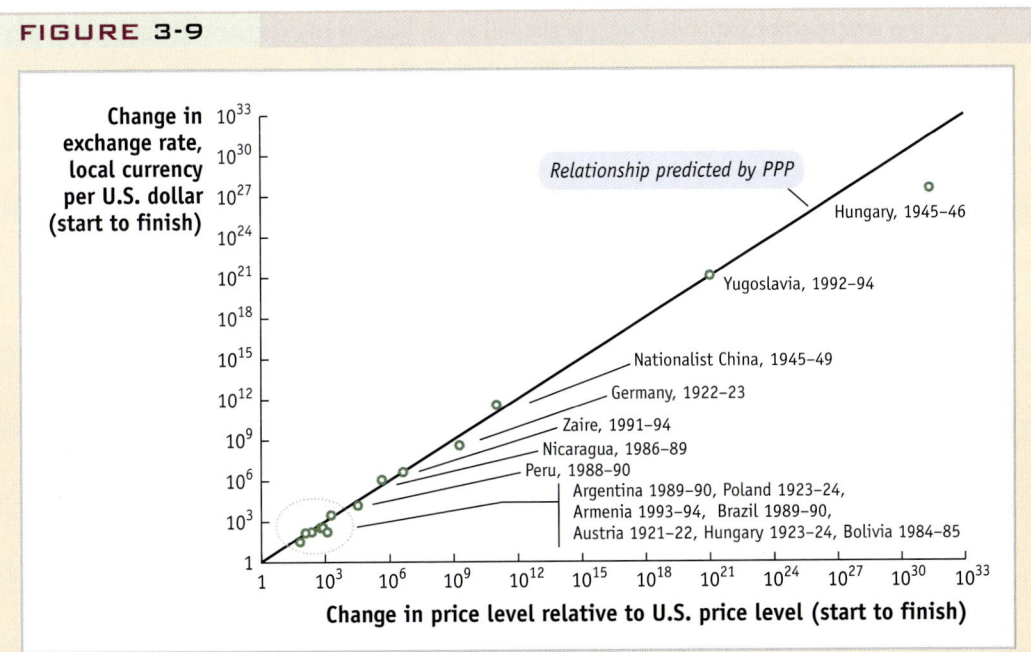

Purchasing Power Parity during Hyperinflations The scatterplot shows the relationship between the cumulative start-to-finish exchange rate depreciation against the U.S. dollar and the cumulative start-to-finish rise in the local price level for hyperinflations in the twentieth century. Note the use of logarithmic scales. The data show a strong correlation between the two variables and a very close resemblance to the theoretical prediction of PPP that all data points would appear on the 45-degree line.

Sources: IMF, *International Financial Statistics*; Global Financial Data; Phillip Cagan, "The Monetary Dynamics of Hyperinflation," in Milton Friedman, ed., 1956, *Studies in the Quantity Theory of Money* (Chicago: University of Chicago Press), pp. 25–117; Pavle Petrovic and Zorica Mladenovic, 2000, "Money Demand and Exchange Rate Determination under Hyperinflation: Conceptual Issues and Evidence from Yugoslavia," *Journal of Money, Credit and Banking*, 32, 785–806.

Above top to bottom are an Argentine 500,000 austral bill of 1990; a 1923 one billion German mark note (1 German billion = 1 U.S. trillion); and a Hungarian 100 Million B-pengő of 1946, with the "B" denoting the Hungarian billion, or a million million: this 100,000,000,000,000,000,000 pengő note is the highest denomination of currency ever issued by any country.

Some price changes were outrageously large. Austria's hyperinflation of 1921 to 1922 was the first one on record, and prices rose by a factor of about 100 (10^2). In Germany from 1922 to 1923, prices rose by a factor of about 20 billion (2×10^{10}); in the worst month, prices were doubling on average every two days. In Hungary from 1945 to 1946, pengö prices rose by a factor of about 10^{31}, the current record, and in July 1946, prices were doubling on average every 15 hours. Serbia's inflation from 1992 to 1994 came close to breaking the record for cumulative price changes. In comparison, Argentina's 700-fold inflation and Brazil's 200-fold inflation from 1989 to 1990 look deceptively modest.

Money Demand in Hyperinflations There is one other important lesson to be learned from hyperinflations. In our simple monetary model, the money demand parameter L was assumed to be *constant* and equal to $\overline{L}$. This implied that real money balances were proportional to real income, with $M/P = \overline{L}Y$ as shown in Equation (3-5). Is this assumption of stable real money balances justified?

The evidence shown in Figure 3-10 suggests this assumption is not justified, based on a subset of the hyperinflations. For each point, on the horizontal axis of this figure, we see the peak monthly inflation rate (the moment when prices were rising most rapidly); on the vertical axis, we see the level of real money balances in that month relative to their initial level (in the month just before the hyperinflation began). If real money balances were stable, there ought to be no variation in the vertical dimension aside from fluctuations in real income. But there is, and with a clear pattern: the higher the level of inflation, the lower the level of real money balances. These declines are far too severe to be explained by just the fall in real incomes experienced during hyperinflations, though such income declines did occur.

FIGURE 3-10

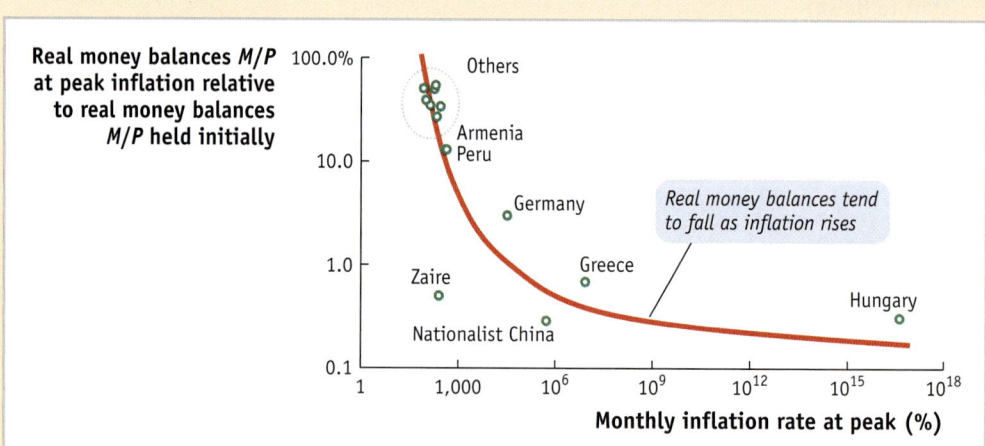

The Collapse of Real Money Balances during Hyperinflations This figure shows that real money balances tend to collapse in hyperinflations as people economize by reducing their holdings of rapidly depreciating notes. The horizontal axis shows the peak monthly inflation rate (%), and the vertical axis shows the ratio of real money balances in that peak month relative to real money balances at the start of the hyperinflationary period. The data are shown using log scales for clarity.

Sources: Global Financial Data; Phillip Cagan, "The Monetary Dynamics of Hyperinflation," in Milton Friedman, ed., 1956, *Studies in the Quantity Theory of Money* (Chicago: University of Chicago Press), pp. 25–117.

HEADLINES

The First Hyperinflation of the Twenty-First Century

By 2007 Zimbabwe was almost at an economic standstill, except for the printing presses churning out the banknotes. A creeping inflation—58% in 1999, 132% in 2001, 385% in 2003, and 586% in 2005—was about to become hyperinflation, and the long-suffering people faced an accelerating descent into even deeper chaos. Three years later, shortly after this news report, the local currency disappeared from use, replaced by U.S. dollars and South African rand.

. . . Zimbabwe is in the grip of one of the great hyperinflations in world history. The people of this once proud capital have been plunged into a Darwinian struggle to get by. Many have been reduced to peddlers and paupers, hawkers and black-market hustlers, eating just a meal or two a day, their hollowed cheeks a testament to their hunger.

Like countless Zimbabweans, Mrs. Moyo has calculated the price of goods by the number of days she had to spend in line at the bank to withdraw cash to buy them: a day for a bar of soap; another for a bag of salt; and four for a sack of cornmeal.

The withdrawal limit rose on Monday, but with inflation surpassing what independent economists say is an almost unimaginable 40 million percent, she said the value of the new amount would quickly be a pittance, too.

"It's survival of the fittest," said Mrs. Moyo, 29, a hair braider who sells the greens she grows in her yard for a dime a bunch. "If you're not fit, you will starve."

Economists here and abroad say Zimbabwe's economic collapse is gaining velocity, radiating instability into the heart of southern Africa. As the bankrupt government prints ever more money, inflation has gone wild, rising from 1,000 percent in 2006 to 12,000 percent in 2007. . . . In fact, Zimbabwe's hyperinflation is probably among the five worst of all time, said Jeffrey D. Sachs, a Columbia University economics professor, along with Germany in the 1920s, Greece and Hungary in the 1940s and Yugoslavia in 1993. . . .

Basic public services, already devastated by an exodus of professionals in recent years, are breaking down on an ever larger scale as tens of thousands of teachers, nurses, garbage collectors and janitors have simply stopped reporting to their jobs because their salaries, more worthless literally by the hour, no longer cover the cost of taking the bus to work. . . .

The bodies of paupers in advanced states of decay were stacking up in the mortuary at Beitbridge District Hospital because not even government authorities were seeing to their burial. . . . Harare Central Hospital slashed admissions by almost half because so much of its cleaning staff could no longer afford to get to work.

Most of the capital, though lovely beneath its springtime canopy of lavender jacaranda blooms, was without water because the authorities had stopped paying the bills to transport the treatment chemicals. Garbage is piling up uncollected. Sixteen people have died in an outbreak of cholera in nearby Chitungwiza, spread by contaminated water and sewage. . . .

Vigilantes in Kwekwe killed a man suspected of stealing two chickens, eggs and a bucket of corn. . . . And traditional chiefs complained about corrupt politicians and army officers who sold grain needed for the hungry to the politically connected instead.

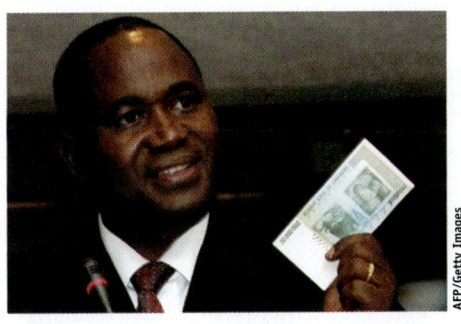

Ink on their hands: Under President Robert Mugabe and Central Bank Governor Gideon Gono (seen clutching a Z$50 million note), Zimbabwe became the latest country to join a rather exclusive club.

Source: Excerpted from Celia W. Dugger, "Life in Zimbabwe: Wait for Useless Money," The New York Times, October 2, 2008.

SIDE BAR

Currency Reform

Hyperinflations help us understand how some currencies become extinct if they cease to function well and lose value rapidly. Dollarization in Ecuador is a recent example. Other currencies survive such travails, only to be reborn. But the low denomination bills—the ones, fives, tens—usually become essentially worthless and normal transactions can require you to be a millionaire. The eradication of a few pesky zeros might then be a good idea. A government may then *redenominate* a new unit of currency equal to 10^N (10 raised to the power N) old units.

Sometimes N can get quite large. In the 1980s, Argentina suffered hyperinflation. On June 1, 1983, the *peso argentino* replaced the (old) peso at a rate of 10,000 to 1. Then on June 14, 1985, the *austral* replaced the peso argentino at 1,000 to 1. Finally, on January 1, 1992, the *convertible peso* replaced the austral at a rate of 10,000 to 1 (i.e., 10,000,000,000 old pesos). After all this, if you had owned 1 new peso in 1983 (and had changed it into the later monies), it would have lost 99.99997% of its U.S. dollar value by 2003.

In 1946 the Hungarian *pengö* became so worthless that the authorities no longer printed the denomination on each note in numbers, but only in words—perhaps to avert distrust (unsuccessful), to hide embarrassment (also unsuccessful), or simply because there wasn't room to print all those zeros. By July 15, 1946, there were 76,041,000,000,000,000,000,000,000 pengö in circulation. A stable new currency, the *forint*, was finally introduced on July 26, 1946, with each forint worth 400,000 quadrillion pengö (4×10^{20} = 400,000,000,000,000,000,000 pengö). The dilution of the Zimbabwean dollar from 2005 to 2009 was even more extreme, as the authorities lopped off 25 zeros in a series of reforms before the currency finally vanished from use.

This finding may not strike you as very surprising. If prices are doubling every few days (or every few hours), the money in people's pockets is rapidly turning into worthless pieces of paper. They will try to minimize their money holdings—and will do so even more as inflation rises higher and higher, just as the figure shows. It becomes just too costly to hold very much money, despite one's need to use it for transactions.

If you thought along these lines, you have an accurate sense of how people behave during hyperinflations. You also anticipated the extensions to the simple model that we make in the next section so it is more realistic. Even during "normal" inflations—situations that are less pathological than a hyperinflation—it is implausible to assume that real money balances are perfectly stable. In our extension of the simple model, we will assume that people make the trade-off highlighted previously: comparing the benefits of holding money for transactions purposes with the costs of holding money as compared with other assets. ∎

4 Money, Interest Rates, and Prices in the Long Run: A General Model

So far we have a long-run theory that links exchange rates to the price levels in each country: PPP. We also have a simple long-run monetary model that links price levels in each country to money supply and demand: the *quantity theory*.

These building blocks provide some basic intuition for the links between price levels, money, and exchange rates. The trouble is that the quantity theory's assumption that the demand for money is stable is implausible. In this section, we explore a more general model that addresses this shortcoming by allowing money demand to vary with the nominal interest rate. But this theory, in turn, brings another variable into play: How is the nominal interest rate determined in the long run? Answering this question will lead us to consider the links between inflation and the nominal interest rate in an open economy. With these new models in hand, we then return to the question of how best to understand what determines exchange rates in the long run.

The Demand for Money: The General Model

The general model of money demand is motivated by two insights, the first of which carries over from the quantity theory, the simple model we studied earlier in this chapter.

- *There is a benefit from holding money.* As is true in the simple quantity theory, the benefit of money is that individuals can conduct transactions with it, and we continue to assume that transactions demand is in proportion to income, all else equal.

- *There is a cost to holding money.* The nominal interest rate on money is zero, $i_{money} = 0$. By holding money and not earning interest, people incur the opportunity cost of holding money. For example, an individual could hold an interest-earning asset paying $i_\$$. The difference in nominal returns between this asset and money would be $i_\$ - i_{money} = i_\$ > 0$. This is one way of expressing the opportunity cost.

Moving from the individual or household level up to the macroeconomic level, we can infer that aggregate money demand in the economy as a whole will behave similarly:

All else equal, a rise in national dollar income (nominal income) will cause a proportional increase in transactions and, hence, in aggregate money demand.

All else equal, a rise in the nominal interest rate will cause the aggregate demand for money to fall.

Thus, we arrive at a general model in which money demand is proportional to nominal income, and is a decreasing function of the nominal interest rate:

$$\underbrace{M^d}_{\text{Demand for money (\$)}} = \underbrace{L(i)}_{\text{A decreasing function}} \times \underbrace{P \times Y}_{\text{Nominal income (\$)}}$$

Recall that, formerly, in the quantity theory, the parameter L (the liquidity ratio, the amount of money needed for transactions per dollar of nominal GDP) was a constant. In this general model, we assume that L is a decreasing function of the nominal interest rate i. Dividing by P, we can derive the demand for real money balances:

$$\underbrace{\frac{M^d}{P}}_{\text{Demand for real money}} = \underbrace{L(i)}_{\text{A decreasing function}} \times \underbrace{Y}_{\text{Real income}}$$

Figure 3-11(a) shows a typical **real money demand function** of this form, with the quantity of real money balances demanded on the horizontal axis and the nominal interest rate on the vertical axis. The downward slope of the demand curve reflects the inverse relationship between the demand for real money balances and the nominal interest rate *at a given level of real income* (Y).

Figure 3-11(b) shows what happens when real income increases from Y_1 to Y_2. When real income increases (by $x\%$), the demand for real money balances increases (by $x\%$) at each level of the nominal interest rate and the curve shifts.

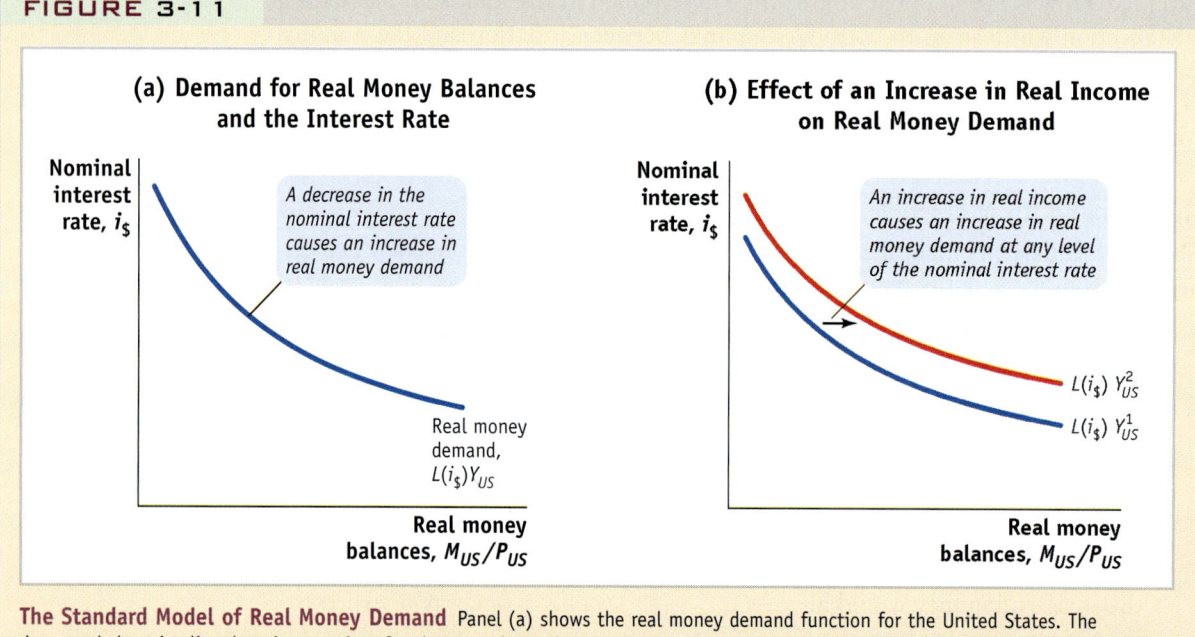

FIGURE 3-11

The Standard Model of Real Money Demand Panel (a) shows the real money demand function for the United States. The downward slope implies that the quantity of real money demand rises as the nominal interest rate $i_\$$ falls. Panel (b) shows that an increase in real income from Y_{US}^1 to Y_{US}^2 causes real money demand to rise at all levels of the nominal interest rate $i_\$$.

Long-Run Equilibrium in the Money Market

The money market is in equilibrium when the real money supply (determined by the central bank) equals the demand for real money balances (determined by the nominal interest rate and real income):

$$\underbrace{\frac{M}{P}}_{\text{Real money supply}} = \underbrace{L(i)Y}_{\text{Real money demand}} \quad (3\text{-}7)$$

We will continue to assume that prices are flexible in the long run and that they adjust to ensure that equilibrium is maintained.

We now have a model that describes equilibrium in the money market which will help us on the way to understanding the determination of the exchange rate. Before we arrive at the long-run exchange rate, however, we need one last piece to the puzzle. Under the quantity theory, the nominal interest rate was ignored. Now, in our general model, it is a key variable in the determination of money demand. So we need a theory to tell us what the level of the nominal interest rate i will be in the long run. Once we have solved this problem, we will be able to apply this new, more complex, but more realistic model of the money market to the analysis of exchange rate determination in the long run.

Inflation and Interest Rates in the Long Run

The tools we need to determine the nominal interest rate in an open economy are already at hand. So far in this chapter, we have developed the idea of purchasing power parity (PPP), which links prices and exchange rates. In the last chapter, we developed another parity idea, uncovered interest parity (UIP), which links exchange rates and interest rates. With only these two relationships in hand, PPP and UIP, we can derive a powerful and striking result concerning interest rates that has profound implications for our study of open economy macroeconomics.

Relative PPP, as indicated in Equation (3-2), states that the rate of depreciation equals the inflation differential at time t. When market actors use this equation to forecast future exchange rates, we use a superscript e to denote such expectations. Equation (3-2) is recast to show expected depreciation and inflation at time t:

$$\underbrace{\frac{\Delta E^e_{\$/€}}{E_{\$/€}}}_{\text{Expected rate of dollar depreciation}} = \underbrace{\pi^e_{US} - \pi^e_{EUR}}_{\text{Expected inflation differential}}$$

Next we recall that uncovered interest parity (UIP) in the approximate form (Equation 3-3) can be rearranged to show that the expected rate of depreciation equals the interest differential at time t:

$$\underbrace{\frac{\Delta E^e_{\$/€}}{E_{\$/€}}}_{\text{Expected rate of dollar depreciation}} = \underbrace{i_\$}_{\text{Net dollar interest rate}} - \underbrace{i_€}_{\text{Net euro interest rate}}$$

This way of writing the UIP equation says that traders will be indifferent to a higher U.S. interest rate relative to the euro interest rates (making U.S. deposits look more attractive) only if the higher U.S. rate is offset by an expected dollar depreciation (making U.S. deposits look less attractive). For example, if the U.S. interest rate is 4% and the euro interest rate is 2%, the interest differential is 2% and the forex market can be in equilibrium only if traders expect a 2% depreciation of the U.S. dollar against the euro, which would exactly offset the higher U.S. interest rate.

The Fisher Effect

Because the left sides of the previous two equations are equal, the right sides must also be equal. Thus, the nominal interest differential equals the expected inflation differential:

$$\underbrace{i_\$ - i_€}_{\text{Nominal interest rate differential}} = \underbrace{\pi^e_{US} - \pi^e_{EUR}}_{\text{Nominal inflation rate differential (expected)}} \quad (3\text{-}8)$$

What does this important result say? To take an example, suppose expected inflation is 4% in the United States and 2% in Europe. The inflation differential on the right is then +2% (4%−2% = +2%). If interest rates in Europe are 3%, then to make the interest differential the same as the inflation differential, +2%, the interest rate in the United States must equal 5% (5%−3% = +2%).

Now suppose expected inflation in the United States changes, rising by one percentage point to 5%. If nothing changes in Europe, then the U.S. interest rate must also rise by one percentage point to 6% for the equation to hold. In general, this equation predicts that changes in the expected rate of inflation will be fully incorporated (one for one) into changes in nominal interest rates.

All else equal, a rise in the expected inflation rate in a country will lead to an equal rise in its nominal interest rate.

This result is known as the **Fisher effect,** named for the American economist Irving Fisher (1867–1947). Note that because this result depends on an assumption of PPP, it is therefore likely to hold only in the long run.

The Fisher effect makes clear the link between inflation and nominal interest rates under flexible prices, a finding that is widely applicable. For a start, it makes sense of the evidence we just saw on money holdings during hyperinflations (see Figure 3-10). As inflation rises, the Fisher effect tells us that the nominal interest rate i must rise by the same amount; the general model of money demand then tells us that $L(i)$ must fall because it is a decreasing function of i. Thus, for a given level of real income, real money balances must fall as inflation rises.

In other words, the Fisher effect predicts that the change in the opportunity cost of money is equal not just to the change in the nominal interest rate but also to the change in the inflation rate. In times of very high inflation, people should, therefore, want to reduce their money holdings—and they do.

Real Interest Parity

As just described, the Fisher effect tells us something about nominal interest rates, but we can quickly derive the implications for real interest rates, too. Rearranging the last equation, we find

$$i_\$ - \pi^e_{US} = i_\euro - \pi^e_{EUR}$$

The expressions on either side of this equation might look familiar from previous courses in macroeconomics. When the inflation rate (π) is subtracted from a *nominal* interest rate (i), the result is a **real interest rate** (r), the inflation-adjusted reurn on an interest-bearing asset. Given this definition, we can simplify the last equation further. On the left is the expected real interest rate in the United States ($r^e_{US} = i_\$ - \pi^e_{US}$). On the right is the expected real interest rate in Europe ($r^e_{EUR} = i_\euro - \pi^e_{EUR}$).

Thus, using only two assumptions, PPP and UIP, we have shown that

$$r^e_{US} = r^e_{EUR} \tag{3-9}$$

This remarkable result states the following: *If PPP and UIP hold, then expected real interest rates are equalized across countries.*

This powerful condition is called **real interest parity** and because it depends on an assumption of PPP, it is therefore likely to hold only in the long run.[10]

We have arrived at a strong conclusion about the potential for globalization to cause convergence in economic outcomes, because real interest parity implies the following: *Arbitrage in goods and financial markets alone is sufficient, in the long run, to cause the equalization of real interest rates across countries.*

We have considered two countries, but this argument applies to all countries integrated into the global capital market. In the long run, they will all share a common expected real interest rate, the long-run expected **world real interest rate** denoted r^*, so

$$r^e_{US} = r^e_{EUR} = r^*$$

---

[10] You may have encountered other theories in which real interest rates are equalized across countries by other means. Countries may share common technologies (due to technology diffusion) or might have similar saving behavior (due to similar preferences). Such assumptions could lead to identical real interest rates even in two *closed* economies. But here we have derived the real interest parity condition *only* from UIP and PPP, meaning that, in *open* economies, these are *sufficient* conditions for real interest rates to be equalized. No other assumptions are needed!

From now on, unless indicated otherwise, we treat r^* as a given, exogenous variable, something outside the control of a policy maker in any particular country.[11]

Under these conditions, the Fisher effect is even clearer, because, by definition,

$$i_\$ = r^e_{US} + \pi^e_{US} = r^* + \pi^e_{US}, \qquad i_\euro = r^e_{EUR} + \pi^e_{EUR} = r^* + \pi^e_{EUR}$$

Thus, in each country, the long-run expected nominal interest rate is the long-run world real interest rate plus that country's expected long-run inflation rate. For example, if the world real interest rate is $r^* = 2\%$, and the country's long-run expected inflation rate goes up by two percentage points from 3% to 5%, then its long-run nominal interest rate also goes up by two percentage points from the old level of $2 + 3 = 5\%$ to a new level of $2 + 5 = 7\%$.

APPLICATION

Evidence on the Fisher Effect

Are the Fisher effect and real interest parity supported by empirical evidence? One might expect a problem here. We derived them from purchasing power parity. The evidence we have seen on PPP offers support only in the long run. Thus, we do not expect the Fisher effect and real interest parity to hold exactly in the short run, but we might expect them to hold (at least approximately) in the long run.

Figure 3-12 shows that the Fisher effect is close to reality in the long run: on average, countries with higher inflation rates tend to have higher nominal interest rates, and the data line up fairly well with the predictions of the theory. Figure 3-13 shows that, for

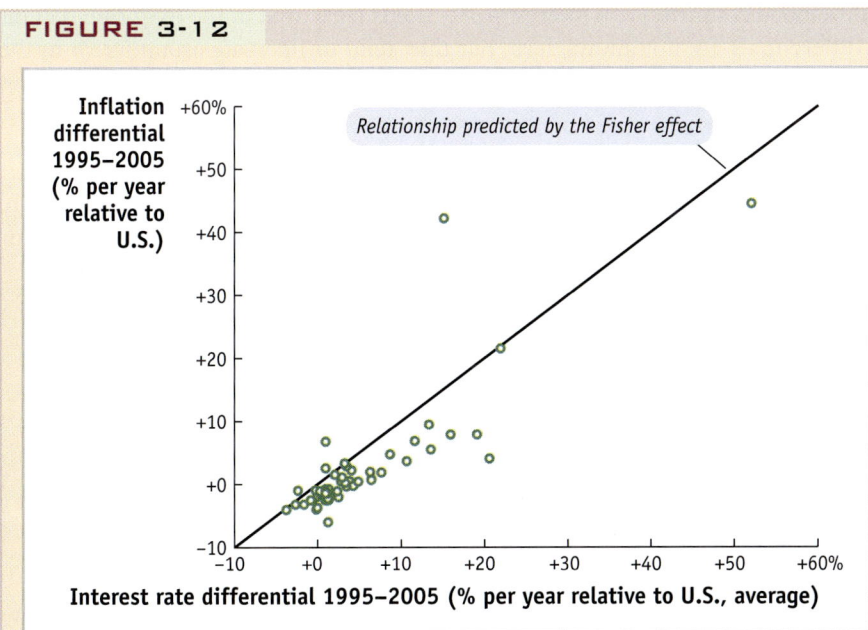

FIGURE 3-12

Inflation Rates and Nominal Interest Rates, 1995–2005 This scatterplot shows the relationship between the average annual nominal interest rate differential and the annual inflation differential relative to the United States over a ten-year period for a sample of 62 countries. The correlation between the two variables is strong and bears a close resemblance to the theoretical prediction of the Fisher effect that all data points would appear on the 45-degree line.

Source: IMF, International Financial Statistics.

---

[11] In advanced economic theories, the determinants of the world real interest rate are explored, with reference to consumption preferences of households and the extent to which they discount the future.

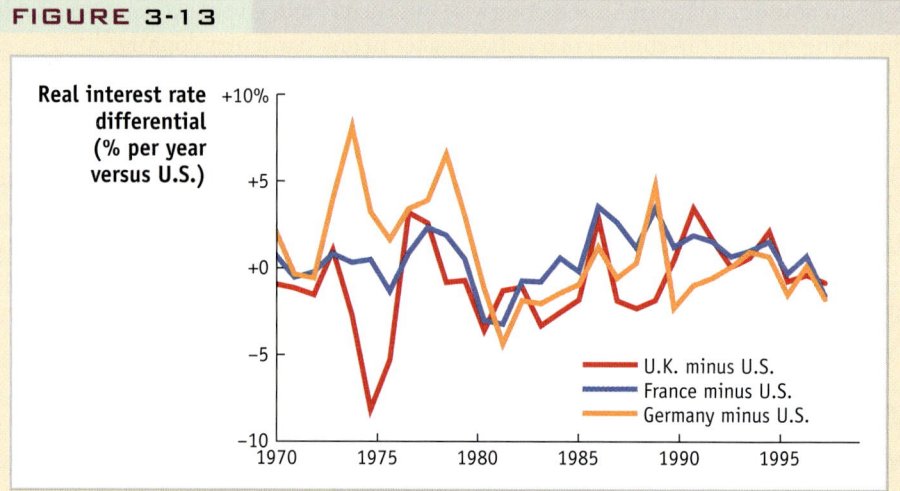

FIGURE 3-13

Real Interest Rate Differentials, 1970–1999 This figure shows actual real interest rate differentials over three decades for the United Kingdom, Germany, and France relative to the United States. These differentials were not zero, so real interest parity did not hold continuously. But the differentials were on average close to zero, meaning that real interest parity (like PPP) is a general long-run tendency in the data.

Source: Maurice Obstfeld and Alan M. Taylor, 2004, Global Capital Markets: Integration, Crisis, and Growth, Japan-U.S. Center Sanwa Monographs on International Financial Markets (Cambridge, UK: Cambridge University Press).

three developed countries, real interest parity holds fairly well in the long run: real interest differentials are not always zero, but they tend to fluctuate around zero in the long run. This could be seen as evidence in favor of long-run real interest parity. ∎

The Fundamental Equation under the General Model

Now that we understand how the nominal interest rate is determined in the long run, our general model is complete. This model differs from the simple model (the quantity theory) *only* by allowing L to vary as a function of the nominal interest rate i.

We can therefore update our fundamental equations to allow for this change in how we treat L. For example, the fundamental equation of the monetary approach to exchange rates, Equation (3-3), can now be suitably modified:

$$\underbrace{E_{\$/\euro}}_{\text{Exchange rate}} = \underbrace{\frac{P_{US}}{P_{EUR}}}_{\substack{\text{Ratio of} \\ \text{price levels}}} = \frac{\left(\dfrac{M_{US}}{L_{US}(i_\$)Y_{US}}\right)}{\left(\dfrac{M_{EUR}}{L_{EUR}(i_\euro)Y_{EUR}}\right)} = \underbrace{\frac{(M_{US}/M_{EUR})}{(L_{US}(i_\$)Y_{US}/L_{EUR}(i_\euro)Y_{EUR})}}_{\substack{\text{Relative nominal money supplies} \\ \text{divided by relative real money demands}}} \quad (3\text{-}10)$$

What have we gained from this refinement? We know that the simple model will remain valid for cases in which nominal interest rates remain unchanged in the long run. It is only when nominal interest rates change that the general model has different implications, and we now have the right tools for that situation. To put those tools to work, we revisit the example of an exchange rate forecasting problem we encountered earlier in this chapter.

Exchange Rate Forecasts Using the General Model

Earlier in the chapter, we looked at two forecasting problems *under the assumption of flexible prices*. The first was a one-time unanticipated change in an otherwise constant U.S. money supply. Under the assumptions we made (stable real income in both countries and stable European money supply), this change caused a one-time increase in the U.S. price level but did not lead to a change in U.S. inflation (which was zero before and after the event).

The Fisher effect tells us that if inflation rates are unchanged, then, in the long run, nominal interest rates remain unchanged. Thus, the predictions of the simple model remain valid. But in the second and more complex forecasting problem, there was a one-time unanticipated change in the U.S. money growth rate that *did* lead to a change in inflation. It is here that the general model makes different predictions.

Earlier we assumed that U.S. and European real income growth rates are identical and equal to zero (0%), so real income levels are constant. We also assumed that the European money supply is constant, so that the European price level is constant, too. This allowed us to focus on changes on the U.S. side of the model, all else equal.

We now reexamine the forecasting problem for the case in which there is an increase in the U.S. rate of money growth. We learn at time T that the United States is raising the rate of money supply growth from some fixed rate μ to a slightly higher rate $\mu + \Delta\mu$.

For example, imagine an increase from 2% to 3% growth, so $\Delta\mu = 1\%$. How will the exchange rate behave in the long run? To solve the model, we make a provisional assumption that U.S. inflation rates and interest rates are constant before and after time T and focus on the differences between the two periods caused by the change in money supply growth. The story is told in Figure 3-14:

a. The money supply is growing at a constant rate. If the interest rate is constant in each period, then real money balances M/P remain constant, by assumption, because $L(i)Y$ is then a constant. If real money balances are constant, then M and P grow at the same rate. Before T that rate is $\mu = 2\%$; after T that rate is $\mu + \Delta\mu = 3\%$. That is, the U.S. inflation rate rises by an amount $\Delta\mu = 1\%$ at time T.

b. As a result of the Fisher effect, U.S. interest rates also rise by $\Delta\mu = 1\%$ at time T. Consequently, real money balances M/P must fall at time T because $L(i)Y$ will decrease as i increases.

c. In (a) we have described the path of M. In (b) we found that M/P is constant up to T, then drops suddenly, and then is constant after time T. What path must the price level P follow? Up to time T, it is a constant multiple of M; the same applies after time T, but the constant has increased. Why? The nominal money supply grows smoothly, without a jump. So if real money balances drop down discontinuously at time T, the price level must jump up discontinuously at time T. The intuition for this is that the rise in inflation and interest rates at time T prompts people to instantaneously demand less real money, but because the supply of nominal money is unchanged, the price level has to jump up. Apart from this jump, P grows at a constant rate; before T that rate is $\mu = 2\%$; after T that rate is $\mu + \Delta\mu = 3\%$.

d. PPP implies that E and P must move in the same proportion, so E is always a constant multiple of P. Thus, E jumps like P at time T. Apart from this jump, E grows at a constant rate; before T that rate is $\mu = 2\%$; after T that rate is $\mu + \Delta\mu = 3\%$.

FIGURE 3-14

An Increase in the Growth Rate of the Money Supply in the Standard Model Before time T, money, prices, and the exchange rate all grow at rate μ. Foreign prices are constant. In panel (a), we suppose at time T there is an increase $\Delta\mu$ in the rate of growth of home money supply M. This causes an increase $\Delta\mu$ in the rate of inflation; the Fisher effect means that there will be a $\Delta\mu$ increase in the nominal interest rate; as a result, as shown in panel (b), real money demand falls with a discrete jump at T. If real money balances are to fall when the nominal money supply expands continuously, then the domestic price level must make a discrete jump up at time T, as shown in panel (c). Subsequently, prices grow at the new higher rate of inflation; and given the stable foreign price level, PPP implies that the exchange rate follows a similar path to the domestic price level, as shown in panel (d).

Corresponding to these four steps, Figure 3-14 illustrates the path of the key variables in this example. (Our provisional assumption of constant inflation rates and interest rates in each period is satisfied, so the proposed solution is internally consistent.)

Comparing Figure 3-14 with Figure 3-6, we can observe the subtle qualitative differences between the predictions of the simple quantity theory and those of the more general model. Shifts in the interest rate introduce jumps in real money demand. Because money supplies evolve smoothly, these jumps end up being reflected in the price levels and hence—via PPP—in exchange rates. The Fisher effect tells us that these interest rate effects are ultimately the result of changes in expected inflation.

Looking Ahead We can learn a little more by thinking through the market mechanism that produces this result. People learn at time T that money growth will be more rapid in the United States. This creates expectations of higher inflation in the United States. If people believe PPP holds in the long run, they will believe higher future inflation will cause the U.S. currency to depreciate in the future. This prospect makes holding dollars less attractive, by UIP. People try to sell dollars, and invest in euros. This creates immediate downward pressure on the dollar—even though at time T itself the supply of dollars does not change at all! This lesson underlines yet again the importance of expectations in determining the exchange rate. *Even if actual economic conditions today are completely unchanged, news about the future affects today's exchange rate.* This crucial insight can help us explain many phenomena relating to the volatility and instability in spot exchange rates, an idea we develop further in the chapters that follow.

5 Monetary Regimes and Exchange Rate Regimes

The monetary approach shows that, in the long run, all nominal variables—the money supply, interest rate, price level, and exchange rate—are interlinked. Hence, monetary policy choices can radically affect some important economic outcomes, notably prices and inflation, about which policy makers, governments, and the people they represent deeply care. The approach therefore highlights issues that must be taken into account in long-run economic policy design, and we will explore these important connections between theory and policy in this final section of the chapter.

We have repeatedly stressed the importance of inflation as an economic variable. Why is it so important? High or volatile inflation rates are considered undesirable. They may destabilize an economy or retard its growth.[12] Economies with low and stable inflation generally grow faster than those with high or volatile inflation. Inflationary crises, in which inflation jumps to a high or hyperinflationary level, are very damaging indeed.[13]

Thus, an overarching aspect of a nation's economic policy is the desire to keep inflation within certain bounds. To achieve such an objective requires that policy makers be subject to some kind of constraint in the long run. Such constraints are called **nominal anchors** because they attempt to tie down a nominal variable that is potentially under the policy makers' control.

Policy makers cannot directly control prices, so the attainment of price stability in the *short run* is not feasible. The question is what can policy makers do to promote price stability in the long run and what types of flexibility, if any, they will allow themselves in the short run. Long-run nominal anchoring and short-run flexibility are the

---

[12] Macroeconomists can list numerous potential costs of inflation. Expected inflation generates a cost of holding money, a tax on transactions that adds friction to the economy; firms and workers use nominal contracts for prices and would have to change prices and recontract more often; inflation also distorts the economy when a tax system has significant nominal provisions (e.g., fixed deductions and exemptions). Unexpected inflation creates arbitrary redistributions from creditors to debtors, and this introduces risk into borrowing and lending, making interest rates and investment more costly. In short, if inflation is other than low and stable, economic life becomes at best inconvenient and at worst (as in a hyperinflation) dysfunctional. See N. Gregory Mankiw, 2007, *Macroeconomics*, 6th ed., Chap. 4 (New York: Worth).
[13] This evidence is merely suggestive: high inflation and slow growth may each be caused by other factors, such as weak institutions. Some studies have used sophisticated econometrics to address this problem. See Stanley Fischer, 1993, "The Role of Macroeconomic Factors in Growth," *Journal of Monetary Economics*, 32, 485–511; Robert J. Barro, 1997, *Determinants of Economic Growth* (Cambridge, MA: MIT Press); Michael Bruno and William Easterly, 1998, "Inflation Crises and Long-Run Growth," *Journal of Monetary Economics*, 41, 3–26.

characteristics of the policy framework that economists call the **monetary regime.** In this section, we examine different types of monetary regimes and what they mean for the exchange rate.

The Long Run: The Nominal Anchor

Which variables could policy makers use as anchors to achieve an inflation objective in the long run? To answer this key question, all we have to do is go back and rearrange the equations for relative PPP at Equation (3-2), the quantity theory in rates of change at Equation (3-6), and the Fisher effect at Equation (3-8), to obtain alternative expressions for the rate of inflation in the home country. To emphasize that these findings apply generally to all countries, we relabel the countries Home (H) and Foreign (F) instead of United States and Europe.

The three main nominal anchor choices that emerge are as follows:

- **Exchange rate target:** Relative PPP at Equation (3-2) says that the rate of depreciation equals the inflation differential, or $\Delta E_{H/F}/E_{H/F} = \pi_H - \pi_F$. Rearranging this expression suggests one way to anchor inflation is as follows:

$$\underbrace{\pi_H}_{\text{Inflation}} = \underbrace{\frac{\Delta E_{H/F}}{E_{H/F}}}_{\substack{\text{Rate of} \\ \text{depreciation} \\ | \\ \boxed{\text{Anchor variable}}}} + \underbrace{\pi_F}_{\substack{\text{Foreign} \\ \text{inflation}}}$$

Relative PPP says that home inflation equals the rate of depreciation plus foreign inflation. A simple rule would be to set the rate of depreciation equal to a constant. Under a fixed exchange rate, that constant is set at zero (a peg). Under a crawl, it is a nonzero constant. Alternatively, there may be room for movement about a target (a band). Or there may be a vague goal to allow the exchange rate "limited flexibility." Such policies can deliver stable home inflation if PPP works well and if policy makers keep their commitment. The drawback is the final term in the equation: PPP implies that over the long run the home country "imports" inflation from the foreign country over and above the chosen rate of depreciation. For example, under a peg, if foreign inflation rises by 1% per year, then so, too, does home inflation. Thus, countries almost invariably peg to a country with a reputation for price stability (e.g., the United States). This is a common policy choice: fixed exchange rates of some form are in use in more than half of the world's countries.

- **Money supply target:** The quantity theory suggests another way to anchor because the fundamental equation for the price level in the monetary approach says that inflation equals the excess of the rate of money supply growth over and above the rate of real income growth:

$$\underbrace{\pi_H}_{\text{Inflation}} = \underbrace{\mu_H}_{\substack{\text{Money supply growth} \\ | \\ \boxed{\text{Anchor variable}}}} - \underbrace{g_H}_{\text{Real output growth}}$$

A simple rule of this sort is: set the growth rate of the money supply equal to a constant, say, 2% a year. The printing presses should be put on automatic pilot, and no human interference should be allowed. Essentially, the central bank is run by robots. This would be difficult to implement. Again the drawback is the final term in the previous equation: real income growth can be unstable. In periods of high growth, inflation will be below the desired level. In periods of low growth, inflation will be above the desired level. For this reason, money supply targets are waning in popularity or are used in conjunction with other targets. For example, the European Central Bank claims to use monetary growth rates as a partial guide to policy, but nobody is quite sure how serious it is.

- **Inflation target plus interest rate policy:** The Fisher effect suggests yet another anchoring method:

$$\underbrace{\pi^e_H}_{\text{Inflation (expected)}} = \underbrace{i_H}_{\substack{\text{Nominal interest rate} \\ | \\ \text{Anchor variable}}} - \underbrace{r^*}_{\text{World real interest rate}}$$

The Fisher effect says that home inflation is the home nominal interest rate minus the foreign real interest rate. If the latter can be assumed to be constant, then as long as the average home nominal interest rate is kept stable, inflation can also be kept stable. This type of nominal anchoring framework is an increasingly common policy choice. Assuming a stable world real interest rate is not a bad assumption. (And in principle, the target level of the nominal interest rate could be adjusted if necessary.) More or less flexible versions of inflation targeting can be implemented. A central bank could in theory set the nominal interest rate at a fixed level at all times, but such rigidity is rarely seen and central banks usually adjust interest rates in the short run to meet other goals. For example, if the world real interest rate is $r^* = 2.5\%$, and the country's long-run inflation target is 2%, then its long-run nominal interest rate ought to be on average equal to 4.5% (because 2.5% = 4.5% − 2%). This would be termed the *neutral* level of the nominal interest rate. But in the short run, the central bank might desire to use some flexibility to set interest rates above or below this neutral level. How much flexibility is a matter of policy choice, as is the question of what economic objectives should drive deviations from the neutral rate (e.g., inflation performance alone, or other factors like output and employment that we shall consider in later chapters).

The Choice of a Nominal Anchor and Its Implications
Under the assumptions we have made, any of the three nominal anchor choices are valid. If a particular long-run inflation objective is to be met, then, all else equal, the first equation says it will be consistent with one particular rate of depreciation; the second equation says it will be consistent with one particular rate of money supply growth; the third equation says it will be consistent with one particular rate of interest. But if policy makers announced targets for all three variables, they would be able to match all three consistently only by chance. Two observations follow.

First, using more than one target may be problematic. Under a fixed exchange rate regime, policy makers cannot employ any target other than the exchange rate.

TABLE 3-2

Exchange Rate Regimes and Nominal Anchors This table illustrates the possible exchange rate regimes that are consistent with various types of nominal anchors. Countries that are dollarized or in a currency union have a "superfixed" exchange rate target. Pegs, bands, and crawls also target the exchange rate. Managed floats have no preset path for the exchange rate, which allows other targets to be employed. Countries that float freely or independently are judged to pay no serious attention to exchange rate targets; if they have anchors, they will involve monetary targets or inflation targets with an interest rate policy. The countries with "freely falling" exchange rates have no serious target and have high rates of inflation and depreciation. It should be noted that many countries engage in implicit targeting (e.g., inflation targeting) without announcing an explicit target and that some countries may use a mix of more than one target.

	COMPATIBLE EXCHANGE RATE REGIMES				
Type of Nominal Anchor	Countries without a Currency of Their Own	Pegs/ Bands/Crawls	Managed Floating	Freely Floating	Freely Falling (rapid depreciation)
Exchange rate target	✓	✓	✓		
Money supply target			✓	✓	
Inflation target (plus interest rate policy)			✓	✓	
None				✓	✓

However, they may be able to use a mix of different targets if they adopt an intermediate regime, such as a managed exchange rate with limited flexibility. Table 3-2 illustrates the ways in which the choice of a target as a nominal anchor affects the choice of exchange rate regime. Obviously, these are not independent choices. But a variety of choices do exist. Thus, *nominal anchoring is possible with a variety of exchange rate regimes.*

Second, whatever target choice is made, a country that commits to a target as a way of nominal anchoring is committing itself to set future money supplies and interest rates in such a way as to meet the target. Only one path for future policy will be compatible with the target in the long run. Thus, *a country with a nominal anchor sacrifices monetary policy autonomy in the long run.*

APPLICATION

Nominal Anchors in Theory and Practice

An appreciation of the importance of nominal anchors has transformed monetary policy making and inflation performance throughout the global economy in recent decades.

In the 1970s, most of the world was struggling with high inflation. An economic slowdown prompted central banks everywhere to loosen monetary policy. In advanced countries, a move to floating exchange rates allowed great freedom for them to loosen their monetary policy. Developing countries had already proven vulnerable to high inflation and now many of them were exposed to even worse inflation. Those who were pegged to major currencies imported high inflation via PPP. Those who weren't pegged struggled to find a credible nominal anchor as they faced economic downturns of their own. High oil prices everywhere contributed to inflationary pressure.

TABLE 3-3

Global Disinflation Cross-country data from 1980 to 2004 show the gradual reduction in the annual rate of inflation around the world. This disinflation process began in the advanced economies in the early 1980s. The emerging markets and developing countries suffered from even higher rates of inflation, although these finally began to fall in the 1990s.

	ANNUAL INFLATION RATE (%)				
	1980–1984	1985–1989	1990–1994	1995–1999	2000–2004
World	14.1%	15.5	30.4	8.4	3.9
Advanced economies	8.7	3.9	3.8	2.0	1.8
Emerging markets and developing countries	31.4	48.0	53.2	13.1	5.6

Source: Kenneth Rogoff, 2003, "Globalization and Global Disinflation," *Economic Review*, Federal Reserve Bank of Kansas City, IV, 45–78.

In the 1980s, inflationary pressure continued in many developed countries, and in many developing countries high levels of inflation, and even hyperinflations, were not uncommon. Governments were forced to respond to public demands for a more stable inflation environment. In the 1990s, policies designed to create effective nominal anchors were put in place in many countries.

One study found that the use of explicit targets grew markedly in the 1990s, replacing regimes in which there had previously been no explicit nominal anchor. The number of countries in the study with exchange rate targets increased from 30 to 47. The number with money targets increased from 18 to 39. The number with inflation targets increased most dramatically, almost sevenfold, from 8 to 54. Many countries had more than one target in use: in 1998, 55% of the sample announced an explicit target (or monitoring range) for more than one of the exchange rate, money, and inflation.[14]

Looking back from the present we can see that most, but not all, of those policies have turned out to be credible, too, thanks to political developments in many countries that have fostered **central-bank independence.** Independent central banks stand apart from the interference of politicians: they have operational freedom to try to achieve the inflation target, and they may even play a role in setting that target.

Overall, these efforts are judged to have achieved some success, although in many countries inflation had already been brought down substantially in the early to mid-1980s before inflation targets and institutional changes were implemented. Table 3-3 shows a steady decline in average levels of inflation since the early 1980s. The lowest levels of inflation are seen in the advanced economies, although developing countries have also started to make some limited progress. In the industrial countries, central-bank independence is now commonplace (it was not in the 1970s), but in developing countries it is still relatively rare.

---

[14] Gabriel Sterne, August 1999, "The Use of Explicit Targets for Monetary Policy: Practical Experiences of 91 Economies in the 1990s," *Bank of England Quarterly Bulletin*, 39(3), 272–281.

Still, one can have too much of a good thing, and the crisis of 2008–2010 prompted some second thoughts about inflation targets. Typically, such targets have been set at about 2% in developed countries, and with a world real interest rate of 2% this implies a neutral nominal interest rate of 4%. In terms of having room to maneuver, this rate permits central banks to temporarily cut their interest rates up to four percentage points below the neutral level. Prior to the crisis this range was considered ample room for central banks to take short-run actions as needed (e.g., to stimulate output or the rate of inflation if either fell too low). In the crisis, however, central banks soon hit the lower bound of zero rates and could not prevent severe output losses and declines in inflation rates to low or, at times, negative levels (*deflation*). As Irving Fisher famously noted, deflation is very damaging economically—it drives up real interest rates when nominal rates can fall no further as an offset, and falling prices make the real burden of nominal debts higher. These problems have led some economists, among them the IMF's Chief Economist, Olivier Blanchard, to question whether inflation targets should be set higher (e.g., at 4% rather than 2%).[15] The idea received a lukewarm reception, however: moving to a higher inflation target is in principle easy, but many feared its potential abuse could place at risk the hard-won credibility gains that central banks have earned for themselves in the last three decades. Indeed, even as inflation rates fell almost to zero in major economies like the United States and Eurozone, many central bankers continued to speak of their vigilance in guarding against inflation. ■

6 Conclusions

This chapter emphasized the determinants of exchange rates in the long run using the monetary approach. We employed purchasing power parity and a simple monetary model (the quantity theory) to study an equilibrium in which goods are arbitraged and prices are flexible. Under these assumptions, in the home country, changes in the money supply pass through into proportional changes in the price level and the exchange rate.

We also found that uncovered interest parity and purchasing power parity implied that real interest rates are equalized across countries. This helped us develop a monetary model that was more complex—and more realistic—because it allowed money demand to fluctuate in response to changes in the interest rate. In that setting, increases in money growth lead to higher inflation and a higher nominal interest rate and, hence, via decreases in money demand, to even higher price levels. Still, the same basic intuition holds, and one-time changes in the money supply still lead to proportionate changes in prices and exchange rates.

The monetary approach to exchange rates provides a basis for certain kinds of forecasting and policy analysis using the flexible-price model in the long run. But such forecasts matter even in the short run because today's spot exchange rate depends, like all asset prices, on the exchange rate expected to prevail in the future. To make these connections clear, in the next chapter we bring together the key ideas of arbitrage (from the previous chapter) and expectations (from this chapter) to form a complete model of the exchange rate.

---

[15] Olivier Blanchard, Giovanni Dell'Ariccia, and Paolo Mauro, "Rethinking Macroeconomic Policy," *IMF Staff Position Note*, SPN/10/03, February 12, 2010.

KEY POINTS

1. Purchasing power parity (PPP) implies that the exchange rate should equal the relative price level in the two countries, and the real exchange rate should equal 1.

2. Evidence for PPP is weak in the short run but more favorable in the long run. In the short run, deviations are common and changes in the real exchange rate do occur. The failure of PPP in the short run is primarily the result of market frictions, imperfections that limit arbitrage, and price stickiness.

3. A simple monetary model (the quantity theory) explains price levels in terms of money supply levels and real income levels. Because PPP can explain exchange rates in terms of price levels, the two together can be used to develop a monetary approach to the exchange rate.

4. If we can forecast money supply and income, we can use the monetary approach to forecast the level of the exchange rate at any time in the future. However, the monetary approach is valid only under the assumption that prices are flexible. This assumption is more likely to hold in the long run, so the monetary approach is not useful in the short run forecast. Evidence for PPP and the monetary approach is more favorable in the long run.

5. PPP theory, combined with uncovered interest parity, leads to the strong implications of the Fisher effect (interest differentials between countries should equal inflation differentials). The Fisher effect says that changes in local inflation rates pass through one for one into changes in local nominal interest rates. The result implies real interest parity (expected real interest rates should be equalized across countries). Because these results rest on PPP, they should be viewed only as long-run results, and the evidence is somewhat favorable.

6. We can augment the simple monetary model (quantity theory) to allow for the demand for real money balances to decrease as the nominal interest rate rises. This leads to the general monetary model. Its predictions are similar to those of the simple model, except that a one-time rise in money growth rates leads to a one-time rise in inflation, which leads to a one-time drop in real money demand, which in turn causes a one-time jump in the price level and the exchange rate.

7. The monetary approach to exchange rate determination in the long run has implications for economic policy. Policy makers and the public generally prefer a low-inflation environment. Various policies based on exchange rates, money growth, or interest rates have been proposed as nominal anchors. Recent decades have seen a worldwide decline in inflation thanks to the explicit recognition of the need for nominal anchors.

KEY TERMS

monetary approach to exchange rates, p. 64
law of one price (LOOP), p. 65
purchasing power parity (PPP), p. 66
absolute PPP, p. 66
real exchange rate, p. 67
real depreciation, p. 67
real appreciation, p. 67
overvalued, p. 67
undervalued, p. 67
inflation, p. 68
relative PPP, p. 69

money, p. 76
central bank, p. 77
money supply, p. 77
money demand, p. 78
quantity theory of money, p. 78
fundamental equation of the monetary model of the price level, p. 79
fundamental equation of the monetary approach to exchange rates, p. 80
hyperinflation, p. 86
real money demand function, p. 91

Fisher effect, p. 94
real interest rate, p. 94
real interest parity, p. 94
world real interest rate, p. 94
nominal anchors, p. 99
monetary regime, p. 100
exchange rate target, p. 100
money supply target, p. 100
inflation target plus interest rate policy, p. 101
central-bank independence, p. 103

PROBLEMS

1. Suppose that two countries, Vietnam and Côte d'Ivoire, produce coffee. The currency unit used in Vietnam is the dong (VND). Côte d'Ivoire is a member of Communaute Financiere Africaine (CFA), a currency union of West African countries that use the CFA franc (XOF). In Vietnam, coffee sells for 5,000 dong (VND) per pound. The exchange rate is 30 VND per 1 CFA franc, $E_{VND/XOF} = 30$.

    a. If the law of one price holds, what is the price of coffee in Côte d'Ivoire, measured in CFA francs?

    b. Assume the price of coffee in Côte d'Ivoire is actually 160 CFA francs per pound of coffee. Compute the relative price of coffee in Côte d'Ivoire versus Vietnam. Where will coffee traders buy coffee? Where will they sell coffee in this case? How will these transactions affect the price of coffee in Vietnam? In Côte d'Ivoire?

2. Consider each of the following goods and services. For each, identify whether the law of one price will hold, and state whether the relative price $q^g_{US/Foreign}$ is greater than, less than, or equal to 1. Explain your answer in terms of the assumptions we make when using the law of one price.

    a. Rice traded freely in the United States and Canada
    b. Sugar traded in the United States and Mexico; the U.S. government imposes a quota on sugar imports into the United States
    c. The McDonald's Big Mac sold in the United States and Japan
    d. Haircuts in the United States and the United Kingdom

3. Use the table that follows to answer this question. Treat the country listed as the home country, and treat the United States as the foreign country. Suppose the cost of the market basket in the United States is $P_{US} = \$190$. Check to see whether purchasing power parity (PPP) holds for each of the countries listed, and determine whether we should expect a real appreciation or real depreciation for each country (relative to the United States) in the long run. For the answer, create a table similar to the one shown and fill in the blank cells. (Hint: Use a spreadsheet application such as Excel.)

Country (currency measured in FX units)	Per $, $E_{FX/\$}$	Price of Market Basket (in FX)	Price of U.S. Basket in FX (P_{us} times $E_{FX/\$}$)	Real Exchange Rate, $q_{COUNTRY/US}$	Does PPP Hold? (yes/no)	Is FX Currency Overvalued or Undervalued?	Is FX Currency Expected to Have Real Appreciation or Depreciation?
Brazil (real)	2.1893	520					
India (rupee)	46.6672	12,000					
Mexico (peso)	11.0131	1,800					
South Africa (rand)	6.9294	800					
Zimbabwe (Z$)	101,347	4,000,000					

4. Table 3-1 in the text shows the percentage undervaluation or overvaluation in the Big Mac, based on exchange rates in July 2009. Suppose purchasing power parity holds and in the long run, so that these deviations would be expected to disappear. Suppose the local currency prices of the Big Mac remained unchanged. Exchange rates in January 4, 2010, were as follows (source: IMF):

Country	Per U.S. $
Australia (A$)	0.90
Brazil (real)	1.74
Canada (C$)	1.04
Denmark (krone)	5.17
Eurozone (euro)	0.69
India (rupee)	46.51
Japan (yen)	93.05
Mexico (peso)	12.92
Sweden (krona)	7.14

Based on these data and Table 3-1, calculate the change in the exchange rate from July to January, and state whether the direction of change was consistent with the PPP-implied exchange rate using the Big Mac Index. How might you explain the failure of the Big Mac Index to correctly predict the change in the nominal exchange rate between July 2009 and January 2010?

5. You are given the following information. The current dollar-pound exchange rate is $2 per pound. A U.S. basket that costs $100 would cost $120 in the United Kingdom. For the next year, the Fed is predicted to keep U.S. inflation at 2% and the Bank of England is predicted to keep U.K. inflation at 3%. The speed of convergence to absolute PPP is 15% per year.

a. What is the expected U.S. minus U.K. inflation differential for the coming year?
b. What is the current U.S. real exchange rate $q_{US/UK}$ with the United Kingdom?
c. How much is the dollar overvalued/undervalued?
d. What do you predict the U.S. real exchange rate with the United Kingdom will be in one year's time?
e. What is the expected rate of real depreciation for the United States (versus the United Kingdom)?
f. What is the expected rate of nominal depreciation for the United States (versus the United Kingdom)?
g. What do you predict will be the dollar price of one pound a year from now?

6. Describe how each of the following factors might explain why PPP is a better guide for exchange rate movements in the long run, versus the short run: (i) transactions costs, (ii) nontraded goods, (iii) imperfect competition, (iv) price stickiness. As markets become increasingly integrated, do you suspect PPP will become a more useful guide in the future? Why or why not?

7. Consider two countries: Japan and Korea. In 1996 Japan experienced relatively slow output growth (1%), while Korea had relatively robust output growth (6%). Suppose the Bank of Japan allowed the money supply to grow by 2% each year, while the Bank of Korea chose to maintain relatively high money growth of 12% per year.

For the following questions, use the simple monetary model (where L is constant). You will find it easiest to treat Korea as the home country and Japan as the foreign country.

a. What is the inflation rate in Korea? In Japan?
b. What is the expected rate of depreciation in the Korean won relative to the Japanese yen (¥)?
c. Suppose the Bank of Korea increases the money growth rate from 12% to 15%. If nothing in Japan changes, what is the new inflation rate in Korea?
d. Using time series diagrams, illustrate how this increase in the money growth rate affects the money supply M_K, Korea's interest rate, prices P_K, real money supply, and $E_{won/¥}$ over time. (Plot each variable on the vertical axis and time on the horizontal axis.)
e. Suppose the Bank of Korea wants to maintain an exchange rate peg with the Japanese yen. What money growth rate would the Bank of Korea have to choose to keep the value of the won fixed relative to the yen?
f. Suppose the Bank of Korea sought to implement policy that would cause the Korean won to appreciate relative to the Japanese yen. What ranges of the money growth rate (assuming positive values) would allow the Bank of Korea to achieve this objective?

8. This question uses the general monetary model, where L is no longer assumed constant, and money demand is inversely related to the nominal interest rate. Consider the same scenario described at the beginning of the previous question. In addition, the bank deposits in Japan pay a 3% interest rate, $i_¥ = 3\%$.

   a. Compute the interest rate paid on Korean deposits.
   b. Using the definition of the real interest rate (nominal interest rate adjusted for inflation), show that the real interest rate in Korea is equal to the real interest rate in Japan. (Note that the inflation rates you computed in the previous question will be the same in this question.)
   c. Suppose the Bank of Korea increases the money growth rate from 12% to 15% and the inflation rate rises proportionately (one for one) with this increase. If the nominal interest rate in Japan remains unchanged, what happens to the interest rate paid on Korean deposits?
   d. Using time series diagrams, illustrate how this increase in the money growth rate affects the money supply M_K; Korea's interest rate; prices P_K; real money supply; and $E_{won/¥}$ over time. (Plot each variable on the vertical axis and time on the horizontal axis.)

9. Both advanced economics and developing countries have experienced a decrease in inflation since the 1980s (see Table 3-3 in the text). This question considers how the choice of policy regime has influenced such global disinflation. Use the monetary model to answer this question.

   a. The Swiss Central Bank currently targets its money growth rate to achieve policy objectives. Suppose Switzerland has output growth of 3% and money growth of 8% each year. What is Switzerland's inflation rate in this case? Describe how the Swiss Central Bank could achieve an inflation rate of 2% in the long run through the use of a nominal anchor.
   b. Like the Federal Reserve, the Reserve Bank of New Zealand uses an interest rate target.

Suppose the Reserve Bank of New Zealand maintains a 6% interest rate target and the world *real* interest rate is 1.5%. What is the New Zealand inflation rate in the long run? In 1997 New Zealand adopted a policy agreement that required the bank to maintain an inflation rate no higher than 2.5%. What interest rate targets would achieve this objective?

c. The central bank of Lithuania maintains an exchange rate band relative to the euro. This is a prerequisite for joining the Eurozone. Lithuania must keep its exchange rate within ±15% of the central parity of 3.4528 litas per euro. Compute the exchange rate values corresponding to the upper and lower edges of this band. Suppose PPP holds. Assuming Eurozone inflation is currently 2% per year and inflation in Lithuania is 5%, compute the rate of depreciation of the lita. Will Lithuania be able to maintain the band requirement? For how long? Does your answer depend on where in the band the exchange rate currently sits? A primary objective of the European Central Bank is price stability (low inflation) in the current and future Eurozone. Is an exchange rate band a necessary or sufficient condition for the attainment of this objective?

10. Several countries that have experienced hyperinflation adopt dollarization as a way to control domestic inflation. For example, Ecuador has used the U.S. dollar as its domestic currency since 2000. What does dollarization imply about the exchange rate between Ecuador and the United States? Why might countries experiencing hyperinflation adopt dollarization? Why might they do this rather than just fixing their exchange rate?

11. You are the central banker for a country that is considering the adoption of a new nominal anchor. When you take the position as chairperson, the inflation rate is 4% and your position as the central bank chairperson requires that you achieve a 2.5% inflation target within the next year. The economy's growth in real output is currently 3%. The world real interest rate is currently 1.5%. The currency used in your country is the lira. *Assume prices are flexible.*

   a. Why is having a nominal anchor important for you to achieve the inflation target? What is the drawback of using a nominal anchor?

   b. What is the growth rate of the money supply in this economy? If you choose to adopt a money supply target, which money supply growth rate will allow you to meet your inflation target?

   c. Suppose the inflation rate in the United States is currently 2% and you adopt an exchange rate target relative to the U.S. dollar. Compute the percent appreciation/depreciation in the lira needed for you to achieve your inflation target. Will the lira appreciate or depreciate relative to the U.S. dollar?

   d. Your final option is to achieve your inflation target using interest rate policy. Using the Fisher equation, compute the current nominal interest rate in your country. What nominal interest rate will allow you to achieve the inflation target?

NETWORK

The Big Mac Index isn't the only popular PPP gauge. In 2004 the *Economist* made a Starbuck's Tall Latte Index, which you can try to find online. (*Hint:* Google "cnn tall latte index.") In 2007 two new indices appeared: the iPod Index (based on the local prices of Apple's iPod music player) and iTunes Index (based on the local prices of a single song downloaded from Apple's iTunes store). Find those indices online and the discussions surrounding them. (*Hint:* Google "ipod itunes index big mac.") Do you think that either the iPod Index or iTunes Index is a better guide to currency overvaluation/undervaluation than the Big Mac Index? Explain your answer.

Visit the websites of some central banks around the world, for example, the U.S. Federal Reserve (http://www.federalreserve.gov/) and the European Central Bank (http://www.ecb.int/). Read their main statements of policy. Try to find out what their policy goals are *in the long run*. Who sets them? Is there more than one goal? What about a nominal anchor—is controlling inflation a long-run goal? If so, what policy is used to try to ensure that the long-run inflation goal will be met? In the short run, is the main tool they use for implementing their policy the quantity of money, the exchange rate, or the interest rate?

4

Exchange Rates II: The Asset Approach in the Short Run

1 Exchange Rates and Interest Rates in the Short Run: UIP and FX Market Equilibrium

2 Interest Rates in the Short Run: Money Market Equilibrium

3 The Asset Approach: Applications and Evidence

4 A Complete Theory: Unifying the Monetary and Asset Approaches

5 Fixed Exchange Rates and the Trilemma

6 Conclusions

The long run is a misleading guide to current affairs. In the long run we are all dead. Economists set themselves too easy, too useless a task if in tempestuous seasons they can only tell us that when the storm is past the ocean is flat again.
John Maynard Keynes, *A Tract on Monetary Reform*, 1923

As we saw in the last chapter, the monetary approach to exchange rates may work in the long run, but it is a poor guide to what happens in the short run. To recap this distinction, let's return to the Canada–U.S. comparison with which we opened the last chapter—only this time we'll focus on developments in the short run.

From March 2005 to March 2006, the Canadian price level (measured by the consumer price index) rose from 126.5 to 129.3, an increase of 2.2%. The U.S. price level rose from 193.3 to 199.8, an increase of 3.4%. U.S. prices therefore increased 1.2% more than Canadian prices. But over the same period, the loonie (Canadian dollar) rose in value from $0.8267 to $0.8568, an appreciation of 3.6%.[1]

Because Canadian baskets cost 2.2% more in loonie terms, *and* each loonie cost 3.6% more in U.S. dollar terms, the change in the U.S. dollar price of the Canadian basket was approximately the sum of these two changes, or about 5.8%. But over the same period, the U.S. dollar price of U.S. baskets rose only 3.4%. Taking the difference, Canadian baskets ended up 2.4% more expensive than U.S. baskets, meaning that the U.S. *real* exchange rate with Canada rose by 2.4%, a real depreciation. This pattern was not unusual. In the previous year from March 2004 to March 2005, the real depreciation had been even larger, at 7.5%, so over two years Canadian goods rose in price by about 10% compared with U.S. goods.

---

[1] Data for this example are taken from the Bank of Canada and U.S. Bureau of Labor Statistics.

As we have already noted, evidence of this kind suggests that substantial deviations from purchasing power parity (PPP) occur in the short run: the same basket of goods generally does not cost the same everywhere at all times. These short-run failures of the monetary approach prompted economists to develop an alternative theory to explain exchange rates in the short run: the **asset approach to exchange rates,** the subject of this chapter.

The asset approach is based on the idea that currencies are assets. The price of the asset in this case is the spot exchange rate, the price of one unit of foreign exchange. Here we can draw on what we learned about how arbitrage plays a major role in the forex market by forcing the expected returns of two assets in different currencies to be equal. This insight led us to derive the uncovered interest parity (UIP) condition. Because it characterizes a forex market equilibrium, UIP is further explored and extensively applied in this chapter.

The asset approach differs from the monetary approach in its time frame and assumptions. In the monetary approach, we envisage a long run that takes several years; in the asset approach, we are typically thinking of a short run of a matter of a few months, or perhaps a year or so at most. In the monetary approach, we treat goods prices as perfectly flexible, a plausible assumption in the long run; in the asset approach, we assume that goods prices are sticky, a more appropriate assumption in the short run. Each theory is valid but only in the right context. Thus, rather than supplanting the monetary approach, the asset approach complements it, and provides us with the final building blocks necessary to construct a complete theory of exchange rates.

So far, we have assumed that exchange rates are determined by market forces in the goods, money, and foreign exchange markets—so our theory is relevant when the exchange rate floats, and the authorities leave it to find its own market-determined level. Can our theory also tell us anything about fixed exchange rates? Yes. At the end of the chapter, we see how the same theoretical framework can be applied to a fixed exchange rate regime.

1 Exchange Rates and Interest Rates in the Short Run: UIP and FX Market Equilibrium

To begin our study of exchange rates in the short run, let's recap the crucial equilibrium condition for the forex (or FX) market. In our earlier presentation, we considered a U.S. investor with two alternative investment strategies: a one-year investment in a U.S. dollar account with an interest rate $i_\$$, or a one-year investment in a euro account with an interest rate $i_€$. Here are the essentials.

Risky Arbitrage

For the case of risky arbitrage, the foreign exchange market is in equilibrium when there is no expected difference in the rates of return on each type of currency investment. As before, we assume the Home country is the United States (US); the Foreign country is Europe (EUR, meaning the Eurozone). As we saw in the approximate uncovered interest parity condition—Equation (2-3), and repeated in this section as Equation (4-1)—this outcome requires that the dollar rate of return on the Home investment (the dollar deposit) equal the expected dollar rate of return on the Foreign investment (the euro deposit),

$$\underbrace{i_\$}_{\substack{\text{Interest rate} \\ \text{on dollar deposits} \\ = \\ \text{Dollar rate of return} \\ \text{on dollar deposits}}} = \underbrace{\underbrace{i_\euro}_{\substack{\text{Interest rate} \\ \text{on euro deposits}}} + \underbrace{\frac{(E^e_{\$/\euro} - E_{\$/\euro})}{E_{\$/\euro}}}_{\substack{\text{Expected rate of depreciation} \\ \text{of the dollar}}}}_{\substack{\text{Expected dollar rate of return} \\ \text{on euro deposits}}} \qquad (4\text{-}1)$$

where each interest rate is an annual rate, $E_{\$/\euro}$ is today's exchange rate (the spot rate), and $E^e_{\$/\euro}$ is the expected future exchange rate that will prevail one year ahead.

The uncovered interest parity (UIP) equation is the **fundamental equation of the asset approach to exchange rates,** and from now on, we use it in the form of Equation (4-1). As we have seen, by rearranging this equation, we can solve it for the spot exchange rate, provided we know all of the other variables. Thus, the asset approach employs the UIP equation to determine today's spot exchange rate, as illustrated in Figure 4-1. Hence, the theory is useful only if we can assume knowledge of interest rates and the future expected exchange rate. Where does that knowledge come from?

Exchange Rate Expectations First, we need a forecast of the future level of the exchange rate $E^e_{\$/\euro}$. The asset approach itself does not provide the answer, so we must look elsewhere. Where to look? In the long-run monetary approach to the exchange rate presented in the previous chapter. We can now see how the asset approach and monetary approach fit together.

Short-Term Interest Rates The second assumption is that we know today's interest rates on deposit accounts in each country, the dollar interest rate $i_\$$, and the euro account interest rate $i_\euro$. Market participants can observe these short-term interest rates. But how are these interest rates determined, and, in particular, what is their relation to economic policy? In the next section, we explore that question to develop a fuller understanding of how exchange rates are determined.

FIGURE 4-1

Building Block: Uncovered Interest Parity—The Fundamental Equation of the Asset Approach In this model, the nominal interest rate and expected future exchange rate are treated as known exogenous variables (in green). The model uses these variables to predict the unknown endogenous variable (in red), the current spot exchange rate.

Equilibrium in the FX Market: An Example

To explore the concepts we've just studied, let's work through a numerical example to show how equilibrium in the foreign exchange market is determined.

Suppose we have made a forecast (using the long-run monetary model of exchange rates) that the expected future exchange rate $E^e_{\$/€}$ (in one year's time) is 1.224 dollars per euro. Suppose also that the current European interest rate $i_€$ is 3%, and the current U.S. interest rate $i_\$$ is 5%.

Now examine Table 4-1 to see how, for various values of the spot exchange rate $E_{\$/€}$, we can calculate the domestic rate of return and expected foreign rate of return in U.S. dollars. (Remember that 5% = 0.05, 3% = 0.03, etc.) As you work through the table, remember that the foreign returns have two components: one due to the European interest rate $i_€$ and the other due to the expected rate of depreciation of the dollar, as in Equation (4-1).

Figure 4-2 presents an **FX market diagram,** a graphical representation of these returns in the forex market. We plot the expected domestic and foreign returns (on the vertical axis) against today's spot exchange rate (on the horizontal axis). The domestic dollar return (DR) (which is just the Home nominal interest rate) is fixed at 5% = 0.05 and is independent of the spot exchange rate.

The foreign expected dollar return (FR) depends on the spot exchange rate according to Equation (4-1) and it varies as we just saw in Table 4-1. For example, we can infer from the table that a spot exchange rate of 1.224 implies a foreign return of

TABLE 4-1

Interest Rates, Exchange Rates, Expected Returns, and FX Market Equilibrium: A Numerical Example The foreign exchange (FX) market is in equilibrium when the domestic and foreign returns are equal. In this example, the dollar interest rate is 5%, the euro interest rate is 3%, and the expected future exchange rate (one year ahead) is = 1.224 $/€. The equilibrium is highlighted in bold type, where both returns are 5% in annual dollar terms. Figure 4-2 plots the domestic and foreign returns (columns 1 and 6) against the spot exchange rate (column 3). Figures are rounded in this table.

(1)	(2)	(3)	(4)	(5)	(6) = (2) + (5)
Interest Rate on Dollar Deposits (annual)	Interest Rate on Euro Deposits (annual)	Spot Exchange Rate (today)	Expected Future Exchange Rate (in 1 year)	Expected Euro Appreciation against Dollar (in 1 year)	Expected Dollar Return on Euro Deposits (annual)
Domestic Return ($)					Foreign Expected Return ($)
$i_\$$	$i_€$	$E_{\$/€}$	$E^e_{\$/€}$	$\dfrac{E^e_{\$/€} - E_{\$/€}}{E_{\$/€}}$	$i_€ + \dfrac{E^e_{\$/€} - E_{\$/€}}{E_{\$/€}}$
0.05	0.03	1.16	1.224	0.0552	0.0852
0.05	0.03	1.18	1.224	0.0373	0.0673
0.05	**0.03**	**1.20**	**1.224**	**0.02**	**0.05**
0.05	0.03	1.22	1.224	0.0033	0.0333
0.05	0.03	1.24	1.224	−0.0129	0.0171

Market equilibrium (highlighted in the third data row)

FIGURE 4-2

FX Market Equilibrium: A Numerical Example
The returns calculated in Table 4-1 are plotted in this figure. The dollar interest rate is 5%, the euro interest rate is 3%, and the expected future exchange rate is 1.224 $/€. The foreign exchange market is in equilibrium at point 1, where the domestic returns DR and expected foreign returns FR are equal at 5% and the spot exchange rate is 1.20 $/€.

3% = 0.03. Hence, the point (1.224, 0.03) is on the *FR* line, as shown. This is the special case in which there is no expected depreciation (spot and expected future exchange rates are equal to 1.224), so the foreign return equals the Foreign interest rate, 3%.

More generally, we see that the foreign return falls as the spot exchange rate $E_{\$/€}$ increases, all else equal. Why? This is clear mathematically from the right side of Equation (4-1). The intuition is as follows. If the dollar depreciates today, $E_{\$/€}$ rises; a euro investment is then a more expensive (and, thus, less attractive) proposition, all else equal. That is, $1 moved into a European account is worth fewer euros today; this, in turn, leaves fewer euro proceeds in a year's time after euro interest has accrued; and if expectations are fixed so that the future euro-dollar exchange rate $E^e_{\$/€}$ is known and unchanged, then those fewer future euros will be worth fewer future dollars. Hence, the foreign return (in dollars) goes down as $E_{\$/€}$ rises, *all else equal*. The *FR* curve is therefore downward sloping.

What is the equilibrium level of the spot exchange rate? According Table 4-1, the equilibrium exchange rate is 1.20 $/€. Only at that exchange rate are domestic returns and foreign returns equalized. To illustrate the solution graphically, domestic and foreign returns are plotted in Figure 4-2. The FX market is in equilibrium, and foreign and domestic returns are equal, at the point at which the *FR* and *DR* curves intersect. This is labeled as point 1.

Adjustment to FX Market Equilibrium

Our FX market equilibrium condition and its graphical representation should now be clear. But how is this equilibrium reached? It turns out that arbitrage automatically pushes the level of the exchange rate toward its equilibrium value.

To see this, suppose that the market is initially out of equilibrium, with the spot $E_{\$/€}$ exchange rate at a level too low, so that the foreign return—the right-hand side of Equation (4-1)—exceeds the domestic return (the left-hand side).

At point 2 in Figure 4-2, foreign returns are well above domestic returns. With the spot exchange rate of 1.16 $/€ and (from Table 4-1) an expected future exchange rate as high as 1.224 $/€, the euro is expected to *appreciate* by 5.5% = 0.055 [= (1.224/1.16) − 1]. In addition, euros earn at an interest rate of 3%, for a whopping foreign expected return of 5.5% + 3% = 8.5% = 0.085, which far exceeds the domestic return of 5%. At point 2, in other words, the euro offers too high a return; equivalently, it is too cheap. Traders want to sell dollars and buy euros. These market pressures bid up the price of a euro: the dollar starts to depreciate against the euro, causing $E_{\$/€}$ to rise, which moves foreign and domestic returns into equality and forces the exchange rate back toward equilibrium at point 1.

The same idea applies to a situation in which the spot exchange rate $E_{\$/€}$ is initially too high. At point 3 in Figure 4-2, foreign and domestic returns are not equal: the exchange rate is 1.24 $/€. Given where the exchange rate is expected to be in a year's time (1.224 $/€), paying a high price of 1.24 $/€ today means the euro is expected to *depreciate* by about 1.3% = 0.013 [= 1.224/1.24 − 1]. If euro deposits pay 3%, and euros are expected to depreciate 1.3%, this makes for a net foreign return of just 1.7%, well below the domestic return of 5% = 0.05. In other words, at point 3, the euro offers too low a return; equivalently, it is too expensive today. Traders will want to sell euros.

Only at point 1 is the euro trading at a price at which the foreign return equals the domestic return. At point 1, the euro is neither too cheap nor too expensive—its price is just right for uncovered interest parity to hold, for arbitrage to cease, and for the FX market to be in equilibrium.

Changes in Domestic and Foreign Returns and FX Market Equilibrium

When economic conditions change, the two curves depicting domestic and foreign returns shift. In the case of the domestic return curve, the movements are easy to understand because the curve is a horizontal line that intersects the vertical axis at the domestic interest rate. If the domestic interest changes, the curve shifts up or down. Shifts in the foreign returns curve are a bit more complicated because there are two parts to the foreign return: the foreign interest rate plus any expected change in the exchange rate.

To gain greater familiarity with the model, let's see how the FX market example shown in Figure 4-2 responds to three separate shocks:

- A higher domestic interest rate, $i_\$ = 7\%$
- A lower foreign interest rate, $i_€ = 1\%$
- A lower expected future exchange rate, $E^e_{\$/€} = 1.20$ $/€

These three cases are shown in Figure 4-3, panels (a), (b), and (c). In all three cases, the shocks make dollar deposits more attractive than euro deposits, but for different reasons. Regardless of the reason, however, the shocks we examine all lead to dollar appreciations.

A Change in the Domestic Interest Rate In Figure 4-3, panel (a), when $i_\$$ rises to 7%, the domestic return is increased by 2% so the domestic return curve *DR* shifts up by 2% = 0.02 from DR_1 to DR_2. The foreign return is unaffected. Now, at the initial equilibrium spot exchange rate of 1.20 $/€, the domestic return (point 4) is higher than the foreign return. Traders sell euros and buy dollars; the dollar appreciates to 1.177 $/€ at the new equilibrium, point 5. The foreign return and domestic return are equal once again and UIP holds once more.

FIGURE 4-3

(a) A Change in the Home Interest Rate A rise in the dollar interest rate from 5% to 7% increases domestic returns, shifting the DR curve up from DR_1 to DR_2. At the initial equilibrium exchange rate of 1.20 $/€ on DR_2, domestic returns are above foreign returns at point 4. Dollar deposits are more attractive and the dollar appreciates from 1.20 $/€ to 1.177 $/€. The new equilibrium is at point 5.

(b) A Change in the Foreign Interest Rate A fall in the euro interest rate from 3% to 1% lowers foreign expected dollar returns, shifting the FR curve down from FR_1 to FR_2. At the initial equilibrium exchange rate of 1.20 $/€ on FR_2, foreign returns are below domestic returns at point 6. Dollar deposits are more attractive and the dollar appreciates from 1.20 $/€ to 1.177 $/€. The new equilibrium is at point 7.

(c) A Change in the Expected Future Exchange Rate A fall in the expected future exchange rate from 1.224 to 1.20 lowers foreign expected dollar returns, shifting the FR curve down from FR_1 to FR_2. At the initial equilibrium exchange rate of 1.20 $/€ on FR_2, foreign returns are below domestic returns at point 6. Dollar deposits are more attractive and the dollar appreciates from 1.20 $/€ to 1.177 $/€. The new equilibrium is at point 7.

A Change in the Foreign Interest Rate In Figure 4-3, panel (b), when $i_€$ falls to 1%, euro deposits now pay a lower interest rate (1% versus 3%). The foreign return curve FR shifts down by 2% = 0.02 from FR_1 to FR_2. The domestic return is unaffected. Now, at the old equilibrium rate of 1.20 $/€, the foreign return (point 6) is lower than the domestic return. Traders sell euros and buy dollars; the dollar appreciates to 1.177 $/€ at the new equilibrium, point 7, and UIP holds once more.

A Change in the Expected Future Exchange Rate In Figure 4-3, panel (c), a decrease in the expected future exchange rate $E^e_{\$/€}$ lowers the foreign return because a future euro is expected to be worth fewer dollars in the future. The foreign return curve FR shifts down from FR_1 to FR_2. The domestic return is unaffected. At the old equilibrium rate of 1.20 $/€, the foreign return (point 6) is lower than the domestic return. Again, traders sell euros and buy dollars, causing the dollar to appreciate and the spot exchange rate to fall to 1.177 $/€. The new equilibrium is point 7.

Summary

The FX market diagram, with its representation of domestic returns and foreign returns, is central to our analysis in this chapter and later in the book. Be sure that you understand that domestic returns depend only on the Home interest rate $i_\$$, but that foreign returns depend on both the Foreign interest rate $i_€$ *and* the expected future exchange rate $E^e_{\$/€}$. Remember that any change which raises (lowers) the foreign return relative to the domestic return makes euro deposits more (less) attractive to investors, so that traders will buy (sell) euro deposits. The traders' actions push the FX market toward a new equilibrium at which the dollar will have depreciated (appreciated) against the euro.

To check your understanding, you might wish to rework the three examples and the figures for the opposite cases of a *decrease* in $i_\$$, an *increase* in $i_€$, and an *increase* in $E^e_{\$/€}$; constructing the equivalent of Table 4-1 for each case may also prove helpful.

2 Interest Rates in the Short Run: Money Market Equilibrium

The previous section laid out the essentials of the asset approach to exchange rates. Figure 4-1 sums up the uncovered interest parity relationship at the heart of the asset approach. The spot exchange rate is the output (endogenous variable) of this model, and the expected future exchange rate and the home and foreign interest rates are the inputs (exogenous variables). But where do these inputs come from? In the last chapter, we developed a theory of the long-run exchange rate, the monetary approach, which can be used to forecast the future exchange rate. That leaves us with just one unanswered question: How are current interest rates determined?

Money Market Equilibrium in the Short Run: How Nominal Interest Rates Are Determined

Having seen how the supply and demand for money work in the previous chapter, we can build on that foundation here. We consider two money markets in two locations: the United States and Europe. Both markets are in equilibrium with money demand equal to money supply. In both locations, the money supply is controlled by a central bank and is taken as given; the demand for real money balances $M/P = L(i)Y$ is a function of the interest rate i and real income Y.

The Assumptions It is important to understand the key difference between the way we approach money market equilibrium in the short run (in this chapter) and the way we approached it in the long run (in the last chapter).

In the last chapter, we made the following *long-run* assumptions:

- In the long run, the price level P is fully flexible and adjusts to bring the money market to equilibrium.
- In the long run, the nominal interest rate i equals the world real interest rate plus domestic inflation.

In this chapter, we make *short-run* assumptions that are quite different:

- In the short run, the price level is sticky; it is a known predetermined variable, fixed at $P = \overline{P}$ (the bar indicates a fixed value).
- In the short run, the nominal interest rate i is fully flexible and adjusts to bring the money market to equilibrium.

Why do we make different assumptions in the short run?

First, why assume prices are now sticky? The assumption of sticky prices, also called **nominal rigidity,** is common to the study of macroeconomics in the short run. Economists have many explanations for price stickiness. Nominal wages may be sticky because of long-term labor contracts. Nominal product prices may be sticky because of *menu costs;* that is, firms may find it costly to frequently change their output prices. Thus, while it is reasonable to assume that all prices are flexible in the long run, they may not be in the short run.

Second, why assume that interest rates are now flexible? In the previous chapter, we showed that nominal interest rates are pinned down by the Fisher effect (or real interest parity) in the long run: in that case, the home nominal interest rate was equal to the world real interest rate plus the home rate of inflation. However, recall that this result does not apply in the short run because it is derived from purchasing power parity—which, as we know, only applies in the long run. Indeed, we saw evidence that in the short run real interest rates fluctuate in ways that deviate from real interest parity.

The Model With these explanations of our short-run assumptions in hand, we can now use the same general monetary model of the previous chapter and write down expressions for money market equilibrium in the two countries as follows:

$$\underbrace{\frac{M_{US}}{\overline{P}_{US}}}_{\text{U.S. supply of real money balances}} = \underbrace{L(i_\$) \times Y_{US}}_{\text{U.S. demand for real money balances}} \qquad (4\text{-}2)$$

$$\underbrace{\frac{M_{EUR}}{\overline{P}_{EUR}}}_{\text{European supply of real money balances}} = \underbrace{L(i_€) \times Y_{EUR}}_{\text{U.S. demand for real money balances}} \qquad (4\text{-}3)$$

To recap: In the long run, prices adjust to clear the money market and bring money demand and money supply into line. In the short run, when prices are sticky, such adjustment is not possible. However, nominal interest rates *are* free to adjust. In the short run, the nominal interest rate in each country adjusts to bring money supply and money demand into equilibrium.

Money Market Equilibrium in the Short Run: Graphical Solution

Figure 4-4 represents the U.S. money market (a similar diagram applies to the European market). On the horizontal axis is the quantity of U.S. real money balances M_{US}/P_{US} and on the vertical axis is the U.S. nominal interest rate $i_\$$. The vertical line represents the supply of real money balances; this supply is fixed by the central bank at the level $M^1_{US}/\overline{P}^1_{US}$ and is independent of the level of the interest rate. The downward-sloping line represents the demand for real money balances, $L(i_\$) \times Y_{US}$. Demand decreases as the U.S. nominal interest rate increases because the opportunity cost of holding money rises and people don't want to hold high money balances. The money market is in equilibrium at point 1: the demand and supply of real money balances are equal at $M^1_{US}/\overline{P}^1_{US}$ and at a nominal interest rate $i^1_\$$.

Adjustment to Money Market Equilibrium in the Short Run

If interest rates are flexible in the short run, as we assume they are, there is nothing to prevent them from adjusting to clear the money market. But how do market forces ensure that a nominal interest rate $i^1_\$$ is attained? The adjustment process works as follows.

Suppose instead that the interest rate was $i^2_\$$, so that we were at point 2 on the real money demand curve. At this interest rate, real money demand is less than real money supply. In the aggregate, the central bank has put more money in the hands of the public than the public wishes to hold. The public will desire to reduce its cash holdings by ex-

FIGURE 4-4

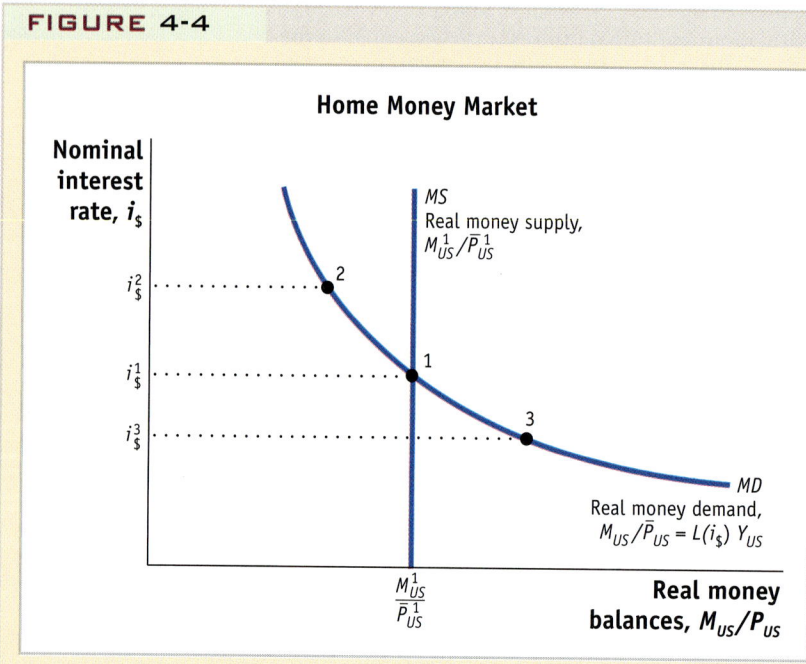

Equilibrium in the Home Money Market The supply and demand for real money balances determine the nominal interest rate. The money supply curve (MS) is vertical at $M^1_{US}/\overline{P}^1_{US}$ because the quantity of money supplied does not depend on the interest rate. The money demand curve (MD) is downward-sloping because an increase in the interest rate raises the cost of holding money, thus lowering the quantity demanded. The money market is in equilibrium when the nominal interest rate $i^1_\$$ is such that real money demand equals real money supply (point 1). At points 2 and 3, demand does not equal supply and the interest rate will adjust until the money market returns to equilibrium.

changing money for interest-bearing assets such as bonds, saving accounts, and so on. That is, they will save more and seek to lend their money to borrowers. But borrowers will not want to borrow more unless the cost of borrowing falls. So the interest rate will be driven down as eager lenders compete to attract scarce borrowers. As this happens, back in the money market, in Figure 4-4, we move from point 2 back toward equilibrium at point 1.

A similar story can be told if the money market is initially at point 3, where there is an excess demand for money. In this case, the public wishes to reduce their savings in the form of interest-bearing assets and turn them into cash. Now fewer loans are extended. The loan market will suffer an excess demand. But borrowers will not want to borrow less unless the cost of borrowing rises. So the interest rate will be driven up as eager borrowers compete to attract scarce lenders. These adjustments end only when point 1 is reached and there is no excess supply of real money balances.

Another Building Block: Short-Run Money Market Equilibrium

This model of the money market may be familiar from previous courses in macroeconomics. The lessons that are important for our theory of exchange rates are summed up in Figure 4-5. We treat the price level in each country as fixed and known in the short run. We also assume that the money supply and real income in each country are known. The equilibrium equations for the money market, Equations (4-2) and (4-3), then tell us the interest rates in each country. Once these are known, we can put them to use in another building block seen earlier: the interest rates can be plugged into the fundamental equation of the asset approach to exchange rate determination, Equation (4-1), along with the future expected exchange rate derived from a forecast based on the long-run monetary model of the previous chapter. In that way, the spot exchange rate can finally be determined.

Changes in Money Supply and the Nominal Interest Rate

Money market equilibrium depends on money supply and money demand. If either changes, the equilibrium will change. To help us better understand how exchange rates are determined, we need to understand how these changes occur.

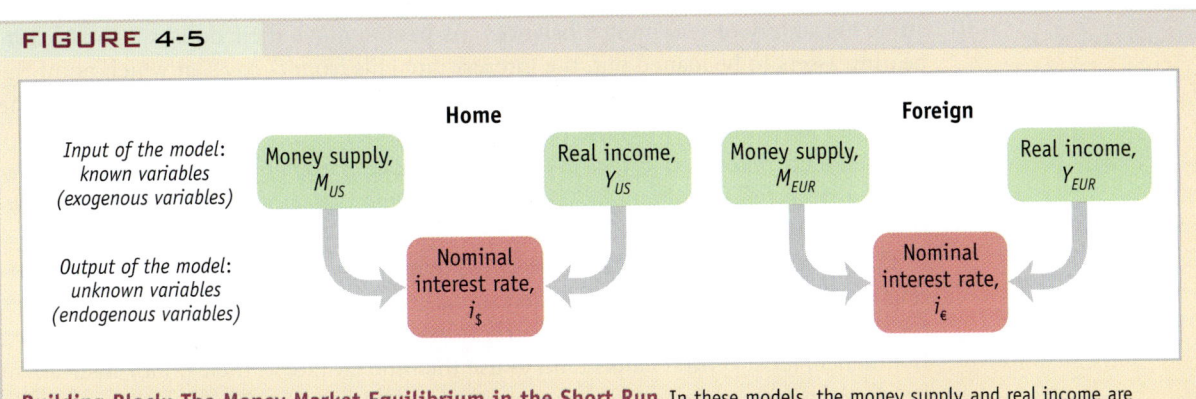

FIGURE 4-5

Building Block: The Money Market Equilibrium in the Short Run In these models, the money supply and real income are known exogenous variables (in green boxes). The models use these variables to predict the unknown endogenous variables (in red boxes), the nominal interest rates in each country.

Home Money Market with Changes in Money Supply and Money Demand In panel (a), with a fixed price level $\overline{P}^1_{US}$, an increase in nominal money supply from M^1_{US} to M^2_{US} causes an increase in real money supply from $M^1_{US}/\overline{P}^1_{US}$ to $M^2_{US}/\overline{P}^1_{US}$. The nominal interest rate falls from $i^1_\$$ to $i^2_\$$ to restore equilibrium at point 2. In panel (b), with a fixed price level $\overline{P}^1_{US}$, an increase in real income from Y^1_{US} to Y^2_{US} causes real money demand to increase from MD_1 to MD_2. To restore equilibrium at point 2, the interest rate rises from $i^1_\$$ to $i^2_\$$.

Figure 4-6, panel (a), shows how the money market responds to a monetary policy change consisting of an increase in the Home (U.S.) nominal money supply from M^1_{US} to M^2_{US}. Because, by assumption, the U.S. price level is fixed in the short run at $\overline{P}^1_{US}$, the increase in nominal money supply causes an increase in real money supply from $M^1_{US}/\overline{P}^1_{US}$ to $M^2_{US}/\overline{P}^1_{US}$. In the figure, the money supply curve shifts to the right from MS_1 to MS_2. Point 1 is no longer an equilibrium; at the interest rate $i^1_\$$, there is now an excess supply of real money balances. As people move their dollars into interest-bearing assets to be loaned out, the interest rate falls from $i^1_\$$ to $i^2_\$$, at which point the money market is again in equilibrium at point 2. By the same logic, a reduction in the nominal money supply will raise the interest rate.

To sum up, *in the short run, all else equal, an increase in a country's money supply will lower the country's nominal interest rate; a decrease in a country's money supply will raise the country's nominal interest rate.*

Fortunately, our graphical analysis shows that, for a *given* money demand curve, setting a money supply level uniquely determines the interest rate and vice versa. Hence, for many purposes, *the money supply or the interest rate may be used as a policy instrument*. In practice, most central banks tend to use the interest rate as their policy instrument because the money demand curve may not be stable, and the fluctuations caused by this instability would lead to unstable interest rates if the money supply were set at a given level as the policy instrument.

APPLICATION

Can Central Banks Always Control the Interest Rate? A Lesson from the Crisis of 2008–2009

In our analyses so far, we have assumed that central banks can control the money market interest rate, and that they can effectively do so whether they set the interest rate or the money supply. These assumptions are critical in this chapter and in the rest of this book. But are they really true? In general, perhaps, but policy operations by central banks can be undermined by financial market disruptions. Recent events in many countries illustrate the problem.

In the United States, for example, the Federal Reserve sets as its *policy rate* the interest rate that it charges banks for overnight loans. In normal times, changes in this cost of short-term funds for the banks are usually passed through into the *market rates* the banks charge to borrowers on loans such as mortgages, corporate loans, auto loans, etc., as well as on interbank loans between the banks themselves. This process is one of the most basic elements in the so-called *transmission mechanism* through which the effects of monetary policy are eventually felt in the real economy.

In the recent crisis, however, banks regarded other banks and borrowers (and even themselves) as facing potentially catastrophic risks. As a result, they lent much less freely and when they did loan, they charged much higher interest rates to compensate themselves for the risk of the loan suffering a loss or default. Thus, although the Fed brought its policy rate all the way down from 5.25% to 0% in 2007 and 2008, there was no similar decrease in market rates. In fact, market interest rates barely moved at all.

A second problem arose once policy rates hit the *zero lower bound* (ZLB). At that point, the central banks' capacity to lower interest rate further was exhausted. However, many central banks wanted to keep applying downward pressure to market rates to calm financial markets. The Fed's response was a policy of *quantitative easing*.

Usually, the Fed expands base money M0 by either lending to banks which put up safe government bonds as collateral, or by buying government bonds outright in open-market operations—although these actions are taken only in support of the Fed's interest rate target. But in the crisis, and with interest rates stuck at a floor, the Fed engaged in a number of extraordinary policy actions to push more money out more quickly:

1. It expanded the range of credit securities it would accept as collateral to include lower-grade, private-sector bonds.

2. It expanded the range of securities that it would buy outright to include private-sector credit instruments such as commercial paper and mortgage-backed securities.

3. It expanded the range of counterparties from which it would buy securities to include some nonbank institutions such as primary dealers and money market funds.

As a result of massive asset purchases along these lines, M0 in the United States more than doubled to over a trillion dollars. However, there was very little change in M1 or M2, indicating that banks had little desire to translate the cash they were receiving from the Fed into the new loans and new deposits that would expand the broad money supply.

Similar crisis actions were taken by the Bank of England and, eventually, by the European Central Bank; both expanded their collateral rules, although their outright purchase programs were more narrowly focused on aggressive use of open-market

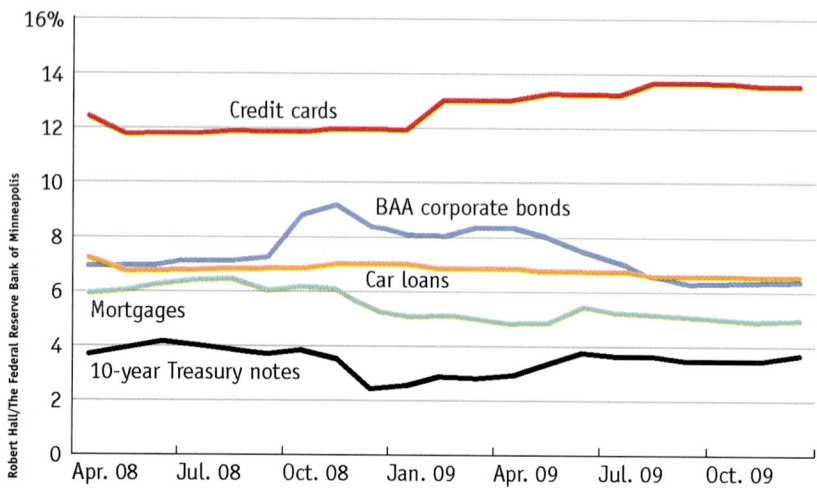

A broken transmission: the Fed's extraordinary interventions did little to change private credit market interest rates in 2008–2009.

operations to purchase large quantities of U.K. and Eurozone government bonds (though in the ECB's case this did include low-grade bonds from crisis countries such as Greece and Portugal).

To sum up, with the traditional transmission mechanism broken, central banks had to find different tools. In the Fed's case, by directly intervening in markets for different types of private credit at different maturities, policy makers hoped to circumvent the impaired transmission mechanism. Would matters have been much worse if the central banks had done nothing at all? It's hard to say (and we may not be able to attempt an answer until all the data are in once the crisis and recession are over). However, if the aim was to lower market interest rates in a meaningful way and expand broader monetary aggregates, it is as yet unclear whether these policies have had significant economic effects. ■

Changes in Real Income and the Nominal Interest Rate

Figure 4-6, panel (b), shows how the money market responds to an increase in Home (U.S.) real income from Y^1_{US} to Y^2_{US}. The increase in real income causes real money demand to increase as reflected in the shift from MD_1 to MD_2. At the initial interest rate $i^1_\$$, there is now an excess demand for real money balances. To restore equilibrium at point 2, the interest rate rises from $i^1_\$$ to $i^2_\$$ to encourage people to hold lower dollar balances. Similarly, a reduction in real income will lower the interest rate.

To sum up, *in the short run, all else equal, an increase in a country's real income will raise the country's nominal interest rate; a decrease in a country's real income will lower the country's nominal interest rate.*

The Monetary Model: The Short Run versus the Long Run

The short-run implications of the model we have just discussed differ from the long-run implications of the monetary approach we presented in the previous chapter. It is important that we look at these differences, and understand how and why they arise.

Consider the following example: the Home central bank that previously kept the money supply constant suddenly switches to an expansionary policy. In the following year, it allows the money supply to grow at a rate of 5%.

- If such expansions are expected to be a permanent policy in the long run, the predictions of the long-run monetary approach and Fisher effect are clear. All else equal, a five-percentage-point increase in the rate of Home money growth causes a five-percentage-point increase in the rate of Home inflation and a five-percentage-point increase in the Home nominal interest rate. The Home interest rate *rises* in the long run when prices are flexible.

- If this expansion is expected to be temporary, then the short-run model we have just studied in this chapter tells a very different story. All else equal, if the Home money supply expands, the immediate effect is an excess supply of real money balances. The home interest rate will then *fall* in the short run when prices are sticky.

These different outcomes illustrate the importance of the assumptions we make about price flexibility. They also underscore the importance of the nominal anchor in monetary policy formulation and the constraints that central banks have to confront.

The different outcomes also explain some apparently puzzling linkages among money, interest rates, and exchange rates. In both of the previous cases, an expanded money supply leads to a weaker currency. However, in the short run, low interest rates and a weak currency go together, whereas in the long run, high interest rates and a weak currency go together.

What is the intuition for these findings? In the short run, when we study the impact of a lower interest rate and we say "all else equal," we have assumed that expectations have not changed concerning future exchange rates (or money supply or inflation). In other words, we envisage (implicitly) a temporary policy that does not tamper with the nominal anchor. In the long run, if the policy turns out to be permanent, this assumption is inappropriate; prices are flexible and money growth, inflation, and expected depreciation now all move in concert—in other words, the "all else" is no longer equal.

A good grasp of these key differences between the short- and long-run approaches is essential to understanding the determinants of exchange rates. To cement our understanding, in the rest of the chapter we will explore the different implications of temporary and permanent policy changes. To facilitate our applied work, we now lay out the short-run model in a succinct, graphical form.

3 The Asset Approach: Applications and Evidence

To simplify the graphical presentation of the asset approach, we focus on conditions in the Home economy; a similar approach can be used for the Foreign economy. For illustration we again assume that Home is the United States and Foreign is Europe.

The Asset Approach to Exchange Rates: Graphical Solution

Figure 4-7 shows two markets: panel (a) shows the Home money market (for the United States), and panel (b) shows the FX market diagram (for the dollar-euro market). This figure summarizes the asset approach in the short run.

The U.S. Money Market Panel (a) depicts equilibrium in the U.S. money market. The horizontal axis shows the quantity of U.S. real money balances demanded or supplied, M_{US}/P_{US}. The vertical axis shows the U.S. nominal interest rate $i_\$$. Two relationships are shown:

1. The vertical line *MS* represents the U.S. real money supply. The line is vertical because (i) the nominal U.S. money supply M_{US} is treated as exogenous (known), because it is set by the Home central bank, and (ii) the U.S. price level $\bar{P}_{US}$ is treated as exogenous (known) in the short run due to price stickiness.

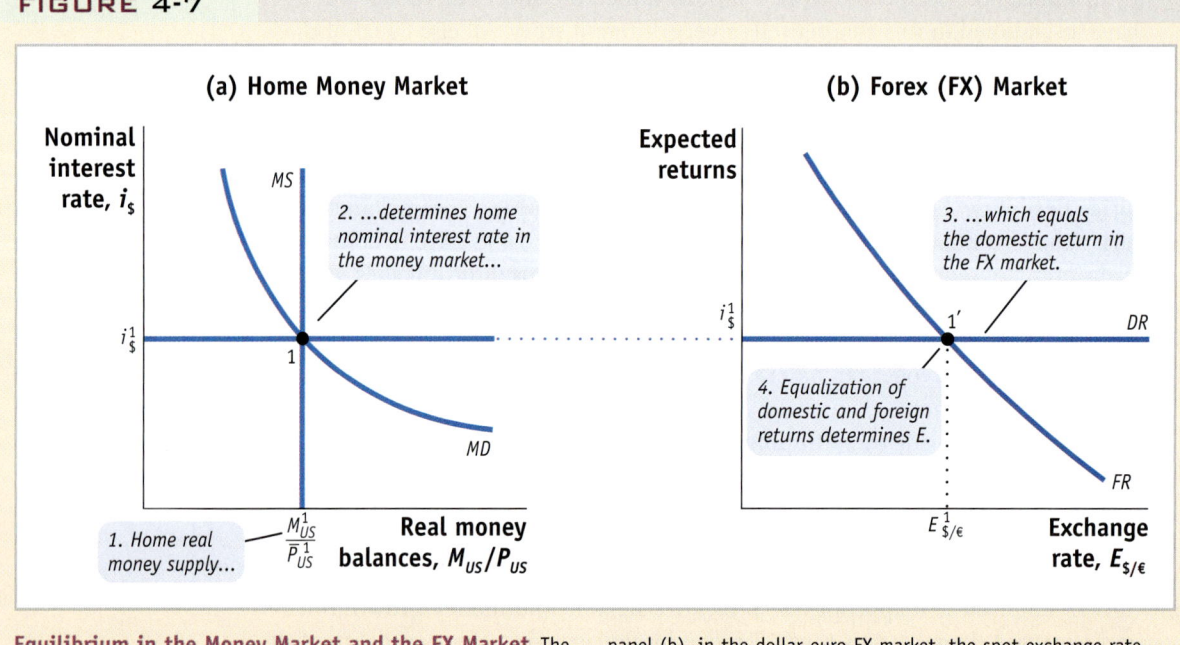

Equilibrium in the Money Market and the FX Market The figure summarizes the equilibria in the two asset markets in one diagram. In panel (a), in the home (U.S.) money market, the home nominal interest rate $i_\$^1$ is determined by the levels of real money supply MS and demand MD with equilibrium at point 1. In panel (b), in the dollar-euro FX market, the spot exchange rate $E_{\$/€}^1$ is determined by foreign and domestic expected returns, with equilibrium at point 1'. Arbitrage forces the domestic and foreign returns in the FX market to be equal, a result that depends on capital mobility.

2. The curve MD on the diagram represents the U.S. demand for real money balances, $L(i_\$)Y_{US}$. It slopes down because, when the Home nominal interest rate $i_\$$ rises, the opportunity cost of holding money increases, and demand falls. For now, we also assume that the U.S. real income level Y_{US} is exogenous (given) and fixed in the short run.

In equilibrium, money demand equals money supply, the quantity of real money demanded and supplied is $M_{US}^1/\overline{P}_{US}^1$, and the nominal interest rate is $i_\$^1$ (point 1).

The Market for Foreign Exchange Panel (b) depicts equilibrium in the FX market. The horizontal axis shows the spot exchange rate, $E_{\$/€}$. The vertical axis shows U.S. dollar returns on Home and Foreign deposits. Two relationships are shown:

1. The downward-sloping foreign return curve FR shows the relationship between the exchange rate and the expected dollar rate of return on Foreign deposits $[i_€ + (E_{\$/€}^e - E_{\$/€})/E_{\$/€}]$. The European interest rate $i_€$ is treated as exogenous (given); it is determined in the European money market, which is not shown in this figure. The expected future exchange rate $E_{\$/€}^e$ is treated as exogenous (given); it is determined by a forecast obtained from the long-run model we developed in the previous chapter.

2. The horizontal domestic return line DR shows the dollar rate of return on U.S. deposits, which is the U.S. nominal interest rate $i_\$$. It is horizontal at $i_\$^1$ because this is the U.S. interest rate determined in the Home money market in panel (a), and it is the same regardless of the spot exchange rate.

In equilibrium, foreign and domestic returns are equal (uncovered interest parity holds) and the FX market is in equilibrium at point 1′.

Capital Mobility Is Crucial We assume that the FX market is subject to the arbitrage forces we have studied and that uncovered interest parity will hold. But this is true only if there are no capital controls: as long as capital can move freely between Home and Foreign capital markets, domestic and foreign returns will be equalized. Our assumption that DR equals FR depends on capital mobility. If capital controls are imposed, there is no arbitrage and no reason why DR has to equal FR.

Putting the Model to Work With this graphical apparatus in place, it is relatively straightforward to solve for the exchange rate given knowledge of all the known (exogenous) variables we have specified previously.

To solve for the exchange rate, we start in the Home money market in panel (a) on the horizontal axis, at the level of real money supply $M^1_{US}/\overline{P}^1_{US}$; we trace upward along MS to MD at point 1, to find the current Home interest rate $i^1_\$$. We then trace right and move across from the Home money market to the FX market in panel (b), since the Home interest rate is the same as domestic return DR in the FX market. We eventually meet the FR curve at point 1′. We then trace down and read off the equilibrium exchange rate $E^1_{\$/€}$.

Our graphical treatment shows that solving the model is as simple as tracing a path around the diagrams. While we gain in simplicity, we also lose some generality because one market, the foreign money market, has been left out of the analysis. However, the same analysis also applies to the foreign country. As a quick check that you understand the logic of the asset approach to exchange rates, you might try to construct the equivalent of Figure 4-7 under the assumption that Europe is the Home economy and the United States is the Foreign economy. (Hint: In the FX market, you will need to treat the Home [European] expected future exchange rate $E^e_{€/\$}$ and the Foreign [U.S.] interest rate $i_\$$ as given. Take care with the currency units of every variable when making the switch.)

Short-Run Policy Analysis

The graphical exposition in Figure 4-7 shows how the asset approach works to determine the exchange rate. This approach can be used to analyze the impacts of economic policy or other shocks to the economy.

The most straightforward shocks we can analyze are temporary shocks because they affect only the current state of the money and foreign exchange markets and do not affect expectations about the future. In this section, we use the model to see what happens when there is a temporary, short-run increase in the money supply by the central bank.

A Temporary Shock to the Home Money Supply We take the model of Figure 4-7 and assume that, apart from the Home money supply, all exogenous variables remain unchanged and fixed at the same level. Thus, Foreign money supply, Home and Foreign real income and price levels, and the expected future exchange rate are all fixed.

The initial state of all markets is shown in Figure 4-8. The Home money market is in equilibrium at point 1 where Home money supply MS and money demand MD are equal at the Home nominal interest rate $i^1_\$$. The foreign exchange market is in

FIGURE 4-8

Temporary Expansion of the Home Money Supply In panel (a), in the Home money market, an increase in Home money supply from M_{US}^1 to M_{US}^2 causes an increase in real money supply from $M_{US}^1/\overline{P}_{US}^1$ to $M_{US}^2/\overline{P}_{US}^1$. To keep real money demand equal to real money supply, the interest rate falls from to $i_\$^1$ to $i_\$^2$, and the new money market equilibrium is at point 2. In panel (b), in the FX market, to maintain the equality of domestic and foreign expected returns, the exchange rate rises (the dollar depreciates) from $E_{\$/€}^1$ to $E_{\$/€}^2$, and the new FX market equilibrium is at point 2'.

equilibrium at point 1', where domestic return DR equals foreign return FR, where $i_\$^1 = i_€^1 + (E_{\$/€}^e − E_{\$/€}^1)/E_{\$/€}^1$, and the spot exchange rate is $E_{\$/€}^1$.

Suppose the U.S. money supply is increased temporarily from M_{US}^1 to M_{US}^2. Under the assumption of sticky prices, $\overline{P}_{US}^1$ does not change, so the U.S. real money supply will increase to $M_{US}^2/\overline{P}_{US}^1$, and the real money supply curve shifts from MS_1 to MS_2 in panel (a). U.S. real money demand is unchanged, so the money market equilibrium shifts from point 1 to point 2 and the nominal interest rate falls from $i_\$^1$ to $i_\$^2$. The expansion of the U.S. money supply causes the U.S. nominal interest rate to fall.

A *temporary* monetary policy shock leaves the long-run expected exchange rate $E_{\$/€}^e$ unchanged. Assuming all else equal, European monetary policy is also unchanged, and the euro interest rate remains fixed at $i_€$. If $E_{\$/€}^e$ and $i_€$ are unchanged, then the foreign return FR curve in panel (b) is unchanged and the new FX market equilibrium is at point 2'. The lower domestic return $i_\$^2$ is matched by a lower foreign return. The foreign return is lower because the U.S. dollar has depreciated from $E_{\$/€}^1$ to $E_{\$/€}^2$.

The result is intuitive, and we have seen each of the steps previously. We now just put them all together: a Home monetary expansion lowers the Home nominal interest rate, which is also the domestic return in the FX market. This makes Foreign deposits more attractive and makes traders wish to sell Home deposits and buy Foreign deposits. This, in turn, makes the Home exchange rate increase (depreciate). However, this depreciation makes Foreign deposits less attractive (all else equal). Eventually, the equality of foreign and domestic returns is restored, uncovered interest parity holds again, and the foreign exchange market reaches a new short-run equilibrium.

A Temporary Shock to the Foreign Money Supply We now repeat the previous analysis for a shock to the *Foreign* money supply. All other exogenous variables remain unchanged and fixed at their initial levels. Thus, Home money supply, Home and Foreign real income and price levels, and the expected future exchange rate are all fixed. The initial state of all markets is shown in Figure 4-9: the Home money market is in equilibrium at point 1 and the FX market is in equilibrium at point 2.

Let's see what happens when the Foreign money supply increases temporarily. Because changes in the Foreign money supply have no effect on the Home money market in panel (a), equilibrium remains at point 1 and the Home nominal interest rate stays at $i_\$^1$.

The shock is temporary, so long-run expectations are unchanged, and the expected exchange rate $E_{\$/€}^e$ stays fixed in panel (b). However, because the Foreign money supply has expanded temporarily, the euro interest rate falls from $i_€^1$ to $i_€^2$. Foreign returns are diminished, all else equal, by a fall in euro interest rates, so the foreign return curve FR shifts downward from FR_1 to FR_2. On the horizontal axis in panel (b), we can see that at the new FX market equilibrium (point 2′) the Home exchange rate has decreased (the U.S. dollar has appreciated) from $E_{\$/€}^1$ to $E_{\$/€}^2$.

FIGURE 4-9

Temporary Expansion of the Foreign Money Supply In panel (a), there is no change in the Home money market. In panel (b), an increase in the Foreign money supply causes the Foreign (euro) interest rate to fall from $i_€^1$ to $i_€^2$. For a U.S. investor, this lowers the foreign return $i_€ + (E_{\$/€}^e - E_{\$/€})/E_{\$/€}$, all else equal. To maintain the equality of domestic and foreign returns in the FX market, the exchange rate falls (the dollar appreciates) from $E_{\$/€}^1$ to $E_{\$/€}^2$, and the new FX market equilibrium is at point 2′.

This result is also intuitive. A Foreign monetary expansion lowers the Foreign nominal interest rate, which lowers the foreign return in the FX market. This makes Foreign deposits less attractive and makes traders wish to buy Home deposits and sell Foreign deposits. This, in turn, makes the Home exchange rate decrease (appreciate). However, this appreciation makes Foreign deposits more attractive (all else equal). Eventually, the equality of foreign and domestic returns is restored, uncovered interest parity holds again, and the foreign exchange market reaches a new short-run equilibrium.

To ensure you have grasped the model fully, you might try two exercises. First, derive the predictions of the model for temporary *contractions* in the Home or Foreign money supplies. Second, go back to the version of Figure 4-7 that you constructed from the European perspective and generate predictions using that version of the model, first for a temporary expansion of the money supply in Europe and then for a temporary expansion in the United States. Do you get the same answers?

APPLICATION

The Rise and Fall of the Dollar, 1999–2004

In the 1990s, many developed countries adopted monetary policies that established clear, long-run nominal anchors. The European Central Bank (ECB), for example, adopted an explicit inflation target. The Federal Reserve in the United States operated with a more implicit target, but nonetheless could claim to have a credible anchor, too.

The Fisher effect tells us that nominal anchoring of this kind ought to keep nominal interest rate differentials between the United States and the Eurozone roughly constant in the long run. But in the short run, this constraint does not apply, so central banks have some freedom to temporarily change their monetary policies. In the years 2000 to 2004, such flexibility was put to use and interest rates in the United States and Europe followed very different tracks.

In later chapters, we study in more detail why central banks alter monetary policy in the short run, but for now we focus on how such changes affect exchange rates. As Figure 4-10 shows, the Fed raised interest rates from 1999 to 2001 faster than the ECB (the Fed was more worried about the U.S. economy "overheating" with higher inflation). In this period of global economic boom, the ECB's policy also tightened over time, as measured by changes in the Euro interest rate—the refinancing rate set by the ECB. But the changes were more restrained and slower in coming.

As Figure 4-10 also shows, the Fed then lowered interest rates aggressively from 2001 to 2004, with rates falling as low as 1% in 2003 to 2004 (the U.S. economy had slowed after the boom and the Fed hoped that lower interest rates would avert a recession; the terrorist attacks of September 11, 2001, led to fears of a more serious economic setback and encouraged further monetary easing). The ECB also acted similarly to lower interest rates, but again the ECB did not move rates as far or as fast as the Fed.

As a result, the ECB's interest rate, previously lower than the Fed's rate, was soon higher than the U.S. rate in 2001 and remained higher through 2004. Investors most likely viewed these policy changes as a temporary shift in monetary policy in both countries. Hence, they might be considered as an example of temporary monetary policy shocks. Do our model's predictions accord well with reality?

Up until 2001, the policy of higher rates in the United States could be seen as a temporary Home monetary contraction (relative to Foreign), and our model would predict a dollar appreciation in the short run. After 2001 the aggressive reductions in

FIGURE 4-10

U.S.–Eurozone Interest Rates and Exchange Rates, 1999–2004 From the euro's birth in 1999 until 2001, the dollar steadily appreciated against the euro, as interest rates in the United States were raised well above those in Europe. In early 2001, however, the Federal Reserve began a long series of interest rate reductions. By 2002 the Fed Funds rate was well below the ECB's refinancing rate. Theory predicts a dollar appreciation (1999–2001) when U.S. interest rates were relatively high, followed by a dollar depreciation (2001–2004) when U.S. interest rates were relatively low. Looking at the figure, you will see that this is what occurred.

Sources: Websites of central banks; OANDA. Exchange rate is monthly average.

U.S. interest rates could be seen as a temporary Home monetary expansion (relative to Foreign), and our model predicts a dollar depreciation in the short run. Looking at the path of the dollar-euro exchange rate in the figure, we can see that the model accords well with reality. ■

4 A Complete Theory: Unifying the Monetary and Asset Approaches

In this section, we extend our analysis from the short run to the long run, and examine permanent as well as temporary shocks. To do this, we put together a complete theory of exchange rates that couples the long-run and short-run approaches, as shown schematically in Figure 4-11:

- We need the asset approach (this chapter)—short-run money market equilibrium and uncovered interest parity:

$$\left.\begin{array}{l} \overline{P}_{US} = M_{US}/[L_{US}(i_\$)Y_{US}] \\ \overline{P}_{EUR} = M_{EUR}/[L_{EUR}(i_\euro)Y_{EUR}] \\ i_\$ = i_\euro + \dfrac{E^e_{\$/\euro} - E_{\$/\euro}}{E_{\$/\euro}} \end{array}\right\} \text{The asset approach.} \quad (4\text{-}4)$$

There are three equations and three unknowns (two short-run nominal interest rates and the spot exchange rate). The future expected exchange rate must be known, as must the current levels of money and real income. (The price level is also treated as given.)

- But to forecast the future expected exchange rate, we also need the long-run monetary approach from the previous chapter—a long-run monetary model and purchasing power parity:

$$\left.\begin{array}{l} P^e_{US} = M^e_{US}/[L_{US}(i^e_\$)Y^e_{US}] \\ P^e_{EUR} = M^e_{EUR}/[L_{EUR}(i^e_\euro)Y^e_{EUR}] \\ E^e_{\$/\euro} = P^e_{US}/P^e_{EUR} \end{array}\right\} \quad \text{The monetary approach.} \quad (4\text{-}5)$$

There are three equations and three unknowns (two price levels and the exchange rate). Note that all variables here have a superscript e to denote future expected values or forecasts. We assume that forecasts of future money, real income, and nominal interest rates are known. This model can then be applied to obtain price forecasts and, hence, a forecast of the future expected exchange rate.[2]

Figure 4-11 sums up all the theory we have learned so far in the past two chapters. It shows how all the pieces fit together. In total we have six equations and six unknowns.

It is only now, with all the building blocks in place, that we can fully appreciate how the two key mechanisms of *expectations* and *arbitrage* operate in a variety of ways to determine exchange rates in both the short run and the long run. Ensure you are comfortable with all of the building blocks—how they work individually and how they connect.

After no little effort, we have arrived at a complete theory to explain exchange rates in the short run and the long run. The model incorporates all of the key economic fundamentals that affect exchange rates and, in practice, although forex markets exhibit a great deal of turbulence and uncertainty, there is evidence that these fundamentals play a major role in shaping traders' decisions (see **Side Bar: Confessions of a Forex Trader**).

Long-Run Policy Analysis

When and how can we apply the complete model? The downside of working with the complete model is that we have to keep track of multiple mechanisms and variables; the upside is that the theory is fully developed and can be applied to short-run and long-run policy shocks.

The temporary shocks we saw in the last section represent only one kind of monetary policy change, one that does not affect the long-run nominal anchor. The fact that these shocks were temporary allowed us to conduct all of the analysis under

---

[2] Recall that the previous chapter also showed us how real interest parity can be used to solve for the long-run nominal interest rate i in each country, the so-called *neutral level* of the nominal interest rate. For example, restricting our attention to the case of a stable long-run inflation rate (e.g., under nominal anchoring in which an announced inflation target is expected to be hit in each country), we have

$$\left.\begin{array}{l} i_\$ = \pi_{US,target} + r^* \\ i_\euro = \pi_{EUR,target} + r^* \end{array}\right\} \quad \text{Real interest parity.}$$

FIGURE 4-11

A Complete Theory of Floating Exchange Rates: All the Building Blocks Together Inputs to the model are known exogenous variables (in green boxes). Outputs of the model are unknown endogenous variables (in red boxes). The levels of money supply and real income determine exchange rates.

the assumption that the long-run expected level of the exchange rate remained unchanged.

When the monetary authorities decide to make a *permanent* change, however, this assumption of unchanged expectations is no longer appropriate. Under such a change, the authorities would cause an enduring change in all nominal variables; that is, they would be electing to change their nominal anchor policy in some way. Thus, when a monetary policy shock is permanent, the long-run expectation of the level of the exchange rate has to adjust. This change will, in turn, cause the exchange rate predictions of the short-run model to differ from those made when the policy shock was only temporary.

SIDE BAR

Confessions of a Forex Trader

Trying to forecast exchange rates is a major enterprise in financial markets and serves as the basis of any trading strategy. A tour of the industry would find many firms offering forecasting services at short, medium, and long horizons. Forecasts are generally based on three methodologies (or some mix of all three):

1. *Economic fundamentals.* Forecasts are based on ideas developed in the past two chapters. Exchange rates are determined by factors such as money, output, interest rates, and so on; hence, forecasters try to develop long- and short-range predictions of these "fundamental" variables. Example: "The exchange rate will depreciate because a looser monetary policy is expected."

2. *Politics.* Forecasts recognize that some factors that are not purely economic can affect exchange rates. One is the outbreak of war (see the application at the end of this chapter). Political crises might matter, too, if they affect perceptions of risk. Changes in risk interfere with simple interest parity and can move exchange rates. Making such forecasts is more qualitative and subjective, but is still concerned with fundamental determinants in our theory. Example: "The exchange rate will depreciate because a conflict with a neighboring state raises the probability of war and inflation."

3. *Technical methods.* Forecasts rely on extrapolations from past behavior. Trends may be assumed to continue ("momentum"), or recent maximum and minimum values may be assumed to be binding. These trading strategies assume that financial markets exhibit some persistence and, if followed, may make such an assumption self-fulfilling for a time. Nonetheless, large crashes that return asset prices back to fundamental levels can burst such bubbles. Example: "The exchange rate has hit this level three times this year but never gone further; it will not go further this time."

A recent survey of U.K. forex traders provided some interesting insights into this world.* One-third described their trading as "technically based," and one-third said their trades were "fundamentals-based"; others were jobbing or trading for clients.

The survey revealed that insights from economic theory mattered little from one hour to the next. In the very short run, within the day, traders confessed that many factors unrelated to economic fundamentals affected exchange rates in the market: 29% cited "bandwagon effects," and 33% mentioned "overreaction to news." Concerning within-day changes in exchange rates, when asked, "Do you believe exchange rate movements accurately reflect changes in the fundamental value," fully 97% of the traders responded no and only 3% yes. However, in the medium run, described as within six months, 58% responded yes. And in the long run, described as more than six months, 87% thought that changes reflected fundamentals.

Which economic fundamentals mattered? News about money supplies, interest rates, and GDP levels was quickly incorporated into trading, usually in less than a minute or even in a matter of seconds. All of these are key variables in our complete model. As we would expect, PPP was deemed irrelevant within the day, but 16% thought it mattered in the medium run, and 44% in the long run. The lack of unanimity about PPP may reflect legitimate concerns about its shortcomings (which we examined in the previous chapter).

---
* Yin-Wong Cheung, Menzie D. Chinn, and Ian W. Marsh, 2004, "How Do UK-Based Foreign Exchange Dealers Think Their Market Operates?" *International Journal of Finance and Economics*, 9(4), 289–306.

These insights guide our analysis of permanent policy shocks. They also tell us that we cannot approach such analysis chronologically. Before we can figure out what happens in the short run, we have to know expectations; that is, what is going to happen in the long run. Thus, we have to use a technique that is common in forward-looking economic problems: we must *solve backward* from the future to the present. (This ordering mirrors the presentation of the material in this textbook—we must understand the long run before we can understand the short run.)

A Permanent Shock to the Home Money Supply We start our analysis of the Home (United States) and Foreign (Europe) economies with each economy currently at a long-run equilibrium in which all variables are steady. In this equilibrium, we assume that each country has a fixed real income, a fixed money supply, and a zero rate of inflation. Hence, there is a zero rate of depreciation because the equilibrium is characterized by purchasing power parity, and interest rates in each country are the same because the equilibrium is characterized by uncovered interest parity.

Our analysis is shown Figure 4-12. Panels (a) and (b) show the short-run impacts of a permanent increase in the money supply in the Home (U.S.) money and FX markets; panels (c) and (d) show the long-run impacts and the adjustment from the short run to the long run. We examine each of these three aspects in turn.

As shown in panels (a), (b), (c), and (d), we suppose the Home economy starts with initial equilibria in the home money and FX markets shown by points 1 and 1′, respectively. In the money market, in panels (a) and (c), at point 1, the home money market is initially in equilibrium: MS_1 corresponds to an initial real money supply of $M^1_{US}/\overline{P}^1_{US}$; given real money demand MD, the nominal interest rate is $i^1_\$$. In the FX market, in panels (b) and (d), at point 1′, the domestic return DR_1 is the nominal interest rate $i^1_\$$. Given the foreign return curve FR_1, the equilibrium exchange rate is $E^1_{\$/€}$. If both economies are at a long-run equilibrium with zero depreciation, then this is also the expected future exchange rate $E^{e1}_{\$/€} = E^1_{\$/€}$.

We now start to figure out what happens after the policy shock hits today, working backward from the future to the present.

The Long Run Refer to panels (c) and (d) of Figure 4-12. In the long run, we know from the monetary approach that an increase in the money supply will eventually lead to a proportionate increase in the price level and the exchange rate. If the money supply increases from M^1_{US} to M^2_{US} today, then the price level will *eventually* increase by the same proportion from P^1_{US} to P^2_{US}, and, to maintain PPP, the exchange rate will *eventually* rise by the same proportion (and the dollar will depreciate) from $E^1_{\$/€}$ to its long-run level $E^4_{\$/€}$, in panel (d), where $E^4_{\$/€}/E^1_{\$/€} = P^2_{US}/P^1_{US} = M^2_{US}/M^1_{US} > 1$. (We use "4" to denote long-run exchange rate values because there will be some short-run responses to consider in just a moment.)

Thus, in the long run, in panel (c), if money and prices both rise in the same proportion, then the real money supply will be unchanged at its original level $M^1_{US}/P^1_{US} = M^2_{US}/P^2_{US}$, the real money supply curve will still be in its original position MS_1, and the nominal interest rate will again be $i^1_\$$. In the long run, the money market returns to where it started: long-run equilibrium is at point 4 (which is the same as point 1).

In the FX market, however, a permanent money supply shock causes some permanent changes in the long run. One thing that does not change is the domestic return, DR_1, since in the long run it returns to $i^1_\$$. But the exchange rate will rise from the initial long-run exchange rate, $E^1_{\$/€}$, to a new long-run level $E^4_{\$/€}$. Because $E^4_{\$/€}$ is a long-run stable level, it is also the new expected level of the exchange rate $E^4_{\$/€}$ that will prevail in the future. That is, the future will look like the present, under our assumptions, except that the exchange rate will be sitting at $E^4_{\$/€}$ instead of $E^1_{\$/€}$. What does this change do to the foreign return curve FR? As we know, when the expected exchange rate increases, foreign returns are higher, so the FR curve shifts up, from FR_1 to FR_2. Because in the long run $E^4_{\$/€}$ is the new stable equilibrium exchange rate, and $i^1_\$$ is the interest rate, the new FX market equilibrium is at point 4′ where FR_2 intersects DR_1.

FIGURE 4-12

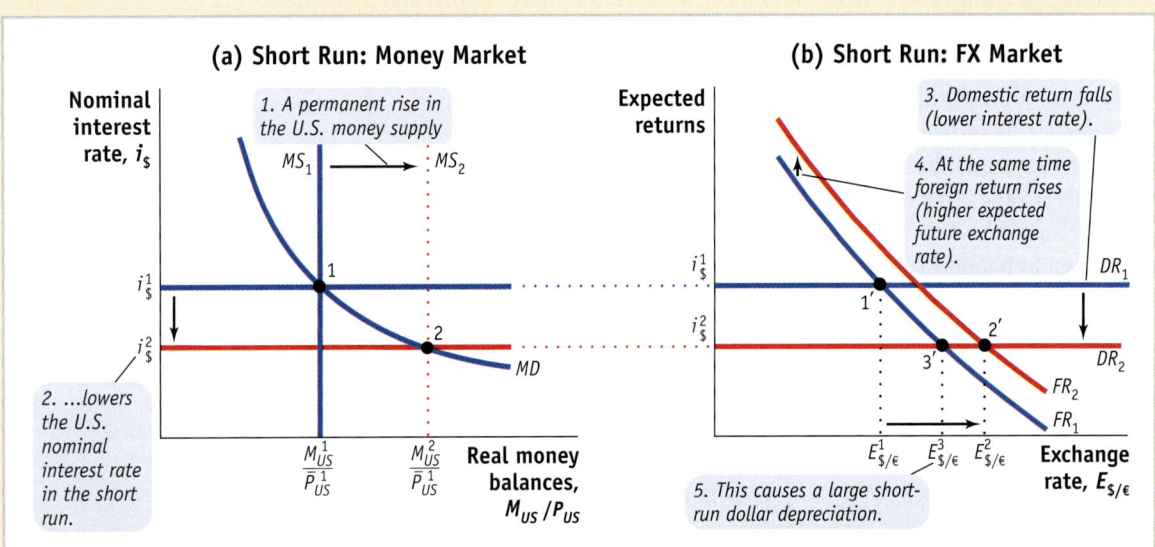

Permanent Expansion of the Home Money Supply Short-Run Impact: In panel (a), the home price level is fixed, but the supply of dollar balances increases and real money supply shifts out. To restore equilibrium at point 2, the interest rate falls from $i_\$^1$ to $i_\$^2$. In panel (b), in the FX market, the home interest rate falls, so the domestic return decreases and DR shifts down. In addition, the permanent change in the home money supply implies a permanent, long-run depreciation of the dollar. Hence, there is also a permanent rise in $E_{\$/€}^e$, which causes a permanent increase in the foreign return $i_€ + (E_{\$/€}^e - E_{\$/€})/E_{\$/€}$, all else equal; FR shifts up from FR_1 to FR_2. The simultaneous fall in DR and rise in FR cause the home currency to depreciate steeply, leading to a new equilibrium at point 2' (and not at 3', which would be the equilibrium if the policy were temporary).

Long-Run Adjustment: In panel (c), in the long run, prices are flexible, so the home price level and the exchange rate both rise in proportion with the money supply. Prices rise to P_{US}^2, and real money supply returns to its original level M_{US}^1/P_{US}^1. The money market gradually shifts back to equilibrium at point 4 (the same as point 1). In panel (d), in the FX market, the domestic return DR, which equals the home interest rate, gradually shifts back to its original level. The foreign return curve FR does not move at all: there are no further changes in the Foreign interest rate or in the future expected exchange rate. The FX market equilibrium shifts gradually to point 4'. The exchange rate falls (and the dollar appreciates) from $E_{\$/€}^2$ to $E_{\$/€}^4$. Arrows in both graphs show the path of gradual adjustment.

The Short Run Only now that we have changes in expectations worked out can we work back through panels (a) and (b) of Figure 4-12 to see what will happen in the short run.

Look first at the FX market in panel (b). Because expectations about the future exchange rate have changed with today's policy announcement, the FX market is affected immediately. Everyone knows that the exchange rate will be $E^4_{\$/€}$ in the future. The foreign return curve shifts when the expected exchange rate changes; it rises from FR_1 to FR_2. This is the same shift we just saw in the long-run panel (d). The dollar is expected to depreciate to $E^4_{\$/€}$ (relative to $E^1_{\$/€}$) in the future, so euro deposits are more attractive today.

Now consider the impact of the change in monetary policy in the short run. Look at the money market in panel (a). In the short run, if the money supply increases from M^1_{US} to M^2_{US} but prices are sticky at P^1_{US}, then real money balances rise from M^1_{US}/P^1_{US} to M^2_{US}/P^1_{US}. The real money supply shifts from MS_1 to MS_2 and the home interest rate falls from $i^1_\$$ to $i^2_\$$, leading to a new short-run money market equilibrium at point 2.

Now look back to the FX market in panel (b). If this were a *temporary* monetary policy shock, expectations would be unchanged, and the FR_1 curve would still describe foreign returns, but domestic returns would fall from DR_1 to DR_2 as the interest rate fell and the home currency would depreciate to the level $E^3_{\$/€}$. The FX market equilibrium, after a temporary money supply shock, would be at point 3', as we have seen before.

But this is not the case now. This time we are looking at a permanent shock to money supply. It has *two* effects on today's FX market. One impact of the money supply shock is to lower the home interest rate, decreasing domestic returns in today's FX market from DR_1 to DR_2. The other impact of the money supply shock is to increase the future expected exchange rate, increasing foreign returns in today's FX market from FR_1 to FR_2. Hence, the FX market equilibrium in the short run is where DR_2 and FR_2 intersect, now at point 2', and the exchange rate depreciates all the way to $E^2_{\$/€}$.

Note that the short-run equilibrium level of the exchange rate ($E^2_{\$/€}$) is higher than the level that would be observed under a temporary shock ($E^3_{\$/€}$) and also higher than the level that will be observed in the long run ($E^4_{\$/€}$). To sum up, *in the short run, the permanent shock causes the exchange rate to depreciate more than it would under a temporary shock and more than it will end up depreciating in the long run.*

Adjustment from Short Run to Long Run The arrows in panels (c) and (d) of Figure 4-12 trace what happens as we move from the short run to the long run. Prices that were initially sticky in the short run become unstuck. The price level rises from P^1_{US} to P^2_{US}, and this pushes the real money supply back to its initial level, from MS_2 back to MS_1. Money demand MD is unchanged. Hence, in the home money market of panel (c), the economy moves from the short-run equilibrium at point 2 to the long-run equilibrium, which is again at point 1, following the path shown by the arrows. Hence, the interest rate gradually rises from $i^2_\$$ back to $i^1_\$$. This raises the domestic returns over in the FX market of panel (d) from DR_2 back to DR_1. So the FX market moves from the short-run equilibrium at point 2' to the long-run equilibrium, which is again at point 4'.

An Example Let's make this very tricky experiment a bit more concrete with a numerical example. Suppose you are told that, all else equal, (i) the home money supply permanently increases by 5% today; (ii) prices are sticky in the short run, so this also causes an increase in real money supply that lowers domestic interest rates by four percentage points from 6% to 2%; (iii) prices will fully adjust in one year's time to today's monetary expansion and PPP will hold again. Based on this information, can you predict what will happen to prices and the exchange rate today and in a year's time?

Yes. Work backward from the long run to the short run, as before. In the long run, a 5% increase in M means a 5% increase in P that will be achieved in one year. By PPP, this 5% increase in P implies a 5% rise in E (a 5% depreciation in the dollar's value) over the same period. In other words, over the next year E will rise at 5% per year, which will be the rate of depreciation. Finally, in the short run, UIP tells us what happens to the exchange rate today: to compensate investors for the four-percentage-point decrease in the domestic interest rate, arbitrage in the FX market requires that the value of the home currency be expected to appreciate at 4% per year; that is, E must fall 4% in the year ahead. However, if E has to fall 4% in the next year and still end up 5% above its level at the start of today, then it must jump up 9% today: it overshoots its long-run level.

Overshooting

Compared with the temporary expansion of money supply we studied before, the permanent shock has a much greater impact on the exchange rate in the short run.

Under the temporary shock, domestic returns go down; traders want to sell the dollar for one reason only—temporarily lower dollar interest rates make dollar deposits less attractive. Under the permanent shock, domestic returns go down and foreign returns go up; traders want to sell the dollar for two reasons—temporarily lower dollar interest rates and an expected dollar depreciation make dollar deposits *much* less attractive. In the short run, the interest rate and exchange rate effects combine to create an instantaneous "double whammy" for the dollar, which gives rise to a phenomenon that economists refer to as exchange rate **overshooting.**

To better visualize the overshooting phenomenon, we show in Figure 4-13 the time path over which the key economic variables change after the permanent shock we just studied using Figure 4-12. We see the following in the four panels of Figure 4-13:

a. The nominal money supply is subject to a one-time increase at time T.

b. Real money balances rise instantaneously but revert to their initial level in the long run; the nominal interest rate falls instantaneously but reverts to its initial level in the long run.

c. The price level is sticky in the short run but rises to a new higher level in the long run, increasing in the same proportion as the nominal money supply.

d. The exchange rate rises (depreciates) to a new higher level in the long run, rising in the same proportion as the nominal money supply. In the short run, however, the exchange rate rises even more, overshooting its long-run level, then gradually decreasing to its long-run level (which is still higher than the initial level).

The overshooting result adds yet another argument for the importance of a sound long-run nominal anchor: without it, exchange rates are likely to be more volatile,

FIGURE 4-13

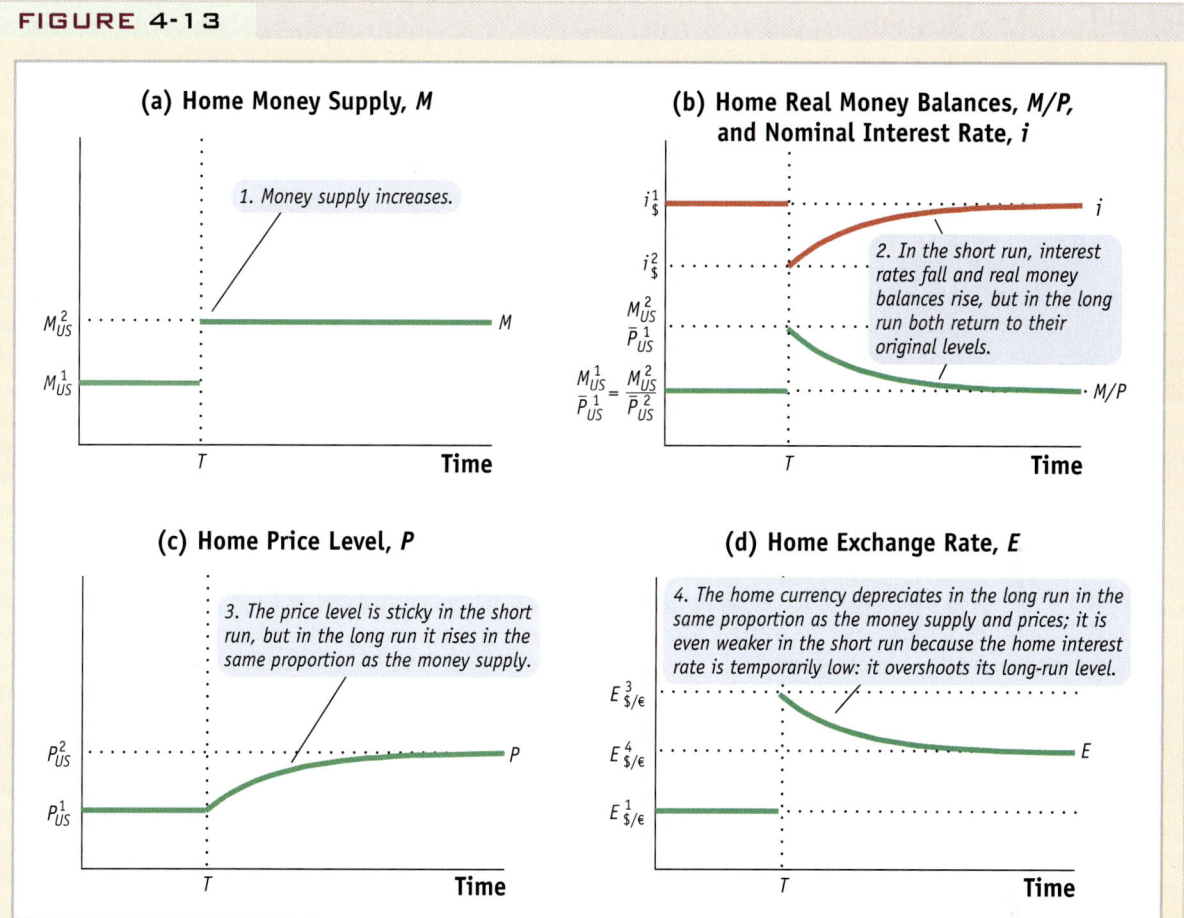

Responses to a Permanent Expansion of the Home Money Supply In panel (a), there is a one-time permanent increase in home (U.S.) nominal money supply at time T. In panel (b), prices are sticky in the short run, so there is a short-run increase in the real money supply and a fall in the home interest rate. In panel (c), in the long run, prices rise in the same proportion as the money supply. In panel (d), in the short run, the exchange rate overshoots its long-run value (the dollar depreciates by a large amount), but in the long run, the exchange rate will have risen only in proportion to changes in money and prices.

creating instability in the forex market and possibly in the wider economy. The wild fluctuations of exchange rates in the 1970s, at a time when exchange rate anchors were ripped loose, exposed these linkages with great clarity (see **Side Bar: Overshooting in Practice**). And new research provides evidence that the shift to a new form of anchoring, inflation targeting, might be helping to bring down exchange rate volatility in recent years.[3]

---

[3] Andrew K. Rose, 2007, "A Stable International Monetary System Emerges: Inflation Targeting Is Bretton Woods, Reversed," *Journal of International Money and Finance*, 26(5), 663–681.

SIDE BAR

Overshooting in Practice

Overshooting can happen in theory, but does it happen in the real world? The model tells us that if there is a tendency for monetary policy shocks to be more permanent than temporary, then there will be a tendency for the exchange rate to be more volatile. Thus, we might expect to see a serious increase in exchange rate volatility whenever a nominal anchoring system breaks down. Indeed, such conditions were seen in the 1970s, which is precisely when the overshooting phenomenon was discovered. How did this happen?

From the 1870s until the 1970s, except during major crises and wars, the world's major currencies were fixed against one another. Floating rates were considered anathema by policy makers and economists. Later in this book, we study the gold standard regime that began circa 1870 and fizzled out in the 1930s and the subsequent "dollar standard" of the 1950s and 1960s that was devised at a conference at Bretton Woods, New Hampshire, in 1944. As we shall see, the Bretton Woods system did not survive long for various reasons.

When floating rates reappeared in the 1970s, fears of instability returned. Concern mounted as floating exchange rates proved much more volatile than could be explained according to the prevailing flexible-price monetary approach: the models said that money supplies and real income were simply too stable to be able to generate such large fluctuations (as seen in Figure 4-14). Some feared that this was a case of *animal spirits,* John Maynard Keynes's term for irrational forces, especially in asset markets like that for foreign exchange. The challenge to economists was to derive a new model that could account for the wild swings in exchange rates.

Enter economist Rudiger Dornbusch of MIT. Building on Keynesian foundations, he published a paper in 1976 in which he showed that sticky prices and flexible exchange rates implied exchange rate overshooting.[*] Dornbusch's seminal work was a fortuitous case of a theory arriving at just the right time. In the 1970s, countries abandoned exchange rate anchors and groped for new ways to conduct monetary policy in a new economic environment. Policies varied and inflation rates grew, diverged, and persisted. Overshooting helps make sense of all this: if traders saw policies as having no well-defined anchor, monetary policy shocks might no longer be guaranteed to be temporary, so long-run expectations could swing wildly with every piece of news.

---

[*] Rudiger Dornbusch, December 1976, "Expectations and Exchange Rate Dynamics," *Journal of Political Economy,* 84, 1161–1176.

FIGURE 4-14

Exchange Rates for Major Currencies before and after 1973 Under the Bretton Woods system of fixed but adjustable dollar pegs, exchange rates were mostly stable from 1950 until 1970. The system was declared officially dead in 1973. From then on, all of these currencies have fluctuated against the dollar.

Source: International Monetary Fund (IMF), International Financial Statistics.

5 Fixed Exchange Rates and the Trilemma

We have developed a complete theory of exchange rates, based on the assumption that market forces in the money market and the foreign exchange market determine exchange rates. Our models have the most obvious application to the case of floating exchange rate regimes. But as we have seen, not every country floats. Can our theory also be applied to the equally important case of fixed exchange rate regimes and to other intermediate regimes? The answer is yes, and we conclude this chapter by adapting our existing theory for the case of fixed regimes.

What Is a Fixed Exchange Rate Regime?

To understand the crucial difference between fixing and floating, we contrast the polar cases of tight fixing (hard pegs including narrow bands) and free floating, and ignore, for now, intermediate regimes. We also set aside regimes that include controls on arbitrage (*capital controls*) because such extremes of government intervention render our theory superfluous. Instead, we focus on the case of a fixed rate regime without controls so that capital is mobile and arbitrage is free to operate in the foreign exchange market.

Here the government itself becomes an actor in the foreign exchange market and uses intervention in the market to influence the market rate. Exchange rate intervention takes the form of the central bank buying and selling foreign currency at a fixed price, thus holding the market exchange rate at a fixed level denoted $\overline{E}$.

We can explore the implications of that policy in the short run and the long run using the familiar building blocks of our theory. To give a concrete flavor to these analyses, we replace the United States and the Eurozone (whose currencies float against each other) with an example of an actual fixed exchange rate regime. The Foreign country remains the Eurozone, and the Home country is now Denmark.

We examine the implications of Denmark's decision to peg its currency, the krone, to the euro at a fixed rate $\overline{E}_{DKr/€}$.[4]

In the long run, fixing the exchange rate is one kind of nominal anchor. Yet even if it allowed the krone to float but had *some* nominal anchor, Denmark's monetary policy would still be constrained in the long run by the need to achieve its chosen nominal target. We have seen that any country with a nominal anchor faces long-run monetary policy constraints of some kind. *What we now show is that a country with a fixed exchange rate faces monetary policy constraints not just in the long run but also in the short run.*

Pegging Sacrifices Monetary Policy Autonomy in the Short Run: Example

By assumption, equilibrium in the krone-euro foreign exchange market requires that the Danish interest rate be equal to the Eurozone interest rate plus the expected rate of depreciation of the krone. But under a peg, the expected rate of depreciation is zero.

---

[4] The actual arrangement is a "narrow band" centered on 7.46038 DKr/€ and officially of width ±2.25%, according to the ERM arrangement between Denmark and the Eurozone that has been in effect since 1999. In practice, the peg is much tighter and krone usually stays within ±0.5% of the central rate.

Here uncovered interest parity reduces to the simple condition that the Danish central bank must set its interest rate equal to $i_€$, the rate set by the European Central Bank (ECB):

$$i_{DKr} = i_€ + \underbrace{\frac{E^e_{DKr/€} - E_{DKr/€}}{E_{DKr/€}}}_{\text{Equals zero for a credible fixed exchange rate}} = i_€$$

Denmark has lost control of its monetary policy: it cannot independently change its interest rate under a peg.

The same is true of money supply policy. Short-run equilibrium in Denmark's money market requires that money supply equal money demand, but once Denmark's interest rate is set equal to the Eurozone interest rate $i_€$, there is only one feasible level for money supply, as we see by imposing $i_€$ as the Danish interest rate in money market equilibrium:

$$M_{DEN} = \overline{P}_{DEN} L_{DEN}(i_{DKr}) Y_{DEN} = \overline{P}_{DEN} L_{DEN}(i_€) Y_{DEN}$$

The implications are stark. The final expression contains the euro interest rate (exogenous, as far as the Danes are concerned), the fixed price level (exogenous by assumption), and output (also exogenous by assumption). No variable in this expression is under the control of the Danish authorities in the short run, and this is the only level of the Danish money supply consistent with equilibrium in the money and forex markets at the pegged rate $\overline{E}_{DKr/€}$. If the Danish central bank is to maintain the peg, then in the short run it must choose the level of money supply implied by the last equation.

What's going on? Arbitrage is the key force. For example, if the Danish central bank tried to supply more krone and lower interest rates, they would be foiled by arbitrage. Danes would want to sell krone deposits and buy higher-yield euro deposits, applying downward pressure on the krone. To maintain the peg, whatever krone the Danish central bank had tried to pump into circulation, it would promptly have to buy them back in the foreign exchange market.

Thus, *our short-run theory still applies, but with a different chain of causality*:

- Under a float, the home monetary authorities pick the money supply M. In the short run, the choice of M determines the interest rate i in the money market; in turn, via UIP, the level of i determines the exchange rate E. The money supply is an input in the model (an exogenous variable), and the exchange rate is an output of the model (an endogenous variable).

- Under a fix, this logic is reversed. Home monetary authorities pick the fixed level of the exchange rate E. In the short run, a fixed E pins down the home interest rate i via UIP (forcing i to equal the foreign interest rate i^*); in turn, the level of i determines the level of the money supply M necessary to meet money demand. The exchange rate is an input in the model (an exogenous variable), and the money supply is an output of the model (an endogenous variable).

This reversal of short-run causality is shown in a new schematic in the top part of Figure 4-15.

FIGURE 4-15

A Complete Theory of Fixed Exchange Rates: Same Building Blocks, Different Known and Unknown Variables Unlike in Figure 4-11, the Home country is now assumed to fix its exchange rate with the Foreign country. Inputs to the model are known exogenous variables (in green boxes). Outputs of the model are unknown endogenous variables (in red boxes). The levels of real income and the fixed exchange rate determine the Home money supply levels, given outcomes in the Foreign country.

Pegging Sacrifices Monetary Policy Autonomy in the Long Run: Example

As we have noted, choosing a nominal anchor implies a loss of long-run monetary policy autonomy. Let's quickly see how that works when the anchor is a fixed exchange rate.

Following our discussion of the standard monetary model, we must first ask what the nominal interest rate is going to be in Denmark in the long run. But we have already answered that question; it is going to be tied down the same way as in the short run, at the level set by the ECB, namely $i_€$. We might question, in turn, where *that* level $i_€$ comes from (the answer is that it will be related to the "neutral" level of the nominal interest rate consistent with the ECB's own nominal anchor, its inflation target for the Eurozone). But that is beside the point: all that matters is that $i_€$ is as much out of Denmark's control in the long run as it is in the short run.

Next we turn to the price level in Denmark, which is determined in the long run by PPP. But if the exchange rate is pegged, we can write long-run PPP for Denmark as

$$P_{DEN} = \overline{E}_{DKr/€} P_{EUR}$$

Here we encounter another variable that is totally outside of Danish control in the long run. Under PPP, pegging to the euro means that the Danish price level is a fixed multiple of the Eurozone price level (which is exogenous, as far as the Danes are concerned).

With the long-run nominal interest and price level outside of Danish control, we can show, as before, that monetary policy autonomy is out of the question. We just substitute $i_{DKr} = i_€$ and $P_{DEN} = \overline{E}_{DKr/€} P_{EUR}$ into Denmark's long-run money market equilibrium to obtain

$$M_{DEN} = P_{DEN} L_{DEN}(i_{DKr}) Y_{DEN} = \overline{E}_{DKr/€} P_{EUR} L_{DEN}(i_€) Y_{DEN}$$

The final expression contains the long-run euro interest rate and price levels (exogenous, as far as the Danes are concerned), the fixed exchange rate level (exogenous by assumption), and long-run Danish output (also exogenous by assumption). Again, no variable in the final expression is under the control of the Danish authorities in the long run, and this is the only level of the Danish money supply consistent with equilibrium in the money and foreign exchange market at the pegged rate of $\overline{E}_{DKr/€}$.

Thus, *our long-run theory still applies, just with a different chain of causality*:

- Under a float, the home monetary authorities pick the money supply M. In the long run, the growth rate of M determines the interest rate i via the Fisher effect and also the price level P; in turn, via PPP, the level of P determines the exchange rate E. The money supply is an input in the model (an exogenous variable), and the exchange rate is an output of the model (an endogenous variable).

- Under a fix, this logic is reversed. Home monetary authorities pick the exchange rate E. In the long run, the choice of E determines the price level P via PPP, and also the interest rate i via UIP; these, in turn, determine the necessary level of the money supply M. The exchange rate is an input in the model (an exogenous variable), and the money supply is an output of the model (an endogenous variable).

This reversal of long-run causality is also shown in the new schematic in the bottom part of Figure 4-15.

The Trilemma

Our findings lead to the conclusion that policy makers face some tough choices. Not all desirable policy goals can be simultaneously met. These constraints are summed up in one of the most important principles in open-economy macroeconomics.

Consider the following three equations and parallel statements about desirable *policy goals*. For illustration we return to the Denmark–Eurozone example:

---

1. $\dfrac{E^e_{DKr/€} - E_{DKr/€}}{E_{DKr/€}} = 0$ *A fixed exchange rate*
   - May be desired as a means to promote stability in trade and investment
   - Represented here by zero expected depreciation

---

2. $i_{DKr} = i_€ + \dfrac{E^e_{DKr/€} - E_{DKr/€}}{E_{DKr/€}}$ *International capital mobility*
   - May be desired as a means to promote integration, efficiency, and risk sharing
   - Represented here by uncovered interest parity, which results from arbitrage

---

3. $i_{DKr} \neq i_€$ *Monetary policy autonomy*
   - May be desired as a means to manage the Home economy's business cycle
   - Represented here by the ability to set the Home interest rate independently of the Foreign interest rate

---

For a variety of reasons, as noted, governments may want to pursue all three of these policy goals. But they can't: formulae 1, 2, and 3 show that it is a *mathematical impossibility* as shown by the following statements:

- 1 and 2 imply not 3 (1 and 2 imply interest equality, contradicting 3).
- 2 and 3 imply not 1 (2 and 3 imply an expected change in *E*, contradicting 1).
- 3 and 1 imply not 2 (3 and 1 imply a difference between domestic and foreign returns, contradicting 2).

This result, known as the **trilemma,** is one of the most important ideas in international macroeconomics.[5] It tells us that the three policy goals just outlined are mutually incompatible: you cannot have all three at once. You must choose to drop one of the three (or, equivalently, you must adopt one of three pairs: 1 and 2, 2 and 3, or 3 and 1). Sadly, there is a long history of macroeconomic disasters stemming from the failure of some policy that ignored this fundamental lesson.

The trilemma can be illustrated graphically as in Figure 4-16. Each corner of the triangle represents a viable policy choice. For each corner, the label at the vertex indicates the goal that has been sacrificed, while the labels on each adjacent edge of the triangle explain the goals that can be attained (see **Side Bar: Intermediate Regimes**).

---

[5] A definition: Trilemma *noun* 1. a quandary posed by three alternative courses of action (*Collins English Dictionary* online).

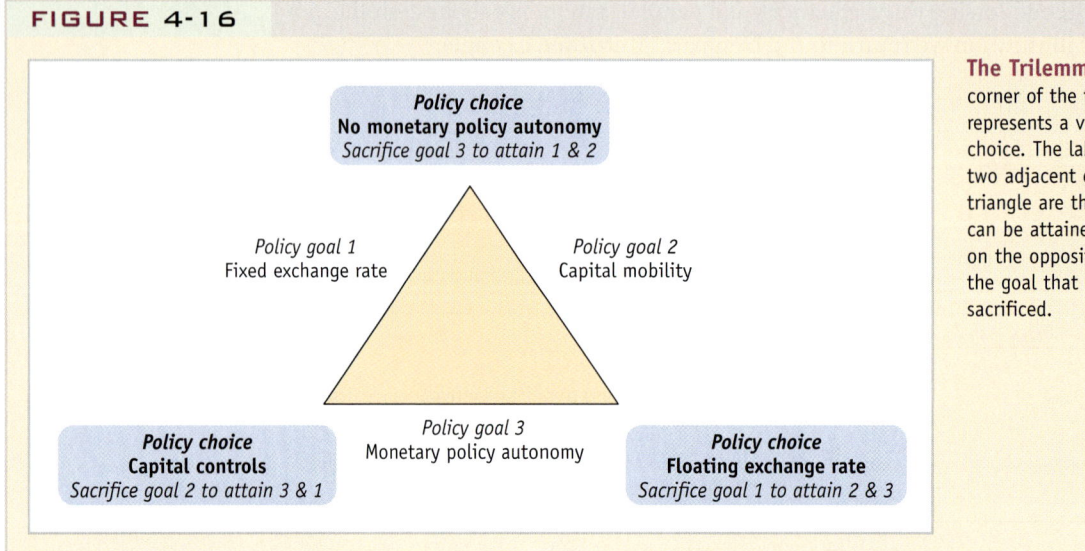

FIGURE 4-16

The Trilemma Each corner of the triangle represents a viable policy choice. The labels on the two adjacent edges of the triangle are the goals that can be attained; the label on the opposite edge is the goal that has to be sacrificed.

SIDE BAR

Intermediate Regimes

The lessons of the trilemma most clearly apply when the policies are at the ends of a spectrum: a hard peg or a float, perfect capital mobility or immobility, complete autonomy or none at all. But sometimes a country may not be fully in one of the three corners: the rigidity of the peg, the degree of capital mobility, and the independence of monetary policy could be partial rather than full.

For example, in a band arrangement, the exchange rate is maintained within a range of ±X% of some central rate. The significance of the band is that some expected depreciation (i.e., a little bit of floating) is possible. As a result, a limited interest differential can open up between the two countries. For example, suppose the band is 2% wide (i.e., ±1% around a central rate). To compute home interest rates, UIP tells us that we must add the foreign interest rate (let's suppose it is 5%) to the expected rate of depreciation (which is ±2% if the exchange rate moves from one band edge to the other). Thus, Home may "fix" this way and still have the freedom to set 12-month interest rates in the range between 3% and 7%. But the home country cannot evade the trilemma forever: on average, over time, the rate of depreciation will have to be zero to keep the exchange rate within the narrow band, meaning that the Home interest rate must track the Foreign interest rate apart from small deviations.

Similar qualifications to the trilemma could result from partial capital mobility, in which barriers to arbitrage could also lead to interest differentials. And with such differentials emerging, the desire for partial monetary autonomy can be accommodated.

In practice, once these distinctions are understood, it is usually possible to make some kind of judgment about which corner best describes the country's policy choice. For example, in 2007 both Slovakia and Denmark were supposedly pegged to the euro as members of the EU's Exchange Rate Mechanism (ERM). But the similarities ended there. The Danish krone was operating in ERM bands of official width ±2.25%, but closer to ±0.5% in practice, a pretty hard peg with almost no movement. The Slovak koruna was operating with ±15% bands and at one point even shifted that band by appreciating its central rate by 8.5% in March 2007. With its perpetual narrow band, Denmark's regime was clearly fixed. With its wide and adjustable bands, Slovakia's regime was closer to managed floating.[*]

---

[*] Note that Slovakia has since joined the euro as of 2009.

APPLICATION

The Trilemma in Europe

We motivated the trilemma with the case of Denmark, which has chosen policy goals 1 and 2. As a member of the European Union (EU), Denmark adheres to the single-market legislation that requires free movement of capital within the bloc. It also unilaterally pegs its krone to the euro under the EU's Exchange Rate Mechanism (ERM), an arrangement that ostensibly serves as a stepping-stone to Eurozone membership. Consequently, UIP predicts that the Danish central bank must set an interest rate at the same level as that set by the ECB; it has lost option 3.

The Danes could make one of two politically difficult choices if they wished to gain monetary independence from the ECB: they could abandon their commitment to the EU treaties on capital mobility (drop 2 to get 3), which is extremely unlikely, or they could abandon their ERM commitment and let the krone float against the euro (drop 1 to get 3), which is also fairly unlikely. Floating is, however, the choice of the United Kingdom, an EU country that has withdrawn from the ERM and that allows the pound to float against the euro.

Figure 4-17 shows evidence for the trilemma. Since 1999 the United Kingdom has had the ability to set interest rates independently of the ECB. But Denmark

FIGURE 4-17

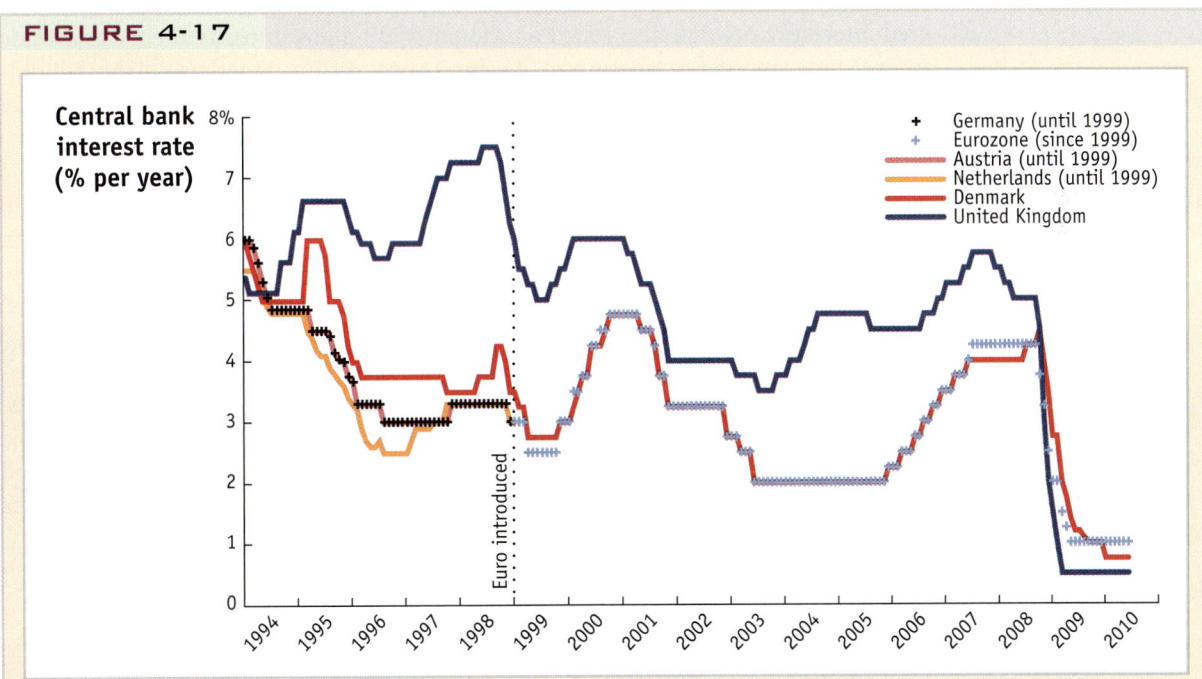

The Trilemma in Europe The figure shows selected central banks' base interest rates for the period 1994 to 2010 with reference to the German mark and euro base rates. In this period, the British made a policy choice to float against the German mark and (after 1999) against the euro. This permitted monetary independence because interest rates set by the Bank of England could diverge from those set in Frankfurt. No such independence in policy making was afforded by the Danish decision to peg the krone first to the mark and then to the euro. Since 1999 the Danish interest rate has moved almost exactly in line with the ECB rate. Similar forces operated pre-1999 for other countries pegging to the mark, such as the Netherlands and Austria. Until they joined the Eurozone in 1999, their interest rates, like that of Denmark, closely tracked the German rate.

Sources: Websites of the central banks.

has not: since 1999 the Danish interest rate has tracked the ECB's rate almost exactly. (Most of the departures from equality reflect uncertainty about the euro project and Denmark's peg at two key moments: at the very start of the euro project in 1999, and during the credibility crisis of the Eurozone following the financial crash of 2008.)

These monetary policy ties to Frankfurt even predate the euro itself. Before 1999 Denmark, and some countries such as Austria and the Netherlands, pegged to the German mark with the same result: their interest rates had to track the German interest rate, but the U.K. interest rate did not. The big difference is that Austria and the Netherlands have formally abolished their national currencies, the schilling and the guilder, and have adopted the euro—an extreme and explicit renunciation of monetary independence. Meanwhile, the Danish krone lives on, showing that a national currency can suggest monetary sovereignty in theory but may deliver nothing of the sort in practice. ■

6 Conclusions

In this chapter, we drew together everything we have learned so far about exchange rates. We built on the concepts of arbitrage and equilibrium in the foreign exchange (FX) market in the short run, taking expectations as given and applying uncovered interest parity. We also relied on the purchasing power parity theory as a guide to exchange rate determination in the long run. Putting together all these building blocks provides a complete and internally consistent theory of exchange rate determination.

Exchange rates are an interesting topic in and of themselves, but at the end of the day, we also care about what they mean for the wider economy, how they relate to macroeconomic performance, and the part they play in the global monetary system. That is our goal in the next chapters in which we apply our exchange rate theories in a wider framework to help us understand how exchange rates function in the national and international economy.

The theory we've developed in the past three chapters is the first tool that economists and policy makers pick up when studying a problem involving exchange rates. This theory has served well in rich and poor countries, whether in periods of economic stability or turbulence. Remarkably, it has even been applied in wartime, and to round off our discussion of exchange rates. we digress into some colorful applications of the theory from conflicts past and present.

APPLICATION

News and the Foreign Exchange Market in Wartime

Our theory of exchange rates places expectations at center stage, but demonstrating the effect of changing expectations empirically is a challenge. However, wars dramatically expose the power of expectations to change exchange rates. War raises the risk that a currency may depreciate in value rapidly in the future, possibly all the way to zero. For one thing, the government may need to print money to finance its war effort, but how much inflation this practice will generate may be unclear. In addition, there is a risk of defeat and a decision by the victor to impose new economic arrangements such as a new currency; the existing currency may then be converted into the new currency at a rate dictated by the victors or, in a worst-case scenario, it may be declared totally worthless; that is, not legal tender. Demand for the currency will then collapse to nothing and so will its value. Investors in the foreign exchange market are continually updating their forecasts about a war's possible outcomes, and, as a result, the path of an exchange rate during wartime usually reveals a clear influence of the effects of news.

The U.S. Civil War, 1861–1865 For four years, beginning April 12, 1861, a war raged between the Union (Northern) and Confederate (Southern) forces. An important economic dimension of this conflict was the decision by the Confederate states to issue their own currency, the Confederate dollar, to help gain economic autonomy from the North and finance their war effort. The exchange rate of the Confederate dollar against the U.S. dollar is shown in Figure 4-18.

How should we interpret these data? The two currencies differed in one important respect. If the South had won, and the Confederate states had gained independence, they would have kept their Confederate dollar, and the Northern United States would have kept their U.S. dollar, too. Instead, the South was defeated, and, as expected in these circumstances, the U.S. dollar was imposed as the sole currency of the unified country; the Confederate dollar, like all liabilities of the Confederate nation, was repudiated by the victors and, hence, became worthless.

FIGURE 4-18

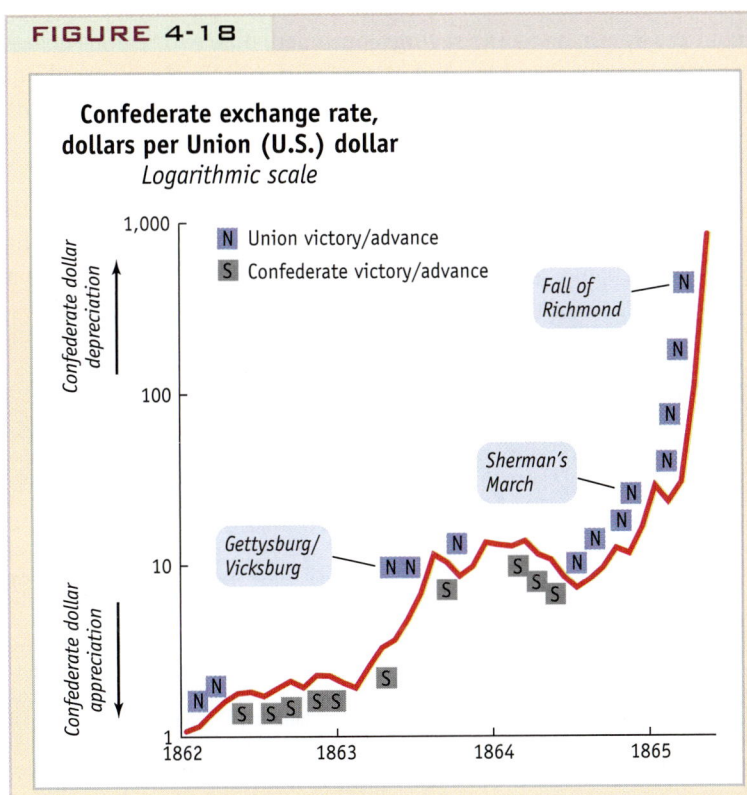

Exchange Rates and News in the U.S. Civil War The value of the Confederate dollar fluctuated against the U.S. dollar and is shown on a logarithmic scale. Against the backdrop of a steady trend, victories and advances by the North (N) were generally associated with faster depreciation of the Confederate currency, whereas major Southern successes (S) usually led to a stronger Confederate currency.

Sources: Global Financial Data; George T. McCandless Jr., 1996, "Money, Expectations, and U.S. Civil War," *American Economic Review,* 86(3), 661–671.

War news regularly influenced the exchange rate.[6] As the South headed for defeat, the value of the Confederate dollar shrank. The overall trend was driven partly by inflationary war finance and partly by the probability of defeat. Major Northern victories marked "N" tended to coincide with depreciations of the Confederate dollar. Major Southern victories marked "S" were associated with appreciations or, at least, a slower depreciation. The key Union victory at Gettysburg, July 1–3, 1863, and the near simultaneous fall of Vicksburg on July 4 were followed by a dramatic depreciation of the Confederate dollar. By contrast, Southern victories (in the winter of 1862 to 1863 and the spring of 1864) were periods when the Southern currency held steady or even appreciated. But by the fall of 1864, and particularly after Sherman's March, the writing was on the wall, and the Confederate dollar began its final decline.

Currency traders in New York did good business either way. They were known to whistle "John Brown's Body" after a Union victory and "Dixie" after Confederate success, making profits all the while as they traded dollars for gold and vice versa. Abraham Lincoln was not impressed, declaring, "What do you think of those fellows in Wall Street, who are gambling in gold at such a time as this? . . . For my part, I wish every one of them had his devilish head shot off."

The Iraq War, 2002–2003

The Civil War is not the only example of such phenomena. In 2003 Iraq was invaded by a U.S.-led coalition of forces intent on overthrowing the regime of Saddam Hussein, and the effects of war on currencies were again visible.[7]

Our analysis of this case is made a little more complicated by the fact that at the time of the invasion there were *two* currencies in Iraq. Indeed, some might say there were two Iraqs. Following a 1991 war, Iraq had been divided: in the North, a de facto Kurdish government was protected by a no-fly zone enforced by the Royal Air Force and U.S. Air Force; in the South, Saddam's regime continued. The two regions developed into two distinct economies, and each had its own currency. In the North, Iraqi dinar notes called "Swiss" dinars circulated.[8] In the South, a new currency, the "Saddam" or "print" dinar, was introduced.[9]

Figure 4-19 shows the close correlation between wartime news and exchange rate movements for this modern episode. We can compare exchange rate movements with well-known events, but panel (a) allows another interesting comparison. In 2002 a company called TradeSports Exchange allowed bets on Saddam's destiny by setting up a

---

[6] This correlation was noted by Wesley Mitchell, 1903, *A History of the Greenbacks* (Chicago: University of Chicago Press). For recent econometric studies that examine this phenomenon, see George T. McCandless Jr., 1996, "Money, Expectations, and U.S. Civil War," *American Economic Review*, 86(3), 661–671; and Kristen L. Willard, Timothy W. Guinnane, and Harvey S. Rosen, 1996, "Turning Points in the Civil War: Views from the Greenback Market," *American Economic Review*, 86(4), 1001–1018.

[7] This case study draws on Mervyn King, May 2004, "The Institutions of Monetary Policy," *American Economic Review*, 94(2), 1–13.

[8] The notes were printed in Britain using plates of Swiss manufacture. The Kurds issued no new notes of their own; indeed, they had no means to do so and simply used this legacy currency after 1991. No new Swiss dinars were issued after 1989 in the South either.

[9] Once economic sanctions were imposed after the 1991 war, Baghdad had no access to the high-security technology and papers used to make modern banknotes. Instead, the Swiss dinar was retired, and the Saddam regime issued new legal tender notes in a form that it *could* print, using low-technology offset litho techniques that your local printer might use. These were the so-called Saddam or print dinars. Circulation of these notes exploded: a large volume of notes were printed by the Iraqi Central Bank and counterfeits added to this number. For these reasons, the northern currency, the Swiss dinar, was much more stable in the 1990s than the Saddam dinar.

FIGURE 4-19

(a) Online Bookmaker's Odds

TradeSports contract: Saddam deposed by end Jun 2003

TradeSports contract: Saddam captured by end Dec 2003

1. "Good news" for the Kurds

3. "Bad news" for the Kurds

(b) Exchange Rates for the Kurdish Region

Swiss dinars per U.S. dollar

Swiss dinars per 1000 Saddam dinars (right scale)

2. Swiss dinar appreciates

4. Swiss dinar depreciates

Exchange Rates and News in the Iraq War As regime change looked more likely from 2002 to 2003, as reflected in panel (a), the Swiss dinar, the currency used by the Kurds, appreciated against the U.S. dollar and the Saddam dinar, the currency used in the south, as shown in panel (b). When the U.S. invasion ended, the difficult postwar transition began. Insurgencies and the failure to find Saddam Hussein became a cause for concern, as reflected in panel (a). The Swiss dinar depreciated against the dollar until December 2003, as shown in panel (b).

Notes: Panel (a) shows two contract prices: the value in cents of a TradeSports contract that paid 100¢ if Saddam were deposed by the end of June 2003 and 0 otherwise, and the value in cents of a contract that paid 100¢ if Saddam were captured by the end of December 2003 and 0 otherwise.

Source: Mervyn King, 2004, "The Institutions of Monetary Policy," American Economic Review, 94(2), 1–13.

Currencies in wartime: A Confederate 2 dollar note of 1864 issued in Richmond; an Iraqi "Swiss" 25 dinar from the Kurdish region; a widely forged post-1991 Iraqi "Saddam" 25 dinar note; a post-2003 250 new Iraqi dinar note.

market in contracts that paid $1 if he was deposed by a certain date, and the prices of these contracts are shown using the left scale. After he was deposed, contracts that paid out upon his capture were traded, and these are also shown. If such a contract had a price of, say, 80¢, then this implied that "the market" believed the probability of overthrow or apprehension was 80%.

In panel (b), we see the exchange rates of the Swiss dinar against the U.S. dollar and the Saddam dinar from 2002 to 2003. The Kurds' Swiss dinar–U.S. dollar rate had held at 18 per U.S. dollar for several years but steadily appreciated in 2002 and 2003 as the prospect of a war to depose Saddam became more likely. By May 2003, when the invasion phase of the war ended and Saddam had been deposed, it had appreciated as far as 6 to the dollar. The war clearly drove this trend: the more likely the removal of Saddam, the more durable would be Kurdish autonomy, and the more likely it was that a postwar currency would be created that respected the value of the Kurds' Swiss dinars. Notice how the rise in the value of the Swiss dinar tracked the odds of regime change until mid-2003.

After Baghdad fell, the coalition sought to capture Saddam, who had gone into hiding. As the hunt wore on, and a militant/terrorist insurgency began, fears mounted that he would never be found and his regime might survive underground and reappear. The odds on capture fell, and, moving in parallel, so did the value of the Swiss dinar. The Kurds now faced a rising probability that the whole affair would end badly for them and their currency. (However, when Saddam Hussein was captured on December 14, 2003, the Swiss dinar appreciated again.)

We can also track related movements in the Swiss dinar against the Saddam or print dinar. Before and during the war, while the Swiss dinar was appreciating against the U.S. dollar, it was also appreciating against the Saddam dinar. It strengthened from around 10 Swiss dinars per 1,000 Saddam in early 2002 to about 3 Swiss dinars per 1,000 Saddam in mid-2003. Then, as the postwar operations dragged on, this trend was reversed. By late 2003, the market rate was about 6 Swiss dinars per 1,000 Saddam. Again, we can see how the Kurds' fortunes appeared to the market to rise and fall.

What became of all these dinars? Iraqis fared better than the holders of Confederate dollars. A new dinar was created under a currency reform announced in July 2003 and implemented from October 15, 2003, to January 15, 2004.[10] Exchange rate expectations soon moved into line with the increasingly credible official conversion rates and U.S. dollar exchange rates for the new dinar. ■

---

[10] Under this reform, all the Swiss and Saddam notes were retired and a newly designed, secure currency for Iraq was brought into circulation nationally. As long as this currency reform was seen as credible, and the market believed it would successfully take place, the market rate would have to converge to the fixed rate set in advance by the authorities for note replacement. As the reform date approached, this convergence occurred, except for what appears to be a small "forgery risk premium" on the Saddam notes—detecting a fake among these notes was by no means simple.

KEY POINTS

1. Our theory of exchange rates builds on two ideas: arbitrage and expectations. First, we developed the theory for the case of floating exchange rates.

2. In the short run, we assume prices are sticky and the asset approach to exchange rates is valid. Interest-bearing accounts in different currencies may offer different rates of nominal interest. Currencies may be expected to depreciate or appreciate against one another. There is an incentive for arbitrage: investors will shift funds from one country to another until the expected rate of return (measured in a common currency) is equalized. Arbitrage in the foreign exchange (FX) market determines today's spot exchange rate, and the FX market is in equilibrium when the uncovered interest parity condition holds. To apply the UIP condition, however, we need a forecast of the expected exchange rate in the long run.

3. In the long run, we assume prices are flexible and the monetary approach to exchange rates is valid. This approach states that in the long run, purchasing power parity (PPP) holds so that the exchange rate must equal the ratio of the price levels in the two countries. Each price level, in turn, depends on the ratio of money supply to money demand in each country. The monetary approach can be used to forecast the long-run future expected exchange rate, which, in turn, feeds back into short-run exchange rate determination via the UIP equation.

4. Putting together all of these ingredients yields a complete theory of how exchange rates are determined in the short run and the long run.

5. This model can be used to analyze the impact of changes to monetary policy, as well as other shocks to the economy.

6. A temporary home monetary expansion causes home interest rates to fall and the home exchange rate to depreciate. This temporary policy can be consistent with a nominal anchor in the long run.

7. A permanent home monetary expansion causes home interest rates to fall and the home exchange rate to depreciate and, in the short run, overshoot what will eventually be its long-run level. This permanent policy is inconsistent with a nominal anchor in the long run.

8. The case of fixed exchange rates can also be studied using this theory. Under capital mobility, interest parity becomes very simple. In this case, the home interest rate equals the foreign interest rate. Home monetary policy loses all autonomy compared with the floating case. The only way to recover it is to impose capital controls. This is the essence of the trilemma.

KEY TERMS

asset approach to exchange rates, p. 112
fundamental equation of the asset approach to exchange rates, p. 113
FX market diagram, p. 114
nominal rigidity, p. 119
overshooting, p. 138
trilemma, p. 145

PROBLEMS

1. Use the money market and foreign exchange (FX) diagrams to answer the following questions about the relationship between the British pound (£) and the U.S. dollar ($). The exchange rate is in U.S. dollars per British pound $E_{\$/£}$. We want to consider how a change in the U.S. money supply affects interest rates and exchange rates. On all graphs, label the initial equilibrium point A.

   a. Illustrate how a *temporary* decrease in the U.S. money supply affects the money and FX markets. Label your short-run equilibrium point B and your long-run equilibrium point C.

   b. Using your diagram from (a), state how each of the following variables changes in the *short run* (increase/decrease/no change): U.S. interest rate, British interest rate, $E_{\$/£}$, $E^e_{\$/£}$, and the U.S. price level P.

   c. Using your diagram from (a), state how each of the following variables changes in the *long run* (increase/decrease/no change relative to their initial values at point A): U.S. interest rate, British interest rate, $E_{\$/£}$, $E^e_{\$/£}$, and U.S. price level P.

2. Use the money market and foreign exchange (FX) diagrams to answer the following questions. This question considers the relationship between the Indian rupee (Rs) and the U.S. dollar ($). The exchange rate is in rupees per dollar, $E_{Rs/\$}$. On all graphs, label the initial equilibrium point A.

   a. Illustrate how a *permanent* increase in India's money supply affects the money and FX markets. Label your short-run equilibrium point B and your long-run equilibrium point C.

   b. By plotting them on a chart with time on the horizontal axis, illustrate how each of the following variables changes over time (for India): nominal money supply M_{IN}, price level P_{IN}, real money supply M_{IN}/P_{IN}, interest rate i_{Rs}, and the exchange rate $E_{Rs/\$}$.

   c. Using your previous analysis, state how each of the following variables changes in the *short run* (increase/decrease/no change): India's interest rate i_{Rs}, $E_{Rs/\$}$, expected exchange rate $E^e_{Rs/\$}$, and price level P_{IN}.

   d. Using your previous analysis, state how each of the following variables changes in the *long run* (increase/decrease/no change relative to their initial values at point A): India's interest rate i_{Rs}, $E_{Rs/\$}$, $E^e_{Rs/\$}$, and India's price level P_{IN}.

   e. Explain how overshooting applies to this situation.

3. Is overshooting (in theory and in practice) consistent with purchasing power parity? Consider the reasons for the usefulness of PPP in the short run versus the long run and the assumption we've used in the asset approach (in the short run versus the long run). How does overshooting help to resolve the empirical behavior of exchange rates in the short run versus the long run?

4. Use the money market and foreign exchange (FX) diagrams to answer the following questions. This question considers the relationship between the euro (€) and the U.S. dollar ($). The exchange rate is in U.S. dollars per euro, $E_{\$/€}$. Suppose that with financial innovation in the United States, real money demand in the United States decreases. On all graphs, label the initial equilibrium point A.

   a. Assume this change in U.S. real money demand is temporary. Using the FX/money market diagrams, illustrate how this change affects the money and FX markets. Label your short-run equilibrium point B and your long-run equilibrium point C.

   b. Assume this change in U.S. real money demand is permanent. Using a new diagram, illustrate how this change affects the money and FX markets. Label your short-run equilibrium point B and your long-run equilibrium point C.

   c. Illustrate how each of the following variables changes over time in response to a permanent reduction in real money demand: nominal money supply M_{US}, price level P_{US}, real money supply M_{US}/P_{US}, U.S. interest rate $i_\$$, and the exchange rate $E_{\$/€}$.

5. This question considers how the foreign exchange (FX) market will respond to changes in monetary policy in South Korea. For these questions, define the exchange rate as South Korean won per Japanese yen, $E_{won/¥}$. Use the FX and money market diagrams to answer the following questions. On all graphs, label the initial equilibrium point A.

   a. Suppose the Bank of Korea permanently decreases its money supply. Illustrate the short-run (label equilibrium point B) and long-run effects (label equilibrium point C) of this policy.
   b. Now, suppose the Bank of Korea announces it plans to permanently decrease its money supply but doesn't actually implement this policy. How will this affect the FX market in the short run if investors believe the Bank of Korea's announcement?
   c. Finally, suppose the Bank of Korea permanently decreases its money supply, but this change is not anticipated. When the Bank of Korea implements this policy, how will this affect the FX market in the short run?
   d. Using your previous answers, evaluate the following statements:
      - If a country wants to increase the value of its currency, it can do so (temporarily) without raising domestic interest rates.
      - The central bank can reduce both the domestic price level and value of its currency in the long run.
      - The most effective way to increase the value of a currency is through surprising investors.

6. In the late 1990s, several East Asian countries used limited flexibility or currency pegs in managing their exchange rates relative to the U.S. dollar. This question considers how different countries responded to the East Asian currency crisis (1997–1998). For the following questions, treat the East Asian country as the home country and the United States as the foreign country. Also, for the diagrams, you may assume these countries maintained a currency peg (fixed rate) relative to the U.S. dollar. Also, for the following questions, you need consider only the short-run effects.

   a. In July 1997, investors expected that the Thai baht would depreciate. That is, they expected that Thailand's central bank would be unable to maintain the currency peg with the U.S. dollar. Illustrate how this change in investors' expectations affects the Thai money market and FX market, with the exchange rate defined as baht (B) per U.S. dollar, denoted $E_{B/\$}$. Assume the Thai central bank wants to maintain capital mobility and preserve the level of its interest rate, and abandons the currency peg in favor of a floating exchange rate regime.
   b. Indonesia faced the same constraints as Thailand—investors feared Indonesia would be forced to abandon its currency peg. Illustrate how this change in investors' expectations affects the Indonesian money market and FX market, with the exchange rate defined as rupiahs (Rp) per U.S. dollar, denoted $E_{Rp/\$}$. Assume that the Indonesian central bank wants to maintain capital mobility and the currency peg.
   c. Malaysia had a similar experience, except that it used capital controls to maintain its currency peg and preserve the level of its interest rate. Illustrate how this change in investors' expectations affects the Malaysian money market and FX market, with the exchange rate defined as ringgit (RM) per U.S. dollar, denoted $E_{RM/\$}$. You need show only the short-run effects of this change in investors' expectations.
   d. Compare and contrast the three approaches just outlined. As a policy maker, which would you favor? Explain.

7. Several countries have opted to join currency unions. Examples include those in the Euro area, the CFA franc union in West Africa, and the Caribbean currency union. This involves sacrificing the domestic currency in favor of using a single currency unit in multiple countries. Assuming that once a country joins a currency union, it will not leave, do these countries face the policy trilemma discussed in the text? Explain.

8. During the Great Depression, the United States remained on the international gold standard longer than other countries. This effectively

meant that the United States was committed to maintaining a fixed exchange rate at the onset of the Great Depression. The U.S. dollar was pegged to the value of gold, along with other major currencies, including the British pound, French franc, and so on. Many researchers have blamed the severity of the Great Depression on the Federal Reserve and its failure to react to economic conditions in 1929 and 1930. Discuss how the policy trilemma applies to this situation.

9. On June 20, 2007, John Authers, investment editor of the *Financial Times*, wrote the following in his column "The Short View":

> The Bank of England published minutes showing that only the narrowest possible margin, 5–4, voted down [an interest] rate hike last month. Nobody foresaw this. . . . The news took sterling back above $1.99, and to a 15-year high against the yen.

Can you explain the logic of this statement? Interest rates in the United Kingdom had remained unchanged in the weeks since the vote and were still unchanged after the minutes were released. What news was contained in the minutes that caused traders to react? Explain using the asset approach.

10. We can use the asset approach to both make predictions about how the market will react to current events and understand how important these events are to investors. Consider the behavior of the Union/Confederate exchange rate during the Civil War. How would each of the following events affect the exchange rate, defined as Confederate dollars per Union dollar, $E_{C\$/\$}$?

   a. The Confederacy increases the money supply by 2,900% between July and December 1861.
   b. The Union Army suffers a defeat in Battle of Chickamauga in September 1863.
   c. The Confederate Army suffers a major defeat with Sherman's March in the autumn of 1864.

NET WORK

Search the Internet for websites and services offering exchange rate forecasts. (*Hint:* Google "exchange rate forecast.") How far ahead is the forecast made? What do the forecasters say about the methods that they use, if anything? Is the forecast based on fundamentals or technical methods? How much credence would you give to the forecast?

National and International Accounts: Income, Wealth, and the Balance of Payments

Money is sent from one country to another for various purposes: such as the payment of tributes or subsidies; remittances of revenue to or from dependencies, or of rents or other incomes to their absent owners; emigration of capital, or transmission of it for foreign investment. The most usual purpose, however, is that of payment for goods. To show in what circumstances money actually passes from country to country for this or any of the other purposes mentioned, it is necessary briefly to state the nature of the mechanism by which international trade is carried on, when it takes place not by barter but through the medium of money.

John Stuart Mill, 1848

1 Measuring Macroeconomic Activity: An Overview

2 Income, Product, and Expenditure

3 The Balance of Payments

4 External Wealth

5 Conclusions

In Chapter 2, we encountered George, the hypothetical American tourist in Paris. We learned about his use of exchange rate conversion—but how did he pay for his expenses? He traded some of his assets (such as dollar cash converted into euros, or charges on his debit card against his bank account) for goods and services (hotel, food, wine, etc.). Every day households and firms routinely trade goods, services, and assets, but when such transactions cross borders, they link the home economy with the rest of the world. In the upcoming chapters, we study economic transactions between countries, how they are undertaken, and what impact they have on the macroeconomy.

To that end, the first task of any macroeconomist is to measure economic transactions. The collection and analysis of such data can help improve research and policy formulation. In a closed economy there are important aggregate flows to consider, such as national output, consumption, investment, and so on. When an economy is open to transactions with the rest of the world, there are a host of additional economic transactions that take place across borders. In today's world economy these international flows of trade and finance have reached unprecedented levels.

Beyond barter: international transactions involve not just goods and services but also financial assets.

Cross-border flows of good, services, and capital are measured in various ways and are increasingly important subjects of discussion for economists and policy makers, for businesses, and for the well-educated citizen. There are debates about the size of the U.S. trade deficit, trade surpluses in emerging economies like China and India, the growing indebtedness of the United States to the rest of the world, and how these trends might be related to national saving and the government's budget. To understand such debates, we must first know what is being talked about. What do all these measures mean and how are they related? How does the global economy actually function?

The goals of this chapter are to explain the international system of trade and payments, to discover how international trade in *goods and services* is complemented and balanced by a parallel trade in *assets*, and to see how these transactions relate to national income and wealth. In the remainder of the book, we will use these essential tools to understand the macroeconomic linkages between nations.

1 Measuring Macroeconomic Activity: An Overview

To understand macroeconomic accounting in an open economy, we build on the principles used to track payments in a closed economy. As you may know from previous courses in economics, a closed economy is characterized by a *circular flow of payments*, in which economic resources are exchanged for payments as they move through the economy. At various points in this flow, economic activity is measured and recorded in the **national income and product accounts.** In an open economy, however, such measurements are more complicated because we have to account for cross-border flows. These additional flows are recorded in a nation's **balance of payments accounts.** In this opening section, we survey the principles behind these measurements. In later sections, we define the measurements more precisely and explore how they work in practice.

The Flow of Payments in a Closed Economy: Introducing the National Income and Product Accounts

Figure 5-1 shows how payments flow in a closed economy. At the top is **gross national expenditure (GNE),** the total expenditure on final goods and services by home entities in any given period of measurement (usually a calendar year, unless otherwise noted). It is made up of three parts: personal consumption C, investment I, and government spending G. The sum of these variables equals GNE.

Once GNE is spent, where do the payments flow next? All of this spending constitutes all payments for final goods and services within the nation's borders. Because the economy is closed, the nation's expenditure must be spent on the final goods and services it produces. More specifically, a country's **gross domestic product (GDP)** is the value of all (*intermediate* and *final*) goods and services produced as output by firms, minus the value of all goods and services purchased as inputs by firms. (GDP is also

FIGURE 5-1

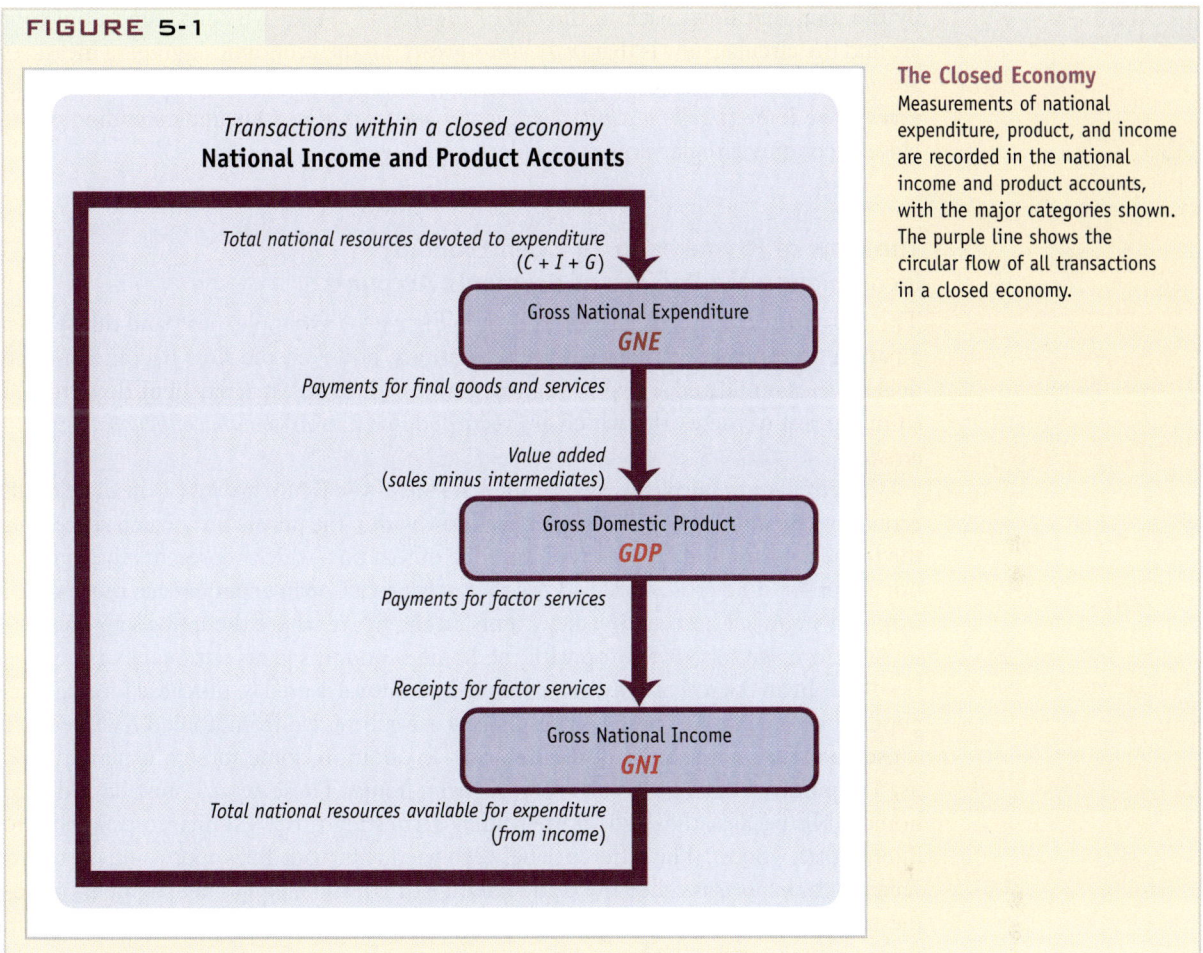

The Closed Economy
Measurements of national expenditure, product, and income are recorded in the national income and product accounts, with the major categories shown. The purple line shows the circular flow of all transactions in a closed economy.

known as *value added*.) GDP is a product measure, in contrast to GNE, which is an expenditure measure. In a closed economy, intermediate sales must equal intermediate purchases, so in GDP these two terms cancel out, leaving only the value of final goods and services produced, which equals the expenditure on final goods and services, or GNE. Thus, GDP equals GNE.

Once GDP is sold, where do the payments flow next? Because GDP measures the value of firm outputs minus the cost of firm inputs, and this remaining flow is paid by firms as income to factors such as the owners of labor, capital, and land employed by the firms. The factors may, in turn, be owned by households, government, or firms, but such distinctions are not important. The key thing in a closed economy is that all such income is paid to domestic entities. It thus equals the total income resources of the economy, also known as **gross national income (GNI).** By this point in our circular flow, we can see that in a closed economy the expenditure on total goods and services GNE equals GDP, which is then paid as income to productive factors GNI.

Once GNI is received by factors, where do the payments flow next? Clearly, there is no way for a closed economy to finance expenditure except out of its own income, so total income is, in turn, spent and must be the same as total expenditure. This is shown by the loop that flows back to the top of Figure 5-1. What we have seen in our tour around the circular flow is that *in a closed economy*, all the economic aggregate measures are equal: GNE equals GDP which equals GNI which equals GNE. *In a closed economy, expenditure is the same as product, which is the same as income.* Our understanding of the closed economy circular flow is complete.

The Flow of Payments in an Open Economy: Incorporating the Balance of Payments Accounts

The closed-economy circular flow shown in Figure 5-1 is simple, neat, and tidy. When a nation opens itself to trade with other nations, however, the flow becomes a good deal more complicated. Figure 5-2 incorporates all of the extra payment flows to and from the rest of the world, which are recorded in a nation's *balance of payments (BOP) accounts.*

The circulating purple arrows on the left side of the figure are just as in the closed-economy case in Figure 5-1. These arrows flow within the purple box, which represents the home country, and do not cross the edge of that box, which represents the international border. The cross-border flows that occur in an open economy are represented by green arrows. There are five key points on the figure where these flows appear.

As before, we start at the top with the home economy's gross national expenditure, $C + I + G$. In an open economy, some home expenditure is used to purchase foreign final goods and services. At point 1, these *imports* are subtracted from home GNE because those goods are not sold by domestic firms. In addition, some foreign expenditure is used to purchase final goods and services from home. These *exports* must be added to home GNE because those goods are sold by domestic firms. (A similar logic applies to intermediate goods.) The difference between payments made for imports and payments received for exports is called the **trade balance (TB),** and it equals net payments to domestic firms due to trade. GNE plus TB equals GDP, the total value of production in the home economy.

At point 2, some home GDP is paid to foreign entities for *factor service imports*, that is, domestic payments to capital, labor, and land owned by foreign entities. Because this income is not paid to factors at home, it is subtracted when computing home income. Similarly, some foreign GDP may be paid to domestic entities as payment for *factor service exports*, that is, foreign payments to capital, labor, and land owned by domestic entities. Because this income is paid to factors at home, it is added when computing home income. The value of factor service exports minus factor service imports is known as **net factor income from abroad (NFIA),** and thus GDP plus NFIA equals GNI, the total income earned by domestic entities from all sources, domestic and foreign.

At point 3, we see that the home country may not retain all of its earned income GNI. Why? Domestic entities might give some of it away—for example, as foreign aid or remittances by migrants to their families back home. Similarly, domestic entities might receive gifts from abroad. Such gifts may take the form of income transfers or be "in kind" transfers of goods and services. They are considered nonmarket transactions, and are referred to as *unilateral transfers.* **Net unilateral transfers (NUT)** equals the value of unilateral transfers the country receives from the rest of the world minus those it gives to the rest of the world. These net transfers have to be added to GNI to calculate **gross national disposable income (GNDI),** and thus GNI plus NUT equals GNDI, which represents the total income resources available to the home country.

FIGURE 5-2

The Open Economy Measurements of national expenditure, product, and income are recorded in the national income and product accounts, with the major categories shown on the left. Measurements of international transactions are recorded in the balance of payments accounts, with the major categories shown on the right. The purple line shows the flow of transactions within the home economy; the green lines show all cross-border transactions.

The balance of payments accounts collect together the trade balance, net factor income from abroad, and net unilateral transfers and report their sum as the **current account (CA),** which is a tally of all international transactions in goods, services, and income (occurring through market transactions or transfers). The current account is not, however, a complete picture of international transactions. Resource flows of goods, services, and income are not the only items that flow between open economies. Financial assets such as stocks, bonds, or real estate are also traded across international borders.

At point 4, we see that a country's capacity to spend is not restricted to be equal to GNDI, but instead can be increased or decreased by trading assets with other countries. When foreign entities pay to acquire assets from home entities, the value of these *asset exports* increases resources available for spending at home. Conversely, when domestic entities pay to acquire assets from the rest of the world, the value of the *asset imports* decreases resources available for spending. The value of asset exports minus asset imports is called the **financial account (FA).** These net asset exports are added to home GNDI when calculating the total resources available for expenditure in the home country.

Finally, at point 5, we see that a country may not only buy and sell assets but also transfer assets as gifts. Such asset transfers are measured by the **capital account (KA),** which is the value of capital transfers from the rest of the world minus those to the rest of the world. These net asset transfers must also be added to home GNDI when calculating the total resources available for expenditure in the home country.

After some effort, at the bottom of Figure 5-2, we have finally computed the entire value of the resources, including home and foreign sources, that are available for home to use for total spending, or gross national expenditure, as the flow loops back to the top. We have now fully modified the circular flow to account for international transactions.[1]

These modifications to the circular flow in Figure 5-2 tell us something very important about the balance of payments. We start at the top with GNE. We add the trade balance to get GDP, we add net factor income from abroad to get GNI, and then we add net unilateral transfers received to get GNDI. We then add net asset exports measured by the financial account and net capital transfers measured by the capital account, and we get back to GNE. That is, we start with GNE, add in *everything* in the balance of payments accounts, and still end up with GNE. What does this tell us? The sum of all the items in the balance of payments account, the net sum of all those cross-border flows, must amount to zero! The balance of payments account *does* balance. We shall explore the implications of this important result later in this chapter.

2 Income, Product, and Expenditure

In the previous section, we sketched out all the important national and international transactions that occur in an open economy. With that overview in mind, we now formally define the key accounting concepts in the two sets of accounts and put them to use.

---

[1] In the past, both the financial and capital accounts were jointly known as "the capital account." This change should be kept in mind not only when consulting older documents but also when listening to contemporary discussion because not everyone cares for the new (and somewhat confusing) nomenclature.

Three Approaches to Measuring Economic Activity

There are three main approaches to the measurement of aggregate economic activity within a country:

- The *expenditure approach* looks at the demand for goods: it examines how much is spent on demand for final goods and services. The key measure is GNE.
- The *product approach* looks at the supply of goods: it measures the value of all goods and services produced as output minus the value of goods used as inputs in production. The key measure is GDP.
- The *income approach* focuses on payments to owners of factors: it tracks the amount of income they receive. The key measures are gross national income GNI and gross national disposable income GNDI (which includes net transfers).

It is crucial to note that in a closed economy the three approaches generate the same number: In a closed economy, GNE = GDP = GNI. In an open economy, however, this is not true.

From GNE to GDP: Accounting for Trade in Goods and Services

As before, we start with gross national expenditure, or GNE, which is *by definition* the sum of consumption C, investment I, and government consumption G. Formally, these three elements are defined, respectively, as follows:

- *Personal consumption expenditures* (usually called "consumption") equal total spending by private households on final goods and services, including nondurable goods such as food, durable goods such as a television, and services such as window cleaning or gardening.
- *Gross private domestic investment* (usually called "investment") equals total spending by firms or households on final goods and services to make additions to the stock of capital. Investment includes construction of a new house or a new factory, the purchase of new equipment, and net increases in inventories of goods held by firms (i.e., unsold output).
- *Government consumption expenditures and gross investment* (often called "government consumption") equal spending by the public sector on final goods and services, including spending on public works, national defense, the police, and the civil service. It does *not* include any transfer payments or income redistributions, such as Social Security or unemployment insurance payments—these are *not* purchases of goods or services, just rearrangements of private spending power.

As for GDP, it is *by definition* the value of all goods and services produced as output by firms, minus the value of all intermediate goods and services purchased as inputs by firms. It is thus a product measure, in contrast to the expenditure measure GNE. Because of trade, not all of the GNE payments go to GDP, and not all of GDP payments arise from GNE.

To adjust GNE and find the contribution going into GDP, we must *subtract* the value of final goods imported (home spending that goes to foreign firms) and we must *add* the value of final goods exported (foreign spending that goes to home firms). In addition, we can't forget about intermediate goods: we must *subtract* the value of imported intermediates (in GDP they also count as home's purchased inputs) and we must *add* the value of exported intermediates (in GDP they also count as home's produced output).[2] So, adding it all up, to get from GNE to GDP, we must add the value of *all* exports denoted EX and subtract the value of *all* imports IM. Thus,

$$\underbrace{GDP}_{\text{Gross domestic product}} = \underbrace{C + I + G}_{\substack{\text{Gross national expenditure} \\ GNE}} + \underbrace{\left(\underbrace{EX}_{\substack{\text{All exports,} \\ \text{final \& intermediate}}} - \underbrace{IM}_{\substack{\text{All imports,} \\ \text{final \& intermediate}}}\right)}_{\substack{\text{Trade balance} \\ TB}} \quad (5\text{-}1)$$

This important formula for GDP says that *gross domestic product is equal to gross national expenditure (GNE) plus the trade balance (TB)*.

Although the adjustments for final goods trade might be more obvious or familiar in the above derivation, it is also crucial to understand and account for intermediate goods transactions properly because, due to globalization and outsourcing, trade in intermediate goods has surged in recent decades. For example, according to the 2010 *Economic Report of the President*, some estimates suggest that one-third of the growth of world trade from 1970 to 1990 was driven by intermediate trade arising from the growth of "vertically specialized" production processes (outsourcing, offshoring, etc.). More strikingly, as of 2010, it appears that—probably for the first time in world history—total world trade now consists rather more of trade in intermediate goods (60%) than in final goods (40%).

The trade balance, TB, is also often referred to as *net exports*. Because it is the net value of exports minus imports, it may be positive or negative.

If $TB > 0$, exports are greater than imports and we say a country has a *trade surplus*.

If $TB < 0$, imports are greater than exports and we say a country has a *trade deficit*.

In 2009 the United States had a trade deficit because its trade balance was −$392 billion.

From GDP to GNI: Accounting for Trade in Factor Services

Trade in factor services occurs when, say, the home country is paid income by a foreign country as compensation for the use of labor, capital, and land owned by home entities but in service in the foreign country. We say the home country is exporting factor services to the foreign country and receiving factor income in return.

An example of a labor service export is a home country professional temporarily working overseas, say, a U.S. architect freelancing in London. The wages she earns in the United Kingdom are factor income for the United States. An example of trade in capital services is *foreign direct investment*. For example, U.S.-owned factories in Ireland generate income for their U.S. owners; Japanese-owned factories in the United States generate income for their Japanese owners. Other examples of payments for

---

[2] Note that intermediate inputs sold by home firms and purchased by other home firms cancel out in GDP, in both closed and open economies. For example, suppose there are two firms A and B, and Firm A makes a $200 table (a final good) and buys $100 in wood (an intermediate input) from Firm B, and there is no trade. Total sales are $300; but GDP or value added is total sales of $300 minus the $100 of inputs purchased; so GDP is equal to $200. Now suppose Firm B makes and exports $50 of extra wood. After this change, GDP is equal to $250. You can see here that GDP *is not equal to* the value of final goods produced in an economy (although it is quite often claimed, mistakenly, that this is a definition of GDP).

capital services include income from overseas *financial* assets such as foreign securities, real estate, or loans to governments, firms, and households.

These payments are accounted for as additions to and subtractions from home GDP. Some home GDP is paid out as *income payments* to foreign entities for factor services imported by the home country IM_{FS}. In addition, domestic entities receive some income payments from foreign entities as *income receipts* for factor services exported by the home country EX_{FS}.

Accounting for these income flows, gross national income (GNI), the total income earned by domestic entities, is given by GDP plus the income from overseas EX_{FS}, minus the income going overseas IM_{FS}.[3] The last two terms, income receipts minus income payments, are the home country's *net factor income from abroad*, $NFIA = EX_{FS} - IM_{FS}$. This may be a positive or negative number, depending on whether income receipts are larger or smaller than income payments.

With the help of the GDP expression in Equation (5-1), we obtain the key formula for GNI that says the *gross national income equals gross domestic product (GDP) plus net factor income from abroad (NFIA)*.

$$GNI = \underbrace{\underbrace{C + I + G}_{\substack{\text{Gross national expenditure} \\ GNE}} + \underbrace{(EX - IM)}_{\substack{\text{Trade balance} \\ TB}}}_{GDP} + \underbrace{(EX_{FS} - IM_{FS})}_{\substack{\text{Net factor income from abroad} \\ NFIA}} \quad (5\text{-}2)$$

In 2009 the United States received income payments from foreigners EX_{FS} of $589 billion and made income payments to foreigners IM_{FS} of $484 billion, so the net factor income from abroad NFIA was +$105 billion. Earlier in this chapter, we computed U.S. GDP to be $14,256 billion; because of net factor income from abroad, U.S. GNI was a little higher at $14,361 billion.

APPLICATION

Celtic Tiger or Tortoise?

International trade in factor services (as measured by NFIA) can generate a difference between the product and income measures in a country's national accounts. In the United States, this difference is typically small, but at times NFIA can play a major role in the measurement of a country's economic activity.

In the 1970s, Ireland was one of the poorer countries in Europe, but over the next three decades it experienced speedy economic growth with an accompanying investment boom now known as the Irish Miracle. From 1980 to 2007, Irish real GDP per person grew at a phenomenal rate of 4.1% per year—not as rapid as in some developing countries but extremely rapid by the standards of the rich countries of the European Union (EU) or the Organization for Economic Cooperation and Development (OECD). Comparisons with fast-growing Asian economies—the "Asian Tigers"—soon had people speaking of the "Celtic Tiger" when referring to Ireland.

---

[3] GNI is the accounting concept formerly known as GNP, or *gross national product*. The term GNP is still often used, but GNI is technically more accurate because the concept is a measurement of income rather than product. Note that taxes and subsidies on production and imports are counted in GNE (both) and GDP (production taxes only). This treatment ensures that the tax income paid to the home country is properly counted as a part of home income. We simplify the presentation in this textbook by assuming there are no taxes and subsidies.

Did Irish citizens enjoy all of these gains? No. Figure 5-3 shows that in 1980 Ireland's annual net factor income from abroad was virtually nil—about €–70 per person (in 2007 real euros) or –0.5% of GDP. Yet by 2000, around 15% to 20% of Irish GDP was being used to make net factor income payments to foreigners who had invested heavily in the Irish economy by buying stocks and bonds and by purchasing land and building factories on it. (By some estimates, 75% of Ireland's industrial-sector GDP originated in foreign-owned plants in 2004.) These foreign investors expected their big Irish investments to generate income, and so they did, in the form of net factor payments abroad amounting to almost one-fifth of Irish GDP. This meant that Irish GNI (the income paid to Irish people and firms) was a lot smaller than Irish GDP.[4] Ireland's net factor income from abroad has remained large and negative ever since.

This example shows how GDP can be a misleading measure of economic performance. When ranked by GDP per person, Ireland was the 4th richest OECD economy

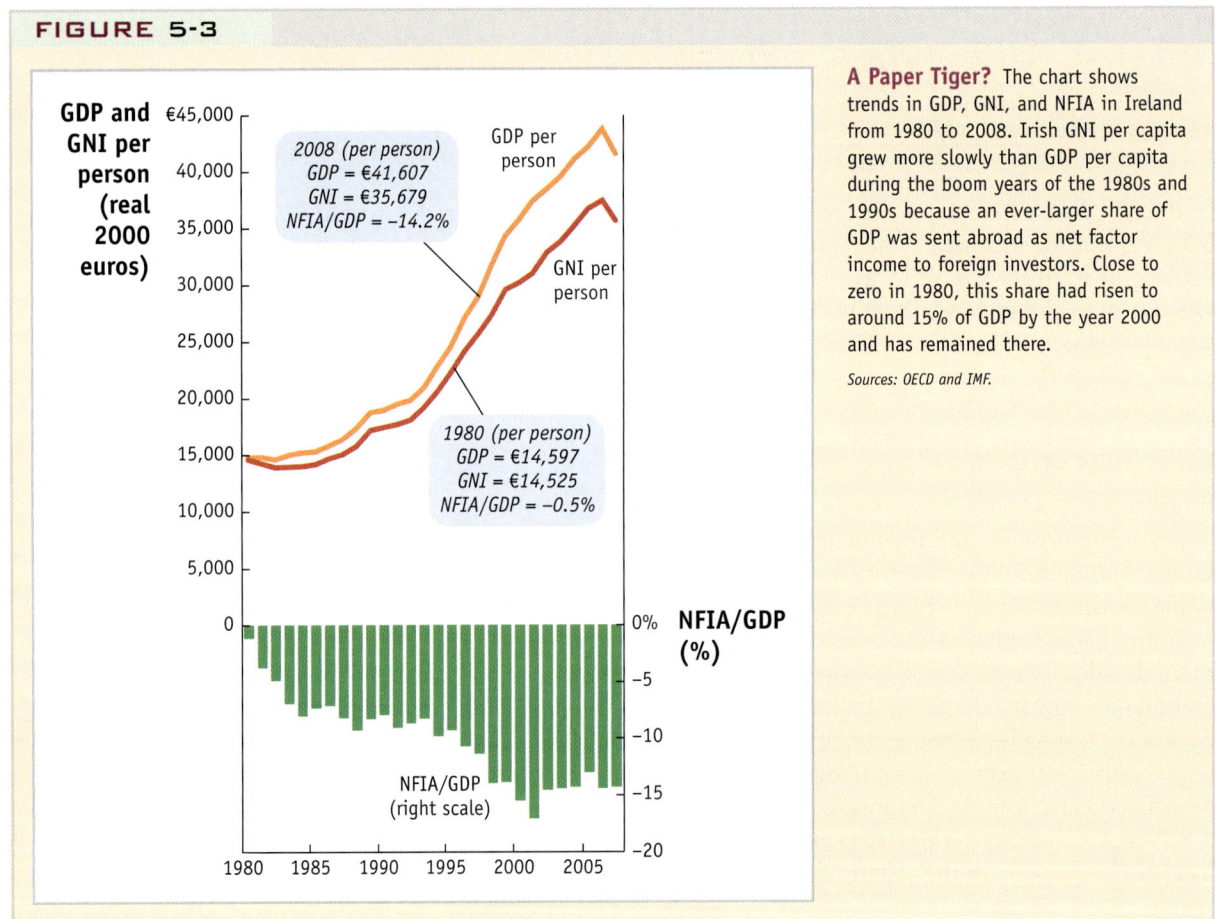

FIGURE 5-3

A Paper Tiger? The chart shows trends in GDP, GNI, and NFIA in Ireland from 1980 to 2008. Irish GNI per capita grew more slowly than GDP per capita during the boom years of the 1980s and 1990s because an ever-larger share of GDP was sent abroad as net factor income to foreign investors. Close to zero in 1980, this share had risen to around 15% of GDP by the year 2000 and has remained there.

Sources: OECD and IMF.

---

[4] Irish GDP might have been inflated as a result of various accounting problems. Some special factors exacerbated the difference between GDP and GNI in Ireland, such as special tax incentives that encouraged foreign firms to keep their accounts in a way which generated high profits "on paper" at their low-tax Irish subsidiaries rather than in their high-tax home country. For these reasons, many economists believe that Irish GNI, despite being more conservative, might be a truer measure of the economy's performance.

in 2004; when ranked by GNI per person, it was only 17th richest.[5] The Irish outflow of net factor payments is certainly an extreme case, but it serves to underscore an important point about income measurement in open economies. Any country that relies heavily on foreign investment to generate economic growth is not getting a free lunch. Irish GNI per person grew at "only" 3.6% from 1980 to the peak in 2007; this was 0.5% per year less than the growth rate of GDP per person over the same period. Living standards grew impressively, but the more humble GNI figures may give a more accurate measure of what the Irish Miracle actually meant for the Irish. ∎

From GNI to GNDI: Accounting for Transfers of Income

So far, we have fully described market transactions in goods, services, and income. However, many international transactions take place outside of markets. International nonmarket transfers of goods, services, and income include such things as foreign aid by governments in the form of *official development assistance* (ODA) and other help, private charitable gifts to foreign recipients, and income remittances sent to relatives or friends in other countries. These transfers are "gifts" and may take the form of goods and services (food aid, volunteer medical services) or income transfers.

If a country receives transfers worth UT_{IN} and gives transfers worth UT_{OUT}, then its net unilateral transfers, NUT, are $NUT = UT_{IN} - UT_{OUT}$. Because this is a net amount, it may be positive or negative.

In general, net unilateral transfers play a small role in the income and product accounts for most high-income countries (net outgoing transfers are typically no more than 5% of GNI). But they are an important part of the gross national disposable income (GNDI) for many low-income countries that receive a great deal of foreign aid or migrant remittances, as seen in Figure 5-4.

Measuring national generosity is highly controversial and a recurring theme of current affairs (see **Headlines: Are Rich Countries "Stingy" with Foreign Aid?**). You might think that net unilateral transfers are in some ways a better measure of a country's generosity toward foreigners than official development assistance, which is but one component. For example, looking at the year 2000, a USAID report, *Foreign Aid in the National Interest*, claimed that while U.S. ODA was only $9.9 billion, other U.S. government assistance (such as contributions to global security and humanitarian assistance) amounted to $12.7 billion, and assistance from private U.S. citizens totaled $33.6 billion—for total foreign assistance equal to $56.2 billion, more than five times the level of ODA.

To include the impact of aid and all other transfers in the overall calculation of a country's income resources, we must add net unilateral transfers to gross national income. Using the definition of GNI in Equation (5-2), we obtain a full measure of national income in an open economy, known as gross national disposable income (GNDI), henceforth denoted Y:

$$\underbrace{Y}_{GNDI} = \underbrace{C + I + G}_{GNE} + \underbrace{(EX - IM)}_{\substack{\text{Trade balance} \\ TB}} + \underbrace{(EX_{FS} - IM_{FS})}_{\substack{\text{Net factor income} \\ \text{from abroad} \\ NFIA}} + \underbrace{(UT_{IN} - UT_{OUT})}_{\substack{\text{Net unilateral} \\ \text{transfers} \\ NUT}} \quad (5\text{-}3)$$

$$\underbrace{\phantom{C + I + G + (EX - IM) + (EX_{FS} - IM_{FS})}}_{GNI}$$

In general, economists and policy makers prefer to use GNDI to measure national income. Why? GDP is not a true measure of income because, unlike GNI, it does not

---

[5] Joe Cullen, "There's Lies, Damned Lies, and Wealth Statistics," *Irish Times*, May 1, 2004.

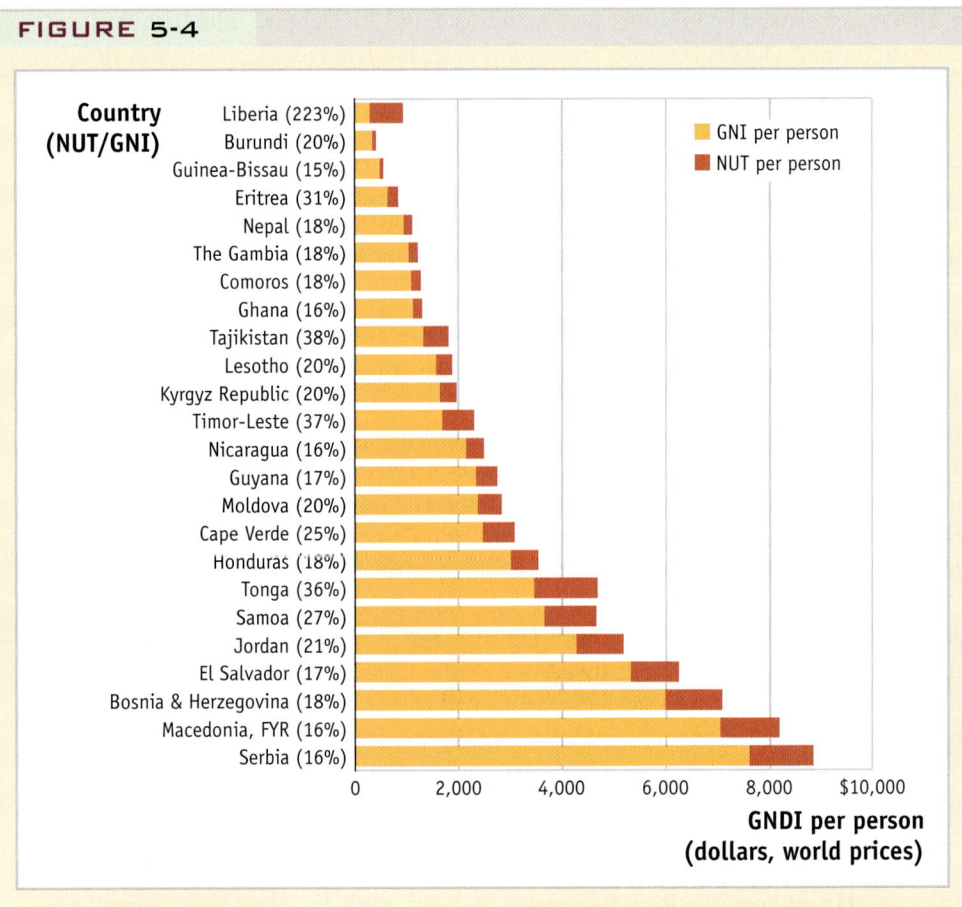

FIGURE 5-4

Major Transfer Recipients The chart shows average figures for 2000 to 2008 for all countries in which net unilateral transfers exceeded 15% of GNI. Many of the countries shown were heavily reliant on foreign aid, including some of the poorest countries in the world such as Liberia, Burundi, Eritrea, and Nepal. Some countries with higher incomes also have large transfers because of substantial migrant remittances from a large number of emigrant workers overseas, for example, Tonga, Jordan, El Salvador, and Cape Verde.

Source: World Bank, World Development Indicators.

include net factor income from abroad. GNI is not a perfect measure either because it leaves out international transfers. GNDI is a preferred measure because it most closely corresponds to the resources available to the nation's households, and national welfare depends most closely on this accounting measure.

What the National Economic Aggregates Tell Us

We have explained all the international flows shown in Figure 5-2 and have developed three key equations that link the important national economic aggregates in an open economy:

- To get from GNE to GDP, we add TB (Equation 5-1).
- To get from GDP to GNI, we add NFIA (Equation 5-2).
- To get from GNI to GDNI, we add NUT (Equation 5-3).

HEADLINES

Are Rich Countries "Stingy" with Foreign Aid?

The Asian tsunami on December 26, 2004, was one of the worst natural disasters of modern times. Hundreds of thousands of people were killed and billions of dollars of damage was done. Some aftershocks were felt in international politics. Jan Egeland, UN undersecretary general for humanitarian affairs and emergency relief, declared, "It is beyond me why we are so stingy." His comments rocked the boat in many rich countries, especially in the United States where official aid fell short of the UN goal of 0.7% of GNI. However, the United States gives in other ways, making judgments about stinginess far from straightforward.

Is the United States stingy when it comes to foreign aid? . . . The answer depends on how you measure. . . .

In terms of traditional foreign aid, the United States gave $16.25 billion in 2003, as measured by the Organization of Economic Cooperation and Development (OECD), the club of the world's rich industrial nations. That was almost double the aid by the next biggest net spender, Japan ($8.8 billion). Other big donors were France ($7.2 billion) and Germany ($6.8 billion).

But critics point out that the United States is much bigger than those individual nations. As a group, member nations of the European Union have a bit larger population than the United States and give a great deal more money in foreign aid—$49.2 billion altogether in 2003.

In relation to affluence, the United States lies at the bottom of the list of rich donor nations. It gave 0.15% of gross national income to official development assistance in 2003. By this measure, Norway at 0.92% was the most generous, with Denmark next at 0.84%.

Bring those numbers down to an everyday level and the average American gave 13 cents a day in government aid, according to David Roodman, a researcher at the Center for Global Development (CGD) in Washington. Throw in another nickel a day from private giving. That private giving is high by international standards, yet not enough to close the gap with Norway, whose citizens average $1.02 per day in government aid and 24 cents per day in private aid. . . .

[Also], the United States has a huge defense budget, some of which benefits

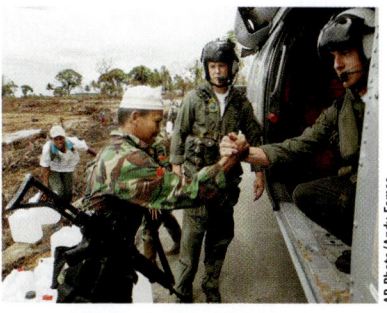

An Indonesian soldier thanks two U.S. airmen after a U.S. Navy helicopter delivered fresh water to Indonesian tsunami victims. The normal operating costs of military assets used for humanitarian purposes are not fully counted as part of official development assistance.

developing countries. Making a judgment call, the CGD includes the cost of UN peacekeeping activities and other military assistance approved by a multilateral institution, such as NATO. So the United States gets credit for its spending in Kosovo, Australia for its intervention in East Timor, and Britain for military money spent to bring more stability to Sierra Leone. . . .

"Not to belittle what we are doing, we shouldn't get too self-congratulatory," says Frederick Barton, an economist at the Center for Strategic and International Studies in Washington.

Source: "Foreign Aid: Is the U.S. Stingy?" Christian Science Monitor/MSN Money, January 6, 2005.

To go one step further, we can group the three cross-border terms into an umbrella term that is called the current account, CA:

$$\underbrace{Y}_{GNDI} = \underbrace{C + I + G}_{GNE} + \underbrace{\{\underbrace{(EX - IM)}_{\substack{\text{Trade balance}\\TB}} + \underbrace{(EX_{FS} - IM_{FS})}_{\substack{\text{Net factor income}\\\text{from abroad}\\NFIA}} + \underbrace{(UT_{IN} - UT_{OUT})}_{\substack{\text{Net unilateral}\\\text{transfers}\\NUT}}\}}_{\substack{\text{Current account}\\CA}} \quad (5\text{-}4)$$

It is important to understand the intuition for this expression. On the left is our full income measure, GNDI. The first term on the right is GNE, which measures payments by home entities. The other terms on the right, combined into CA, measure all net payments to home arising from the full range of international transactions in goods, services, and income.

Remember that in a closed economy, there are no international transactions so TB and NFIA and NUT (and hence CA) are all zero. Therefore, in a closed economy, the four main aggregates GNDI, GNI, GDP, and GNE are exactly equal. In an open economy, however, each of these four aggregates can differ from the others.

Understanding the Data for the National Economic Aggregates

Now that we've learned how a nation's principal economic aggregates are affected by international transactions in theory, let's see how this works in practice. In this section, we take a look at some data from the real world to see how they are recorded and presented in official statistics.

Table 5-1 shows data for the United States in 2009 reported by the Bureau of Economic Analysis in the official national income and product accounts.

Lines 1 to 3 of the table show the components of gross national expenditure, GNE. Personal consumption expenditures C were $10,089 billion, gross private domestic investment I was $1,629 billion, and government consumption G was $2,931 billion. Summing up, GNE was equal to $14,649 billion, which is shown on line 4.

On line 5 appears the trade balance, TB, which was the net export of goods and services, in the amount of −$392 billion. (That net exports are negative means that the United States imported more goods and services than it exported.) Adding this to GNE gives gross domestic product GDP on line 6, which amounted to $14,256 billion. Next we account for net factor income from abroad NFIA, equal to +$105 billion on line 7.

TABLE 5-1

U.S. Economic Aggregates in 2009 The table shows the computation of GDP, GNI, and GNDI in 2009 in billions of dollars using the components of gross national expenditure, the trade balance, international income payments, and unilateral transfers.

Line	Category	Symbol	$ billions
1	Consumption (personal consumption expenditures)	C	$10,089
2	+ Investment (gross private domestic investment)	I	1,629
3	+ Government consumption (government expenditures)	G	2,931
4	= Gross national expenditure	GNE	14,649
5	+ Trade balance	TB	−392
6	= Gross domestic product	GDP	14,256
7	+ Net factor income from abroad	NFIA	105
8	= Gross national income	GNI	14,361
9	+ Net unilateral transfers	NUT	−125
10	= Gross national disposable income	GNDI	14,236

Note: Details may not add to totals because of rounding.

Source: U.S. Bureau of Economic Analysis, NIPA Tables 1.1.5 and 4.1, using the NIPA definition of the United States.

Adding this to GDP gives gross national income GNI, equal to $14,361 billion as shown on line 8.

Finally, to get to the bottom line, we account for the fact that the United States receives net unilateral transfers from the rest of the world of −$125 billion (i.e., the United States makes net transfers to the rest of the world of $125 billion) on line 9. Adding these negative transfers to GNI results in a gross national disposable income GNDI of $14,236 billion on line 10.

Some Recent Trends Figures 5-5 and 5-6 show recent trends in various components of U.S. national income. Examining these breakdowns gives us a sense of the relative magnitude and economic significance of each component.

In Figure 5-5, GNE is shown as the sum of consumption C, investment I, and government consumption G. Consumption accounts for about 70% of GNE, while government consumption G accounts for about 15%. Both of these components are relatively stable. Investment accounts for the rest (about 15% of GNE), but investment tends to fluctuate more than C and G (e.g., it fell steeply in the great recession of 2008–2010). Over the period shown, GNE grew from $6,000 billion to about $15,000 billion in current dollars.

Figure 5-6 shows the trade balance (TB), net factor income from abroad (NFIA), and net unilateral transfers (NUT), which constitute the current account (CA). In the United States, the trade balance is the dominant component in the current account. For the entire period shown, the trade balance has been in deficit and has grown larger

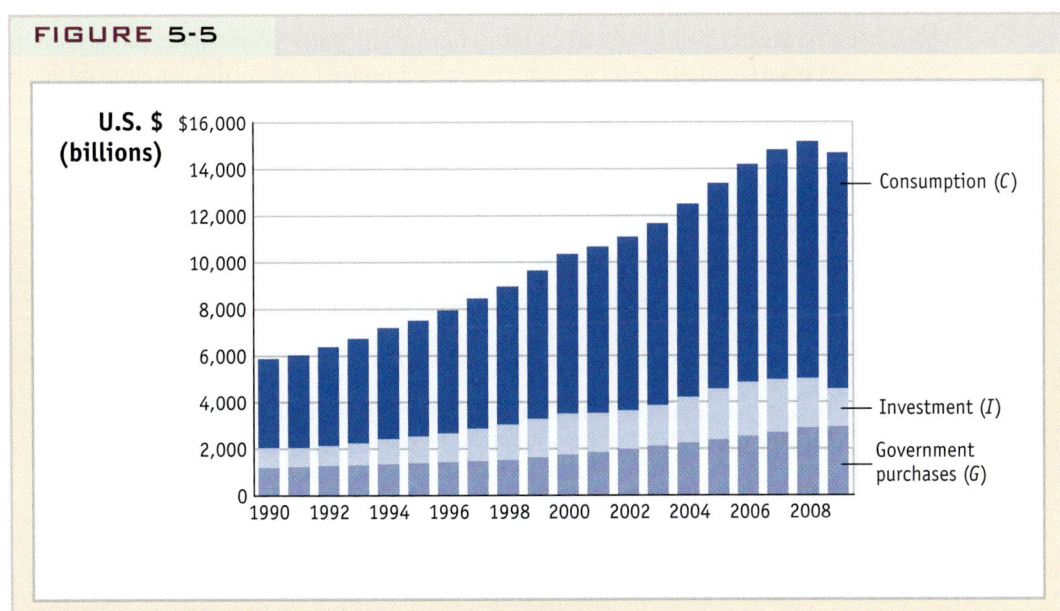

FIGURE 5-5

U.S. Gross National Expenditure and Its Components, 1990–2009 The figure shows consumption (*C*), investment (*I*), and government purchases (*G*), in billions of dollars.

Source: U.S. Bureau of Economic Analysis, using the NIPA definition of the United States, which excludes U.S. territories.

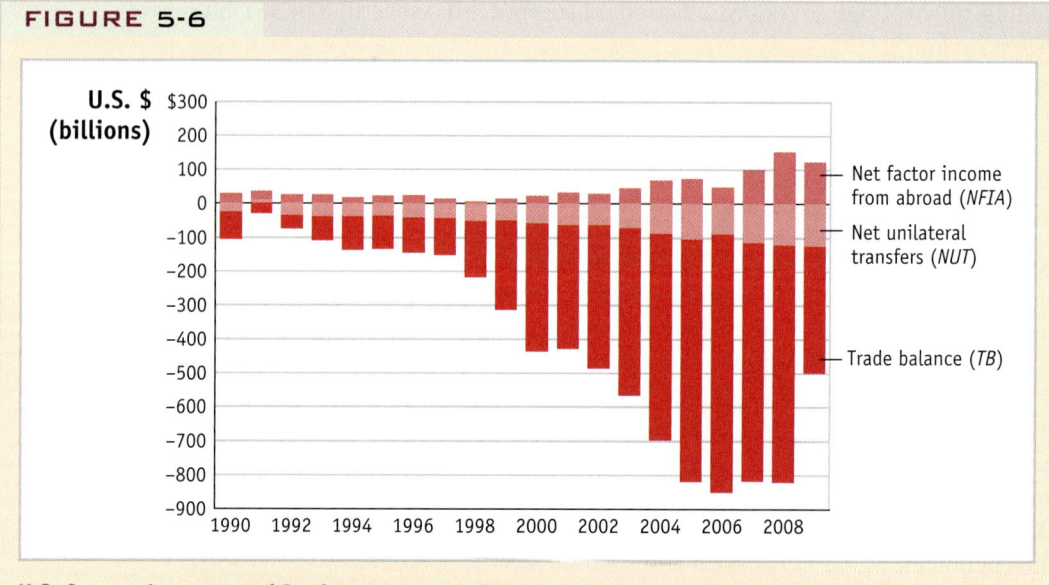

U.S. Current Accounts and Its Components, 1990–2009 The figure shows the trade balance (*TB*), net factor income from abroad (*NFIA*), and net unilateral transfers (*NUT*), in billions of dollars.

Source: U.S. Bureau of Economic Analysis, using the ITA definition of the United States, which includes U.S. territories.

over time. From 2004 to 2008, the trade balance was close to –$800 billion, but it fell during the recession as global trade declined. Net unilateral transfers, a smaller figure, have been between –$100 and –$125 billion in recent years.[6] Net factor income from abroad was positive in all years shown, and has recently been in the range of $100 to $150 billion.

What the Current Account Tells Us

Because it tells us, in effect, whether a nation is spending more or less than its income, the current account plays a central role in economic debates. In particular, it is important to remember that Equation (5-4) can be concisely written as

$$Y = C + I + G + CA \qquad (5\text{-}5)$$

This equation is the open-economy **national income identity.** It tells us that the current account represents the difference between national income Y (or GNDI) and gross national expenditure GNE (or $C + I + G$). Hence,

GNDI is greater than GNE if and only if CA is positive, or in surplus.

GNDI is less than GNE if and only if CA is negative, or in deficit.

---

[6] In 1991 the United States was a net recipient of unilateral transfers, as a result of transfer payments from other rich countries willing to help defray U.S. military expenses in the Gulf War.

Subtracting $C + G$ from both sides of the last identity, we can see that the current account is also the difference between **national saving** ($S = Y - C - G$) and investment:

$$\underbrace{S}_{Y-C-G} = I + CA \qquad (5\text{-}6)$$

where national saving is defined as income minus consumption minus government consumption. This equation is called the **current account identity** even though it is just a rearrangement of the national income identity. Thus,

S is greater than I if and only if CA is positive, or in surplus.

S is less than I if and only if CA is negative, or in deficit.

These last two equations give us two ways of interpreting the current account, and tell us something important about a nation's economic condition. A current account deficit measures how much a country spends in excess of its income or—equivalently—how it saves too little relative to its investment needs. (Surpluses mean the opposite.) We can now understand the widespread use of the current account deficit in the media as a measure of how a country is "spending more than it earns" or "saving too little" or "living beyond its means."

APPLICATION

Global Imbalances

We can apply what we have learned to study some remarkable features of financial globalization in recent years, including the explosion in *global imbalances:* the widely discussed current account surpluses and deficits (seen in various countries and regions) that have been of great concern to policy makers.

Figure 5-7 shows trends since 1980 in saving, investment, and the current account for four groups of industrial countries. All flows are expressed as ratios relative to each region's GDP. Some trends stand out. First, in all regions, saving and investment have been on a marked downward trend for the past 30 years. From its peak, the ratio of saving to GDP fell by about 8 percentage points in the United States, about 15 percentage points in Japan, and about 6 percentage points in the Euro zone and other countries. Investment ratios typically followed a downward path in all regions, too. In Japan, this decline was steeper than the savings, but in the United States, there was hardly any decline in investment.

On some level, these trends reflect the recent history of the industrialized countries. The U.S. economy grew rapidly after 1990 and the Japanese economy grew very slowly, with other countries in between. The fast-growing U.S. economy generated high investment demand, while in slumping Japan investment collapsed; other regions maintained middling levels of growth and investment. Saving in all the countries reflects the demographic shift toward aging populations with fewer workers for each elderly person. This trend is commonly associated with decreased saving as the "demographic burden" of the unproductive retirees raises consumption relative to income.

The current account identity tells us that *CA* equals *S* minus *I*. Thus, investment and saving trends have a predictable impact on the current accounts of industrial countries. Because saving fell faster than investment in the United States, the current account

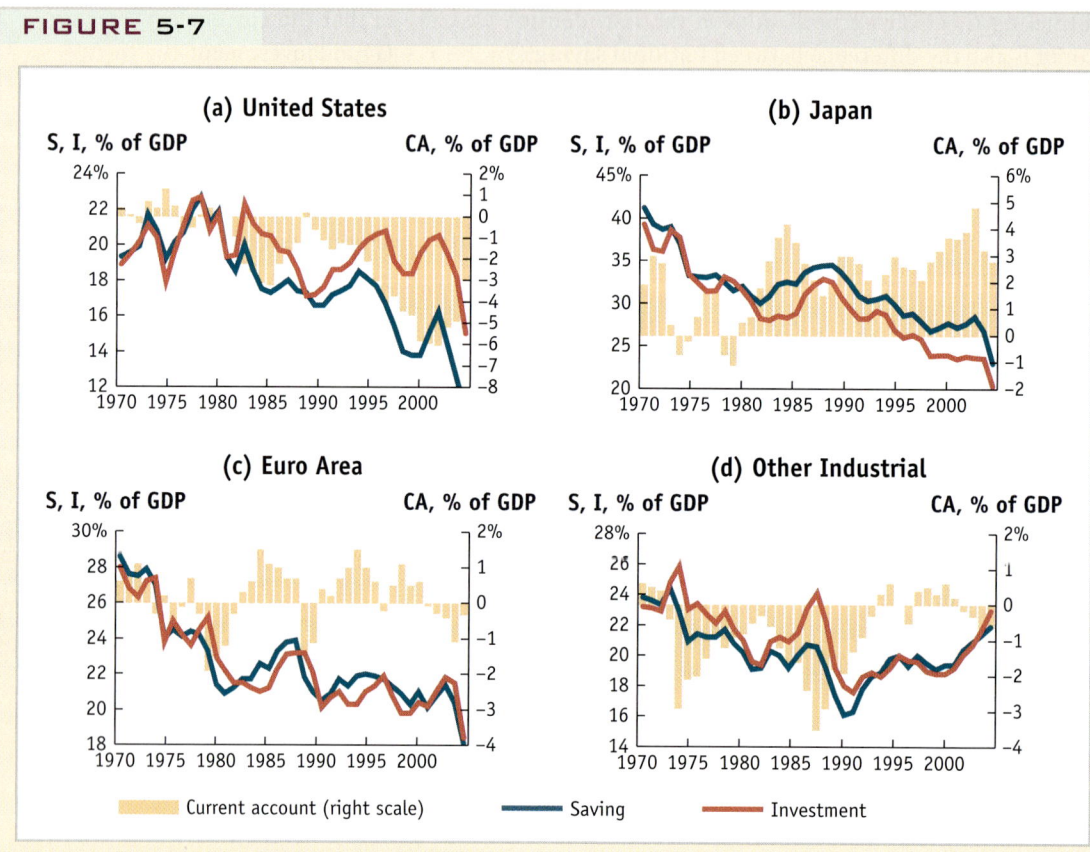

FIGURE 5-7

Saving, Investment, and Current Account Trends: Industrial Countries The charts show saving, investment, and the current account as a percent of each subregion's GDP for four groups of advanced countries. The United States has seen both saving and investment fall since 1980, but saving has fallen further than investment, opening up a large current account deficit approaching 6% of GDP in recent years. Japan's experience is the opposite: investment fell further than saving, opening up a large current account surplus of about 3% to 5% of GDP. The Euro area has also seen saving and investment fall but has been closer to balance overall. Other advanced countries (e.g., non-Euro area EU countries, Canada, Australia, etc.) have tended to run large current account deficits which have recently moved toward balance.

Source: IMF, World Economic Outlook, September 2005, and updates.

moved sharply into deficit, a trend that was only briefly arrested in the early 1990s. By 2003–2005 the U.S. current account was at a record deficit level close to –6% of U.S. GDP. In Japan, saving fell less than investment, so the opposite happened: a very big current account surplus opened up in the 1980s and 1990s, and it is currently near 4% of Japanese GDP. In the other industrial regions, saving and investment did not diverge so much, so the current account has recently remained closer to balance.

To uncover the sources of the trends in total saving, Figure 5-8 examines two of its components, public and private saving. We define **private saving** as that part of *after-tax* private sector disposable income that is *not* devoted to private consumption C. After-tax private sector disposable income, in turn, is defined as national income Y minus the net taxes T paid by households to the government. Hence, private saving S_p is

$$S_p = Y - T - C \qquad (5\text{-}7)$$

FIGURE 5-8

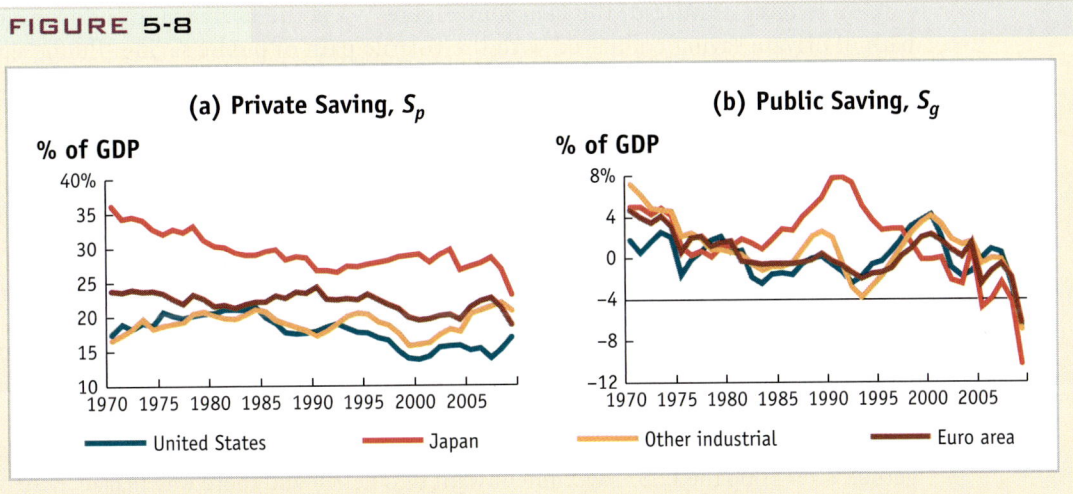

Private and Public Saving Trends: Industrial Countries The chart on the left shows private saving and the chart on the right public saving, both as a percent of GDP. Private saving has been declining in the industrial countries, especially in Japan (since the 1970s) and in the United States (since the 1980s). Private saving has been more stable in the Euro area and other countries. Public saving is clearly more volatile than private saving. Japan has been mostly in surplus and massively so in the late 1980s and early 1990s. The United States briefly ran a government surplus in the late 1990s but has now returned to a deficit position.

Source: IMF, World Economic Outlook, September 2005, and updates.

Private saving can be a positive number, but if the private sector consumption exceeds after-tax disposable income, then private saving will be negative. (Here, the private sector includes households and private firms, which are ultimately owned by households.)

Similarly, we define **government saving** or **public saving** as the difference between tax revenue T received by the government and government purchases G.[7] Hence, public saving S_g equals

$$S_g = T - G \tag{5-8}$$

Government saving is positive when tax revenue exceeds government consumption ($T > G$) and the government runs a *budget surplus*. If the government runs a *budget deficit*, however, government consumption exceeds tax revenue ($G > T$), and public saving is negative.

If we add these last two equations, we see that private saving plus government saving equals total national saving, since

$$S = Y - C - G = \underbrace{(Y - T - C)}_{\text{Private saving}} + \underbrace{(T - G)}_{\text{Government saving}} = S_p + S_g \tag{5-9}$$

In this last equation, taxes cancel out and do not affect saving in the aggregate because they are simply a transfer from the private sector to the public sector.

---

[7] Here, the government includes all levels of government: national/federal, state/regional, local/municipal, and so on.

One striking feature of the charts in Figure 5-8 is the fairly smooth downward path of private saving compared with the volatile path of public saving. Public saving is government tax revenue minus spending, and it fluctuates greatly as economic conditions change. We see that over the years private saving (by firms and households) has dropped the most in Japan, with a smaller drop seen in the United States. In other countries, the trend has been a little steadier. As for public saving, the most noticeable feature is the very large surpluses run up in Japan in the boom of the 1980s and early 1990s that subsequently disappeared during the long slump in the mid- to late 1990s and early 2000s. In other regions, surpluses in the 1970s soon gave way to deficits in the 1980s, and despite occasional improvements in the fiscal balance (as in the late 1990s), deficits have been the norm in the public sector. The United States witnessed a particularly sharp move from surplus to deficit after the year 2000.

Do government deficits cause current account deficits? Sometimes they do go together: after 2000 the U.S. government went into deficit and there was a large increase in the current account deficit as seen in Figure 5-7. But these "twin deficits" are not inextricably linked, as is sometimes believed. We can use the equation just given and the current account identity to write

$$CA = S_p + S_g - I \tag{5-10}$$

Now suppose the government lowers your taxes by $100 this year and borrows to finance the resulting deficit but also says you will be taxed by an extra $100 plus interest next year to pay off the debt. The theory of *Ricardian equivalence* asserts that you and other households will save the tax cut to pay next year's tax increase, so a fall in public saving is fully offset by a contemporaneous rise in private saving—and in the last equation the current account is *unchanged*. However, empirical studies do not support this theory: private saving does not fully offset government saving in practice.[8]

How large is the effect of a government deficit on the current account deficit? Research suggests that a change of 1% of GDP in the government deficit (or surplus) coincides with a 0.2% to 0.4% of GDP change in the current account deficit (or surplus), a result consistent with a partial Ricardian offset.

A second reason why the current account might move independently of saving (public or private) is that there may be a contemporaneous change in the level of investment in the last equation. A comparison of Figures 5-7 and 5-8 shows this effect at work. For example, we can see from Figure 5-7 that the large U.S. current account deficits of the early to mid-1990s were driven by an investment boom, even as total saving rose slightly, driven by an increase in public saving seen in Figure 5-8. Here there was no correlation between government deficit (falling) and current account deficit (rising).

Finally, Figure 5-9 shows global trends in saving, investment, and the current account for industrial countries, developing countries that are most financially integrated into the world economy (emerging markets and oil exporters), and all countries. The large weight of the U.S. economy means that in aggregate, the industrial countries have shifted into current account deficit over this period, a trend that has been offset by a shift toward surplus in the developing countries. The industrialized

---

[8] Menzie D. Chinn and Hiro Ito, 2007, "Current Account Balances, Financial Development and Institutions: Assaying the World 'Saving Glut,'" *Journal of International Money and Finance*, 26(4): 546–569.

FIGURE 5-9

Global Imbalances The charts show saving (blue), investment (red), and the current account (yellow) as a percent of GDP. In the 1990s, emerging markets moved into current account surplus and this financed the overall trend toward current account deficit of the industrial countries. For the world as a whole since the 1970s, global investment and saving rates have declined as a percent of GDP, falling from a high of near 26% to lows near 20%. Notes: Oil producers include Norway.

Source: IMF, *World Economic Outlook*, September 2005, and updates.

countries all followed a trend of declining investment and saving ratios, but the developing countries saw the opposite trend: rising investment and saving ratios. For the developing countries, however, the saving increase was larger than the investment increase, allowing a current account surplus to open up. For the world as a whole, however, the industrial country trend dominates—because the GDP weight of those countries is still so large. Globally, saving and investment ratios have fallen in the past 30 years. ■

3 The Balance of Payments

In the previous section, we saw that the current account summarizes the flow of all international market transactions in goods, services, and factor services plus nonmarket transfers. In this section, we look at what's left: international transactions in assets. These transactions are of great importance because they tell us how the current account is financed and, hence, whether a country is becoming more or less indebted to the rest of the world. We begin by looking at how transactions in assets are accounted for, once again building on the intuition developed in Figure 5-2.[9]

Accounting for Asset Transactions: the Financial Account

The financial account (FA) records transactions between residents and nonresidents that involve financial assets. The total value of financial assets that are received by the rest of the world from the home country is the home country's *export of assets*, denoted EX_A (the subscript "A" stands for asset). The total value of financial assets that are received by the home country from the rest of the world in all transactions is the home country's *import of assets*, denoted IM_A.

The financial account measures all "movement" of financial assets across the international border. By this, we mean a movement from home to foreign ownership, or vice versa, even if the assets do not physically move. This definition also covers all types of assets: real assets such as land or structures, and financial assets such as debt (bonds, loans) or equity. The financial account also includes assets issued by any entity (firms, governments, households) in any country (home or overseas). Finally, the financial account includes market transactions as well as transfers, or gifts of assets.

Subtracting asset imports from asset exports yields the home country's net overall balance on asset transactions, which is known as the financial account, where $FA = EX_A - IM_A$. A negative FA means that the country has imported more assets than it has exported; a positive FA means the country has exported more assets than it has imported. The financial account therefore measures how the country accumulates or decumulates assets through international transactions.

Accounting for Asset Transactions: the Capital Account

The capital account (KA) covers two remaining areas of asset movement of minor quantitative significance. One is the acquisition and disposal of nonfinancial, nonproduced assets (e.g., patents, copyrights, trademarks, franchises, etc.). They have to be included here because such nonfinancial assets do not appear in the financial account, although like financial assets, they can be bought and sold with resulting payments flows. The other important item in the capital account is capital transfers (i.e., gifts of assets), an example of which is the forgiveness of debts.[10]

---

[9] Officially, following the 1993 revision to the System of National Accounts by the U.N. Statistical Office, the place where international transactions are recorded should be called "rest of the world account" or the "external transactions account." The United States calls it the "international transactions account." However, the older terminology was the "balance of payments account," and this usage persists, so we adopt it here.

[10] The capital account does *not* include involuntary debt cancellation, such as results from unilateral defaults. Changes in assets and liabilities due to defaults are counted as capital losses, or valuation effects, which are discussed later in this chapter.

As with unilateral income transfers, capital transfers must be accounted for properly. For example, the giver of an asset must deduct the value of the gift in the capital account to offset the export of the asset, which is recorded in the financial account, because in the case of a gift the export generates no associated payment. Similarly, recipients of capital transfers need to record them to offset the import of the asset recorded in the financial account.

Using similar notation to that employed with unilateral transfers of income, we denote capital transfers received by the home country as KA_{IN} and capital transfers given by the home country as KA_{OUT}. The capital account, $KA = KA_{IN} - KA_{OUT}$, denotes net capital transfers received. A negative KA indicates that more capital transfers were given by the home country than it received; positive KA indicates that the home country received more capital transfers than it made.

The capital account is a minor and technical accounting item for most developed countries. In some developing countries, however, the capital account can play an important role because in some years nonmarket debt forgiveness can be large, whereas market-based international financial transactions may be small.

Accounting for Home and Foreign Assets

Asset trades in the financial account can be broken down into two types: assets issued by home entities (home assets) and assets issued by foreign entities (foreign assets). This is of economic interest, and sometimes of political interest too, because the breakdown makes clear the distinction between the location of the asset issuer and the location of the asset owner, that is, who owes what to whom.

From the home perspective, a foreign asset is a claim on a foreign country. When a home entity holds such an asset, it is called an **external asset** of the home country because it represents an obligation owed to the home country by the rest of the world. Conversely, from the home country's perspective, a home asset is a claim on the home country. When a foreign entity holds such an asset, it is called an **external liability** of the home country because it represents an obligation owed by the home country to the rest of the world. For example, when a U.S. firm invests overseas and acquires a computer factory located in Ireland, the acquisition is an external asset for the United States (and an external liability for Ireland). When a Japanese firm acquires an automobile plant in the United States, the acquisition is an external liability for the United States (and an external asset for Japan). A moment's thought reveals that all other assets traded across borders have a nation in which they are located and a nation by which they are owned—this is true for bank accounts, equities, government debt, corporate bonds, and so on. (For some examples, see the **Side Bar: Double-Entry Bookkeeping in the Balance of Payments.**)

If we use superscripts "H" and "F" to denote home and foreign assets, we can break down the financial account as the sum of the net exports of each type of asset:

$$FA = \underbrace{(EX_A^H - IM_A^H)}_{\substack{\text{Net export of} \\ \text{home assets}}} + \underbrace{(EX_A^F - IM_A^F)}_{\substack{\text{Net export of} \\ \text{foreign assets}}} = \underbrace{(EX_A^H - IM_A^H)}_{\substack{\text{Net export of} \\ \text{home assets} \\ = \\ \text{Net additions to} \\ \text{external liabilities}}} - \underbrace{(IM_A^F - EX_A^F)}_{\substack{\text{Net import of} \\ \text{foreign assets} \\ = \\ \text{Net additions to} \\ \text{external assets}}} \quad (5\text{-}11)$$

In the last part of this formula, we use the fact that net imports of foreign assets are just *minus* net exports of foreign assets, allowing us to change the sign. This reveals to us that FA equals *the additions to external liabilities* (the home-owned assets moving into foreign ownership, net) *minus the additions to external assets* (the foreign-owned assets moving into home ownership, net). This is our first indication of how flows of assets have implications for changes in a nation's wealth, a topic to which we return shortly.

How the Balance of Payments Accounts Work: A Macroeconomic View

To make further progress in our quest to understand the links between flows of goods, services, income, and assets, we have to understand how the current account, capital account, and financial account are related and why, in the end, the balance of payments accounts must, indeed, balance as suggested by the workings of the open-economy circular flow in Figure 5-2.

Recall from Equation (5-4) that gross national disposable income is

$$Y = GNDI = GNE + TB + NFIA + NUT = \underbrace{GNE + CA}_{\text{Resources available to home country from income}}$$

Does this expression represent all of the resources that are available to the home economy to finance expenditure? No. It represents only the income resources, the resources obtained from the market sale and purchase of good, services, and factor services and nonmarket transfers. In addition, the home economy can free up (or use up) resources in another way: by engaging in net sales (or purchases) of assets. We can calculate these extra resources using our previous definitions:

$$[\underbrace{EX_A}_{\substack{\text{Value of}\\\text{all assets}\\\text{exported}}} - \underbrace{KA_{OUT}}_{\substack{\text{Value of}\\\text{all assets}\\\text{exported}\\\text{as gifts}}}] - [\underbrace{IM_A}_{\substack{\text{Value of}\\\text{all assets}\\\text{imported}}} - \underbrace{KA_{IN}}_{\substack{\text{Value of}\\\text{all assets}\\\text{imported}\\\text{as gifts}}}] = EX_A - IM_A + KA_{IN} - KA_{OUT} = \underbrace{FA + KA}_{\substack{\text{Extra resources}\\\text{available to the}\\\text{home country due}\\\text{to asset trades}}}$$

$$\underbrace{}_{\substack{\text{Value of all assets}\\\text{exported via sales}}} \underbrace{}_{\substack{\text{Value of all assets}\\\text{imported via purchases}}}$$

Adding the last two expressions, we arrive at the value of the total resources available to the home country for expenditure purposes. This total value must equal the total value of home expenditure on final goods and services, GNE:

$$\underbrace{GNE + CA}_{\substack{\text{Resources available}\\\text{to home country}\\\text{due to income}}} + \underbrace{FA + KA}_{\substack{\text{Extra resources available}\\\text{to the home country}\\\text{due to asset trades}}} = GNE$$

We can cancel GNE from both sides of this expression to obtain the important result known as the balance of payments identity or **BOP identity**:

$$\underbrace{CA}_{\text{Current account}} + \underbrace{KA}_{\text{Capital account}} + \underbrace{FA}_{\text{Financial account}} = 0 \qquad (5\text{-}12)$$

The balance of payments sums to zero: it does balance!

How the Balance of Payments Accounts Work: A Microeconomic View

We have just found that at the macroeconomic level, $CA + KA + FA = 0$, a very simple equation that summarizes, in three variables, every single one of the millions of international transactions a nation engages in. This is one way to look at the BOP accounts.

Another way to look at the BOP is to look behind these three variables to the specific flows we saw in Figure 5-2, and the individual transactions within each flow.

$$CA = (EX - IM) + (EX_{FS} - IM_{FS}) + (UT_{IN} - UT_{OUT})$$
$$KA = (KA_{IN} - KA_{OUT}) \qquad (5\text{-}13)$$
$$FA = (EX_A^H - IM_A^H) + (EX_A^F - IM_A^F)$$

Written this way, the components of the BOP identity allow us to see the details behind why the accounts must balance. As you can observe from these equations, there are 12 transaction types (each preceded by either a plus or minus sign) and 3 accounts (CA, KA, FA) in which they can appear.

If an item has a plus sign, it is called a balance of payments credit or **BOP credit.** Six types of transactions receive a plus (+) sign as follows:

Current account (CA):	Exports of goods and services (+EX);
	Exports of factor services (+EX_{FS});
	Unilateral transfers received (+UT_{IN}).
Capital account (KA):	Capital transfers received (+KA_{IN}).
Financial account (FA):	Exports of home and foreign assets (+EX_A^H, +EX_A^F).

If an item has a minus sign, it is called a balance of payments debit or **BOP debit.** Six types of transactions receive a minus (−) sign as follows:

Current account (CA):	Imports of goods and services (−IM);
	Imports of factor services (−IM_{FS});
	Unilateral transfers given (−UT_{OUT}).
Capital account (KA):	Capital transfers given (−KA_{OUT}).
Financial account (FA):	Imports of home and foreign assets (−IM_A^H, −IM_A^F).

Now, to see why the BOP accounts balance in aggregate, we have to understand one simple principle: *every market transaction (whether for goods, services, factor services, or assets) has two parts. If party A engages in a transaction with a counterparty B, then A receives from B an item of a given value, and in return B receives from A an item of equal value.*[11]

Thus, whenever a transaction generates a credit somewhere in the BOP account, it must also generate a corresponding debit somewhere else in the BOP account. Similarly, every debit generates a corresponding credit. It might not be obvious where the offsetting item is, but it must exist somewhere *if* the accounts have been measured properly. Of course, this is a big if, and we will see the consequences of mismeasurement shortly. (For more detail on this topic, see **Side Bar: Double-Entry Bookkeeping in the Balance of Payments.**)

---

[11] This principle applies not only to market transactions, but also to nonmarket transactions such as gifts and foreign aid that enter into the BOP accounts as "net unilateral transfers" or in the capital account. For example, a $100 export of food aid is not a market transaction, but appears as a credit item in total exports. This credit is offset in the BOP accounts by a −$100 debit in net unilateral transfers. In this way, nonmarket gifts, for which nothing is offered in return, are properly recorded and yet leave the BOP accounts in balance.

SIDE BAR

The Double-Entry Principle in the Balance of Payments

We can make the double-entry principle more concrete by looking at some (mostly) hypothetical international transactions and figuring out how they would be recorded in the U.S. BOP accounts.

1. Recall from Chapter 2 that our friend George was in Paris in 2003. Suppose he spent $110 (€100) on French wine one evening. This is a U.S. import of a foreign service. George pays with his American Express card. The bar is owed $110 (or €100) by American Express (and Amex is owed by George). The United States has exported an asset to France: the bar now has a claim against American Express. From the U.S. perspective, this represents an increase in U.S. assets owned by foreigners. The double entries in the U.S. BOP appear in the current account and the financial account:

CA: Drinks in Paris bar	$-IM$	$-\$110$
FA: Bar's claim on AMEX	$+EX_A^H$	$+\$110$

2. George was in the bar to meet his Danish cousin Georg. They both work as wine merchants. After a few bottles of Bordeaux, George enthuses about Arkansas chardonnay and insists Georg give it a try. Georg counters by telling George he should really try some Jutland rosé. Each cousin returns home and asks his firm to ship a case of each wine (worth $36) to the other. This barter transaction (involving no financial activity) would appear solely as two entries in the U.S. current account:

CA: Arkansas wine exported to Denmark	EX	$+\$36$
CA: Jutland wine imported to United States	$-IM$	$-\$36$

3. Later that night, George met a French entrepreneur in a smoky corner of the bar. George vaguely remembers the story: the entrepreneur's French tech company was poised for unbelievable success with an upcoming share issue. George decides to invest $10,000 to buy the French stock; he imports a French asset. The stock is sold to him through the French bank BNP, and George sends them a U.S. dollar check. BNP then has a claim against Citibank, an export of a home asset to France. Both entries fall within the financial account:

FA: George's French tech stocks	$-IM_A^F$	$-\$10,000$
FA: BNP claim against Citibank	$+EX_A^H$	$+\$10,000$

4. Rather surprisingly, George's French stocks do quite well. By December 2003 they have doubled in value. George makes a $5,000 donation to charity. His charity purchases U.S. relief supplies that will be exported to Bam, Iran, following a devastating earthquake in that city. The two entries here are entirely in the U.S. current account. The supplies are a nonmarket export of goods offset by the value of the unilateral transfer:

CA: Relief supplies exported to Bam	EX	$+\$5,000$
CA: George's charitable gift	$-UT_{OUT}$	$-\$5,000$

5. George was also pleased to see that some poor countries were benefiting from another kind of foreign assistance, debt forgiveness. In June 2003 the U.S. secretary of state announced that the United States would forgive $1 billion of debt owed by the government of Pakistan. This would decrease U.S.-owned assets overseas. The United States was exporting Pakistani assets: it hands the canceled debts back to Pakistan, a credit in the financial account. The double entries would be seen in the capital and financial accounts:

KA: U.S. grant of debt relief	$-KA_{OUT}$	$-\$1,000,000,000$
FA: Decline in U.S. external assets	$-EX_A^F$	$+\$1,000,000,000$

Understanding the Data for the Balance of Payments Account

To illustrate all the principles we've learned, let's look at the United States' balance of payments account. Table 5-2 shows an extract of the U.S. BOP accounts for 2009.[12]

---

[12] The BOP account is published each year as the "international transactions account (ITA)" by the BEA. The ITA uses a different definition of the United States territory than the national income and product accounts (NIPA), so these figures do not exactly match those in Table 5-1.

TABLE 5-2

The U.S. Balance of Payments in 2009 The table shows U.S. international transactions in 2009 in billions of dollars. Major categories are in bold type.

Major Account	Line	Category or Subcategory	Symbol	$ billions
Current Account	1	**Exports of goods and services**	$+EX$	**$1,571**
	1a	Of which: Goods		1,068
	1b	Services		502
	2	**Income receipts [= exports of factor services]**	$+EX_{FS}$	**588**
	3	**Imports of goods and services (−)**	$-IM$	**−1,946**
	3a	Of which: Goods (−)		−1,575
	3b	Services (−)		−370
	4	**Income payments [= imports of factor services] (−)**	$-IM_{FS}$	**−467**
	5	**Net unilateral transfers**	NUT	**−125**
Capital and Financial Account	6	**Capital account net**	KA	**0**
	7	**U.S.-owned assets abroad net increase (−)**		**−140**
		[= net imports of ROW assets or financial outflow (−)]		
	7a	Of which: U.S. official reserve assets		−52
	7b	Other assets		−88
	8	**Foreign-owned assets in U.S. net increase (+)**		**306**
		[= net exports of U.S. assets or financial inflow (+)]		
	8a	Of which: Foreign official assets		450
	8b	Other assets		−144
Statistical Discrepancy	9	**Statistical discrepancy (sum of 1 to 8, sign reversed)**	SD	**213**
Summary Items		**Balance on current account** (lines 1, 2, 3, 4, and 5)	CA	**−378**
		Of which: Balance on goods and services (lines 1 and 3)	TB	−375
		Balance on income (lines 2 and 4)	NFIA	121
		Balance on financial account (lines 7 and 8)	FA	**165**
		Of which: Official settlements balance (lines 7a and 8a)		398
		Nonreserve financial account (lines 7b and 8b)		−233

Notes: Details may not add to totals because of rounding. The statistical discrepancy shown here includes financial derivatives.

Source: U.S. Bureau of Economic Analysis, ITA Table 1, using the ITA definition of the United States. This includes U.S. territories, so these figures are slightly different from those in Table 5-1.

In the current account, in the top part of the table, we look first at the trade in goods and services on lines 1 and 3. Overall exports, EX, were +$1,571 billion (line 1, a credit), and imports, IM, were −$1,946 billion (line 3, a debit). In the summary items, we see the balance on goods and services, the trade balance, TB, was −$375 billion (line 1 plus line 3, or exports minus imports). Exports and imports and the trade balance are also broken down even further into goods and service components (lines 1ab and 3ab).

The next part of the current account on lines 2 and 4 deals with trade in factor services, also known as the *income account* (referring to the income paid to those factors). Income receipts for factor service exports, EX_{FS}, generated a credit of +$588 billion and income payments for factor service imports, IM_{FS}, generated a debit of −$467 billion.

Adding these two items resulted in net factor income from abroad NFIA equal to +$121 billion (line 2 plus line 4), a net credit.

Lastly, we see that net unilateral transfers, NUT, were −$125 billion, a net debit (line 5); the United States was a net donor as measured by the net transfer of goods, services, and income to the rest of the world. (Typically, in summary tables like these, unilateral transfers are shown only in net form.)

Overall, summing lines 1 through 5, the 2009 U.S. current account balance, CA, was −$378 billion, that is, a deficit of $378 billion, as shown in the summary items at the foot of the table.

A country that has a current account surplus is called a **(net) lender.** By the BOP identity, we know that it must have a deficit in its asset accounts, so like any lender, it is, on net, buying assets (acquiring IOUs from borrowers). For example, China is a large net lender. A country that has a current account deficit is called a **(net) borrower.** By the BOP identity, we know that it must have a surplus in its asset accounts, so like any borrower, it is, on net, selling assets (issuing IOUs to lenders). As we can see, the United States is a large net borrower.

Now we move to the capital and financial accounts. Typically, in summary tables like these, the capital account is shown only in net form. The United States in 2009 had a negligible capital account, KA, of less than $0.5 billion, reported as zero (line 6).

Lastly, we move to the financial account. As explained, this account can be broken down in terms of the exports and imports of two kinds of assets: U.S. assets (U.S. external liabilities) and rest of the world assets (U.S. external assets). In this summary the net trades are shown for each kind of asset.

We see that the United States was engaged in the net import of foreign assets, so that external assets (U.S.-owned assets abroad) increased by $140 billion. This net import of foreign assets is recorded as a debit of −$140 billion (line 7). Note that the minus sign maintains the convention that imports are debits.

At the same time, the United States was engaged in the net export of U.S. assets to the rest of the world so that external liabilities (foreign-owned assets in the United States) increased by $306 billion; the net export of U.S. assets is duly recorded as a credit of +$306 billion (line 8).

The sum of lines 7 and 8 gives the financial account balance, FA, of +$165 billion, recorded in the summary items.

For further information on interventions by central banks, financial account transactions are often also broken down into reserve and nonreserve components. Changes in reserves arise from official intervention in the forex market—that is, purchases and sales by home and foreign monetary authorities. The balance on all reserve transactions is called the *official settlements balance*, and the balance on all other asset trades is called the *nonreserve financial account*. We see here that U.S. authorities intervened a little: a net import of $52 billion of U.S. official reserves (line 7a) means that the Federal Reserve bought $52 billion in foreign (i.e., nondollar) exchange reserves from foreigners. In contrast, foreign central banks intervened a lot: U.S. entities sold them $450 billion in U.S. dollar reserve assets (line 8a).

Adding up the current account, the capital account, and the financial account (lines 1 through 8), we find that the total of the three accounts was −$213 billion (−$378 + $0 + $165 = −$213). The BOP accounts are supposed to balance by adding to zero—in reality, they never do. Why not? Because the statistical agencies tasked with gathering BOP data find it impossible to track every single international transaction correctly, due to measurement errors and omissions. Some problems result from the smuggling of goods or trade tax evasion. Larger errors are likely due to the mismeasured, concealed, or illicit movement of financial income flows and assets movements (e.g., money laundering and capital tax evasion).

The Statistical Discrepancy To "account" for this error, statistical agencies create an accounting item, the *statistical discrepancy* (SD) equal to minus the error $SD = -(CA + KA + FA)$. With that "correction," the amended version of the BOP identity will hold true in practice, sweeping away the real-world measurement problems. In the table, the statistical discrepancy is shown on line 9.[13] Once the statistical discrepancy is included, the balance of payments accounts always balance.

Some Recent Trends in the U.S. Balance of Payments Figure 5-10 shows recent trends in various components of the U.S. balance of payments. The sharp downward trend

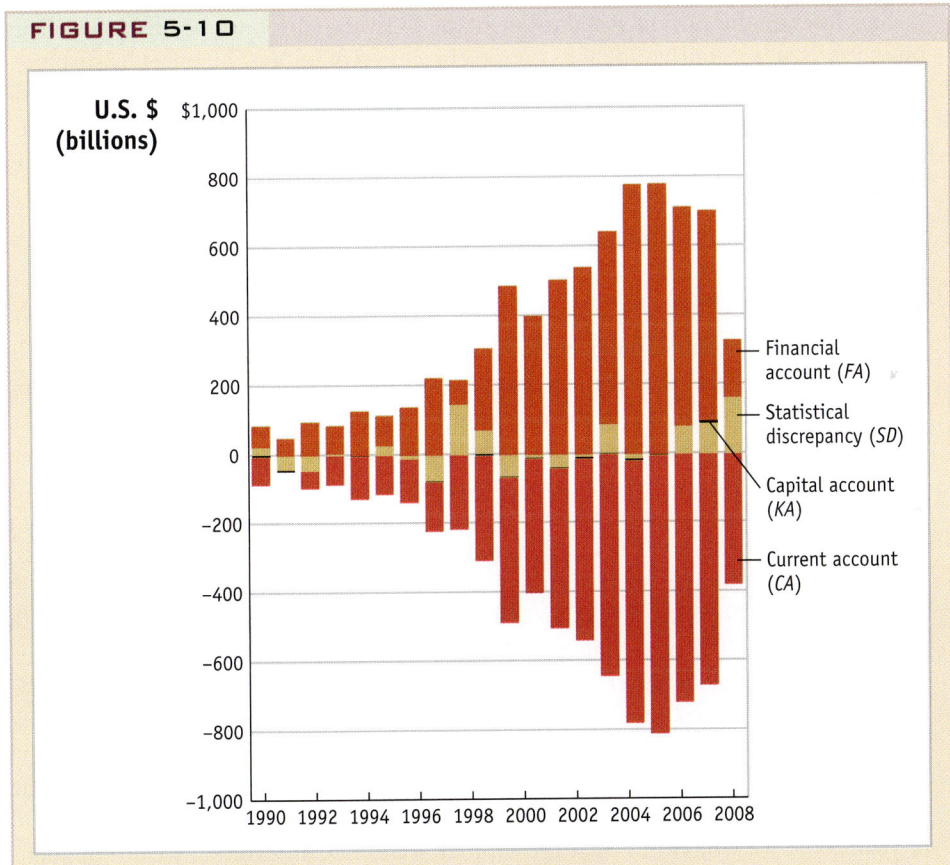

FIGURE 5-10

U.S. Balance of Payments and Its Components, 1990–2009 The figure shows the current account balance (CA), the capital account balance (KA, barely visible), the financial account balance (FA), and the statistical discrepancy (SD), in billions of dollars.

Source: U.S. Bureau of Economic Analysis, using the ITA definition of the United States, which includes U.S. territories.

---

[13] Prior to 2007, the U.S. statistical discrepancy included unmeasured financial derivatives transactions. Starting in 2007, the BEA estimates these transactions, but they are not as yet broken down in detail into home and foreign assets. For clarity, they are not reported here and are included in the statistical discrepancy in Table 5-2.

of the current account is as previously shown in Figure 5-6, so for the balance of payments identity to hold, there must be an offsetting upward trend in other parts of the BOP accounts. This is indeed the case. We can see that the United States has been financing its growing deficit on the current account primarily by running an expanding surplus on the financial account. In the mid-1990s, there was close to a $100 billion current account deficit and a comparable financial account surplus. A decade later, both figures were in the region of $800 billion, with a substantial decline only after the global financial crisis.

What the Balance of Payments Account Tells Us

The balance of payments accounts consist of the current account, which measures external imbalances in goods, services, factor services, and unilateral transfers. The financial and capital accounts measure asset trades. Using the principle that market transactions must consist of a trade of two items of equal value, we find that the balance of payments accounts really do balance.

Surpluses on the current account side of the BOP accounts must be offset by deficits on the asset side. Similarly, deficits on the current account must be offset by surpluses on the asset side. By telling us how current account imbalances are financed, the balance of payments makes the connection between a country's income and spending decisions and the evolution of that country's wealth, an important connection we develop further in the final section of this chapter.

4 External Wealth

The measurement of a nation's income flow is not the only important economic variable that must be adapted to the open-economy environment. Economists and policy makers, and the general public, also care about a nation's stock of *wealth*. And so, probably, do you.

For example, Anne has income and expenditures of $50,000 each year and savings in the bank of $10,000. But she also has a credit card debt of $20,000. Beth's life is identical to Anne's in almost every respect: she has income and expenditures of $50,000 each year and savings of $10,000, but she has no credit card debt. Who is better off? Clearly, Beth is. Her income is the same as Anne's. But Anne's wealth or "net worth" is −$10,000 (savings of $10,000 minus debt of $20,000), whereas Beth has a net worth of +$10,000. Anne's wealth is −20% of her income; Beth's wealth is +20% of her income.

Just as a household is better off with higher wealth, all else equal, so is a country. We can calculate a home country's "net worth" or **external wealth** with respect to the rest of the world (ROW) by adding up all of the home assets owned by ROW (foreigners' claims against home) and then subtracting all of the ROW assets owned by the home country (home claims against foreigners). Doing this for the United States at the end of year 2009, we would find that the United States had an external wealth of about −$2,866 billion. This made the United States the world's biggest debtor in history at the time of this writing. The United States' net debt to the rest of the world was about $9,300 for every American. Because GDP per person in the United States was about $46,400 in 2009, the external wealth of the U.S. was about −20% of GDP.

Why is U.S. external wealth at this level? How did it get there and what will happen next? To understand how the wealth levels of countries evolve, in this final section of the chapter we build on what we have learned from the national income and balance of payments accounts.

The Level of External Wealth

First, we give a definition of the level of a country's external wealth (W):

$$\underbrace{\text{External wealth}}_{W} = \underbrace{\begin{bmatrix} \text{ROW assets} \\ \text{owned by home} \end{bmatrix}}_{A} - \underbrace{\begin{bmatrix} \text{Home assets} \\ \text{owned by ROW} \end{bmatrix}}_{L} \quad (5\text{-}14)$$

External wealth equals the value of total external assets (A) minus the value of total external liabilities (L). The former is what is owed to the home country by the rest of the world, and the latter is what is owed to the rest of the world by the home country. A country's level of external wealth is also called its *net international investment position* or *net foreign assets*. It is a stock measure, not a flow measure.

If $W > 0$, home is a **net creditor** *country: external assets exceed external liabilities.*

If $W < 0$, home is a **net debtor** *country: external liabilities exceed external assets.*

External wealth is only one part of a nation's total wealth. The other part of a nation's wealth is internal wealth, which corresponds to the total value of all nonfinancial assets in the home country. (The links between external wealth and total wealth are explored further in the appendix to this chapter.)

Because we are focusing on international economic relationships, our main emphasis is on external wealth because it measures the outstanding obligations of one country to another. Those obligations, and when and how they are paid, can be the source of great economic and political stress. Moreover, the net debts of nations, like those of individuals, ultimately carry a cost. To understand external wealth, let's look at how it is measured and how it evolves.

Changes in External Wealth

There are two reasons a country's level of external wealth changes over time.

1. *Financial flows:* As a result of asset trades, the country can increase or decrease its external assets and liabilities. How? Net exports of foreign assets cause an equal decrease in the level of external assets and hence a corresponding decrease in external wealth. Net exports of home assets cause an equal increase in the level of external liabilities and hence a corresponding decrease in external wealth. For example, if net exports of assets (whether home or foreign) are +$1 billion, then the change in external wealth is –$1 billion. The net export of assets of all kinds is measured by the financial account (FA), and this has a *negative* effect on external wealth in any period.

2. *Valuation effects:* The value of existing external assets and liabilities may change over time because of capital gains or losses. In the case of external wealth, this change in value could be due to price effects or exchange rate effects. For example, suppose, a U.S. citizen buys 100 shares of BP on the London Stock Exchange at £7 each. Suppose the exchange rate is $1.8 per pound. These U.S. external assets are worth $12.60 each (1.8 times 7), for a total of $1,260. Suppose the price of these shares then falls to £6, and the exchange rate stays the same. Each share is now worth $10.80 (1.8 times 6) and the 100 shares are valued at $1,080. Their value has fallen in dollar terms by $180 (£1 times 1.8 times 100), which is a capital loss. This is an example of a price effect. Now suppose the exchange rate rises to $2 per pound. Each share is still worth £6 in

U.K. currency but $12 in U.S. currency (2 times 6), so the total value of the shares rises to $1,200, which, relative to the $1,080 they were previously worth, implies a capital gain of $120. This is an example of an exchange rate effect. Similar effects can change the value of external liabilities.

Adding up these two contributions to the change in external wealth (ΔW), we find

$$\underbrace{\begin{bmatrix} \text{Change in} \\ \text{external wealth} \end{bmatrix}}_{\Delta W} = -\underbrace{\begin{bmatrix} \text{Financial} \\ \text{account} \end{bmatrix}}_{\substack{\text{Net export of assets} \\ = \\ FA}} + \underbrace{\begin{bmatrix} \text{Capital gains on} \\ \text{external wealth} \end{bmatrix}}_{\substack{\text{Valuation effects} \\ = \\ \text{Capital gains} \\ \text{minus capital losses}}} \quad (5\text{-}15)$$

We gain a deeper understanding of this expression if we recall the BOP identity: the current account plus the capital account plus the financial account equals zero. Hence, minus the financial account equals the current account plus the capital account, or $-FA = CA + KA$. Substituting this identity into Equation (5-15), we obtain

$$\underbrace{\begin{bmatrix} \text{Change in} \\ \text{external wealth} \end{bmatrix}}_{\Delta W} = \underbrace{\begin{bmatrix} \text{Current} \\ \text{account} \end{bmatrix}}_{\substack{CA \\ = \\ \text{Unspent} \\ \text{income}}} + \underbrace{\begin{bmatrix} \text{Capital} \\ \text{account} \end{bmatrix}}_{\substack{KA \\ = \\ \text{Net capital} \\ \text{transfers received}}} + \underbrace{\begin{bmatrix} \text{Capital gains on} \\ \text{external wealth} \end{bmatrix}}_{\substack{\text{Valuation effects} \\ = \\ \text{Capital gains} \\ \text{minus capital losses}}} \quad (5\text{-}16)$$

This fundamental formula tells us that a country can increase its external wealth in one of only three ways:

- Through its own thrift (a CA surplus, so expenditure is less than income)
- By the charity of others (a KA surplus, by receiving net gifts of wealth)
- With the help of windfalls (having positive capital gains)

Similarly, a country can reduce its external wealth by doing any of the opposites.

Understanding the Data on External Wealth

To track external wealth accurately, statisticians apply Equation (5-15). They face the challenge of not only keeping tabs on every trade in assets but also correctly assessing the impact of changing financial market conditions around the world on the value of the country's external assets and liabilities.

Measures of levels and changes in national external wealth are tabulated in an account known as the net international investment position. To illustrate with an example, a simplified version of this account for the United States appears in Table 5-3. The data in the table show a clear distinction between the contribution of financial flows to changes in external wealth—net trade in assets, in column (a)—and the impact of various kinds of valuation effects—columns (b), (c), and (d).

Table 5-3, line 3, column (a), shows that in 2009 the United States, on net, exported $165 billion in assets (exports of $306 billion on line 2, minus imports of $140 billion on line 1). On their own, these financial flows would have reduced U.S. external wealth by $165 billion in just one year. Yet nothing of the sort happened because more-than-offsetting valuation effects of +$953 billion—columns (b), (c), and (d)—boosted U.S. external wealth over the same period. These valuation effects were mainly driven by +$523 billion in price change effects and $277 billion in exchange rate effects.

TABLE 5-3

U.S. External Wealth in 2008–2009 The table shows changes in the U.S. net international investment position during the year 2009 in billions of dollars. The net result in row 3 equals row 1 minus row 2.

Category	Position, end 2008 ($ billions)	Changes in Position during 2009 ($ billions)					Position, end 2009 ($ billions)
		Financial Flows (a)	Of Which Valuation Effects			Total (a + b + c + d)	
			Price Changes (b)	Exchange Rate Changes (c)	Other Changes (d)		
1. External Assets	$13,117	140	1,066	358	185	1,750	14,867
= U.S.-owned assets abroad, of which:							
U.S. official reserve assets	294	52	57	1	0	110	404
U.S. government assets, other	624	−541	—	0	0	−541	83
U.S. private assets	12,200	630	1,009	357	185	2,181	14,380
2. External Liabilities	16,771	306	534	81	32	962	17,733
= Foreign-owned assets in the United States, of which:							
Foreign official assets in the United States	3,940	450	−14	0	−3	434	4,374
Other foreign assets	12,831	−144	557	81	35	528	13,359
3. External Wealth							
= Line 1 minus Line 2	−3,654	−165	523	277	153	788	−2,866
= Net international investment position of the United States							
Symbol	W (end 2008)	−FA	Capital gains				W (end 2009)

Note: Financial derivatives are excluded.

Source: U.S. Bureau of Economic Analysis.

Thus, while the United States borrowed an additional $165 billion from various nations in 2009, its external wealth actually rose by $788 billion as shown on line 3. Talk about a free lunch.

So what happened in 2009? Two main factors were at work. First, equity values rose worldwide, as the global financial crisis abated. But U.S. external assets include a larger share of equities than U.S. external liabilities, which consist of a great deal of U.S. debt. This difference in the composition of the two portfolios means that rising equity markets boosted the values of U.S. external assets much more than U.S. external liabilities. Second, about 95% of U.S. external liabilities were denominated in U.S. dollars, including vast foreign holdings of U.S. Treasury bills, held either as foreign official assets in central banks or as low-risk assets by foreign investors. These assets tended to have a stable value in dollar terms and did not experience any exchange rate valuation effects because they are denominated in dollars. In contrast, about two-thirds of U.S. external assets (foreign direct investment, bank loans, government debt) are denominated in foreign currencies, such as the euro, that were appreciating against the dollar.[14]

Some Recent Trends Over the longer run, the changes in external wealth in Equation (5-16) gradually cumulate. In the case of the United States, for the past three decades, the financial account has been almost always in surplus, reflecting a net export of assets to the rest of the world to pay for chronic current account deficits (the capital account has been negligibly small).

If there were no valuation effects, then Equation (5-15) would make a simple prediction. The change in the level of external wealth between two dates should equal the cumulative net import of assets (minus the financial account) over the intervening period. For example, if we had taken the U.S. external wealth level at the end of 1988 and added to that level all subsequent financial flows until the end of 2009, we would have estimated U.S. external wealth in 2009 at –$6,741 billion. The actual 2009 figure was a lot smaller: –$2,738 billion.

Why? Valuation effects or capital gains generated the difference of $4,003 billion in external wealth over the period, and from 1988 to 2009 these effects reduced U.S. net external indebtedness in 2009 by more than half compared with the level that financial flows alone would have predicted. The flip side of these valuation effects is that the rest of the world outside the United States suffered an equal and opposite capital loss over the same period. Why? Capital gains always have a "zero sum" property—by symmetry, an increase in the dollar value of the home country's external assets is simultaneously an increase in the dollar value of the rest of the world's external liabilities.

What External Wealth Tells Us

External wealth data tell us the net credit or debit position of a country with respect to the rest of the world. They include data on external assets (foreign assets owned by the home country) and external liabilities (home assets owned by foreigners). A creditor country has positive external wealth, a debtor country negative external wealth.

What drives external wealth? The current account told us about the imbalances in a country's external flows of goods, services, factor services, and income. The balance of payments accounts told us how these imbalances require offsetting financial flows of assets between countries. Countries with a current account surplus (deficit) must be net buyers (sellers) of assets. This buying and selling of assets has implications for external wealth. An increase in a country's external wealth results from every net import of assets; conversely, a decrease in external wealth results from every net export of assets. In addition, countries can experience capital gains or losses on their external assets and liabilities that cause changes in external wealth. All of these changes are summarized in the statement of a country's net international investment position.

---

[14] Data on the currency composition of U.S. external wealth from Cedric Tille, 2005, "Financial Integration and the Wealth Effect of Exchange Rate Fluctuations," Staff Reports 226, Federal Reserve Bank of New York.

5 Conclusions

The science of macroeconomics would be impossible without data, and the vast majority of the data we employ emerge from the efforts of official statisticians around the world. Notwithstanding the inevitable statistical discrepancies, and even the occasional errors of omission and commission (see **Side Bar: Beware of Greeks Bearing Statistics**), we would be lost without these measures of macroeconomic activity.

This chapter has illustrated some important accounting concepts and has highlighted some unusual and intriguing features of the current international economic system. We have seen how a consistent system of national income and product accounts allow for the tracking of international trade flows (including trade in intermediate goods), cross-border factor income flows, and unilateral transfers. We have also seen how these net resource flows of goods and services can be matched against a parallel set of net payment activities involving assets in the balance of payments

SIDE BAR

Beware of Greeks Bearing Statistics

It is important, but rather sad, to note that when it comes to national statistics, one cannot believe everything one reads. Over the years numerous governments have been suspected of fiddling with their official data for various purposes, as indicated by the following examples:

- *Greece*. In 2001 Greece was allowed to join the Eurozone. One of the criteria it had to meet in order to join was that its budget deficit could not be over 3% of its GDP. Greece met this requirement according to its official statistics. In November 2004, after it had been allowed to join the Eurozone, Greece admitted its 2003 budget deficit was really 3.4%, twice as large as it had previously claimed. In fact, the budget deficit had not been below 3% since 1999. The EU was not amused. Greece continued to publish incorrect or manipulated data (including a 25% upward adjustment to GDP to take into account "black economy" activity such as prostitution). By inflating its GDP, Greece made its budget deficit position look better than it was, which may have allowed Greece to borrow from other countries on favorable terms. When the euro crisis hit in 2008–2009, the full horror of Greece's weak economic and fiscal position become clear, by which point the fiasco had forced other Eurozone nations to provide emergency funding and threatened the survival of the euro project itself.
- *Italy*. In 1987 Italy was considered much poorer than northern European countries. But its statisticians also decided to increase GDP by 15% after some guesswork to account for the black economy. Instantly, Italians had a higher official GDP per person than the British, an event known as *il sorpasso*. Not that this made any Italians actually feel richer.
- *Argentina*. After its 2001 crisis, a new populist government took over but faced problems with high and persistent inflation. To "solve" this problem, the government "reorganized" its official statistical bureau, which then started publishing much lower, and highly suspicious inflation data. Lower inflation also helped the government avoid larger costs of indexed benefits and allowed the government to claim it had solved the inflation problem. Few believed these published data were true.
- *China*. In the latest International Comparison Project by the World Bank, China's own estimate of its yuan price level came in much higher than had been expected. This had various implications: dividing nominal yuan income by the price level made China look quite a bit poorer. And higher prices made China's real exchange rate less undervalued, or even overvalued. Since poorer countries usually have lower price levels, both of these impacts had the effect of making China's exchange rate look more fairly valued, given its standard of living. This came about at a time when China was under considerable political pressure to appreciate its currency. But skeptics doubted whether the data were totally plausible, because the change in the yuan price level since the previous ICP was much larger than that implied by China's own official inflation data over the same period.

accounts. Finally, we have seen how the flow of trades in assets can be combined with capital gains and losses to track the evolution of a nation's stock of external wealth, an important part of its total wealth, as recorded in the statement of the net international investment position.

We presented a fuller exposition using as an example the United States' accounts of income, balance of payments, and external wealth. In the remainder of the book, we make extensive use of the concepts introduced in this chapter to develop theories that explore the global macroeconomic linkages between nations.

KEY POINTS

1. National flows of expenditure, product, income, and wealth, and international flows of goods, services, income, and assets, together measure important aspects of a country's economic performance and describe its economy's relationship to economies in rest of the world. The records kept in the national income and product accounts, the balance of payments account, and the net international investment position track these data.

2. The key measures of economic activity are:
   - Gross national expenditure (GNE) measures an economy's total spending on final goods and services. It is the sum of consumption, investment, and government consumption: GNE = $C + I + G$.
   - Gross domestic product (GDP) measures total production (value of all output minus value of all purchased inputs).
   - Gross national income (GNI) measures the total payments to an economy's domestic factors.
   - Gross national disposable income (GNDI, also denoted Y) measures an economy's disposable income including transfers.

   In a closed economy, GNE = GDP = GNI = GNDI.

3. In an open economy, GDP need not equal GNE. When nations can trade, the sum of goods and services demanded by domestic residents need not be the same as the sum of goods and services supplied by domestic firms. The difference between GDP and GNE is the trade balance TB: GDP = GNE + TB. The trade balance is the difference between a nation's imports and exports of goods and services.

4. In an open economy, GDP need not equal GNI because imports and exports of factor services (measured by net factor income from abroad or NFIA) imply that factor income received by domestic residents need not be the same as factor payments made by domestic firms. Thus, GNI = GDP + NFIA.

5. In an open economy, the true level of disposable income is best measured by gross national disposable income or Y = GNDI. GNDI need not equal GNI because net unilateral transfers (NUT) to foreigners may be positive, due to foreign aid and other nonmarket gifts. Thus, Y = GNDI = GNI + NUT.

6. The sum of all the aforementioned international transactions, TB + NFIA + NUT, is called the current account (CA).

7. From the relationships just outlined, we find that $Y = C + I + G + CA$. This expression is known as the *national income identity*.

8. National saving S is defined as $Y - C - G$. From the national income identity, we can derive the current account identity: $S = I + CA$. The current account equals saving minus investment. Movements in investment or saving, all else equal, feed directly into the current account.

9. All international trades in goods and services and in assets are recorded in an account known as the balance of payments (BOP). As a result of double-entry bookkeeping, and allowing for gifts and transfers, the BOP must sum to zero.

10. The BOP contains the following:

    - Net exports of goods and services, TB, called the trade balance
    - Net exports of factor services, NFIA, called the net factor income from abroad
    - Net unilateral transfers received, NUT, called the net unilateral transfers
    - Net transfers of assets received, KA, called the capital account
    - Net exports of assets, FA, called the financial account

11. The first three items are the current account CA. Since the BOP accounts sum to zero, this implies the balance of payments identity: $CA + FA + KA = 0$.

12. External wealth is a measure of a country's credit or debt position versus the rest of the world. It equals external assets—rest of world (ROW) assets owned by home—minus external liabilities (home assets owned by ROW). The net export (import) of assets lowers (raises) a country's external wealth. External wealth is one part of a country's total wealth.

13. External wealth can change for one of two reasons: the export or import of assets (called financial flows) or changes in the value of existing assets due to capital gains or losses (called valuation effects). Both of these channels affect net external wealth.

KEY TERMS

national income and product accounts, p. 158
balance of payments accounts, p. 158
gross national expenditure (GNE), p. 158
gross domestic product (GDP), p. 158
gross national income (GNI), p. 159
trade balance (TB), p. 160
net factor income from abroad (NFIA), p. 160
net unilateral transfers (NUT), p. 160
gross national disposable income (GNDI), p. 160
current account (CA), p. 162
financial account (FA), p. 162
capital account (KA), p. 162
national income identity, p. 172
national saving, p. 173
current account identity, p. 173
private saving, p. 174
government saving, p. 175
public saving, p. 175
external asset, p. 179
external liability, p. 179
BOP identity, p. 180
BOP credit, p. 181
BOP debit, p. 181
(net) lender, p. 184
(net) borrower, p. 184
external wealth (W), p. 186
net creditor, p. 187
net debtor, p. 187

PROBLEMS

1. Below is a partial table of the OECD's 2004 ranking of member countries based on their GDP per capita. Compute the ratio of GNI to GDP in each case. What does this imply about net factor income from abroad in each country? Compute the GNI rankings of these countries. Are there any major differences between the GDP and GNI rankings? What do these differences imply? Indicate?

		GDP per Person	GNI per Person
1	Luxembourg	$64,843	$53,299
2	Norway	$41,880	$42,062
3	United States	$39,660	$39,590
4	Ireland	$36,536	$31,151
5	Switzerland	$34,740	$37,638
6	Netherlands	$33,571	$34,527
7	Iceland	$33,271	$31,897
8	Austria	$33,235	$32,843
9	Australia	$32,643	$31,462
10	Canada	$32,413	$31,751
11	Denmark	$32,335	$32,232
12	Belgium	$31,985	$31,675
13	United Kingdom	$31,780	$32,470
14	Sweden	$31,072	$31,007
15	Germany	$29,916	$28,732
16	Finland	$29,833	$30,361
17	Japan	$29,173	$29,739
18	France	$29,006	$29,287
19	Italy	$27,744	$27,586
20	Greece	$27,691	$27,412
21	Spain	$26,018	$25,672
22	New Zealand	$24,834	$23,205
23	Slovenia	$21,527	$21,268
24	Korea	$20,723	$20,771
25	Czech Republic	$19,426	$18,314
26	Portugal	$19,324	$19,029
27	Hungary	$16,519	$15,548
28	Slovak Republic	$14,651	$14,708
29	Poland	$13,089	$12,511
30	Mexico	$10,145	$9,989
31	Turkey	$7,212	$7,186

2. Note the following accounting identity for gross national income (GNI):

$$GNI = C + I + G + TB + NFIA$$

Using this expression, show that in a closed economy, gross domestic product (GDP), gross national income (GNI), and gross national expenditures (GNE) are the same. Show that domestic investment is equal to domestic savings.

3. Show how each of the following would affect the U.S. balance of payments. Include a description of the debit and credit items, and in each case identify which specific account is affected (e.g., imports of goods and services, IM; exports of assets, EX_A; and so on. (For this question, you may find it helpful to refer to the Appendix.)

   a. A California computer manufacturer purchases a $50 hard disk from a Malaysian company, paying the funds from a bank account in Malaysia.

   b. A U.S. tourist to Japan sells his iPod to a local resident for yen worth $100.

   c. The U.S. central bank sells $500 million of its holdings of U.S. Treasury bonds to a British financial firm and purchases pound sterling foreign reserves.

   d. A foreign owner of Apple shares receives $10,000 in dividend payments, which are paid into a New York bank.

   e. The central bank of China purchases $1 million of export earnings from a firm that has sold $1 million of toys to the United States, and the central bank holds these dollars as reserves.

   f. The U.S. government forgives a $50 million debt owed by a developing country.

4. In 2010 the country of Ikonomia has a current account deficit of $1 billion and a nonreserve financial account surplus of $750 million. Ikonomia's capital account is in a $100 million surplus. In addition, Ikonomian factories located in foreign countries earn $700 million. Ikonomia has a trade deficit of $800 million. Assume Ikonomia neither gives nor receives unilateral transfers. Ikonomia's GDP is $9 billion.

   a. What happened to Ikonomia's net foreign assets during 2010? Did it acquire or lose foreign assets during the year?

b. Compute the official settlements balance (OSB). Based on this number, what happened to the central bank's (foreign) reserves?
c. How much income did foreign factors of production earn in Ikonomia during 2010?
d. Compute net factor income from abroad (NFIA).
e. Using the identity $BOP = CA + FA + KA$, show that $BOP = 0$.
f. Compute Ikonomia's gross national expenditure (GNE), gross national income (GNI), and gross national disposable income (GNDI).

5. To answer this question, you must obtain data from the Bureau of Economic Analysis (BEA), http://www.bea.gov, on the U.S. balance of payments (BOP) tables. Go to interactive tables to obtain *annual* data for 2008 (the default setting is for quarterly data). It may take you some time to become familiar with how to navigate the website. *You need only refer to Table 1 on the BOP accounts.* Using the BOP data, compute the following for the United States:

   a. Trade balance (TB), net factor income from abroad (NFIA), net unilateral transfers (NUT), and current account (CA)
   b. Financial account (FA)
   c. Official settlements balance (OSB), referred to as "U.S. official reserve assets" and "Foreign official assets in the U.S."
   d. Nonreserve financial account (NRFA)
   e. Balance of payments (BOP). Note that this may not equal zero because of statistical discrepancy. Verify that the discrepancy is the same as the one reported by the BEA.

6. Continuing from the previous question, find nominal GDP for the United States in 2008 (you can find it elsewhere on the BEA site). Use this information along with your previous calculations to compute the following:

   a. Gross national expenditure (GNE), gross national income (GNI), and gross national disposable income (GNDI)
   b. In macroeconomics, we often assume the U.S. economy is a closed economy when building models that describe how changes in policy and shocks affect the economy. Based on the previous data (BOP and GDP), do you think this is a reasonable assumption to make? Do international transactions account for a large share of total transactions (involving goods and services, or income) involving the United States?

7. During the 1980s, the United States experienced "twin deficits" in the current account and government budget. Since 1998 the U.S. current account deficit has grown steadily along with rising government budget deficits. Do government budget deficits lead to current account deficits? Identify other possible sources of the current account deficits. Do current account deficits necessarily indicate problems in the economy?

8. Consider the economy of Opulenza. In Opulenza, domestic investment of $400 million earned $20 million in capital gains during 2009. Opulenzans purchased $120 million in new foreign assets during the year; foreigners purchased $160 million in Opulenzan assets. Assume the valuation effects total $1 million in capital gains.

   a. Compute the change in domestic wealth in Opulenza.
   b. Compute the change in external wealth for Opulenza.
   c. Compute the total change in wealth for Opulenza.
   d. Compute domestic savings for Opulenza.
   e. Compute Opulenza's current account. Is the CA in deficit or surplus?
   f. Explain the intuition for the CA deficit/surplus in terms of savings in Opulenza, financial flows, and its domestic/external wealth position.
   g. How would a depreciation in Opulenza's currency affect its domestic, external, and total wealth? Assume that foreign assets owned by Opulenzans are denominated in foreign currency.

9. This question asks you to compute valuation effects for the United States in 2004, using the same methods mentioned in the chapter. Use the bea.gov website to collect the data needed for this question: look under the "International" heading.

Visit the BEA's balance of payments data page and obtain the U.S. balance of payments for 2004 in billions of dollars. Be sure to get the correct year, and annual data, not quarterly.

Visit the BEA's net international investment position data page and obtain the U.S. net international investment position for end 2003 to end 2004.

a. What was the U.S. current account for 2004?
b. What was the U.S. financial account for 2004?
c. What was the U.S. change in external wealth for 2004?
d. What was the U.S. total valuation effect for 2004?
e. Does the answer to part (d) equal the answer to part (e) minus the answer to part (c)? Why?
f. What do the BEA data indicate was the U.S. valuation effect due to exchange rate changes for 2004?

You may now assume that the U.S. dollar depreciated by 10% against major currencies in 2004, and use this average to estimate valuation effects.

g. What were end-2003 U.S. external liabilities? If 5% of these liabilities were in foreign currency and were subject to a 10% exchange rate appreciation, what decrease in U.S. external wealth resulted?
h. What were end-2003 U.S. external assets? If 65% of these assets were subject to a 10% exchange rate appreciation, what increase in U.S. external wealth resulted?
i. Using the answers to parts (g) and (h), what was the 2004 U.S. valuation effect due to exchange rate changes according to your rough calculation? Is it close to the BEA figure in part (f)?

NETWORK

Go to the UN website and find out what the Millennium Development Goals are (http://www.un.org/millenniumgoals). Go to the Gleneagles summit website and examine the promises made (http://www.g8.gov.uk/). Use the Web to check up on how well these G8 promises are being kept, such as the UN goal of 0.7% of GDP in official development assistance, the promise to eradicate export subsidies, and the aim to double aid by 2010. (*Hint:* Google sites such as Oxfam or the Jubilee Debt Campaign, or look for the World Bank Tools for Monitoring the Millennium Development Goals.)

Use the Web to locate the official macroeconomic statistics for your country. (In the United States, go to http://www.bea.gov.) Find the latest annual data corresponding to the measures discussed in this section. Was your country's GDP higher or lower than its GNE? Why? Was your country's GNI higher or lower than its GDP? Why? What about GNDI—was your country a net giver or receiver of transfers?

APPENDIX TO CHAPTER 5

External Wealth and Total Wealth

In this chapter, we studied external wealth. But individuals and countries care about their total wealth. How does external wealth relate to total wealth?

External wealth is only part of a country's *total wealth*, the sum of the home capital stock (all nonfinancial assets in the home economy, denoted K) plus amounts owed to home by foreigners (A) minus amounts owed foreigners by home (L):

$$\text{Total wealth} = \underbrace{K}_{\text{Home nonfinancial assets}} + \underbrace{(A-L)}_{\text{External wealth}}$$

In this definition, note that we deliberately exclude financial assets owed by one home entity to another home entity because in the aggregate these cancel out and form no part of a country's total wealth.

Changes in the value of total wealth can then be written as follows:

$$\begin{bmatrix}\text{Change in}\\ \text{total wealth}\end{bmatrix} = \underbrace{\begin{bmatrix}\text{Additions}\\ \text{to } K\end{bmatrix} + \begin{bmatrix}\text{Additions}\\ \text{to } A-L\end{bmatrix}}_{\text{Additions (acquisitions minus disposals)}} + \underbrace{\begin{bmatrix}\text{Capital gains}\\ \text{on } K\end{bmatrix} + \begin{bmatrix}\text{Capital gains}\\ \text{on } A-L\end{bmatrix}}_{\text{Valuation effects (gains minus losses)}}$$

There are two kinds of terms in this expression. The total value of wealth (of a person or a country) may change due to *additions* of assets (such as purchases, sales, or net gifts) or due to valuation effects (capital gains—or, if they are negative, capital losses—arising from changes in the prices of assets).

The previous equation can be simplified by two observations. First, additions to the domestic capital stock K have a simpler expression: they are known as investment, denoted I. (Strictly, this is the gross addition to the capital stock; the net addition would require the subtraction of depreciation, and in the previous notation that would be accounted for under valuation effects since depreciating assets fall in value.)

Second, additions to external wealth, $A - L$, also have a simpler expression: they are equal to net additions to external assets minus net additions to external liabilities, and as we saw in the main chapter, these are equal to *minus* the financial account, $-FA$.

Substituting, we can rewrite the last equations as

$$\begin{bmatrix}\text{Change in}\\ \text{total wealth}\end{bmatrix} = \underbrace{I}_{\substack{\text{Additions to } K\\ =\\ \text{Additions to}\\ \text{assets in the}\\ \text{home economy}}} + \underbrace{(-FA)}_{\substack{\text{Additions to}\\ A-L\\ =\\ \text{Net import of}\\ \text{assets into the}\\ \text{home economy}}} + \underbrace{\begin{bmatrix}\text{Capital gains}\\ \text{on } K\end{bmatrix} + \begin{bmatrix}\text{Capital gains}\\ \text{on } A-L\end{bmatrix}}_{\text{Valuation effects (gains minus losses)}}$$

Now, using the BOP identity, we know that $CA + KA + FA = 0$ so that minus the financial account $-FA$ must equal $CA + KA$; hence, we can write

$$\begin{bmatrix}\text{Change in}\\ \text{total wealth}\end{bmatrix} = I + CA + KA + \underbrace{\begin{bmatrix}\text{Capital gains}\\ \text{on } K\end{bmatrix} + \begin{bmatrix}\text{Capital gains}\\ \text{on } A-L\end{bmatrix}}_{\text{Valuation effects (gains minus losses)}}$$

Notice what has happened here. The BOP identity makes the connection between external asset trade and activity in the current account. We take the connection one step further using the current account identity, $S = I + CA$, which allows us to write

$$\begin{bmatrix} \text{Change in} \\ \text{total wealth} \end{bmatrix} = S + KA + \underbrace{\begin{bmatrix} \text{Capital gains} \\ \text{on } K \end{bmatrix} + \begin{bmatrix} \text{Capital gains} \\ \text{on } A - L \end{bmatrix}}_{\text{Valuation effects (gains minus losses)}}$$

The message of this expression is clear. As we all probably know from personal experience, there are only three ways to get more (or less) wealthy: do more (or less) saving (S), receive (or give) gifts of assets (KA), or enjoy the good (bad) fortune of capital gains (losses) on your portfolio. What is true about individuals' wealth is also true for the wealth of a nation in the aggregate.

Balance of Payments I: The Gains from Financial Globalization

Save for a rainy day.

Make hay while the sun shines.

Don't put all your eggs in one basket.

1. The Limits on How Much a Country Can Borrow: The Long-Run Budget Constraint
2. Gains from Consumption Smoothing
3. Gains from Efficient Investment
4. Gains from Diversification of Risk
5. Conclusions

How does your household cope with economic shocks and the financial challenges they pose? Let's take an extreme example. Suppose you are self-employed and own a business. A severe storm appears and a flood overwhelms your town. This is bad news on several fronts. As people recover from the disaster, businesses, including yours, suffer and your income is lower for several months. If your business premises are damaged, you must also plan to make new investments to repair the damage.

If you have no financial dealings with anyone, your household, as a little closed economy, faces a difficult trade-off as your income falls. Your household income has to equal its consumption plus investment. Would you try to maintain your level of consumption, and neglect the need to invest? Or would you invest, and let your household suffer as you cut back drastically on consumption? Faced with an emergency like this, most of us look for help beyond our own household, if we can: We might hope for transfers (gifts from friends and family, or the government), or we might rely on financial markets (dip into savings, apply for a loan, rely on an insurance payout, etc.).

What does this story have to do with international economics? If we redraw the boundaries of this experiment and expand from the household unit, to the local, regional, and finally national level, the same logic applies. Countries face shocks all the time, and how they are able cope with them depends on whether they are open or closed to economic interactions with other nations.

To get a sense of how countries can deal with shocks, we can look at data from Caribbean and Central American countries that have faced the same kinds of shock as

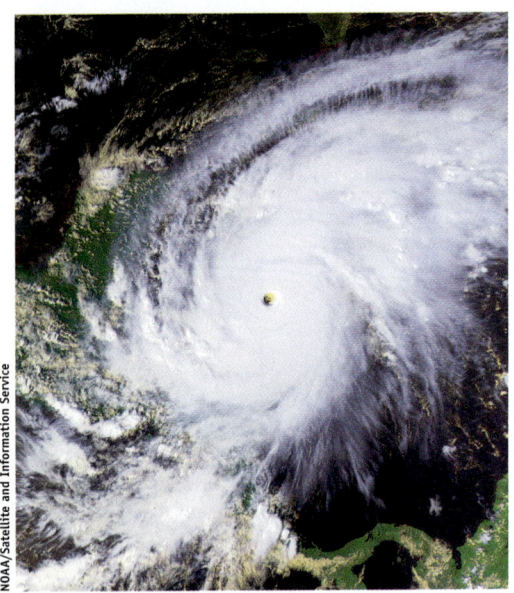

Hurricane Mitch battered Central America from October 22, 1998, to November 5, 1998. It was the deadliest hurricane in more than 200 years and the second deadliest ever recorded.

the household we just described. Every year many tropical storms, some of them of hurricane strength, sweep through this region. The storms are large—hundreds of miles across—and most countries in the region are much smaller in size, some no more than little islets. For them, a hurricane is the town flood blown up to a national scale. The worst storms cause widespread destruction and loss of life.

Hurricanes are tragic human events, but they provide an opportunity for research. Economists study them because such an "act of God"—in economics jargon, a "natural experiment"—provides a laboratory-like test of economic theory. Figure 6-1 shows the average macroeconomic response in these countries after they were hit by a hurricane. In the aftermath, these countries do some of the things we would expect households to do: accept nonmarket gifts (transfers from foreign countries) and borrow (by running a current account deficit). If we subtract nonmarket transfers and examine market behavior alone, the patterns are striking. As a fraction of GDP, investment is typically 3% to 6% higher than normal in the three years after a hurricane, and saving is 1% to 5% lower (excluding transfers). Combining the two effects, the current account (saving minus investment) falls dramatically and is 6% to 10% more in deficit than normal.

Hurricanes are extreme examples of economic shocks. They are not representative of the normal fluctuations that countries experience, but their very size and randomness expose important macroeconomic responses. The countries' responses illustrate some of the important financial mechanisms that help open economies cope with all types of shocks, large and small.

In this chapter, we see how financially open economies can, in theory, reap gains from financial globalization. We first look at the factors that limit international

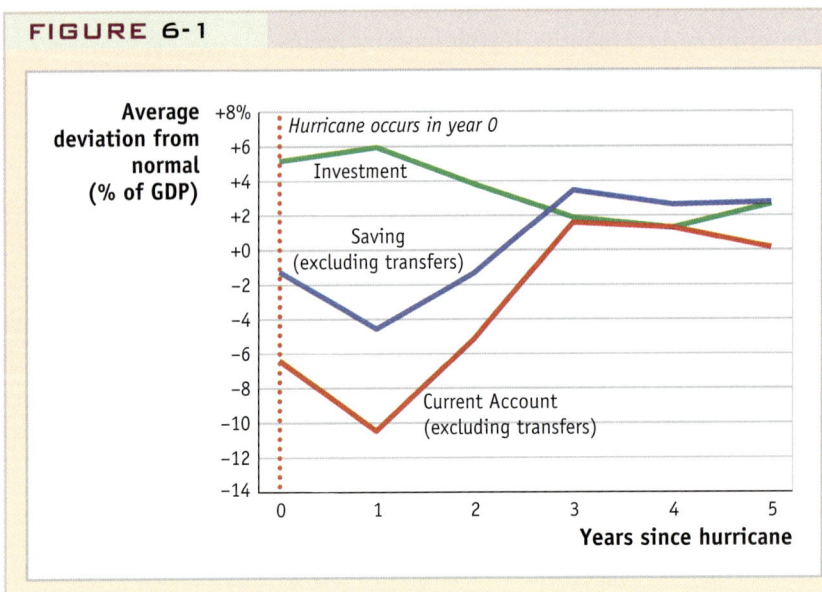

FIGURE 6-1

The Macroeconomics of Hurricanes The figure shows the average response (excluding transfers) of investment, saving, and the current account in a sample of Caribbean and Central American countries in the years during and after severe hurricane damage. The responses are as expected: investment rises (to rebuild), and saving falls (to limit the fall in consumption); hence, the current account moves sharply toward deficit.

Note: Transfers are excluded from saving and the current account, and the saving measure is calculated as $S - NUT = I + CA - NUT$.

Source: John C. Bluedorn, 2005, Hurricanes: Intertemporal Trade and Capital Shocks, Oxford Economics Working Paper No. 2005-241.

borrowing and lending. Then, in the remaining sections of the chapter, we see how a nation's ability to use international financial markets allows it to accomplish three different goals:

- consumption smoothing (steadying consumption when income fluctuates);
- efficient investment (borrowing to build a productive capital stock); and
- diversification of risk (by trading of stocks between countries).

Along the way, we look at how well the theoretical gains from financial globalization translate into reality (an area of some dispute among economists) and find that many of these gains have yet to be realized. In advanced countries, the gains from financial globalization are often large and more attainable, but in poorer countries the gains may be smaller and harder to realize. We want to understand why these differences exist, and what risks may arise for poor countries that attempt to capture the gains from financial globalization.

1 The Limits on How Much a Country Can Borrow: The Long-Run Budget Constraint

Our introductory examples show how borrowing can help countries (like households) better cope with shocks. But, also like households, there is a limit to how much a country can borrow (or, how much lenders will lend). Understanding the constraints on how countries might borrow and lend to one another is our critical first task in this chapter. With this understanding we can then examine how financial globalization shapes the economic choices available to a country as economic conditions change over time. The ability to borrow in times of need and lend in times of prosperity has profound effects on a country's well-being.

When we study an economy as it evolves over time, we are taking a *dynamic approach* to macroeconomics rather than a static approach. The dynamic approach is also known as the *intertemporal approach* to macroeconomics. One key element in this approach is to keep track of whether a country is managing its wealth sustainably. The intertemporal approach makes use of the key lessons from the end of the last chapter, which taught us how to account for the change in external wealth from one period to the next.

In this section, we use changes in an open economy's external wealth to derive the key constraint that limits its borrowing in the long run: the *long-run budget constraint* (LRBC). The LRBC tells us precisely how and why a country must, in the long run, "live within its means." A country's ability to adjust its external wealth through borrowing and lending provides a buffer against economic shocks, but the long-run budget constraint places limits on the use of this buffer.

To develop some intuition, let's look at a simple household analogy. This year (year 0) you borrow $100,000 from the bank at an interest rate of 10% annually. You have no other wealth and inflation is zero. Once you borrow the $100,000, assume that there are two different ways in which you can deal with your debt each year.

> **Case 1** *A debt that is serviced.* Every year you pay the 10% interest due on the principal amount of the loan, $10,000, but you never pay any principal. At the end of each year, the bank renews the loan (a rollover), and your wealth remains constant at –$100,000.

Case 2 *A debt that is not serviced.* You pay neither interest nor principal but ask the bank to roll over the principal plus the interest due on it each year. In year 1, the overdue interest is $10,000, and your debt grows by 10% to $110,000. In year 2, the overdue interest is 10% of $110,000, or $11,000, and your debt grows by 10% again to $121,000. Assuming this process goes on and on, your level of debt grows by 10% every year.

Case 2 is not sustainable. If the bank allows it, your debt level will explode to infinity as it grows by 10% every year forever. This case, sometimes called a rollover scheme, a pyramid scheme, or a *Ponzi game*,[1] illustrates the limits or constraints on the use of borrowing, which implies negative external wealth. In the long run, lenders will simply not allow the debt to grow beyond a certain point. Debts must be paid off eventually. This requirement is the essence of the long-run budget constraint.

How The Long-Run Budget Constraint Is Determined

As is usual when building an economic model, we start with a basic model that makes a number of simplifying assumptions, but yields lessons that can be extended to more complex cases. Here are the assumptions we make about various conditions that affect our model:

- Prices are perfectly flexible. Under this assumption, all analyses in this chapter can be conducted in terms of real variables, and all monetary aspects of the economy can be ignored. (To adjust for inflation and convert to real terms, we could divide all nominal quantities by an index of prices.)

- The country is a **small open economy.** The country trades goods and services with the rest of the world through exports and imports and can lend or borrow overseas, but only by issuing or buying debt (bonds). Because it is small, the country cannot influence prices in world markets for goods and services.

- All debt carries a real interest rate r^*, the **world real interest rate,** which we assume to be constant. Because the country is small, it takes the world real interest rate as given, and we assume it can lend or borrow an unlimited amount at this interest rate.

- The country pays a real interest rate r^* on its start-of-period debt liabilities L and is paid the same interest rate r^* on its start-of-period debt assets A. In any period, the country earns net interest income payments equal to r^*A minus r^*L or, more simply, r^*W, where W is external wealth $(A - L)$ at the start of the period. External wealth may vary over time.

- There are no unilateral transfers ($NUT = 0$), no capital transfers ($KA = 0$), and no capital gains on external wealth. Under these assumptions, there are only two nonzero items in the current account: the trade balance and net factor income from abroad, r^*W. If r^*W is positive, the country is earning interest and is a lender/creditor with positive external wealth. If r^*W is negative, the country is paying interest and is a borrower/debtor with negative external wealth.

---

[1] This type of borrowing strategy is named after the infamous swindler Charles Ponzi who engaged in a "pyramid" or "chain letter" operation of this type in Boston in 1919 and 1920, borrowing new money from an expanding base of creditors to pay off past debt.

Calculating the Change in Wealth Each Period In the previous balance of payments chapter, we saw that the change in external wealth equals the sum of three terms: the current account, the capital account, and capital gains on external wealth. In the special case we are studying, our assumptions tell us that the last two terms are zero, and that the current account equals the sum of just two terms: the trade balance TB plus any net interest payments r^*W at the world interest rate on the external wealth held at the end of the last period.

Mathematically, we can write the change in external wealth from end of year $N-1$ to end of year N as follows (where subscripts denote periods, here years):

$$\underbrace{\Delta W_N}_{\text{Change in external wealth this period}} = \underbrace{W_N - W_{N-1}}_{} = \underbrace{TB_N}_{\text{Trade balance this period}} + \underbrace{r^* W_{N-1}}_{\text{Interest paid/received on last period's external wealth}}$$

In this simplified world, external wealth can change for only two reasons: surpluses or deficits on the trade balance in the current period, or surpluses and deficits on net factor income arising from interest received or paid.

Calculating Future Wealth Levels Now that we have a formula for wealth changes, and assuming we know the initial level of wealth in year $N-1$, we can compute the level of wealth at any time in the future by repeated application of the formula.

To find wealth at the end of year N, we rearrange the preceding equation:

$$\underbrace{W_N}_{\text{External wealth at the end of this period}} = \underbrace{TB_N}_{\text{Trade balance this period}} + \underbrace{(1 + r^*)W_{N-1}}_{\text{Last period's external wealth plus interest paid/received}}$$

This equation presents an important and intuitive result: it shows that wealth at the end of a period is the sum of two terms. The trade balance this period captures an addition to wealth due to net exports (exports minus imports). Wealth at the end of last period times $(1 + r^*)$ captures the wealth from last period plus the interest earned on that wealth. The examples in the following sections will help us become familiar with using this kind of expression to understand the dynamics of a country's external wealth and the role of the trade balance.

The Budget Constraint in a Two-Period Example

We first put these ideas to work in a simplified two-period example. Suppose we start in year 0, so $N = 0$. Suppose further that a country has some initial external wealth from year -1 (an inheritance from the past), and can borrow or lend in the present period (year 0). We also impose the following limits: by the end of year 1, the country must end all external borrowing and lending. All debts owed or owing must be paid off, and the country must end that year with zero external wealth.

By the formula given earlier, $W_0 = (1 + r^*)W_{-1} + TB_0$. At the end of year 0, the country carries over from the last period (year -1) its initial wealth level, plus any interest accumulated on it. If the country runs a trade deficit, it has to run its external wealth down by adding liabilities (borrowing) or cashing in external assets (dissaving); conversely, if it runs a trade surplus, it lends that amount to the rest of the world.

Where do things stand at the end of year 1? Earlier, we imposed the limitation that at the end of year 1 the country must have zero external wealth. Applying the preceding formula to year 1, we know that $W_1 = 0 = (1 + r^*)W_0 + TB_1$. We can substitute $W_0 = (1 + r^*)W_{-1} + TB_0$ into this formula to obtain

$$W_1 = 0 = (1 + r^*)^2 W_{-1} + (1 + r^*)TB_0 + TB_1$$

In addition to its initial level of external wealth W_{-1}, two years later at the end of year 1 the country has accumulated wealth equal to the trade balance in years 0 and 1 plus the one year of interest earned (or paid) on the year 0 trade balance, plus the two years of interest earned (or paid) on its initial wealth.

But now, because we have stated that the final wealth level W_1 must be zero, the right-hand side of the last equation must be zero, too. For that to be the case, the present (TB_0) and future (TB_1) trade balances (and accumulated interest on those balances) must be equal and opposite to initial wealth (W_{-1}) (and accumulated interest on that):

$$-(1 + r^*)^2 W_{-1} = (1 + r^*)TB_0 + TB_1$$

This equation is the *two-period budget constraint*. It tells us that a creditor country with positive initial wealth (left-hand-side negative) can afford to run trade deficits "on average" in future; conversely, a debtor country (left-hand-side positive) is required to run trade surpluses "on average" in future.

Present Value Form By dividing the previous equation by $(1 + r^*)$, we find a much more intuitive expression for the two-period budget constraint:

$$\underbrace{-(1 + r^*)W_{-1}}_{\text{Minus the present value of wealth from last period}} = \underbrace{TB_0 + \frac{TB_1}{(1 + r^*)}}_{\text{Present value of all present and future trade balances}}$$

Every element in this statement of the two-period budget constraint represents a quantity expressed in present value terms.

By definition, the **present value** of X in period N is the amount that would have to be set aside now, so that, with accumulated interest, X is available in N periods. If the interest rate is r^*, then the present value of X is $X/(1 + r^*)^N$. For example, if you are told that you will receive $121 at the end of year 2 and the interest rate is 10%, then the present value of that $121 now, in year 0, is $100 because $100 × 1.1 (adding interest earned in year 1) × 1.1 (adding interest earned in year 2) = $121.

A Two-Period Example Let's put some numbers into the last equation. Suppose a country starts in debt, with a wealth level of −$100 million at the end of year −1: $W_{-1} = -\$100$ million. At a real interest rate of 10%, how can the country satisfy the two-period budget constraint that it must have zero external wealth at the end of year 1? To pay off $110 million (initial debt plus the interest accruing on this debt during period 0), the country must ensure that the present value of future trade balances is +$110 million.

The country has many ways to do this. It could run a trade surplus of $110 million in period 0, pay off its debt at the end of period 0, and then have balanced trade in period 1; or it could wait to pay off the debt until the end of period 1, which would require the country to run a trade surplus of $121 million in period 1 after having balanced trade in period 0. Or it could have any other combination of trade balances in periods 0 and 1 that allows it to pay off the debt and accumulated interested so that external wealth at the end of period 1 is zero and the budget constraint is satisfied.

Extending the Theory to the Long Run By extending the two-period model to N periods, and allowing N to run to infinity, we can extend and transform the two-period budget constraint into the **long-run budget constraint (LRBC).** Repeating the two-period logic N times, external wealth after N periods is initial wealth (and accumulated interest on that wealth, whether positive or negative) plus all intervening trade balances (and accumulated interest on those positive or negative balances). If external wealth is to be zero at the end of N periods, then the sum of the present values of N present and future trade balances must equal minus the present value of external wealth. If N runs to infinity, we get an infinite sum and arrive at the equation of the LRBC:[2]

$$\text{LRBC:} \underbrace{-(1+r^*)W_{-1}}_{\substack{\text{Minus the present value of} \\ \text{wealth from last period}}} = \underbrace{TB_0 + \frac{TB_1}{(1+r^*)} + \frac{TB_2}{(1+r^*)^2} + \frac{TB_3}{(1+r^*)^3} + \frac{TB_4}{(1+r^*)^4} + \cdots}_{\text{Present value of all present and future trade balances}} \quad (6\text{-}1)$$

This equation generalizes the result from the two-period case, to many periods. A debtor (surplus) country must have future trade balances that are offsetting and positive (negative) in present value terms.

This expression for the LRBC plays an important role in our analysis of how countries can lend or borrow because it imposes a condition that rules out choices that would lead to exploding positive or negative external wealth.

A Long-Run Example: The Perpetual Loan

The following example helps us understand the long-run budget constraint and apply it to a case that we revisit in the rest of the chapter to explore how countries that take out an initial loan must make payments to service that loan in the future.

Suppose today is year 0 and a country is to pay (e.g., to its creditors) a constant amount X every year starting next year, year 1. What is the present value (PV) of that sequence of payments (X)?

$$PV(X) = \frac{X}{(1+r^*)} + \frac{X}{(1+r^*)^2} + \frac{X}{(1+r^*)^3} + \cdots$$

This expression for $PV(X)$ is an infinite sum. If we multiply this equation by $(1+r^*)$ we obtain:

$$PV(X)(1+r^*) = X + \frac{X}{(1+r^*)} + \frac{X}{(1+r^*)^2} + \frac{X}{(1+r^*)^3} + \cdots$$

---

[2] We can take the basic equation for the change in external wealth, $W_0 = (1+r^*)W_{-1} + TB_0$, and apply it N times with repeated substitution to obtain wealth at the end of period N:

$$W_N = (1+r^*)^{N+1}W_{-1} + (1+r^*)^N TB_0 + (1+r^*)^{N-1} TB_1 + (1+r^*)^{N-2} TB_2 + \cdots + (1+r^*)TB_{N-1} + TB_N$$

If we divide the previous equation by $(1+r^*)^N$, we get

$$\frac{W_N}{(1+r^*)^N} = (1+r^*)W_{-1} + TB_0 + \frac{TB_1}{(1+r^*)} + \frac{TB_2}{(1+r^*)^2} + \cdots + \frac{TB_N}{(1+r^*)^N}.$$

As we saw earlier, in a Ponzi game, external wealth W_N explodes, growing by a factor $(1+r^*)$ every period. To prevent this, external wealth W_N (whether positive or negative) must grow more slowly in the long run than the factor $(1+r^*)^N$. In this case, as N approaches infinity, the left-hand side of the equation will approach zero. This in turn would imply that the right-hand side of the last equation must also approach zero. This leads directly to the LRBC Equation (6–1) in the text.

If we now subtract the first equation from the second, all of the terms on the right cancel out except X, so we get $r^* PV(X) = X$, which we can rearrange to find a simple expression for $PV(X)$:

$$\underbrace{\frac{X}{(1+r^*)} + \frac{X}{(1+r^*)^2} + \frac{X}{(1+r^*)^3} + \cdots}_{PV(X)} = \frac{X}{r^*} \quad (6\text{-}2)$$

This formula helps us compute $PV(X)$ for any stream of constant payments, something we often need to do to verify the long-run budget constraint.

For example, if the constant payment is $X = 100$ and the interest rate is 5% ($r^* = 0.05$), Equation (6-2) says that the present value of a stream of payments of 100 starting in year 1 is $100/0.05 = 2,000$:

$$\frac{100}{(1+0.05)} + \frac{100}{(1+0.05)^2} + \frac{100}{(1+0.05)^3} + \cdots = \frac{100}{0.05} = 2,000$$

This example, which recurs later in this chapter, shows the stream of interest payments on a **perpetual loan** (i.e., an interest-only loan or, equivalently, a sequence of loans for which *only* the principal is refinanced or rolled over every year). If the amount loaned by the creditor is $2,000 in year 0, and this principal amount is outstanding forever, then the interest that must be paid each year to service the debt is 5% of $2,000, or $100. Under these conditions, the present value of the future interest payments equals the value of the amount loaned in year 0 and the LRBC is satisfied.

Implications of the LRBC for Gross National Expenditure and Gross Domestic Product

In economics, a budget constraint always tells us something about the limits to expenditure, whether for a person, firm, or government. The LRBC is no different—it tells us that in the long run, a country's national expenditure (GNE) is limited by how much it produces (GDP).

To see how, recall from the previous chapter that the trade balance is equal to the difference between gross domestic product and gross national expenditure, $TB = GDP - GNE$. If we insert this expression into the LRBC equation (6-1) and collect terms, we see that

$$\underbrace{\underbrace{+(1+r^*)W_{-1}}_{\substack{\text{Present value of}\\\text{wealth from}\\\text{last period}}} + \underbrace{GDP_0 + \frac{GDP_1}{(1+r^*)} + \frac{GDP_2}{(1+r^*)^2} + \cdots}_{\text{Present value of present and future } GDP}}_{\text{Present value of the country's resources}} \quad (6\text{-}3)$$

$$= \underbrace{GNE_0 + \frac{GNE_1}{(1+r^*)} + \frac{GNE_2}{(1+r^*)^2} + \cdots}_{\text{Present value of present and future } GNE}$$

=
Present value of the country's spending

The left side of this equation is the present value of resources of the country in the long run: the present value of any inherited wealth plus the present value of present and future product. The right side is the present value of all present and future spending $(C + I + G)$ as measured by *GNE*.

We have arrived at the following, very important result: *the long-run budget constraint says that in the long run, in present value terms, a country's expenditures (GNE) must equal its production (GDP) plus any initial wealth.*

The LRBC therefore shows quite precisely how an economy must live within its means in the long run.

Summary

The key lesson of our intertemporal model is that a closed economy is subject to a tighter budget constraint than an open economy. In a closed economy, "living within your means" requires a country to have balanced trade each and every year. In an open economy, "living within your means" requires only that a country must maintain a balance between its trade deficits and surpluses that satisfies the long-run budget constraint—they must balance only in a present value sense, rather than year by year.

This conclusion implies that an open economy ought to be able to do better (or no worse) than a closed economy in achieving its desired pattern of expenditure over time. This is the essence of theoretical argument that there are gains from financial globalization.

In the next section, we now examine this argument in greater detail and consider whether—or more precisely, under what circumstances—it is valid in the real world. But first, we consider some situations in which the assumptions of the model might need to be modified.

APPLICATION

The Favorable Situation of the United States

Two assumptions greatly simplified our intertemporal model. We assumed that the same real rate of interest r^* applied to income received on assets and income paid on liabilities, and we assumed that there were no capital gains on external wealth. However, these assumptions are not satisfied for the United States.

"Exorbitant Privilege" The United States has since the 1980s been a net debtor with $W = A - L < 0$. Under the model's simplifying assumptions, negative external wealth would lead to a deficit on net factor income from abroad with $r^*W = r^*(A - L) < 0$. Yet as we saw in the last chapter, U.S. net factor income from abroad has been positive throughout this period (although this situation may be about to change). How can this be?

The only way a net debtor can earn positive net interest income is by receiving a higher rate of interest on its assets than it pays on its liabilities. The data show that this has been consistently true for the United States since the 1960s. The interest the United States has received on its assets has been higher by about 1.5 to 2 percentage points per year on average (with a slight downward trend) than the interest it pays on its liabilities.

To develop a framework to make sense of this finding, suppose the United States receives interest at the world real interest rate r^* on its external assets but pays interest at a lower rate r^0 on its liabilities. Then its net factor income from abroad is $r^*A - r^0L = r^*W + (r^* - r^0)L$. The final term, the interest rate difference times total liabilities, is an income bonus the United States earns as a "banker to the world"—like any other bank, it borrows low and lends high.

Understandably, the rest of the world may resent this state of affairs from time to time. In the 1960s French officials complained about the United States' "exorbitant privilege" of being able to borrow cheaply by issuing external liabilities in the form of reserve assets (Treasury debt) while earning higher returns on U.S. external assets such as foreign equity and foreign direct investment. This conclusion is not borne out in the data, however. U.S. Bureau of Economic Analysis (BEA) data suggest that most of the interest rate difference is due not to the low interest paid on Treasury debt, but to the low interest rate on U.S. equity liabilities (i.e., low profits earned on foreign investment in the United States).[3]

"Manna from Heaven" The difference between interest earned and interest paid isn't the only deviation from our simple model that benefits the United States. BEA statistics reveal that the country has long enjoyed positive capital gains, KG, on its external wealth. This gain, which started in the 1980s, comes from a difference of two percentage points between large capital gains on several types of external assets and smaller capital losses on external liabilities

It is hard to pin down the source of these capital gains because the BEA data suggest that these effects are not the result of price or exchange rate effects, and they just reflect capital gains that cannot be otherwise measured. As a result, some skeptics call these capital gains "statistical manna from heaven." As with the "exorbitant privilege," this financial gain for the United States is a loss for the rest of the world. As a result, some economists describe the United States as more like a "venture capitalist to the world" than a "banker to the world," given the large contribution of differential profits and capital gains (rather than pure interest) on equity to this persistent beneficial wealth effect.[4]

Summary When we add the 2% capital gain differential to the 1.5% interest differential, we end up with a U.S. total return differential (interest plus capital gains) of about 3.5% per year since the 1980s. For comparison, in the same period, the total return differential was close to zero in every other G7 country.

To include the effects of the total return differential in our model, we have to incorporate the effect of the extra "bonuses" on external wealth, as well as the conventional terms that reflect the trade balance and interest payments:

$$\Delta W_N = \underbrace{W_N - W_{N-1}}_{\substack{\text{Change in} \\ \text{external wealth} \\ \text{this period}}} = \underbrace{TB_N}_{\substack{\text{Trade} \\ \text{balance} \\ \text{this period}}} + \underbrace{r^* W_{N-1}}_{\substack{\text{Interest paid/received} \\ \text{on last period's} \\ \text{external wealth}}} + \underbrace{(r^* - r^0)L}_{\substack{\text{Income due to} \\ \text{interest rate} \\ \text{differential}}} + \underbrace{KG}_{\substack{\text{Capital gains} \\ \text{on external} \\ \text{wealth}}}$$

$$\underbrace{\hphantom{TB_N + r^* W_{N-1}}}_{\text{Conventional effects}} \quad \underbrace{\hphantom{(r^* - r^0)L + KG}}_{\text{Additional effects}}$$

---

[3] John Kitchen, 2007, "Sharecroppers or Shrewd Capitalists? Projections of the U.S. Current Account, International Income Flows, and Net International Debt," *Review of International Economics*, 15(5), 1036–1061; Barry Bosworth, Susan M. Collins, and Gabriel Chodorow Reich, 2007, "Returns on FDI: Does the US Really Do Better?" *Brookings Trade Forum*, 177–210.
[4] William R. Cline, 2005, *The United States as a Debtor Nation* (Washington, D.C.: Institute for International Economics and Center for Global Development); Pierre-Olivier Gourinchas and Hélène Rey, 2007, "From World Banker to World Venture Capitalist: US External Adjustment and the Exorbitant Privilege," in Richard Clarida, ed., *G7 Current Account Imbalances: Sustainability and Adjustment* (Chicago: University of Chicago Press).

Too Good to Be True? With this equation, the implications of the final two terms become clearer for the U.S. economy. When positive, they offset wealth losses due to trade deficits. Thus, if these terms increase in value by 1% of GDP, for example, then the United States could run an additional 1% of GDP in trade deficit forever and still satisfy its LRBC.

As Figure 6-2 shows, the United States has seen these offsets increase markedly in recent years, rising from 1% of GDP in the late 1980s to an average of about 4% of GDP in the 2000s. These large offsets have led some economists to take a relaxed view of the swollen U.S. trade deficit because they finance a large chunk of the country's trade deficit—with luck, in perpetuity.[5] However, we may not be able to count on these offsets forever: longer-run evidence suggests that they are not stable and may be diminishing over time.[6]

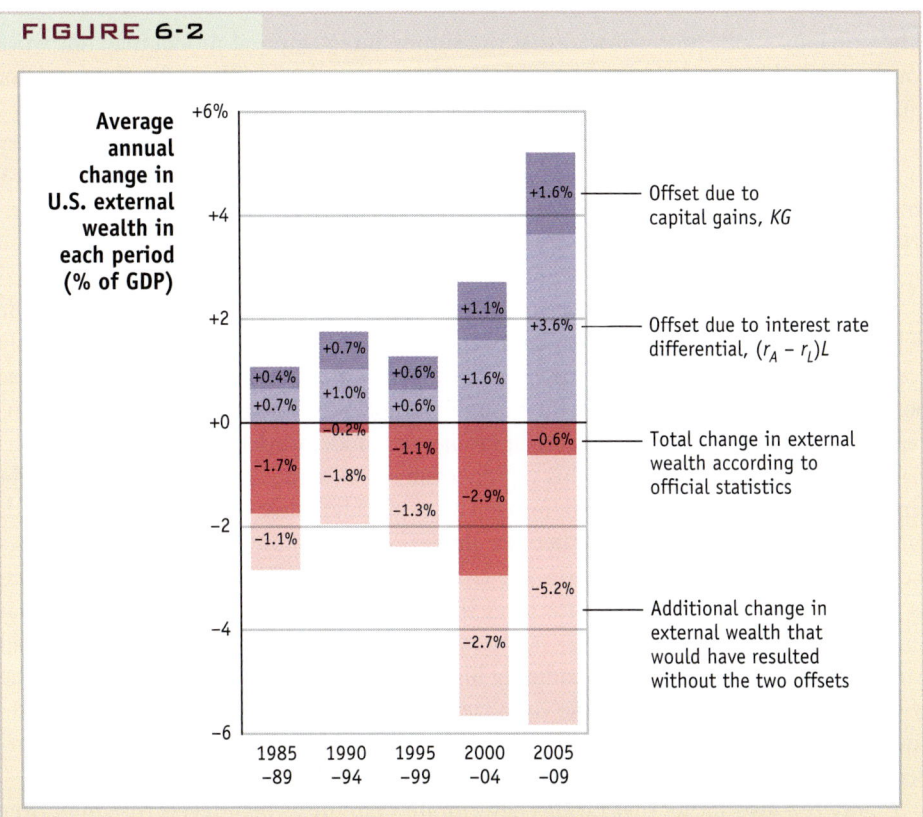

FIGURE 6-2

How Favorable Interest Rates and Capital Gains on External Wealth Help the United States The total average annual change in U.S. external wealth each period is shown by the dark red columns. Negative changes were offset in part by two positive effects. One effect was due to the favorable interest rate differentials on U.S. assets (high) versus liabilities (low). The other effect was due to favorable rates of capital gains on U.S. assets (high) versus liabilities (low). Without these two offsetting effects, the declines in U.S. external wealth would have been much bigger.

Notes: Interest rate differential effects are computed assuming that counterfactual liability yields would have been equal to asset yields. Capital gains are computed as the difference between financial flows and changes in external wealth.

Source: U.S. Bureau of Economic Analysis, Balance of Payments Accounts and Net International Investment Position.

---

[5] Ricardo Hausmann and Federico Sturzenegger, "'Dark Matter' Makes the US Deficit Disappear," *Financial Times*, December 7, 2005.
[6] Christopher M. Meissner and Alan M. Taylor, 2008, "Losing Our Marbles in the New Century? The Great Rebalancing in Historical Perspective," in *Global Imbalances and the Evolving World Economy*, J. S. Little, ed. (Boston: Federal Reserve Bank of Boston).

Others warn that, given the likely presence of errors in these data, we really have no idea what is going on. In 2006 economist Daniel Gros calculated that the United States had borrowed $5,500 billion over 20 years, even though its external wealth had fallen by "only" $2,800 billion. Have $2.7 trillion dollars been mislaid? Gros argued that most of this difference can be attributed to poor U.S. measurement of the assets foreigners own and investment earnings foreigners receive. Correcting these errors would make all of the additional offset terms disappear—and roughly double the estimated current level of U.S. net indebtedness to the rest of the world.[7] ■

APPLICATION

The Difficult Situation of the Emerging Markets

The previous application showed that the simple intertemporal model may not work for the United States. In this section, we see that its assumptions may also not work for emerging markets and developing countries.

As in the U.S. example, the first assumption we might question is that the country faces the same real interest rate on assets and liabilities. The United States borrows low and lends high. For most poorer countries, the opposite is true. Because of country risk, investors typically expect a risk premium before they will buy any assets issued by these countries, whether government debt, private equity, or FDI profits.

Figure 6-3 plots government credit ratings (from Standard & Poor's) against public debt levels using historical data for a large sample of countries. Bond ratings were highly correlated with risk premiums. At the top of the figure are the advanced countries whose bonds were rated AA or better. (At the time this sample was constructed, before the financial crisis, these countries had high credit ratings and moderate debt levels; after the financial crisis and Great Recession, this rapidly changed as some advanced countries' debt rapidly ballooned and their credit ratings fell quite quickly). Most advanced-country bonds carried very small-risk premiums because investors were confident that these countries would repay their debts. In addition, the risk premiums did not increase markedly even as these countries went further into debt. In the bottom half of the figure, we see that emerging markets and developing countries inhabited a very different world. They had worse credit ratings and correspondingly higher-risk premiums. Only about half of the government bonds issued by these countries were considered investment grade, BBB– and above; the rest were considered junk bonds. Investors demanded extra profit as compensation for the perceived risks of investing in many of these countries.

Figure 6-3 also shows that ratings deteriorated rapidly as debt levels rose in poorer countries, an effect that is not as strong in the advanced countries. This observation shows the sharp limits to borrowing for poorer countries: at some stage, the cost of borrowing becomes prohibitive, if it is possible at all.

This example brings us to the other assumption of the simple model that sometimes fails to hold in poorer countries, the assumption that the country can borrow or lend as much as it wants at the prevailing world real interest rate. On the lending side, it usually isn't a problem to save as much as you want. On the borrowing side, however, lenders often tell borrowers that they have reached a debt limit and can borrow no more. When that happens, access to external credit ceases, and anything additional a country wants to consume or invest has to be taken out of its own domestic output.

---

[7] Daniel Gros, "Discrepancies in US Accounts Hide Black Hole," *Financial Times*, June 14, 2006.

FIGURE 6-3

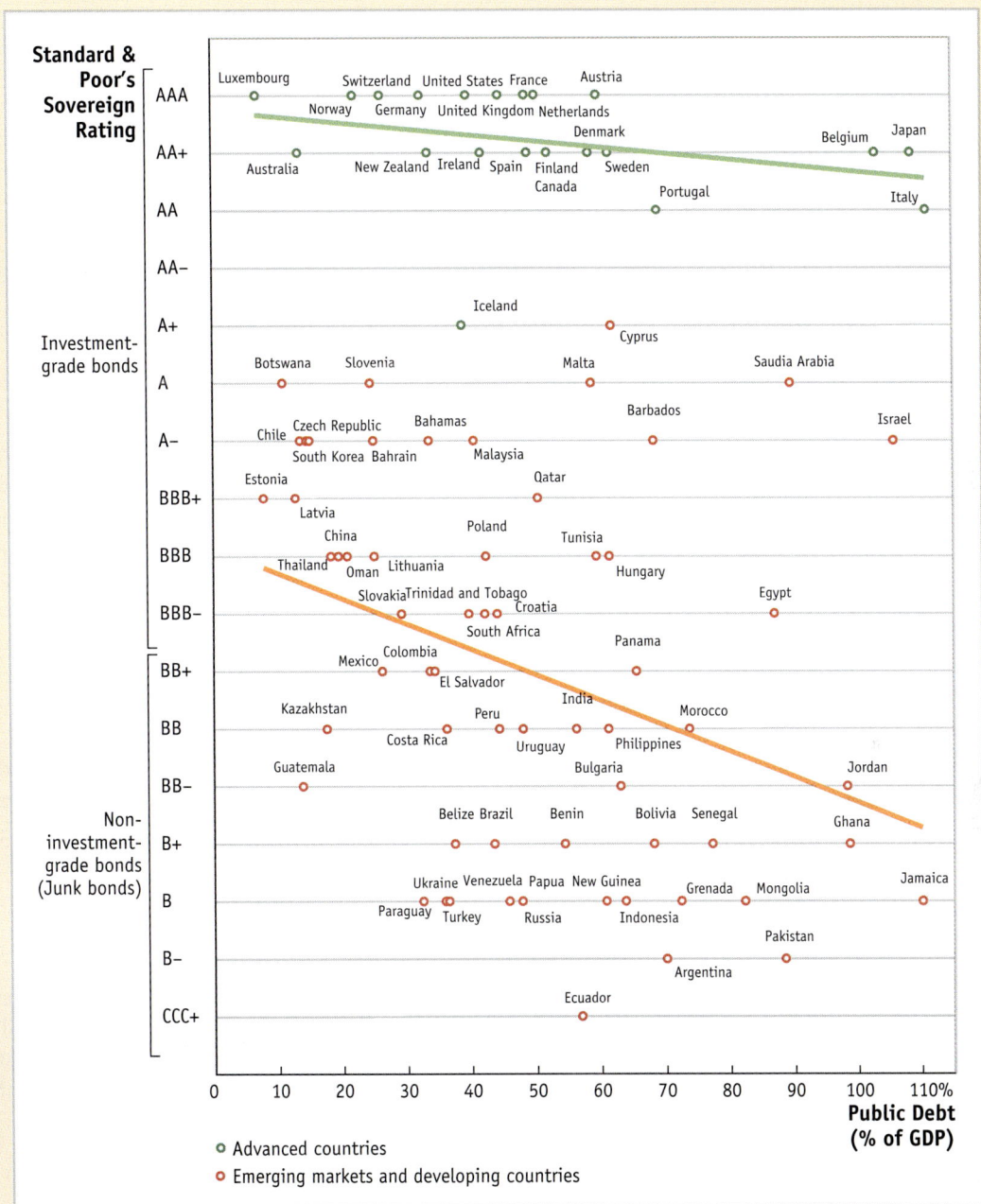

Sovereign Ratings and Public Debt Levels: Advanced Countries versus Emerging Markets and Developing Countries The data shown are for the period from 1995 to 2005. The advanced countries (green) are at the top of the chart. Their credit ratings (vertical axis) do not drop very much in response to an increase in debt levels (horizontal axis). And ratings are always high investment grade. The emerging markets and developing countries (orange) are at the bottom of the graph. Their ratings are low or junk, and their ratings deteriorate as debt levels rise.

Note: The data shown are from the period before the global financial crisis. Since that event, many advanced countries have seen large increases in public debt and ratings downgrades, and in some cases the impacts have been serious, e.g. Iceland, Ireland, Portugal, and Spain.

Source: Inter-American Development Bank, 2006, "How to Live with Debt," Ideas for Development in the Americas 11 (September–December), Figure 2.

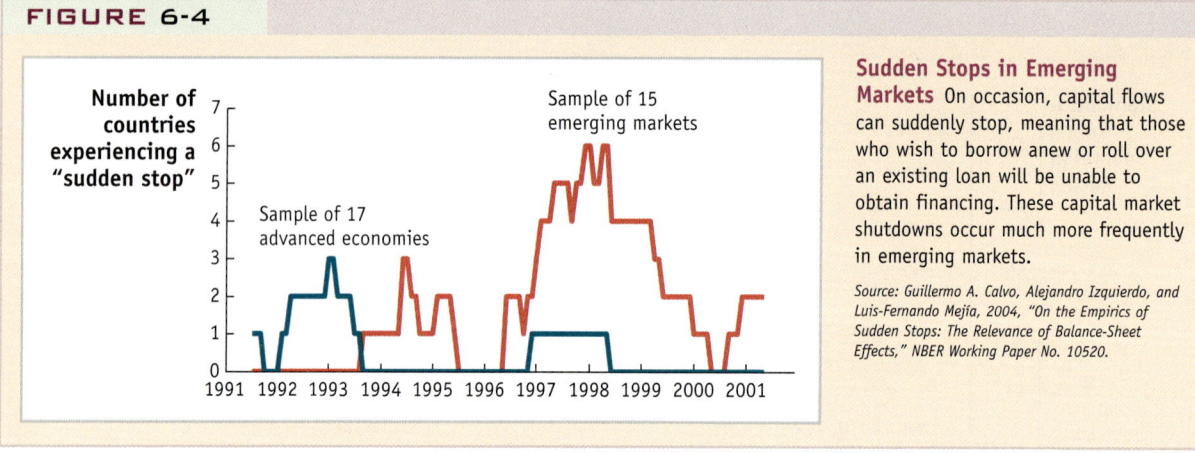

FIGURE 6-4

Sudden Stops in Emerging Markets On occasion, capital flows can suddenly stop, meaning that those who wish to borrow anew or roll over an existing loan will be unable to obtain financing. These capital market shutdowns occur much more frequently in emerging markets.

Source: Guillermo A. Calvo, Alejandro Izquierdo, and Luis-Fernando Mejía, 2004, "On the Empirics of Sudden Stops: The Relevance of Balance-Sheet Effects," NBER Working Paper No. 10520.

Figure 6-4 illustrates the remarkable frequency with which emerging market countries experience this kind of isolation from global capital markets. Research by economists Guillermo Calvo and Carmen Reinhart has focused attention on sudden stops in the flow of external finance, especially in emerging markets.[8] In a **sudden stop,** a borrower country sees its financial account surplus rapidly shrink (suddenly nobody wants to buy any more of its domestic assets) and so the current account deficit also must shrink (because there is no way to finance a trade imbalance). Reaching a debt limit can be a jolting macroeconomic shock for any economy, because it necessitates sudden and possibly large adjustments to expenditure and to the composition of expenditure. Most seriously, output may drop if domestic investment is curtailed as a result of lack of access to external credit. As the constraints arising from hitting a debt limit begin to bite, the upside of financial globalization recedes, and the downside of economic instability may take its place. In later chapters, we examine why credit market disruptions happen by looking in more detail at financial problems, crises, and default. ∎

2 Gains from Consumption Smoothing

In the next two sections of this chapter, we bring together the long-run budget constraint and a simplified model of an economy to see how gains from financial globalization can be achieved in theory. In this section, we focus on the gains that result when an open economy uses external borrowing and lending to eliminate an important kind of risk, namely, undesirable fluctuations in aggregate consumption.

The Basic Model

We retain all of the assumptions we made when developing the long-run budget constraint. There are no international transfers of income or capital, and the price level is

---

[8] On the disruptions and costs caused by sudden stops, see Guillermo Calvo and Carmen M. Reinhart, 2000, "When Capital Inflows Suddenly Stop: Consequences and Policy Options," in *Reforming the International Monetary and Financial System*, Peter B. Kenen and Alexander K. Swoboda, eds. (Washington, D.C.: International Monetary Fund), pp. 175–201; Pablo E. Guidotti, Federico Sturzenegger, and Agustín Villar, 2004, "On the Consequences of Sudden Stops," *Economía*, 4(2), 171–214; Michael M. Hutchison and Ilan Noy, 2006, "Sudden Stops and the Mexican Wave: Currency Crises, Capital Flow Reversals and Output Loss in Emerging Markets," *Journal of Development Economics*, 79(1), 225–248.

perfectly flexible, so all nominal values are also real values, and so on. We also adopt some additional assumptions. These hold whether the economy is closed or open.

- The economy's GDP or output is denoted Q. It is produced each period using labor as the only input. Production of GDP may be subject to shocks; depending on the shock, the same amount of labor input may yield different amounts of output.

- Households, which consume, are identical. This means we can think of a representative household, and use the terms "household" and "country" interchangeably. Preferences of the country/household are such that it will choose a level of consumption C that is constant over time, or smooth. This level of smooth consumption must be consistent with the country/household's long-run budget constraint.

- To keep the rest of the model simple—for now—we assume that consumption is the only source of demand. Both investment I and government spending G are zero. Under these assumptions, GNE equals personal consumption expenditures C. In this simple case, if the country is open, the trade balance (GDP minus GNE) equals Q minus C. The trade balance is positive only if Q, output, is greater than consumption C.

- Our analysis begins at time 0, and we assume the country begins with zero initial wealth inherited from the past, so that W_{-1} is equal to zero.

- When the economy is open, we look at its interaction with the rest of the world (ROW). We assume that the country is small, ROW is large, and the prevailing world real interest rate is constant at r^*. In the numerical examples that follow, we will assume $r^* = 0.05 = 5\%$ per year.

Taken all together, these assumptions give us a special case of the LRBC that requires the present value of current and future trade balances to equal zero (because initial wealth is zero):

$$0 = \underbrace{\text{Present value of } TB}_{\text{Initial wealth is zero}} = \underbrace{\text{Present value of } Q}_{\text{Present value of GDP}} - \underbrace{\text{Present value of } C,}_{\text{Present value of GNE}}$$

or equivalently,

$$\underbrace{\text{Present value of } Q}_{\text{Present value of GDP}} = \underbrace{\text{Present value of } C.}_{\text{Present value of GNE}} \qquad (6\text{-}4)$$

Remember, this equation says that the LRBC will hold, and the present value of current and future TB will be zero, if and only if the present value of current and future Q equals the present value of current and future C.

Consumption Smoothing: A Numerical Example and Generalization

Now that we've clarified the assumptions for our model, we can explore how countries smooth consumption by examining two cases:

- A closed economy, in which $TB = 0$ in all periods, external borrowing and lending are not possible, and the LRBC is automatically satisfied
- An open economy, in which TB does not have to be zero, borrowing and lending are possible, and we must verify that the LRBC is satisfied

Let's begin with a numerical example that illustrates the gains from consumption smoothing. We will generalize the result later.

Closed versus Open Economy: No Shocks Table 6-1 provides a numerical example for our model economy when it is closed and experiences no shocks. Output Q is 100 units in each period, and all output is devoted to consumption. The present value of 100 in each period starting in year 0 equals the present value of 100 in year 0, which is simply 100, plus the present value of 100 in every subsequent year, which is 100/0.05 = 2,000 [using Equation (6-2), from the case of a perpetual loan]. Thus, the present value of present and future output is 2,100.

If this economy were open rather than closed, nothing would be different. The LRBC is satisfied because there is a zero trade balance at all times. Consumption C is perfectly smooth: every year the country consumes all 100 units of its output, and this is the country's preferred consumption path. There are no gains from financial globalization because this open country prefers to consume only what it produces each year, and thus has no need to borrow or lend to achieve its preferred consumption path.

Closed versus Open Economy: Shocks The smooth path for the closed economy cannot be maintained if it suffers shocks to output, such as one of the hurricanes discussed at the start of the chapter. Suppose there is a temporary unanticipated output shock of –21 units in year 0. Output Q falls to 79 in year 0 and then returns to a level of 100 thereafter. The change in the present value of output is simply the drop of 21 in year 0. The present value of output falls from 2,100 to 2,079, a drop of 1%.

Over time, will consumption in an open economy respond to this shock in the same way closed-economy consumption does? In the closed economy, there is no doubt what happens. Because all output is consumed and there is no possibility of a trade imbalance, consumption necessarily falls to 79 in year 0 and then rises back to 100 in year 1 and stays there forever. The path of consumption is no longer smooth, as shown in Table 6-2.

In the open economy, however, a smooth consumption path is still attainable because the country can borrow from abroad in year 0, and then repay over time. The country can't afford its original smooth consumption path of 100 every period, because the present value of output is now less. So what smooth consumption path can it afford?

In the first section of this chapter, we spent some time deriving the LRBC. Now we can see why: the LRBC, given by Equation (6-4), is the key to determining a smooth

TABLE 6-1

A Closed or Open Economy with No Shocks Output equals consumption. Trade balance is zero. Consumption is smooth.

		Period							Present Value
		0	1	2	3	4	5	...	($r^* = 0.05$)
Output GDP	Q	100	100	100	100	100	100	...	2,100
Expenditure GNE	C	100	100	100	100	100	100	...	2,100
Trade balance	TB	0	0	0	0	0	0	...	0

Note: All variables take the same values from period 1 onward.

TABLE 6-2

A Closed Economy with Temporary Shocks Output equals consumption. Trade balance is zero. Consumption is volatile.

		\multicolumn{6}{c}{Period}		Present Value
		0	1	2	3	4	5	...	($r^* = 0.05$)
Output GDP	Q	79	100	100	100	100	100	...	2,079
Expenditure GNE	C	79	100	100	100	100	100	...	2,079
Trade balance	TB	0	0	0	0	0	0	...	0

Note: All variables take the same values from period 1 onward.

consumption path in the face of economic shocks. Once we establish the present value of output, we know the present value of consumption, because these must be the same; from this fact we can figure out the feasible smooth level of consumption.

In this example, the present value of output Q has fallen 1% (from 2,100 to 2,079), so the present value of consumption must also fall by 1%. How will this be achieved? Consumption can remain smooth, and satisfy the LRBC, if it falls by 1% (from 100 to 99) in every year. To double-check this logic, we compute the present value of C, using the perpetual loan formula again: $99 + 99/0.05 = 99 + 1,980 = 2,079$. Because the present value of C and the present value of Q are equal, the LRBC is indeed satisfied.

Table 6-3 shows the path of all the important macroeconomic aggregates for the open economy. In year 0, the country runs a trade balance of $TB = -20$ (a deficit), because output Q is 79 and consumption C is 99. In subsequent years, when output is 100, the country keeps consumption at 99, and has a trade balance $TB = +1$ (a surplus). Offsetting this +1 trade balance, the country must make net factor income from abroad payments $NFIA = -1$ in the form of interest paid. The country must borrow 20 in year 0, and then make, in perpetuity, 5% interest payments of 1 unit on the 20 units borrowed.

TABLE 6-3

An Open Economy with Temporary Shocks A trade deficit is run when output is temporarily low. Consumption is smooth.

		\multicolumn{6}{c}{Period}		Present Value
		0	1	2	3	4	5	...	($r^* = 0.05$)
Output GDP	Q	79	100	100	100	100	100	...	2,079
Expenditure GNE	C	99	99	99	99	99	99	...	2,079
Trade balance	TB	−20	+1	+1	+1	+1	+1	...	0
Net factor income from abroad	NFIA	0	−1	−1	−1	−1	−1	...	—
Current account	CA	20	0	0	0	0	0	...	—
External wealth	W	20	−20	−20	−20	−20	−20	...	—

Note: All variables take the same values from period 1 onward.

In year 0, the current account $CA (= TB + NFIA)$ is −20. In all subsequent years, net factor income from abroad is −1 and the trade balance is +1, implying that the current account is 0, with no further borrowing. The country's external wealth W is therefore −20 in all periods, corresponding to the perpetual loan taken out in year 0. External wealth is constant at −20; it does not explode because interest payments are made in full each period and no further borrowing is required.

The lesson is clear. When output fluctuates, a closed economy cannot smooth consumption, but an open one can.

Generalizing The lesson of our numerical example applies to any situation in which a country wants to smooth its consumption when confronted with shocks. Suppose, more generally, that output Q and consumption C are initially stable at some value with $Q = C$ and external wealth of zero. The LRBC is satisfied because the trade balance is zero at all times.

Now suppose output unexpectedly falls in year 0 by an amount ΔQ, and then returns to its prior value for all future periods. The loss of output in year 0 reduces the present value of output (GDP) by the amount ΔQ. To meet the LRBC, the country must lower the present value of consumption by the same amount. A closed economy accomplishes this by lowering its consumption by the whole amount of ΔQ in year 0. That is its only option! An open economy, however, lowers its consumption uniformly (every period) by a smaller amount, $\Delta C < \Delta Q$. But how big a reduction is needed to meet the LRBC?

Because consumption falls less than output in year 0, the country will run a trade deficit of $\Delta Q - \Delta C < 0$ in year 0. The country must borrow from other nations an amount equal to this trade deficit, and external wealth falls by the amount of that new debt. In subsequent years, output returns to its normal level but consumption stays at its reduced level, so trade surpluses of ΔC are run in all subsequent years.

Because the LRBC requires that these surpluses be large enough to service the debt, we know how large the drop in consumption must be. A loan of $\Delta Q - \Delta C$ in year 0 requires interest payments of $r^*(\Delta Q - \Delta C)$ in later years. If the subsequent trade surpluses of ΔC are to cover these interest payments, then we know that ΔC must be chosen so that

$$\underbrace{r^* \times \underbrace{(\Delta Q - \Delta C)}_{\text{Amount borrowed in year 0}}}_{\text{Interest due in subsequent years}} = \underbrace{\Delta C}_{\text{Trade surplus in subsequent years}}$$

To find out how big a cut in consumption is necessary, we rearrange and find that

$$\Delta C = \frac{r^*}{1 + r^*} \Delta Q$$

Note that the fraction in the above equation is between zero and 1. Thus, the generalized lesson is that an open economy only needs to lower its steady consumption level by a *fraction* of the size of the temporary output loss. [E.g., in the previous numerical example, $\Delta C = (0.05/1.05) \times (21) = 1$, so consumption had to fall by 1 unit.]

Smoothing Consumption when a Shock Is Permanent We just showed how an open economy uses international borrowing to smooth consumption in response to a temporary shock to output. When the shock is permanent, however, the outcome is different. With a permanent shock, output will be lower by ΔQ in all years, so the only way either a closed or open economy can satisfy the LRBC while keeping consumption smooth is to cut consumption by $\Delta C = \Delta Q$ in all years. This is optimal, even in an open economy, because consumption remains smooth, although at a reduced level.

Comparing the results for a temporary shock and a permanent shock, we see an important point: consumers can smooth out temporary shocks—they have to adjust a bit, but the adjustment is far smaller than the shock itself—but they must adjust immediately and fully to permanent shocks. For example, if your income drops by 50% just this month, you might borrow to make it through this month with minimal adjustment in spending; however, if your income is going to remain 50% lower in every subsequent month, then you need to cut your spending permanently.

Summary: Save for a Rainy Day

Financial openness allows countries to "save for a rainy day." This section's lesson has a simple household analogy. If you cannot use financial institutions to lend (save) or borrow (dissave), you have to spend what you earn each period. If you have unusually low income, you have little to spend. If you have a windfall, you have to spend it all. Using financial transactions to smooth consumption fluctuations makes a household better off. The same applies to countries.

In a closed economy, consumption must equal output in every period, so output fluctuations immediately generate consumption fluctuations. In an open economy, the desired smooth consumption path can be achieved by running a trade deficit during bad times and a trade surplus during good times. By extension, deficits and surpluses can also be used to finance extraordinary and temporary emergency spending needs, such as the costs of war (see **Side Bar: Wars and the Current Account**).

SIDE BAR

Wars and the Current Account

Our theory of consumption smoothing can take into account temporary and "desired" consumption shocks. The most obvious example of such a shock is war.

Although we assumed zero government spending above, in reality, countries' consumption includes private consumption C and public consumption G. It is simple to augment the model to include G as well as C. Under this circumstance, the constraint is that the present value of GNE ($C + G$) must equal the present value of GDP. A war means a temporary increase in G.

Borrowing internationally to finance war-related costs goes back centuries. Historians have long argued about the importance of the creation of the British public debt market as a factor in the country's rise to global leadership compared with powerful continental rivals like France. From the early 1700s (which saw rapid financial development led by major financiers like the Rothschilds) to the end of the Napoleonic Wars in 1815, the British were able to maintain good credit; they could borrow domestically and externally cheaply and easily (often from the Dutch) to finance the simultaneous needs of capital formation for the Industrial Revolution and high levels of military spending.

In the nineteenth century borrowing to finance war-related costs became more commonplace. In the 1870s the defeated French issued bonds in London to finance a reparation payment to the triumphant Germans. World War I and II saw massive lending by the United States to other Allied countries. More recently, when the United States went to war in Afghanistan (2001) and Iraq (2003), there was a sharp increase in the U.S. current account deficit and in external debt due in part to war-related borrowing.

Better at raising armies than finance, the French fought with one hand tied behind their back.

APPLICATION

Consumption Volatility and Financial Openness

Does the evidence show that countries avoid consumption volatility by embracing financial globalization? A simple test might be to compute the volatility of a country's consumption divided by the volatility of its output (where volatility equals the standard deviation of the growth rate). If more consumption smoothing is achieved, the computed ratio ought to fall. In fact, in our simple model of a small, open economy that can borrow or lend without limit, and that prefers a perfectly smooth path of consumption, this ratio should fall to zero when the gains from financial globalization are realized. In practice, this will not be true if all countries are affected by common global shocks. For example, if every country suffers a negative shock, every country will want to borrow, but that is simply infeasible. In practice, however, not all shocks are global, so countries ought to be able to achieve some reduction in consumption volatility through external finance. (We consider the importance of local and global shocks later in this chapter.)

With this in mind, Figure 6-5 presents some discouraging evidence. On the horizontal axis, countries are sorted into ten groups (deciles) from those that participate least in financial globalization (are least financially liberalized) to those that participate

FIGURE 6-5

Consumption Volatility Relative to Output Volatility For a very large sample of 170 countries over the period 1995 to 2004, we compute the ratio of consumption volatility to output volatility, expressed as a percentage. A ratio less than 100% indicates that some consumption smoothing has been achieved. Countries are then grouped into ten groups (deciles), ordered from least financially open (1) to most financially open (10). The average volatility in each group is shown. Only the most financially open countries have volatility ratios less than 100%. The high ratios in groups 1 to 8 show, perversely, that consumption is even more volatile than output in these countries.

Note: Volatility is measured by the standard deviation of real output or consumption growth according to the Penn World Tables.

Source: Index of financial openness from Sebastian Edwards, "Capital Controls, Sudden Stops and Current Account Reversals," in Sebastian Edwards, ed., 2007, *International Capital Flows* (Chicago: University of Chicago Press).

most. On the left are more closed countries with tight capital controls (generally poorer countries), on the right are the more open countries that permit free movement of capital (mostly advanced countries). For all these countries, we assess their ability to smooth total consumption ($C + G$) in the period from 1995 to 2004 using annual data. In closed countries, we would expect that the volatility of consumption would be similar to the volatility of output (GDP); the ratio of the two would be close to 100%. But if an open country were able to smooth consumption in line with our simple model, this ratio ought to be lower than 100%.

The figure shows that most groups of countries have an average consumption-to-output volatility ratio well above 100%. Moreover, as financial liberalization increases, this ratio shows little sign of decrease until fairly high levels of liberalization are reached (around the seventh or eighth decile). Indeed, until we get to the ninth and tenth deciles, all of these ratios are above 100%. Similar findings have been found using a variety of tests, and it appears that only at a very high threshold of financial liberalization does financial globalization deliver any consumption-smoothing benefits.[9]

Why are these findings so far from the predictions of our simple model? In poorer countries, some of the relatively high consumption volatility must be unrelated to financial openness—it is there even in closed countries. In the real world, households are not identical and global capital markets do not reach every person. Some people and firms do not or cannot participate in even domestic financial markets, perhaps due to backward financial systems. Other problems may stem from the way financial markets operate (e.g., poor transparency and regulation) in emerging market countries that are partially open and/or have partially developed their financial systems.

The evidence may not imply a failure of financial globalization, but it does not provide a ringing endorsement either. Consumption-smoothing gains may prove elusive for emerging markets until they advance further by improving poor governance and weak institutions, developing their financial systems, and pursuing further financial liberalization. ∎

APPLICATION

Precautionary Saving, Reserves, and Sovereign Wealth Funds

One obstacle to consumption smoothing in poorer countries is the phenomenon of sudden stops, which we noted earlier. If poorer countries can't count on credit lines to be there when they need them, they may fall back on an alternative strategy of engaging in **precautionary saving,** whereby the government acquires a buffer of external assets, a "rainy day" fund. That is, rather than allowing external wealth to fluctuate around an average of zero, with the country sometimes being in debt and sometimes being a creditor, the country maintains a higher positive "average balance" in its external wealth account to reduce or even eliminate the need to go into a net debt

---

[9] M. Ayhan Kose, Eswar S. Prasad, and Marco E. Terrones, 2007, "How Does Financial Globalization Affect Risk Sharing? Patterns and Channels," IZA Discussion Papers 2903, Institute for the Study of Labor (IZA).

position. This approach is costly, because a sacrifice of consumption is needed to build up the buffer. However, a poor country may deem the cost to be worthwhile if it allows them to smooth consumption more reliably once the buffer is established.

In the world economy today, precautionary saving is on the rise and takes two forms. The first is the accumulation of **foreign reserves** by central banks. These reserves may be used to achieve other goals, such as maintaining a fixed exchange rate, so a conflict of goals may sometimes arise. As external assets on the nation's balance sheet, however, these reserves can be deployed during a sudden stop to cushion the blow to the domestic economy. Many economists argue that some part or even the greater part of reserve accumulation in recent years in emerging markets is driven by this precautionary motive.[10]

The second form of precautionary saving by governments is through what are called **sovereign wealth funds,** state-owned asset management companies that invest some government savings (possibly including central bank reserves) overseas. Often, the asset management companies place the government savings in safe assets; increasingly, the funds are being placed in riskier assets such as equity and foreign direct investment (FDI). Some countries, such as Norway (which had an oil boom in the 1970s), use such funds to save windfall gains from the exploitation of natural resources for future needs. Many newer funds have appeared in emerging markets and developing countries (such as Singapore, China, Malaysia, and Taiwan), but these funds have been driven more by precautionary saving than resource booms.

As of 2010, the countries with the biggest sovereign wealth funds were in China ($831 billion), Abu Dhabi ($654 billion), Norway ($471 billion), and Saudi Arabia ($415 billion), with other large funds (between $50 and $150 billion each) in Kuwait, Russia Singapore, Qatar, Libya, Australia, and Algeria.[11]

Most observers believe it is likely that sovereign wealth funds will continue to grow in size, and that their use will spread to other countries (see **Headlines: Copper-Bottomed Insurance**). It is interesting that, despite having a legitimate economic rationale, these funds may generate international tensions, as they already have, by attempting to acquire politically sensitive equity and FDI assets from advanced countries. ■

3 Gains from Efficient Investment

Suppose an economy has opened up, and is taking full advantage of the gains from consumption smoothing. Has it completely exploited the benefits of financial globalization? The answer is no, because openness delivers gains not only on the consumption side but also on the investment side by improving a country's ability to augment its capital stock and take advantage of new production opportunities.

---

[10] Joshua Aizenman and Jaewoo Lee, 2005, "International Reserves: Precautionary versus Mercantilist Views, Theory and Evidence," NBER Working Paper No. 11366; Romain Ranciere and Olivier Jeanne, 2006, "The Optimal Level of International Reserves for Emerging Market Countries: Formulas and Applications," IMF Working Paper No. 06/229; Ceyhun Bora Durdu, Enrique G. Mendoza, and Marco E. Terrones, 2007, "Precautionary Demand for Foreign Assets in Sudden Stop Economies: An Assessment of the New Merchantilism," NBER Working Paper No. 13123.

[11] Data from http://www.swfinstitute.org/fund-rankings/.

HEADLINES

Copper-Bottomed Insurance

Many developing countries experience output volatility. Sovereign wealth funds can buffer these shocks, as recent experience in Chile has shown.

Thousands of government workers marched on downtown Santiago last November [2008], burning an effigy of Chilean Finance Minister Andres Velasco and calling him "disgusting" as a strike for higher wages paralyzed public services.

Five months later, polls show that Velasco is President Michelle Bachelet's most popular minister. During a three-year copper boom he and central bank President Jose De Gregorio set aside $48.6 billion, more than 30 percent of the country's gross domestic product, that he is now using for tax cuts, subsidies and cash handouts to poor families.

The Chilean peso has risen almost 10 percent against the dollar this year to become the best-performing currency among emerging markets. The country's economy is expected to grow 0.1 percent in 2009, as the region contracts 1.5 percent, according to the International Monetary Fund. . . .

Velasco, 48, applied the lessons learned from decades of economic failure in Latin America—ones he said could also help the U.S. The current crisis followed "a massive regulatory failure in many advanced financial markets over the last decade or so," Velasco said in an interview April 21 [2009] in his office overlooking the presidential palace in downtown Santiago.

"This is a movie that may be novel to some Americans, but this is a movie that people in other places of the world, Chile included, know we have seen," said Velasco, who is scheduled to meet April 25 with Federal Reserve Chairman Ben S. Bernanke in Washington. "We know how it begins, how it unfolds and how it ends." . . .

Commodity-driven swings of boom and bust have defined Latin America's economic history for the past 100 years.

"That is a cycle that needs to be ended," Velasco said. "We have been out to show that a Latin American country can manage properly, and not mismanage, a commodity cycle. You save in times of abundance, and you invest in lean times."

When Velasco joined Bachelet's new cabinet in March 2006, the price of copper had risen by more than half in 12 months to $2.25 a pound. Taxes and profits from state-owned Codelco, the world's largest copper producer, provide about 15 percent of government revenue. Bachelet, 57, Chile's second consecutive socialist president, came under almost immediate pressure to start spending the revenue.

Students went on strike in May of that year, demanding more money for education. More than 800,000 people protested at high schools and universities, and police with water cannons and tear gas arrested more than 1,000. Velasco reiterated his commitment to "prudent fiscal policies" as politicians from the governing coalition demanded he resign. . . .

In his first three years in office, Velasco posted the biggest budget surpluses since the country returned to democracy in 1990. In 2007, Chile became a net creditor for the first time since independence from Spain in 1810.

Last July [2008], copper reached a record of $4.08 a pound. By year-end, the central bank had built $23.2 billion of reserves. The government had $22.7 billion in offshore funds and about $2.8 billion in its own holdings.

After Lehman Brothers Holdings Inc.'s September 15 bankruptcy sparked a global credit freeze, Velasco and De Gregorio had the equivalent of more than 30 percent of GDP available if needed to shore up Chile's banks and defend the peso.

The price of copper plummeted 52 percent from September 30 to year-end, and Velasco dusted off his checkbook. In the first week of January, he and Bachelet unveiled a $4 billion package of tax cuts and subsidies.

"He has been vindicated," said Luis Oganes, head of Latin American research at JPMorgan Chase & Co. in New York, who studied under Velasco. . . .

Velasco's stimulus spending, including 40,000-peso ($68.41) handouts to 1.7 million poor families, has paid off politically. His approval rating almost doubled to 57 percent in March from a low of 31 percent in August, according to Adimark GfK, a Santiago-based polling company. He is now the most well-liked member of the government, second only to the president at 62 percent.

"People finally understood what was behind his 'stinginess' of early years," said Sebastian Edwards, a Chilean economist at the University of California, Los Angeles. "That explains the rise in his popularity."

Source: Excerpted from Sebastian Boyd, Harvard Peso Doctor Vindicated as Chile Evades Slump, bloomberg.com, April 23, 2009.

The Basic Model

To illustrate these investment gains, we must refine the model we have been using by abandoning the assumption that output can be produced using only labor. We now assume that producing output requires labor and capital, which is created over time by investing output. When we make this change, the LRBC Equation (6-4) must be modified to include investment I as a component of GNE. For simplicity, however, we still assume that government consumption G is zero. With this change, the LRBC becomes

$$\underbrace{0}_{\text{Initial wealth is zero}} = \text{Present value of } TB$$

Because the TB is output (Q) minus consumption + investment ($C + I$), we can rewrite this last equation in the following form:

$$\underbrace{\text{Present value of } Q}_{\text{Present value of GDP}} = \underbrace{\text{Present value of } C + \text{Present value of } I}_{\text{Present value of GNE}} \quad (6\text{-}5)$$

The LRBC will hold if and only if the present value of output Q equals the present value of expenditure ($C + I$).

Using this modified LRBC, we now study investment and consumption decisions in two cases:

- A closed economy, in which external borrowing and lending are not possible, the trade balance is zero in all periods, and the LRBC is automatically satisfied.
- An open economy, in which borrowing and lending are possible, the trade balance can be more or less than zero, and we must verify that the LRBC is satisfied.

Efficient Investment: A Numerical Example and Generalization

Let's start with a country that has output of 100, consumption C of 100, no investment, a zero trade balance, and zero external wealth. If that state persisted, the LRBC would be satisfied, as in the previous numerical example above. This describes the optimal path of consumption in both the closed and open economies when output is constant and there are no shocks.

But now suppose there is a shock in year 0 that takes the form of a new investment opportunity. For example, it could be that in year 0 engineers discover that by building a new factory with a new machine, the country can produce a certain good much more cheaply than current technology allows. Or perhaps there is a resource discovery, but a mine must first be built to extract the minerals from the earth. What happens next? We turn first to a numerical example and then supply a more general answer.

We assume that undertaking the investment (in machines or factories or mines) would require an expenditure of 16 units, and that in return the investment will pay off in future years by increasing the country's output by 5 units in year 1 and all subsequent years (but not in year 0).

The country now faces some choices. Should it undertake this investment? And if it does, will it make out better if it is open or closed? We find the answers to these questions by looking at how an *open* economy would deal with the opportunity to invest, and then showing why a country would make itself worse off by choosing to be closed, thereby relinquishing at least some of the gains the investment opportunity affords.

As in the previous example, the key to solving this problem is to work with the LRBC and see how the choices a country makes to satisfy it have to change as circumstances do. Before the investment opportunity shock, output and consumption were each 100 in all periods, and had a present value of 2,100. Investment was zero in every period, and the LRBC given by Equation (6-5) was clearly satisfied. If the country decides to not act on the investment opportunity, this situation continues unchanged whether the economy is closed or open.

Now suppose the open economy undertakes the investment. First, we must calculate the difference this would make to the country's resources, as measured by the present value of output. Output would be 100 today and then 105 in every subsequent year. The present value of this stream of output is 100 plus 105/0.05 or 2,200. This is an increase of 100 over the old present value of output (2,100). Note that the present value of the increment to output is 100.

Can all of this additional output be devoted to consumption? No. To obtain this stream of additional output, the country has had to invest 16 units in the current period. In this scenario, because all investment occurs in the current period, 16 is also the present value of investment in the modified LRBC given by Equation (6-5).

Looking at that LRBC, we've calculated the present value of output (2,200), and now we have the present value of investment (16). We can see that the present value of consumption must equal 2,200 minus 16, or 2,184. This is 4% higher than it was without the investment. Even allowing for the fact that some expenditure has to be devoted to investment, the resources available for consumption have risen by 4% in present value terms (from 2,100 without the investment, to 2,184 with it).

We can now find the new level of smooth consumption each period that satisfies the LRBC. Because the present value of C has risen by 4% from 2,100 to 2,184, the country can afford to raise consumption C in all periods by 4% from 100 to 104. (As a check, note that $104 + 104/0.05 = 2,184$.) Is the country better off if it makes the investment? Yes—not only does its consumption remain smooth, but it is also 4% higher in all periods.

Table 6-4 lays out the details of this case. In year 0, consumption C is 104, investment I is 16, and GNE is 120. The trade balance is –20 because output Q is only 100.

TABLE 6-4

An Open Economy with Investment and a Permanent Shock The economy runs a trade deficit to finance investment and consumption in period 0 and runs a trade surplus when output is higher in later periods. Consumption is smooth.

			Period							Present Value
			0	1	2	3	4	5	...	($r^* = 0.05$)
Output GDP	Q		100	105	105	105	105	105	...	2,200
Expenditure GNE	C		104	104	104	104	104	104	...	2,184
	I		16	0	0	0	0	0	...	16
Trade balance	TB		–20	+1	+1	+1	+1	+1	...	0
Net factor income from abroad	$NFIA$		0	–1	–1	–1	–1	–1	...	—
Current account	CA		–20	0	0	0	0	0	...	—
External wealth	W		–20	–20	–20	–20	–20	–20	...	—

Note: All variables take the same values from period 1 onward.

The country must borrow 20 units in year 0 to fund the investment of 16 *and* the 4 additional units of consumption the country can afford as a result of the investment. In all future years, consumption C is 104, and because there is no subsequent investment, *GNE* is also 104. Output Q is 105, and the trade balance is +1.

The initial trade deficit of 20 in year 0 results in an external debt of 20. As a perpetual loan, with an interest rate of 5%, this debt of 20 must be serviced by net interest payments of –1 in each subsequent year if the LRBC is to be satisfied. The interest payment of –1 offsets the trade surplus of +1 each period forever. Hence, the current account is zero in all future years, with no further borrowing, and the country's external wealth is –20 in all periods. External wealth does not explode, and the LRBC is satisfied.

This outcome is preferable to any outcome the closed economy can achieve. To attain an output level of 105 from year 1 on, the closed economy would have to cut consumption to 84 in year 0 to free up 16 units for investment. Although the country would then enjoy consumption of 105 in all subsequent years, this is not a smooth consumption path! The open economy *could* choose this path (cutting consumption to 84 in year 0), because it satisfies the LRBC. It won't choose this path, however, because by making the investment, it cannot only smooth its consumption but also do so *at a higher level*. The open economy is better off making the investment *and* smoothing consumption, two goals that the closed economy cannot simultaneously achieve.

Generalizing The lesson of our numerical example applies to any situation in which a country confronts new investment opportunities. Suppose that a country starts with zero external wealth, constant output Q, consumption C equal to output, and investment I equal to zero. A new investment opportunity appears requiring ΔK units of output in year 0. This investment will generate an additional ΔQ units of output in year 1 and all later years (but not in year 0).

Ultimately, consumers care about consumption. In an open economy, they can smooth their consumption, given future output. The constant level of consumption is limited only by the present value of available resources, as expressed by the LRBC. Maximizing the level of consumption is the same as maximizing the present value of consumption. Rearranging Equation (6-5), the LRBC requires that the present value of consumption must equal the present value of output minus the present value of investment. How is this present value maximized?

The increase in the present value of output $PV(Q)$ comes from extra output in every year but year 0, and the present value of these additions to output is, using Equation (6-2),

$$\text{Change in present value of output} = \frac{\Delta Q}{(1+r^*)} + \frac{\Delta Q}{(1+r^*)^2} + \frac{\Delta Q}{(1+r^*)^3} + \cdots = \frac{\Delta Q}{r^*}$$

The change in the present value of investment $PV(I)$ is simply ΔK.

This means the investment will increase the present value of consumption—and hence will be undertaken—if and only if $\Delta Q/r^* \geq \Delta K$. There are two ways to look at this conclusion. Rearranging, investment is undertaken when

$$\underbrace{\Delta Q}_{\substack{\text{Output increase in} \\ \text{subsequent periods}}} \geq \underbrace{r^* \times \Delta K}_{\substack{\text{Interest payment due in} \\ \text{subsequent periods to} \\ \text{finance initial investment}}}$$

The intuition here is that investment occurs up to the point at which the annual benefit from the marginal unit of capital (ΔQ) equals or exceeds the annual cost of borrowing the funds to pay for that capital ($r^* \Delta K$).

Putting it another way, dividing by ΔK, investment is undertaken when

$$\underbrace{\frac{\Delta Q}{\Delta K}}_{\text{Marginal product of capital}} \geq \underbrace{r^*}_{\text{World real interest rate}} \qquad (6\text{-}6)$$

This is a standard formula for the optimal or efficient level of investment and may look familiar from other courses in economics. Firms will take on investment projects as long as the **marginal product of capital,** or **MPK,** is at least as great as the real interest rate.

Summary: Make Hay While the Sun Shines

In an open economy, firms borrow and repay to undertake investment that maximizes the present value of output. Households also borrow and lend to smooth consumption, but these borrowing and lending decisions are separate from those of firms.

When investing, an open economy sets its *MPK* equal to the world real rate of interest. If conditions are unusually good (high productivity), it makes sense to invest more capital and produce more output. Conversely, when conditions turn bad (low productivity), it makes sense to lower capital inputs and produce less output. This strategy maximizes the present value of output minus investment. Households then address the separate problem of how to smooth the path of consumption when output changes. A closed economy must be self-sufficient. Any resources invested are resources not consumed. More investment implies less consumption. This creates a trade-off. When investment opportunities are good, the country wants to invest to generate higher output in the future. Anticipating that higher output, the country wants to consume more today, but it cannot—it must consume less to invest more.

Proverbially, financial openness helps countries to "make hay while the sun shines"— and, in particular, to do so without having to engage in a trade-off against the important objective of consumption smoothing. The lesson here has a simple household analogy. Suppose you find a great investment opportunity. If you have no financial dealings with the outside world, you would have to sacrifice consumption and save to finance the investment.

APPLICATION

Delinking Saving from Investment

The story of the Norwegian oil boom provides a good illustration of our theory about investment and financial openness. North Sea oil was discovered in the 1960s, but the mass exploitation of this resource was unprofitable as long as cheap and plentiful supplies of oil were being produced elsewhere, primarily in the Persian Gulf. Then came the first "oil shock" in the early 1970s, when the cartel of Oil Producing and Exporting Countries (OPEC) colluded to raise world oil prices dramatically, a shock that was (correctly) viewed as permanent. At these higher oil prices, it suddenly made sense to exploit North Sea oil. Starting in the early 1970s, oil platforms, pipelines, refineries, and terminals were sprouting offshore and along the coast of Norway, causing its capital stock to permanently increase in response to a new productive investment opportunity.

Figure 6-6 shows the path of saving (S) and investment (I) measured as ratios of GDP in Norway from 1965 to 1990. The oil boom is clearly visible in the investment share of GDP, which in the 1970s rose about 10 percentage points above its typical level. Had Norway been a closed economy, this additional investment would have been financed by a decrease in the share of output devoted to public and private consumption. As you can see, no such sacrifice was necessary. Norway's saving rate was flat in this period or even fell slightly. In Norway's open economy, saving and investment were delinked and the difference was made up by the current account $CA = S - I$, which moved sharply into deficit, approaching minus 15% of GDP at one point. Thus, all of the short-run increase in investment was financed by foreign investment in Norway, much of it by multinational oil companies.

Is Norway a special case? Economists have examined large international datasets to see whether there is general evidence that countries can delink investment decisions from saving decisions as the Norwegians did. One approach follows the pioneering work of Martin Feldstein and Charles Horioka.[12] They estimated what fraction β of each additional dollar saved tended to be invested in the same country. In other words, in their model, if saving rose by an amount ΔS, they estimated that investment would rise by an amount $\Delta I = \beta \Delta S$. In a closed economy, the "savings retention" measure β would equal 1, but they argued that increasing financial openness would tend to push β below 1.

For example, suppose one were to estimate β for the period 1980 to 2000 for three groups of countries with differing degrees of financial integration within the group: in

FIGURE 6-6

The Oil Boom in Norway Following a large increase in oil prices in the early 1970s, Norway invested heavily to exploit oil fields in the North Sea. Norway took advantage of openness to finance a temporary increase in investment by running a very large current account deficit, thus increasing its indebtedness to the rest of the world. At its peak, the current account deficit was more than 10% of GDP.

Source: Alan M. Taylor, 2002, "A Century of Current Account Dynamics," *Journal of International Money and Finance*, 21(6), 725–748.

---

[12] Martin Feldstein and Charles Horioka, 1980, "Domestic Saving and International Capital Flows," *Economic Journal*, 90(358), 314–329.

a sample of countries in the European Union, where international financial integration had advanced furthest, the estimated value of β is 0.26, meaning that 26% of each additional dollar saved tended to be invested in the same country; in a sample of all developed countries with a somewhat lower level of financial integration, the estimate of β is 0.39; and in a sample of emerging markets, where financial integration was lower still, the estimate of β is 0.67.[13] These data thus indicate that financially open countries seem to have a greater ability to delink saving and investment, in that they have a much lower "savings retention" measure β. ∎

Can Poor Countries Gain from Financial Globalization?

Our analysis shows that if the world real interest rate is r^* and a country has investment projects for which the marginal product of capital MPK exceeds r^*, then the country should borrow from the rest of the world to finance investment in these projects. Keep this conclusion in mind as we now examine an enduring question in international macroeconomics: Why doesn't more capital flow to poor countries?

Production Function Approach To look at this question carefully, economists must take a stand on what determines a country's marginal product of capital. For this purpose, economists usually employ a version of a **production function** that maps available capital per worker, $k = K/L$, and the prevailing level of **productivity** A to the level of output per worker, $q = Q/L$, where Q is GDP.

A simple and widely used production function takes the form

$$\underbrace{q}_{\text{Output per worker}} = \underbrace{A}_{\text{Productivity level}} \times \underbrace{k^\theta}_{\text{Capital per worker}}$$

where θ is a number between 0 and 1 that measures the contribution of capital to production.[14] Specifically, θ is the elasticity of output with respect to capital (i.e., a 1% increase in capital per worker generates a θ% increase in output per worker). In the real world, θ has been estimated to be approximately one-third, and this is the value we employ here.[15] An illustration is given in the top part of Figure 6-7, panel (a), which graphs the production function for the case in which $\theta = 1/3$ and the productivity level is set at a reference level of 1, so $A = 1$. Thus, for this case $q = k^{1/3}$.

With this production function, what is the marginal product of capital, MPK? It is the slope of the production function, the incremental change in output per worker Δq divided by the incremental change in capital per worker Δk. As we can see from the figure, capital's marginal product MPK (the extra output we get by increasing capital per worker) decreases as k increases. Indeed, from the preceding formula, we can find that MPK, or the slope of the production function, is given by

$$MPK = \frac{\Delta q}{\Delta k} = \underbrace{\theta A k^{\theta - 1}}_{\text{Slope of the production function}} = \theta \times \frac{q}{k}$$

---

[13] Author's calculations based on International Monetary Fund, *International Financial Statistics*, with investment and saving measured as a share of GDP.
[14] This is called the Cobb–Douglas production function.
[15] Douglas Gollin, April 2002, "Getting Income Shares Right," *Journal of Political Economy*, 110(2), 458–474.

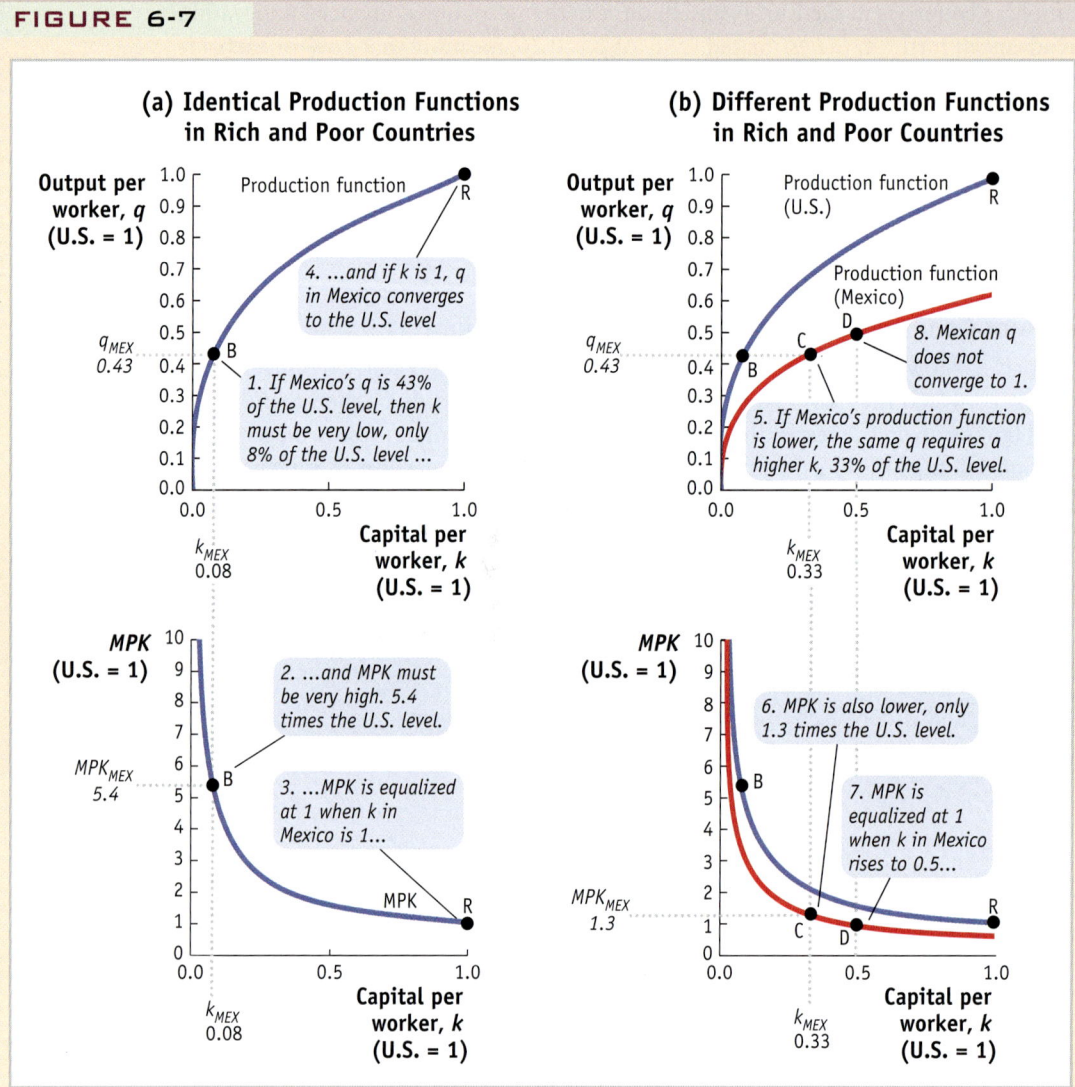

FIGURE 6-7

Why Doesn't Capital Flow to Poor Countries? If poor and rich countries share the same level of productivity (a common production function), then MPK must be very high in poor countries, as shown in panel (a). For example, if B represents Mexico and R the United States, we would expect to see large flows of capital to poor countries, until their capital per worker k and, hence, output per worker q rise to levels seen in the rich world (movement from point B to point R). The result is convergence. This doesn't happen in reality. Poor and rich countries have different levels of productivity (different production functions) and so MPK may not be much higher in poor countries than it is in rich countries, as shown in panel (b). The poor country (Mexico) is now at C and not at B. Now investment occurs only until MPK falls to the rest of the world level at point D. The result is divergence. Capital per worker k and output per worker q do not converge to the levels seen in the rich country.

Thus, in this special case, the *marginal product of capital* is proportional to output per worker divided by capital per worker (the output-capital ratio) or the *average product of capital*. The MPK for the case we are studying, in which $\theta = 1/3$ and $A = 1$, is shown in the bottom part of Figure 6-7, panel (a).

A Benchmark Model: Countries Have Identical Productivity Levels To see how a country responds to the possibilities opened up by financial globalization, let's look at what determines the incentive to invest in small open economies of the type we are studying, assuming they all have access to the same level of productivity, $A = 1$.

To understand when such a country will invest, we need to understand how its *MPK* changes as k changes. For example, suppose the country increases k by a factor of 8. Because $q = k^{1/3}$, q increases by a factor of 2 (the cube root of 8). Let's suppose this brings the country up to the U.S. level of output per worker. Because $MPK = q/k$ and because q has risen by a factor of 2, while k has risen by a factor of 8, *MPK* changes by a factor of 1/4; that is, it falls to 1/4 its previous level.

This simple model says that poor countries with output per worker of 1/2 the U.S. level have an *MPK* of four times the U.S level. Countries with one-quarter the U.S. per worker output level have an *MPK* of 16 times the U.S level, and so on.

To make the model concrete, let's see how well it applies to a comparison of the United States and Mexico in the late 1980s.[16] During this time, the United States produced approximately twice as much GDP per worker as Mexico. Now let's choose units such that all U.S. variables take the value 1, and Mexican variables are proportions of the corresponding U.S. variables. For example, with these units, q was 0.43 in Mexico in the late 1980s (i.e., output per worker in Mexico was 43% of output per worker in the United States).

Now consider the implications of assuming that the economies of Mexico and the United States were described by the same production function with a common productivity level, $A = 1$. In Figure 6-7, panel (a), the United States is at point R (for rich) and Mexico is at point B, and its low output implies a capital per worker k that is only 8% of the U.S. level. What is Mexico's marginal product of capital? It is 5.4 times the U.S. marginal product of capital. Why? As above, *MPK* is θ (a constant for both countries equal to 1/3) times q/k. In the United States, $q/k = 1$; in Mexico, $q/k = 0.43/0.08 = 5.4$.

We can think of the United States and other rich countries as representing the rest of the world—a large financially integrated region, from Mexico's point of view. The world real interest rate r^* is the opportunity cost of capital for the rest of the world, that is, the rich world's *MPK*. If the real interest rate r^* is, say, 10% in rich countries like the United States, then their *MPK* is 10%, and Mexico has an *MPK* of 54%!

To take an even more dramatic example, we could look at India, a much poorer country than Mexico. India's output per worker was just 8.6% of the U.S. level in 1988. Using our simple benchmark model, we would infer that the *MPK* in India was 135 times the U.S. level![17]

To sum up, the simple model says that the poorer the country, the higher its *MPK*, because of the twin assumptions of diminishing marginal product and a common productivity level. Investment ought to be very profitable in Mexico (and India, and all poor countries). Investment in Mexico should continue until Mexico is at point R. Economists

---

[16] In 1985 levels of GDP per worker were $23,256 in Mexico and $48,164 in the United States (in 1996 international dollars), according to the reference source for such data, the Penn World Tables. By 1995 this gap had widened a little. The data in this example are based on Robert E. Hall and Charles I. Jones, 1999, "Why Do Some Countries Produce So Much More Output per Worker Than Others?" *Quarterly Journal of Economics*, 114(1), 83–116.

[17] First solve for the relative level of capital per worker in India: $k_{IND}/k_{US} = [q_{IND}/q_{US}]^{1/\theta} = [0.086]^3 = 0.000636$. The relative MPK in India would then equal $[q_{IND}/q_{US}]/[k_{IND}/k_{US}] = [0.086]/[0.086]^3 = 1/[0.086]^2 = 135$.

would describe such a trajectory for Mexico as **convergence.** If the world is characterized by convergence, countries can reach the level of capital per worker and output per worker of the rich country through investment and capital accumulation alone.

The Lucas Paradox: Why Doesn't Capital Flow from Rich to Poor Countries?

Twenty or thirty years ago, a widespread view among economists was that poor countries had access to exactly the same technologies as rich countries, given the flow of ideas and knowledge around a globalizing world. This led economists to assume that if policies shifted to allow greater international movement of capital, foreign investment would flood into poor countries because their very poverty implied that capital was scarce in these countries, and therefore its marginal product was high.

But as Nobel laureate Robert Lucas wrote in his widely cited article "Why Doesn't Capital Flow from Rich to Poor Countries?":

> If this model were anywhere close to being accurate, and if world capital markets were anywhere close to being free and complete, it is clear that, in the face of return differentials of this magnitude, investment goods would flow rapidly from the United States and other wealthy countries to India and other poor countries. Indeed, one would expect no investment to occur in the wealthy countries. . . . The assumptions on technology and trade conditions that give rise to this example must be drastically wrong, but exactly what is wrong with them, and what assumptions should replace them?[18]

What was drastically wrong was the assumption of identical productivity levels A across countries, as represented by the single production function in Figure 6-7, panel (a). Although this model is often invoked, it is generally invalid. Can we do better?

An Augmented Model: Countries Have Different Productivity Levels

To see why capital does not flow to poor countries, we now suppose that A, the productivity level, is different in the United States and Mexico, as denoted by country subscripts:

$$\underbrace{q_{US}}_{\substack{\text{Output per worker} \\ \text{in the United States}}} = \underbrace{A_{US} k_{US}^{\theta}}_{\text{U.S. production function}} \qquad \underbrace{q_{MEX}}_{\substack{\text{Output per worker} \\ \text{in Mexico}}} = \underbrace{A_{MEX} k_{MEX}^{\theta}}_{\text{Mexican production function}}$$

Countries have potentially different production functions and different *MPK* curves, depending on their relative levels of productivity, as shown in Figure 6-7, panel (b). The Mexican curves are shown here as lower than the U.S. curves. We now show that this augmented model is a much better match with reality.

The earlier *MPK* equation holds for each country, so we can compute the ratios of country *MPK*s as

$$\frac{MPK_{MEX}}{MPK_{US}} = \frac{[\theta q_{MEX}/k_{MEX}]}{[\theta q_{US}/k_{US}]} = \frac{q_{MEX}/q_{US}}{k_{MEX}/k_{US}}$$

Using this equation, we can see the importance of allowing productivity levels to differ across countries. We know that $q_{MEX}/q_{US} = 0.43$, but we can also obtain data on capital per worker that show $k_{MEX}/k_{US} = 0.33$. Plugging these numbers into the last

---

[18] Robert E. Lucas Jr., May 1990, "Why Doesn't Capital Flow from Rich to Poor Countries?" *American Economic Review*, 80(2), 92–96. Lucas presented the India example with the assumption that capital's share was 0.4 rather than one-third, and that India's output per worker was one-fifteenth of the U.S. level. In that case, India's *MPK* is "only" 58 times the U.S. level, an equally absurd conclusion.

expression says that *MPK* in Mexico is not 5.4 times the U.S. level, as we had earlier determined, but only about 1.3 times (0.43/0.33) the U.S. level. The smaller multiple is due to the lower productivity level that our model attaches to Mexico.

Put another way, the data show that Mexico's capital per worker is about one-third that of the United States. If the simple model were true, Mexico would have a level of output level per worker of $(1/3)^{1/3} = 0.69$ or 69% of the U.S. level. However, Mexico's output per worker was much less, only 0.43 or 43% of the U.S. level. This gap can only be explained by a lower productivity level in Mexico. We infer that *A* in Mexico equals 0.43/0.69 = 0.63, or 63% of that in the United States.

This means that Mexico's production function and *MPK* curves are lower than those for the United States. This more accurate representation of reality is shown in Figure 6-7, panel (b). Mexico is not at point B, as was assumed in panel (a); it is at point C, on a different (lower) production function and a different (lower) *MPK* curve. The *MPK* gap between Mexico and the United States is much smaller, which greatly reduces the incentive for capital to migrate to Mexico from the United States.

The measured *MPK* differentials in the augmented model do not seem to indicate a major failure of global capital markets to allocate capital efficiently. But the augmented model has very different implications for convergence. Mexico would borrow only enough to move from point C to point D, where its *MPK* equals r^*. This investment would raise its output per worker a little, but it would still be far below that of the United States.

APPLICATION

A versus *k*

In our previous calculations, we found that Mexico did not have a high level of *MPK* relative to the United States. Hence, we would not expect large flows of capital into Mexico but would expect Mexico to remain relatively poor even with access to global financial markets.

Is this conclusion true in general? What about other developing countries? Table 6-5 repeats the same exercise we just did for many developing countries, including Mexico. In all cases, predicted GDP gains due to financial globalization are large with the benchmark model, but disappointingly small once we augment the model to correct for productivity differences. Moreover, if we were to allow for the fact that gross national income (GNI) gains are less than GDP gains as a result of factor payments to foreign capital that would be due on foreign investment, then the net GNI gains would be smaller still.

This is a profound result. Once we allow for productivity differences, investment will not cause poor countries to reach the same level of capital per worker or output per worker as rich countries. Economists describe this outcome as one of long-run **divergence** between rich and poor countries. Unless poor countries can lift their levels of productivity (raise *A*), access to international financial markets is of limited use. They may be able to usefully borrow capital, thereby increasing output per worker by some amount, but there are not enough opportunities for productive investment for complete convergence to occur.

In the developing world, global capital markets typically are not failing. Rather, low levels of productivity *A* make investment unprofitable, leading to low output levels that do not produce convergence. But what exactly does *A* represent?

An older school of thought focused on *A* as reflecting a country's **technical efficiency,** construed narrowly as a function of its technology and management capabilities.

TABLE 6-5

Why Capital Doesn't Flow to Poor Countries The table shows data on output and capital per worker (columns 1 and 2). Column 3 shows the level of productivity relative to the United States that is implied by the data. Productivity differences are large for poor countries. If these differences are assumed away, then the gains from financial globalization in poor countries could be large (columns 4, 5). But if they remain, the gains will be small (columns 6, 7).

	(a) Data		(b) Implied Productivity (U.S. = 1)	(c) Outcomes with Financial Globalization			
				With U.S. Productivity Level, A_{us} Increase in:		With Actual Productivity, A Increase in:	
Country, Group, or Region	$\frac{q}{q_{us}}$ (1)	$\frac{k}{k_{us}}$ (2)	$\frac{A}{A_{us}}$ (3)	Capital k (4)	Output q (5)	Capital k (6)	Output q (7)
Latin America							
Argentina	0.42	0.38	0.58	+163%	+139%	+15%	+5%
Brazil	0.32	0.24	0.51	+311	+214	+50	+15
Chile	0.26	0.26	0.41	+289	+280	+4	+1
Mexico	0.43	0.33	0.63	+207	+131	+53	+15
Asia							
China	0.06	0.05	0.17	+2,001	+1,569	+41	+12
India	0.09	0.04	0.24	+2,213	+1,064	+180	+41
Indonesia	0.11	0.09	0.24	+980	+805	+30	+9
Pakistan	0.13	0.04	0.37	+2,202	+679	+408	+72
Africa							
Congo	0.12	0.06	0.32	+1,677	+722	+218	+47
Kenya	0.06	0.03	0.18	+3,078	+1,674	+140	+34
Nigeria	0.05	0.04	0.14	+2,259	+1,970	+22	+7
South Africa	0.25	0.23	0.41	+334	+300	+13	+4
	Group Average			Based on Group Average			
Per Capita Income Quintiles							
1st (Poorest 20% of countries)	0.04	0.02	0.15	+5,371	+2,474	+210	+46
2nd (2nd Poorest 20%)	0.10	0.07	0.25	+1,426	+907	+86	+23
3rd (Middle 20%)	0.21	0.18	0.38	+463	+368	+32	+10
4th (2nd Richest 20%)	0.40	0.37	0.56	+167	+148	+12	+4
5th (Richest 20%)	0.75	0.85	0.80	+17	+32	−17	−6
Major Groups							
Developing	0.15	0.11	0.31	+836	+572	+65	+18
Emerging	0.29	0.23	0.48	+329	+241	+41	+12

Source: Robert E. Hall and Charles I. Jones, February 1999, "Why Do Some Countries Produce So Much More Output per Worker Than Others?" Quarterly Journal of Economics, 114(1), 83–116.

Today, many economists believe there is very little obstacle to the flow of such knowledge between countries, and that the problem must instead be one of implementation. These economists believe that the level of A may primarily reflect a country's **social efficiency,** construed broadly to include institutions, public policies, and even cultural conditions such as the level of trust. Low productivity might then follow from low levels of human capital (poor education policies) or poor-quality institutions (bad governance, corruption, red tape, and poor provision of public goods including infrastructure). And indeed there is some evidence that, among poorer countries, more capital does tend to flow to the countries with better institutions.[19]

More Bad News? The augmented model shows that as long as productivity gaps remain, investment will be discouraged, and, regrettably, poor countries will not see their incomes converge to rich levels. If we now take some other factors into account, the predictions of the model about convergence are even less optimistic.

- The model makes no allowance for risk premiums. Suppose the *MPK* is 10% in the United States and 13% in Mexico. The differential may be a risk premium Mexico must pay to foreign lenders that compensates them for the risk of investing in an emerging market (e.g., risks of regulatory changes, tax changes, expropriation, and other political risks). In this case, no additional capital flows into Mexico. In Figure 6-7, panel (b), Mexico stays at point C and its income does not increase at all.

- Risk premiums may be large enough to cause capital to flow "uphill" from poor to rich. If world capital markets impose a risk premium higher than 3%, say, 7%, then capital would actually leave Mexico for the United States, moving from the higher to the lower *MPK* region, in search of a "safe haven" that provides higher risk-adjusted returns. In Figure 6-7, panel (b), Mexico would move left of point C as capital flowed out, and per capita output would fall. Is this a relevant case? Yes. Figure 6-8 shows that risk premiums can be substantial in

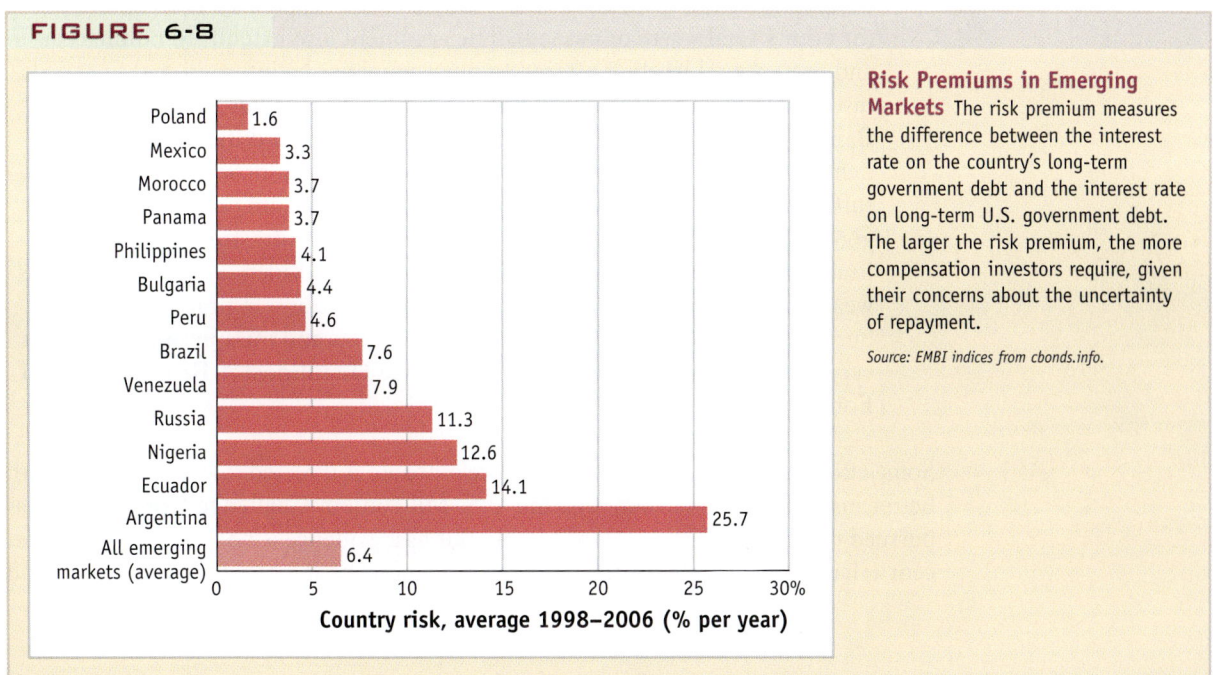

FIGURE 6-8

Risk Premiums in Emerging Markets The risk premium measures the difference between the interest rate on the country's long-term government debt and the interest rate on long-term U.S. government debt. The larger the risk premium, the more compensation investors require, given their concerns about the uncertainty of repayment.

Source: EMBI indices from cbonds.info.

---

[19] James R. Lothian, April 2006, "Institutions, Capital Flows and Financial Integration," *Journal of International Money and Finance*, 25(3), 358–369; Laura Alfaro, Sebnem Kalemli-Ozcan, and Vadym Volosovych, 2008, "Why Doesn't Capital Flow from Rich to Poor Countries? An Empirical Investigation," *Review of Economics and Statistics*, 90(2), 347–368.

emerging markets, including Mexico. And U.S. Treasury securities data indicate that from 1994 to 2006, U.S. holdings of Mexican assets rose from $50 billion to $65 billion, but Mexican holdings of U.S. assets rose from $5 billion to $95 billion; on net, capital moved north.

- The model assumes that investment goods can be acquired at the same relative price in output terms everywhere. In fact, the model treats one unit of investment as the same as one unit of output. But in developing countries, it often costs much more than one unit of output to purchase one unit of capital goods. Poor countries often are ill-equipped to efficiently supply nontraded capital goods (such as buildings or bridges), and their imported capital goods (such as machinery and equipment) are often quite expensive because of trade costs (such as tariffs and transport costs).[20]

- The model assumes that the contribution of capital to production is equal across countries. In our estimates, we used 1/3 as the elasticity of output with respect to capital. But recent research suggests that capital's share may be much lower in many developing countries, where a large part of GDP is derived from natural resources with little use of physical capital. This lowers the MPK even more.[21]

- The model suggests that **foreign aid** may do no better than foreign investors in promoting growth. The model doesn't care where additional capital comes from. Investments paid for by transfers (aid or debt relief) rather than private investments face the same low MPK and the same divergence result holds. Economists dispute whether foreign aid can make a difference to long-term development and growth, or if it is only an act of charity to prop up the poor (or even a total waste of money). The argument also extends to nonmarket and preferential lending offered to poor countries by international financial institutions such as the **World Bank** (see **Side Bar: What Does the World Bank Do?**). In support of the case that aid can make a difference, aid proponents argue that aid can finance public goods that can provide externalities sufficient to jolt a poor country out of a bad equilibrium or "poverty trap"—goods that private markets cannot provide (such as infrastructure, public health, and education). Aid skeptics reply that the evidence for such effects is weak, either because the links are not there or because in practice aid is so bureaucratized and subject to so many diversions and misappropriations that very little of it actually gets spent wisely (see **Headlines: A Brief History of Foreign Aid**).

Some efforts are now being made to ensure more aid is directed toward countries with better institutional environments: the U.S. Millennium Challenge Corporation has pursued this goal, as has the World Bank. But past evidence is not encouraging: A recent exhaustive study of aid and growth by economists Raghuram Rajan and Arvind

---

[20] Alan M. Taylor, 1998, "On the Costs of Inward-Looking Development: Price Distortions, Growth, and Divergence in Latin America," *Journal of Economic History*, 58(1), 1–28; Jonathan Eaton and Samuel Kortum, 2001, "Trade in Capital Goods," *European Economic Review*, 45(7), 1195–1235.

[21] Francesco Caselli and James Feyrer, 2007, "The Marginal Product of Capital," *Quarterly Journal of Economics*, 122(2), 535–568.

SIDE BAR

What Does the World Bank Do?

The World Bank (worldbank.org), based in Washington, D.C., is one of the Bretton Woods "twins" established in 1944 (the other is the International Monetary Fund). Its main arm, the International Bank for Reconstruction and Development, has 185 member countries. Its principal purpose is to provide financing and technical assistance to reduce poverty and promote sustained economic development in poor countries. A country's voting weight in the governance of the World Bank is based on the size of its capital contributions. The World Bank can raise funds at low interest rates and issue AAA-rated debt as good as that of any sovereign nation. It then lends to poor borrowers at low rates. Because the borrower nations could not obtain loans on these terms (or even any terms) elsewhere, the loans are a form of aid or transfer. In return for the preferential rate, the bank may approve a loan for a particular development purpose (building infrastructure, e.g.) or to support a policy reform package. Controversially, conditions may also be imposed on the borrowing nation, such as changes in trade or fiscal policy. As a result of sovereignty, the implementation of the conditions and the use of the loans have in some cases not turned out as intended, although outright default on these preferential loans is almost unheard of.

HEADLINES

A Brief History of Foreign Aid

Foreign aid is frequently on the political agenda. But can it make any difference?

In 1985, when Bob Geldof organized the rock spectacular Live Aid to fight poverty in Africa, he kept things simple. "Give us your fucking money" was his famous (if apocryphal) command to an affluent Western audience—words that embodied Geldof's conviction that charity alone could save Africa. He had no patience for complexity: we were rich, they were poor, let's fix it. As he once said to a luckless official in the Sudan, after seeing a starving person, "I'm not interested in the bloody system! Why has he no food?"

Whatever Live Aid accomplished, it did not save Africa. Twenty years later, most of the continent is still mired in poverty. So when, earlier this month, Geldof put together Live 8, another rock spectacular, the utopian rhetoric was ditched. In its place was talk about the sort of stuff that Geldof once despised—debt-cancellation schemes and the need for "accountability and transparency" on the part of African governments—and, instead of fund-raising, a call for the leaders of the G-8 economies to step up their commitment to Africa. (In other words, don't give us your fucking money; get interested in the bloody system.) Even after the G-8 leaders agreed to double aid to Africa, the prevailing mood was one of cautious optimism rather than euphoria.

That did not matter to the many critics of foreign aid, who mounted a lively backlash against both Live 8 and the G-8 summit. For them, continuing to give money to Africa is simply "pouring billions more down the same old ratholes," as the columnist Max Boot put it. At best, these critics say, it's money wasted; at worst, it turns countries into aid junkies, clinging to the World Bank for their next fix. Instead of looking for help, African countries need to follow the so-called Asian Tigers (countries like South Korea and Taiwan), which overcame poverty by pursuing what Boot called "superior economic policies."

Skepticism about the usefulness of alms to the Third World is certainly in order. Billions of dollars have ended up in the pockets of kleptocratic rulers—in Zaire alone, Mobutu Sese Soko stole at least four billion—and still more has been misspent on massive infrastructure boondoggles, like the twelve-billion-dollar Yacyreta Dam, between Argentina and Paraguay, which Argentina's former President called "a monument to corruption." And historically there has been little correlation between aid and economic growth.

This checkered record notwithstanding, it's a myth that aid is doomed to failure. Foreign aid funded the campaign to eradicate smallpox, and in the sixties it brought the Green Revolution in agriculture to countries like India and Pakistan, lifting living standards and life expectancies for hundreds of millions of

Continued on next page

people. As for the Asian nations that Africa is being told to emulate, they may have pulled themselves up by their bootstraps, but at least they were provided with boots. In the postwar years, South Korea and Taiwan had the good fortune to become, effectively, client states of the U.S. Between 1946 and 1978, in fact, South Korea received nearly as much U.S. aid as the whole of Africa. Meanwhile, the billions that Taiwan got allowed it to fund a vast land-reform program and to eradicate malaria. And the U.S. gave the Asian Tigers more than money; it provided technical assistance and some military defense, and it offered preferential access to American markets.

Coincidence? Perhaps. But the two Middle Eastern countries that have shown relatively steady and substantial economic growth—Israel and Turkey—have also received tens of billions of dollars in U.S. aid. The few sub-Saharan African countries that have enjoyed any economic success at all of late—including Botswana, Mozambique, and Uganda—have been major aid recipients, as has Costa Rica, which has the best economy in Central America. Ireland (which is often called the Celtic Tiger) has enjoyed sizable subsidies from the European Union. China was the World Bank's largest borrower for much of the past decade.

Nobody doubts that vast amounts of aid have been squandered, but there are reasons to think that we can improve on that record. In the first place, during the Cold War aid was more often a geopolitical tool than a well-considered economic strategy, so it's not surprising that much of the money was wasted. And we now understand that the kind of aid you give, and the policies of the countries you give it to, makes a real difference. A recent study by three scholars at the Center for Global Development found that, on average, foreign aid that was targeted at stimulating immediate economic growth (as opposed to, say, dealing with imminent crises) has had a significantly beneficial effect, even in Africa.

There's still a lot wrong with the way that foreign aid is administered. Too little attention is paid to figuring out which programs work and which don't, and aid still takes too little advantage of market mechanisms, which are essential to making improvements last. There's plenty we don't know about what makes one country succeed and another fail, and, as the former World Bank economist William Easterly points out, the foreign-aid establishment has often promised in the past that things would be different. So we should approach the problem of aid with humility. Yet humility is no excuse for paralysis. In 2002, President Bush created the Millennium Challenge Account, which is designed to target assistance to countries that adopt smart policies, and said that the U.S. would give five billion dollars in aid by 2006. Three years later, a grand total of $117,500 has been handed out. By all means, let's be tough-minded about aid. But let's not be hardheaded about it.

Source: James Surowiecki, "A Farewell to Alms?" *New Yorker,* July 25, 2005.

Subramanian concluded: "We find little robust evidence of a positive (or negative) relationship between aid inflows into a country and its economic growth. We also find no evidence that aid works better in better policy or geographical environments, or that certain forms of aid work better than others. Our findings suggest that for aid to be effective in the future, the aid apparatus will have to be rethought."[22]

---

[22] Raghuram G. Rajan and Arvind Subramanian, 2008, "Aid and Growth: What Does the Cross-Country Evidence Really Show?" *Review of Economics and Statistics,* 90(4), 643–665.

4 Gains from Diversification of Risk

In the second section of this chapter, we studied consumption smoothing using a simplified model. We used a borrowing and lending approach, we considered a small open economy, we assumed that countries owned their own output, and we treated output shocks as given. We then saw how debt can be used to smooth the impact of output shocks on consumption. However, we also discussed the finding that in practice, countries seem to be unable to eliminate the effects of output volatility. The problems seem to be especially difficult in emerging markets and developing countries. We also saw that reliance on borrowing and lending may create problems because there may be limits to borrowing, risk premiums, and sudden stops in the availability of credit.

Are there other ways for a country to cope with shocks to output? Yes. In this final section, we show how **diversification,** another facet of financial globalization, can help smooth shocks by promoting risk sharing. With diversification, countries own not only the income stream from their own capital stock, but also income streams from capital stocks located in other countries. We see how, by using financial openness to trade such rights—for example, in the form of capital equity claims like stocks and shares—countries may be able to reduce the volatility of their incomes (and hence their consumption levels) without *any* net lending or borrowing whatsoever.

Diversification: A Numerical Example and Generalization

To keep things simple and to permit us to focus on diversification, we assume there is no borrowing (the current account is zero at all times). To illustrate the gains from diversification, we examine the special case of a world with two countries, A and B, which are identical except that their respective outputs fluctuate asymmetrically; that is, they suffer equal and opposite shocks.

We now explore how this world economy performs in response to the output shocks. We examine the special case in which there are two possible "states of the world," which are assumed to occur with an equal probability of 50%. In terms of output levels, state 1 is a bad state for A and a good state for B; state 2 is a good state for A and a bad state for B.

We assume that all output is consumed, and that there is no investment or government spending. As we know from the previous chapter, output is distributed to factors in the form of income. We assume output is divided 60-40 between labor income and capital income in each country. The key question for us will be, who owns this income? Domestic residents or foreigners?

Home Portfolios To begin, both countries are closed, and households in each country own the entire capital stock of their own country. Thus, A owns 100% of A's capital, and B owns 100% of B's capital. Under these assumptions, output (as measured by gross domestic product, GDP) is the same as income (as measured by gross national income, GNI) in A and B.

A numerical example is given in Table 6-6, panel (a). In state 1, A's output is 90, of which 54 units are payments to labor and 36 units are payments to capital; in state 2, A's output rises to 110, and factor payments rise to 66 for labor and 44 units for capital. The opposite is true in B: in state 1, B's output is higher than it is in state 2. Using our national accounting definitions, we know that in each closed economy, consumption C, income GNI, and output GDP are equal. In both A and B, all of these quantities are volatile. GNI, and hence consumption, flips randomly between 90 and 110 in

TABLE 6-6

Portfolio Diversification Choices: Diversifiable Risks In countries A and B, GDP is allocated 60% to labor income and 40% to capital income. There are two "states of the world": state 1 is bad for A and good for B; state 2 is the opposite. On average, GDP equals 100, but in the good state, GDP is 110, and in the bad state it is only 90. Thus, world GDP and GNI always equal 200, world labor income is always 120, and world capital income is always 80. When each country holds only its own assets as in panel (a), GNI equals GDP and is very volatile. When each country holds a 50% share of the world portfolio as in panel (b), GNI volatility decreases because capital income is now smoothed. When each country holds a portfolio made up only of the other country's capital as in panel (c), GNI volatility falls even further by making capital income vary inversely with labor income.

(a) When Countries Hold 100% Home Portfolios
Each Country Owns 100% of Its Own Capital

	COUNTRY A			COUNTRY B			WORLD		
	Capital Income	Labor Income	GDP = GNI	Capital Income	Labor Income	GDP = GNI	Capital Income	Labor Income	GDP = GNI
State 1	36	54	90	44	66	110	80	120	200
State 2	44	66	110	36	54	90	80	120	200
Variation about mean	∓ 4	∓ 6	∓ 10	± 4	± 6	± 10	0	0	0

(b) When Countries Hold World Portfolios
Each Country Owns 50% A Capital and 50% B Capital with Payoffs as in Panel (a)

	COUNTRY A			COUNTRY B			WORLD		
	Capital Income	Labor Income	GNI	Capital Income	Labor Income	GNI	Capital Income	Labor Income	GDP = GNI
State 1	40	54	94	40	66	106	80	120	200
State 2	40	66	106	40	54	94	80	120	200
Variation about mean	0	∓ 6	∓ 6	0	± 6	± 6	0	0	0

(c) When Countries Hold 100% Foreign Portfolios
Each Country Owns 100% of the Other Country's Capital with Payoffs as in Panel (a)

	COUNTRY A			COUNTRY B			WORLD		
	Capital Income	Labor Income	GNI	Capital Income	Labor Income	GNI	Capital Income	Labor Income	GDP = GNI
State 1	44	54	98	36	66	102	80	120	200
State 2	36	66	102	44	54	98	80	120	200
Variation about mean	± 4	∓ 6	∓ 2	∓ 4	± 6	± 2	0	0	0

both countries. The variation of GNI about its mean of 100 is plus or minus 10 in each country. Because households prefer smooth consumption, this variation is undesirable.

World Portfolios Notice that when one country's capital income is up, the other's is down. World GDP equals world GNI and is always 200. World labor income is always 120 and world capital income is always 80.

It is apparent from Figure 6-9 that the two countries can achieve partial income smoothing if they diversify their portfolios of capital assets. For example, each country could own half of the domestic capital stock, and half of the other country's capital stock. Indeed, this is what standard portfolio theory says that investors should try to do. The results of this portfolio diversification are shown in Table 6-6, panel (b).

Now each country owns one-half of its own capital stock but sells the other half to the other country in exchange for half of the other country's capital stock.[23] Each country's output or GDP is still as it was described in panel (a). But now country incomes or GNI can differ from their outputs or GDP. Owning 50% of the world portfolio means that each country has a capital income of 40 every period. However, labor income still varies between 54 and 66 in the bad and good states, so total income (and hence consumption) varies between 94 and 106. Thus, as Table 6-6, panel (b), shows, capital income for each country is smoothed at 40 units, the average of A and B capital income in panel (a), as also illustrated in Figure 6-9.

How does the balance of payments work when countries hold the world portfolio? Consider country A. In state 1 (bad for A, good for B), A's income or GNI exceeds A's output, GDP, by 4 (94 − 90 = +4). Where does the extra income come from? The extra is net factor income from abroad of +4. Why is it +4? This is precisely equal to the difference between the income earned on A's external assets (50% of B's payments to capital of 44 = 22) and the income paid on A's external liabilities (50% of A's payments to capital of 36 = 18). What does A do with that net factor income? A runs a trade balance of −4, which means that A can consume 94, even when its output is only 90. Adding the trade balance of −4 to net factor income from abroad of +4 means that the current account is 0, and there is still no need for any net borrowing or lending, as assumed. These flows are reversed in state 2 (which is good for A, bad for B).

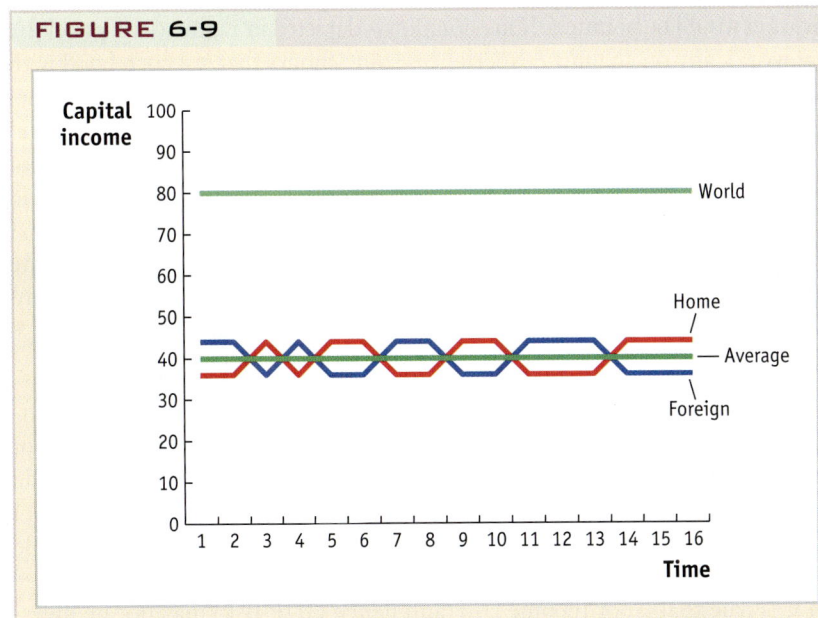

FIGURE 6-9

Portfolio Diversification and Capital Income: Diversifiable Risks The figure shows fluctuations in capital income over time for different portfolios, based on the data in Table 6-6. Countries trade claims to capital income by trading capital assets. When countries hold the world portfolio, they each earn a 50-50 split (or average) of world capital income. World capital income is constant if shocks in the two countries are asymmetrical and cancel out. All capital income risk is then fully diversifiable.

---

[23] Note that this financial transaction would balance in the financial account, as a pure asset trade, so no borrowing or lending is needed and the current account remains zero, as we have assumed.

Note that after diversification, income or GNI varies in A and B by plus or minus 6 (around a mean of 100), which is less than the range of plus or minus 10 seen in Table 6-6, panel (a). This is because 40% of income is capital income and so 40% of the A income fluctuation of 10 can be smoothed by the portfolio diversification.

Generalizing Let us try to generalize the concept of capital income smoothing through diversification. Consider the volatility of capital income by itself, in the example we have just studied. Each country's payments to capital are volatile. A portfolio of 100% country A's capital or 100% of country B's capital has capital income that varies by plus or minus 4 (between 36 and 44). But a 50-50 mix of the two leaves the investor with a portfolio of minimum, zero volatility (it always pays 40).

This outcome is summed up in Figure 6-10, panel (a), which refers to either country, A or B. There is an identical high level of capital income volatility when the country holds either a 100% home portfolio or a 100% foreign portfolio. However, holding a mix of the two reduces capital income volatility, and a minimum volatility of zero can be achieved by holding the 50-50 mix of the world capital income portfolio.

To generalize this result to the real world, we need to recognize that not all shocks are asymmetric as we have assumed here. The outputs of countries A and B may not be equal and opposite (with correlation −1) as we have assumed here. In general, there will be some common shocks, which are identical shocks experienced by both countries. The impact of common shocks cannot be lessened or eliminated by any form of asset trade. For example, suppose we add an additional shock determined by two new states of the world, X and Y (these states of the world are independent of states of the world 1 and 2). We shall assume that in state X, the new shock adds five units to each country's output; in state Y, it subtracts five units from each. There is no way to avoid this shock by portfolio diversification. The X-Y shocks in each country are perfectly positively correlated (correlation +1). If this were the only shock, the countries' outputs would move up and down together and diversification would be pointless. This situation is depicted in Figure 6-10, panel (b).

In the real world, any one country experiences some shocks that are correlated with those of other countries, either positively or negatively, and some of which are uncorrelated. As long as some shocks are asymmetric, or country-specific, and not common between the home and foreign country, then the two countries can take advantage of gains from the diversification of risk. In this more general case in which symmetric and asymmetric shocks are combined, as depicted in Figure 6-10, panel (c), holding a 100% portfolio of domestic (or foreign) assets generates a volatile income. But holding the 50-50 world portfolio will lower the volatility of income, albeit not all the way to zero (see the appendix at the end of the chapter for a detailed discussion).

Limits to Diversification: Capital versus Labor Income As we saw in Table 6-6, panel (b), elimination of total income risk cannot be achieved by holding the world portfolio, even in the case of purely asymmetric shocks of capital assets. Why? Because labor income risk is not being shared. Admittedly, the same theory would apply if one could trade labor like an asset, but this is impossible because ownership rights to labor cannot be legally traded in the same way as one can trade capital or other property (that would be slavery).

Although it is true that labor income risk (and hence GDP risk) may not be diversifiable through the trading of claims to labor assets or GDP, this is not quite the end of our story—in theory at least. We saw in Table 6-6, panel (a), that capital and labor income in each country are perfectly correlated in this example: A good state raises

FIGURE 6-10

Return Correlations and Gains from Diversification The charts plot the volatility of capital income against the share of the portfolio devoted to foreign capital. The two countries are identical in size and experience shocks of similar amplitude. In panel (a), shocks are perfectly asymmetric (correlation = −1), capital income in the two countries is perfectly *negatively* correlated. Risk can be eliminated by holding the world portfolio, and there are large gains from diversification. In panel (b), shocks are perfectly symmetric (correlation = +1), capital income in the two countries is perfectly *positively* correlated. Risk cannot be reduced, and there are no gains from diversification. In panel (c), when both types of shock are present, the correlation is neither perfectly negative nor positive. Risk can be partially eliminated by holding the world portfolio, and there are still some gains from diversification.

both capital and labor income, and a bad state lowers both. This is not implausible—in reality, shocks to production do tend to raise and lower incomes of capital and labor simultaneously. This means that, as a risk-sharing device, trading claims to capital income can substitute for trading claims to labor income.

To illustrate this, imagine an unrealistic scenario in which the residents of each country own no capital stock in their own country but own the entire capital stock of the other country. As shown in Table 6-6, panel (c), owning only the other country's portfolio achieves more risk sharing than holding 50% of the world portfolio.

For example, when A is in the good state (state 2), A's labor income is 66 but A's capital income is 36 (assumed now to be 100% from B, which is in the bad state). This adds up to a portfolio of 102. In the bad state for A (state 2), A's labor income is 54, but A's capital income is 44 (from B, which is in a good state), for a total GNI of 98. So A's income (and consumption) vary by plus or minus 2, between 98 and 102 in panel (c). Compare this fluctuation of ±2 around the mean of 100 to the fluctuations of ±10 (home portfolio) and ±6 (the world portfolio) in panels (a) and (b).

You can see how additional risk reduction has been achieved. A would like to own claims to 50% of B's total income. It could achieve this by owning 50% of B's capital and 50% of B's labor. But labor can't be owned, so A tries to get around the restriction of owning 0% of B's labor by acquiring much more than 50% of B's capital. Because labor's share of income in both countries is more than half in this example—a realistic ratio—this strategy allows for the elimination of some, but not all, risk.

APPLICATION

The Home Bias Puzzle

So much for theory. In practice, we do not observe countries owning foreign-biased portfolios or even the world portfolio. Countries tend to own portfolios that suffer from a strong **home bias,** a tendency of investors to devote a disproportionate fraction of their wealth to assets from their own home country, when a more globally diversified portfolio might protect them better from risk.

To illustrate this, economist Karen Lewis compared the risk and return for sample portfolios from which U.S. investors could have chosen for the period 1970 to 1996. She imagined an experiment in which some assets are allocated to a domestic portfolio (the S&P 500) and the remainder to an overseas portfolio (Morgan Stanley's EAFE fund). In this stylized problem, the question is what weight to put on each portfolio, when the weights must sum to 100%. In reality, U.S. investors picked a weight of about 8% on foreign assets. Was this a smart choice?

Figure 6-11 shows the risk and return for every possible weight between 0% and 100%. Return is measured by the mean rate of return (annualized percent per year); risk is measured by the standard deviation of the return (its root mean square deviation from its mean).

With regard to returns, the foreign portfolio had a slightly higher average return than the home portfolio during this period, so increasing the weight in the foreign portfolio would have increased the returns: the mean return line slopes up slightly from left to right. What about risk? A 100% foreign portfolio (point E) would have generated higher risk than the home U.S. portfolio (point A); thus, E is above A. However, we know that some mix of the two portfolios ought to produce a lower volatility than either extreme because the two returns are not perfectly correlated. This minimum volatility will not be zero because there are some undiversifiable, symmetric shocks, but it will be lower than the volatility of the 100% home and 100% foreign portfolios: overseas and domestic returns are not perfectly correlated, implying that substantial country-specific diversifiable risks exist.

In fact, Lewis showed that a U.S. investor with a 0% weight on the overseas portfolio (point A) could have raised that weight to as much as 39% (point C), while simultaneously raising the average of her total return and lowering its risk. Even moving to the right of C (toward D) would make sense, though how far would depend on how the investor viewed the risk-return trade-off. Choosing a weight as low as 8% (point B) would seem to be a puzzle.

Broadly speaking, economists have had one of two reactions to the emergence of the "home bias puzzle" in the 1990s. One is to propose many different theories to explain it away: Perhaps it is costly to acquire foreign assets, or get information about them? Perhaps there are asymmetries between home and foreign countries' consumption patterns (due to nontraded goods or trade frictions or even tastes) that make domestic assets a better hedge against domestic consumption risk? Perhaps home investors worry about regulatory barriers and the problems of corporate governance in foreign

FIGURE 6-11

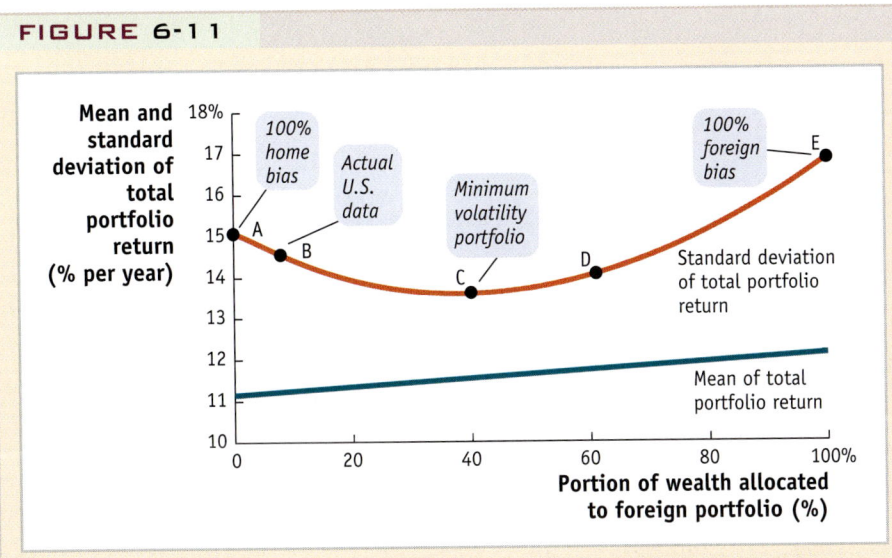

Portfolio Diversification in the United States The figure shows the return (mean of monthly return) and risk (standard deviation of monthly return) for a hypothetical portfolio made up from a mix of a pure home U.S. portfolio (the S&P 500) and a pure foreign portfolio (the Morgan Stanley EAFE) using data from the period 1970 to 1996. U.S. investors with a 0% weight on the overseas portfolio (point A) could have raised that weight as high as 39% (point C) and still raised the return and lowered risk. Even moving to the right of C (toward D) would make sense, though how far would depend on how the investor viewed the risk-return trade-off. The actual weight seen was extremely low at just 8% (point B) and was considered a puzzle.

Source: Karen K. Lewis, 1999, "Trying to Explain Home Bias in Equities and Consumption," Journal of Economic Literature, 37(2), 571–608.

markets? These and many other solutions have been tried in extremely complex economic models, but none has been judged a complete success.

The other reaction of economists has been to look at the evidence of home bias in the period from the 1970s to the 1990s (the period of the Lewis study) as a legacy of the pronounced deglobalization of financial markets in the postwar period that might slowly disappear. Recent evidence suggests that this might be happening to some degree. There has been a dramatic increase in overseas equity investments in a sample of advanced countries from 1970 to 2003, with a very strong upward trend after 1985 in IMF data. For example, in the United States, the foreign share of the U.S. portfolio has risen from 5.6% in 1990 to 12.7% in 2003. Over the same period, the U.K. portfolio saw its foreign share rise from 33.1% to 52.4%. Figure 6-12 shows the massive extent of cross-border holdings of assets in today's global economy.

Furthermore, these figures might understate the true extent to which residents have diversified away from home capital because many large multinational firms have capital income streams that flow from operations in many countries. For example, an American purchasing a share of Intel or Ford, or a Briton purchasing a share of BP, or a Japanese purchasing a share of Sony, is really purchasing shares of income streams from the globally diversified operations of these companies. Technically, Intel is recorded in the data as a 100% U.S. "home" stock, but this makes the home bias puzzle look much

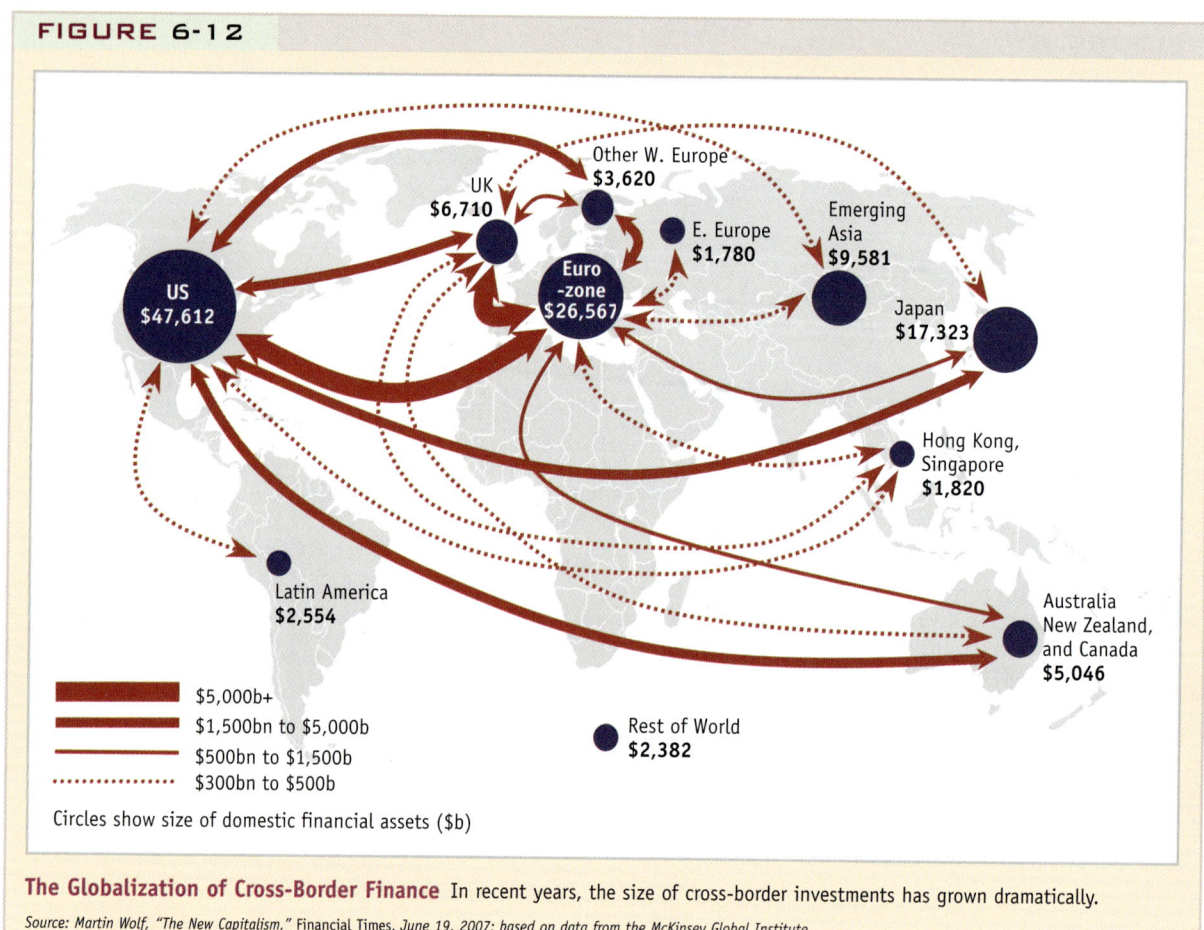

The Globalization of Cross-Border Finance In recent years, the size of cross-border investments has grown dramatically.

Source: Martin Wolf, "The New Capitalism," *Financial Times,* June 19, 2007; based on data from the McKinsey Global Institute.

worse than it really is because investors do seem to invest heavily in firms such as these that provide an indirect foreign exposure.[24]

Recent trends in diversification within portfolios and within companies may mean that even if the puzzle cannot be explained away, perhaps it will gradually go away. ■

Summary: Don't Put All Your Eggs in One Basket

If countries were able to borrow and lend without limit or restrictions in an efficient global capital market, our discussions of consumption smoothing and efficient investment would seem to suggest that they should be able to cope quite well with the array of possible shocks, in order to smooth consumption. In reality, as the evidence shows, countries are not able to fully exploit the intertemporal borrowing mechanism.

In this environment, diversification of income risk through the international trading of assets can deliver substantial benefits. In theory, if countries were able to pool their income streams and take shares from that common pool of income, all country-specific shocks would be averaged out, leaving countries exposed only to common global shocks to income, the sole remaining undiversifiable shocks that cannot be avoided.

---

[24] Fang Cai and Francis E. Warnock, 2006, "International Diversification at Home and Abroad," NBER Working Paper No. 12220.

Financial openness allows countries—like households—to follow the old adage "Don't put all your eggs in one basket." The lesson here has a simple household analogy. Think of a self-employed person who owns a ski shop. If the only capital she owns is her own business capital, then her capital income and labor income move together, and go up in good times (winter) and down in bad times (summer). Her total income could be smoothed if she sold some stock in her company and used the proceeds to buy stock in another company that faced asymmetric shocks (a surf shop, perhaps).

In practice, however, risk sharing through asset trade is limited. For one thing, the number of assets is limited. The market for claims to capital income is incomplete because not all capital assets are traded (e.g., many firms are privately held and are not listed on stock markets), and trade in labor assets is legally prohibited. Moreover, even with the traded assets available, investors have shown very little inclination to invest their wealth outside their own country, although that may be slowly changing in an environment of ongoing financial globalization.

5 Conclusions

If a firm or household were to retreat from the national financial markets by keeping its money in a bag in a closet and paying cash for all its purchases (house, cars, appliances, toothpaste, gum, etc.), we would regard it as a strange and potentially costly move. By allowing households to save and borrow, financial markets help households smooth consumption in the face of shocks to their income (such as a debilitating illness, the loss of a job, destruction of property by floods or other acts of nature). Likewise, financial markets allow firms to borrow to invest efficiently in productive projects and permit investors to diversify their portfolios across a wide range of assets.

On the global scale, the same principles apply in theory to countries, subject to the long-run budget constraint. They, too, face income shocks, new investment opportunities, and country-specific risks. We have seen how they can similarly benefit from access to an external capital market—the global capital market.

Theory proves to be far from reality, however: The extent to which countries make use of global financial markets is still limited. Even in the most financially open advanced countries, consumption shocks remain, investment is often financed out of domestic saving, and a home bias persists in investors' portfolios. In poorer countries, we see no consumption smoothing gains realized, and there is little scope for development based on external finance until current low productivity levels are improved.

Are global capital markets failing? To the criticism that financial globalization doesn't work, one could respond that it hasn't really been fully tried yet. Many emerging markets and most developing countries are still on the road to full financial liberalization, and large barriers remain. Even so, deeper institutional weaknesses in these countries may hinder the efficient operation of the mechanisms we have studied. One could argue that such weaknesses may be corrected or diminished by the stimulus to competition, transparency, accountability, and stability that financial openness may provide.[25] But absent further institutional improvements, the benefits of financial globalization are likely to be much smaller for these countries, and they must also be weighed against potential offsetting costs, such as the risk of crises, which will be discussed in later chapters.

---

[25] M. Ayhan Kose, Eswar Prasad, Kenneth S. Rogoff, and Shang-Jin Wei, 2006, "Financial Globalization: A Reappraisal," NBER Working Paper No. 12484.

KEY POINTS

1. Countries can use their external wealth as a buffer to smooth consumption in the face of fluctuations in output or investment. However, this process is not without its limits. The country must service its debts and must not allow debts to roll over and grow without limit at the real rate of interest.

2. The condition that guarantees that debts are serviced is the long-run budget constraint, or LRBC: the present value of future trade deficits must equal minus the present value of initial wealth.

3. The long-run budget constraint can be put another way: The present value of GDP plus the present value of initial wealth (the country's resources) must equal the present value of GNE (the country's spending).

4. In a closed economy, the country must satisfy $TB = 0$ in every period as there is no external trade in goods or assets. In an open economy, the economy has to satisfy only the long-run budget constraint, which states that TB equals minus the present value of initial wealth. The former is a tighter constraint than the latter—implying that there can be gains from financial globalization.

5. The current account may be lower than normal in any period when there is unusually high private or public consumption (during a war, e.g.), unusually low output (such as occurs after a natural disaster), or unusually high investment (such as that following a natural resource discovery).

6. If poor countries had the same productivity as rich countries, there would be substantial gains from investing in poor countries where the marginal product of capital, or MPK, would be much higher. However, this is not the case, and there is little evidence of investment inefficiency at the global level as measured by MPK gaps between countries. What gaps there are may be due to risk premiums. Consequently, large-scale investment (and foreign aid) in poor countries may not accelerate economic growth.

7. In addition to lending and borrowing, a country can reduce its risk by the international diversification of income claims. In practice, only capital income claims (capital assets) are tradable. Labor is not a tradable asset.

8. When assets are traded internationally, two countries can eliminate the income risk arising from country-specific or idiosyncratic shocks; such risk is called diversifiable risk. However, they can do nothing to eliminate the global risk, the shock common to both countries, called undiversifiable risk.

9. In practice, the use of the current account as a buffer and the extent of diversification fall far short of theory's prediction even in advanced countries. Consumption volatility persists, domestic investment is mostly financed from domestic saving, and portfolios display pronounced home bias.

10. In emerging markets and developing countries, financial openness has progressed more slowly and access to global capital markets is more limited and often on worse terms. The gains from financial openness appear weaker, and there is the downside risk of sudden stops and other crises. For gains to be realized, countries may require deeper institutional changes and further liberalization.

CHAPTER 6 ■ BALANCE OF PAYMENTS I: THE GAINS FROM FINANCIAL GLOBALIZATION

KEY TERMS

long-run budget constraint (LRBC), p. 201
small open economy, p. 202
world real interest rate, p. 202
present value, p. 204
perpetual loan, p. 206
sudden stop, p. 212
precautionary saving, p. 219
foreign reserves, p. 220
sovereign wealth funds, p. 220
marginal product of capital (MPK), p. 225
production function, p. 227
productivity, p. 227
convergence, p. 230
divergence, p. 231
technical efficiency, p. 231
social efficiency, p. 232
foreign aid, p. 234
World Bank, p. 234
diversification, p. 237
home bias, p. 242

PROBLEMS

1. Using the notation from the text, answer the following questions. You may assume that net labor income from abroad is zero, there are no capital gains on external wealth, and there are no unilateral transfers.

   a. Express the change in external wealth (ΔW_0) at the end of period 0 as a function of the economy's trade balance (TB), the real interest rate (a constant r^*), and initial external wealth (W_{-1}).

   b. Using (a), write an expression for the stock of external wealth at the end of period 0 (W_0). This should be written as a function of the economy's trade balance (TB_0), the real interest rate, and initial external wealth (W_{-1}).

   c. Using (a) and (b), write an expression for the stock of external wealth at the end of period 1 (W_1). This should be written as a function of the economy's trade balance (TB) each period, the real interest rate, and initial external wealth (W_{-1}).

   d. Using your answers from (a), (b), and (c), write an expression for the stock of external wealth at the end of period 2 (W_2). This should be written as a function of the economy's trade balance (TB) each period, the real interest rate, and initial external wealth (W_{-1}).

   e. Suppose we require that W_2 equal zero. Write down the condition that the three trade balances (in periods 0, 1, and 2) must satisfy. Arrange the terms in present value form.

2. Using the assumptions and answers from the previous question, complete the following:

   a. Write an expression for the *future value* of the stock of external wealth in period N (W_N). This should be written as a function of the economy's trade balance (TB) each period, the real interest rate r^*, and initial external wealth.

   b. Using the answer from (a), write an expression for the *present value* of the stock of external wealth in period N (W_N).

   c. The "no Ponzi game" conditions force the present value of W_N to tend to zero as N gets large. Explain why this implies that the economy's initial external wealth is equal to the present value of future trade deficits.

   d. How would the expressions in parts (a) and (b) change if the economy had net labor income (positive or negative) to/from abroad or net unilateral transfers? Explain briefly.

3. *In this question assume all dollar units are real dollars in billions, so, for example, $150 means $150 billion. It is year 0. Argentina thinks it can find $150 of domestic investment projects with an MPK of 10% (each $1 invested pays off $0.10 in every later year). Argentina invests $84 in year 0 by borrowing $84 from the rest of the world at a world real interest rate r^* of 5%. There is no further borrowing or investment after this.*

Use the standard assumptions: Assume initial external wealth W (W in year -1) is 0. Assume $G = 0$ always; and assume $I = 0$ except in year 0. Also, assume $NUT = KA = 0$ and that there is no net labor income from abroad so $NFIA = r^*W$.

The projects start to pay off in year 1 and continue to pay off all years thereafter. Interest is paid in perpetuity, in year 1 and every year thereafter. In addition, assume that if the projects are not done, then $GDP = Q = C = \$200$ in all years, so that $PV(Q) = PV(C) = 200 + 200/0.05 = 4,200$.

a. Should Argentina fund the $84 worth of projects? Explain your answer.

b. Why might Argentina be able to borrow only $84 and not $150?

c. From this point forward, assume the projects totaling $84 are funded and completed in year 0. If the MPK is 10%, what is the total payoff from the projects in future years?

d. Assume this is added to the $200 of GDP in all years starting in year 1. In dollars, what is Argentina's $Q = GDP$ in year 0, year 1, and later years?

e. At year 0, what is the new $PV(Q)$ in dollars? *Hint:* To ease computation, calculate the value of the increment in $PV(Q)$ due to the extra output in later years.

f. At year 0, what is the new $PV(I)$ in dollars? Therefore, what does the LRBC say is the new $PV(C)$ in dollars?

g. Assume that Argentina is consumption smoothing. What is the percent change in $PV(C)$? What is the new level of C in all years? Is Argentina better off?

h. For the year the projects go ahead, year 0, explain Argentina's balance of payments as follows: state the levels of CA, TB, $NFIA$, and FA.

i. What happens in later years? State the levels of CA, TB, $NFIA$, and FA in year 1 and every later year.

4. Continuing from the previous question, we now consider Argentina's external wealth position.

a. What is Argentina's external wealth W in year 0 and later? Suppose Argentina has a one-year debt (i.e., not a perpetual loan) that must be rolled over every year. After a few years, in year N, the world interest rate rises to 15%. Can Argentina stick to its original plan? What are the interest payments due on the debt if $r^* = 15\%$? If $I = G = 0$, what must Argentina do to meet those payments?

b. Suppose Argentina decides to unilaterally default on its debt. Why might Argentina do this? State the levels of CA, TB, $NFIA$, and FA in year N and all subsequent years. What happens to the Argentine level of C in this case?

c. When the default occurs, what is the change in Argentina's external wealth W? What happens to the rest of the world's (ROW's) external wealth?

d. External wealth data for Argentina and ROW are recorded in the account known as the net international investment position. Is this change in wealth recorded as a financial flow, a price effect, or an exchange rate effect?

5. Using production function and MPK diagrams, answer the following questions. For simplicity, assume there are two countries: a poor country (with low living standards) and a rich country (with high living standards).

a. Assuming that poor and rich countries have the same production function, illustrate how the poor country will converge with the rich country. Describe how this mechanism works.

b. In the data, countries with low living standards have capital-to-worker ratios that are too high to be consistent with the model used in (a). Describe and illustrate how we can modify the model used in (a) to be consistent with the data.

c. Given your assumptions from (b), what does this suggest about the ability of poor countries to converge with rich countries? What do we expect to happen to the gap between rich and poor countries over time? Explain.

Using the model from (b), explain and illustrate how convergence works in the following cases.

d. The poor country has a marginal product of capital that is higher than that of the rich country.

e. The marginal products in each country are equal. Then, the poor country experiences an increase in human capital through government funding of education.

f. The marginal products in each country are equal. Then, the poor country experiences political instability such that investors require a risk premium to invest in the poor country.

6. Assume that Brazil and the United States have different production functions $q = f(k)$, where q is output per worker and k is capital per worker. Let $q = Ak^{1/3}$. You are told that relative to the U.S. = 1, Brazil has an output per worker of 0.32 and capital per worker of 0.24. Can A be the same in Brazil as in the United States? If not, compute the level of A for Brazil. What is Brazil's *MPK* relative to the United States?

7. Use production function and *MPK* diagrams to examine Turkey and the EU. Assume that Turkey and the EU have different production functions $q = f(k)$, where q is output per worker and k is capital per worker. Let $q = Ak^{1/3}$. Assume that the productivity level A in Turkey is lower than that in the EU.

   a. Draw a production function diagram (with output per worker y as a function of capital per worker k) and *MPK* diagram (*MPK* versus k) for the EU. (*Hint:* Be sure to draw the two diagrams with the production function directly above the *MPK* diagram so that the level of capital per worker k is consistent on your two diagrams.)

   b. For now, assume capital cannot flow freely in and out of Turkey. On the same diagrams, plot Turkish production function and *MPK* curves, assuming that the productivity level A in Turkey is half the EU level and that Turkish *MPK* exceeds EU *MPK*. Label the EU position in each chart *EU* and the Turkish position *T1*.

   c. Assume capital can now flow freely between Turkey and the EU and the rest of the world, and that the EU is already at the point where $MPK = r^*$. Label r^* on the vertical axis of the *MPK* diagram. Assume no risk premium. What will Turkey's capital per worker level k be? Label this outcome point *T2* in each diagram. Will Turkey converge to the EU level of q? Explain.

8. This question continues from the previous problem, focusing on how risk premiums explain the gaps in living standards across countries.

   a. Investors worry about the rule of law in Turkey and also about the potential for hyperinflation and other bad macroeconomic policies. Because of these worries, the initial gap between *MPK* in Turkey and r^* is a risk premium *RP*. Label *RP* on the vertical axis of the *MPK* diagram. Now where does Turkey end up in terms of k and q?

   b. In light of (a), why might Turkey be keen to join the EU?

   c. Some EU countries are keen to exclude Turkey from the EU. What might be the *economic* arguments for that position?

9. In this chapter, we saw that financial market integration is necessary for countries to smooth consumption through borrowing and lending. Consider two economies: those of the Czech Republic and France. For each of the following shocks, explain how and to what extent each country can trade capital to better smooth consumption.

   a. The Czech Republic and France each experience an EU-wide recession.

   b. A strike in France leads to a reduction in French income.

   c. Floods destroy a portion of the Czech capital stock, lowering Czech income.

10. Assume that a country produces an output Q of 50 every year. The world interest rate is 10%. Consumption C is 50 every year, and $I = G = 0$. There is an unexpected drop in output in year 0, so output falls to 39 and is then expected to return to 50 in every future year. If the country desires to smooth consumption, how much should it borrow in period 0? What will the new level of consumption be from then on?

11. Assume that a country produces an output Q of 50 every year. The world interest rate is 10%. Consumption C is 50 every year, and $I = G = 0$. There is an unexpected war in year 0, which costs 11 units and is predicted to last one year. If the country desires to smooth consumption, how much should it borrow in period 0? What will the new level of consumption be from then on?

The country wakes up in year 1 and discovers that the war is still going on and will eat up another 11 units of expenditure in year 1. If the country still desires to smooth consumption looking forward from year 1, how much should it borrow in period 1? What will the new level of consumption be from then on?

12. Consider a world of two countries: Highland (H) and Lowland (L). Each country has an average output of 9 and desires to smooth consumption. All income takes the form of capital income and is fully consumed each period.

   a. Initially, there are two states of the world: Pestilence (P) and Flood (F). Each happens with 50% probability. Pestilence affects Highland and lowers the output there to 8, leaving Lowland unaffected with an output of 10. Flood affects Lowland and lowers the output there to 8, leaving Highland unaffected with an output of 10. Devise a table with two rows corresponding to each state (rows marked P and F). In three columns, show income to three portfolios: the portfolio of 100% H capital, the portfolio of 100% L capital, and the portfolio of 50% H + 50% L capital.

   b. Two more states of world appear: Armageddon (A) and Utopia (U). Each happens with 50% probability but is uncorrelated with the P-F state. Armageddon affects both countries equally and lowers income in each country by a further four units, whatever the P-F state. Utopia leaves each country unaffected. Devise a table with four rows corresponding to each state (rows marked PA, PU, FA, and FU). In three columns, show income to three portfolios: the portfolio of 100% H capital, the portfolio of 100% L capital, and the portfolio of 50% H + 50% L capital.

Compare your answers to parts (a) and (b), and consider the optimal portfolio choices. Does diversification eliminate consumption risk in each case? Explain.

N E T W O R K

1. Go the BEA website (bea.gov). Find the latest annual balance of payments data for the United States.
   a. Compute income earned on (1) external assets and (2) income paid on external liabilities.
   b. Find the latest net international investment position data for the United States. Compute (3) external assets and (4) external liabilities for the end of the prior year.
   c. Divide (1) by (3) and then divide (2) by (4) to find the implied rates of interest on external assets and liabilities. Is the United States still privileged?
2. To learn more about the aid debate, download some of the conflicting arguments made by two prominent figures: Jeffrey Sachs and William Easterly (Google "sachs easterly"). See, for example, their "Foreign Aid Face Off" in the *Los Angeles Times* (latimes.com, April 30, 2006, and May 7, 2006). For some impartial views, download and read two articles: one by Nicholas Kristof ("Aid: Can It Work," *New York Review of Books,* October 5, 2006) and one by Martin Wolf ("Aid Is Well Worth Trying," *Financial Times,* July 5, 2005); neither should require a subscription. After weighing all these arguments, do you feel more or less optimistic about what aid can achieve?

APPENDIX TO CHAPTER 6

Common versus Idiosyncratic Shocks

In reality, home and foreign incomes will not have a perfect inverse correlation as we have assumed in the text. Let us generalize a bit more for our two countries, and focus on capital income.

A More General Case Suppose the shocks to capital income are a and b, for countries A and B, respectively, and that these take a random value each period. The common shock is the *average shock* in the two countries: $\frac{1}{2}(a+b)$. In the chapter, we assumed the average shock was zero, so the shocks were equal and opposite. In the real world, however, this need not be the case.

We can define the A-specific shock as the shock a minus the average shock: $a - \frac{1}{2}(a+b) = \frac{1}{2}(a-b)$. Similarly, the B-specific shock is b minus the average shock: $b - \frac{1}{2}(a+b) = \frac{1}{2}(b-a)$. These *idiosyncratic shocks* are nonzero as long as the A shock is not the same as the B shock, that is, as long as a is not equal to b.

By doing this algebraic manipulation, the A shock can be written as the common shock plus the A-specific shock:

$$a = \underbrace{\frac{1}{2}(a+b)}_{\text{Common shock}} + \underbrace{\frac{1}{2}(a-b)}_{\text{A-specific shock}}$$

Similarly, the B shock can be written as the common shock plus the B-specific shock:

$$b = \underbrace{\frac{1}{2}(a+b)}_{\text{Common shock}} + \underbrace{\frac{1}{2}(b-a)}_{\text{A-specific shock}}$$

We see that the country-specific shocks are the exact opposites of each other: $\frac{1}{2}(a-b)$ and $\frac{1}{2}(b-a)$. The good news is that country-specific shocks are a *diversifiable* risk and satisfy the conditions of the simple case examined in the chapter. So the income risk they generate can be eliminated by diversification: in the world portfolio, the country-specific shocks cancel out, as we can see by adding up the last two equations.

But the common shock is $\frac{1}{2}(a+b)$. As long as this is nonzero, these shocks matter; that is, as long as the shocks are not equal and opposite, pure asymmetric country-specific shocks. The bad news is, the global shocks are an *undiversifiable* risk—no matter which assets you own, you get hit with the global shock, so asset trade offers no escape from these risks.

Numerical Example Figure 6-A1 (an extension of Figure 6-9) provides an illustration of the partial reduction in risk that can be achieved in this case. In Figure 6-9, each country owned 50% of the world portfolio. Thus, capital incomes in each state were as follows: in state 1, A = 36, B = 44; in state 2, A = 44, B = 36. The occurrence of states 1 and 2 was random with 50-50 odds. If A and B diversified by each holding 50% of the world portfolio, they had stable capital income of 40 every period.

In Figure 6-A1, we add an extra "global" shock, which has two states, X and Y, that occur at random with 50-50 odds. However, the random X-Y shock is *independent* of the 1-2 shock. We suppose that when the global shock is in state X, both countries receive an extra five units of capital income. When the global shock is in state Y, both countries receive five units less of capital income.

There are now four possible states of the world: 1X, 1Y, 2X, and 2Y. Each has a 25% chance of occurring. For the four states, the capital incomes of the portfolios are as follows:

1X	Home = 41	Foreign = 49	World = 90	Average = 45
2X	Home = 49	Foreign = 41	World = 90	Average = 45
1Y	Home = 31	Foreign = 39	World = 70	Average = 35
2Y	Home = 39	Foreign = 31	World = 70	Average = 35

From this table, and the example shown in Figure 6-A1, we see, as expected, that in this world, holding half of the world portfolio eliminates the risk associated with fluctuations between states 1 and 2. The best that each country can do is to have an income that fluctuates between 45 (half of 90, state X) and 35 (half of 70, state Y). In state X, all income risk associated with states 1 and 2 is gone. And in state Y, all income risk associated with states 1 and 2 is gone. But nothing can be done to eliminate the risk associated with fluctuations between states X and Y.

This more general result does not overturn our basic findings. Holding a 100% home portfolio generates a volatile capital income. So does holding a 100% foreign portfolio. Holding a mix of the two lowers the volatility of capital income, at least when some of the shocks are country-specific shocks, which is always the case in the real world.

FIGURE 6-A1

Portfolio Diversification and Capital Income: Undiversifiable Risks We take the example from Table 6-6 and Figure 6-9, and we add a common "global" shock to each country. With probability 50%, each country experiences a five-unit increase in capital income, and with probability 50% experiences a five-unit decrease in capital income. Holding half of the world portfolio reduces *but does not eliminate* capital income risk entirely because the global shock is an undiversifiable risk for the world as a whole.

Balance of Payments II: Output, Exchange Rates, and Macroeconomic Policies in the Short Run

If demand shifts from the products of country B to the products of country A, a depreciation by country B or an appreciation by country A would correct the external imbalance and also relieve unemployment in country B and restrain inflation in country A. This is the most favorable case for flexible exchange rates based on national currencies.

Robert Mundell, 1961

It is easy to understand the dislike . . . for a [fixed exchange rate] system which dictated that a slump must be aggravated by monetary reactions, although, doubtless, [people] had forgotten that the same system served to enhance booms.

Alec Ford, 1962

1 Demand in the Open Economy

2 Goods Market Equilibrium: The Keynesian Cross

3 Goods and Forex Market Equilibria: Deriving the IS Curve

4 Money Market Equilibrium: Deriving the LM Curve

5 The Short-Run IS-LM-FX Model of an Open Economy

6 Stabilization Policy

7 Conclusions

In November 2004, the president of the European Central Bank, Jean-Claude Trichet, declared that the large and persistent depreciation of the U.S. dollar against the euro was "not welcome from the standpoint of the ECB." He also called the exchange rate movements "brutal," the same adjective he had used a few months before. However, later the same month, Alan Greenspan, then chairman of the U.S. Federal Reserve, seemed perfectly at ease as he hinted that movements in the dollar's exchange rate were most likely to continue as an acceptable means of macroeconomic adjustment for the U.S. economy. Why was the ECB president so fretful? Why was his American counterpart so relaxed? Clearly—in the view of at least one of the central bankers—the exchange rate must matter for the economy as a whole.

Thus far our study of exchange rates has been largely disconnected from real activity and the rest of the economy. Chapters 2 through 4 developed a theory of exchange rates, in which the economy's level of output was taken as given. To gain a more complete understanding of how an open economy works, we now extend our theory and explore what happens when exchange rates and output fluctuate in the short run.

To do this, we build on the accounting framework we learned in the balance of payments chapter to understand how macroeconomic aggregates (including output, income, consumption, investment, and the trade balance) move together and in response to shocks in an open economy.

The model we study is an open-economy variant of the well-known IS-LM model that is widely used in the study of closed-economy macroeconomics. The key assumption of this type of Keynesian model is that prices are "sticky" in the short run so that output is determined by shifts in demand in the goods market. When we are finished, we will have a model that explains the relationships among all the major macroeconomic variables in an open economy in the short run.

Naturally, such a model can shed light on many policy issues. We can see how monetary and fiscal policies affect the economy, and discuss how they can be used to stabilize the economy and maintain full employment. One key lesson we learn in this chapter is that the feasibility and effectiveness of macroeconomic policies depend crucially on the type of exchange rate regime in operation.

1 Demand in the Open Economy

To understand macroeconomic fluctuations, we need to grasp how short-run disturbances affect three important markets in an economy: the goods market, the money market, and the forex market. In earlier chapters, we studied the forex market and the money market, so we will recap and apply here what we learned in those chapters. But what about the goods market? In the forex chapters, we assumed that output was fixed at a level $\overline{Y}$. We took this to be the full-employment level of output that would be expected to prevail in the long run, when all factor market prices have adjusted to ensure that all factors like labor and capital are employed. But these assumptions about output and employment are valid only in the long run. To understand short-run fluctuations in economic activity, we now develop a short-run, sticky-price Keynesian model and show how fluctuations in demand can create fluctuations in real economic activity. To start building this model, we first make our assumptions clear and then look at how demand is defined and why it fluctuates.

Preliminaries and Assumptions

Our interest in this chapter is to study short-run fluctuations in a simplified, abstract world of two countries. Our main focus is on the home economy. We use an asterisk to denote foreign variables when we need them. For our purposes, the foreign economy can be thought of as "the rest of the world" (ROW). The key assumptions we make are as follows:

- Because we are examining the short run, we assume that home and foreign price levels, $\overline{P}$ and $\overline{P}^*$, are fixed due to price stickiness. As a result of price stickiness, expected inflation is fixed at zero, $\overline{\pi}^e = 0$. If prices are fixed, all quantities can be viewed as both real and nominal quantities in the short run because there is no inflation.

- We assume that government spending $\overline{G}$ and taxes $\overline{T}$ are fixed at some constant level, which are subject to policy change.

- We assume that conditions in the foreign economy such as foreign output $\overline{Y}^*$ and the foreign interest rate $\overline{i}^*$ are fixed and taken as given. Our main interest is in the equilibrium and fluctuations in the home economy.

- We assume that income Y is equivalent to output: that is, gross domestic product (GDP) equals gross national disposable income (GNDI). From our study of the national accounts, we know that the difference between the two equals net factor income from abroad plus net unilateral transfers. The analysis in this chapter could easily be extended to include these additional sources of income, but this added complexity would not offer any additional significant insights. We further assume that net factor income from abroad ($NFIA$) and net unilateral transfers (NUT) are zero, which implies that the current account (CA) equals the trade balance (TB); for the rest of this chapter, we shall just refer to the trade balance.

Our main objective is to understand how output (income) is determined in the home economy in the short run. As we learned from the national accounts, total expenditure or demand for home-produced goods and services is made up of four components: consumption, investment, government consumption, and the trade balance. In the following section, we see how each component is determined in the short run, and use the fact that the demand must equal supply to characterize the economy's short-run equilibrium.

Consumption

The simplest model of aggregate private consumption relates household **consumption** C to **disposable income** Y^d. As we have learned in Chapter 5, disposable income is the level of total pretax income Y received by households minus the taxes paid by households $\overline{T}$, so that $Y^d = Y - \overline{T}$. Consumers tend to consume more as their disposable income rises, a relationship that can be represented by an increasing function, called the *consumption function*:

$$\text{Consumption} = C = C(Y - \overline{T})$$

A typical consumption function of this form is graphed in Figure 7-1; it slopes upward because consumption increases when disposable income increases.

This equation is known as the *Keynesian consumption function*. In some economic theories, consumption smoothing is both desirable and feasible. That is, in any given year consumption need not depend on income in that year, but rather on total lifetime resources (wealth). In contrast, the Keynesian consumption function assumes that private consumption expenditure *is* sensitive to changes in current income. This assumption

FIGURE 7-1

The Consumption Function The consumption function relates private consumption, C, to disposable income, $Y - \overline{T}$. The slope of the function is the marginal propensity to consume, MPC.

seems to be a more reasonable match with reality, at least in the short run, given the empirical finding that there is very little consumption smoothing seen in practice, either at the household or national level.

Marginal Effects The consumption function relates the level of consumption to the level of disposable income, but we are more often interested in the response of such variables to small changes in equilibrium, due to policy or other shocks. For that purpose, the slope of the consumption function is called the **marginal propensity to consume (MPC),** and it tells us how much of every extra $1 of disposable income received by households is spent on consumption. We generally assume that MPC is between 0 and 1: when consumers receive an extra unit of disposable income (whether it's a euro, dollar, or yen), they will consume only a fraction of it and save the remainder. For example, if you elect to spend $0.75 of every extra $1 of disposable income you receive, your MPC is 0.75. We can also define the *marginal propensity to save (MPS)* as $1 - MPC$, so in this example $MPS = 0.25$, meaning that $0.25 of every extra $1 of disposable income is saved.

Investment

The simplest model of aggregate investment makes two key assumptions: firms face an array of possible investment projects, each of which earns a different real return; and a firm will invest capital in a project only if the real returns exceed the firm's cost of borrowing capital. The firm's borrowing cost is the **expected real interest rate** r^e, which equals the nominal interest rate i minus the expected rate of inflation π^e: $r^e = i - \pi^e$. It is important to note that, in general, the expected real interest rate depends not only on the nominal interest rate but also on expected inflation. However, under our simplifying assumption that expected inflation is zero, the expected real interest rate equals the nominal interest rate, $r^e = i$.

When the expected real interest rate in the economy falls, we expect more investment projects to be undertaken. For example, at a real interest rate of 10%, there may be only $1 billion worth of profitable investment projects that firms wish to undertake; but if the real interest rate falls to 5%, there may now be $2 billion worth of profitable projects. Hence, our model assumes that investment I is a decreasing function of the real interest rate; that is, investment falls as the real interest rate rises.

$$\text{Investment} = I = I(i)$$

Remember that this is true only because when expected inflation is zero, the real interest rate equals the nominal interest rate. Figure 7-2 shows a typical investment function of this type. It slopes downward because as the real interest rate falls, the quantity of investment rises.

The Government

To develop a basic model of economic activity in the short run, we will assume that the government's role is simple. It collects an amount T of **taxes** from private households and spends an amount G on **government consumption** of goods and services.

Note that the latter includes only actual spending on goods and services bought by the public sector at all levels. For example, G includes military equipment and personnel, transport and infrastructure, public universities and schools, and so forth. Excluded from this concept are the often huger sums involved in government **transfer programs,** such as social security, medical care, or unemployment benefit systems, that

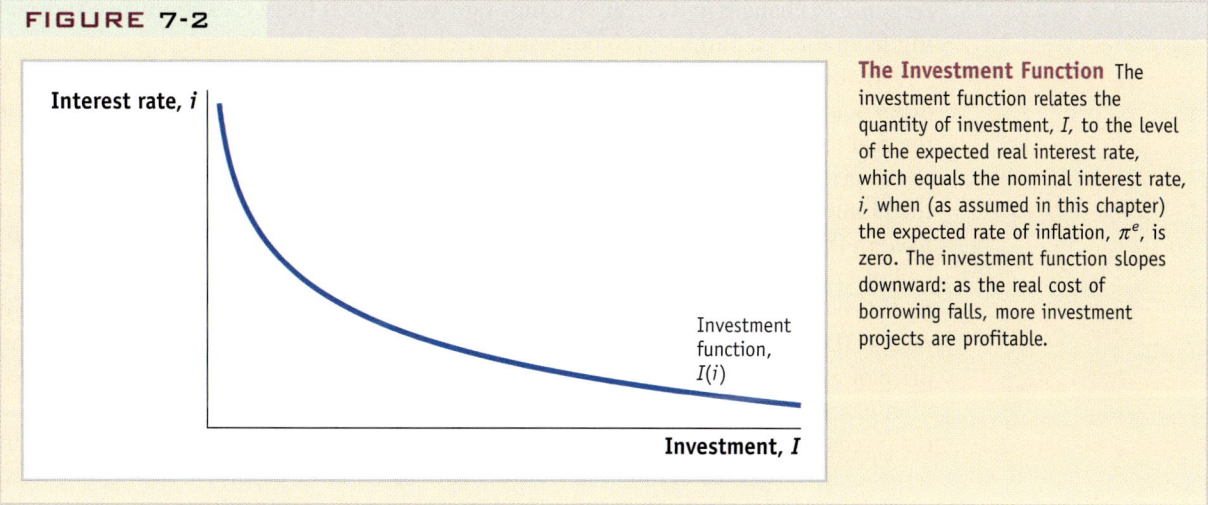

FIGURE 7-2

The Investment Function The investment function relates the quantity of investment, I, to the level of the expected real interest rate, which equals the nominal interest rate, i, when (as assumed in this chapter) the expected rate of inflation, π^e, is zero. The investment function slopes downward: as the real cost of borrowing falls, more investment projects are profitable.

redistribute income between households. Such transfers are excluded because we assume that *in the aggregate* they do not generate any change in the total expenditure on goods and services; they merely change who gets to engage in the act of spending.

In the unlikely event that $G = T$ exactly, government spending exactly equals taxes and we say that the government has a *balanced budget*. If $T > G$, the government is said to be running a *budget surplus* (of size $T - G$); if $G > T$, a *budget deficit* (of size $G - T$ or, equivalently, a negative surplus of $T - G$).

Fiscal policy is concerned with the levels of taxes T and spending G set by the government. In this chapter, we do not study in detail why or how governments make such policy choices; we make the simple assumption that in the short run the levels of taxes and spending are set exogenously at some fixed levels, denoted by an overbar:

$$\text{Government purchases} = G = \overline{G}$$
$$\text{Taxes} = T = \overline{T}$$

Policy makers may change these levels of taxes and spending at any time. We analyze the impact of such changes on the economy later in this chapter.

The Trade Balance

In the balance of payments chapter, we saw from an accounting standpoint that the trade balance (equal to exports minus imports) measures the impact of foreign trade on the demand for domestic output. To develop a model, however, we need to know what drives these flows, so in our simple model we now explore three key determinants of the trade balance: the real exchange rate and the level of home and foreign incomes.

The Role of the Real Exchange Rate
What is the role of the real exchange rate? Recall George, the American tourist we met at the start of our study of exchange rates, who had to deal with a weaker dollar during his visits to Paris over the course of several years. If U.S. and French prices are sticky (constant in euro and U.S. dollar terms), then as the U.S. exchange rate depreciates, the prices of French goods and services became more and more expensive in dollar terms. In the end, George was ready to take a vacation in California instead. In the aggregate, when spending patterns change in

response to changes in the real exchange rate, we say that there is **expenditure switching** from foreign purchases to domestic purchases.

Expenditure switching is a major factor in determining the level of a country's exports and imports. When learning about exchange rates in the long run, we saw that the real exchange rate is the price of goods and services in a foreign economy relative to the price of goods and services in the home economy. If Home's exchange rate is E, the Home price level is $\overline{P}$ (fixed in the short run), and the Foreign price level is $\overline{P}^*$ (also fixed in the short run), then the real exchange rate q of Home is defined as $q = E\overline{P}^*/\overline{P}$.

For example, suppose that the home country is the United States, and the reference basket costs $100; suppose that in Canada the same basket costs C$120 and the exchange rate is $0.90 per Canadian dollar. In the expression $q = E\overline{P}^*/\overline{P}$, the numerator $E\overline{P}^*$ is the price of foreign goods converted into home currency terms, $108 = 120 × 0.90$; the denominator $\overline{P}$ is the home currency price of home goods, $100; the ratio of the two is the real exchange rate, $q = \$108/\$100 = 1.08$. This is the relative price of foreign goods in terms of home goods. In this case, Canadian goods are more expensive than U.S. goods.

A rise in the home real exchange rate (a real depreciation) signifies that foreign goods have become more expensive relative to home goods. As the real exchange rate rises, both home and foreign consumers will respond by *expenditure switching:* the home country will import less (as *home* consumers switch to buying home goods) and export more (as *foreign* consumers switch to buying home goods). These concepts are often seen in economic debates and news coverage (see **Headlines: Expenditure Switching and the Dollar Devaluation** and **The Curry Trade**) and they provide us with the following insight:

- *We expect the trade balance of the home country to be an increasing function of the home country's real exchange rate. That is, as the home country's real exchange rate rises (depreciates), it will export more and import less, and the trade balance rises.*

The Role of Income Levels The other determinant of the trade balance we might wish to consider is the income level in each country. As we argued earlier in our discussion of the consumption function, when domestic disposable income increases, consumers tend to spend more on all forms of consumption, including consumption of foreign goods. These arguments provide a second insight:

- *We expect an increase in home income to be associated with an increase in home imports and a fall in the home country's trade balance.*

Symmetrically, from the rest of the world's standpoint, an increase in rest of the world income ought to be associated with an increase in rest of the world spending on home goods, resulting in an increase in home exports. This is our third insight:

- *We expect an increase in rest of the world income to be associated with an increase in home exports and a rise in the home country's trade balance.*

Combining the three insights above, we can write the trade balance as a function of three variables: the real exchange rate, home disposable income, and rest of the world disposable income:

$$TB = TB(\underbrace{E\overline{P}^*/\overline{P}}_{\text{Increasing function}}, \underbrace{Y - \overline{T}}_{\text{Decreasing function}}, \underbrace{Y^* - \overline{T}^*}_{\text{Increasing function}})$$

We show the relationship between the trade balance and the real exchange rate in Figure 7-3, for the home country, all else equal—that is, holding home and foreign disposable income fixed. The trade balance is an *increasing* function of the real

HEADLINES

Expenditure Switching and the Dollar Devaluation

From 2001 to 2004, the U.S. dollar began a sustained depreciation against many currencies. The economic impacts were reflected in the following string of pronouncements—in the space of just one week—from all corners of the globe and found in The Financial Times.

DOLLAR'S DIVE SET TO DELIGHT EXPORTERS AS WELL AS TOURISTS

January 9, 2004. Listen carefully to the crowds shuffling down New York's Fifth Avenue, and the more immediate effects of the plummeting dollar are obvious in the voices of European shoppers enjoying dramatic increases in purchasing power. One couple from London caused a stir at Saks department store by walking in and spending $25,000 on a single diamond necklace. . . . By the fourth quarter of this year, the National Association of Manufacturers expects exports to be up by 12 per cent, with its members also benefiting from falling imports as rivals abroad struggle with the other side of the exchange rate coin.

EURO'S RAPID RISE WORRIES ECB

January 9, 2004. The European Central Bank yesterday signaled its growing unease over the rapid rise of the euro against the dollar. . . . Jean Claude Trichet, bank president, said repeatedly the bank did not like "excessive volatility" in foreign exchange markets. . . . Pascal Lamy, the EU's trade commissioner, said the euro was approaching a level that could be worrying for the competitiveness of the eurozone's exporters.

EURO ERODES GERMANY'S ROLE AS AN INDUSTRIAL POWERHOUSE

January 13, 2004. The currency's seemingly unstoppable ascent against the dollar is speeding an industrial decline.

. . . Economists expect even more jobs to go as German companies struggle to cut costs and boost productivity.

STRONG CURRENCY HITS AUSTRALIANS

January 13, 2004. Almost one in five Australian manufacturers are considering moving production offshore because of the strengthening of the Australian dollar in the past two years, says a report. . . . The study, based on a survey of 800 manufacturers, found that lost sales due to import penetration were at least as significant as lower export returns. . . . "At this level exports struggle to compete on world markets," it said.

FIGURE 7-3

The Trade Balance and the Real Exchange Rate The trade balance is an increasing function of the real exchange rate, $E\bar{P}^*/\bar{P}$. When there is a real depreciation (a rise in q), foreign goods become more expensive relative to home goods, and we expect the trade balance to increase as exports rise and imports fall (a rise in TB). The trade balance may also depend on income. If home income levels rise, then some of the increase in income may be spent on the consumption of imports. For example, if home income rises from Y_1 to Y_2, then the trade balance will decrease, whatever the level of the real exchange rate, and the trade balance function will shift down.

HEADLINES

The Curry Trade

In 2009, a dramatic weakening of the pound against the euro sparked an unlikely boom in cross-Channel grocery deliveries.

If carrying coals to Newcastle is judged a pointless exercise, then importing croissants, baguettes and bottles of claret into France might seem even more absurd. But, due to the strength of the euro against the pound, hundreds of Britons living in France are now using the internet to order their food, including many French specialties, from British supermarkets.

Simon Goodenough, the director of Sterling Shopping, a delivery firm based in Brackley, Northamptonshire, says his company has 2,500 British customers in France and is running five delivery vans full of food to France each week.

"We deliver food from Waitrose, Sainsbury's and Marks and Spencer, but by far the biggest is Asda," said Goodenough ". . .We sit in our depot sometimes looking at the things people have bought and just laugh at the craziness of it all. We have seen croissants and baguettes in people's shopping bags. And we have delivered bottles of Bergerac wine bought from Sainsbury's to a customer in Bergerac. We even have a few French customers who have now heard about what we do. They love things like curries and tacos, which they just can't get in France.". . .

Goodenough said many of his company's British customers hold pensions or savings in sterling rather than euros: "They have seen a 30% drop in their spending power over the past 18 months."

John Steventon owns La Maison Removals, a delivery company based in Rayleigh, Essex. It takes food from its warehouse to about 1,000 British customers in central France.

"We just can't cope with demand at the moment," he said. . . . "We found that friends in France were asking us to bring over British food for them so we just thought it made sense to set up a food delivery service. . . . The savings for buying food, in particular, are amazing due to the strength of the euro. Customers tell us that for every £100 they would spend in France buying food, they save £30 buying through us, even with our 15% commission. A lot of people are using us to get things they really miss, such as bacon and sausages."

Nikki Bundy, 41, has lived near Périgueux in the Dordogne with her family for four years. . . . "It's just so much cheaper for us to buy our food this way. . . . The food in France is lovely, but you can come out of a supermarket here with just two carrier bags having spent €100. I still try and buy my fresh fruit and veg in France, but most other things I now buy from Asda."

Source: Excerpted from Leo Hickman, "Expat Orders for British Supermarket Food Surge on Strength of euro," *The Guardian*, June 9, 2010.

---

exchange rate $E\overline{P}^*/\overline{P}$. Thus, the relationship shown in Figure 7-3 is upward-sloping. The reason is that an increase in the real exchange rate (a real depreciation) increases TB by raising exports and lowering imports, implying a movement along the curve drawn.

The effect of the real exchange rate on the trade balance is now clear. What about the effects of changes in output? An illustration of the impact of an increase in home output on the trade balance is shown in Figure 7-3. At any level of the real exchange rate, an increase in home output leads to more spending on imports, lowering the trade balance. This change would be represented as a downward shift in the trade balance curve, that is, a reduction in TB for a given level of Y.

Marginal Effects Once More The impact of changes in output on the trade balance can also be thought of in terms of the marginal propensity to consume. Suppose home output (which equals home income, because of the assumptions we've made) rises by an amount $\Delta Y = \$1$ and that, all else equal, this leads to an increase in home imports of $\Delta IM = \$MPC_F$, where $MPC_F > 0$. We refer to MPC_F as the *marginal propensity to consume foreign imports*. For example, if $MPC_F = 0.1$, this means that out of every additional $1 of income, $0.10 are spent on imports.

How does MPC_F relate to the MPC seen earlier? After a $1 rise in income, any additional goods consumed have to come from somewhere, home or abroad. The fraction

MPC of the $1 increment spent on all consumption must equal the sum of the incremental spending on home goods plus incremental spending on foreign goods. Let $MPC_H > 0$ be the *marginal propensity to consume home goods*. By assumption $MPC = MPC_H + MPC_F$. For example, if $MPC_F = 0.10$ and $MPC_H = 0.65$, then $MPC = 0.75$; for every extra dollar of disposable income, home consumers spend 75 cents, 10 cents on imported foreign goods and 65 cents on home goods (and they save 25 cents).[1]

APPLICATION

The Trade Balance and the Real Exchange Rate

Our theory assumes that the trade balance increases when the real exchange rate rises. Is there evidence to support this proposition? In Figure 7-4, we examine the evolution of the U.S. trade balance (as a share of GDP) in recent years as compared with the U.S. real exchange rate with the rest of the world.

FIGURE 7-4

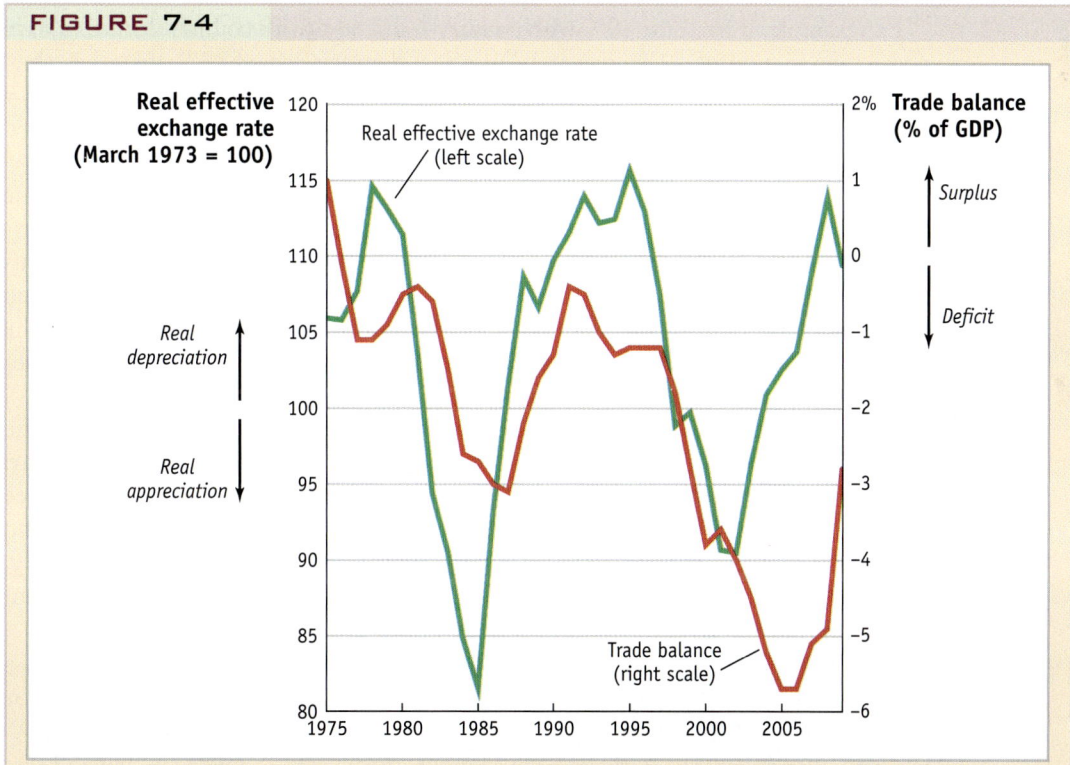

The Real Exchange Rate and the Trade Balance: United States, 1975–2006 Does the real exchange rate affect the trade balance in the way we have assumed? The data show that the U.S. trade balance is correlated with the U.S. real effective exchange rate index. Because the trade balance also depends on changes in U.S. and rest of the world disposable income (and other factors), it may respond with a lag to changes in the real exchange rate, so the correlation is not perfect (as seen in the years 2000–2006).

Sources: U.S. Federal Reserve; Bureau of Economic Analysis NIPA.

---

[1] A similar calculation can be applied to the export function, where exports will depend on the marginal propensity to consume imports in the foreign country.

By considering the home country to be the United States and the foreign "country" to be the rest of the world, we cannot use data on the *bilateral* real exchange rate q for any individual foreign country. We need a composite or weighted-average measure of the price of goods in all foreign countries relative to the price of U.S. goods. To accomplish this, economists construct *multilateral* measures of real exchange rate movement.

The most common weighting scheme uses a weight equal to that country's share in the home country's trade. If there are N foreign countries, we can write home's total trade as the sum of its trade with each foreign country: Trade = Trade$_1$ + Trade$_2$ + $\cdots$ + Trade$_N$. Applying a trade weight to each bilateral real exchange rate's percentage change, we obtain the percentage change in home's multilateral real exchange rate or **real effective exchange rate:**

$$\underbrace{\frac{\Delta q_{\text{effective}}}{q_{\text{effective}}}}_{\text{Real effective exchange rate change (in \%)}} = \underbrace{\left(\frac{\text{Trade}_1}{\text{Trade}} \frac{\Delta q_1}{q_1}\right) + \left(\frac{\text{Trade}_2}{\text{Trade}} \frac{\Delta q_2}{q_2}\right) + \cdots + \left(\frac{\text{Trade}_N}{\text{Trade}} \frac{\Delta q_N}{q_N}\right)}_{\text{Trade-weighted average of bilateral real exchange rate changes (in \%)}}$$

For example, if we trade 40% with country 1 and 60% with country 2, and we have a real appreciation of 10% against 1 but a real depreciation of 30% against 2, then the change in our real effective exchange rate is (40% × −10%) + (60% × 30%) = (0.4 × −0.1) + (0.6 × 0.3) = −0.04 + 0.18 = 0.14 = + 14%. That is, we have experienced an effective trade-weighted real depreciation of 14%.

Figure 7-4 shows that the U.S. multilateral real exchange rate and the U.S. trade balance have been mostly positively correlated, as predicted by our model. In periods when the United States has experienced a real depreciation, the U.S. trade balance has tended to increase. Conversely, real appreciations have usually been associated with a fall in the trade balance. However, the correlation between the real exchange rate and the trade balance is not perfect. There appears to be lag between, say, a real depreciation and a rise in the trade balance (as in the mid-1980s). Why? Import and export flows may react only slowly or weakly to changes in the real exchange rate, so the trade balance can react in unexpected ways (see **Side Bar: Barriers to Expenditure Switching: Pass-Through and J Curve**). We can also see that the trade balance and real exchange rate did not move together as much during the years 2000 to 2008 because other factors, such as tax cuts and wartime spending, may have created extra deficit pressures that spilled over into the U.S. current account during this period. ∎

Exogenous Changes in Demand

We have already treated as given, or exogenous, the changes or *shocks* in demand that originate in changes to government purchases or taxes. However, other exogenous changes in demand can affect consumption, investment, or the trade balance, and it is important to know how to analyze these, too. Examples of such changes are illustrated in Figure 7-6.

- *An exogenous change in consumption.* Suppose that at any given level of disposable income, consumers decide to spend more on consumption. After this shock, the consumption function would shift up as in Figure 7-6, panel (a). For example, an increase in household wealth following a stock market or housing market boom (as seen in expansions since 1990) could lead to a shift of this sort. This is a change in consumption demand unconnected to disposable income.

SIDE BAR

Barriers to Expenditure Switching: Pass-Through and the J Curve

The basic analysis in the text assumes that two key mechanisms are operating. First, we assume that a nominal depreciation causes a real depreciation and raises the price of foreign imports relative to home exports. Second, we assume that such a change in relative prices will lower imports, raise exports, and increase the trade balance. In reality, there are reasons why both mechanisms operate weakly or with a lag.

Trade Dollarization, Distribution, and Pass-Through

One assumption we made was that prices are sticky in local currency. But what if some *home* goods prices are set in *foreign* currency?

For example, let the foreign country be the United States and suppose a share d of the home-produced basket of goods is priced in U.S. dollars at a sticky *dollar* price $\overline{P}_1^*$. Suppose the remaining share, $1 - d$, is priced, as before, in local currency at a sticky *local currency* price $\overline{P}_2$. Hence,

$$\left.\begin{array}{l}\text{Price of foreign goods}\\ \text{relative to dollar-priced}\\ \text{home goods}\end{array}\right\} = \frac{E \times \overline{P}^*}{E \times \overline{P}_1} = \frac{\overline{P}^*}{\overline{P}_1} \text{ has a weight} = d$$

$$\left.\begin{array}{l}\text{Price of foreign goods}\\ \text{relative to local-currency-}\\ \text{priced home goods}\end{array}\right\} = \frac{E \times \overline{P}^*}{\overline{P}_2} \text{ has a weight} = 1 - d$$

What now is the price of all foreign-produced goods relative to all home-produced goods (the real exchange rate)? It is the weighted sum of the relative prices of the two parts of the basket. Hence, we find

$$q = \text{Home real exchange rate} = d\frac{\overline{P}^*}{\overline{P}_1} + (1 - d)\frac{E\overline{P}^*}{\overline{P}_2}$$

The first term with a weight d does not contain E because both numerator and denominator are dollar prices (already expressed in a common currency). Only the second term with a weight $(1 - d)$ contains E, since the prices are in different currencies. Thus, a 1% increase in E will lead to only a $(1 - d)$% increase in the real exchange rate.

When d is 0, all home goods are priced in local currency and we have our basic model. A 1% rise in E causes a 1% rise in q. There is full **pass-through** from changes in the nominal exchange rate to changes in the real exchange rate. But as d rises, pass-through falls. If d is 0.5, then a 1% rise in E causes just a 0.5% rise in q. The real exchange rate becomes less responsive to changes in the nominal exchange rate, and this means that expenditure switching effects will be muted.

It turns out that many countries around the world conduct a large fraction of their trade in a currency other than their own, such as U.S. dollars. The most obvious examples of goods with dollar prices are the major commodities: oil, copper, wheat, and so on. In some Persian Gulf economies, a nominal depreciation of the exchange rate does almost nothing to change the price of exports (more than 90% of which is oil priced in dollars) relative to the price of imports (again, overwhelmingly priced in dollars).

But dollar invoicing—and in Greater Europe, euro invoicing—extends around the world, as shown in Table 7-1. Over 90% of U.S. imports are priced in dollars: all else equal, a U.S. depreciation will hardly change the prices of these imports at all. Some

TABLE 7-1

Trade Dollarization The table shows the extent to which the dollar and the euro were used in the invoicing of payments for exports and imports of different countries in the 2002–2004 period. In the United States, for example, 100% of exports are invoiced and paid in U.S. dollars but so, too, are 93% of imports. In Asia, U.S. dollar invoicing is very common, accounting for 48% of Japanese exports and more than 75% of exports and imports in Korea, Malaysia, and Thailand. In Europe the euro figures more prominently as the currency used for trade, but the U.S. dollar is still used in a sizable share of transactions.

	Exports Denominated in		Imports Denominated in	
	U.S. Dollar	Euro	U.S. Dollar	Euro
United States	100%	—	93%	—
United Kingdom	26	21%	37	27%
Australia	70	1	50	9
Asia				
Japan	48	10	9	5
Korea	83	7	80	5
Malaysia	90	—	90	—
Thailand	85	3	76	4
Eurozone				
France	34	52	47	45
Germany	24	63	34	55
Italy	18	75	25	70
Greece	46	47	55	40
Spain	30	61	36	60
EU New Accession Countries				
Czech Republic	13	70	18	66
Hungary	12	83	19	73
Latvia	27	57	—	49
Slovakia	12	74	21	60

Source: Selected data from Linda Goldberg and Cédric Tille, "The Internationalization of the Dollar and Trade Balance Adjustment," Federal Reserve Bank of New York Staff Report 255, August 2006.

Asian countries have trade flows that are 70% to 90% dollarized. Much of this is intra-Asian trade; if, say, a Korean supplier sells to a Japanese manufacturer, very often they conduct the trade not in yen or won, but entirely in U.S. dollars, which is the currency of neither the exporter nor the importer! The table also shows that many new EU member states in Eastern Europe have export shares largely denominated in euros.

Trade dollarization is not the only factor limiting pass-through in the real world. Even after an import has arrived at the port, it still has to pass through various intermediaries. The retail, wholesale, and other distribution activities all add a local currency cost or markup to the final price paid by the ultimate buyer. Suppose the markup is $100 on an import that costs $100 at the port, so the good retails for $200 in shops. Suppose a 10% depreciation of the dollar raises the port price to $110. All else equal, the retail price will rise to just $210, only a 5% increase at the point of final sale. Thus, expenditure switching by final users will be muted by the limited pass-through from port prices to final prices.

How large are these effects? A recent study of 76 developed and developing countries found that, over the period of one year, a 10% exchange rate depreciation resulted in a 6.5% rise in imported goods prices at the port of arrival but perhaps only a 4% rise in the retail prices of imported goods.[*]

The J Curve

Our model of the trade balance assumes that a real depreciation improves a country's trade balance by increasing exports and reducing imports. In reality, however, these effects may be slow to appear because orders for export and import goods are placed months in advance. Thus, at the moment of depreciation there will be no instantaneous change in export and import volumes.

What does this slow adjustment imply? Exports will continue to sell for a time in the same quantity and at the same domestic price, and so total export earnings remain fixed. What will change is the domestic price paid for the import goods. They will have become more expensive in domestic currency terms. If the same quantity of imports flows in but costs more per unit, then the home country's total import bill will rise.

As a result, if export earnings are fixed but import expenditures are rising, the trade balance will initially *fall* rather than rise, as shown in Figure 7-5. Only after time passes, and export and import orders adjust to the new relative prices, will the trade balance move in the positive direction we have assumed. Because of its distinctive shape, the curve traced out by the trade balance over time in Figure 7-5 is called the **J Curve**. Some empirical studies find that the effects of the J Curve last up to a year after the initial depreciation. Hence, the assumption that a depreciation boosts spending on the home country's goods may not hold in the very short run.

---

[*] Jeffrey A. Frankel, David C. Parsley, and Shang-Jin Wei, 2005, "Slow Passthrough around the World: A New Import for Developing Countries?" National Bureau of Economic Research (NBER) Working Paper No. 11199.

FIGURE 7-5

1. A nominal depreciation occurs at time T; prices are sticky, so this is also a real depreciation.
2. At first the quantity of exports is unchanged. Eventually, after a lag, orders for home exports are boosted by the depreciation.
3. At first the quantity of imports is unchanged, but their price rises (foreign goods cost more in terms of home output). Eventually, after a lag, the quantity of imports declines.
4. At first, the trade balance falls due to price effects (more expensive imports, with unchanged import and export quantities). Gradually quantities adjust and the trade balance rises. This is the J Curve.

The J Curve When prices are sticky and there is a nominal and real depreciation of the home currency, it may take time for the trade balance to move toward surplus. In fact, the initial impact may be toward deficit. If firms and households place orders in advance, then import and export quantities may react sluggishly to changes in the relative price of home and foreign goods. Hence, just after the depreciation, the value of home exports, EX, will be unchanged. However, home imports now cost more due to the depreciation. Thus, the value of imports, IM, would actually *rise* after a depreciation, causing the trade balance TB = EX − IM to fall. Only after some time would exports rise and imports fall, allowing the trade balance to rise relative to its pre-depreciation level. The path traced by the trade balance during this process looks vaguely like a letter J.

FIGURE 7-6

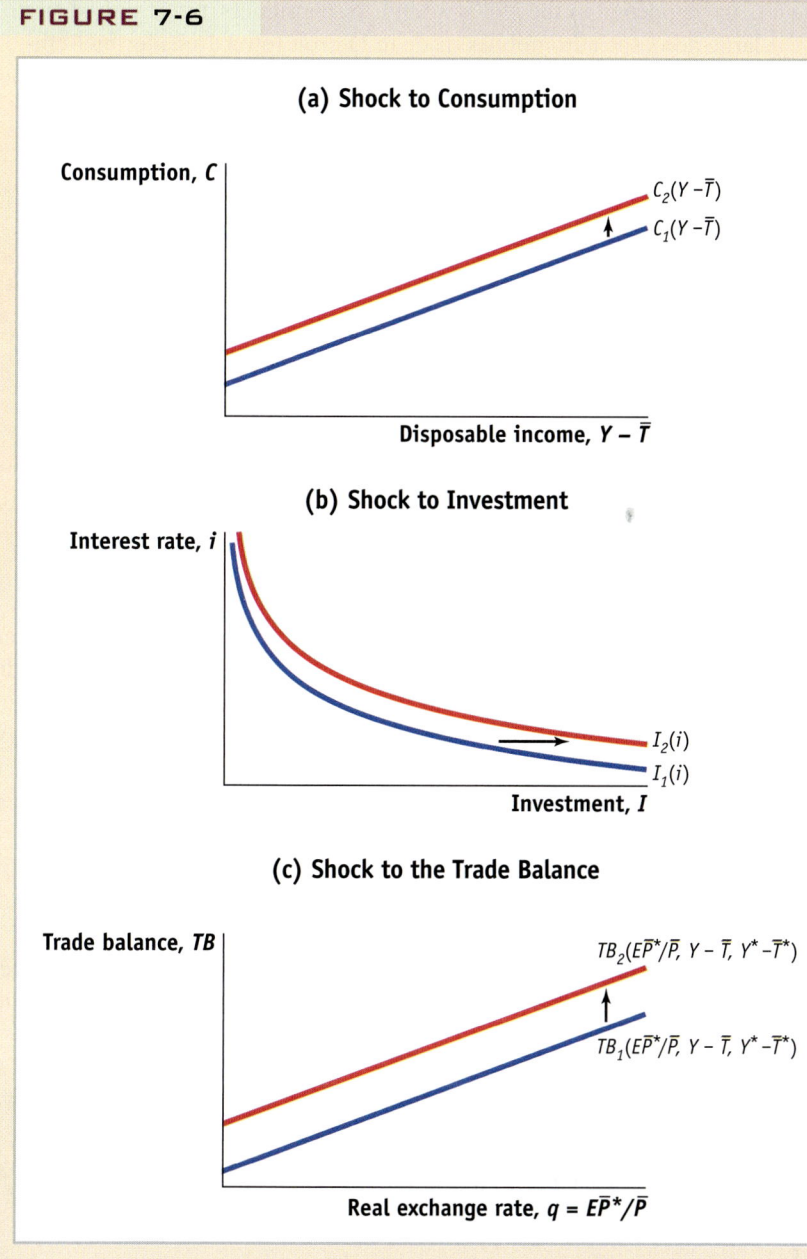

Exogenous Shocks to Consumption, Investment, and the Trade Balance (a) When households decide to consume more at any given level of disposable income, the consumption function shifts up. (b) When firms decide to invest more at any given level of the interest rate, the investment function shifts right. (c) When the trade balance increases at any given level of the real exchange rate, the trade balance function shifts up.

- *An exogenous change in investment.* Suppose that at any given level of the interest rate, firms decide to invest more. After this shock, the investment function would shift up as in Figure 7-6, panel (b). For example, a belief that high-technology companies had great prospects for success led to a large surge in investment in this sector in many countries in the 1990s. This is a change in investment demand unconnected to the interest rate.

- *An exogenous change in the trade balance.* Suppose that at any given level of the real exchange rate, export demand rises and/or import demand falls. After one of these shocks, trade balance function would shift up as in Figure 7-6, panel (c).

Such a change happened in the 1980s when U.S. consumers' tastes shifted away from the large domestic automobiles made in Detroit toward smaller fuel-efficient imported cars manufactured in Japan. This is a switch in demand away from U.S. and toward Japanese products unconnected with the real exchange rate.

2 Goods Market Equilibrium: The Keynesian Cross

We have now studied the determinants of each component of demand. We next put all the components together and show that the goods market is in equilibrium when total demand from all these components is equal to total supply.

Supply and Demand

The total aggregate *supply* of final goods and services is equal to total national output measured by GDP. Given our assumption that the current account equals the trade balance, gross national income Y equals GDP:

$$\text{Supply} = GDP = Y$$

Aggregate demand, or just "demand," consists of all the possible sources of demand for this supply of output. In the balance of payments chapter, we studied the expenditure side of the national income accounts and saw that supply is absorbed into different uses according to the national income identity. This accounting identity *always* holds true. But an identity is not an economic model. A model must explain how, in equilibrium, the observed demands take on their desired or planned values and still satisfy the accounting identity. How can we construct such a model?

We may write total demand for GDP as

$$\text{Demand} = D = C + I + G + TB$$

We can substitute the formulae for consumption, investment, and the trade balance presented in the first section of this chapter into this total demand equation to obtain

$$D = C(Y - \overline{T}) + I(i) + \overline{G} + TB(E\overline{P}^*/\overline{P}, Y - \overline{T}, Y^* - \overline{T}^*)$$

Finally, in an equilibrium, demand D must equal supply Y, so from the preceding two equations we can see that the **goods market equilibrium condition** is

$$Y = \underbrace{C(Y - \overline{T}) + I(i) + \overline{G} + TB(E\overline{P}^*/\overline{P}, Y - \overline{T}, Y^* - \overline{T}^*)}_{D} \tag{7-1}$$

Determinants of Demand

The right-hand side of Equation (7-1) shows that many factors can affect demand: home and foreign output (Y and Y^*), home and foreign taxes (T and T^*), the home nominal interest rate (i), government spending ($\overline{G}$), and the real exchange rate ($E\overline{P}^*/\overline{P}$). Let us examine each of these in turn. We start with home output Y, and assume that all other factors remain fixed.

A rise in output Y (all else equal) will cause the right-hand side to increase. For example, suppose output increases by $\Delta Y = \$1$. This change causes consumption spending C to increase by $+\$MPC$. The change in imports will be $+MPC_F$, causing the trade balance to change by −MPC_F. So the total change in D will be $(MPC − MPC_F) = $MPC_H > 0$, a positive number. This is an intuitive result: an extra $1 of output generates some spending on home goods (an amount MPC_H), with the remainder either spent on foreign goods (an amount MPC_F) or saved (an amount MPS).

Using this result, Figure 7-7, panel (a), plots demand D, the right-hand side of Equation (7-1), as a function of income or output Y only. For the moment, we hold fixed all other determinants of D. Because D increases as Y increases, the demand function has a positive slope MPC_H, a number between 0 and 1.

Also drawn is the 45-degree line, which represents Y, the left-hand side of Equation (7-1). The 45-degree line has a slope of 1, so it is steeper than the demand function.

FIGURE 7-7

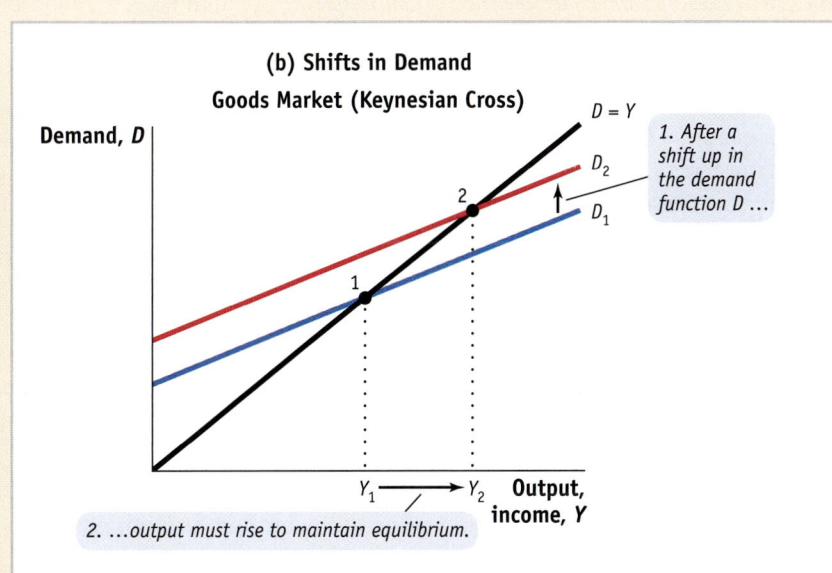

Panel (a): The Goods Market Equilibrium and the Keynesian Cross Equilibrium is where demand, D, equals real output or income, Y. In this diagram, equilibrium is a point 1, at an income or output level of Y_1. The goods market will adjust toward this equilibrium. At point 2, the output level is Y_2 and demand, D, exceeds supply, Y; as inventories fall, firms expand production and output rises toward Y_1. At point 3, the output level is Y_3 and supply Y exceeds demand; as inventories rise, firms cut production and output falls toward Y_1.

Panel (b): Shifts in Demand The goods market is initially in equilibrium at point 1, at which demand and supply both equal Y_1. An increase in demand, D, at all levels of real output, Y, shifts the demand curve up from D_1 to D_2. Equilibrium shifts to point 2, where demand and supply are higher and both equal Y_2. Such an increase in demand could result from changes in one or more of the components of demand: C, I, G, or TB.

This diagram is often called the **Keynesian cross.** It depicts the goods market equilibrium: the goods market is in equilibrium at point 1 where the two lines intersect, for that is the unique point where $D = Y$. This corresponds to an income or output level of Y_1.

Why does the goods market adjust to an equilibrium at this point? To the right of point 1, output tends to fall; to the left of point 1, output tends to rise. Why? At point 2, the output level is Y_2 and demand D exceeds supply Y; as inventories fall, firms expand production and output rises toward Y_1. At point 3, the output level is Y_3 and supply Y exceeds demand; as inventories rise, firms cut production and output falls toward Y_1. Only at point 1 are firms in an equilibrium in which production levels are stable in the short run.

Note the crucial assumptions in this model are that prices are fixed and firms are willing to adjust their production and employment to meet whatever the desired level of demand happens to be. These assumptions may be plausible in the short run, but they do not apply in the long run, when prices can adjust and output and employment are determined by the economy's ability to fully employ its technology and resources.

Factors That Shift the Demand Curve

The Keynesian cross also allows us to examine the impact of the other factors in Equation (7-1) on goods market equilibrium. Let's look at four important cases:

- *A change in government spending.* An exogenous rise in government purchases $\overline{G}$ (all else equal) increases demand at every level of output, as seen in Equation (7-1). More government purchases directly add to the total demand in the economy. This change causes an upward shift in the demand function D, as in Figure 7-7, panel (b). Goods market equilibrium shifts from point 1 to point 2, to an output level Y_2.

The lesson: any exogenous change in G (due to changes in the government budget) will cause the demand curve to shift.

- *A change in taxes (or other factors affecting consumption).* A fall in taxes $\overline{T}$ (all else equal) increases disposable income. When consumers have more disposable income, they spend more on consumption. This change raises demand at every level of output Y, because C increases as disposable income increases. This is seen in Equation (7-1) and in Figure 7-7, panel (a). Thus, a fall in taxes shifts the demand function upward from D_1 to D_2, as shown again in Figure 7-7, panel (b). The increase in D causes the goods market equilibrium to shift from point 1 to point 2, and output rises to Y_2.

The lesson: any exogenous change in C (due to changes in taxes, tastes, etc.) will cause the demand curve to shift.

- *A change in the home interest rate (or other factors affecting investment).* A fall in the interest rate i (all else equal) will lead to an increase in I, as firms find it profitable to engage in more investment projects, and spend more. This change leads to an increase in demand D at every level of output Y. The demand function D shifts upward, as seen in Figure 7-7, panel (b). The increase in demand causes the goods market equilibrium to shift from point 1 to point 2, and output rises to Y_2.

The lesson: any exogenous change in I (due to changes in interest rates, the expected profitability of investment, changes in tax policy, etc.) will cause the demand curve to shift.

- *A change in the home exchange rate.* A rise in the nominal exchange rate E (all else equal) implies a rise in the real exchange rate EP^*/P (due to sticky prices). This is a real depreciation, and through its effects on the trade balance TB via expenditure switching, it will increase demand D at any given level of home output Y. For example, spending switches from foreign goods to American goods when the U.S. dollar depreciates. This change causes the demand function D to shift up, as seen yet again in Figure 7-7, panel (b).

The lesson: any change in the exchange rate will cause the demand curve to shift.

- *A change in the home or foreign price level.* If prices are flexible, then a *rise* in foreign prices or a *fall* in domestic prices causes a home real depreciation, raising $q = E\overline{P}^*/\overline{P}$. This real depreciation causes TB to rise and, all else equal, it will increase demand D at any given level of home output Y. For example, spending switches from foreign goods to American goods when the U.S. prices fall. This change causes the demand function D to shift up, as seen yet again in Figure 7-7, panel (b).

The lesson: any change in P^* or P will cause the demand curve to shift.

Summary

An increase in output Y causes a move along the demand curve. But any increase in demand that is *not* due to a change in output Y will instead cause the demand curve itself to shift upward in the Keynesian cross diagram, as in Figure 7-7, panel (b). Similarly, any contraction in demand not due to output changes will cause the demand function to shift downward.

To conclude, the main factors that shift the demand curve out are as follows:

The opposite changes lead to a decrease in demand and shift the demand curve in.

3 Goods and Forex Market Equilibria: Deriving the IS Curve

We have made an important first step in our study of the short-run behavior of exchange rates and output. Our analysis of demand shows how the level of output adjusts to ensure a goods market equilibrium, given the levels of each component of demand. Each component, in turn, has its own particular determinants, and we have examined how shifts in these determinants (or in other exogenous factors) might shift the level of demand and, hence, change the equilibrium level of output.

But there is more than one market in the economy, and a *general equilibrium* requires equilibrium in all markets—that is, equilibrium in the goods market, the money market, and the forex market. We need to bring all three markets into the analysis, and we do that next by developing a tool of macroeconomic analysis known as the IS-LM diagram. A version of this may be familiar to you from the study of closed-economy macroeconomics, but in this chapter we develop a variant of this approach for an open economy.

Analyzing equilibria in three markets simultaneously is a tall order, but it is made more manageable by proceeding one step at a time. Our first step builds on the depiction of goods market equilibrium developed in the last section using the Keynesian cross and adds on the depiction of forex market equilibrium that we developed in the earlier exchange rate chapters.

Equilibrium in Two Markets

We begin by defining the **IS curve,** which is one part of the IS-LM diagram.

The IS curve shows combinations of output Y and the interest rate i for which the goods and forex markets are in equilibrium.

In Figure 7-8, panel (b), we derive the IS curve by using the Keynesian cross to analyze goods market equilibrium. In panel (c), we impose the uncovered interest parity relationship that ensures the forex market is in equilibrium.

Before we continue, let's take a closer look at why the various graphs in this figure are oriented as they are. The Keynesian cross in panel (a) and the IS diagram in panel (b) share a common horizontal axis, the level of output or income. Hence, these figures are arranged one above the other so that these common output axes line up.

The forex market in panel (c) and the IS diagram in panel (b) share a common vertical axis, the level of the interest rate. Hence, these figures are arranged side by side so that these common interest rate axes line up.

We thus know that if output Y is at a level consistent with demand equals supply, shown in the Keynesian cross in panel (a), and if the interest rate i is at a level consistent with uncovered interest parity, shown in the forex market in panel (c), then in panel (b) we must have a combination of Y and i that is consistent with equilibrium in both goods and forex markets.

Forex Market Recap

In earlier chapters we learned that the forex market is in equilibrium when the expected returns expressed in domestic currency are the same on foreign and domestic interest-bearing (money market) bank deposits. Equation (10-3) described this condition, known as uncovered interest parity (UIP):

$$\underbrace{\underbrace{i}_{\text{Domestic interest rate}} = \underbrace{i^*}_{\text{Foreign interest rate}} + \underbrace{\left(\frac{E^e}{E} - 1\right)}_{\substack{\text{Expected rate of depreciation} \\ \text{of the domestic currency}}}}_{\substack{\text{Domestic return} \hspace{3cm} \text{Expected foreign return}}}$$

The expected return on the foreign deposit *measured in home currency* equals the foreign interest rate plus the expected rate of depreciation of the home currency.

Taking the foreign interest rate i^* and expectations of the future exchange rate E^e as given, we know that the right-hand side of this expression decreases as E increases: the

Deriving the IS Curve The Keynesian cross is in panel (a), IS curve in panel (b), and forex (FX) market in panel (c). The economy starts in equilibrium with output, Y_1; interest rate, i_1; and exchange rate, E_1. Consider the effect of a decrease in the interest rate from i_1 to i_2, all else equal. In panel (c), a lower interest rate causes a depreciation; equilibrium moves from 1' to 2'. A lower interest rate boosts investment and a depreciation boosts the trade balance. In panel (a), demand shifts up from D_1 to D_2, equilibrium from 1" to 2", output from Y_1 to Y_2. In panel (b), we go from point 1 to point 2. The IS curve is thus traced out, a downward-sloping relationship between the interest rate and output. When the interest rate falls from i_1 to i_2, output rises from Y_1 to Y_2. The IS curve describes all combinations of i and Y consistent with goods and FX market equilibria in panels (a) and (c).

intuition for this is that the more expensive it is to purchase foreign currency today, the lower the expected return must be, all else equal.

The inverse relationship between E and the expected foreign return on the right-hand side of the previous equation is shown by the *FR* (foreign returns) line in panel (b) of Figure 7-8. The domestic return *DR* is the horizontal line corresponding to the level of the domestic interest rate i.

Deriving the IS Curve

Using the setup in Figure 7-8, we can now derive the shape of the IS curve by considering how changes in the interest rate affect output *if the goods and forex markets are to remain in equilibrium.*

Initial Equilibrium Let us suppose that the goods market and forex markets are initially in equilibrium at an interest rate i_1, an output or income level Y_1, and an exchange rate E_1.

In panel (a) by assumption, at an output level Y_1, demand equals supply, so the output level Y_1 must correspond to the point 1″, which is at the intersection of the Keynesian cross, and the figure is drawn accordingly.

In panel (c) by assumption, at an interest rate i_1 and an exchange rate E_1, the domestic and foreign returns must be equal, so this must be the point 1′, which is at the intersection of the DR_1 and FR curves, and the figure is drawn accordingly.

Finally, in panel (b) by assumption, at an interest rate i_1 and an output level Y_1, both goods and forex markets are in equilibrium. Thus, the point 1 is on the IS curve, *by definition*.

Lines are drawn joining the equal output levels Y_1 in panels (a) and (b). The domestic return line DR_1 traces out the home interest rate level from panel (b) across to panel (c).

A Fall in the Interest Rate Now in Figure 7-8, let us suppose that the home interest rate falls from i_1 to i_2. What happens to equilibria in the good and forex markets?

We first look at the forex market in panel (c). From our analysis of UIP in earlier chapters we know that when the home interest rate falls, domestic deposits have a lower return and look less attractive to investors. To maintain forex market equilibrium, the exchange rate must rise (the home currency must depreciate) until domestic and foreign returns are once again equal. In our example, when the home interest rate falls to i_2, the exchange rate must rise from E_1 to E_2 to equalize FR and DR_2 and restore equilibrium in the forex market at point 2′.

How do the changes in the home interest rate and the exchange rate affect demand? As shown in panel (a), demand will increase (shift up) for two reasons, as we learned earlier in this chapter.

First, when the domestic interest rate falls, firms are willing to engage in more investment projects, and their increased investment augments demand. The increase in investment, all else equal, *directly* increases demand D at any level of output Y.

Second, the exchange rate E has risen (depreciated). Because prices are sticky in the short run, this rise in the nominal exchange rate E also causes a rise in the real exchange rate $E\overline{P}^*/\overline{P}$. That is, the nominal depreciation causes a real depreciation. This increases demand D via expenditure switching. At any level of output Y consumers switch expenditure from relatively more expensive foreign goods toward relatively less expensive domestic goods. Thus, the fall in the interest rate *indirectly* boosts demand via exchange rate effects felt through the trade balance TB.

One important observation is in order: in an open economy, the phenomenon of expenditure switching operates as an additional element in demand that is not present in a closed economy. *In an open economy, lower interest rates stimulate demand through the traditional closed-economy investment channel and through the trade balance. The trade balance effect occurs because lower interest rates cause a nominal depreciation, which in the short run is also a real depreciation, which stimulates external demand via the trade balance.*

To summarize, panel (a) shows clearly that in response to a decrease in the interest rate, demand has shifted up to D_2 and the Keynesian cross goods market equilibrium is restored by a rise in output to Y_2, which corresponds to point $2''$.

In panel (b), we can now derive the shape of the IS curve. At an interest rate i_1 and output level Y_1 and at an interest rate i_2 and an output level Y_2, both the goods and forex markets are in equilibrium. *We have now derived the shape of the IS curve, which describes goods and forex market equilibrium. When the interest rate falls from i_1 to i_2, output rises from Y_1 to Y_2. The IS curve is downward-sloping, which illustrates the negative relationship between the interest rate i and output Y.*

Factors That Shift the IS Curve

In deriving the IS curve, we treated various demand factors as exogenous, including fiscal policy, price levels, and the exchange rate. If any factors other than the interest rate and output change, the position of the IS curve would have to change. These effects are central in any analysis of changes in an economy's equilibrium. We now explore several changes that result in an increase in demand; that is, an upward shift in the demand curve in Figure 7-9, panel (a). (A decrease in demand would result from changes in the opposite direction.)

- *A change in government spending.* If demand shifts up because of a *rise* in $\overline{G}$, a fiscal expansion, all else equal, what happens to the IS curve? The initial equilibrium point (Y_1, i_1) would no longer be a goods market equilibrium: if the interest rate is unchanged at i_1, then I is unchanged, as are the exchange rate E and hence TB. Yet demand has risen due to the change in G. That demand has to be satisfied somehow, so more output has to be produced. Some—but not all—of that extra output will be consumed, but the rest can meet the extra demand generated by the rise in government spending. At the interest rate i_1, output must rise to Y_2 for the goods market to once again be in equilibrium. Thus, the IS curve must shift right as shown in Figure 7-9, panel (b).

The lesson: a rise in government spending shifts the IS curve out.

- *A change in taxes.* Suppose taxes were to decrease. With all other factors remaining unchanged, this tax cut makes demand shift up by boosting private consumption, all else equal. We assume that the interest rate i_1, the exchange rate E_1, and government's spending policy are all fixed. Thus, neither I nor TB nor G change. With an excess of demand, supply has to rise, so output must again increase to Y_2 and the IS curve shifts right.

The lesson: a reduction in taxes shifts the IS curve out.

- *A change in the foreign interest rate or expected future exchange rate.* A *rise* in the foreign interest rate i^* or a *rise* in the future expected exchange rate E^e causes a depreciation of the home currency, all else equal (recall that in the forex market, the FR curve shifts out because the return on foreign deposits has increased; if the home interest rate is unchanged, E must rise). A rise in E causes the real exchange rate to depreciate, because prices are sticky. As a result, TB rises via expenditure switching, and demand increases. Because C, I, and G do not change, there is an excess of demand, and supply has to rise to restore equilibrium. Output Y increases, and the IS curve shifts right.

The lesson: an increase in the foreign return (via i^* or E^e) shifts the IS curve out.

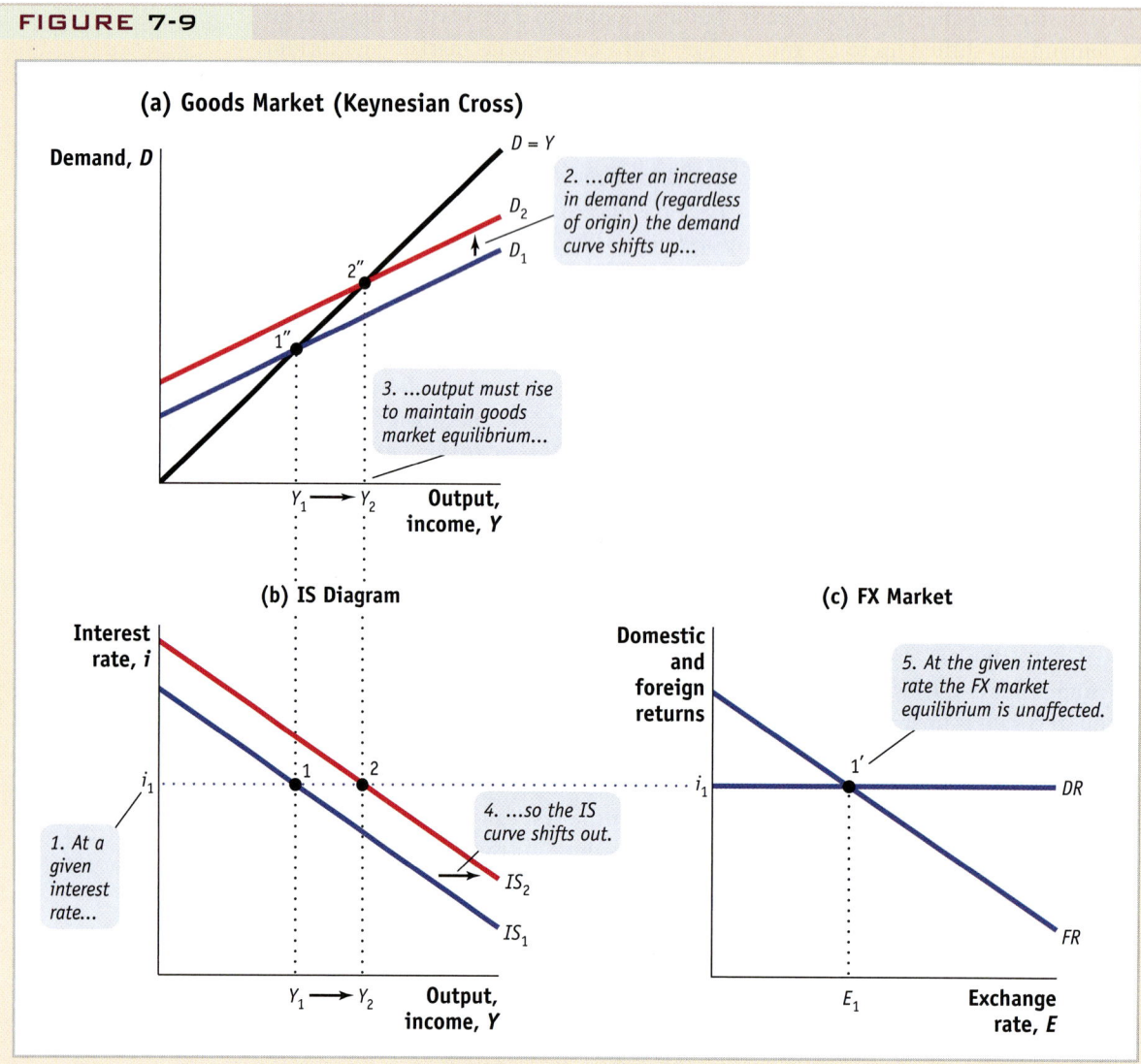

Exogenous Shifts in Demand Cause the IS Curve to Shift In the Keynesian cross in panel (a), when the interest rate is held constant at i_1, an exogenous increase in demand (due to other factors) causes the demand curve to shift up from D_1 to D_2 as shown, all else equal. This moves the equilibrium from 1" to 2", raising output from Y_1 to Y_2. In the IS diagram in panel (b), output has risen, with no change in the interest rate. The IS curve has therefore shifted right from IS_2 to IS_1. The nominal interest rate and hence the exchange rate are unchanged in this example, as seen in panel (c).

- *A change in the home or foreign price level.* If prices are flexible, then a *rise* in foreign prices or a *fall* in domestic prices causes a home real depreciation, raising $q = E\bar{P}^*/\bar{P}$. This real depreciation causes TB to rise and, all else equal, demand will rise to a position like D_2. With an excess of demand, supply has to rise to restore equilibrium. Output Y must increase, and the IS curve shifts right.

The lesson: an increase P^* or a decrease in P shifts the IS curve out.

These examples show that the position of the IS curve depends on various factors that we treat as given (or exogenous). We may write this observation using the notation

$$IS = IS(G, T, i^*, E^e, P^*, P)$$

There are many other exogenous shocks to the economy that can be analyzed in a similar fashion—for example, a sudden exogenous change in consumption, investment, or the trade balance. How will the IS curve react in each case? You may have detected a pattern from the preceding discussion.

The general rule is as follows: *any type of shock that increases demand at a given level of output will shift the IS curve to the right; any shock that decreases demand will shift the IS curve down.*

Summing Up the IS Curve

When prices are sticky, the IS curve summarizes the relationship between output Y and the interest rate i necessary to keep the goods and forex markets in short-run equilibrium. The IS curve is downward-sloping. Why? Lower interest rates stimulate demand via the investment channel and, through exchange rate depreciation, via the trade balance. Higher demand can be satisfied in the short run only by higher output. Thus, when the interest rate falls, output rises, and the economy moves along the IS curve.

As for shifts in the IS curve, we have found that any factor which increases demand D at a given home interest rate i must cause the demand curve to shift up, leading to higher output Y and, as a result, an outward shift in the IS curve.

To conclude, the main factors that shift the IS curve out can be summed up as follows:

The opposite changes lead to a decrease in demand and shift the demand curve down and the IS curve to the left.

4 Money Market Equilibrium: Deriving the LM Curve

The IS curve links the forex market and the goods market as depicted by the Keynesian cross. It summarizes combinations of Y and i at which goods demand equals goods supply in a way that is consistent with forex market equilibrium. We have now taken care of equilibria in two out of three markets, so there is only one market left to worry about. In this section, we derive a set of combinations of Y and i that ensures equilibrium in the money market, a concept that can be represented graphically as the **LM curve**.

The LM curve is more straightforward to derive than the IS curve for a couple of reasons. First, the money market is something we have already studied in earlier chapters, so we already have all the tools we need to build the LM curve. Second, unlike the IS curve, the open-economy LM curve is no different from the closed-economy LM curve, so there will be no new material here if you have previously studied the closed-economy IS-LM model in another course.

Money Market Recap

In our earlier study of the money market, we assumed that the level of output or income Y was given. In deriving the LM curve, we now face a new question: What happens in the money market when an economy's output changes?

In the short-run, the price level is assumed to be sticky at a level $\overline{P}$, and the money market is in equilibrium when the demand for real money balances $L(i)Y$ equals the real money supply $M/\overline{P}$:

$$\underbrace{\frac{M}{\overline{P}}}_{\text{Real money supply}} = \underbrace{L(i)Y}_{\text{Real money demand}} \qquad (7\text{-}2)$$

Figure 7-10, panel (a), shows that real money demand MD varies inversely with the nominal interest rate. As a result of this relationship, the demand curve for real money balances slopes downward. The real money supply MS is assumed to be fixed

FIGURE 7-10

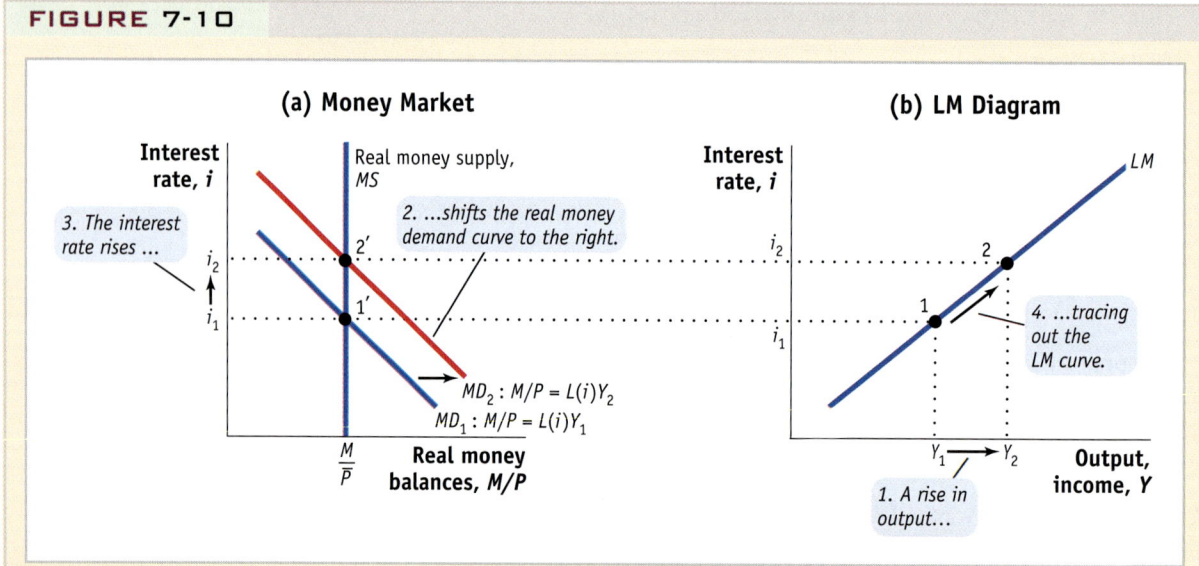

Deriving the LM Curve If there is an increase in real income or output from Y_1 to Y_2 in panel (b), the effect in the money market in panel (a) is to shift the demand for real money balances to the right, all else equal. If the real supply of money, MS, is held fixed at $M/\overline{P}$, then the interest rate rises from i_1 to i_2 and money market equilibrium moves from point 1' to point 2'. The relationship thus described between the interest rate and income, all else equal, is known as the LM curve and is depicted in panel (b) by the shift from point 1 to point 2. The LM curve is upward-sloping: when the output level rises from Y_1 to Y_2, the interest rate rises from i_1 to i_2. The LM curve in panel (b) describes all combinations of i and Y that are consistent with money market equilibrium in panel (a).

for now. Initially, the level of output is Y_1 at and the money market is in equilibrium at 1′, where real money demand is on MD_1 at $M/\overline{P} = L(i_1)Y_1$.

If output changes, the real money demand curve shifts. For example, if output rises to Y_2 and the real money supply $M/\overline{P}$ remains fixed, then real money demand increases because more output implies a larger number of transactions in the economy for which money is needed. The real money demand curve shifts right to MD_2. To keep money supply and demand equal, $M/\overline{P} = L(i_2)Y_2$, the interest rate rises from $i = i_1$ to $i = i_2$. Equilibrium moves from 1′ to 2′.

Deriving the LM Curve

This exercise can be repeated for any level of output Y. Doing so will generate a combination of interest rates i and outputs Y for which the money market is in equilibrium. This set of points, called the *LM curve*, is drawn in Figure 7-10, panel (b).

For example, if the real money supply is fixed at $M/\overline{P}$, an increase in output from Y_1 to Y_2 generates a rise in the nominal interest rate from i_1 to i_2 in panel (a), as we have just seen. This change can also be depicted as a move from point 1 to point 2 along the *LM* curve, as shown in panel (b).

We have now derived the shape of the LM curve, which describes money market equilibrium. When output rises from Y_1 to Y_2, the interest rate rises from i_1 to i_2. The LM curve is an upward-sloping relationship between the interest rate i and output Y.

The two ways of depicting the money market equilibrium are entirely equivalent. The money market diagram shows the relationship between real money balances demanded and supplied at different interest rates, holding output fixed. The *LM* curve diagram shows the relationship between output and the interest rate holding real money balances as fixed. Because the *LM* curve does *not* hold output fixed, it is important to developing our model of how output, interest rates, and exchange rates fluctuate in the short run.

Factors That Shift the LM Curve

An important reason for a shift in the LM curve is a change in the real money supply. (Changes in output result in a move *along* a given LM curve.) The LM curve tells us the interest rate i that equilibrates the money market at any given level of output Y. Given Y, we know that the equilibrium interest rate i depends on real money supply $M/\overline{P}$, and so the position of the LM curve depends on $M/\overline{P}$.

The effect of the real money supply on a nation's output or income is important because we are often interested in the impact of monetary policy changes on overall economic activity. To see how this effect operates via the LM curve, we can examine the money market diagram in Figure 7-11, panel (a). An increase in the nominal money supply M with sticky prices raises real money supply from $M_1/\overline{P}$ to $M_2/\overline{P}$ and shifts the real money supply curve *MS* to the right.

What happens in the LM diagram if the exogenous real money supply $M/\overline{P}$ changes in this way? For a given level of output Y, the increased supply of real money drives the interest rate down to i_2, and equilibrium in the money market shifts from point 1′ to point 2′. A decrease in the interest rate to i_2 when the level of output is unchanged at Y means that we cannot be on the same LM curve as before. There must have been a downward shift of the LM curve from LM_1 to LM_2 in Figure 7-11, panel (b).

We have shown the following: *an increase in real money supply shifts the LM curve down or to the right; a decrease in the real money supply shifts the LM curve up or to the left.*

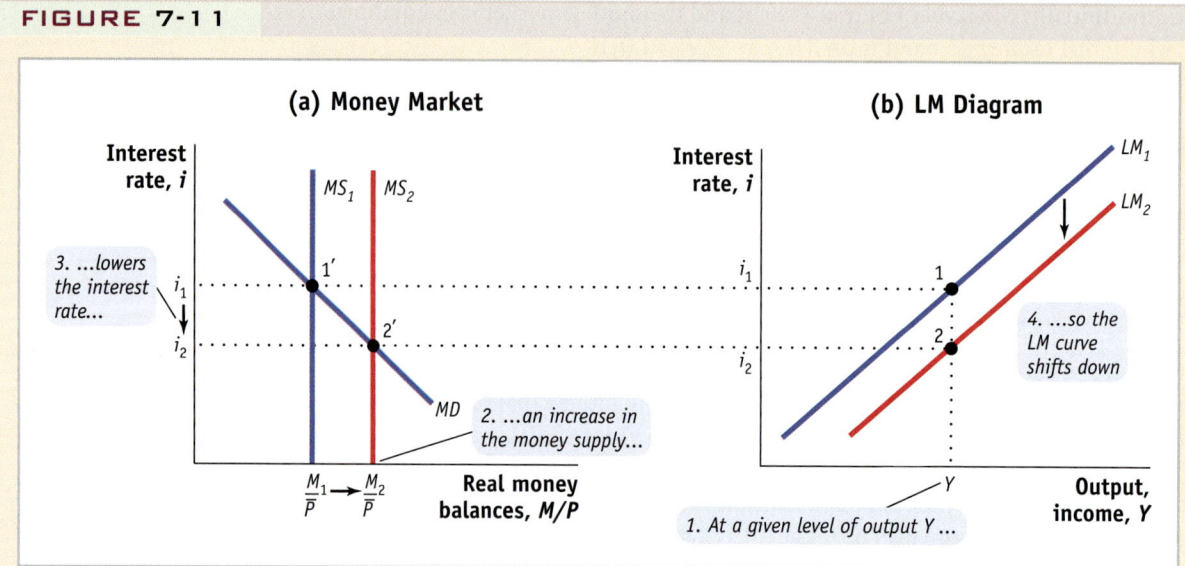

Change in the Money Supply Shifts the LM Curve In the money market, shown in panel (a), we hold fixed the level of real income or output, Y, and hence real money demand, MD. All else equal, we show the effect of an increase in money supply from M_1 to M_2. The real money supply curve moves out from MS_1 to MS_2. This moves the equilibrium from 1′ to 2′, lowering the interest rate from i_1 to i_2. In the LM diagram, shown in panel (b), the interest rate has fallen, with no change in the level of income or output, so the economy moves from point 1 to point 2. The LM curve has therefore shifted down from LM_1 to LM_2.

Thus, the position of the LM curve is a function of real money supply:

$$LM = LM(M/\overline{P})$$

Remember that in this short-run model of the economy, prices are sticky and treated as given, so any change in the real money supply in the short run is caused by changes in the nominal money supply M, which for now we take as given or exogenous.

Other factors can influence the position of the LM curve. In addition to changes in the money supply, exogenous changes in real money demand will also cause the LM curve to shift. For example, for a given money supply, a decrease in the demand for real money balances (an increase in the L function) at a given level of output Y will tend to lower the interest rate, all else equal, which would be depicted as a shift down or to the right in the LM curve.

Summing Up the LM Curve

When prices are sticky, the LM curve summarizes the relationship between output Y and interest rate i necessary to keep the money market in short-run equilibrium for a given level of the real money supply. The LM curve is upward-sloping. Why? In a money market equilibrium, if real money supply is constant, then real money demand must also be constant. If output rises, real money demand rises and to maintain equilibrium, real money demand must contract. This contraction in real money demand is accomplished by a rise in the interest rate. Thus, on the LM curve, when output rises, so, too, does the interest rate.

The following factors shift the LM curve:

The opposite changes lead to an increase in the home interest rate and shift the LM curve up or to the left.

5 The Short-Run IS-LM-FX Model of an Open Economy

We are now in a position to fully characterize an open economy that is in equilibrium in goods, money, and forex markets, as shown in Figure 7-12. This IS-LM-FX figure combines the goods market (the IS curve), the money market (the LM curve), and the forex (FX) market diagrams.

The *IS* and *LM* curves are both drawn in panel (a). The goods and forex markets are in equilibrium if and only if the economy is on the *IS* curve. The money market is in equilibrium if and only if the economy is on the *LM* curve. Thus, all three markets are in equilibrium if and only if the economy is at point 1, where *IS* and *LM* intersect.

FIGURE 7-12

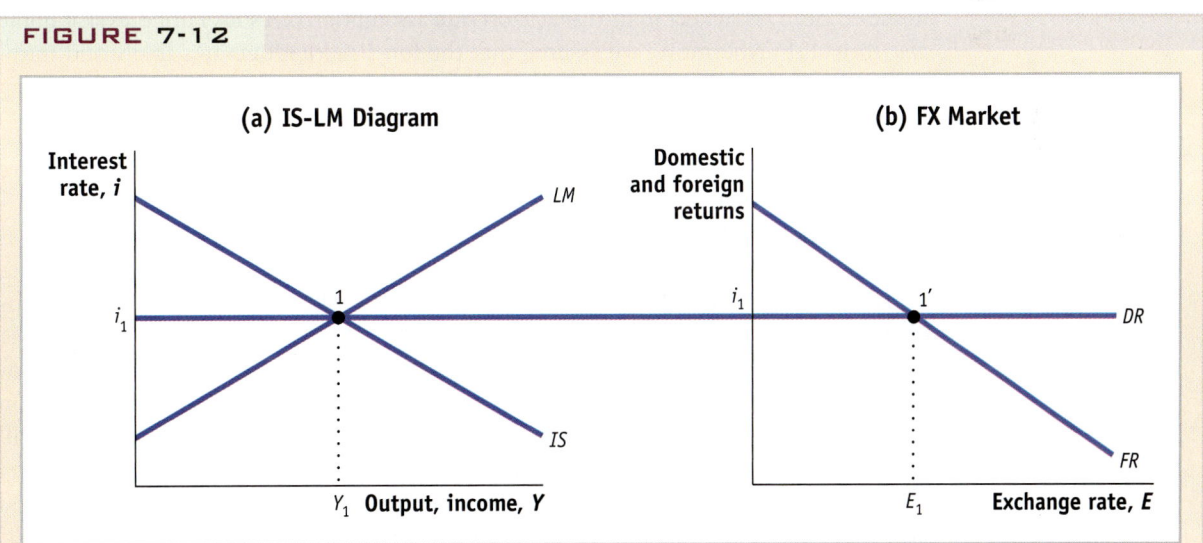

Equilibrium in the IS-LM-FX Model In panel (a), the *IS* and *LM* curves are both drawn. The goods and forex markets are in equilibrium when the economy is on the *IS* curve. The money market is in equilibrium when the economy is on the *LM* curve. Both markets are in equilibrium if and only if the economy is at point 1, the unique point of intersection of *IS* and *LM*. In panel (b), the forex (FX) market is shown. The domestic return, *DR*, in the forex market equals the money market interest rate. Equilibrium is at point 1′ where the foreign return *FR* equals domestic return, *i*.

The forex market, or FX market, is drawn in panel (b). The domestic return DR in the forex market equals the money market interest rate. Equilibrium is at point 1′ where the foreign return FR is equal to domestic return i.

In the remainder of this chapter, and in the rest of this book, we make extensive use of this graphical depiction of the open-economy equilibrium to analyze the short-run response of an open economy to various types of shocks. In particular, we look at how government policies affect the economy and the extent to which they can be employed to enhance macroeconomic performance and stability.

Macroeconomic Policies in the Short Run

Now that we understand the open-economy IS-LM-FX model and all the factors that influence an economy's short-run equilibrium, we can use the model to look at how a nation's key macroeconomic variables (output, exchange rates, trade balance) are affected in the short run by changes in government macroeconomic policies.

We focus on the two main policy actions: changes in **monetary policy,** implemented through changes in the money supply, and changes in **fiscal policy,** involving changes in government spending or taxes. Of particular interest is the question of whether governments can use such policies to insulate the economy from fluctuations in output.

We will see that the impact of these policies is profoundly affected by a nation's choice of exchange rate regime, and we will consider the two polar cases of fixed and floating exchange rates. Many countries are on some kind of flexible exchange rate regime and many are on some kind of fixed regime, so considering policy effects under both fixed and floating systems is essential.

The key assumptions of this section are as follows. The economy begins in a state of long-run equilibrium. We then consider policy changes in the home economy, assuming that conditions in the foreign economy (i.e., the rest of the world) are unchanged. The home economy is subject to the usual short-run assumption of a sticky price level at home *and* abroad. Furthermore, we assume that the forex market operates freely and unrestricted by capital controls and that the exchange rate is determined by market forces.

Temporary Policies, Unchanged Expectations Finally, we examine only *temporary* changes in policies. We will assume that long-run expectations about the future state of the economy are unaffected by the policy changes. In particular, the future expected exchange rate E^e is held fixed. The reason for studying temporary policies is that we are primarily interested in how governments use fiscal and monetary policies to handle temporary shocks and business cycles in the short run, and our model is applicable only in the short run.[2]

The key lesson of this section is that policies matter and can have significant macroeconomic effects in the short run. Moreover, their impacts depend in a big way on the type of exchange rate regime in place. Once we understand these linkages, we will better understand the contentious and ongoing debates about exchange rates and macroeconomic policies, including the never-ending arguments over the merits of fixed and floating exchange rates (a topic covered in detail in the next chapter).

---

[2] Moreover, permanent changes may not be truly feasible given realistic constraints on governments. For example, a permanent increase in money supply, all else equal, would lead to a permanent increase in the price level, violating a money, exchange rate, or inflation target (the nominal anchor). A permanent increase in government spending, with no increase in taxes, would not be feasible given the government's long-run budget constraint.

Monetary Policy under Floating Exchange Rates

In this policy experiment, we consider a temporary monetary expansion in the home country when the exchange rate is allowed to float. Because the expansion is not permanent, we assume there is no change in long-run expectations so that the expected future exchange rate remains steady at E^e. This means that there is no change in the expected foreign return curve in the forex market.

Figure 7-13 illustrates the predictions of the model. In panel (a) in the IS-LM diagram, the goods and money markets are initially in equilibrium at point 1. The interest rate in the money market is also the domestic return DR_1 that prevails in the forex market. In panel (b), the forex market is initially in equilibrium at point 1'.

A temporary monetary expansion that increases the money supply from M_1 to M_2 would shift the LM curve to the right in panel (a) from LM_1 to LM_2, causing the interest rate to fall from i_1 to i_2. The domestic return falls from DR_1 to DR_2. In panel (b), the lower interest rate would imply that the exchange rate must depreciate, rising from E_1 to E_2. As the interest rate falls (increasing investment I) and the exchange rate depreciates (increasing the trade balance), demand increases, which corresponds to the move down the IS curve from point 1 to point 2. Output expands from Y_1 to Y_2. The new equilibrium corresponds to points 2 and 2'.

The intuition for this result is as follows: monetary expansion tends to lower the home interest rate, all else equal. A lower interest rate stimulates demand in two ways. First, directly in the goods market, it causes investment demand I to increase. Second, indirectly, it causes the exchange rate to depreciate in the forex market, which in turn

FIGURE 7-13

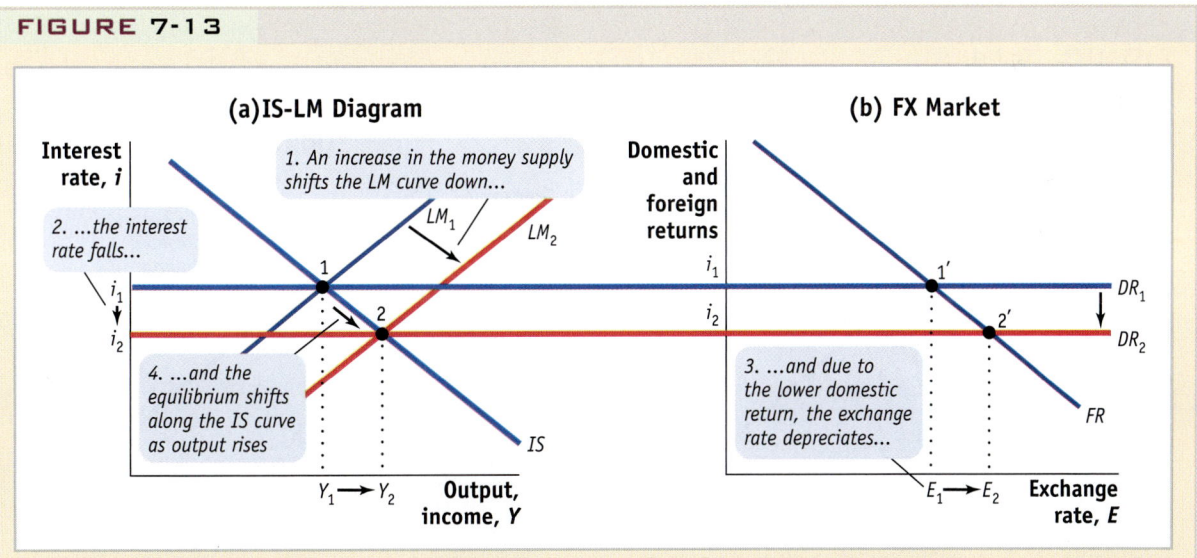

Monetary Policy under Floating Exchange Rates In panel (a) in the IS-LM diagram, the goods and money markets are initially in equilibrium at point 1. The interest rate in the money market is also the domestic return, DR_1, that prevails in the forex market. In panel (b), the forex market is initially in equilibrium at point 1'. A temporary monetary expansion that increases the money supply from M_1 to M_2 would shift the LM curve down in panel (a) from LM_1 to LM_2, causing the interest rate to fall from i_1 to i_2. DR falls from DR_1 to DR_2. In panel (b), the lower interest rate implies that the exchange rate must depreciate, rising from E_1 to E_2. As the interest rate falls (increasing investment, I) and the exchange rate depreciates (increasing the trade balance), demand increases, which corresponds to the move down the IS curve from point 1 to point 2. Output expands from Y_1 to Y_2. The new equilibrium corresponds to points 2 and 2'.

causes expenditure switching in the goods market, which causes the trade balance TB to increase. Both I and TB are sources of demand and both increase.

To sum up: a temporary monetary expansion under floating exchange rates is effective in combating economic downturns by boosting output. It raises output at home, lowers the interest rate, and causes a depreciation of the exchange rate. What happens to the trade balance cannot be predicted with certainty: increased home output will decrease the trade balance as the demand for imports will rise, but the real depreciation will increase the trade balance, because expenditure switching will tend to raise exports and diminish imports. In practice, economists tend to assume that the latter outweighs the former, so a temporary expansion of the money supply is usually predicted to increase the trade balance. (The case of a temporary contraction of monetary policy has opposite effects. As an exercise, work through this case using the same graphical apparatus.)

Monetary Policy under Fixed Exchange Rates

Now let's look at what happens when a temporary monetary expansion occurs in a home country that pegs its exchange rate with respect to the foreign country at $\bar{E}$. The key to understanding this experiment is to recall the uncovered interest parity condition: *the home interest rate must equal the foreign interest rate under a fixed exchange rate.*

Figure 7-14 puts the model to work. In panel (a) in the IS-LM diagram, the goods and money markets are initially in equilibrium at point 1. In panel (b), the forex market is initially in equilibrium at point 1'.

FIGURE 7-14

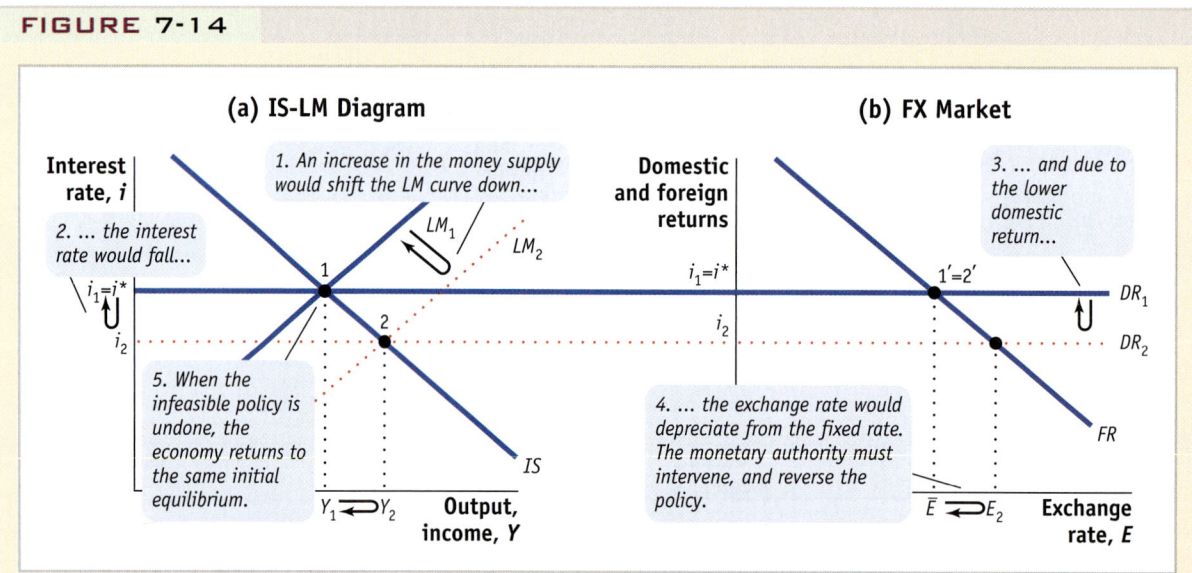

Monetary Policy under Fixed Exchange Rates In panel (a) in the IS-LM diagram, the goods and money markets are initially in equilibrium at point 1. In panel (b), the forex market is initially in equilibrium at point 1'. A temporary monetary expansion that increases the money supply from M_1 to M_2 would shift the LM curve down in panel (a). In panel (b), the lower interest rate would imply that the exchange rate must depreciate, rising from $\bar{E}$ to E_2. This depreciation is inconsistent with the pegged exchange rate, so the policy makers cannot move LM in this way. They must leave the money supply equal to M_1. Implication: under a fixed exchange rate, autonomous monetary policy is not an option.

A temporary monetary expansion that increases the money supply from M_1 to M_2 would shift the LM curve down and to the right in panel (a), and the interest rate would tend to fall, as we have just seen. In panel (b), the lower interest rate would imply that the exchange rate would tend to rise or depreciate toward E_2. This is inconsistent with the pegged exchange rate $\overline{E}$, so the policy makers cannot alter monetary policy and shift the LM curve in this way. They must leave the money supply equal to M_1 and the economy cannot deviate from its initial equilibrium.

This example illustrates a key lesson: under a fixed exchange rate, autonomous monetary policy is not an option. What is going on? Remember that under a fixed exchange rate, the home interest rate must exactly equal the foreign interest rate, $i = i^*$, according to the uncovered interest parity condition. Any shift in the LM curve would violate this restriction and break the fixed exchange rate.

To sum up: monetary policy under fixed exchange rates is impossible to undertake. Fixing the exchange rate means giving up monetary policy autonomy. In an earlier chapter, we learned about the trilemma: countries cannot simultaneously allow capital mobility, maintain fixed exchange rates, and pursue an autonomous monetary policy. We have now just seen the trilemma at work in the IS-LM-FX framework. By illustrating a potential benefit of autonomous monetary policy (the ability to use monetary policy to increase output), the model clearly exposes one of the major costs of fixed exchange rates. Monetary policy, which in principle could be used to influence the economy in the short run, is ruled out by a fixed exchange rate.

Fiscal Policy under Floating Exchange Rates

We now turn to fiscal policy under a floating exchange rate. In this example, we consider a temporary increase in government spending from $\overline{G}_1$ to $\overline{G}_2$ in the home economy. Again, the effect is not permanent, so there are no changes in long-run expectations, and in particular the expected future exchange rate remains steady at E^e. Figure 7-15 shows what happens in our model. In panel (a) in the IS-LM diagram, the goods and money markets are initially in equilibrium at point 1. The interest rate in the money market is also the domestic return DR_1 that prevails in the forex market. In panel (b), the forex market is initially in equilibrium at point 1'.

A temporary fiscal expansion that increases government spending from $\overline{G}_1$ to $\overline{G}_2$ would shift the IS curve to the right in panel (a) from IS_1 to IS_2, causing the interest rate to rise from i_1 to i_2. The domestic return rises from DR_1 to DR_2. In panel (b), the higher interest rate would imply that the exchange rate must appreciate, falling from to E_1 to E_2. As the interest rate rises (decreasing investment I) and the exchange rate appreciates (decreasing the trade balance TB), demand falls, which corresponds to the move up the LM curve from point 1 to point 2. Output expands from Y_1 to Y_2. The new equilibrium is at points 2 and 2'.

What is happening here? The fiscal expansion raises output as the IS curve shifts right. But the increases in output will raise interest rates, all else equal, given a fixed money supply. The resulting higher interest rates will reduce the investment component of demand, and this limits the rise in demand to less than the increase in government spending. This impact of fiscal expansion on investment is often referred to as *crowding out* by economists.

The higher interest rate also causes the home currency to appreciate. As home consumers switch their consumption to now less expensive foreign goods, the trade balance will fall. Thus, the higher interest rate also (indirectly) leads to a *crowding out* of net

Fiscal Policy under Floating Exchange Rates In panel (a) in the IS-LM diagram, the goods and money markets are initially in equilibrium at point 1. The interest rate in the money market is also the domestic return, DR_1, that prevails in the forex market. In panel (b), the forex market is initially in equilibrium at point 1'. A temporary fiscal expansion that increases government spending from $\bar{G}_1$ to $\bar{G}_2$ would shift the IS curve to the right in panel (a) from IS_1 to IS_2, causing the interest rate to rise from i_1 to i_2. The domestic return shifts up from DR_1 to DR_2. In panel (b), the higher interest rate would imply that the exchange rate must appreciate, falling from E_1 to E_2. As the interest rate rises (decreasing investment, I) and the exchange rate appreciates (decreasing the trade balance), demand falls, which corresponds to the move along the LM curve from point 1 to point 2. Output expands from Y_1 to Y_2. The new equilibrium corresponds to points 2 and 2'.

exports, and this too limits the rise in output to less than the increase in government spending. Thus, in an open economy, fiscal expansion not only crowds out investment (by raising the interest rate) but also crowds out net exports (by causing the exchange rate to appreciate).

To sum up: a temporary expansion of fiscal policy under floating exchange rates is effective. It raises output at home, raises the interest rate, causes an appreciation of the exchange rate, and decreases the trade balance. (A temporary contraction of fiscal policy has opposite effects. As an exercise, work through the contraction case using the same graphical apparatus.)

Fiscal Policy under Fixed Exchange Rates

Now let's see how the outcomes differ when the home country pegs its exchange rate with respect to the foreign country at $\bar{E}$. The key is to recall the parity condition: the home interest rate must remain exactly equal to the foreign interest rate for the peg to hold.

Figure 7-16 shows what happens in this case. In panel (a) in the IS-LM diagram, the goods and money markets are initially in equilibrium at point 1. The interest rate in the money market is also the domestic return DR_1 that prevails in the forex market. In panel (b), the forex market is initially in equilibrium at point 1'.

FIGURE 7-16

(a) IS-LM Diagram

1. An increase in government spending shifts the IS curve right...
5. The money supply expands, so the LM curve shifts down.
2. ... which would tend to raise the interest rate...
6. The interest rate is unchanged, so the peg holds.
7. Output rises dramatically.

(b) FX Market

3. ... and raise the domestic return.
4. The exchange rate would tend to appreciate away from the fixed rate. The monetary authority must intervene.

Fiscal Policy under Fixed Exchange Rates In panel (a) in the IS-LM diagram, the goods and money markets are initially in equilibrium at point 1. The interest rate in the money market is also the domestic return, DR_1, that prevails in the forex market. In panel (b), the forex market is initially in equilibrium at point 1′. A temporary fiscal expansion on its own increases government spending from $\overline{G}_1$ to $\overline{G}_2$ and would shift the IS curve to the right in panel (a) from IS_1 to IS_2, causing the interest rate to rise from i_1 to i_2. The domestic return would then rise from DR_1 to DR_2. In panel (b), the higher interest rate would imply that the exchange rate must appreciate, falling from $\overline{E}$ to E_2. To maintain the peg, the monetary authority must now intervene, shifting the LM curve down, from LM_1 to LM_2. The fiscal expansion thus prompts a monetary expansion. In the end, the interest rate and exchange rate are left unchanged, and output expands *dramatically* from Y_1 to Y_2. The new equilibrium corresponds to points 2 and 2′.

A temporary fiscal expansion that increases government spending from $\overline{G}_1$ to $\overline{G}_2$ would shift the IS curve to the right in panel (a) from IS_1 to IS_2, causing the interest rate to rise from i_1 to i_2. The domestic return would rise from DR_1 to DR_2. In panel (b), the higher interest rate would imply that the exchange rate must appreciate, falling from $\overline{E}$ to E_2. To maintain the peg, the monetary authority must intervene, shifting the LM curve to the right also, from LM_1 to LM_2. The fiscal expansion thus prompts a monetary expansion. In the end, the interest rate and exchange rate are left unchanged, and output expands *dramatically* from Y_1 to Y_2. The new equilibrium corresponds to points 2 and 2′.

What is happening here? From the last example, we know that there is appreciation pressure associated with a fiscal expansion if the currency is allowed to float. To maintain the peg, the monetary authority must immediately alter its monetary policy at the very moment the fiscal expansion occurs so that the LM curve shifts from LM_1 to LM_2. The way to do this is to expand the money supply, and this generates pressure for depreciation, offsetting the appreciation pressure. If the monetary authority pulls this off, the market exchange rate will stay at the initial pegged level $\overline{E}$.

Thus, when a country is operating under a fixed exchange, fiscal policy is super-effective because any fiscal expansion by the government forces an immediate monetary expansion by the central bank to keep the exchange rate steady. The double, and simultaneous, expansion of demand by the fiscal and monetary authorities imposes a huge stimulus on the economy, and output rises from Y_1 to Y_2 (beyond the level achieved by the same fiscal expansion under a floating exchange rate).

To sum up: a temporary expansion of fiscal policy under fixed exchange rates raises output at home by a considerable amount. (The case of a temporary contraction of fiscal policy would have similar but opposite effects. As an exercise, work through this case using the same graphical apparatus.)

Summary

We have now examined the operation of fiscal and monetary policies under both fixed and flexible exchange rates and have seen how the impacts of these policies differ dramatically depending on the exchange rate regime. The outcomes can be summarized as follows:

Responses to Policy Shocks in the IS-LM-FX Model

Exchange Rate Regime	Policy	Impact on:				
		i	E	I	TB	Y
Floating	Monetary expansion	↓	↑	↑	↑?	↑
	Fiscal expansion	↑	↓	↓	↓	↑
Fixed	Monetary expansion	0	0	0	0	0
	Fiscal expansion	0	0	0	↓	↑

In this table, an up arrow ↑ indicates that the variable rises; a down arrow ↓, indicates that the variables falls; and a zero indicates no effect. The effects would be reversed for contractionary policies. The row of zeros for monetary expansion under fixed rates reflects the fact that this infeasible policy cannot be undertaken.

In a floating exchange rate regime, autonomous monetary and fiscal policy is feasible. The power of monetary policy to expand demand comes from two forces in the short run: lower interest rates boost investment and a depreciated exchange rate boosts the trade balance, all else equal. In the end, though, the trade balance will experience downward pressure from an import rise due to the increase in home output and income. The net effect on output and investment is positive, and the net effect on the trade balance is unclear—but in practice it, too, is likely to be positive.

Expansionary fiscal policy is also effective under a floating regime, even though the impact of extra spending is offset by crowding out in two areas: investment is crowded out by higher interest rates, and the trade balance is crowded out by an appreciated exchange rate. Thus, on net, investment falls and the trade balance also falls, and the latter effect is unambiguously amplified by additional import demand arising from increased home output.

In a fixed exchange rate regime, monetary policy loses its power for two reasons. First, interest parity implies that the domestic interest rate cannot move independently of the foreign rate, so investment demand cannot be manipulated. Second, the peg means that there can be no movement in the exchange rate, so the trade balance cannot be manipulated by expenditure switching.

Only fiscal policy is feasible under a fixed regime. Tax cuts or spending increases by the government can generate additional demand. But fiscal expansion then requires a monetary expansion to keep interest rates steady and maintain the peg. Fiscal policy becomes ultra-powerful in a fixed exchange rate setting—the reason for this is that if interest rates and exchange rates are held steady by the central bank, investment and the trade balance are never crowded out by fiscal policy. Monetary policy follows fiscal policy and amplifies it.

6 Stabilization Policy

We now have seen that macroeconomic policies can effect economic activity in the short run. These effects open up the possibility that the authorities can use changes in policies to try to keep the economy at or near its full-employment level of output. This is the essence of **stabilization policy.** If the economy is hit by a temporary adverse shock, policy makers could use expansionary monetary and fiscal policies to prevent a deep recession. Conversely, if the economy is pushed by a shock above its full employment level of output, contractionary policies could tame the boom.

For example, suppose a temporary adverse shock such as a sudden decline in investment, consumption, or export demand shifts the IS curve to the left. Or suppose an adverse shock such as a sudden increase in money demand suddenly moves the LM curve up. Either shock would cause home output to fall. In principle, the home policy makers could offset these shocks by using fiscal policy to shift either the IS curve or LM curve (or both) to cause an offsetting increase in output. When used judiciously, monetary and fiscal policies can thus be used to stabilize the economy and absorb shocks.

The policies must be used with care, however. If the economy is stable and growing, an additional temporary monetary or fiscal stimulus may cause an unsustainable boom that will, when the stimulus is withdrawn, turn into an undesirable bust. In their efforts to do good, policy makers must be careful not to destabilize the economy through the ill-timed, inappropriate, or excessive use of monetary and fiscal policies.

APPLICATION

Australia, New Zealand, and the Asian Crisis of 1997

At the end of 1997, many observers would have predicted economic difficulties for Australia and New Zealand in the short run. Both countries were very open to trade, and a large part of the demand for their exports was generated by a group of industrializing East Asian economies, including Korea, Thailand, and Indonesia. The problem was that all of these major trading partners suffered serious economic crises in 1997, which caused a large economic contraction in each country characterized by significant declines in output and the demand for foreign goods. To some extent, the East Asian and Pacific region as a whole was likely to be dragged into recession by these events.

In our framework, the demand for Australia's and New Zealand's exports declined as a result of a contraction in foreign output Y^*. All else equal, they would have suffered an exogenous decline in their trade balance: at every real exchange rate, the demand for exports declined, and demand fell. These events would be represented by a leftward shift of Australia's and New Zealand's IS curves, which we show in Figure 7-17.

Our model tells us that if the governments of Australia and New Zealand had chosen to ignore the Asian crisis, their economies would have contracted, home interest rates would have fallen, and the value of their currencies would have fallen. In

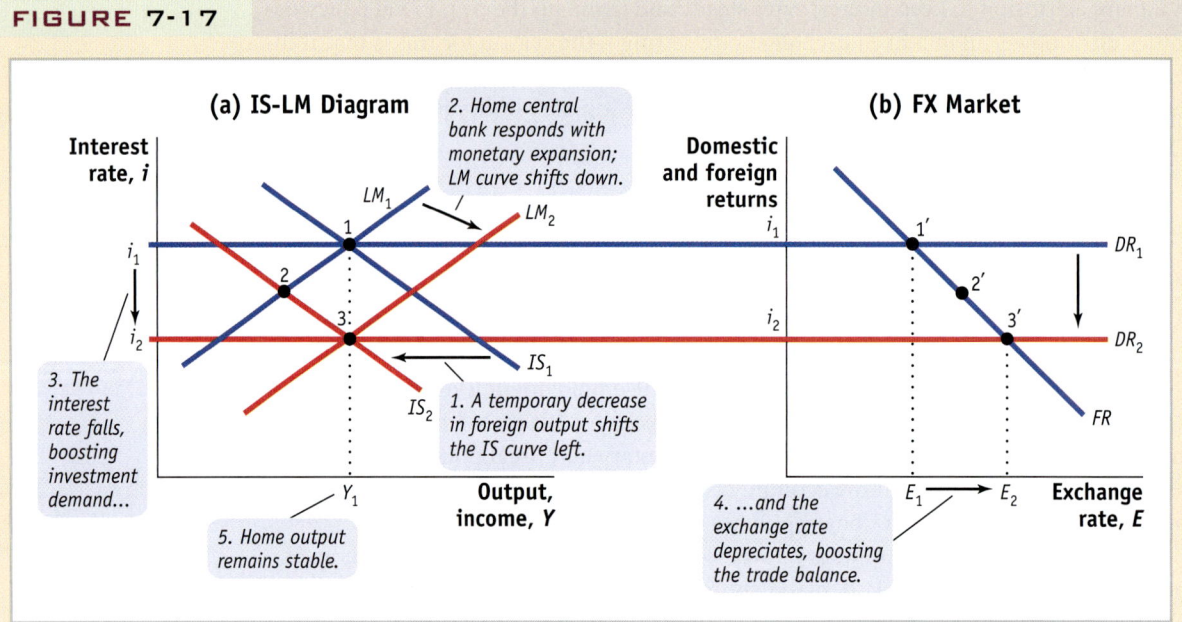

Stabilization Policy under Floating Exchange Rates In panel (a) in the IS-LM diagram, the goods and money markets are initially in equilibrium at point 1. The interest rate in the money market is also the domestic return, DR_1, that prevails in the forex market. In panel (b), the forex market is initially in equilibrium at point 1'. An exogenous negative shock to the trade balance (e.g., due to a collapse in foreign income) causes the IS curve to shift in from IS_1 to IS_2. Without further action, output and interest rates would fall and the exchange rate would tend to depreciate. The central bank can stabilize output at its former level by responding with a monetary policy expansion, increasing the money supply from M_1 to M_2. This causes the LM curve to shift down from LM_1 to LM_2. The new equilibrium corresponds to points 3 and 3'. Output is now stabilized at the original level Y_1. The interest rate falls further. The domestic return falls from DR_1 to DR_2, and the exchange rate depreciates all the way from E_1 to E_2.

Figure 7-17, panel (a), the IS-LM equilibrium shifts from point 1 to point 2, and the initial deterioration in trade balance would be only partially offset by the induced depreciation and increased investment. The forex market equilibrium would be at 2'. In the end, demand would still be below its initial level and a recession would result.

However, this did not happen. The central banks of both Australia and New Zealand responded to the Asian crisis with expansionary monetary policy. This would be depicted in our model by a down or right shift in the LM curve. The IS-LM equilibrium in the economy shifts from point 2 to point 3 in Figure 7-17, panel (a). At point 3, the further reduction in the home interest rate exacerbates the depreciation of the currency and stimulates demand through both the investment and expenditure-switching channels. Recession is avoided and output is sustained at its original level. The forex market in panel (b) ends up at 3' with a large depreciation.

Figure 7-18 shows data for the Australian and New Zealand economies in this period. The home exchange rates were allowed to depreciate substantially, and as a result, the trade balances in both countries held up, partly due to export growth to non-Asian markets that was made possible by the temporary weakening of the real exchange rate. This episode provides a good example of how policy makers can use a floating exchange rate to cushion the blows of external macroeconomic shocks. Policy makers in Australia and New Zealand knew that after the Asian crisis had passed—in a few years'

FIGURE 7-18

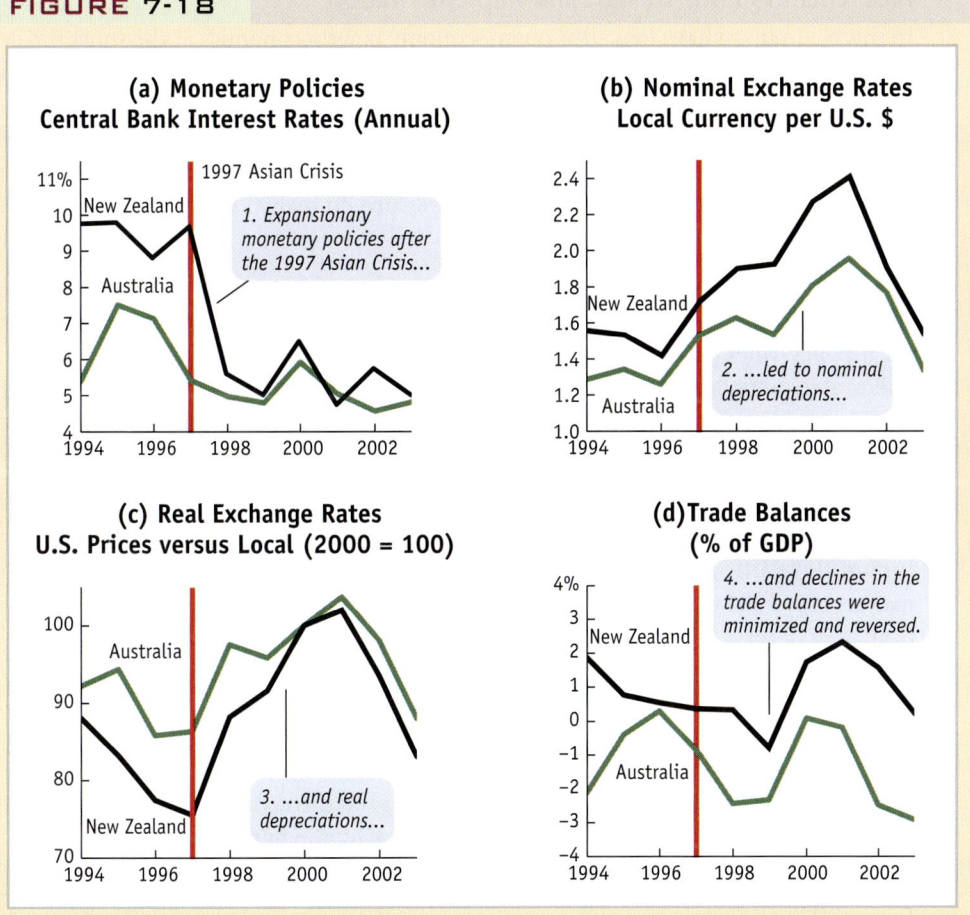

Demand Shocks Down Under Australian and New Zealand exports were likely to be badly hit after the 1997 Asian crisis as the incomes of their key trading partners contracted. Both countries were operating on a floating exchange rate, however. To bolster demand, the central banks in both countries pursued an expansionary monetary policy, lowering interest rates, as shown in panel (a), and allowing the domestic currency to depreciate about 30% in nominal terms, as shown in panel (b). This contributed to a real depreciation of about 20% to 30% in the short run, panel (c). As a result, the trade balance of both countries moved strongly toward surplus, illustrated in panel (d), and thus demand was higher than it would otherwise have been. In each country, a recession was avoided.

Sources: IMF, International Financial Statistics; World Bank, World Development Indicators.

time—there would be renewed demand for their goods. In the short run, the problem was to manage a temporary drop in aggregate demand.

This response was widely praised in economic policy-making circles, as in the following quotation from the OECD's 1999 *Economic Survey of Australia*:

> Australia has continued to grow above its trend rate over the past two years with the economy proving to be remarkably resilient in the face of significant weakness in many of its trading partners, especially in Asia. At the same time, inflation remained low and the rate of unemployment was reduced further. This performance was helped by dynamic growth of domestic demand at the time when the crisis broke out, and a credible mix of macro-policies which allowed the exchange rate to move freely, kept monetary conditions expansionary and maintained fiscal retrenchment. ■

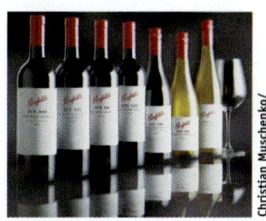

A case study: exports of wine and other Australian goods boomed after the real depreciation.

Problems in Policy Design and Implementation

In this chapter, we have looked at open-economy macroeconomics in the short run and at the role that monetary and fiscal policies can play in determining economic outcomes. The simple models we used have clear consequences. On the face of it, if policy makers were really operating in such an uncomplicated environment, they would have the ability to exert substantial control and could always keep output steady with no unemployed resources and no inflation pressure. In reality, life is more complicated for policy makers for a variety of reasons.

Policy Constraints Policy makers may not always be free to apply the policies they desire. A fixed exchange rate rules out any use of monetary policy. Other firm monetary or fiscal policy rules, such as interest rate rules or balanced-budget rules, place limits on policy. Even if policy makers decide to act, other constraints may bind them. While it is always feasible to print money, it may not be possible (technically or politically) to raise the real resources necessary for a fiscal expansion. Countries with weak tax systems or poor creditworthiness—problems that afflict developing countries—may find themselves unable to tax or borrow to finance an expansion of spending even if they wished to do so.

Incomplete Information and the Inside Lag Our models assume that the policy makers have full knowledge of the state of the economy before they take corrective action: they observe the economy's IS and LM curves and know what shocks have hit. In reality, macroeconomic data are compiled slowly and it may take weeks or months for policy makers to fully understand the state of the economy today. Even then, it will take time to formulate a policy response (the lag between shock and policy actions is called the *inside lag*). On the monetary side, there may be a delay between policy meetings. On the fiscal side, it may take time to pass a bill through the legislature and then enable a real change in spending or taxing activity by the public sector.

Policy Response and the Outside Lag Even if they finally receive the correct information, policy makers then have to formulate the right response given by the model. In particular, they must not be distracted by other policies or agendas, nor subject to influence by interest groups that might wish to see different policies enacted. Finally, it takes time for whatever policies are enacted to have any effect on the economy, through the spending decisions of the public and private sectors (the lag between policy actions and effects is called the *outside lag*).

Long-Horizon Plans Other factors may make investment and the trade balance less sensitive to policy. If the private sector understands that a policy change is temporary, then there may be reasons not to change consumption or investment expenditure. Suppose a firm can either build and operate a plant for several years or else not build at all (e.g., the investment might be of an irreversible form). For example, a firm may not care about a higher real interest rate this year and may base its decision on the expected real interest rate that will affect its financing over many years ahead. Similarly, a temporary real appreciation may have little effect on whether a firm can profit in the long run from sales in the foreign market. In such circumstances, firms' investment and export activities may not be very sensitive to short-run policy changes.

Weak Links from the Nominal Exchange Rate to the Real Exchange Rate Our discussion assumed that changes in the nominal exchange rate lead to real exchange rate changes, but the reality can be somewhat different for some goods and services. For example, the dollar depreciated 42% against the euro from 2002 to 2004, but the U.S.

prices of German cars, like BMWs, barely changed. Why? There are a number of reasons for this weak *pass-through* phenomenon, including the dollarization of trade and the distribution margins that separate retail prices from port prices (as we saw in **Side Bar: Barriers to Expenditure Switching: Pass-Through and the J Curve**). The forces of arbitrage may also be weak as a result of noncompetitive market structures: for example, BMW sells through exclusive dealers and government regulation requires that cars meet different standards in Europe versus the United States. These obstacles allow a firm like BMW to *price to market:* to charge a steady U.S. price even as the exchange rate moves temporarily. If a firm can bear (or hedge) the exchange rate risk, it might do this to avoid the volatile sales and alienated customers that might result from repeatedly changing its U.S. retail price list.

Pegged Currency Blocs Our model's predictions are also affected by the fact that for some major countries in the real world, their exchange rate arrangements are characterized—often not as a result of their own choice—by a mix of floating and fixed exchange rate systems with different trading partners. From 2002 to 2004, the dollar depreciated markedly against the euro, pound, and several other floating currencies, but in the "Dollar Bloc" (Japan, China, India, and others), the monetary authorities have ensured that the variation in the value of their currencies against the dollar is small or zero. When a large bloc of other countries pegs to the U.S. dollar, this limits the ability of the United States to engineer a real effective depreciation.

Weak Links from the Real Exchange Rate to the Trade Balance Our discussion also assumed that real exchange rate changes lead to changes in the trade balance. There may be several reasons why these linkages are weak in reality. One major reason is transaction costs in trade. Suppose the exchange rate is $1 per euro and an American is consuming a domestic good that costs $100 as opposed to a European good costing €100 = $100. If the dollar appreciates to $0.95 per euro, then the European good looks cheaper on paper, only $95. Should the American switch to the import? Yes, if the good can be moved without cost—but there are few such goods! If shipping costs $10, it still makes sense to consume the domestic good until the exchange rate falls below $0.90 per euro. Practically, this means that expenditure switching may be a nonlinear phenomenon: it will be weak at first and then much stronger as the real exchange rate change grows larger. This phenomenon, coupled with the J Curve effects discussed earlier, may cause the response of the trade balance in the short run to be small or even in the wrong direction.

APPLICATION

Macroeconomic Policies in the Liquidity Trap

Undoubtedly, one of the most controversial experiments in macroeconomic policymaking began in 2008–2010 as monetary and fiscal authorities around the world tried to respond to the major recession that followed the global financial crisis. In this application, even as the story continues to unfold, we look at the initial U.S. policy response and interpret events using the IS-LM-FX model of this chapter.

The unusual aspect of this crisis was the very rapid realization that monetary policy alone could not fully offset the magnitude of the shock to demand. In the context of our IS-LM-FX model, as consumption and investment fell for exogenous reasons, the shock moved the IS curve very far leftward. One major source of the demand shock was that, as we saw in an earlier chapter, banks were very afraid of taking on risk and sharply reduced their lending to firms and households—and even when they did lend, they were still charging very high interest rates. Thus, even with very expansionary monetary policy, that is, large rightward shifts of the LM curve, low policy rates did not translate into cheap borrowing for the private sector. Once the U.S. Federal Reserve had brought its policy rate to zero in December 2008, there was little more it could do to stimulate demand using conventional monetary policies.

This peculiar situation is depicted by the blue lines in Figure 7-19 and differs from the normal IS-LM-FX setup we have seen so far. After the demand shock and the Fed's response to it, the IS curve has moved so far in (to IS_1) and the LM curve has moved so far out (to LM_1), that the IS and LM curves now intersect at a very low interest rate: so low that it is equal to zero. In the money market, nominal interest rates can't fall below zero, so another way of describing this situation is to say that the economy was at an IS-LM equilibrium at which the LM curve was absolutely flat and resting on the horizontal axis (at a 0% interest rate) in the diagram.

[Note that in the FX diagram this would place the domestic return DR at zero. Also, note that interest rates were by this time at zero in all developed countries, for similar

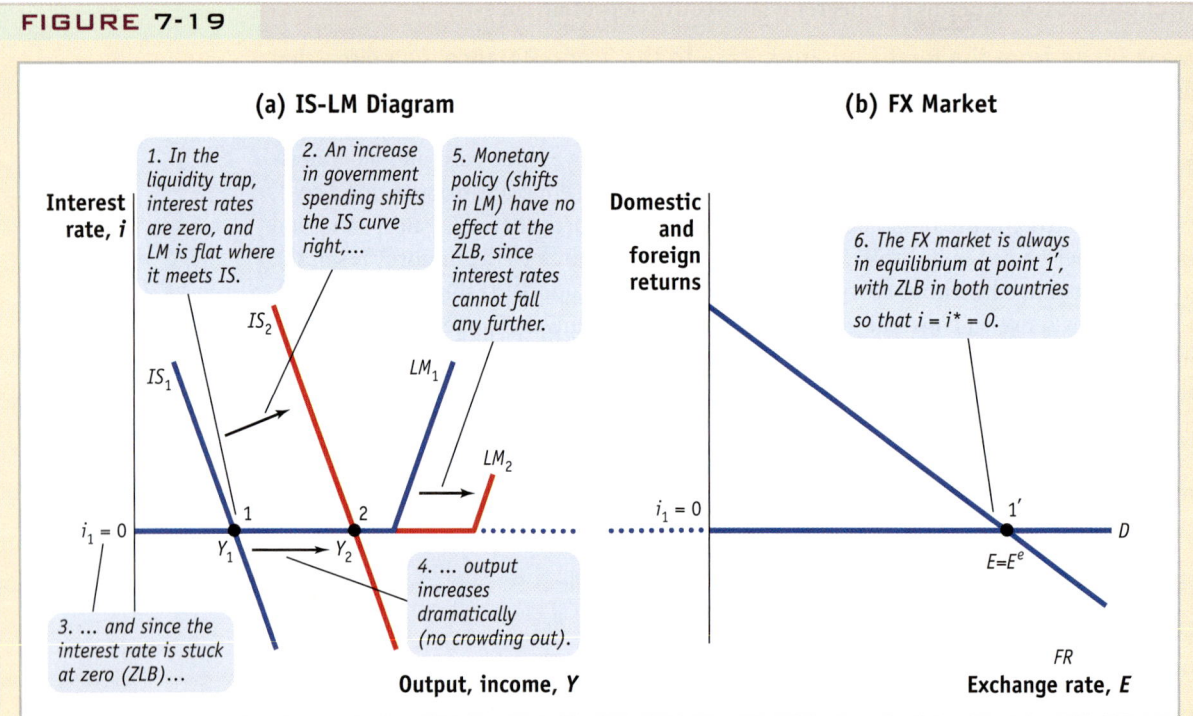

FIGURE 7-19

Macroeconomic Policies in the Liquidity Trap After a severe negative shock to demand, the *IS* curve may move very far to the left (IS_1). The nominal interest rate may then fall all the way to the zero lower bound (ZLB), with IS_1 intersecting the flat portion of the LM_1 curve at point 1, on the horizontal axis, in panel (a). Output is depressed at a level Y_1. In this scenario, monetary policy is impotent because expansionary monetary policy (e.g., a rightward shift from LM_1 to LM_2) cannot lower the interest rate any further. However, fiscal policy may be very effective, and a shift right from IS_1 to IS_2 leaves the economy still at the ZLB, but with a higher level of output Y_2. (The figure is drawn assuming the ZLB holds in both home and foreign economies, so the FX market is in equilibrium at point 1' with $E = E^e$ at all times.)

reasons. Thus, it is also appropriate to think of the foreign (e.g., euro) interest rate as also stuck at zero, which in the FX diagram would lower the foreign return *FR*.]

The situation just described is unusual in several ways. First, monetary policy is powerless in this situation: it cannot be used to lower interest rates because interest rates can't go any lower. In the diagram, moving the LM curve out to LM_2 does not dislodge the economy from the horizontal portion of the LM curve. We are still stuck on the IS_1 curve at a point 1 and a 0% percent interest rate. This unfortunate state of affairs is known as the *zero lower bound* (*ZLB*). It is also known as a *liquidity trap* because liquid money and interest-bearing assets have the same interest rate of zero, so there is no opportunity cost to holding money, and thus changes in the supply of central bank money have no effect on the incentive to switch between money and interest-bearing assets.

Can anything be done? Yes. The bad news is that fiscal policy is the only tool now available to increase demand. The good news is that fiscal policy has the potential to be super powerful in this situation. The reason is that as long as interest rates are stuck at zero, and the monetary authorities keep them there, government spending will not crowd out investment or net exports, in contrast to the typical situation we studied earlier in this chapter.[3] In 2009 because the Fed and the private sector anticipated more than a year or two of very high unemployment and falling inflation, everyone had expectations of zero interest rates for a long period.

Did the United States use fiscal policy to try to counteract the recession? Yes. Did it work? Not as well as one might have hoped.

The government's fiscal response took two forms. First was the *automatic stabilizer* built into existing fiscal policies. In the models that we have studied so far in this chapter, we have assumed that taxes and spending are fixed. In reality, however, they are not fixed, but vary systematically with income. Most importantly, when income *Y* falls in a recession, receipts from income taxes, sales taxes, and so on, all tend to fall as well. In addition, transfer expenditures (like unemployment benefits) tend to go up: a rise in negative taxes, as it were. This decline does not depend on any policy response, and in the 2008–2010 period the fall in tax revenues (plus the rise in transfers) was enormous.

The second fiscal response was a discretionary policy, the American Recovery and Reinvestment Act (ARRA), better known as the "stimulus" bill. This policy was one of the first actions undertaken by the Obama administration and it was signed into law on February 17, 2009. Some of the president's advisors had originally hoped for a $1.4 trillion package, mostly for extra government consumption and investment spending, and also for aid to states. This was to be spread over 2 to 3 years from 2009–2011. However, the final compromise deal with Congress was only half as big, $787 billion over three years, and was tilted more toward temporary tax cuts. Most of the stimulus was scheduled to take effect in 2010, not 2009, reflecting the policy lags we noted above. On average, the package amounted to about 1.5% of GDP in spending and tax cuts.

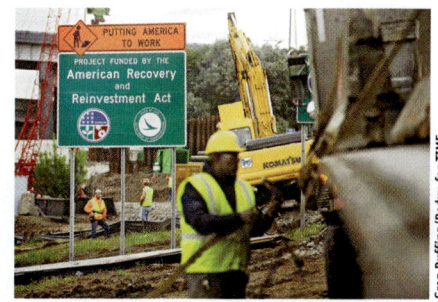

Construction work on an interstate highway in Cleveland, Ohio, funded by government stimulus money.

Some key outcomes are shown in Figure 7-20. As panel (a) shows, the size of the gap between actual and potential output left a huge hole to be filled by fiscal policy. By mid-2009 this hole was about 6% of potential GDP or over $1 trillion at an annual rate. *Even if the entire stimulus was spent*, the fiscal package could at best have filled only

---

[3] Note that, at the ZLB, the model resembles the fixed exchange rate model, not the floating exchange rate model, because being stuck at the ZLB pegs the interest rate (in this case at zero, rather than at i^*).

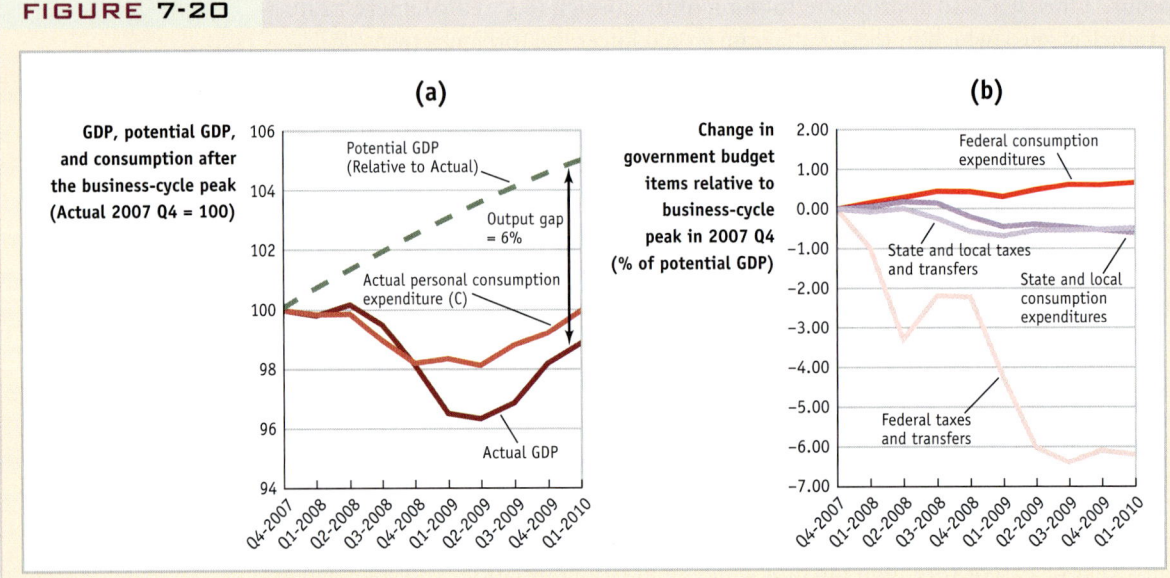

FIGURE 7-20

Fiscal Policy in the Great Recession: Didn't Work or Wasn't Tried? In the U.S. economic slump of 2008–2010, output had fallen 6% below the estimate of potential (full-employment) level of GDP by the first quarter of 2009, as seen in panel (a). This was the worst U.S. recession since the 1930s. Policy responses included automatic fiscal expansion (increases in spending and reductions in taxes), plus an additional discretionary stimulus (the 2009 American Recovery and Reinvestment Act or ARRA). The tax part of the stimulus appeared to do very little: significant reductions in taxes seen in panel (b) were insufficient to prop up consumption expenditure, as seen in panel (a), as consumers saved the extra disposable income. And on the government spending side there was no stimulus at all in the aggregate: increases in federal government expenditure were fully offset by cuts in state and local government expenditure, as seen in panel (b).

Sources: Federal Reserve Economic Indicators (FRED). Potential output from Congressional Budget Office; all other data from the Bureau of Economic Analysis.

about one-quarter of the collapse in demand or 1.5% of GDP. Policy makers in the government, and many observers, knew the package was too small, but politics stood in the way of a larger package.

The data in panel (a) also show that private consumption fell precipitously. One intention of ARRA was to support private spending through tax cuts. Tax revenues T did fall considerably [largely at the federal level as shown in panel (b), because states were getting some offsetting transfers via ARRA]. But tax cuts did not appear to generate much extra private spending, certainly not enough to offset the initial collapse in consumption expenditure. Many consumers were unsure about the economic recovery, worried about the risks of unemployment, and trying to use whatever "extra" money they got from tax cuts to pay down their debts or save. In addition, because people were trying to hold onto their money (precautionary motives were high), the marginal propensity to consume was probably low. Furthermore, for non-Keynesian consumers, the temporary nature of many of the tax cuts meant that anyone following the principles of *Ricardian equivalence* would be likely to save the tax cut to pay off an expected future tax liability.

This left government spending G to do a great deal of the stimulation, but problems arose because of the contrary effects of state and local government policies. As the figure shows, federal expenditures went up, rising by 0.5% of GDP in 2010. Leaving aside the miniscule size of this change, a big source of trouble was that state and local government expenditures went down by just as much. States and localities imposed austerity spending cuts, which were made necessary by calamitous declines in their tax revenues, by their limited ability to borrow, and by the feeble amount of aid to states authorized in the final ARRA package. The net change in overall government expenditures was thus, in the end, zero.

To sum up, the aggregate U.S. fiscal stimulus had four major weaknesses: it was rolled out too slowly, due to policy lags; the overall package was too small, given the magnitude of the decline in aggregate demand; the government spending portion of the stimulus, for which positive expenditure effects were certain, ended up being close to zero, due to state and local cuts; and this left almost all the work to tax cuts (automatic and discretionary) that recipients, for good reasons, were more likely to save rather than spend. With monetary policy impotent and fiscal policy weak and ill designed, the economy remained mired in its worst slump since the 1930s Great Depression.[4] ■

7 Conclusions

The analysis of macroeconomic policy is different in an open economy than in a closed economy. The trade balance generates an additional source of demand, and its fluctuations are driven by changes in output and the real exchange rate. Expenditure switching is a key mechanism at work here: as international relative prices change, demand shifts from foreign to home goods and vice versa.

The open economy IS-LM-FX framework is a workhorse model for analyzing the macroeconomic responses to shocks and to changes in monetary and fiscal policies. Exploring these responses, in turn, draws out some clear contrasts between the operation of fixed and flexible exchange rate regimes.

Under flexible exchange rates, monetary and fiscal policies can be used. Monetary expansions raise output and also lower the interest rate, which stimulates investment and causes a depreciation, which in turn stimulates the trade balance. Fiscal expansions raise output; raise the interest rate, which depresses investment; and cause an appreciation, which in turn lowers the trade balance.

With two policy tools available, the authorities have considerable flexibility. In particular, their ability to let the exchange rate adjust to absorb shocks makes a strong case for a floating exchange rate. Now we can understand the logic behind Robert Mundell's quote at the start of the chapter.

Under fixed exchange rates, monetary policy cannot be used because the home interest rate has to remain equal to the foreign interest rate in order for the exchange rate to remain fixed. But fiscal policy has great power under a fixed exchange rate. Fiscal expansions raise output and force the monetary authority to expand the money supply to prevent any rise in the interest rate and any appreciation of the exchange rate. In contrast to the floating case, in which interest rate increases and exchange rate appreciation put downward pressure on investment and the trade balance, the demand stimulus is even greater.

---

[4] The size of the output gap was understood early on, even before President Obama took office. At the start of January 2009 the Congressional Budget Office forecast that, without a stimulus, unemployment would rise above 9% by early 2010, and remain there for several years, with an output gap projected to be 6.8% of GDP in 2010 and 2011 (numbers very close to what has transpired). In that context, some economists pointed out the problems with the size and design of the ARRA package, especially the use of temporary tax cuts. See, for example, Martin Feldstein, Statement for the House Democratic Steering and Policy Committee, January 7, 2009; and Paul Krugman, "The Obama Gap," *The New York Times*, January 8, 2009.

With only one policy tool available, the authorities in fixed rate regimes have much less flexibility. They also expose the economy to more volatility because any demand shock will entail an immediate and reinforcing monetary shock. The tendency of fixed exchange rate systems to amplify demand shocks helps us understand the logic behind Alec Ford's quote at the start of the chapter.

Whatever the regime, fixed or floating, our findings suggest that macroeconomic policy can *in principle* be used to stabilize an open economy when it suffers from external shocks. Under floating exchange rates, however, more policy options are available (monetary and fiscal policy responses are feasible) than under fixed exchange rates (only a fiscal policy response is feasible).

Despite these relatively simple lessons, real-world policy design is not straightforward. Policy makers have difficulty identifying shocks, devising the right response, and acting quickly enough to ensure that policy actions have a timely effect. Even then, under some conditions, the economy may respond in unusual ways.

KEY POINTS

1. In the short run, we assume prices are sticky at some preset level P. There is thus no inflation, and nominal and real quantities can be considered equivalent. We assume output GDP equals income Y or GDNI and that the trade balance equals the current account (there are no transfers or factor income from abroad).

2. The Keynesian consumption function says that private consumption spending C is an increasing function of household disposable income $Y - T$.

3. The investment function says that total investment I is a decreasing function of the real or nominal interest rate i.

4. Government spending is assumed to be exogenously given at a level G.

5. The trade balance is assumed to be an increasing function of the real exchange rate EP^*/P, where P^* denotes the foreign price level.

6. The national income identity says that national income or output equals private consumption C, plus investment I, plus government spending G, plus the trade balance TB: $Y = C + I + G + TB$. The right-hand side of this expression is called *demand*, and its components depend on income, interest rates, and the real exchange rate. In equilibrium, demand must equal the left-hand side, supply, or total output Y.

7. If the interest rate falls in an open economy, demand is stimulated for two reasons. A lower interest rate directly stimulates investment. A lower interest rate also leads to an exchange rate depreciation, all else equal, which increases the trade balance. This demand must be satisfied for the goods market to remain in equilibrium, so output rises. This is the basis of the IS curve: declines in interest rates must call forth extra output to keep the goods market in equilibrium. Each point on the IS curve represents a combination of output Y and interest rate i at which the goods and FX markets are in equilibrium. Because Y increases as i decreases, the IS curve is downward-sloping.

8. Real money demand arises primarily from transactions requirements. It increases when the volume of transactions (represented by national income Y) increases, and decreases when the opportunity cost of holding money, the nominal interest rate i, increases.

9. The money market equilibrium says that the demand for real money balances L must equal the real money supply: $M/P = L(i)Y$. This equation is the basis for the LM curve: any increases in output Y must cause the interest rate to rise, all else equal (e.g., holding fixed real money M/P). Each point on the LM curve represents a combination of output Y and interest rate i at which the money market is in equilibrium. Because i increases as Y increases, the LM curve is upward-sloping.

10. The IS-LM diagram combines the IS and LM curves on one figure and shows the unique short-run equilibrium for output Y and the interest rate i that describes simultaneous equilibrium in the goods and money markets. The IS-LM diagram can be coupled with the forex market diagram to summarize conditions in all three markets: goods, money, and forex. This combined IS-LM-FX diagram can then be used to assess the impact of various macroeconomic policies in the short run.

11. Under a floating exchange rate, the interest rate and exchange rate are free to adjust to maintain equilibrium. Thus, government policy is free to move either the IS or LM curves. The impacts are as follows:

    - Monetary expansion: LM shifts to the right, output rises, interest rate falls, exchange rate rises/depreciates.
    - Fiscal expansion: IS shifts to the right, output rises, interest rate rises, exchange rate falls/appreciates.

12. Under a fixed exchange rate, the interest rate always equals the foreign interest rate and the exchange rate is pegged. Thus, the government is not free to move the LM curve: monetary policy must be adjusted to ensure that LM is in such a position that these exchange rate and interest rate conditions hold. The impacts are as follows:

    - Monetary expansion: not feasible.
    - Fiscal expansion: IS shifts to the right, LM follows it and also shifts to the right, output rises strongly, interest rate and exchange rate are unchanged.

13. The ability to manipulate the IS and LM curves gives the government the capacity to engage in stabilization policies to offset shocks to the economy and to try to maintain a full-employment level of output. This is easier said than done, however, because it is difficult to diagnose the correct policy response, and policies often take some time to have an impact, so that by the time the policy effects are felt, they may be ineffective or even counterproductive.

KEY TERMS

consumption, p. 255
disposable income, p. 255
marginal propensity to consume (MPC), p. 256
expected real interest rate, p. 256
taxes, p. 256
government consumption, p. 256
transfer programs, p. 256
expenditure switching, p. 258
real effective exchange rate, p. 262
pass-through, p. 263
J Curve, p. 264
goods market equilibrium condition, p. 266
Keynesian cross, p. 268
IS curve, p. 270
LM curve, p. 275
monetary policy, p. 280
fiscal policy, p. 280
stabilization policy, p. 287

PROBLEMS

1. In 2001 President George W. Bush and Federal Reserve Chairman Alan Greenspan were both concerned about a sluggish U.S. economy. They also were concerned about the large U.S. current account deficit. To help stimulate the economy, President Bush proposed a tax cut, while the Fed had been increasing U.S. money supply. Compare the effects of these two policies in terms of their implications for the current account. If policy makers are concerned about the current account deficit, discuss whether stimulatory fiscal policy or monetary policy makes more sense in this case. Then, reconsider similar issues for 2009–2010, when the economy was in a deep slump, the Fed had taken interest rates to zero, and the Obama administration was arguing for larger fiscal stimulus.

2. Suppose that American firms become more optimistic and decide to increase investment expenditure today in new factories and office space.
   a. How will this increase in investment affect output, interest rates, and the current account?
   b. Now repeat part (a), assuming that domestic investment is very responsive to the interest rate so that U.S. firms will cancel most of their new investment plans if the interest rate rises. How will this affect the answer you gave previously?

3. For each of the following situations, use the IS-LM-FX model to illustrate the effects of the shock. For each case, state the effect of the shock on the following variables (increase, decrease, no change, or ambiguous): Y, i, E, C, I, and TB. Assume the government allows the exchange rate to float and makes no policy response.
   a. Foreign output decreases.
   b. Investors expect a depreciation of the home currency.
   c. The money supply increases.
   d. Government spending increases.

4. How would a decrease in the money supply of Paraguay (currency unit is the "guaraní") affect its own output and its exchange rate with Brazil (currency unit is the "real"). Do you think this policy in Paraguay might also affect output across the border in Brazil? Explain.

5. For each of the following situations, use the IS-LM-FX model to illustrate the effects of the shock and the policy response. *Note:* Assume the government responds by using monetary policy to stabilize output, unlike question 3, and assume the exchange rate is floating. For each case, state the effect of the shock on the following variables (increase, decrease, no change, or ambiguous): Y, i, E, C, I, and TB.
   a. Foreign output decreases.
   b. Investors expect a depreciation of the home currency.
   c. The money supply increases.
   d. Government spending increases.

6. Repeat the previous question, assuming the central bank responds in order to maintain a fixed exchange rate. In which case or cases will the government response be the same as in the previous question?

7. This question explores IS and FX equilibria in a numerical example.
   a. The consumption function is $C = 1.5 + 0.75(Y - T)$. What is the marginal propensity to consume MPC? What is the marginal propensity to save MPS?
   b. The trade balance is $TB = 5(1-[1/E]) - 0.25(Y - 8)$. What is the marginal propensity to consume foreign goods $MPCF$? What is the marginal propensity to consume home goods $MPCH$?
   c. The investment function is $I = 2 - 10i$. What is investment when the interest rate i is equal to $0.10 = 10\%$?
   d. Assume government spending is G. Add up the four components of demand and write down the expression for D.

e. Assume forex market equilibrium is given by $i = ([1/E] - 1) + 0.10$, where the two foreign return terms on the right are expected depreciation and the foreign interest rate. What is the foreign interest rate? What is the expected future exchange rate?

8. [More difficult] Continuing the last question, solve for the IS curve: obtain an expression for Y in terms of i, G, and T (eliminate E).

9. Assume that initially the IS curve is given by

$$IS_1: Y = 12 - 1.5T - 30i + 2G$$

and that the price level P is 1, and the LM curve is given by

$$LM_1: M = Y(1 - i)$$

The home central bank uses the interest rate as its policy instrument. Initially, the home interest rate equals the foreign interest rate of 10% or 0.1. Taxes and government spending both equal 2. Call this case 1.

a. According to the IS_1 curve, what is the level of output Y? Assume this is the desired full-employment level of output.
b. According to the LM_1 curve, at this level of output, what is the level of the home money supply?
c. Plot the IS_1 and LM_1 curves for case 1 on a chart. Label the axes, and the equilibrium values.
d. Assume that forex market equilibrium is given by $i = ([1/E] - 1) + 0.10$, where the two foreign return terms on the right are expected depreciation and the foreign interest rate. The expected future exchange rate is 1. What is today's spot exchange rate?
e. There is now a foreign demand shock, such that the IS curve shifts left by 1.5 units at all levels of the interest rate, and the new IS curve is given by

$$IS_2: Y = 10.5 - 1.5T - 30i + 2G$$

The government asks the central bank to stabilize the economy at full employment. To stabilize and return output back to the desired level, according to this new IS curve, by how much must the interest rate be lowered from its initial level of 0.1? (Assume taxes and government spending remain at 2.) Call this case 2.

f. At the new lower interest rate and at full employment, on the new LM curve (LM_2), what is the new level of the money supply?
g. According to the forex market equilibrium, what is the new level of the spot exchange rate? How large is the depreciation of the home currency?
h. Plot the new IS_2 and LM_2 curves for case 2 on a chart. Label the axes, and the equilibrium values.
i. Return to part (e). Now assume that the central bank refuses to change the interest rate from 10%. In this case, what is the new level of output? What is the money supply? And if the government decides to use fiscal policy instead to stabilize output, then, according to the new IS curve, by how much must government spending be increased to achieve this goal? Call this case 3.
j. Plot the new IS_3 and LM_3 curves for case 3 on a chart. Label the axes, and the equilibrium values.

10. In this chapter, we've studied how policy responses affect economic variables in an open economy. Consider each of the problems in policy design and implementation discussed in this chapter. Compare and contrast each problem as it applies to monetary policy stabilization versus fiscal policy stabilization.

APPENDIX 1 TO CHAPTER 7

The Marshall-Lerner Condition

The model developed in this chapter assumes that a depreciation of a country's currency (a rise in q) will cause the trade balance to move toward surplus (a rise in TB). Is this assumption justified?

Let's look at a simple example. Consider a hypothetical two-country world in which trade is initially balanced, so $TB = 0$ or $EX = IM$. The question of how the trade balance changes then simplifies to a question of whether the change in exports is greater or less than the change in imports. Let us consider a small percentage change in the real exchange rate, say, $\Delta q/q = +1\%$, that is, a home real depreciation of 1%. Note that this is, approximately, a foreign real appreciation of 1%, since the foreign real exchange rate $q^* = 1/q$ is simply the inverse of the home real exchange rate, implying that $\Delta q^*/q^* = -1\%$.

As we have argued, when home exports look cheaper to foreigners, the real value of home exports expressed in home units of output will *unambiguously* rise. This effect is described by the elasticity of home exports with respect to the home real exchange rate, denoted η, where

$$\frac{\Delta EX}{EX} = \eta \times \frac{\Delta q}{q} = \eta\%$$

That is, if the home country experiences a 1% real depreciation, its real exports (measured in home units) rise by $\eta\%$.

The same logic applies to the foreign country, with exports EX^*, real exchange rate $q^* = 1/q$, and elasticity η^*, so that

$$\frac{\Delta EX^*}{EX^*} = \eta^* \times \frac{\Delta q^*}{q^*} = \eta^*\%$$

Now consider the trade link between the two countries. Foreign exports must equal home imports, measured in any consistent units. In home real output units

$$\underbrace{\text{Home imports in units of home output}}_{} = \underbrace{IM(q)}_{\text{Home imports (real)}}$$

$$\underbrace{\text{Foreign exports in units of home output}}_{} = \underbrace{\underbrace{(1/P)}_{\substack{\text{Divide by home} \\ \text{price level to} \\ \text{convert to home} \\ \text{output units}}} \times \underbrace{E}_{\substack{\text{Exchange rate} \\ \text{converts} \\ \text{foreign to} \\ \text{domestic} \\ \text{currency}}} \times \underbrace{\underbrace{P^*}_{\substack{\text{Price of} \\ \text{foreign basket} \\ \text{in foreign} \\ \text{currency}}} \times \underbrace{EX^*(q^*)}_{\substack{\text{Foreign exports} \\ \text{(real)}}}}_{\text{Value of foreign exports in foreign currency}}}_{\text{Value of foreign exports in home currency}}$$

Equating these two terms, we find that $IM(q) = (EP^*/P) \times EX^*(q^*)$. Thus,

$$IM(q) = q \times EX^*(q^*)$$

This expression makes intuitive sense for the stylized two-country world that we are studying. It states that *IM*, the quantity of home imports (measured in *home* output units), must equal the quantity of foreign exports EX^* (measured in *foreign* output units) multiplied by a factor q that converts units of foreign goods to units of home goods (since q is the relative price of foreign goods, that is home goods per unit of foreign goods).

For a small change, we may write the percentage change in the previous equation as follows. On the left is the percentage change in imports; on the right is the percentage change in q *times* EX^*, which equals the percentage change in q *plus* the percentage change in EX^*:

$$\frac{\Delta IM}{IM} = \frac{\Delta q}{q} + \frac{\Delta EX^*}{EX^*} = \frac{\Delta q}{q} + \left[\eta^* \times \frac{\Delta q^*}{q^*}\right] = 1\% + [\eta^* \times (-1\%)] = (1 - \eta^*)\%$$

What is going on here? On the home import side, two effects come into play. Foreigners export a lower volume of their more expensive goods measured in foreign output units (a volume effect of $-\eta^*\%$), but those goods will cost more for home importers in terms of home output (a price effect of 1%). The price effect follows because the real exchange rate (the relative price of the foreign goods in terms of domestic goods) has increased (by 1%), and this makes every unit of imports cost more in real terms.

Starting from balanced trade with $EX = IM$, a 1% home real depreciation will cause EX to change by $\eta\%$ and IM to change by $1 - \eta^*\%$. The trade balance (initially zero) will increase (to become positive) if and only if the former impact on EX exceeds the latter impact on IM. This occurs if and only if $\eta > 1 - \eta^*$, or, equivalently,

$$\eta + \eta^* > 1$$

The last expression is known as the *Marshall-Lerner condition:* it says that the trade balance will increase only after a real depreciation if the responsiveness of trade volumes to real exchange rate changes is sufficiently large (or sufficiently elastic) to ensure that the volume effects exceed the price effects.

APPENDIX 2 TO CHAPTER 7

Multilateral Real Exchange Rates

How do the predictions of our model change when a country trades with multiple countries or regions? Can our theory be extended to this more realistic case? Can we make a sensible aggregation of trade flows, trade balances, and real exchange rates across, say, N different countries?

Suppose that for trade with any foreign country (say, country 1), the fractional change in home exports EX_1 and imports IM_1 given a small change in the real exchange rate q_1 is

$$\frac{\Delta EX_1}{EX_1} = \varepsilon \times \frac{\Delta q_1}{q_1}; \qquad \frac{\Delta IM_1}{IM_1} = -\varepsilon \times \frac{\Delta q_1}{q_1}$$

The parameter $\varepsilon > 0$ is an *elasticity*. In this case, it is the elasticity of exports and imports with respect to the real exchange rate. When q rises by 1% (a real depreciation), exports rise by ε% and imports fall by ε%. (A more complicated analysis is needed when the import and export elasticities differ; see the first appendix.)

From these relationships, we find the following by rearranging:

$$\Delta TB_1 = \Delta EX_1 - \Delta IM_1 = \varepsilon \frac{\Delta q_1}{q_1} EX_1 + \varepsilon \frac{\Delta q_1}{q_1} IM_1$$

$$= \varepsilon \times (EX_1 + IM_1) \times \frac{\Delta q_1}{q_1}$$

$$= \varepsilon \times \text{Trade}_1 \times \frac{\Delta q_1}{q_1}$$

where $\text{Trade}_i = [EX_i + IM_i]$ is the total trade of the home country with country i.

Adding up this last equation across all countries, the change in the home trade balance is given by $\Delta TB = \Delta TB_1 + \Delta TB_2 + \cdots + \Delta TB_N$, which we can write as

$$\Delta TB = \varepsilon \times \left[\text{Trade}_1 \frac{\Delta q_1}{q_1} + \text{Trade}_2 \frac{\Delta q_2}{q_2} + \cdots + \text{Trade}_N \frac{\Delta q_N}{q_N} \right]$$

We normalize by total trade, where $\text{Trade} = \text{Trade}_1 + \text{Trade}_2 + \cdots + \text{Trade}_N$, to obtain

$$\Delta TB = \varepsilon \times \text{Trade} \times \left[\frac{\text{Trade}_1}{\text{Trade}} \frac{\Delta q_1}{q_1} + \frac{\text{Trade}_1}{\text{Trade}} \frac{\Delta q_2}{q_2} + \cdots + \frac{\text{Trade}_1}{\text{Trade}} \frac{\Delta q_N}{q_N} \right]$$

The expression in brackets might look familiar. In Chapter 2, we introduced the concept of a *trade-weighted change in the nominal exchange rate*—the change in the value of a currency against a basket of currencies, where the change in each country-pair's nominal exchange rate was weighted by that particular country-pair's share of trade volume. The preceding expression is similar, only with nominal exchange rates replaced by real exchange rates. The expression shows that (with some assumptions) our model can be extended to more realistic scenarios with many countries by using the change in a trade-weighted real exchange rate covering all trading partners.

8

Fixed versus Floating: International Monetary Experience

1. Exchange Rate Regime Choice: Key Issues
2. Other Benefits of Fixing
3. Fixed Exchange Rate Systems
4. International Monetary Experience
5. Conclusions

In truth, the gold standard is already a barbarous relic. All of us, from the Governor of the Bank of England downwards, are now primarily interested in preserving the stability of business, prices, and employment, and are not likely, when the choice is forced on us, deliberately to sacrifice these to the outworn dogma. . . . Advocates of the ancient standard do not observe how remote it now is from the spirit and the requirements of the age.

John Maynard Keynes, 1923

How many more fiascoes will it take before responsible people are finally convinced that a system of pegged exchange rates is not a satisfactory financial arrangement for a group of large countries with independent political systems and independent national policies?

Milton Friedman, 1992

The gold standard in particular—and even pegged exchange rates in general—have a bad name. But the gold standard's having lost her name in the 1920s and 1930s should not lead one to forget her 19th century virtues. . . . Can these lost long-term virtues be retrieved without the world again being in thrall to the barbarous relic? . . . In an integrated world economy, the choice of an exchange rate regime—and thus the common price level—should not be left to an individual country. The spillover effects are so high that it should be a matter of collective choice.

Ronald McKinnon, 2002

A century ago, economists and policy makers may have had their differences of opinion, but—unlike today—they were virtually unanimous in their agreement about the ideal choice of exchange rate regime. Fixed exchange rates were viewed as the best choice. Even if some countries occasionally adopted a floating rate, it was usually with the expectation that they would soon return to a fixed or pegged rate.

The preferred method for fixing the exchange rate was also more or less agreed upon. It was the **gold standard,** a system in which the value of a country's currency was fixed relative to an ounce of gold and, hence, relative to all other currencies that were also pegged to gold. The requirements of the gold standard were strict: although monetary authorities could issue paper money, they were obliged to freely exchange paper currency for gold at the official fixed rate.

Figure 8-1 documents more than 100 years of exchange rate arrangements around the world. From 1870 to 1913, most of the world converged on the gold standard. At the peak in 1913, approximately 70% of countries were part of the gold standard system; very few floated (about 20%) or used other metallic standards (about 10%). Since 1913 much has changed. Adherence to the gold standard weakened during World War I, waxed and waned in the 1920s and 1930s, then was never seen again. John Maynard Keynes and other policy makers designed a new system, but one in which exchange rates were still fixed.

In the period after World War II, the figure shows that many currencies were pegged to the U.S. dollar. The British pound, the French franc, and the German mark were also somewhat popular peg choices. Yet because the pound, franc, and mark were all pegged to the dollar at this time, the vast majority of the world's currencies ended up, directly or indirectly, on what amounted to a "dollar standard" system.

Like the gold standard, the dollar-based system didn't endure either. Beginning in the early 1970s, floating exchange rates became more common, and they now account

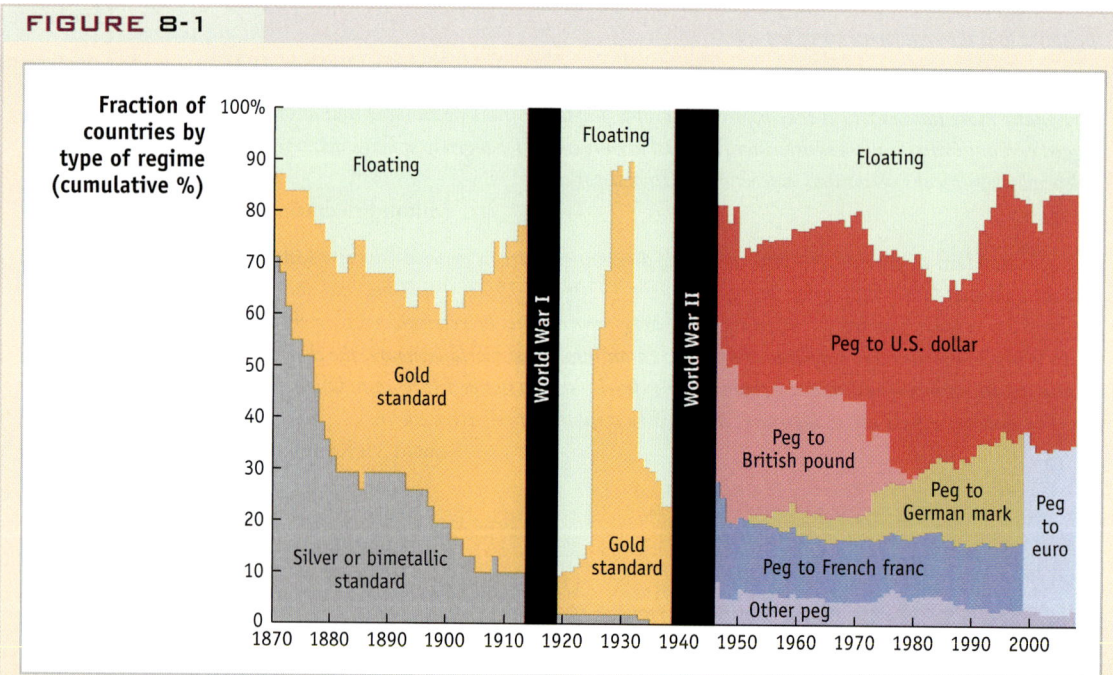

FIGURE 8-1

Exchange Rates Regimes of the World, 1870–2007 The shaded regions show the fraction of countries on each type of regime by year, and they add up to 100%. From 1870 to 1913, the gold standard became the dominant regime. During World War I (1914–1918), most countries suspended the gold standard, and resumptions in the late 1920s were brief. After further suspensions in World War II (1939–1945), most countries were fixed against the U.S. dollar (the pound, franc, and mark blocs were indirectly pegged to the dollar). Starting in the 1970s, more countries opted to float. In 1999 the euro replaced the franc and the mark as the base currency for many pegs.

Sources: Christopher M. Meissner, 2005, "A New World Order: Explaining the International Diffusion of the Gold Standard, 1870–1913," Journal of International Economics, 66(2), 385–406; Christopher M. Meissner and Nienke Oomes, 2006, "Why Do Countries Peg the Way They Peg? The Determinants of Anchor Currency Choice," Cambridge Working Papers in Economics 0643, Faculty of Economics, University of Cambridge, and later updates.

for about 30% of all currency regimes. Remember that these data count all countries' currencies equally, without any weighting for economic size (measured by GDP). In the larger economies of the world, and especially among the major currencies, floating regimes are even more prevalent.

Why do some countries choose to fix and others to float? Why do they change their minds at different times? These are the main questions we confront in this chapter, and they are among the most enduring and controversial questions in international macroeconomics. They have been the cause of conflicts among economists, policy makers, and commentators for many years.

On one side of the debate are those like Milton Friedman (quoted at the start of this chapter) who in the 1950s, against the prevailing gold standard orthodoxy, argued that floating rates are obviously to be preferred, have clear economic advantages, and are the only politically feasible solution. On the opposing side of the debate are figures such as Ronald McKinnon (also quoted above) who think that only a system of fixed rates can prevent noncooperative policy making, keep prices and output stable, and encourage international flows of trade and finance.

What are the pros and cons of different exchange rate regimes? Are the answers black and white? And why should we care?

1 Exchange Rate Regime Choice: Key Issues

In previous chapters, we have examined the workings of the economy under fixed and floating exchange rates. One advantage of understanding the workings of these regimes in such detail is that we are now in a position to address a perennially important macroeconomic policy question: What is the best exchange rate regime choice for a given country at a given time? In this section, we explore the pros and cons of fixed and floating exchange rates by combining the models we have developed with additional theory and evidence. We begin with an application about Germany and Britain in the early 1990s. This story highlights the choices policy makers face as they choose between fixed exchange rates (pegs) and floating exchange rates (floats).

APPLICATION

Britain and Europe: The Big Issues

One way to begin to understand the choice between fixed and floating regimes is to look at countries that have sometimes floated and sometimes fixed and to examine their reasons for switching. In this case study, we look behind the British decision to switch from an exchange rate peg to floating in September 1992.

We start by asking, why did Britain first adopt a peg? The answer derives from Britain's membership in the European Union (EU) since the 1970s and the steps being taken in the 1980s and 1990s by EU member states to move toward a common currency, the euro, which arrived in 1999. For now, we note that the push for a common currency was part of a larger program to create a single market across Europe. Fixed exchange rates, and ultimately a common currency, were seen as a means to promote trade and other forms of cross-border exchange by lowering transaction costs. In addition, it was also felt that an exchange rate anchor might help lower British inflation.

An important stepping-stone along the way to the euro was a fixed exchange rate system created in 1979 called the Exchange Rate Mechanism (ERM), which tied together all member currencies at fixed rates. The most important currency in the ERM was the German mark or deutsche mark (DM). Effectively, in the 1980s and 1990s, the German central bank, the Bundesbank, retained monetary autonomy and had the freedom to set its own money supply levels and nominal interest rates. For other countries, joining the ERM meant that, in effect, they had to *unilaterally* peg to the DM.[1] Thus, we would say that the DM was the **base currency** or **center currency** (or Germany was the *base country* or *center country*) in the fixed exchange rate system.

Britain joined the ERM in 1990. Based on our analysis of fixed exchange rates in the previous chapter, we can understand the implications of that choice using Figure 8-2. This figure shows the familiar one-country IS-LM-FX diagram for Britain and another IS-LM diagram for the center country, Germany. We treat Britain as the home country and Germany as the foreign country, and denote foreign variables with an asterisk.

Panel (a) shows an IS-LM diagram for Germany, with German output on the horizontal axis and the German DM interest rate on the vertical axis. Panel (b) shows the British IS-LM diagram, with British output on the horizontal axis. Panel (c) shows the British forex market, with the exchange rate in pounds per mark. The vertical axes of panels (b) and (c) show returns in pounds, the home currency.

Initially, we suppose the three diagrams are in equilibrium as follows. In panel (b), at point 1, British output is Y_1 and the pound interest rate is i_1. In panel (a), at point 1″, German output is Y_1^* and the DM interest rate i_1^*. In panel (c), at point 1′, the pound is pegged to the DM at the fixed rate $\bar{E}$ and expected depreciation is zero. The trilemma tells us that monetary policy autonomy is lost in Britain: the British interest rate must equal the German interest rate, so there is uncovered interest parity with $i_1 = i_1^*$.

A Shock in Germany With the scene set, our story begins with a threat to the ERM from an unexpected source. The countries of Eastern Europe began their transition away from Communism, a process that famously began with the fall of the Berlin Wall in 1989. After the wall fell, the reunification of East and West Germany was soon under way. Because the economically backward East Germany required significant funds to support social services, pay unemployment benefits, modernize infrastructure, and so on, the reunification imposed large fiscal costs on Germany, but West Germans were willing to pay these costs to see their country united. As we know from the previous chapter, an increase in German government consumption G^* can be represented as a shift to the right in the German IS curve, from IS_1^* to IS_2^* in panel (a). This shift would have moved the German economy's equilibrium from point 1″ to point 3″. All else equal, the model predicts an increase in German interest rates from i_1^* to i_3^* and a boom in German output from Y_1^* to Y_3^*.[2] This was indeed what started to happen.

The next chapter in the story involves the Bundesbank's response to the German government's expansionary fiscal policy. The Bundesbank was deeply afraid that the boom in output might cause an increase in German rates of inflation, and it wished to

---
[1] Officially, all currencies in the ERM pegged to a virtual basket of currencies called the ecu (European currency unit), the precursor of the euro. In practice, though, the DM was the predominant reserve currency and, in effect, the base currency.
[2] All else would not have been equal under this shift, given the ERM; Germany's interest rate increase would have been matched by other ERM members to preserve their pegs. For Germany, those shifts would be increases in the foreign interest rate (from Germany's perspective), and those responses would, in turn, have shifted Germany's IS curve a tiny bit farther. These extra effects make no substantive difference to the analysis, so the extra shift is not shown here, for clarity.

FIGURE 8-2

Off the Mark: Britain's Departure from the ERM in 1992 In panel (a), German reunification raises German government spending and shifts IS^* out. The German central bank contracts monetary policy, LM^* shifts up, and German output stabilizes at Y_1^*. Equilibrium shifts from point 1″ to point 2″, and the German interest rate rises from i_1^* to i_2^*. In Britain, under a peg, panels (b) and (c) show that foreign returns, FR, rise and so the British domestic return, DR, must rise to $i_2 = i_2^*$. The German interest rate rise also shifts out Britain's IS curve slightly from IS_1 to IS_2. To maintain the peg, Britain's LM curve shifts up from LM_1 to LM_2. At the same exchange rate and a higher interest rate, demand falls and output drops from Y_1 to Y_2. Equilibrium moves from point 1 to point 2″. If the British were to float, they could put the LM curve wherever they wanted. For example, at LM_4 the British interest rate holds at i_1 and output booms, but the forex market ends up at point 4′ and there is a depreciation of the pound to E_4. The British could also select LM_3, stabilize output at the initial level Y_1, but the peg still has to break with E rising to E_3.

take steps to head off that risk. Using its policy autonomy, the Bundesbank elected to tighten monetary policy: it contracted the money supply and raised interest rates. This policy change is seen in the upward shift of the German LM curve, from LM_1^* to LM_2^* in panel (a). We suppose that the Bundesbank stabilizes German output at its initial level Y_1^* by raising German interest rates to the even higher level of i_2^*, as shown in the diagram.[3]

---

[3] Interest rate responses in the ERM (described in footnote 2) would, in turn, have moved Germany's IS curve out yet farther, requiring a bit more tightening from the Bundesbank. Again, these indirect effects do not affect the analysis and are not shown, for clarity.

Choices for the Other ERM Countries What happened in the countries of the ERM that were pegging to the DM? We examine what these events implied for Britain, but the other ERM members faced the same problems. The IS-LM-FX model tells us that events in Germany have two implications for the British IS-LM-FX model. First, as the German interest rate i^* rises, the British foreign return curve FR shifts up in the British forex market (to recap: German deposits pay higher interest, all else equal). Second, as the German interest rate i^* rises, the British IS curve also moves out (to recap: at any given British interest rate, the pound has to depreciate more, boosting British demand via expenditure switching). Now we only have to figure out how much the British IS curve shifts, what the British LM curve is up to, and hence how the equilibrium outcome depends on British policy choices.

Choice 1: Float and Prosper? First, let us suppose that the Bank of England had left interest rates unchanged in Britain at i_1 and suppose British fiscal policy had also been left unchanged. In addition, we assume that Britain would allow the pound-DM exchange rate to float in the short run, but for simplicity we also assume that the same expected exchange rate would prevail in the long run, so that the long-run future expected exchange rate E^e remained unchanged at $\overline{E}$.

With these assumptions in place, let's think first about the investment component of demand: I in Britain would be unchanged at $I(i_1)$. But in the forex market in panel (c), with the domestic return DR_1 held at i_1 by the Bank of England and with the foreign return rising from FR_1 to FR_2, the new equilibrium would be at 4′ and the exchange rate would rise temporarily to E_4: the pound would have to depreciate to E_4 against the DM, implying an exit from the ERM system. Now think about the trade balance component of demand: the British trade balance would rise because a nominal depreciation is also a real depreciation in the short run, given sticky prices.[4] As we saw in the previous chapter, British demand would therefore increase, as would British equilibrium output.

To sum up the result after all these adjustments occur, an increase in the foreign interest rate always shifts out the home IS curve, all else equal. We see this in panel (b): British interest rates would still be at i_1, and British output would have risen to Y_4, on the new IS curve IS_2. To keep the interest rate at i_1, as output rises, the Bank of England would have had to expand the money supply and the British LM curve would shift out from LM_1 to LM_4, and the pound would depreciate to E_4. If Britain were to float and depreciate, Britain would experience a boom. But this course of action would not have been compatible with Britain's continued ERM membership.

Choice 2: Peg and Suffer? If Britain's exchange rate were to stay pegged to the DM because of the ERM, however, the outcome for Britain would not be so rosy. In this scenario, the trilemma means that in order to maintain the peg, Britain would have to increase its interest rate and follow the lead of the center country, Germany. In panel (b), the pound interest rate would have to rise to the level $i_2 = i_2^*$ to maintain the peg. In panel (c), the domestic return would rise from DR_1 to DR_2 in step with the foreign return's rise from FR_1 to FR_2, and the new FX market equilibrium would be at 2′. The Bank of England would accomplish this rise in DR by tightening its monetary policy and lowering the British money supply. In panel (b), under a peg, the new position of the IS

---

[4] This is true in a pure two-country model, and, from the British perspective, Germany is the "rest of the world." With many countries, however, the direction of change is still the same. All else equal, a British real depreciation against Germany will still imply a depreciation of the British real effective exchange rate against the rest of the world.

curve at IS_2 would imply an upward shift in the British LM curve, as shown by the move from LM_1 to LM_2. So the British IS-LM equilibrium would now be at point 2, with output at Y_2. The adverse consequences for the British economy now become apparent. At point 2, as compared with the initial point 1, British demand has fallen. Why? British interest rates have risen (depressing investment demand I), but the exchange rate has remained at its pegged level $\bar{E}$ (so there is no change in the trade balance). To sum up, what we have shown in this scenario is that the IS curve may have moved right a bit, but the opposing shift in the LM curve would have been even larger. If Britain were to stay pegged and keep its membership in the ERM, Britain would experience a recession.

In 1992 Britain found itself facing these exact choices. As we have noted, if the British pound had been floating against the DM, then leaving interest rates unchanged would have been an option, and Britain could have achieved equilibrium at point 4 with a higher output, Y_4. Indeed, as we know, the whole range of monetary policy options would have been opened up by floating, including, for example, the choice of a mild monetary contraction, shifting the British LM curve from LM_1 to LM_3, moving equilibrium in panel (b) to point 3, stabilizing U.K. output at its initial level Y_1, with the FX market in panel (c) settling at point 3' with a mild depreciation of the exchange rate to E_3.

What Happened Next? Following an economic slowdown, and after considerable last-minute dithering and chaos, in September 1992 the British Conservative government finally came to the conclusion that the benefits of being in ERM and the euro project were smaller than costs suffered due to a German interest rate hike that was a reaction to Germany-specific events. Two years after joining the ERM, Britain opted out.

Did Britain make the right choice? In Figure 8-3, we compare the economic performance of Britain with that of France, a large EU economy that maintained its ERM peg. After leaving the ERM in September 1992, Britain lowered interest rates [panel (a)]

FIGURE 8-3

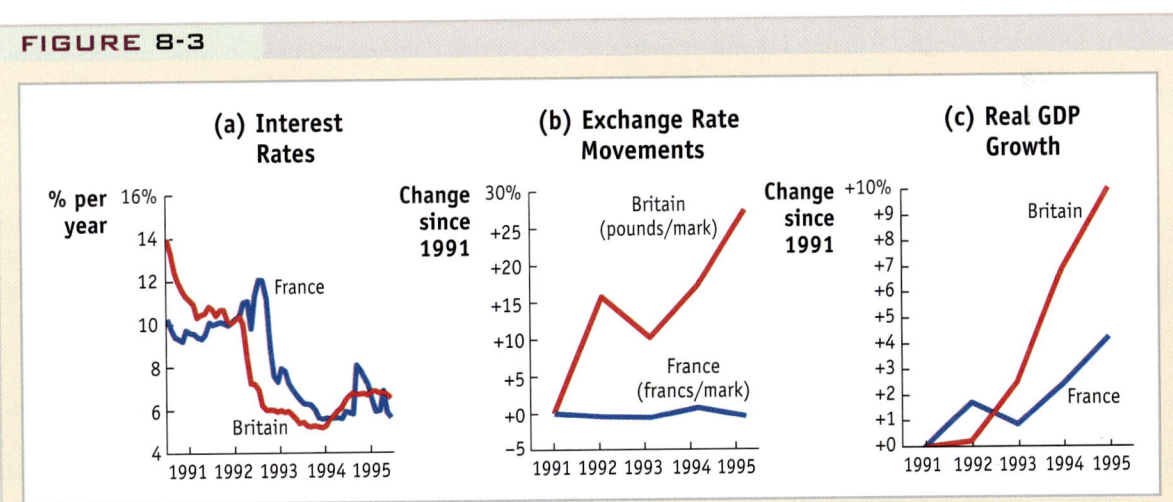

Floating Away: Britain versus France after 1992 Britain's decision to exit the ERM allowed for more expansionary British monetary policy after September 1992. In other ERM countries that remained pegged to the mark, such as France, monetary policy had to be kept tighter to maintain the peg. Consistent with the model, the data show lower interest rates, a more depreciated currency, and faster output growth in Britain compared with France after 1992.

Note: Interest rates are three-month LIBOR, annualized rates.

Sources: Data from Global Financial Data; econstats.com; IMF, International Financial Statistics.

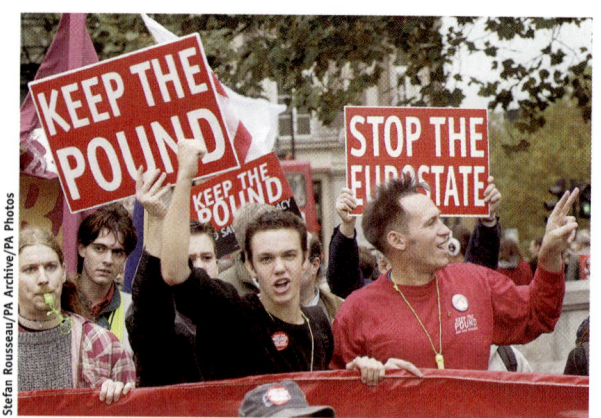

Most Britons are opposed to the euro, some vehemently so.

in the short run and depreciated its exchange rate against the DM [panel (b)]. In comparison, France never depreciated and had to maintain higher interest rates to keep the franc pegged to the DM until German monetary policy eased a year or two later. As our model would predict, the British economy boomed in subsequent years (panel c). The French suffered slower growth, a fate shared by most of the other countries that stayed in the ERM.

The British choice stands to this day. Although the option to rejoin the ERM has remained open since 1992, the British have not shown much interest. The idea of pegging to, much less joining, the euro, is deeply unpopular. All subsequent British governments have decided that the benefits of increased trade and economic integration with Europe were smaller than the associated costs of sacrificing British monetary autonomy.[5] ■

Key Factors in Exchange Rate Regime Choice: Integration and Similarity

We started this chapter with an application about the policy choice and tradeoffs Britain faced in 1992 when it needed to decide between a fixed exchange rate (peg) and a floating exchange rate (float).

At different times and with differing degrees of enthusiasm, British authorities could see the potential benefits of participating fully in an economically integrated single European market, including the gains that would flow from being in the ERM fixed exchange rate system. The fixed exchange rate promised to lower the costs of economic transactions among the members of the ERM zone. But the British could also see—as the events of 1992 made clear—that there would be times when the monetary policy being pursued by authorities in Germany would be out of line with policy that was best for Britain. The fundamental source of this divergence between what Britain wanted and what Germany wanted was that each country faced different shocks. The fiscal shock that Germany experienced after reunification was not felt in Britain or any other ERM country.

To better understand these trade-offs, and hence the decision to fix or float, we now examine the issues that are at the heart of this decision: economic *integration* as measured by trade and other transactions, and economic *similarity*, as measured by the similarity of shocks.

Economic Integration and the Gains in Efficiency

The term "economic integration" refers to the growth of market linkages in goods, capital, and labor markets among regions and countries. We have argued that by lowering transaction costs, a fixed exchange rate might promote integration and hence increase economic efficiency. Why?

---

[5] Even the Liberal Democrats, for a long time pro-euro while just a small party perpetually in opposition, effectively dropped their stance once they had the opportunity to join a coalition government with the Conservatives in 2010.

Trade is the most obvious example of an activity that volatile exchange rates might discourage. Stable exchange rates and prices encourage arbitrage and lower the costs of trade. But trade is not the only type of international economic activity likely to be discouraged by exchange rate fluctuations. Currency-related transaction costs and uncertainty also act as barriers to cross-border capital and labor flows.

- The lesson: *the greater the degree of economic integration between markets in the home country and the base country, the greater will be the volume of transactions between the two, and the greater will be the benefits the home country gains from fixing its exchange rate with the base country. As integration rises, the efficiency benefits of a common currency increase.*

Economic Similarity and the Costs of Asymmetric Shocks

We have also argued that a fixed exchange rate can lead to costs. Our argument depended on the assumption that one country experienced a country-specific shock or **asymmetric shock** that was not shared by the other country: the shocks were dissimilar.

The application on Britain and Germany showed why an *asymmetric* shock causes problems: it leads to a conflict between the policy goals of the two countries. In our example, German policy makers wanted to tighten monetary policy to offset a boom caused by a positive demand shock due to their expansionary fiscal policy. British policy makers did not want to implement the same policy because they had not experienced the same shock.

Now we can begin to see why similar or *symmetric* shocks cause no problems. Imagine a different scenario in which both countries experience an identical demand shock. Both monetary authorities would like to respond identically, raising interest rates in each country by the same amount to stabilize output. Fortunately, this desired symmetric increase in interest rates does not conflict with Britain's fixed exchange rate commitment. If interest rates were initially set at a low common level, $i_1 = i_1^*$, they would just be raised to a new higher level, $i_2 = i_2^*$. Here, Britain can stabilize output *and* stay pegged because uncovered interest parity is still satisfied! The exchange rate $\overline{E}$ does not change, and even though Britain is pegging unilaterally to Germany, Britain has the interest rate it would choose even if it floated and were free to make an independent monetary policy choice.

The simple, general lesson we can draw is that for a home country that unilaterally pegs to a foreign country, asymmetric shocks impose costs in terms of lost output. Desired foreign and home monetary policies will sometimes differ, but the peg means that foreign's policy choice will be imposed on home. In contrast, symmetric shocks do not impose any costs because desired foreign and home monetary policies will be the same, and foreign's imposed choice will suit home perfectly.

In reality, the application of this idea is more complex. The countries may not be identical and the shocks may be a mix of symmetric and asymmetric shocks of different magnitudes. It is possible, although algebraically tedious, to account for these complexities in the same framework. At the end of the day, however, the main point holds true.

- The lesson: *if there is a greater degree of economic similarity between the home country and the base country, meaning that the countries face more symmetric shocks and fewer asymmetric shocks, then the economic stabilization costs to home of fixing its exchange rate to the base become smaller. As economic similarity rises, the stability costs of common currency decrease.*

Simple Criteria for a Fixed Exchange Rate

We can now set out a simple theory of exchange rate regime choice by considering the *net benefits* (benefits minus the costs) of pegging versus floating. Our discussions about integration and similarity have shown the following:

- *As integration rises, the efficiency benefits of a common currency increase.*
- *As symmetry rises, the stability costs of a common currency decrease.*

Our theory says that if market integration or symmetry increases, the net benefits of a fixed exchange rate also increase. If the net benefits are negative, the home country ought to float if the decision is based solely on its economic interests. If the net benefits turn positive, the home country ought to fix.

Figure 8-4 illustrates the theory graphically in an **symmetry-integration diagram** in which the horizontal axis measures the degree of economic integration between a pair of locations, say, A and B, and the vertical axis measures the symmetry of the shocks experienced by the pair A and B.

We use the figure to consider the question of whether A should peg unilaterally to B (or vice versa). Suppose conditions change and the pair moves up and to the right, for example, from point 1 toward point 6. Along this path, integration and symmetry are both increasing, so the net benefits of fixing are increasing. At some critical point (point 2 in the graph), the net benefits turn positive. Before that point, floating is best. After that point, fixing is best.

Our argument is more general: whatever the direction of the path, as long as it moves up and to the right, it must cross some threshold like point 2 beyond which ben-

FIGURE 8-4

A Theory of Fixed Exchange Rates Points 1 to 6 in the figure represent a pair of locations. Suppose one location is considering pegging its exchange rate to its partner. If their markets become more integrated (a move to the right along the horizontal axis) or if the economic shocks they experience become more symmetric (a move up on the vertical axis), the net economic benefits of fixing increase. If the pair moves far enough up or to the right, then the benefits of fixing exceed costs (net benefits are positive), and the pair will cross the fixing threshold shown by the *FIX* line. Above the line, it is optimal for the region to fix. Below the line, it is optimal for the region to float.

efits outweigh costs. Thus, there will exist a set of points—a downward-sloping line passing through point 2—that delineates this threshold. We refer to this threshold as the *FIX* line. Points above the *FIX* line satisfy the economic criteria for a fixed exchange rate.

What might different points on this chart mean? To give an example, if we are at point 6, we might think of A and B as neighborhoods in a city—they are very well integrated and an economic shock is usually felt by all neighborhoods in the city. If A and B were at point 5, they might be two cities. If A and B were at point 4, they might be the regions of a country, still above the *FIX* line. If A and B were at point 3, they might be neighboring, well-integrated countries with few asymmetric shocks. Point 2 is right on the borderline. If A and B were at point 1, they might be less well-integrated countries with more asymmetric shocks and our theory says they ought to float.

The key prediction of our theory is this: *pairs of countries above the FIX line (more integrated, more similar shocks) will gain economically from adopting a fixed exchange rate. Those below the FIX line (less integrated, less similar shocks) will not.*

In a moment, we develop and apply this theory further. But first, let's see if there is evidence to support the theory's two main assumptions: Do fixed exchange rates deliver gains through integration? Do they also impose costs by obstructing stabilization policy?

APPLICATION

Do Fixed Exchange Rates Promote Trade?

Probably the single most powerful argument *for* a fixed exchange rate is that it might boost trade by eliminating trade-hindering frictions. The idea is an old one. In 1878 the United States had yet to rejoin the gold standard following the Civil War. Policy makers were debating whether going back on gold made sense, and J. S. Moore, a U.S. Treasury official testifying before Congress, was questioned on the subject:

> *Question:* Do you not think that the use of a common standard of value has a tendency to promote a free commercial interchange between the various countries using it?
>
> *Answer:* If two countries, be they ever so distant from each other should have the same standard of money . . . there would be no greater harmonizer than such an exchange.

Benefits Measured by Trade Levels As we have noted, this was the conventional wisdom among policy makers in the late nineteenth and early twentieth centuries, and research by economic historians has found strong support for their views: all else equal, a pair of countries adopting the gold standard had bilateral trade levels 30% to 100% higher than comparable pairs of countries that were off the gold standard.[6] Thus, it appears that the gold standard *did* promote trade.

What about fixed exchange rates today? Do they promote trade? Economists have exhaustively tested this hypothesis using increasingly sophisticated statistical methods.

---

[6] J. Ernesto López Córdova and Christopher M. Meissner, March 2003, "Exchange Rate Regimes and International Trade: Evidence from the Classical Gold Standard Era, 1870–1913," *American Economic Review*, 93(1), 344–353; Antoni Estevadeordal, Brian Frantz, and Alan M. Taylor, May 2003, "The Rise and Fall of World Trade, 1870–1939," *Quarterly Journal of Economics*, 118(2), 359–407; Marc Flandreau and Mathilde Maurel, January 2005, "Monetary Union, Trade Integration, and Business Cycles in 19th Century Europe," *Open Economies Review*, 16(2), 135–152. The quotation is cited in an earlier draft of the paper by López Córdova and Meissner.

We can look at some evidence from a recent study in which country pairs A–B were classified in four different ways:

a. The two countries are using a *common currency* (i.e., A and B are in a currency union or A has unilaterally adopted B's currency).

b. The two countries are linked by a *direct* exchange rate peg (i.e., A's currency is pegged to B's).

c. The two countries are linked by an *indirect* exchange rate peg, via a third currency (i.e., A and B have currencies pegged to C but not directly to each other).

d. The two countries are not linked by any type of peg (i.e., their currencies *float* against one another, even if one or both might be pegged to some other third currency).

Using this classification and trade data from 1973 to 1999, economists Jay Shambaugh and Michael Klein compared bilateral trade volumes for all pairs under the three pegged regimes (a) through (c) with the benchmark level of trade under a floating regime (d) to see if there were any systematic differences. They also used careful statistical techniques to control for other factors and to address possible reverse causality (i.e., to eliminate the possibility that higher trade might have caused countries to fix their exchange rates). Figure 8-5 shows their key estimates, according to which currency unions increased bilateral trade by 38% relative to floating regimes. They also found that the adoption of a fixed exchange rate would promote trade, but only for the case of *direct* pegs. Adopting a direct peg increased bilateral trade by 21% compared with a floating exchange rate. Indirect pegs had a negligible and statistically insignificant effect.[7]

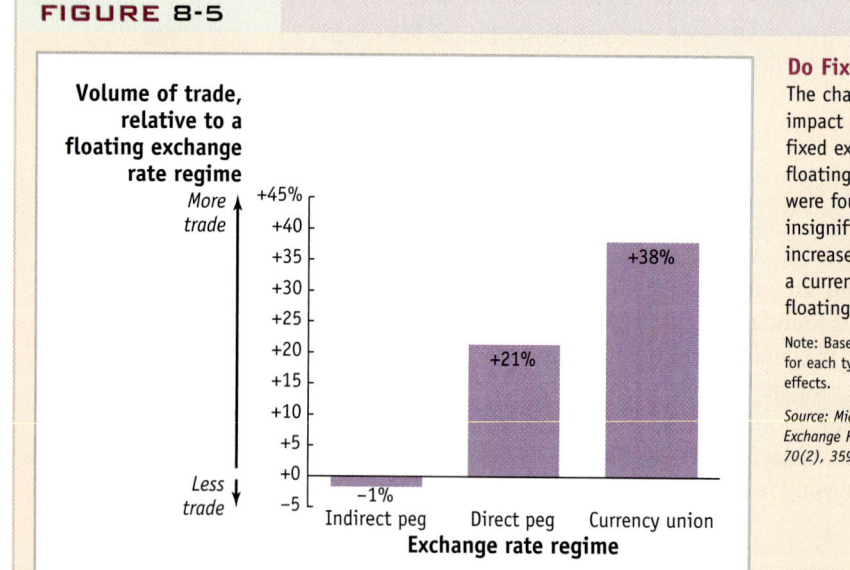

FIGURE 8-5

Do Fixed Exchange Rates Promote Trade? The chart shows one study's estimates of the impact on trade volumes of various types of fixed exchange rate regimes, relative to a floating exchange rate regime. Indirect pegs were found to have a small but statistically insignificant impact on trade, but trade increased under a direct peg by 21%, and under a currency union by 38%, as compared to floating.

Note: Based on a gravity model of trade with binary controls for each type of exchange rate regime using country-pair fixed effects.

Source: Michael W. Klein and Jay C. Shambaugh, 2006, "Fixed Exchange Rates and Trade," *Journal of International Economics*, 70(2), 359–383.

---

[7] Michael W. Klein and Jay C. Shambaugh, 2006, "Fixed Exchange Rates and Trade," *Journal of International Economics*, 70(2), 359–383.

Benefits Measured by Price Convergence Examining the effect of exchange rate regimes on trade levels is just one way to evaluate the impact of currency arrangements on international market integration, and it has been extensively researched. An alternative and growing empirical literature examines the relationship between exchange rate regimes and price convergence. These studies use the law of one price (LOOP) and purchasing power parity (PPP), which we saw first in our exchange rate chapters, as their benchmark criteria for an integrated market. If fixed exchange rates promote trade by lowering transaction costs, then we would expect to find that differences between prices (measured in a common currency) ought to be smaller among countries with pegged rates than among countries with floating rates. In other words, under a fixed exchange rate, we should find that LOOP and PPP are more likely to hold than under a floating regime. (Recall that it is convergence in prices that underlies the gains-from-trade argument.)

Statistical methods can be used to detect how large price differences have to be between two locations before arbitrage begins. Research on prices of baskets of goods shows that as exchange rate volatility increases, the price differences widen and the speed at which prices in the two markets converge decreases. These findings offer support for the hypothesis that fixed exchange rates promote arbitrage and price convergence.[8]

At a more microeconomic level, economists have also studied convergence in the prices of individual goods. For example, several studies focused on Europe have looked at the prices of various goods in different countries (e.g., retail prices of cars and TV sets, and the prices of Marlboro cigarettes in duty-free shops) and have concluded that higher exchange rate volatility is associated with larger price differentials between locations. In particular, while price gaps still remain for many goods, the "in" countries that maintained membership in the ERM (and now the Eurozone) saw prices converge much more than the "out" countries.[9] ■

APPLICATION

Do Fixed Exchange Rates Diminish Monetary Autonomy and Stability?

Probably the single most powerful argument *against* a fixed exchange rate is provided by the trilemma. An economy that unilaterally pegs to a foreign currency sacrifices its monetary policy autonomy.

We have seen the result many times now. If capital markets are open, arbitrage in the forex market implies uncovered interest parity. If the exchange rate is fixed, expected depreciation is zero, and the home interest rate must equal the foreign interest rate. The stark implication is that when a country pegs, it relinquishes its independent monetary policy: it has to adjust the money supply M at all times to ensure that the home interest rate i equals the foreign interest rate i^* (plus any risk premium).

---

[8] Maurice Obstfeld and Alan M. Taylor, 1997, "Nonlinear Aspects of Goods-Market Arbitrage and Adjustment: Heckscher's Commodity Points Revisited," *Journal of the Japanese and International Economies*, 11(4), 441–479.

[9] Marcus Asplund and Richard Friberg, 2001, "The Law of One Price in Scandinavian Duty-Free Stores," *American Economic Review*, 91(4), 1072–1083; Pinelopi Koujianou Goldberg and Frank Verboven, 2004, "Cross-Country Price Dispersion in the Euro Era: A Case Study of the European Car Market," *Economic Policy*, 19(40), 483–521; Jean Imbs, Haroon Mumtaz, Morten O. Ravn, and Hélène Rey, 2009, "One TV, One Price?" NBER Working Papers 15418.

The preceding case study of Britain and the ERM is one more example: Britain wanted to decouple the British interest rate from the German interest rate. To do so, it had to stop pegging the pound to the deutsche mark. Once it had done that, instead of having to contract the British economy as a result of unrelated events in Germany, it could maintain whatever interest rate it thought was best suited to British economic interests.

The Trilemma, Policy Constraints, and Interest Rate Correlations
Is the trilemma truly a binding constraint? Economist Jay Shambaugh tested this proposition, and Figure 8-6 shows some evidence using his data. As we have seen, there are three main solutions to the trilemma. A country can do the following:

1. Opt for open capital markets, with fixed exchange rates (an "open peg").
2. Opt to open its capital market but allow the currency to float (an "open nonpeg").
3. Opt to close its capital markets ("closed").

In case 1, changes in the country's interest rate should match changes in the interest rate of the base country to which it is pegging. In cases 2 and 3, there is no need for the country's interest rate to move in step with the base.

Figure 8-6 displays evidence for the trilemma. On the vertical axis is the annual change in the domestic interest rate; on the horizontal axis is the annual change in the base country interest rate. The trilemma says that in an open peg the two changes should be same and the points should lie on the 45-degree line. Indeed, for open pegs, shown in panel (a), the correlation of domestic and base interest rates is high and the line of best fit has a slope very close to 1. There are some deviations (possibly due to some pegs being more like bands), but these findings show that open pegs have very little monetary policy autonomy. In contrast, for the open nonpegs, shown in panel (b), and closed economies, shown in panel (c), domestic interest rates do not move as much in line with the base interest rate, the correlation is weak, and the slopes are much smaller than 1. These two regimes allow for some monetary policy autonomy.[10]

Costs of Fixing Measured by Output Volatility
The preceding evidence suggests that nations with open pegs have less monetary independence. But it does not tell us directly whether they suffer from greater output instability because their monetary authorities cannot use monetary policy to stabilize output when shocks hit. Some studies have found that, on average, the volatility of output growth *is* much higher under fixed regimes.[11] However, a problem in such studies is that countries

---

[10] The correlation isn't perfect for open pegs, nor is it zero for the other cases. This may not be surprising. Pegs are defined as de facto fixed within a ±2% band. The band allows central banks a little bit of flexibility with their exchange rates and interest rates that would be lacking in a strict peg (a band of zero width). As for nonpegs and closed countries, there may be reasons why their correlation with the base isn't zero. For example, they may have inflation targets or other guides to monetary policy that cause their interest rates to follow paths similar to those of the base country. In other words, these countries have some room for maneuver that open pegs don't have, but how much they choose to use it is another matter.

[11] Atish R. Ghosh, Anne-Marie Gulde, Jonathan D. Ostry, and Holger C. Wolf, 1997, "Does the Nominal Exchange Rate Regime Matter?" NBER Working Paper No. 5874.

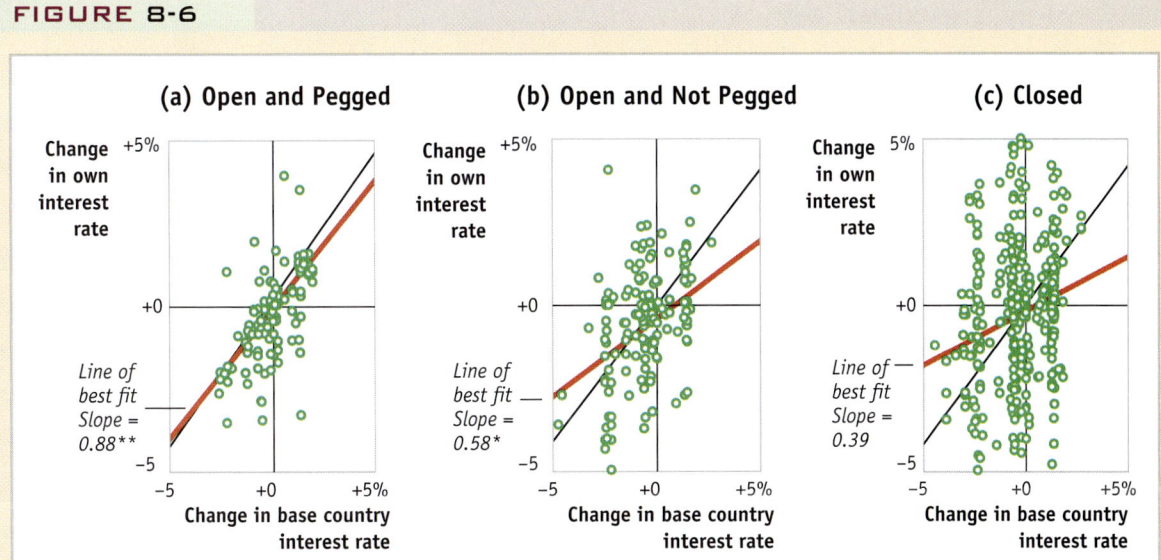

FIGURE 8-6

The Trilemma in Action The trilemma says that if the home country is an open peg, it sacrifices monetary policy autonomy because changes in its own interest rate must match changes in the interest rate of the base country. Panel (a) shows that this is the case. The trilemma also says that there are two ways to get that autonomy back: switch to a floating exchange rate or impose capital controls. Panels (b) and (c) show that either of these two policies permits home interest rates to move more independently of the base country.

Notes: ** Statistically significant at 1% level. * Statistically significant at 5% level. Hyperinflations excluded.

Source: Data from Jay C. Shambaugh, 2004, "The Effect of Fixed Exchange Rates on Monetary Policy," Quarterly Journal of Economics, 119(1), 300–351.

often differ in all kinds of characteristics that may affect output volatility, not just the exchange rate regime—and the results can be sensitive to how one controls for all these other factors.[12]

In the search for cleaner evidence, some recent research has focused on a key prediction of the IS-LM-FX model: all else equal, an increase in the base-country interest rate should lead output to fall in a country that fixes its exchange rate to the base country. This decline in output occurs because countries that fix have to tighten their monetary policy and raise their interest rates to match that of the base country. In contrast, countries that float do not have to follow the base country's rate increase and can use their monetary policy autonomy to stabilize, by lowering their interest rate and/or allowing their currency to depreciate. Economists Julian di Giovanni and Jay Shambaugh looked at changes in base-country interest rates (say, the U.S. dollar or euro rates) and examined the correlation of these base interest rate changes with changes in GDP in a large sample of fixed and floating nonbase countries. The results, shown in Figure 8-7,

---

[12] See, for example, Eduardo Levy-Yeyati and Federico Sturzenegger, September 2003, "To Float or to Fix: Evidence on the Impact of Exchange Rate Regimes on Growth," *American Economic Review*, 93(4), 1173–1193; Kenneth Rogoff, Ashoka Mody, Nienke Oomes, Robin Brooks, and Aasim M. Husain, 2004, "Evolution and Performance of Exchange Rate Regimes," IMF Occasional Paper No. 229, International Monetary Fund.

FIGURE 8-7

Output Costs of Fixed Exchange Rates Recent empirical work finds that shocks which raise base country interest rates are associated with large output losses in countries that fix their currencies to the base, but not in countries that float. For example, as seen here, when a base country raises its interest rate by one percentage point, a country that floats experiences an average increase in its real GDP growth rate of 0.05% (not statistically significantly different from zero), whereas a country that fixes sees its real GDP growth rate slow on average by a significant 0.12%.

Source: Julian di Giovanni and Jay C. Shambaugh, 2008, "The Impact of Foreign Interest Rates on the Economy: The Role of the Exchange Rate Regime," Journal of International Economics, 74(2), 341–361. See Table 3.

clearly confirm the theory's predictions: when a base country hikes its interest rate, it spreads economic pain to those countries pegging to it, but not to the countries that are floating. These findings confirm that one cost of a fixed exchange rate regime is a more volatile level of output, a cost that is consistent with the theory we have developed. ∎

2 Other Benefits of Fixing

We began the chapter by emphasizing two key factors that influence the choice of fixed versus floating rate regimes: economic integration (market linkages) and economic similarity (symmetry of shocks). But other factors can play a role and in this section, we explore some other benefits of a fixed exchange rate regime, benefits that can be particularly important in emerging markets and developing countries.

Fiscal Discipline, Seigniorage, and Inflation

One common argument in favor of fixed exchange rate regimes in developing countries is that an exchange rate peg prevents the government from printing money to finance government expenditure. Under such a financing scheme, the central bank is called upon to *monetize* the government's deficit (i.e., give money to the government in exchange for debt). This process increases the money supply and leads to high inflation. The source of the government's revenue is, in effect, an inflation tax (called *seigniorage*) levied on the members of the public who hold money (see **Side Bar: The Inflation Tax**).

SIDE BAR

The Inflation Tax

How does the inflation tax work? Consider a situation in which a country with a floating exchange rate faces a constant budget deficit and is unable to finance this deficit through domestic or foreign borrowing. To cover the deficit, the treasury department calls on the central bank to "monetize" the deficit by purchasing an amount of government bonds equal to the deficit.

For simplicity, suppose output is fixed at Y, prices are completely flexible, and inflation and the nominal interest rate are constant. At any instant, money grows at a rate $\Delta M/M = \Delta P/P = \pi$, so the price level rises at a rate of inflation π equal to the rate of money growth. The Fisher effect tells us that the nominal interest rate is $i = r^* + \pi$, where r^* is the real world interest rate.

This ongoing inflation erodes the real value of money held by households. If a household holds M/P in real money balances, then a moment later when prices have increased by an amount $\Delta M/M = \Delta P/P = \pi$, a fraction π of the real value of the original M/P is lost to inflation. The cost of the inflation tax to the household is $\pi \times M/P$. For example, if I hold $100, the price level is currently 1, and inflation is 1%, then after one period the initial $100 is worth only $99 in real (inflation-adjusted) terms, and prices are 1.01.

What is the inflation tax worth to the government? It can spend the extra money printed ΔM to buy real goods and services worth $\Delta M/P = (\Delta M/M) \times (M/P) = \pi \times (M/P)$. For the preceding example, the money supply expands from $100 to $101, and this would provide financing worth $1 to the government. The real gain for the government equals the real loss to the households.

The amount that the inflation tax transfers from household to the government is called seigniorage, which can be written as

$$\underbrace{\text{Seigniorage}}_{\text{Inflation tax}} = \underbrace{\pi}_{\text{Tax rate}} \times \underbrace{\frac{M}{P}}_{\text{Tax base}} = \pi \times L(r^* + \pi)Y$$

The two terms are often viewed as the tax rate (here, inflation) and the tax base (the thing being taxed; here, money). The first term rises as inflation π rises, but the second term goes to zero as π gets large because if inflation becomes very high, people try to hold almost no money, and real money demand $L(r^* + \pi)Y$ falls to zero.

Because of these two offsetting effects, the inflation tax tends to hit diminishing returns as a source of real revenue: as inflation increases, the tax generates increasing real revenues at first, but eventually the rise in the first term is overwhelmed by the fall in the second term. Once a country is in a hyperinflation, the economy is usually well beyond the point at which real inflation tax revenues are maximized.

High inflation and hyperinflation (inflation in excess of 50% *per month*) are undesirable. If nothing else (such as fiscal discipline) can prevent them, a fixed exchange rate may start to look more attractive. Does a fixed exchange rate rule out inflationary finance and the abuse of seigniorage by the government? In principle, yes, but this anti-inflationary effect is not unique to a fixed exchange rate. As we saw in an earlier chapter on the monetary approach to exchange rates, any nominal anchor will have the same effect.

If a country's currency floats, its central bank can print a lot or a little money, with very different inflation outcomes. If a country's currency is pegged, the central bank might run the peg well, with fairly stable prices, or run the peg so badly that a crisis occurs, the exchange rate ends up in free fall, and inflation erupts.

Nominal anchors—whether money targets, exchange rate targets, or inflation targets—imply a "promise" by the government to ensure certain monetary policy outcomes in the long run. However, these promises do not guarantee that the country will achieve these outcomes. All policy announcements including a fixed exchange rate are to some extent "cheap talk." If pressure from the treasury to monetize deficits gets too strong, the commitment to any kind of anchor could fail.

The debate over whether fixed exchange rates improve inflation performance cannot be settled by theory alone—it is an empirical question. What has happened in reality? Table 8-1 lays out the evidence on the world inflation performance from 1970 to 1999. Average inflation rates are computed for all countries and for subgroups of countries:

TABLE 8-1

Inflation Performance and the Exchange Rate Regime Cross-country annual data from the period 1970 to 1999 can be used to explore the relationship, if any, between the exchange rate regime and the inflation performance of an economy. Floating is associated with slightly lower inflation in the world as a whole (9.9%) and in the advanced countries (3.5%) (columns 1 and 2). In emerging markets and developing countries, a fixed regime eventually delivers lower inflation outcomes, but not right away (columns 3 and 4).

	Annual Inflation Rate (%)			
Regime Type	World	Advanced Countries	Emerging Markets and Developing Countries	Emerging Markets and Developing Countries (Excluding the Year after a Regime Change)
Fixed	17.4%	4.8%	19.6%	8.8%
Limited flexibility	11.1	8.3	12.4	10.8
Managed floating	14.0	7.8	15.1	14.7
Freely floating	9.9	3.5	21.2	15.8
Freely falling	387.8	47.9	396.1	482.9

Source: Author's calculations based on the dataset from Kenneth Rogoff, Ashoka Mody, Nienke Oomes, Robin Brooks, and Aasim M. Husain, 2004, "Evolution and Performance of Exchange Rate Regimes," IMF Occasional Paper No. 229, International Monetary Fund.

advanced economies (rich countries), emerging markets (middle-income countries integrated in world capital markets), and developing countries (other countries).

For all countries (column 1), we can see that average inflation performance appears largely unrelated to the exchange rate regime, whether the choice is a peg (17.4%), limited flexibility (11.1%), managed floating (14.0%), or freely floating (9.9%). Only the "freely falling" has astronomical rates of inflation (387.8%). Similar results hold for the advanced countries (column 2) and for the emerging markets and developing countries (column 3). Although average inflation rates are higher in the latter sample, the first four regimes have fairly similar inflation rates, with fixed and freely floating almost indistinguishable.

We may conclude that as long as monetary policy is guided by *some* kind of nominal anchor, the particular choice of fixed and floating may not matter that much.[13] Possibly the only place where the old conventional wisdom remains intact is in the developing countries, where fixed exchange rates can help to deliver lower inflation rates after high inflations or hyperinflations. Why? In those situations, people may need to see the government tie its own hands in a very open and verifiable way for expectations of perpetually high inflation to be lowered, and a peg is one way to do that. This can be seen in Table 8-1, column 4. If we exclude the first year after a change in the exchange rate regime, we exclude chaotic periods after high inflations and hyperinflations when inflation (and inflationary expectations) may still persist even after the monetary and exchange rate policies have changed. We can then see that once things settle down in

---

[13] Kenneth Rogoff, Ashoka Mody, Nienke Oomes, Robin Brooks, and Aasim M. Husain, 2004, "Evolution and Performance of Exchange Rate Regimes," IMF Occasional Paper No. 229, International Monetary Fund.

years two and later, fixed exchange rates generally do deliver lower (single-digit) inflation rates than other regimes.

- The lesson: *it appears that fixed exchange rates are neither necessary nor sufficient to ensure good inflation performance in many countries. The main exception appears to be in developing countries beset by high inflation, where an exchange rate peg may be the only credible anchor.*

Liability Dollarization, National Wealth, and Contractionary Depreciations

As we learned in the balance of payments chapter, exchange rate changes can have a big effect on a nation's wealth. External assets and liabilities are never entirely denominated in local currency, so movements in the exchange rate can affect their value. For developing countries and emerging markets afflicted by the problem of *liability dollarization*, the wealth effects can be large and destabilizing, providing another argument for fixing the exchange rate, as we now show.

Suppose there are just two countries and two currencies, Home and Foreign. Home has external assets A_H denominated in Home currency (say, pesos) and A_F denominated in Foreign currency (say, U.S. dollars). Similarly, it has external liabilities L_H denominated in Home currency and L_F denominated in Foreign currency. The nominal exchange rate is E (with the units being Home currency per unit of Foreign currency—here, pesos per dollar).

The value of Home's dollar external assets and liabilities can be expressed in pesos as EA_F and EL_F, respectively, using an exchange rate conversion. Hence, the Home country's total external wealth is the sum total of assets minus liabilities expressed in local currency:

$$W = \underbrace{(A_H + EA_F)}_{\text{Assets}} - \underbrace{(L_H + EL_F)}_{\text{Liabilities}}$$

Now suppose there is a small change ΔE in the exchange rate, all else equal. This does not affect the values of A_H and L_H, but it *does* change the values of EA_F and EL_F expressed in pesos. We can express the resulting change in national wealth as

$$\Delta W = \underbrace{\Delta E}_{\substack{\text{Change in} \\ \text{exchange rate}}} \times \underbrace{[A_F - L_F]}_{\substack{\text{Net international} \\ \text{credit(+) or debit(−)} \\ \text{position in dollar assets}}} \quad (8\text{-}1)$$

The expression is intuitive and revealing. After a depreciation ($\Delta E > 0$), the wealth effect is positive if Foreign currency assets exceed Foreign currency liabilities (the net dollar position in brackets is positive) and negative if Foreign currency liabilities exceed Foreign currency assets (the net dollar position in brackets is negative).

For example, consider first the case in which Home experiences a 10% depreciation, with assets of $100 billion and liabilities of $100 billion. What happens to Home wealth if it has half or $50 billion of assets in dollars and no liabilities in dollars? It has a net credit position in dollars, so it ought to gain. Half of assets and all liabilities are expressed in pesos, so their value does not change. But the value of the half of assets denominated in dollars will rise in peso terms by 10% times $50 billion. In this case, a 10% depreciation increases national wealth by 5% or $5 billion because it increases the value of a net foreign currency credit position.

Now look at the case in which Home experiences a 10% depreciation, as in the preceding example, but now Home has zero assets in dollars and half or $50 billion of liabilities in dollars. All assets and half of liabilities are expressed in pesos, so their value does not change. But the value of the half of liabilities denominated in dollars will rise in peso terms by 10% times $50 billion. In this case, a depreciation decreases national wealth by 5% or $5 billion because it increases the value of a net foreign currency debit position.

Destabilizing Wealth Shocks Why do these wealth effects have implications for stabilization policy? In the previous chapter, we saw that nominal exchange rate depreciation can be used as a short-run stabilization tool in the IS-LM-FX model. In the face of an adverse demand shock in the Home country, for example, a depreciation will boost Home aggregate demand by switching expenditure toward Home goods. Now we can see that exchange rate movements might also affect aggregate demand by affecting wealth.

These impacts matter because it is easy to imagine more complex short-run models of the economy in which wealth affects the demand for goods. For example,

- Consumers might spend more when they have more wealth. In this case, the consumption function would become $C(Y - T,$ Total wealth$)$, and consumption would depend not just on after-tax income but also on wealth.

- Firms might find it easier to borrow if their wealth increases (e.g., wealth increases the net worth of firms, increasing the collateral available for loans). The investment function would then become $I(i,$ Total wealth$)$, and investment would depend on both the interest rate and wealth.

We can now begin to understand the importance of the exchange rate valuation effects summarized in Equation (8-1). This equation says that countries have to satisfy a very special condition to avoid changes in external wealth whenever the exchange rate moves: the value of their foreign currency external assets must exactly equal foreign currency liabilities. If foreign currency external assets do not equal foreign currency external liabilities, the country is said to have a *currency mismatch* on its external balance sheet, and exchange rate changes will affect national wealth.

If foreign currency assets exceed foreign currency liabilities, then the country experiences an increase in wealth when the exchange rate depreciates. From the point of view of stabilization, this is likely to be beneficial: additional wealth will complement the direct stimulus to aggregate demand caused by a depreciation, making the effect of the depreciation *even more* expansionary. This benign scenario applies to only a few countries, most notably the United States.

However, if foreign currency liabilities exceed foreign currency assets, then the country experiences a *decrease* in wealth when the exchange rate depreciates. From the point of view of stabilization policy, this wealth effect is unhelpful because the fall in wealth will tend to offset the conventional stimulus to aggregate demand caused by a depreciation. In principle, if the valuation effects are large enough, the overall effect of a depreciation can be contractionary! For example, while an interest rate cut might boost investment, and the ensuing depreciation might also boost the trade balance, such upward pressure on aggregate demand may well be offset partially or fully (or even outweighed) by adverse wealth changes that put downward pressure on demand.

We now see that if a country has an adverse (i.e., negative) net position in foreign currency assets, then the conventional arguments for stabilization policy (and the need for floating) are at best weak and at worst invalid. For many emerging market and developing economies, this is a serious problem. Most of these poorer countries are net debtors, so their external wealth shows a net debit position overall. But their net position in foreign currency is often just as much in debit, or even more so, because their liabilities are often close to 100% dollarized.

Evidence Based on Changes in Wealth When emerging markets experience large depreciations, they often suffer serious collapses in external wealth. To illustrate the severity of this problem, Figure 8-8 shows the impact of exchange rate valuation effects on wealth in eight countries. All the countries witnessed exchange rate crises during the period in which the domestic currency lost much of its value relative to the U.S. dollar. Following the 1997 Asian crisis, Korea, the Philippines, and Thailand saw their currencies depreciate by about 50%; Indonesia's currency depreciated by 75%. In 1999 the Brazilian real depreciated by almost 50%. In 2001 Turkey's lira depreciated suddenly by about 50%, after a long slide. And in Argentina, the peso depreciated by about 75% in 2002.

All of these countries also had a problem of liability dollarization, with large levels of currency mismatch. In the case of the Asian countries, they had borrowed a great deal in yen and U.S. dollars. In the cases of Turkey, Brazil, and Argentina, they had borrowed extensively in U.S. dollars. We would predict, therefore, that all the countries ought to have seen large declines in external wealth as a result of the valuation effects, and indeed this was the case. Countries such as Brazil and Korea escaped lightly, with wealth falling cumulatively by only 5% to 10% of GDP. Countries with larger exposure to foreign currency debt, or with larger depreciations, suffered much more: in Argentina, the Philippines, and Thailand, the losses were 20% to 30% of one year's GDP and in Indonesia almost 40% of one year's GDP.

Evidence Based on Output Contractions Figure 8-8 tells us that countries with large liability dollarization suffered large wealth effects. But do these wealth effects cause serious economic damage—serious enough to warrant consideration as a factor in exchange rate regime choice?

FIGURE 8-8

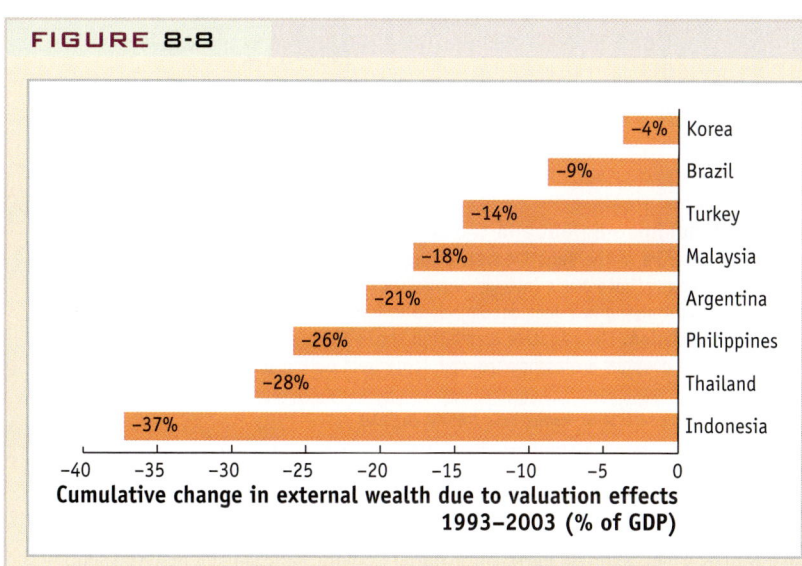

Exchange Rate Depreciations and Changes in Wealth These countries experienced crises and large depreciations of between 50% and 75% against the U.S. dollar and other major currencies from 1993 to 2003. Because large fractions of their external debt were denominated in foreign currencies, all suffered negative valuation effects causing their external wealth to fall, in some cases (such as Indonesia) quite dramatically.

Source: IMF, World Economic Outlook, April 2005, Figure 3.6.

Figure 8-9 suggests that wealth effects are associated with contractions and that the damage is fairly serious. Economists Michele Cavallo, Kate Kisselev, Fabrizio Perri, and Nouriel Roubini looked at the correlation between wealth losses on net foreign currency liabilities suffered during the large depreciations seen after an exchange rate crisis, and a measure of the subsequent fall in real output.[14] There is clearly a strong correlation. For example, after 1992 Britain barely suffered any negative wealth effect and, as we noted earlier, did rather well in its subsequent economic performance: Britain in 1992 sits in the upper left part of this scatterplot (very small wealth loss, no negative impact on GDP). At the other extreme sit cases like Indonesia, where liability dollarization led to massive wealth losses after the 1997 crisis: Indonesia in 1997 sits in the lower right part of this scatterplot (large wealth loss, large negative impact on GDP).

Original Sin Such findings have had a profound influence among professional international macroeconomists in recent years. Previously, external wealth effects were largely ignored and poorly understood. But now, especially after the adverse consequences of recent large depreciations, it is universally recognized that the problem of

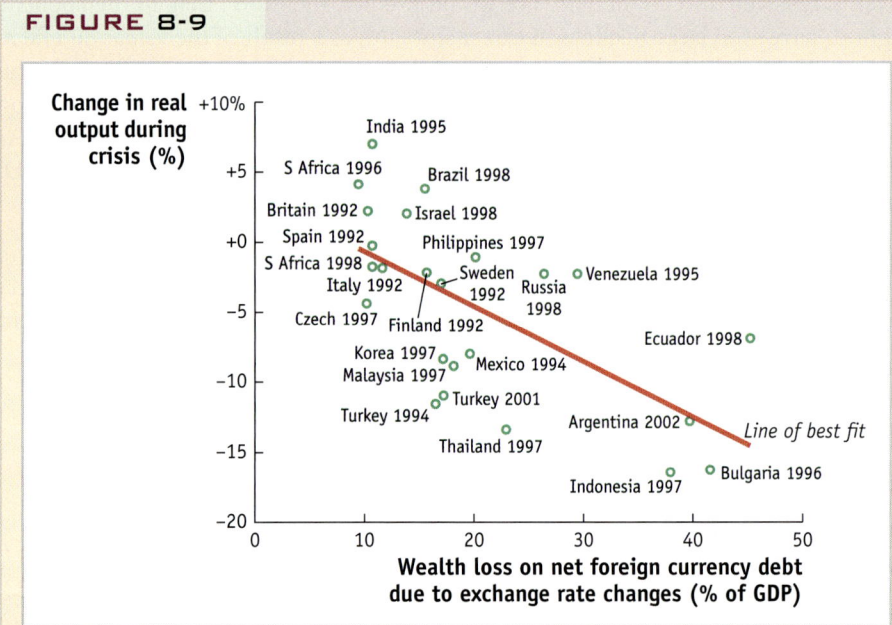

FIGURE 8-9

Foreign Currency Denominated Debt and the Costs of Crises This chart shows the correlation between a measure of the negative wealth impact of a real depreciation and the real output costs after an exchange rate crisis (a large depreciation). On the horizontal axis, the wealth impact is estimated by multiplying net debt denominated in foreign currency (as a fraction of GDP) by the size of the real depreciation. The negative correlation shows that larger losses on foreign currency debt due to exchange rate changes are associated with larger real output losses.

Source: Michele Cavallo, Kate Kisselev, Fabrizio Perri, and Nouriel Roubini, "Exchange Rate Overshooting and the Costs of Floating," Federal Reserve Bank of San Francisco Working Paper Series, Working Paper 2005-07, May 2005.

---

[14] Michele Cavallo, Kate Kisselev, Fabrizio Perri, and Nouriel Roubini, "Exchange Rate Overshooting and the Costs of Floating," Federal Reserve Bank of San Francisco Working Paper Series, Working Paper 2005-07, May 2005.

currency mismatch, driven by liability dollarization, plays a profound role in many developing countries and is a legitimate factor to be considered during any debate over the choice of exchange rate regime.

It is an old problem. In the long history of international investment, one remarkably constant feature has been the inability of most countries—especially poor countries on the periphery of global capital markets—to borrow from abroad in their own currencies. In the late nineteenth century, such countries had to borrow in gold, or in a "hard currency" such as British pounds or U.S. dollars. The same is true today, as is apparent from Table 8-2. In the world's financial centers and the Eurozone, only a small fraction of external liabilities are denominated in foreign currency. In other countries, the fraction is much higher; in developing countries, it is close to 100% on average.

Economists Barry Eichengreen, Ricardo Hausmann, and Ugo Panizza used the term "original sin" to refer to a country's inability to borrow in its own currency.[15] As the provocative name suggests, an historical perspective reveals that the "sin" is highly persistent and originates deep in a country's historical past. Countries that have a weak record of macroeconomic management—often due to institutional or political weakness—have in the past been unable to follow prudent monetary and fiscal policies. Domestic currency debts were frequently diluted in real value by periods of high inflation. Creditors were then unwilling to hold such debt, obstructing the development of a domestic currency bond market. Creditors were then willing to lend only in foreign currency, that is, to hold debt that promised a more stable long-term value.

Still, sinners can find redemption. Another view argues that the problem is one of global capital market failure: for many small countries, the pool of their domestic

TABLE 8-2

Measures of "Original Sin" Only a few developed countries can issue external liabilities denominated in their own currency. In the financial centers and the Eurozone, the fraction of external liabilities denominated in foreign currency is less than 10%. In the remaining developed countries, it averages about 70%. In developing countries, external liabilities denominated in foreign currency are close to 100% on average.

	External Liabilities Denominated in Foreign Currency (average, %)
Financial centers (United States, United Kingdom, Switzerland, Japan)	8%
Eurozone countries	9
Other developed countries	72
Eastern European countries	84
Middle East and African countries	90
Developing countries	93
Asia/Pacific countries	94
Latin American and Caribbean countries	100

Source: Barry Eichengreen, Ricardo Hausmann, and Ugo Panizza, "The Pain of Original Sin." In Barry Eichengreen and Ricardo Hausmann, eds., 2005, *Other People's Money: Debt Denomination and Financial Instability in Emerging-Market Economies* (Chicago: University of Chicago Press).

---

[15] Barry Eichengreen, Ricardo Hausmann, and Ugo Panizza, 2005, "The Pain of Original Sin." In Barry Eichengreen and Ricardo Hausmann, eds., *Other People's Money: Debt Denomination and Financial Instability in Emerging-Market Economies* (Chicago: University of Chicago Press).

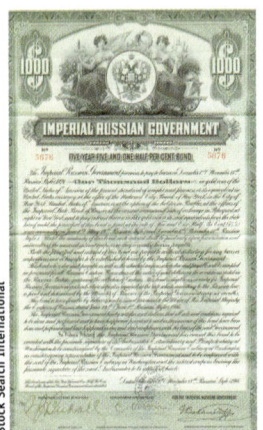

Two Russian bonds: a 100 ruble bond of 1915 and a 1,000 U.S. dollar bond of 1916. Creditors knew the dollar value of the ruble bond could be eroded by ruble depreciation. Only default could erode the value of the dollar bond.

currency liabilities may be too small to offer any significant risk diversification benefits to foreign investors. In this case, multinational institutions might step in to create markets for securities in the currencies of small countries, or in baskets of such currencies. An alternative view argues that as such countries reform—improve their institutional quality, design better policies, secure a low-inflation environment, and develop a better reputation—they will eventually free themselves from original sin and be able to issue external debt in their own currency. Many observers think this is already happening. Habitual "sinners" such as Mexico, Brazil, Colombia, and Uruguay have recently been able to issue some debt in their own currency. In addition, many countries are also reducing currency mismatch by piling up large stocks of foreign currency assets in central bank reserves and sovereign wealth funds. The recent trends indicate substantial progress in reducing this problem as compared with the 1990s.[16]

Yet any optimism must be tempered with caution. Only time will tell whether countries have really turned the corner and put their "sinful" ways behind them. Progress on domestic-currency borrowing is still very slow in many countries, and this still leaves the problem of mismatches in the private sector. While private sector exposure could be insured by the government, that insurance could, in turn, introduce the risk of abuse in the form of *moral hazard*, the risk that an insured entity (here, private borrowers) will engage in excessive risk taking, knowing that it will be bailed out if they incur losses. This could then create massive political problems, because it may not be clear who, in a crisis, would receive a public-sector rescue, and who would not. Why can't the private sector simply hedge all its exchange rate risk? This solution would be ideal, but in many emerging markets and developing countries, currency derivative markets are underdeveloped because many currencies cannot be hedged at all, and for others the markets are poorly developed, and the costs high.

If developing countries are unable to avoid currency mismatches, they must try to cope with them. One option is to reduce or stop external borrowing, but countries are not eager to forsake all borrowing in world capital markets. A more feasible—and perhaps only—alternative is for developing countries to minimize or eliminate valuation effects by limiting the movement of the exchange rate. This is indeed what we observe, and evidence shows that the larger a country's stock of foreign currency liabilities relative to GDP, the more likely that country is to peg its currency to the currency in which the external debt is issued.[17]

- The lesson: *in countries that cannot borrow in their own currency, floating exchange rates are less useful as a stabilization tool and may be destabilizing. This outcome applies particularly to developing countries, and these countries will prefer fixed exchange rates to floating exchange rates, all else equal.*

---

[16] Barry Eichengreen and Ricardo Hausmann, 2005, "Original Sin: The Road to Redemption." In Barry Eichengreen and Ricardo Hausmann, eds., *Other People's Money: Debt Denomination and Financial Instability in Emerging-Market Economies* (Chicago: University of Chicago Press); John D. Burger and Francis E. Warnock, 2003, "Diversification, Original Sin, and International Bond Portfolios," International Finance Discussion Papers 755, Board of Governors of the Federal Reserve System (U.S.); Camilo E. Tovar, 2005, "International Government Debt Denominated in Local Currency: Recent Developments in Latin America," *BIS Quarterly Review*, 109–118; Philip E. Lane and Jay C. Shambaugh, 2007, "Financial Exchange Rates and International Currency Exposures," NBER Working Paper No. 13433.

[17] Ricardo Hausmann, Ugo Panizza, and Ernesto Stein, 2001, "Why Do Countries Float the Way They Float?" *Journal of Development Economics*, 66(2), 387–414; Christopher M. Meissner and Nienke Oomes, 2006, "Why Do Countries Peg the Way They Peg? The Determinants of Anchor Currency Choice," Cambridge Working Papers in Economics 0643, Faculty of Economics, University of Cambridge.

Summary

We began the chapter by emphasizing the two key factors that influence the choice of fixed versus floating rate regimes: economic integration (market linkages) and economic similarity (symmetry of shocks). But we now see that many other factors can affect the benefits of fixing relative to floating.

A fixed exchange rate may have some additional benefits in some situations. It may be the only transparent and credible way to attain and maintain a nominal anchor—which may be particularly important in emerging markets and developing countries with weak institutions, a lack of central bank independence, strong temptations to use the inflation tax, and poor reputations for monetary stability. A fixed exchange rate may also be the only way to avoid large fluctuations in external wealth, which can be a problem in emerging markets and developing countries with high levels of liability dollarization. These may be powerful additional reasons to fix, and they seem to apply with extra force in developing countries. Therefore, such countries may be less willing to allow their exchange rates to float—a situation that some economists describe as a **fear of floating.**

To illustrate the influence of additional costs and benefits in our graphical representation, consider a Home country thinking of pegging to the U.S. dollar as a base currency. Such a Home country with a fear of floating would perceive additional benefits to a fixed exchange rate. So it would be willing to peg its exchange at lower levels of integration and similarity. We would represent this as in Figure 8-10 by an inward shift of the FIX line from FIX_1 to FIX_2. Without fear of floating, based on FIX_1, the Home country would float with symmetry-integration measures given by points 1 and 2, and fix at point 3. But if it had fear of floating, based on FIX_2, it would elect to fix at point 2 because the extra benefits of a fixed rate lower the threshold.

FIGURE 8-10

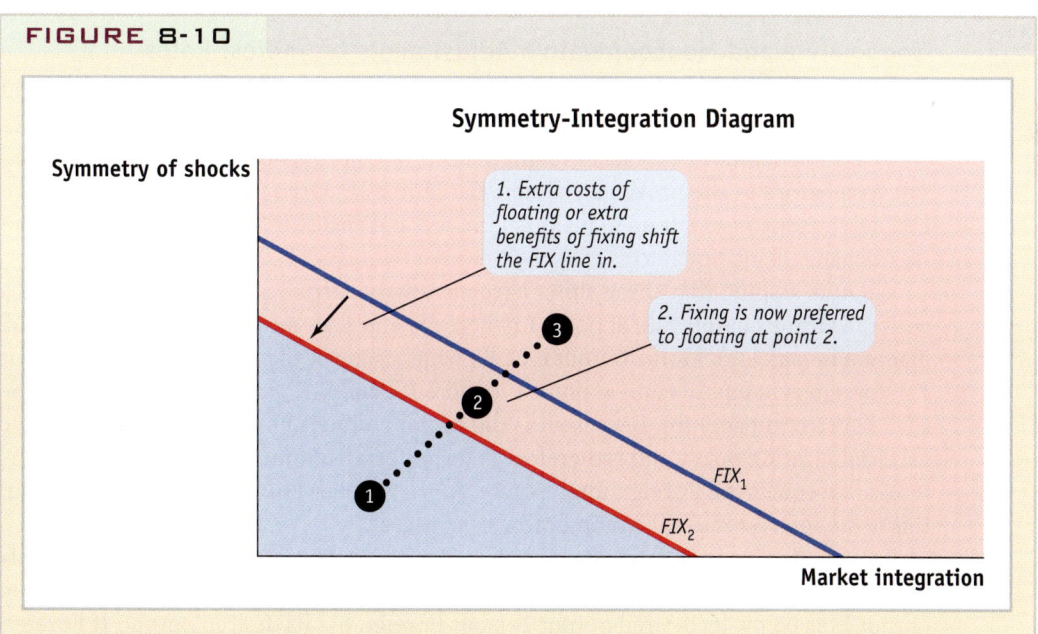

A Shift in the FIX Line Additional benefits of fixing or higher costs of floating will lower the threshold for choosing a fixed exchange rate. The FIX line moves down. Choosing a fixed rate now makes sense, even at lower levels of symmetry or integration (e.g., at point 2).

3 Fixed Exchange Rate Systems

To provide a foundation, our discussion so far has considered only the simplest type of fixed exchange rate: a single home country that unilaterally pegs to a foreign base country. In reality there are more complex arrangements, called **fixed exchange rate systems,** which involve multiple countries. Examples include the global *Bretton Woods system* in the 1950s and 1960s and the European *Exchange Rate Mechanism* (ERM) through which all potential euro members must pass.

These systems were based on a **reserve currency system** in which there are N countries $(1, 2, \ldots, N)$ participating. One of the countries, the center country (the Nth country), provides the reserve currency, which is the base or center currency to which all the other countries peg. In the Bretton Woods system, for example, N was the U.S. dollar; in the ERM, N was the German mark until 1999, and is now the euro.

Throughout this chapter, we have assumed that a country pegs unilaterally to a center country, and we know that this leads to a fundamental asymmetry. The center country has monetary policy autonomy and can set its own interest rate i^* as it pleases. The other noncenter country, which is pegging, then has to adjust its own interest rate so that i equals i^* in order to maintain the peg. The noncenter country loses its ability to conduct stabilization policy, but the center country keeps that power. The asymmetry can be a recipe for political conflict and is known as the *Nth currency problem.*

Are these problems serious? And is there a better arrangement that can be devised? In this section, we show that **cooperative arrangements** may be the answer. We study two kinds of cooperation. One form of cooperation is based on mutual agreement and compromise between center and noncenter countries on the setting of interest rates. The other form of cooperation is based on mutual agreements about adjustments to the levels of the fixed exchange rates themselves.

Cooperative and Noncooperative Adjustments to Interest Rates

Figure 8-11, panel (a), illustrates the possibility of policy conflict between center and noncenter countries. Suppose that Home, which is the noncenter country, experiences an adverse demand shock, but Foreign, the center country, does not. We have studied this case before in the previous chapter: the Home IS curve shifts left and the Home LM curve then must shift up to maintain the peg and ensure that the Home interest rate i is unchanged and equal to i^*.

We now assume that these shifts have already occurred, and we start the analysis with the Home equilibrium at point 1 (where IS_1 and LM_1 intersect) in Home's IS-LM diagram in panel (a). Home output is at Y_1, which is lower than Home's desired output Y_0. Foreign is in equilibrium at point 1' (where IS_1^* and LM_1^* intersect) in Foreign's IS-LM diagram in panel (b). Because it is the center country, Foreign is assumed to have used stabilization policy and is therefore at its preferred output level Y_0^*. The Home interest rate equals the Foreign interest rate, $i_1 = i_1^*$, because Home is pegged to Foreign; this is the interest rate shown on both vertical axes.

Because this is a unilateral peg, only Foreign, the center country, has monetary policy autonomy and the freedom to set nominal interest rates. Home is in recession (its output Y_1 is below its desired output Y_0), but Foreign has its desired output. If Foreign makes no policy concession to help Home out of its recession, this would be the noncooperative outcome. There would be no burden sharing between the two countries: Home is the only country to suffer.

FIGURE 8-11

Cooperative and Noncooperative Interest Rate Policies by the Center Country In panel (a), the noncenter home country is initially in equilibrium at point 1 with output at Y_1, which is lower than desired output Y_0. In panel (b), the center foreign country is in equilibrium at its desired output level Y_0^* at point 1'. Home and foreign interest rates are equal, $i_1 = i_1^*$, and home is unilaterally pegged to foreign. Foreign has monetary policy autonomy. If the center country makes no policy concession, this is the noncooperative outcome.

With cooperation, the foreign country can make a policy concession and lower its interest rate and home can do the same and maintain the peg. Lower interest rates in the other country shift each country's IS curve in, but the easing of monetary policy in both countries shifts each country's LM curve down. The net effect is to boost output in both countries. The new equilibria at points 2 and 2' lie to the right of points 1 and 1'. Under this cooperative outcome, the foreign center country accepts a rise in output away from its desired level, from Y_0^* to Y_2^*. Meanwhile, home output gets closer to its desired level, rising from Y_1 to Y_2.

Now suppose we shift to a cooperative outcome in which the center country makes a policy concession. How? Suppose Foreign lowers its interest rate from to $i_1^* = i_2^*$. Home can now do the same, and indeed must do so to maintain the peg. How do the IS curves shift? A lower Foreign interest rate implies that, *all else equal,* Home demand is lower, so the Home IS curve shifts in to IS_2; similarly, in panel (b), a lower Home interest rate implies that, *all else equal,* Foreign demand is lower, so the Foreign IS^* curve shifts in to IS_2^* in panel (b). However, the easing of monetary policy in both countries means that the LM curves shift down in both countries to LM_2 and LM_2^*.

What is the net result of all these shifts? To figure out the extent of the shift in the IS curve, we can think back to the Keynesian cross and the elements of demand that underlie points on the IS curve. The peg is being maintained. Because the nominal exchange rate is unchanged, the real exchange rate is unchanged, so neither country sees a shift in its Keynesian cross demand curve due to a change in the trade balance. But both countries do see a rise in the Keynesian cross demand curve, as investment demand rises thanks to lower interest rates. The rise in demand tells us that new equilibrium points 2 and 2' lie to the right of points 1 and 1': even though the IS curves have shifted in, the downward shifts in the LM curves dominate, and so output in each country will rise in equilibrium.

Compared with the noncooperative equilibrium outcome at points 1 and 1′, Foreign now accepts a rise in output away from its preferred stable level, as output booms from Y_0^* to Y_2^*. Meanwhile, Home is still in recession, but the recession is not as deep, and output is at a level Y_2 that is higher than Y_1. In the noncooperative case, Foreign achieves its ideal output level and Home suffers a deep recession. In the cooperative case, Foreign suffers a slightly higher output level than it would like and Home suffers a slightly lower output level than it would like. The burden of the adverse shock to Home has been shared with Foreign.

Caveats Why would Home and Foreign agree to a cooperative arrangement in the first place? Cooperation might be possible in principle if neither country wants to suffer too much exchange rate volatility against the other—that is, if they are *close* to wanting to be in a fixed arrangement but neither wants to unilaterally peg to the other. A unilateral peg by either country gives all the benefits of fixing to both countries but imposes a stability cost on the noncenter country alone. If neither country is willing to pay that price, there can be no unilateral peg by either country. They could simply float, but they would then lose the efficiency gains from fixing. But if they can somehow set up a peg with a system of policy cooperation, then they could achieve a lower instability burden than under a unilateral peg and this benefit could tip the scales enough to allow the gains from fixing to materialize for both countries.

Cooperation sounds great on paper. But the historical record casts doubt on the ability of countries to even get as far as announcing cooperation on fixed rates, let alone actually backing that up with true cooperative behavior. Indeed, it is rare to see credible cooperative announcements under *floating* rates, where much less is at stake. Why?

A major problem is that, at any given time, the shocks that hit a group of economies are typically asymmetric. A country at its ideal output level not suffering a shock may be unwilling to change its monetary policies just to help out a neighbor suffering a shock and keep a peg going. In theory, cooperation rests on the idea that my shock today could be your shock tomorrow, and we can all do better if we even out the burdens with the understanding that they will "average out" in the long run. But policy makers have to be able to make credible long-run commitments to make this work and suffer short-run pain for long-run gain. History shows that these abilities are often sadly lacking: short-sighted political goals commonly trump longer-term economic considerations.

For example, consider the European Exchange Rate Mechanism (ERM), which was effectively a set of unilateral pegs to the German mark. The ERM was very clearly built around the idea of safeguarding gains from trade in Europe through fixed rates, but the designers knew that it had to incorporate some burden-sharing measures to ensure that the burden of absorbing shocks didn't fall on every country but Germany. The measures proved inadequate, however, and in the crisis of 1992 the German Bundesbank ignored pleas from Italy, Britain, and other countries for an easing of German monetary policy as recessions took hold in the bloc of countries pegging to the German mark. When the test of cooperation came along, Germany wanted to stabilize Germany's output, not anybody else's. Thus, even in a group of countries as geographically and politically united as the European Union, it was tremendously difficult to make this kind of cooperation work. (This problem was alleviated by true monetary union, with the arrival of the euro and the creation of the European Central Bank.)

The main conclusion is that, in practice, the center country in a reserve currency system has tremendous autonomy, which it may be unwilling to give up lightly, thus making cooperative outcomes hard to achieve consistently.

Cooperative and Noncooperative Adjustments to Exchange Rates

We have studied interest rate cooperation. Is there scope for cooperation in other ways? Yes. Countries may decide to adjust the level of the fixed exchange rate. Such an adjustment is (supposedly) a "one-shot" jump or change in the exchange rate at a particular time, which for now we assume to be unanticipated by investors. Apart from that single jump, at all times before and after the change, the exchange rate is left fixed and Home and Foreign interest rates remain equal.

Suppose a country that was previously pegging at a rate $\overline{E}_1$ announces that it will henceforth peg at a different rate, $\overline{E}_2 \neq \overline{E}_1$. By definition, if $\overline{E}_2 > \overline{E}_1$, there is a **devaluation** of the home currency; if $\overline{E}_2 < \overline{E}_1$, there is a **revaluation** of the home currency.

These terms are similar to the terms "depreciation" and "appreciation," which also describe exchange rate changes. Strictly speaking, the terms "devaluation" and "revaluation" should be used only when pegs are being adjusted; "depreciation" and "appreciation" should be used to describe exchange rates that float up or down. Note, however, that these terms are often used loosely and interchangeably.

A framework for understanding peg adjustment is shown in Figure 8-12. We assume now that both Home and Foreign are noncenter countries in a pegged exchange rate system and that each is pegged to a third center currency, say, the U.S. dollar.

(Why this change in the setup compared with the last section? Interest rate adjustment required us to study moves by the center country to help noncenter countries; with exchange rate adjustment, it is only noncenter countries who change their exchange rates vis-à-vis the center, so in this problem our focus shifts mostly away from the center country.)

We assume that the center (the United States) is a large country with monetary policy autonomy that has set its interest rate at $i_\$$. Home is pegged to the U.S. dollar at $\overline{E}_{\text{home}/\$}$ and Foreign is pegged at $\overline{E}^*_{\text{foreign}/\$}$. In Home's IS-LM diagram in panel (a), equilibrium is initially at point 1 (where IS_1 and LM_1 intersect). Again, due to a prior adverse demand shock, Home output is at Y_1 and is lower than Home's desired output Y_0. In Foreign's IS-LM diagram in panel (b), equilibrium is at Foreign's desired output level Y^*_0 at point 1' (where IS^*_1 and LM^*_1 intersect). Because Home and Foreign peg to the center currency (here, the U.S. dollar), Home and Foreign interest rates equal the dollar interest rate, $i_1 = i^*_1 = i_\$$.

Now suppose that in a cooperative arrangement, Home devalues against the dollar (and against Foreign) and maintains a peg at a new, higher exchange rate. That is, there is an unanticipated rise $\overline{E}_{\text{home}/\$}$. The Home and Foreign interest rates remain equal to the dollar interest rate, $i_1 = i^*_1 = i_\$$, because both countries still peg. We can think back to the IS-LM model, or back to the Keynesian cross that we used to construct the IS curve, if necessary, to figure out the impact of the change. Because the nominal depreciation by Home is also a real depreciation, Home sees demand increase: the Home IS curve shifts out to IS_2. Furthermore, the real depreciation for Home is also a real appreciation for Foreign, so Foreign demand *decreases*: the IS^* curve shifts in to IS^*_2. The outcome is cooperative because the burden of the adverse demand shock is being shared: Home output at Y_2 is lower than the ideal Y_0 but not as low as at Y_1; and Foreign has accepted output lower at Y^*_2 than its ideal Y^*_0.

Why might this kind of cooperation work? Home and Foreign could agree that Home would devalue a little (but not too much) so that both countries would jointly feel the pain. Some other time, when Foreign has a nasty shock, Home would "repay" by feeling some of Foreign's pain.

FIGURE 8-12

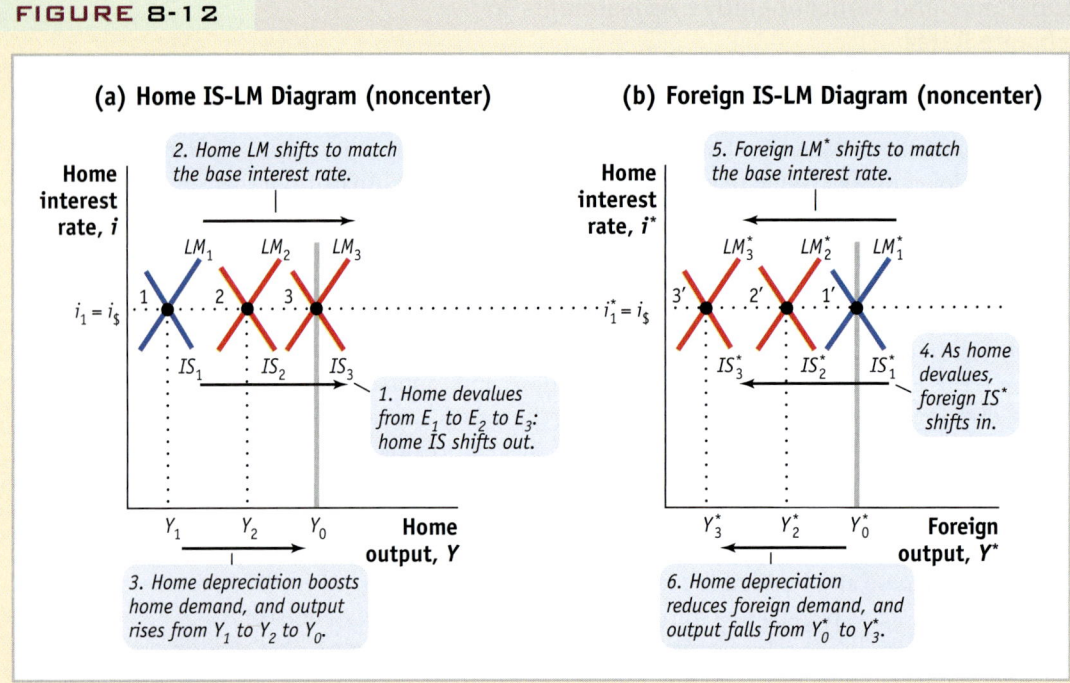

Cooperative and Noncooperative Exchange Rate Adjustments by Noncenter Countries In panel (a), the noncenter home country is initially in equilibrium at point 1 with output at Y_1, which is lower than desired output Y_0. In panel (b), the noncenter foreign country is in equilibrium at its desired output level Y_0^* at point 1'. Home and foreign interest rates are equal to the base (dollar) interest rate and to each other, $i_1 = i_1^* = i_\$^*$, and home and foreign are unilaterally pegged to the base.

With cooperation, home devalues slightly against the dollar (and against foreign) and maintains a peg at a higher exchange rate. The home interest and foreign interest rates remain the same. But the home real depreciation causes home demand to increase: IS shifts out to IS_2. This is also a foreign real appreciation, so foreign demand decreases: IS^* shifts in to IS_2^*. Under this cooperative outcome at points 2 and 2', foreign accepts a fall in output away from its desired level, from Y_0^* to Y_2^*. Meanwhile, home output gets closer to its desired level, rising from Y_1 to Y_2.

With noncooperation, home devalues more aggressively against the dollar. After a large home real depreciation, IS shifts out to IS_3 and IS^* shifts in to IS_3^*. Under this noncooperative outcome at points 3 and 3', home gets its desired output Y_0 by "exporting" the recession to foreign, where output falls all the way to Y_3^*.

Now suppose we shift to a noncooperative outcome in which Home devalues more aggressively against the dollar. After a large real depreciation by Home, Home demand is greatly boosted, and the Home IS curve shifts out a long way to IS_3. Home's real depreciation is also a large real appreciation for Foreign, where demand is greatly reduced, so the Foreign IS^* curve shifts in a long way to IS_3^*. The outcome is noncooperative: Home now gets its preferred outcome with output at its ideal level Y_0; it achieves this by "exporting" the recession to Foreign, where output falls all the way to Y_3^*.

There are two qualifications to this analysis. First, we have only considered a situation in which Home wishes to devalue to offset a negative demand shock. But the same logic applies when Home's economy is "overheating" and policy makers fear that output is above the ideal level, perhaps creating a risk of inflationary pressures. In that case, Home may wish to revalue its currency and export the overheating to Foreign.

Second, we have not considered the center country, here the United States. In reality, the center country also suffers some decrease in demand if Home devalues because the center will experience a real appreciation against Home. However, there is less to worry about in this instance: because the United States is the center country, it has policy autonomy, and can always use stabilization policy to boost demand. Thus, there may be a monetary easing in the center country, a secondary effect that we do not consider here.

Caveats We can now see that adjusting the peg is a policy that may be cooperative or noncooperative in nature. If noncooperative, it is usually referred to as a **beggar-thy-neighbor policy:** Home can improve its position at the expense of Foreign and without Foreign's agreement. When Home is in recession, and its policy makers choose a devaluation and real depreciation, they are engineering a diversion of some of world demand toward Home goods and away from the rest of the world's goods.

This finding brings us to the main drawback of admitting noncooperative adjustments into a fixed exchange rate system. Two can play this game! If Home engages in such a policy, it is possible for Foreign to respond with a devaluation of its own in a tit-for-tat way. Down that road lies exchange rate mayhem, and the pretense of a fixed exchange rate system is over. The countries will no longer be pegging and will be playing a new noncooperative game against each other with floating exchange rates.

Cooperation may be most needed to sustain a fixed exchange rate system with adjustable pegs, so as to restrain beggar-thy-neighbor devaluations. But can it work? Consider continental Europe since World War II, under both the Bretton Woods system and the later European systems such as ERM (which predated the euro). A persistent concern of European policy makers in this period was the threat of beggar-thy-neighbor devaluations. For example, the British pound and the Italian lira devalued against the dollar and later the German mark on numerous occasions from the 1960s to the 1990s. Although some of these peg adjustments had the veneer of official multilateral decisions, some (like the 1992 ERM crisis) occurred when cooperation broke down.

APPLICATION

The Gold Standard

Our analysis in this section has focused on the problems of policy conflict in a reserve currency system in which there is one center country issuing a currency (e.g., the dollar or euro) to which all other noncenter countries peg. As we know from Figure 8-1, this is an apt description of most fixed exchange rate arrangements at the present time and going back as far as World War II. A key issue in such systems is the asymmetry between the center country, which retains monetary autonomy, and the noncenter countries, which forsake it.

Are there symmetric fixed exchange rate systems, in which there is no center country and the asymmetry created by the Nth currency problem can be avoided? In theory the ERM system worked this way before the advent of the euro in 1999, but, as the 1992 crisis showed, there was, in practice, a marked asymmetry between Germany and the other ERM countries. Historically, the only true symmetric systems have been those in which countries fixed the value of their currency relative to some commodity. The most famous and important of these systems was the gold standard, and this system had no center country because countries did not peg the exchange rate at $\overline{E}$, the local currency price of some base currency, but instead they pegged at $\overline{P}_g$, the local currency price of gold.

How did this system work? Under the gold standard, gold and money were seamlessly interchangeable, and the combined value of gold and money in the hands of the public was the relevant measure of money supply (M). For example, consider two countries,

The U.S. gold parity was $20.67 per troy ounce from 1834 to 1933, so a $20 gold coin like this 1907 Saint Gaudens Double Eagle contained 20/20.67 = 0.9675 ounces of gold.

Britain pegging to gold at $\overline{P}_g$ (pounds per ounce of gold) and France pegging to gold at $\overline{P}_g^*$ (francs per ounce of gold). Under this system, one pound cost $1/\overline{P}_g$ ounces of gold, and each ounce of gold cost $\overline{P}_g$ francs, according to the fixed gold prices set by the central banks in each country. Thus, one pound cost $E_{par} = \overline{P}_g^*/\overline{P}_g$ francs, and this ratio defined the *par* exchange rate implied by the gold prices in each country.

The gold standard rested on the principle of free convertibility. This meant that central banks in both countries stood ready to buy and sell gold in exchange for paper money at these mint prices, and the export and import of gold were unrestricted. This allowed arbitrage forces to stabilize the system. How?

Suppose the market exchange rate in Paris (the price of one pound in francs) was E francs per pound and deviated from the par level, with $E < E_{par}$ francs per pound. This would create an arbitrage opportunity. The franc has appreciated relative to pounds, and arbitrageurs could change 1 ounce of gold into $\overline{P}_g^*$ francs at the central bank, and then into $\overline{P}_g^*/E$ pounds in the market, which could be shipped to London and converted into $\overline{P}_g^*/(E\overline{P}_g)$ ounces of gold, which could then be brought back to Paris. Because we assumed that $E < E_{par}$, $\overline{P}_g^*/(E\overline{P}_g) = E_{par}/E > 1$, and the trader ends up with more than an ounce of gold and makes a profit.

As a result of this trade, gold would leave Britain and the British money supply would fall (pounds would be redeemed at the Bank of England by the French traders, who would export the gold back to France). As gold entered France, the French money supply would expand (because the traders could leave it in gold form, or freely change it into franc notes at the Banque de France).

We can note how the result tends to stabilize the foreign exchange market (just as interest arbitrage did in the chapters on exchange rates). Here, the pound was depreciated relative to par and the arbitrage mechanism caused the British money supply to contract and the French money supply to expand. The arbitrage mechanism depended on French investors buying "cheap" pounds. This would bid up the price of pounds in Paris, so E would rise toward E_{par}, stabilizing the exchange rate at its par level.

Four observations are worth noting. First, the process of arbitrage was not really costless, so if the exchange rate deviated only slightly from parity, the profit from arbitrage might be zero or negative (i.e., a loss). Thus, there was a small band around the par rate in which the exchange rate might fluctuate without any arbitrage occurring. However, this band, delineated by limits known as the upper and lower "gold points," was typically small, permitting perhaps at most ±1% fluctuations in E on either side of E_{par}. The exchange rate was, therefore, very stable. For example, from 1879 to 1914, when Britain and the United States were pegged to gold at a par rate of $4.86 per pound, the daily dollar-pound market exchange rate in New York was within 1% of its par value 99.97% of the time (and within half a percent 77% of the time).[18]

Second, in our example we examined arbitrage in only one direction, but, naturally, there would have been a similar profitable arbitrage opportunity—subject to transaction costs—in the opposite direction if E had been above E_{par} and the franc had been depreciated relative to parity. (Working out how one makes a profit in that case, and what the net effect would be on each country's money supply, is left as an exercise.)

Third, gold arbitrage would enforce a fixed exchange rate at E_{par} (plus or minus small deviations within the gold points), thus setting expected depreciation to zero.

---

[18] Eugene Canjels, Gauri Prakash-Canjels, and Alan M. Taylor, 2004, "Measuring Market Integration: Foreign Exchange Arbitrage and the Gold Standard, 1879–1913," *Review of Economics and Statistics*, 86(4), 868–882.

Interest arbitrage between the two countries' money markets would equalize the interest rates in each country (subject to risk premiums). So our earlier approach to the study of fixed exchange rates remains valid, including a central principle, the trilemma.

Fourth, and most important, we see the inherent symmetry of the gold standard system when operated according to these principles. Both countries share in the adjustment mechanism, with the money supply contracting in the gold outflow country (here, Britain) and the money supply expanding in the gold inflow country (here, France). In theory, if these principles were adhered to, neither country has the privileged position of being able to not change its monetary policy, in marked contrast to a center country in a reserve currency system. But in reality, the gold standard did not always operate quite so smoothly, as we see in the next section. ■

4 International Monetary Experience

A vast diversity of exchange rate arrangements have been used throughout history. In the chapter that introduced exchange rates, we saw how different countries fix or float at present; at the start of this chapter, we saw how exchange rate arrangements have fluctuated over more than a century. These observations motivated us to study how countries choose to fix or float.

To try to better understand the international monetary experience and how we got to where we are today, we now apply what we have learned in the book so far.[19] In particular, we rely on the trilemma, which tells us that countries cannot simultaneously meet the three policy goals of a fixed exchange rate, capital mobility, and monetary policy autonomy. With the feasible policy choices thus set out, we draw on the ideas of this chapter about the costs and benefits of fixed and floating regimes to try to understand why various countries have made the choices they have at different times.

The Rise and Fall of the Gold Standard

As we saw in Figure 8-1, the history of international monetary arrangements from 1870 to 1939 was dominated by one story: the rise and fall of the gold standard regime. In 1870 about 15% of countries were on gold, rising to about 70% in 1913 and almost 90% during a brief period of resumption in the 1920s. But by 1939, only about 25% of the world was pegged to gold. What happened? The analysis in this chapter provides insights into one of the grand narratives of economic history.[20]

The period from 1870 to 1914 was the first era of globalization, with increasingly large flows of trade, capital, and people between countries. Depending on the countries in question, some of these developments were attributable to technological developments in transport and communications (such as steamships, the telegraph, etc.); some were a result of policy change (such as tariff reductions). Our model suggests that as the volume of trade and other economic transactions between nations increase, there will be more to gain from adopting a fixed exchange rate (as in Figure 8-4).

---

[19] Barry Eichengreen, 1996, *Globalizing Capital: A History of the International Monetary System* (Princeton, NJ: Princeton University Press); Maurice Obstfeld and Alan M. Taylor, 2004, *Global Capital Markets: Integration, Crisis, and Growth* (Cambridge: Cambridge University Press).
[20] Lawrence Officer, October 1, 2001, "Gold Standard," *EH.Net Encyclopedia*, edited by Robert Whaples, http://eh.net/encyclopedia/article/officer.gold.standard.

Thus, as nineteenth-century globalization proceeded, it is likely that more countries crossed the FIX line and met the economic criteria for fixing.

There were also other forces at work encouraging a switch to the gold peg before 1914. The stabilization costs of pegging were either seen as insignificant—because the pace of economic growth was not that unstable—or else politically irrelevant—because the majority of those adversely affected by business cycles and unemployment were from the mostly disenfranchised working classes. With the exception of some emerging markets, price stability was the major goal and the inflation tax was not seen as useful except in emergencies.

As for the question, why peg to gold? (as opposed to silver, or something else), note that once a gold peg became established in a few countries, the benefits of adoption in other countries would increase further. If you are the second country to go on the gold standard, it lowers your trade costs with one other country; if you are the 10th or 20th country to go on, it lowers your trade costs with 10 or 20 other countries; and so on. This can be thought of as a "snowball effect" (a *network externality*, as economists say), where only one standard can dominate in the end.[21]

This is not to say that all was plain sailing before 1914. Many countries joined gold, only to leave temporarily due to a crisis. Even in countries that stayed on gold, not everyone loved the gold standard. The benefits were often less palpable than the costs, particularly in times of deflation or in recessions. For example, in the United States, prices and output stagnated in the 1890s, drawing support to populists who wanted to leave the gold standard and escape its monetary strictures. The tensions reached a head in 1896 at the Democratic Convention in Chicago, when presidential candidate William Jennings Bryan ended his speech saying: "Having behind us the producing masses of this nation and the world, supported by the commercial interests, the laboring interests and the toilers everywhere, we will answer their demand for a gold standard by saying to them: You shall not press down upon the brow of labor this crown of thorns, you shall not crucify mankind upon a cross of gold." (Bryan lost, the pro-gold McKinley became president, the Gold Standard Act of 1900 was passed to bury any doubts, and tensions defused as economic growth and gold discoveries raised output and prices.)

These trends were upset by World War I. For belligerent countries, the war required financing. The inflation tax was heavily used, and this implied exit from the gold standard. In addition, once a war began in Europe (and later drew in the United States), the majority of global trade was affected by conflict: trade was almost 100% wiped out between belligerents, and fell by 50% between belligerents and neutrals. This effect persisted long after the war ended, and it was exacerbated by protectionism (higher tariffs and quotas) in the 1920s. By the 1930s, world trade had fallen to close to half of its 1914 level. All of these developments meant that the rationale for fixing based on gains from trade was being weakened.[22]

Bryan's "cross of gold."

---

[21] Christopher M. Meissner, 2005, "A New World Order: Explaining the International Diffusion of the Gold Standard, 1870–1913," *Journal of International Economics*, 66(2), 385–406.

[22] Reuven Glick and Alan M. Taylor, 2010, "Collateral Damage: Trade Disruption and the Economic Impact of War," *Review of Economics and Statistics*, 92(1), 102–127; Antoni Estevadeordal, Brian Frantz, and Alan M. Taylor, 2003, "The Rise and Fall of World Trade, 1870–1939," *Quarterly Journal of Economics*, 118(2), 359–407.

Then, from 1929 on, the Great Depression undermined the stability argument for pegging to gold. The 1920s and 1930s featured much more violent economic fluctuations than had been seen prior to 1914, raising the costs of pegging. Moreover, politically speaking, these costs could no longer be ignored. The rise of labor movements and political parties of the left started to give voice and electoral weight to constituencies that cared much more about the instability costs of a fixed exchange rate.[23]

Other factors also played a role. The Great Depression was accompanied by severe deflation, so to stay on gold might have risked further deflation given the slow growth of gold supplies to which all money supplies were linked. Deflation linked to inadequate gold supplies therefore undermined the usefulness of gold as a nominal anchor.[24] Many countries had followed beggar-thy-neighbor policies in the 1920s, choosing to re-peg their currencies to gold at devalued rates, making further devaluations tempting. Among developing countries, many economies were in recession before 1929 because of poor conditions in commodity markets, so they had another reason to devalue (as some did as early as 1929). The war had also left gold reserves distributed in a highly asymmetric fashion, leaving some countries with few reserves for intervention to support their pegs; as backup, many countries now used major currencies as reserves, too, but the value of these reserves depended on everyone else's commitment to the gold peg, a commitment that was increasingly questionable.

All of these weaknesses undermined the confidence and credibility of the commitment to gold pegs in many countries, making the collapse of the pegs more likely. Currency traders would then speculate against various currencies, raising the risk of a crisis. In the face of such speculation, in 1931 both Germany and Austria imposed capital controls, and Britain floated the pound against gold. The gold standard system then unraveled in a largely uncoordinated, uncooperative, and destructive fashion.

In the language of the trilemma, with its three solutions or "corners," the 1930s saw a movement by policy makers away from the "open capital market/fixed exchange rate" corner, and the other two corners came to dominate. Countries unwilling to close their capital markets by imposing controls opted to abandon the gold peg and moved to the open capital market/floating exchange rate solution, allowing them to regain monetary policy autonomy: Britain and the United States among others made this choice. Countries willing to adopt capital controls but unwilling to suffer the volatility of a floating rate moved to the "closed capital market/fixed exchange rate" solution, allowing them to regain monetary policy autonomy in a different way: Germany and many countries in South America made this choice. Gaining monetary autonomy gave all of these countries the freedom to pursue more expansionary monetary policies to try to revive their economies, and most of them did just that. Finally, a few countries remained on the gold standard and did not devalue or impose controls, in part because they were not forced off gold (they had large reserves) and in part because they were worried about the inflationary consequences of floating. France was such a country. Countries that stuck with the gold standard paid a heavy price: compared with 1929, countries that floated had 26% higher output in 1935, and countries that

---

[23] Barry Eichengreen, 1992, *Golden Fetters: The Gold Standard and the Great Depression* (New York: Oxford University Press).
[24] World gold production more or less kept pace with output growth in the nineteenth century, but output grew much faster than gold stocks in the twentieth century. If gold gets scarcer, its relative price must rise. But if the money price of gold is pegged, the only way for the relative price of gold to rise is for all other prices to fall—that is, by economy-wide price deflation.

adopted capital controls had 21% higher output, as compared with the countries that stayed on gold.[25]

Figure 8-13 shows these outcomes diagrammatically. To sum up: although many other factors were important, trade gains and an absence of (or political indifference to) stability costs helped bring the gold standard into being before 1914; reduced trade gains and stability costs that were higher (or more politically relevant) help explain the ultimate demise of the gold standard in the interwar period.

Bretton Woods to the Present

The international monetary system of the 1930s was utterly chaotic. Near the end of World War II, allied economic policy makers gathered in the United States, at Bretton Woods, New Hampshire, to try to ensure that the postwar economy fared better. The architects of the postwar order, notably Harry Dexter White and John Maynard Keynes, constructed a system that preserved one key tenet of the gold standard regime—by keeping fixed rates—but discarded the other by imposing capital controls.

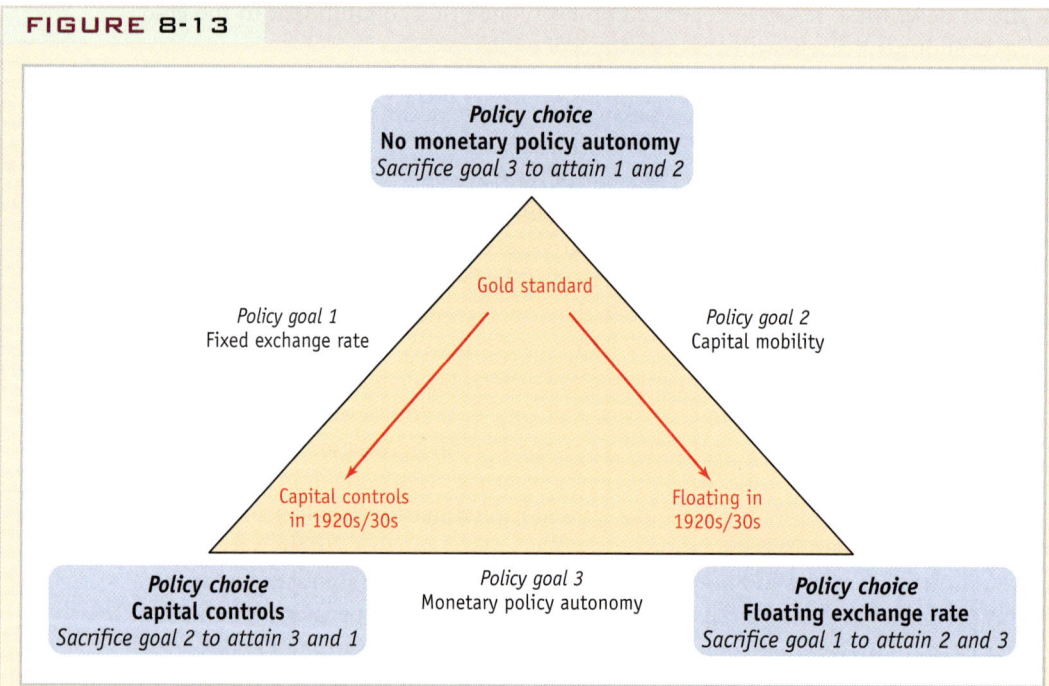

FIGURE 8-13

Solutions to the Trilemma before and after World War I Each corner of the triangle represents a viable policy choice. The labels on the two adjacent edges of the triangle are the goals that can be attained; the label on the opposite edge is the goal that has to be sacrificed. Trade gains and an absence of (or political indifference to) stability costs help explain how the gold standard came into being before 1914 (top corner). Subsequently, reduced trade gains and higher actual (or politically relevant) stability costs help explain the ultimate demise of the gold standard in the 1920s and 1930s. Countries sought new solutions to the trilemma to achieve policy autonomy, either by floating (bottom right corner) or by adopting capital controls (bottom left corner).

---

[25] Maurice Obstfeld and Alan M. Taylor, 2004, *Global Capital Markets: Integration, Crisis, and Growth* (Cambridge: Cambridge University Press). The output cost estimates are from page 143.

The trilemma was resolved in favor of exchange rate stability to encourage the rebuilding of trade in the postwar period. Countries would peg to the U.S. dollar; this made the U.S. dollar the center currency and the United States the center country. The U.S. dollar was, in turn, pegged to gold at a fixed price, a last vestige of the gold standard.

In Figure 8-14, the postwar period starts with the world firmly in the "closed capital market/fixed exchange rate" corner on the left. At Bretton Woods, the interests of international finance were seemingly dismissed, amid disdain for the speculators who had destabilized the gold standard in the 1920s and 1930s: U.S. Treasury Secretary Henry Morgenthau pronounced that the new institutions would "drive . . . the usurious money lenders from the temple of international finance." At the time, only the United States allowed full freedom of international capital movement, but this was soon to change.

It was obvious that to have trade one needed to have payments, so some kind of system for credit was needed, at least on a short-term basis. By the late 1950s, after getting by with half measures, many countries in Europe and elsewhere were ready to liberalize financial transactions related to current account transactions to free up the trade and payments system. At the same time, they sought to limit speculative financial transactions that were purely asset trades within the financial account (e.g., interest arbitrage by forex traders).

FIGURE 8-14

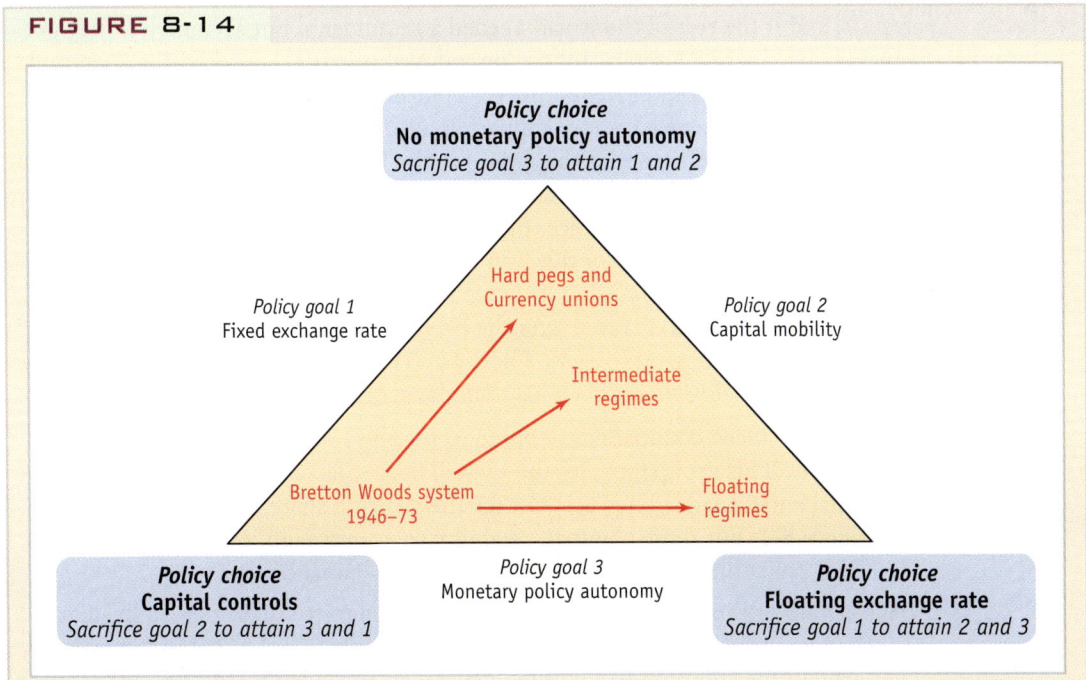

Solutions to the Trilemma since World War II In the 1960s, the Bretton Woods system became unsustainable because capital mobility could not be contained. Thus, countries could no longer have fixed rates and monetary autonomy (bottom left corner). In the advanced countries, the trilemma was resolved by a shift to floating rates, which preserved autonomy and allowed for the present era of capital mobility (bottom right corner). The main exception was the currency union of the Eurozone. In developing countries and emerging markets, the "fear of floating" was stronger; when capital markets were opened, monetary policy autonomy was more often sacrificed and fixed exchange rates were maintained (top corner).

Unfortunately, in practice it proved difficult then (and has proved so ever since) to put watertight controls on financial transactions. Controls in the 1960s were very leaky and investors found ways to circumvent them and move money offshore from local currency deposits into foreign currency deposits. Some used accounting tricks such as over- or underinvoicing trade transactions to move money from one currency to another. Others took advantage of the largely unregulated offshore currency markets that had emerged in London and elsewhere in the late 1950s.

As capital mobility grew and controls failed to hold, the trilemma tells us that countries pegged to the dollar stood to lose their monetary policy autonomy. This was already a reason for them to think about exiting the dollar peg. With autonomy evaporating, the devaluation option came to be seen as the most important way of achieving policy compromise in a "fixed but adjustable" system. But increasingly frequent devaluations (and some revaluations) undermined the notion of a truly fixed rate system, made it more unstable, generated beggar-thy-neighbor policies, and—if anticipated—encouraged speculators.

The downsides became more and more apparent as the 1960s went on. Other factors included a growing unwillingness in many countries to peg to the U.S. dollar, after inflation in the Vietnam War era undermined the dollar's previously strong claim to be the best nominal anchor currency. It was also believed that this inflation would eventually conflict with the goal of fixing the dollar price of gold and that the United States would eventually abandon its commitment to convert dollars into gold, which happened in August 1971. By then it had become clear that U.S. policy was geared to U.S. interests, and if the rest of the world needed a reminder about asymmetry, they got it from U.S. Treasury Secretary John Connally, who in 1971 uttered the memorable words, "The dollar is our currency, but it's your problem."

Figure 8-14 tells us what must happen in an international monetary system once capital mobility reasserts itself, as happened to the Bretton Woods system in the 1960s. The "closed capital market/fixed exchange rate" corner on the left is no longer an option. Countries must make a choice: they can stay fixed and have no monetary autonomy (move to the top corner), or they can float and recover monetary autonomy (move to the right corner).

These choices came to the fore after the Bretton Woods system collapsed from 1971 to 1973. How did the world react? There have been a variety of outcomes, and the tools developed in this chapter help us to understand them:

- Most advanced countries have opted to float and preserve monetary policy autonomy. This group includes the United States, Japan, United Kingdom, Australia, and Canada. They account for the growing share of floating regimes in Figure 8-1. For these countries, stability costs outweigh integration benefits. They are at the bottom right corner of the trilemma diagram.

- A group of European countries instead decided to try to preserve a fixed exchange rate system among themselves, first via the ERM and now "irrevocably" through the adoption of a common currency, the euro. Integration gains in the closely integrated European market might, in part, explain this choice. This group of countries is at the top corner of the trilemma diagram.

- Some developing countries have maintained capital controls, but many of them (especially the emerging markets) have opened their capital markets. Given the "fear of floating" phenomenon, their desire to choose fixed rates (and sacrifice monetary autonomy) is much stronger than in the advanced countries, all else equal. These countries are also at the top corner of the trilemma diagram.

- Some countries, both developed and developing, have camped in the middle ground: they have attempted to maintain intermediate regimes, such as "dirty floats" or pegs with "limited flexibility." India is often considered to be a case of an intermediate regime somewhere between floating or fixed. Such countries are somewhere in the middle on the right side of the trilemma diagram.

- Finally, some countries still impose some capital controls rather than embrace globalization. China has been in this position, although change is afoot. These countries, mostly developing countries, are clinging to the bottom left corner of the trilemma diagram.

5 Conclusions

Exchange rate regimes have varied greatly across countries and across time and continue to do so. Explaining why this is the case, and figuring out the optimal choice of exchange rate regime, are major tasks in international macroeconomics.

We began this chapter by studying the main costs and benefits of fixed versus floating regimes. Fixing enhances the economic efficiency of international transactions. Floating allows authorities to stabilize an economy with monetary policy. The clash between these two goals creates a trade-off. Only with enough economic integration (more gains on transactions) and sufficiently symmetric shocks (less need for policy autonomy) do fixed exchange rates make sense, as shown in the symmetry-integration diagram.

However, other factors also affect the trade-off, especially in emerging markets and developing countries: fixed exchange rates may provide the only credible nominal anchor after a high inflation, and they insulate countries with net foreign currency debt from the adverse wealth effects of depreciations.

Finally, we examined exchange rate systems in theory and in practice. Over the years, fixed rate systems such as the gold standard and the Bretton Woods system have come and gone, with collapses driven, at least in part, by failures of cooperation. That leaves us today with no real international monetary "system" at all, but rather many countries, and occasionally groups of countries, pursuing their own interests and trying to make the best choice of regime given their particular circumstances. As this chapter has shown, there may be good reasons why "one size fits all" will never apply to exchange rate regimes.

KEY POINTS

1. A wide variety of exchange rate regimes have been in operation throughout history to the present.

2. The benefits for the home country from a fixed exchange rate include lower transaction costs and increased trade, investment, and migration with the base or center country.

3. The costs to the home country from a fixed exchange rate arise primarily when the two countries experience different economic shocks and home would want to pursue monetary policies different from those of the base or center country.

4. The costs and benefits of fixing can be summed up on a symmetry-integration diagram. At high levels of symmetry and/or integration, above the FIX line, it makes sense to fix. At low levels of symmetry and/or integration, below the FIX line, it makes sense to float.

5. A fixed rate may confer extra benefits if it is the only viable nominal anchor in a high-inflation country and if it prevents adverse wealth shocks caused by depreciation in countries suffering from a currency mismatch.

6. Using these tools and the trilemma, we can better understand exchange rate regime choices in the past and in the present. Before 1914 it appears the gold standard did promote integration, and political concern for the loss of stabilization policies was limited. In the 1920s and 1930s, increased isolationism, economic instability, and political realignments undermined the gold standard. After 1945 and up to the late 1960s, the Bretton Woods system of fixed dollar exchange rates was feasible, with strict controls on capital mobility, and was attractive as long as U.S. policies were not at odds with the rest of the world. Since 1973 different countries and groups of countries have gone their own way, and exchange rate regimes reflect the sovereign choice of each country.

KEY TERMS

gold standard, p. 303
base currency, p. 306
center currency, p. 306
asymmetric shock, p. 311
symmetry-integration diagram, p. 312
fear of floating, p. 327
fixed exchange rate systems, p. 328
reserve currency system, p. 328
cooperative arrangements, p. 328
devaluation, p. 331
revaluation, p. 331
beggar-thy-neighbor policy, p. 333

PROBLEMS

1. Using the IS-LM-FX model, illustrate how each of the following scenarios affects the home country. Compare the outcomes when the home country has a fixed exchange rate with the outcomes when the home currency floats.
   a. The foreign country increases the money supply.
   b. The home country cuts taxes.
   c. Investors expect a future appreciation in the home currency.

2. The Lithuanian lita is currently pegged to the euro. Using the IS-LM-FX model for Home (Lithuania) and Foreign (Eurozone), illustrate how each of the following scenarios affect Lithuania:
   a. The Eurozone reduces its money supply.
   b. Lithuania cuts government spending to reduce its budget deficit.
   c. The Eurozone countries increase their taxes.

3. Consider two countries that are currently pegged to the euro: Latvia and Comoros. Latvia is a member of the European Union, allowing it to trade freely with other EU countries. Exports to the Eurozone account for the majority of Latvia's outbound trade, which mainly consists of manufacturing goods, services, and wood. In contrast, Comoros is an archipelago of islands off the eastern coast of southern Africa that exports food commodities primarily to the United States and France. Comoros historically maintained a peg with the French franc, switching to the euro when France joined the Eurozone. Compare and contrast Latvia and Comoros in terms of their likely degree of integration symmetry with the Eurozone. Plot Comoros and Latvia on a symmetry-integration diagram as in Figure 8-4.

4. Use the symmetry-integration diagram as in Figure 8-4 to explore the evolution of international monetary regimes from 1870 to 1939—that is, during the rise and fall of the gold standard.
   a. From 1870 to 1913, world trade flows doubled in size relative to GDP, from about 10% to 20%. Many economic historians

believe this was driven by exogenous declines in transaction costs, some of which were caused by changes in transport technology. How would you depict this shift for a pair of countries in the symmetry-integration diagram that started off just below the FIX line in 1870? Use the letter A to label your starting point in 1870 and use B to label the end point in 1913.

b. From 1913 to 1939, world trade flows collapsed, falling in half relative to GDP, from about 20% back to 10%. Many economic historians think this was driven by exogenous increases in transaction costs from rising transport costs and increases in tariffs and quotas. How would you depict this shift for a pair of countries in the symmetry-integration diagram that started off just above the FIX line in 1913? Use the letter B to label your starting point in 1913 and use C to label the end point in 1939.

c. Other economic historians contend that these changes in transaction costs arose endogenously. When countries went on the gold standard, they lowered their transaction costs and boosted trade. When they left gold, costs increased. If this is true, then do points A, B, and C represent unique solutions to the problem of choosing an exchange rate regime?

d. Changes in other factors in the 1920s and 1930s had an impact on the sustainability of the gold standard. These included the following:
   i. An increase in country-specific shocks
   ii. An increase in democracy
   iii. Growth of world output relative to the supply of gold

   In each case, explain why these changes might have undermined commitment to the gold standard.

5. Many countries experiencing high and rising inflation, or even hyperinflation, will adopt a fixed exchange rate regime. Discuss the potential costs and benefits of a fixed exchange rate regime in this case. Comment on fiscal discipline, seigniorage, and expected future inflation.

6. In the late 1970s, several countries in Latin America, notably Mexico, Brazil, and Argentina, had accumulated large external debt burdens. A significant share of this debt was denominated in U.S. dollars. The United States pursued contractionary monetary policy from 1979 to 1982, raising dollar interest rates. How would this affect the value of the Latin American currencies relative to the U.S. dollar? How would this affect their external debt in local currency terms? If these countries had wanted to prevent a change in their external debt, what would have been the appropriate policy response, and what would be the drawbacks?

7. Home's currency is the peso and trades at 1 peso per dollar. Home has external assets of $200 billion, all of which are denominated in dollars. It has external liabilities of $400 billion, 75% of which are denominated in dollars.

   a. Is Home a net creditor or debtor? What is Home's external wealth?
   b. What is Home's net position in dollar-denominated assets?
   c. If the peso depreciates to 1.2 pesos per dollar, what is the change in Home's external wealth in pesos?

8. Evaluate the empirical evidence on how currency depreciation affects wealth and output across countries. How does the decision of maintaining a fixed versus floating exchange rate regime depend on a country's external wealth position?

9. Home signs a free-trade agreement with Foreign, which lowers tariffs and other barriers to trade. Both countries are very similar in terms of economic shocks, as they each produce very similar goods. Use a symmetry-integration diagram as in Figure 8-4 as part of your answer to the following questions:

   a. Initially, trade rises. Does the rise in trade make Home more or less likely to peg its currency to the Foreign currency? Why?
   b. In the longer run, freer trade causes the countries to follow their comparative advantage and specialize in producing very different types of goods. Does the rise in specialization make Home more or less likely to peg its currency to the Foreign currency? Why?

NETWORK

Visit the International Monetary Fund's website (http://www.imf.org) and locate the latest classification of exchange rate regimes in all countries around the world. How many countries are fixing and how many are floating?

Find the photo of the $20 gold coin on page 580 and the specifications in its caption. Calculate the U.S. dollar price of 1 ounce of gold under the pre-1913 gold standard. Now use the Internet to find details, including gold content, of a British gold sovereign coin worth £1 in the same era. Calculate the British pound price of 1 ounce of gold under the pre-1913 gold standard. Now compute the implied pound-dollar exchange rate. Check your answer against the value given in the text.

9
Exchange Rate Crises: How Pegs Work and How They Break

1 Facts About Exchange Rate Crises

2 How Pegs Work: The Mechanics of a Fixed Exchange Rate

3 How Pegs Break I: Inconsistent Fiscal Policies

4 How Pegs Break II: Contingent Monetary Policies

5 Conclusions

Global capital markets pose the same kinds of problems that jet planes do. They are faster, more comfortable, and they get you where you are going better. But the crashes are much more spectacular.
Lawrence Summers, U.S. Secretary of the Treasury, 1999

Either extreme: a fixed exchange rate through a currency board, but no central bank, or a central bank plus truly floating exchange rates; either of those is a tenable arrangement. But a pegged exchange rate with a central bank is a recipe for trouble.
Milton Friedman, Nobel laureate, 1998

In the last chapter, we treated the question "fixed or floating?" as a one-time problem of exchange rate regime choice. We implicitly assumed that, once that choice was made, either option would be a stable and sustainable regime.

Unfortunately, the reality is different. The typical fixed exchange rate succeeds for a few years, only to break. A recent study found that the average duration of any peg was about five years, and the median duration was only two years.[1] When the break occurs, there is often a large and sudden depreciation and burdensome economic and political costs can result. Such a collapse is known as an *exchange rate crisis*. Understanding the causes and consequences of exchange rate crises is a major goal of international macroeconomics because of the damage they do, not only to the country in which the crisis occurs but often to its neighbors and trading partners.

---

[1] Michael W. Klein and Jay C. Shambaugh, 2006, "The Nature of Exchange Rate Regimes," NBER Working Paper No. 12729. Since 1970, with the exception of some peculiar countries (the few destined to join the euro, oil exporters like Saudi Arabia and Bahrain, and tiny microstates like Bhutan and Kiribati), only a handful of pegs have lasted longer than a decade, and only one, Hong Kong's peg to the U.S. dollar, was still surviving. See also Maurice Obstfeld and Kenneth Rogoff, 1995, "The Mirage of Fixed Exchange Rates," *Journal of Economic Perspectives*, 9(4), 73–96.

Still, despite the fragility exposed by these recurrent crises, fixed exchange rate arrangements are not extinct. Typically, after a crisis, a country that prefers to have a fixed exchange rate will try to peg again. Yet there is an important asymmetry in regime changes: the shift from floating to fixed is generally smooth and planned, but the shift from fixed to floating is typically unplanned and catastrophic. Crises imply that there is one additional and significant cost associated with fixing.

1 Facts about Exchange Rate Crises

To understand the importance of exchange rate crises, we spend a few moments examining what crises look like and the costs associated with them.

What Is an Exchange Rate Crisis?

A simple definition of an **exchange rate crisis** would be a "big" depreciation.[2] But how big is big enough to qualify as a crisis? In practice, in an advanced country, a 10% to 15% depreciation might be considered large. In emerging markets, the bar might be set higher, say, 20% to 25%.[3] Examples of such crises are shown in Figure 9-1.

Panel (a) shows the depreciation of six European currencies against the German mark after 1992. Four currencies (the escudo, lira, peseta, and pound) were part of the European Exchange Rate Mechanism (ERM); the other two (the markka and krona) were not in the ERM but were pegging to the German mark. All six currencies lost 15% to 25% of their value against the mark within a year.

In panel (b), we see the depreciation of seven emerging market currencies against the U.S. dollar in various crises that occurred from 1994 to 2002. These depreciations, while also very rapid, were much larger than those in panel (a). These currencies lost 50% to 75% of their value against the dollar in the year following the crisis.

The figure illustrates two important points. First, exchange rate crises can occur in advanced countries as well as in emerging markets and developing countries. Second, the magnitude of the crisis, as measured by the subsequent depreciation of the currency, is often much greater in emerging markets and developing countries.

How Costly Are Exchange Rate Crises?

A mass of evidence has accumulated concerning the potentially damaging effects of exchange rate crises. The economic costs are often large, and the political costs can be even more dramatic (see **Side Bar: The Political Costs of Crises**).

---

[2] We focus on crises thus defined, when the peg actually breaks and there is a sizable depreciation. However, economists sometimes use a broader concept of a *currency crisis* based on other criteria such as reserve losses. See Barry Eichengreen, Andrew K. Rose, and Charles Wyplosz, 1995, "Exchange Market Mayhem: The Antecedents and Aftermath of Speculative Attacks," *Economic Policy*, 10(21), 249–312.

[3] One widely used definition requires at least a 25% depreciation in one year to be sure that such a depreciation is beyond the limits of even a wide band, and a rate of depreciation that is at least 10% higher than in the previous year to ensure that the depreciation is not just part of a broken crawl. Jeffrey A. Frankel and Andrew K. Rose, 1996, "Currency Crashes in Emerging Markets: An Empirical Treatment," *Journal of International Economics*, 41(3-4), 351–366.

FIGURE 9-1

Currency Crashes In recent years, developed and developing countries have experienced exchange rate crises. Panel (a) shows depreciations of six European currencies after crises in 1992. Panel (b) shows depreciations of seven emerging market currencies after crises between 1994 and 2002.

Sources: Global Financial Data; econstats.com.

Some evidence of this sort is presented in Figure 9-2. Annual rates of growth of GDP in years close to crises were compared with growth in other (i.e., "normal") years to obtain a measure of how growth differs during crisis periods. The figure shows that just before a crisis all countries have economic growth that is between 0.5% and 1.0% below that in normal years.

After a typical crisis, advanced countries and emerging markets react differently. In advanced countries, growth accelerates and is above normal by the second and third years after the crisis. Advanced countries tend to bounce back.

Emerging markets do not bounce back, and growth usually plummets: it is 2.5% to 3% below normal in the year of the crisis and the two subsequent years, and is still

FIGURE 9-2

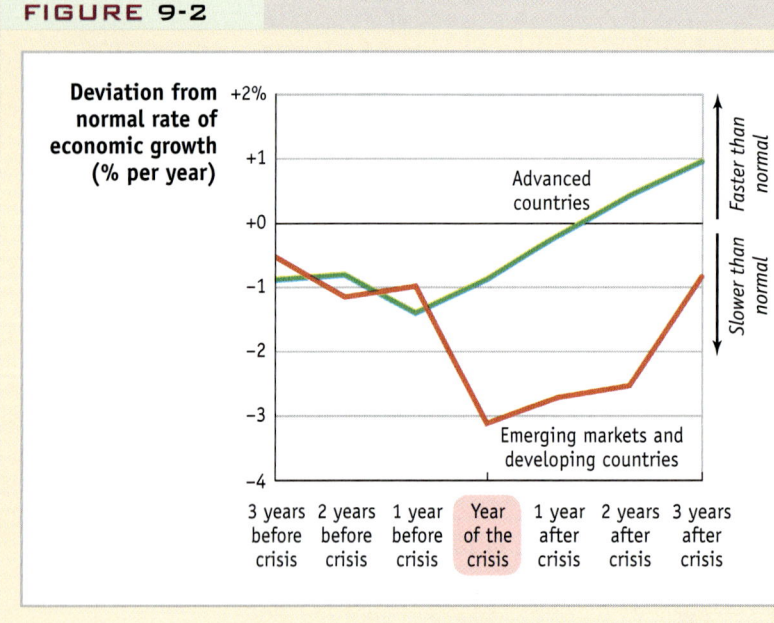

The Economic Costs of Crises

Exchange rate crises can impose large economic costs on a country. After a crisis, growth rates in emerging markets and developing countries are, on average, two to three percentage points lower than normal, an effect that persists for about three years. In advanced countries, a depreciation is typically expansionary, and growth is, on average, faster just after the crisis than it was just before.

Source: Maurice Obstfeld and Alan M. Taylor, 2004, Global Capital Markets: Integration, Crisis and Growth (New York: Cambridge University Press).

1% below normal in the third year. All those reductions in growth add up to about a 10% decline in GDP relative to its typical trend three years after the crisis—a major recession.[4]

The major downturns in emerging markets have serious economic and social consequences. For example, in the aftermath of the Argentina crisis of 2001 to 2002, news reports were filled with shocking tales of unemployment, financial ruin, rising poverty, hunger, and deprivation. After the Asian crisis of 1997, the recoveries were a little faster, but the economic misfortunes were still deep and painful.

Causes: Other Economic Crises Why are exchange rate crises sometimes so damaging? Drawing new lessons from the crises of the 1990s, economists now recognize that exchange rate crises usually go hand in hand with other types of economically harmful financial crises, especially in emerging markets. In the private sector, if banks and other financial institutions face adverse shocks, they may become insolvent, causing them to close or declare bankruptcy: This is known as a **banking crisis.** In the public sector, if the government faces adverse shocks, it may default and be unable or unwilling to pay the principal or interest on its debts: this is known as a *sovereign debt crisis* or **default crisis.** Both banking and default crises can have damaging effects on the economy because they disrupt the flow of credit within and between countries. (In a later chapter, we examine default crises in more detail, including their links to banking and exchange rate crises.)

---

[4] If we were to cumulate these effects over the 7-year time span, we would deduce that advanced countries typically witness a cycle in which they fall perhaps at most 3% below their normal real growth trend but then recover, whereas emerging markets and developing countries typically suffer a deep downturn, with output at times more than 10% below its normal trend and permanently lower.

SIDE BAR

The Political Costs of Crises

Exchange rate crises don't simply have economic consequences—they often have political consequences, too. Figure 9-3 shows that exchange rate crises are often followed by personnel changes at the central bank or finance ministry and not infrequently by a change at the top as well.

At first, this result might seem implausible. As the economist Jeffrey Frankel said, speaking of the Indonesian crisis of 1997: "What is it about devaluation that carries such big political costs? How is it that a strong ruler like Indonesia's Suharto can easily weather 32 years of political, military, ethnic, and environmental challenges, only to succumb to a currency crisis?"*

In emerging markets, we know that the economic costs of exchange rate crises can be large, which helps explain how a Suharto could be undermined. There are many other examples: the Radical Party is the oldest political party in Argentina, but after the exchange rate crisis in 2001 to 2002 under the leadership of President Fernando de la Rúa and Economy Minister Domingo Cavallo, the party faced extinction, polling just 2.3% in the 2003 presidential election.**

Still, why do exchange rate crises carry large political costs in advanced countries where the exit from an exchange rate peg often allows for a depreciation and favorable growth performance? A pertinent example is the decision by Britain's Conservative government to exit the ERM on "Black Wednesday," September 16, 1992. Chancellor Norman Lamont left his job within a year, and Prime Minister John Major tasted defeat at the next general election in 1997, despite faster economic growth after 1992.

Before the crises: Domingo Cavallo, Fernando de la Rúa, Norman Lamont, David Cameron.

The legacy of "Black Wednesday" haunted the Conservatives for years. On the bellwether question of economic competence, the polls gave the new Labour government and its longtime chancellor, Gordon Brown, a massive lead for many years: this was a vital issue of trust that helped keep Labour in power for so long. It was not until 2010 that the Conservatives regained power, under their fifth leader in 13 years, David Cameron (who had been a junior minister working under Lamont at the Treasury on that fateful day in 1992).

Even when a depreciation turns out to be good for the economy, the collapse of a peg typically destroys the reputations of politicians and policy makers for credibility and competence. Regaining the trust of the people can take a very long time.

---

* Jeffrey A. Frankel, "Mundell-Fleming Lecture: Contractionary Currency Crashes in Developing Countries," *IMF Staff Papers*, 52(2), 149–192.

** Cavallo had previously served the rival Peronist Party as economy minister in the Menem administration and had presided over the creation of the fixed exchange rate regime, as well as its collapse.

FIGURE 9-3

Probability of change (%)
- In a normal 12-month period
- In a 12-month period following an exchange rate crisis

Change in head of government: 21% / 29%
Change in Finance Minister and/or Central Bank Governor: 36% / 58%

The Political Costs of Crises

Exchange rate crises usually impose large political costs on those in power. Compared with what is likely to happen during normal, noncrisis times, it is 22% more likely that one of the two main officials with economic responsibilities (the finance minister and central bank governor) will be out of a job the year following a crisis. It is also 9% more likely that the head of government (such as a president, prime minister, or premier) will have to depart for one reason or another.

Note: Data on heads of government are from 1971 to 2003, and data on finance ministers and central bank governors are from 1995 to 1999.

Source: Jeffrey A. Frankel, 2005, "Mundell-Fleming Lecture: Contractionary Currency Crashes in Developing Countries," *IMF Staff Papers*, 52(2), 149–192.

International macroeconomists thus have three crisis types to consider: exchange rate crises, banking crises, and default crises. Evidence shows they are likely to occur simultaneously:

- *The likelihood of a banking or default crisis increases significantly when a country is having an exchange rate crisis.* One study found that the probability of a banking crisis was 1.6 times higher during an exchange rate crisis (16% versus 10% on average). Another study found that the probability of a default crisis was more than 3 times higher during an exchange rate crisis (39% versus 12% on average).[5] Explanations for these impacts focus on valuation effects. As we saw in the last chapter, a big depreciation causes a sudden increase in the local currency value of dollar debts (principal and interest). Because this change in value can raise debt burdens to intolerable levels, it should come as no surprise that exchange rate crises are frequently accompanied by financial distress in both private and public sectors.

- *The likelihood of an exchange rate crisis increases significantly when a country is having a banking or default crisis.* The same two studies just noted found that the probability of an exchange rate crisis was 1.5 times higher during a banking crisis (46% versus 29% on average). The probability of an exchange rate crisis was more than 5 times higher during a default crisis (84% versus 17% on average).

  Explanations for these reverse effects center on the issuance of money by the central bank to bail out banks and governments. Banking crises can be horrendously costly. For example, as seen in Table 9-1, one study found that the fiscal costs of fixing a damaged banking sector (e.g., through the bailout and recapitalization of insolvent institutions) exceeded 25% of GDP in 10 cases and was at least 10% of GDP in another 17 cases. If a country is having a banking crisis, the central bank will be under pressure to extend credit or outright transfers to weak banks to prop them up. If a country is having a default crisis, the government will lose access to foreign and domestic loans and may pressure the central bank to lend to the government. This raises a key question: Why does the extension of credit by the central bank threaten an exchange rate peg? In this chapter, we show how a peg works—and how, if the central bank issues too much money for bailouts, it can place the peg at risk by causing a loss of reserves.

These findings show how crises are likely to happen in pairs, known as **twin crises,** or all three at once, known as **triple crises,** magnifying the costs of any one type of crisis.

Summary

Exchange rate crises have been recurring for more than 100 years, and we have not seen the last of them. They can generate significant economic costs, and policy makers and scholars are seriously concerned about how to prevent them. What is it about fixed exchange rate regimes that make them so fragile? Why and how do crises happen? And how can the risks of such crises be mitigated? These are the questions we address in the rest of this chapter.

---

[5] Graciela L. Kaminsky and Carmen M. Reinhart, 1999, "The Twin Crises: The Causes of Banking and Balance-of-Payments Problems," *American Economic Review,* 89(3), 473–500; Carmen M. Reinhart, 2002, "Default, Currency Crises, and Sovereign Credit Ratings," *World Bank Economic Review,* 16(2), 151–170.

TABLE 9-1

Costly Banking Crises The table shows the estimated costs of major banking crises since the 1970s, in the cases in which costs exceeded 5% of GDP.

Country and Year(s)	Cost (% of GDP)	Country and Year(s)	Cost (% of GDP)
Indonesia 1997	55%	Benin 1988–1990	17%
Argentina 1980–1982	55	Senegal 1988–1991	17
China 1990s	47	Malaysia 1997	16
Jamaica 1995–2000	44	Mauritania 1984–1993	15
Chile 1981–1986	42	Paraguay 1995–1999	13
Thailand 1997	35	Czech Republic 1991	12
Macedonia 1993–1994	32	Taiwan 1997–1998	12
Turkey 2000	31	Finland 1991–1994	11
Israel 1977–1983	30	Hungary 1991–1995	10
South Korea 1997	28	Tanzania 1980s and 1990s	10
Côte d'Ivoire 1988–1991	25	Norway 1987–1993	8
Japan 1991	24	Philippines 1998	7
Uruguay 1981–1985	24	Russia 1998–1999	6
Ecuador 1988	20	Ghana 1982–1989	6
Mexico 1994–1997	19	Colombia 1982–1987	5
Venezuela 1994–1995	18	Sri Lanka 1989–1993	5
Spain 1977–1985	17	Malaysia 1985–1988	5

Source: Gerard Caprio and Daniela Klingebiel, "Episodes of Systemic and Borderline Financial Crises," World Bank, January 2003. Data compiled by Martin Wolf, "Fixing Global Finance," SAIS Lectures, March 2006.

2 How Pegs Work: The Mechanics of a Fixed Exchange Rate

To start, we must first understand how a pegged exchange rate works. Once we know what policy makers have to do to make a peg work, we will then be in a position to understand the factors that make a peg break.

To help us understand the economic mechanisms that operate in a fixed exchange rate system, we develop a simple model of what a central bank does. We then use the model to look at the demands placed on a central bank when a country adopts a fixed exchange rate.

Preliminaries and Assumptions

We consider a small open economy, in which the authorities are trying to peg to some foreign currency. We make the following assumptions, some of which may be relaxed in later analyses:

- For convenience, and without implying that we are referring to any specific country, we assume that the home currency is called the peso. The currency to which home pegs is the U.S. dollar. We assume the authorities have been maintaining a fixed exchange rate, with E fixed at $\overline{E} = 1$ (one peso per U.S. dollar).

- The country's central bank controls the money supply M by buying and selling assets in exchange for cash. The central bank trades only two types of assets: domestic bonds, often government bonds, denominated in local currency (pesos), and foreign assets, denominated in foreign currency (dollars).
- The central bank intervenes in the forex market to peg the exchange rate. It stands ready to buy and sell foreign exchange reserves at the fixed exchange rate $\overline{E}$. If it has no reserves, it cannot do this and the exchange rate is free to float: the peg is broken.
- Unless stated otherwise, we assume that the peg is credible: Everyone believes it will continue to hold. Uncovered interest parity then implies that the home and foreign interest rates are equal: $i = i^*$.
- We also assume for now that the economy's level of output or income is assumed to be exogenous; that is, it is treated as given and denoted Y.
- There is a stable foreign price level $P^* = 1$ at all times. In the short run, the home country's price is sticky and fixed at a level $P = 1$. In the long run, if the exchange rate is kept fixed at 1, then the home price level will be fixed at 1 as a result of purchasing power parity.
- As in previous chapters, the home country's demand for real money balances M/P is determined by the level of output Y and the nominal interest rate i and takes the usual form, $M/P = L(i)Y$. The money market must be in equilibrium, so money demand is always equal to money supply.
- We use the simplest model of a fixed exchange rate, where there is no financial system. The only money is currency, also known as M0 or the monetary base. The monetary base (M0) and broad money (M1) are then the same, so the money supply is denoted M. This assumption allows us to examine the operation of a fixed exchange rate system by considering only the effects of the actions of a central bank.
- If there is no financial system, we do not need to worry about the role of private banks in creating broad money through checking deposits, loans, and so on. A simple generalization would allow for banks by letting broad money be a constant multiple of the currency.[6] Still, the existence of a banking system is important, and even without formal theory, we will see later in the chapter how it affects the operation of a fixed exchange rate.

The Central Bank Balance Sheet

To understand how the home central bank maintains the peg, we must understand how the home central bank manages its assets in relation to its sole liability, the money in circulation.

Suppose the central bank has purchased a quantity B pesos of domestic bonds. By, in effect, loaning money to the domestic economy, the central bank's purchases are usually referred to as **domestic credit** created by the central bank. These purchases are also called the bank's *domestic assets*. Because the central bank purchases these assets

---

[6] Allowing that multiple (the money multiplier) to vary is also possible, but detailed analysis of that mechanism is beyond the scope of this chapter.

with money, this purchase generates part of the money supply. The part of the home money supply created as a result of the central bank's issuing of domestic credit is denoted B.

Now suppose the central bank has also purchased a quantity R dollars of foreign exchange reserves, usually referred to as **reserves** or foreign assets, and that the exchange rate is pegged at a level $\bar{E} = 1$. The central bank also purchases its reserves with money. Thus, given that the exchange rate has always been 1 (by assumption), the part of the money supply created as a result of the central bank's purchase of foreign exchange reserves is $\bar{E} R = R$.[7]

Because the central bank holds only two types of assets, the last two expressions add up to the total money supply in the home economy:

$$\underbrace{M}_{\text{Money supply}} = \underbrace{B}_{\text{Domestic credit}} + \underbrace{R}_{\text{Reserves}} \qquad (9\text{-}1)$$

This equation states that the money supply equals domestic credit plus reserves.

This expression is also useful when expressed not in levels but in changes:

$$\underbrace{\Delta M}_{\substack{\text{Change in}\\\text{money supply}}} = \underbrace{\Delta B}_{\substack{\text{Change in}\\\text{domestic credit}}} + \underbrace{\Delta R}_{\substack{\text{Change in}\\\text{reserves}}} \qquad (9\text{-}2)$$

This expression says that changes in the money supply must result from either changes in domestic credit or changes in reserves.

For example, if the central bank buys additional reserves $\Delta R = 1{,}000$ pesos, the money it spends adds $\Delta M = 1{,}000$ pesos to the money in circulation. If the central bank creates additional domestic credit of $\Delta B = 1{,}000$ pesos, it buys 1,000 pesos of government debt, and this also adds $\Delta M = 1{,}000$ pesos to the money in circulation.

One common way of depicting Equation (9-1) is to write down each entry and construct the **central bank balance sheet.** The domestic debt and foreign reserves purchased by the central bank are its **assets,** $B + R$. The money supply issued by the central bank M is its **liabilities.**

Following is a hypothetical central bank balance sheet. The central bank has purchased 500 million pesos in domestic government bonds and 500 million pesos in foreign exchange reserves. The total money in circulation resulting from these purchases is 1,000 million pesos. As on any balance sheet, total assets equal total liabilities.

SIMPLIFIED CENTRAL BANK BALANCE SHEET (MILLIONS OF PESOS)

Assets		Liabilities	
Reserves R Foreign assets (dollar reserves)	500	**Money supply M** Currency in circulation	1,000
Domestic credit B Domestic assets (peso bonds)	500		

---

[7] In reality, central banks may have acquired reserves in the past at more or less favorable exchange rates, so the current peso value of reserves may be greater than or less than the peso value of the money spent to purchase them. In such cases, the central bank may have positive or negative net worth arising from capital gains or losses on previously purchased reserves (although whether such gains are recorded on the central bank's balance sheet depends on its accounting practices and whether it marks reserves at book value or market value). We ignore this problem because it does not greatly affect the analysis that follows.

Fixing, Floating, and the Role of Reserves

The crucial assumption in our simple model is that the central bank maintains the peg by intervening in the foreign exchange market by buying and selling reserves at the fixed exchange rate. In other words, our model supposes that if the central bank wants to fix the exchange rate, it must have some reserves it can trade to achieve that goal. We also assume, for now, that it holds reserves only for this purpose. Thus:

We are assuming that the exchange rate is fixed if and only if the central bank holds reserves; and the exchange rate is floating if and only if the central bank has no reserves.

These assumptions simplify our analysis by clarifying the correspondence between the central bank balance sheet and the exchange rate regime. In reality, the correspondence may be less clear, but the mechanisms in our model still play a dominant role.

For example, countries may adjust domestic credit as well as reserves. But in no cases does a country attempt to maintain a peg with zero reserves and rely *solely* on domestic credit adjustments. Why? In the very short run, forex market conditions can change so quickly that only direct intervention in that market through reserve trading can maintain the peg. Large adjustments to domestic credit may also pose problems in an emerging market by causing instability in the bond market as the central bank buys or sells potentially large amounts of government bonds.

Countries can also float and yet keep some reserves on hand for reasons that are ignored in our model. They may want reserves on hand for future emergencies, such as war; or as a savings buffer in the event of a sudden stop to financial flows; or so they can peg at some later date.[8] Thus, the minimum level of reserves the central bank will tolerate on its balance sheet may not be at zero, but it would not affect our analysis if we adjusted everything that follows to allow for a higher threshold.

How Reserves Adjust to Maintain the Peg

We now turn to the key questions we need to answer to understand how a peg works. What level of reserves must the central bank have to maintain the peg? And how are reserves affected by changing macroeconomic conditions? If the central bank can maintain a level of reserves above zero, we know the peg will hold. If not, the peg breaks.

We can rearrange Equation (9-1) to solve for the level of reserves, with $R = M - B$. Why do we do that? It is important to remember that reserves are the unknown variable here: by assumption, reserves change as a result of the central bank's interventions in the forex market, which it must undertake to maintain the peg.

Because (in nominal terms) money supply equals money demand, given by $M = \overline{P}L(i)Y$, we can restate and rearrange Equation (9-1) to solve for the level of reserves:

$$\underbrace{R}_{\text{Reserves}} = \underbrace{\overline{P}L(i)Y}_{\text{Money demand}} - \underbrace{B}_{\text{Domestic credit}} \qquad (9\text{-}3)$$

By substituting money demand for money supply, we can investigate how shocks to money demand (say, due to changes in output or the interest rate) or shocks to domestic credit affect the level of reserves.

We can solve this equation. Under our current assumptions, every element on the right-hand side is exogenous and known. The home price level is fixed, the output level

---

[8] Some of these functions may be provided by other reserve-holding agencies within the government (such as the Treasury or a sovereign wealth fund). But often all reserves are held by the central bank, which frequently serves as the financial agent of the country.

is exogenous, interest parity tells us that the home interest rate equals the foreign interest rate, and we can treat domestic credit as predetermined by the central bank's purchases of domestic government debt.

Why is this answer for the reserve level correct and unique? Recall, from the chapter on exchange rates in the short run, how forex market equilibrium is attained. If the central bank bought more reserves than this, home money supply would expand and the home nominal interest rate would fall, the peso would depreciate, and the peg would break. To prevent this, the central bank would need to intervene in the forex market. The central bank would have to offset its initial purchase of reserves to keep the supply of pesos constant and keep the exchange rate holding steady. Similarly, if the central bank sells reserves for pesos, it would cause the peso to appreciate and would have to reverse course and buy back the reserves. The peg means that the central bank must keep the reserves at the level specified in Equation (9-3).

Graphical Analysis of the Central Bank Balance Sheet

Based on this toolkit, we show the mechanics of a pegged exchange rate in Figure 9-4, which illustrates the central bank balance sheet. On the horizontal axis is the money supply M and on the vertical axis is domestic credit B, both measured in pesos. Money demand is initially at the level M_1, and domestic credit is at B_1.

FIGURE 9-4

The Central Bank Balance Sheet Diagram This figure and those that follow present a simplified view of central bank operations. On the 45-degree line, reserves are at zero, and the money supply M equals domestic credit B. Variations in the money supply along this line would cause the exchange rate to float. There is a unique level of the money supply M_1 (here assumed to be 1,000) that ensures the exchange rate is at its chosen fixed value. To fix the money supply at this level, the central bank must choose a mix of assets on its balance sheet that corresponds to points on line XZ, points at which domestic credit B is less than money supply M. At point Z, reserves would be at zero; at point X, reserves would be 100% of the money supply. Any point in between on XZ is a feasible choice. At point 1, for example, domestic credit is $B_1 = 500$, reserves are $R_1 = 500$, and $B_1 + R_1 = M_1 = 1{,}000$.

Two important lines appear in this figure. If reserves R are zero, then all of the money supply is due to domestic credit and Equation (9-1) tells us that $M = B$. The points where $M = B$ are on the 45-degree line. Points on this line, like point Z, correspond to cases in which the central bank balance sheet contains no reserves. By assumption, the country will then have a floating exchange rate, so we call this the **floating line.**

When the assets of the central bank include both reserves and domestic credit, then B and R are both greater than zero and they add up to M. The state of the central bank balance sheet must correspond to a point such as point 1 in this diagram, somewhere on the vertical line XZ. We call this the **fixed line** because on this line the money supply is at the level M_1 necessary to maintain the peg.

If domestic credit is B_1, then reserves are $R_1 = M_1 - B_1$, the vertical (or horizontal) distance between point 1 and the 45-degree floating line. Hence, the distance to the floating line tells us how close to danger the peg is by showing how close we are to the point where reserves run out.[9] The point farthest from danger is X, on the horizontal axis. At this point, domestic credit B is zero and reserves R equal the money supply M. A fixed exchange rate that always operates with reserves equal to 100% of the money supply is known as a **currency board** system.[10]

To sum up: If the exchange rate is floating, the central bank balance sheet must correspond to points on the 45-degree floating line; if the exchange rate is fixed, the central bank balance sheet must correspond to points on the vertical fixed line.

The model is now complete, and with the aid of our key tools—the tabular and graphical representations of the central bank balance sheet—we can see how a central bank that is trying to maintain a peg reacts to two types of shocks. We first look at shocks to the level of money demand and then shocks to the composition of money supply.

Defending the Peg I: Changes in the Level of Money Demand

We first look at shocks to money demand and how they affect reserves by altering the level of money supply M. As we saw in Equation (9-3), money supply is equal to money demand, as given by the equation $M = \overline{P}L(i)Y$. If the price level is fixed, then money demand will fluctuate only in response to shocks in output Y and the home interest rate i (which equals the foreign interest rate i^* if the peg is credible). For now, output is exogenous, and a rise in output will raise money demand. The foreign interest rate is also exogenous, and a rise in the foreign interest rate will raise the home interest rate and thus lower money demand. We assume all else is equal, so domestic credit is constant.

A Shock to Home Output or the Foreign Interest Rate
Suppose output falls or the foreign interest rate rises. We treat either of these events as an exogenous shock for now, all else equal, and suppose it decreases money demand by, say, 10% at the current interest rate.

---

[9] It is important to remember that under our assumptions, all other points in the figure (representing other balance sheet configurations) are ruled out. Floating means having zero reserves and being on the 45-degree line. Other points below the 45-degree line are ruled out because we assume that reserves imply pegging, and these other points would imply a higher or lower level of the money supply and hence an exchange rate other than the pegged rate $\overline{E}$. Points above the 45-degree line are also ruled out: they imply $B > M$ and $R < 0$, which is impossible because reserves cannot be negative.

[10] Strictly speaking, a currency board must satisfy certain other legal and procedural rules. For example, it must own only low-risk interest-bearing foreign assets, not foreign liabilities. It must not perform any function except to exchange domestic currency for foreign currency at a fixed rate. It cannot lend to the domestic banking system to avert banking panics. However, it may hold a bit more than 100% reserve backing, say, 105% to 110%, to guard against fluctuations in the value of its foreign assets. See Kurt Schuler, "Introduction to Currency Boards" (http://users.erols.com/kurrency/intro.htm).

For example, suppose we start with a central bank balance sheet as given earlier. Initially, money supply is $M_1 = 1{,}000$ million pesos. Suppose money demand then falls by 10%. This would lower money demand by 10% to $M_2 = 900$ million pesos. A fall in the demand for money would lower the interest rate in the money market and put depreciation pressure on the home currency. A floating exchange rate would allow the home currency to depreciate in these circumstances. To maintain the peg, the central bank must keep the interest rate unchanged. To achieve this goal, it must sell 100 million pesos ($100 million) of reserves, in exchange for cash, so that money supply contracts as much as money demand. The central bank's balance sheet will then be as follows:

SIMPLIFIED CENTRAL BANK BALANCE SHEET AFTER MONEY DEMAND FALLS (MILLIONS OF PESOS)

Assets		Liabilities	
Reserves R Foreign assets (dollar reserves)	400	**Money supply M** Currency in circulation	900
Domestic credit B Domestic assets (peso bonds)	500		

In Figure 9-5, we can trace the implications of the shock using our graphical apparatus. The demand for money has fallen, so the *fixed line* is still vertical, but it shifts from the initial money demand level $M_1 = 1{,}000$ to a new lower level $M_2 = 900$. There is no change to domestic credit, so it remains constant at the level $B_1 = 500$. Thus, the central bank's balance sheet position shifts from point 1 to point 2. This shift takes the balance sheet position closer to the floating line in the diagram: Reserves are falling. At point 2, reserves have fallen from $R_1 = 500$ to $R_2 = 400$, as shown.

Figure 9-5 also shows what would happen with the opposite shock. If money demand increased by 10% from the initial money demand level $M_1 = 1{,}000$ to a new higher level $M_3 = 1{,}100$, the central bank would need to prevent an interest rate rise and an appreciation by expanding the money supply by 100 pesos. The central bank would need to intervene and increase the money supply by purchasing $100 of reserves. The central bank's balance sheet position would then shift from point 1 to point 3, moving away from the floating line, with reserves rising from $R_1 = 500$ to $R_3 = 600$.

Equation (9-3) confirms these outcomes as a general result when domestic credit is constant (at B_1 in our example). We know that if the change in domestic credit is zero, $\Delta B = 0$, then any change in money supply must equal the change in reserves, $\Delta R = \Delta M$. This is also clear from Equation (9-2).

We have shown the following: *Holding domestic credit constant, a change in money demand leads to an equal change in reserves.*

The Importance of the Backing Ratio In the first example above, money demand and money supply fell by 10% from 1,000 to 900, but reserves fell by 20% from 500 to 400. The proportional fall in reserves was greater than the proportional fall in money because reserves R were initially only 500 and just a fraction (one-half) of the money supply M, which was 1,000. When money demand fell by 100, reserves had to absorb all of the change, with domestic credit unchanged.

The ratio R/M is called the **backing ratio,** and it indicates the fraction of the money supply that is backed by reserves on the central bank balance sheet. It, therefore, tells us

FIGURE 9-5

Shocks to Money Demand If money demand falls, interest rates tend to fall, leading to pressure for an exchange rate to depreciate. To prevent this, the central bank must intervene in the forex market and defend the peg by selling reserves and hence lowering the money supply to keep the interest rate fixed and ensure that money supply equals money demand. As shown here, the money supply declines from $M_1 = 1,000$ to $M_2 = 900$. If domestic credit is unchanged at $B_1 = 500$, the change in the central bank balance sheet is shown by a move from point 1 to point 2, and reserves absorb the money demand shock by falling from $R_1 = 500$ to $R_2 = 400$. An opposite positive shock is shown by the move from point 1 to point 3, where $M_3 = 1,100$ and $R_3 = 600$. In a currency board system, a country maintaining 100% reserves will be on the horizontal axis with zero domestic credit, $B = 0$. A currency board adjusts to money demand shocks by moving from point 1' to points 2' or 3'.

the size of the maximum negative money demand shock that the regime can withstand without running out of reserves *if* domestic credit remains unchanged. In our example, the backing ratio was 0.5 or 50% (reserves were 500 and money supply 1,000 initially), so the central bank could absorb up to a 50% decline in the money supply before all reserves run out. Because reserves were only 500 to start with, a shock of −500 to money demand would cause reserves to just run out.

In general, *for a given size of a shock to money demand, a higher backing ratio will better insulate an economy against running out of reserves, all else equal.*[11]

---

[11] To see this, recall that the change in money supply equals the change in reserves, $\Delta M = \Delta R$; hence, for a given *proportional* size of money demand shock $\Delta M/M$, the proportional loss in reserves $\Delta R/R$ can be computed as

$$\text{\% Change in reserves} = \frac{\Delta R}{R} = \frac{\Delta M}{R} = \frac{\Delta M/M}{R/M} = \frac{\text{\% Change in money supply}}{\text{Backing ratio}}$$

The higher the backing ratio, the smaller the proportional loss of reserves $\Delta R/R$ for a given size of money demand shock $\Delta M/M$. In our example, the backing ratio was 0.5, so a 10% drop in money supply implied a $10\%/0.5 = 20\%$ drop in reserves.

In Figure 9-5, the higher the backing ratio, the higher the level of reserves R and the lower the level of domestic credit B, for a given level of money supply M. In other words, the central bank balance sheet position on this figure would be closer to the horizontal axis and farther away from the floating line. This is the graphical representation of the idea that a high backing ratio makes a peg safer.

Currency Board Operation This maximum backing ratio of 100% is maintained at all times by a currency board. A 100% backing ratio puts the country exactly on the horizontal axis. In Figure 9-5, a currency board would start at point 1′, not point 1. Because reserves would then be 1,000 to start with, a shock of up to −1,000 to money demand could be accommodated without reserves running out. In the face of smaller shocks to money demand such as we have considered, of plus or minus 100, the central bank balance sheet would move to points 2′ or 3′, with reserves equal to money supply equal to money demand equal to 900 or 1,100. These points are as far away from the 45-degree floating line as one can get in this diagram, and they show how a currency board keeps reserves at a maximum 100%. A currency board can be thought of as the safest configuration of the central bank's balance sheet because with 100% backing, the central bank can cope with *any* shock to money demand without running out of reserves. Currency boards are considered a *hard peg* because their high backing ratio ought to confer on them greater resilience in the face of money demand shocks.

Why Does the Level of Money Demand Fluctuate? Our result tells us that to maintain the fixed exchange rate, the central bank must have enough reserves to endure a money demand shock without running out. A shock to money demand is not under the control of the authorities, but they must respond to it. Thus, it is important for policy makers to understand the sources and likely magnitudes of such shocks. Under our assumptions, money demand shocks originate either in shocks to home output Y or the foreign interest rate i^* (because under a credible peg $i = i^*$).

We have studied output fluctuations in earlier chapters, and one thing we observed was that output tends to be much more volatile in emerging markets and developing countries. Thus, the prudent level of reserves is likely to be much higher in these countries. Volatility in foreign interest rates can also be important, whether in U.S. dollars or in other currencies that form the base for pegs.

However, we must also confront a new possibility—that the peg is not fully credible and that simple interest parity fails to hold. In this case, the home interest rate will no longer equal the foreign interest rate, and additional disturbances to home money demand can be caused by the spread between the two. As we now see, this is a vital step toward understanding crises in emerging markets and developing countries.

APPLICATION

Risk Premiums in Advanced and Emerging Markets

So far in the book, we have assumed that uncovered interest parity (UIP) requires that the domestic return (the interest rate on home bank deposits) equal the foreign interest rate plus the expected rate of depreciation of the home currency. However, an important extension of UIP needs to be made when additional risks affect home bank deposits: A **risk premium** is then added to the foreign interest rate to compensate investors for the perceived risk of holding a home domestic currency deposit.

This perceived risk is due to an aversion to exchange rate risk or a concern about default risk:

$$\underbrace{i}_{\substack{\text{Peso}\\\text{interest}\\\text{rate}}} = \underbrace{i^*}_{\substack{\text{Dollar}\\\text{interest}\\\text{rate}}} + \underbrace{\frac{\Delta E^e_{\text{peso}/\$}}{E_{\text{peso}/\$}}}_{\substack{\text{Expected rate of}\\\text{depreciation}\\\text{of the peso}}} + \begin{bmatrix}\text{Exchange rate}\\\text{risk premium}\end{bmatrix} + \begin{bmatrix}\text{Default}\\\text{risk premium}\end{bmatrix} \quad (9\text{-}4)$$

$$\underbrace{\hphantom{\frac{\Delta E^e_{\text{peso}/\$}}{E_{\text{peso}/\$}} + \begin{bmatrix}\text{Exchange rate}\\\text{risk premium}\end{bmatrix} + \begin{bmatrix}\text{Default}\\\text{risk premium}\end{bmatrix}}}_{\substack{\text{Interest rate spread}\\\text{(equal to zero if peg is credible and there are no risk premiums)}}}$$

The left-hand side is still the domestic return, but the right-hand side is now a *risk-adjusted foreign return*. The final three terms are the difference between home and foreign interest rates, and their sum total is known as the **interest rate spread**. What causes these spreads?

The first part of the interest rate spread is the **currency premium:**

$$\text{Currency premium} = \frac{\Delta E^e_{\text{peso}/\$}}{E_{\text{peso}/\$}} + \begin{bmatrix}\text{Exchange rate}\\\text{risk premium}\end{bmatrix}$$

The currency premium should be zero for a credibly pegged exchange rate: The peso is not expected to change in value relative to the dollar. But if a peg is not credible, and investors suspect that the peg may break, there could be a premium reflecting both the size of the expected depreciation and the currency's perceived riskiness. The currency premium therefore reflects the credibility of monetary policy.

The second part of the interest rate spread is known as the **country premium:**

$$\text{Country premium} = \begin{bmatrix}\text{Default}\\\text{risk premium}\end{bmatrix}$$

The country premium is compensation for perceived default risk (settlement or counterparty risk). It will be greater than zero if investors suspect a risk of losses when they attempt to convert a home (peso) asset back to foreign currency (dollars) in the future. Such a loss might occur because of expropriation, bank failure, surprise taxation, delays, capital controls, other regulations, and so on. The country premium therefore reflects the credibility of property rights.

Why does all this matter? Fluctuations in currency and country premiums have the same effect in Equation (9-4) as fluctuations in the foreign interest rate i^*. Sudden increases in the interest rate spread raise the risk-adjusted foreign return and imply sudden increases in the domestic return, here given by the (peso) interest rate i. In some countries, these spreads can be large and volatile—and even more volatile than the foreign interest rate.

Figure 9-6 presents interest rate spreads for two countries with fixed exchange rates. Panel (a) shows an advanced country, Denmark, which pegs to the euro; panel (b) shows an emerging market, Argentina, which pegged to the dollar from 1991 to 2001.

In Denmark, there was some spread in the early years of the euro from 1999 to 2002 (up to about 0.5% per annum), perhaps reflecting a worry that the krone-euro peg might not endure. After 2003 the spread was almost imperceptible (less than 0.1% per annum). Overall, the simple correlation between the krone interest rate and the euro interest rate was very high, equal to 0.99. Investors came to see the peg as credible, eliminating the currency premium almost entirely. They also had no fear of default risk if they invested in Denmark, eliminating the country premium almost entirely. One could therefore make the simple assumption that i was equal to i^* with no spread.

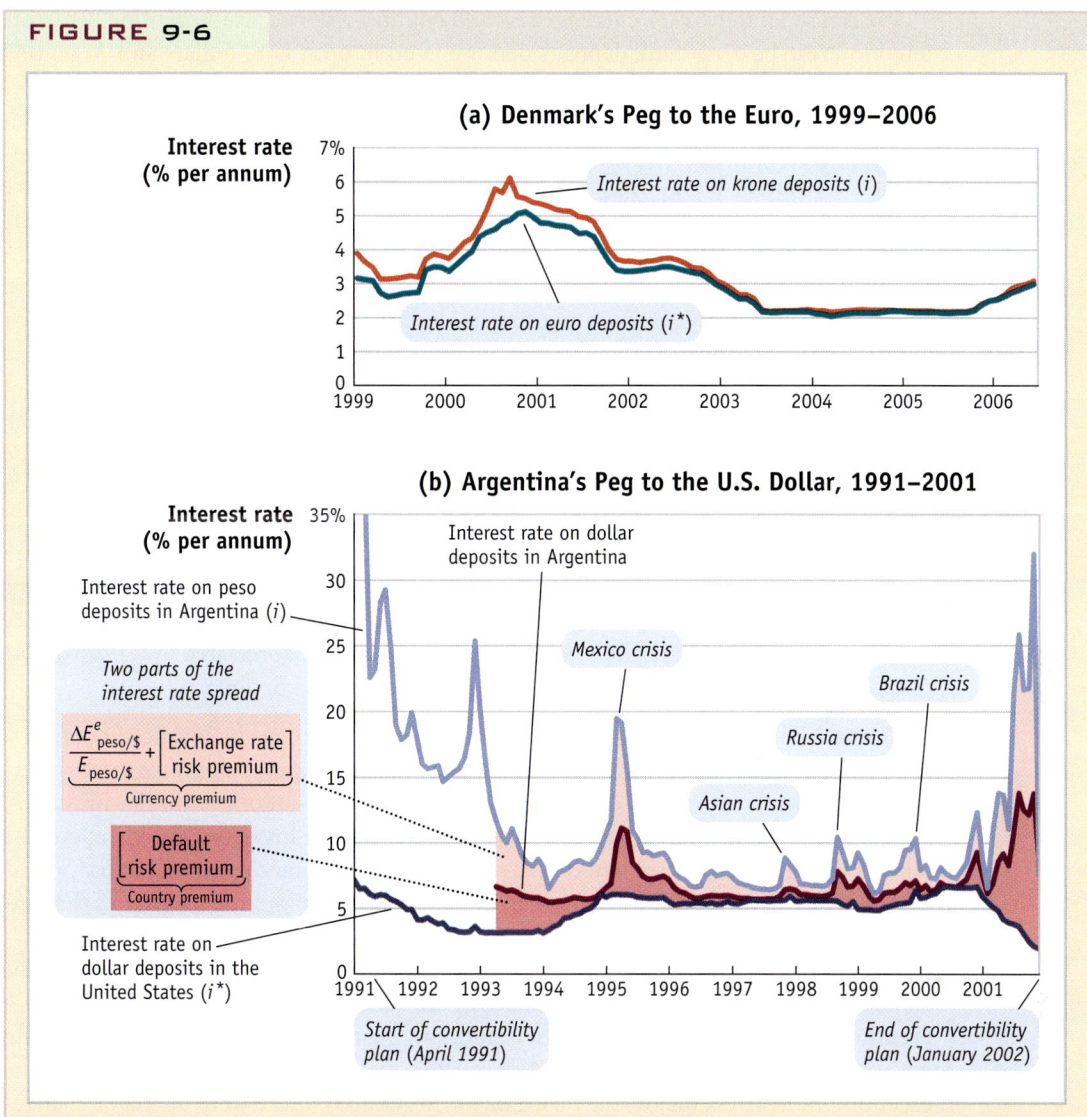

FIGURE 9-6

Interest Rate Spreads: Currency Premiums and Country Premiums When advanced countries peg, the interest rate spread is usually close to zero, and we can assume $i = i^*$. An example is Denmark's peg to the euro in panel (a), where the correlation between the krone and euro interest rates is 0.99. When emerging markets peg, interest rate spreads can be large and volatile, due to both currency and country premiums. An example is Argentina's peg to the U.S. dollar in panel (b), where the correlation between the peso interest rate and the U.S. interest rate is only 0.38.

Note: Three-month interest rates for krone-euro; two-month for peso-dollar.
Source: econstats.com.

In Argentina the spreads were large. The annual peso and dollar interest rates were far apart, often differing by 2 or 3 percentage points and sometimes differing by more than 10 percentage points. Most striking is that changes in the spread were usually more important in determining the Argentine interest rate than were changes in the actual foreign (U.S. dollar) interest rate. Overall, the correlation between the peso interest rate i and the dollar interest rate i^* was low, equal to only 0.38. What was going on?

We can separately track currency risk and country risk because Argentine banks offered interest-bearing bank deposits denominated in both U.S. dollars and Argentine pesos. The lower two lines in panel (b) show the interest rate on U.S. dollar deposits in the United States (i^*) and the interest rate on U.S. dollar deposits in Argentina. Because the rates are expressed in the same currency, the difference between these two interest rates cannot be the result of a currency premium. It represents a pure measure of country premium: investors required a higher interest rate on dollar deposits in Argentina than on dollar deposits in the United States because they perceived that Argentine deposits might be subject to a default risk. (Investors were eventually proved right: In the 2001–2002 crisis, many Argentine banks faced insolvency, some were closed for a time, and a "pesification" law turned many dollar assets into peso assets ex post, a form of expropriation and a contractual default.)

The upper line in panel (b) shows the interest rate on peso deposits in Argentina (i), which is even higher than the interest rate on U.S. dollar deposits in Argentina. Because these are interest rates on bank deposits in the same country, the difference between these two rates cannot be due to a country premium. It represents a pure measure of currency premium. Investors required a higher interest rate on peso deposits in Argentina than on dollar deposits in Argentina because they perceived that peso deposits might be subject to a risk of depreciation; that is, a collapse of the peg. (Investors were eventually proved right: In the 2001–2002 crisis, the peso depreciated by 75% from $1 to the peso to about $0.25 to the peso, or four pesos per U.S. dollar.)

Summary Pegs in emerging markets are different from those in advanced countries. Because of fluctuations in interest rate spreads, they are subject to even greater interest rate shocks than the pegs of advanced countries, as a result of **credibility** problems. Currency premiums may fluctuate because of changes in investors' beliefs about the durability of the peg, a problem of the credibility of monetary policy. Country premiums may fluctuate because of changes in investors' beliefs about the security of their investments, a problem of the credibility of property rights.

Still, not every movement in emerging market spreads is driven by economic fundamentals. For example, in Argentina the figure shows that investors revised their risk premiums sharply upward when other emerging market countries were experiencing crises in the 1990s: Mexico in 1994, Asia in 1997, and later Russia and Brazil. With the exception of Brazil (a major trade partner for Argentina), there were no major changes in Argentine fundamentals during these crises. Thus, many economists consider this to be evidence of **contagion** in global capital markets, possibly even a sign of market inefficiency or irrationality, where crises in some parts of the global capital markets trigger adverse changes in market sentiment in faraway places. ∎

APPLICATION

The Argentine Convertibility Plan Before the Tequila Crisis

The central bank balance sheet diagram helps us to see how a central bank manages a fixed exchange rate and what adjustments need to be made in response to a shock in money demand.

We can gain some familiarity and see the usefulness of this apparatus if we actually put it to use in a concrete example. We will look at the fixed exchange rate system in Argentina known as the Convertibility Plan, which began in 1991 and ended in 2002. In this plan, a peg was maintained as one peso per dollar. With the aid of Figure 9-7,

FIGURE 9-7

Argentina's Central Bank Operations, 1993–1997 In this period, one peso was worth one U.S. dollar. Panel (a) shows the money supply and reserves. The difference between the two is domestic credit. Six key dates are highlighted before, during, and after the Mexican Tequila Crisis. In panel (b), the balance sheet of the central bank at these key dates is shown. Prior to the crisis, domestic credit was essentially unchanged, and reserves grew from $8 billion to $11 billion as money demand grew from M_1 to M_2 in line with rapid growth in incomes (move from point 1 to 2). After the crisis hit in December 1994, interest rate spreads widened, money demand fell from M_2 to M_3, but domestic credit stood still (to point 3) and $1 billion in reserves were lost. In 1995 there was a run on banks and on the currency, and the central bank sterilized by expanding domestic credit by 5 billion pesos and selling $5 billion of reserves as money demand remained constant (to point 4). Reserves reached a low level of $5 billion. By 1996 the crisis had passed and the central bank now replenished its reserves, reversing the earlier sterilization. Domestic credit fell by 5 billion pesos and reserves increased by $5 billion (to point 5, same as point 3). Further sterilized purchases of $4 billion of reserves brought the backing ratio up to 100% in 1997 (to point 6).

Source: IMF, International Financial Statistics. Data compiled by Kurt Schuler.

we focus first on how the central bank managed its balance sheet during an early phase of the plan, in 1993 and 1994. (We will discuss later years shortly.)

Money Demand Shocks, 1993–1994 The evolution of money supply and reserves is shown in panel (a). From point 1 to point 2 (April 1993 to November/December 1994), all was going well. Argentina had recovered from its hyperinflation in 1989 to 1990, prices were stable, and the economy was growing—and so was money demand. But money demand equals money supply. The central bank kept domestic credit more or less unchanged in this period at 4 billion pesos, so reserves expanded (from 8 billion to 11 billion pesos) hand in hand with the base money supply expansion (from 12 billion to 15 billion pesos). The backing ratio rose from about 67% (8/12) to about 73% (11/15). In the central bank balance sheet diagram in panel (b), this is shown by the horizontal move from point 1 to point 2 as the money demand shock causes the fixed line to shift out from M_1 to M_2, so that higher levels of base money supply are now consistent with the peg.

Then a nasty shock happened: a risk premium shock, as we saw earlier. It came about as a result of the so-called Tequila Crisis in Mexico in December 1994. Interest rate spreads widened for Argentina because of currency and country premiums, raising the home interest rate. Argentina's money demand fell. In panel (a), from point 2 to point 3 (November/December 1994 to January/February 1995), base money supply contracted by 1 billion pesos, and this was absorbed almost entirely by a contraction in reserves from 11 billion to 10 billion pesos. The backing ratio fell to about 71% (10/14). In panel (b), this change is shown by the horizontal move from point 2 to point 3 as the money demand shock causes the fixed line to shift in from M_2 to M_3.

To Be Continued Through all of these events, the backing ratio remained high and domestic credit remained roughly steady at around 4 billion pesos, corresponding to our model's assumptions so far. People wanted to swap some pesos for dollars, but nothing catastrophic had happened. However, this was about to change. The shock to Argentina's interest rate proved damaging to the real economy and especially the banking sector. Argentines also became nervous about holding pesos. Foreigners stopped lending to Argentina as the economic situation looked riskier. The central bank stepped in to provide assistance to the ailing banks. But we have yet to work out how a central bank can do this and still maintain a peg. After we complete that task, we will return to the story and see how Argentina managed to survive the Tequila Crisis. ■

Defending the Peg II: Changes in the Composition of Money Supply

So far we have examined changes to the level of money demand. We have assumed that the central bank's policy toward domestic credit was *passive*, and so B has been held constant up to now. In contrast, we now study shocks to domestic credit B, all else equal; and to isolate the effects of changes in domestic credit, we will assume that money demand is constant.

If money demand is constant, then so is money supply. Therefore, the key lesson of this section will be that, on its own, a change in domestic credit cannot affect the level of the money supply, only its composition in terms of domestic credit and reserves. So we will also need to consider why such a policy is ever pursued.

A Shock to Domestic Credit Suppose that the central bank increases domestic credit by an amount $\Delta B > 0$ from B_1 to B_2. This could be the result of an *open market operation* by the bank's bond trading desk to purchase bonds from private parties. Or it could be the result of a demand by the country's economics ministry that the bank directly finance government borrowing. For now we do not concern ourselves with the cause of this policy decision, nor whether it makes any sense. We just ask what implications it has for a central bank trying to peg, all else equal. Domestic output is assumed to be unchanged and the foreign interest rate is also unchanged.

For example, suppose we go back again and start with a central bank balance sheet with money supply at its initial level of $M_1 = 1{,}000$ million pesos. The bank then expands domestic credit from $500 million pesos by buying $\Delta B = \$100$ million of peso bonds. All else equal, this action puts more money in circulation, which lowers the interest rate in the money market and puts depreciation pressure on the exchange rate. A floating rate would depreciate in these circumstances. To defend the peg, the central bank must sell enough reserves to keep the interest rate unchanged. To achieve that, it must sell 100 million pesos ($100 million) of reserves, in exchange for cash, so that the money supply remains unchanged. The central bank's balance sheet will then be as follows:

SIMPLIFIED CENTRAL BANK BALANCE SHEET AFTER EXPANSION OF DOMESTIC CREDIT (MILLIONS OF PESOS)

Assets		Liabilities	
Reserves R Foreign assets (dollar reserves)	400	Money supply M Money in circulation	1,000
Domestic credit B Domestic assets (peso bonds)	600		

What is the end result? Domestic credit B changes by +100 million pesos (rising to 600 million pesos), foreign exchange reserves R change by −100 million pesos (falling to 400 million pesos), and the money supply M remains unchanged (at 1,000 million pesos).

The bond purchases expand domestic credit but also cause the central bank to lose reserves as it is forced to intervene in the forex market. There is no change in monetary policy as measured by home money supply (or interest rates) because the sale and purchase actions by the central bank are perfectly offsetting. Accordingly, this type of central bank action is described as **sterilization** or a sterilized intervention, or a sterilized sale of reserves.

In Figure 9-8, we trace the implications of sterilization policies using our graphical apparatus. On the vertical axis, domestic credit rises from B_1 to B_2. The balance sheet position of the central bank therefore shifts up the fixed line from point 1 to point 2. Reserves fall by ΔB from $R_1 = \$500$ million pesos to $R_2 = \$400$ million pesos. The central bank has moved closer to point Z, the danger point of zero reserves on the 45-degree line. The backing ratio falls from 50% to 40%.

Figure 9-8 also shows what would happen with the opposite shock. If domestic credit fell by 100 million pesos to 400 million pesos at B_3, with an unchanged money demand, then reserves would rise by 100 million pesos. The central bank's balance sheet ends up at point 3. Reserves rise from $R_1 = 500$ to $R_3 = 600$. The backing ratio now rises from 50% to 60%.

FIGURE 9-8

Sterilization If domestic credit rises, money supply rises, all else equal, interest rates tend to fall, putting pressure on the exchange rate to depreciate. To prevent this depreciation, keep the peg, and stay on the fixed line, the central bank must intervene and defend the peg by selling reserves to keep the money supply fixed. As shown here, the money supply is $M_1 = 1,000$. If domestic credit increases from $B_1 = 500$ to $B_2 = 600$, the central bank balance sheet moves from point 1 to point 2, and reserves fall from $R_1 = 500$ to $R_2 = 400$. An opposite shock is shown by the move from point 1 to point 3, where $B_3 = 400$ and $R_3 = 600$. If the country maintains 100% reserves, it has to stay at point 1': A currency board cannot engage in sterilization.

We also see in Figure 9-8 that sterilization is impossible in the case of a currency board because a currency board requires that domestic credit always be zero and that reserves be 100% of the money supply at all times.

Equation (9-3) confirms this as a general result. We know that if the change in money demand is zero, then so is the change in money supply, $\Delta M = 0$; hence, the change in domestic credit, $\Delta B > 0$, must be offset by an equal and opposite change in reserves, $\Delta R = -\Delta B < 0$. This is also clear from Equation (9-2).

We have shown the following: *Holding money demand constant, a change in domestic credit leads to an equal and opposite change in reserves, which is called a sterilization.*

Why Does the Composition of the Money Supply Fluctuate?
Our model tells us that sterilization has no effect on the level of money supply and hence no effect on interest rates and the rest of the economy. This begs the question, why would central banks bother to do this? In the case of buying and selling government bonds, which is the predominant form of domestic credit, the effects are controversial but are generally thought to be small. The only possible effect would be indirect, via portfolio changes in the bond market. If the central bank absorbs some government

debt, it leaves less peso debt for the private sector to hold, and this could change the risk premium on the domestic interest rate. But evidence for that type of effect is rather weak.[12]

However, there is another type of domestic credit that can have very important effects on the wider economy. This is domestic credit caused by a decision by the central bank to lend to private commercial banks in difficulty. Here, the central bank would be fulfilling one of its traditional responsibilities as the protector of the domestic financial system. This has real effects because a domestic banking crisis, if allowed to happen, can cause serious economic harm by damaging the economy's payments system and credit markets.

In theory, when it comes to banks that are having difficulties, economists distinguish between banks that are illiquid and those that are insolvent. Let's see how loans from the central bank to private commercial banks affect the central bank balance sheet for these two important cases, where we are careful to note that for this case we can no longer assume that M0 (currency or base money) is the same as M1 (narrow money, which includes checking deposits) or M2 (broad money, which includes saving deposits).

- *Insolvency and bailouts.* A private bank is **insolvent** if the value of its liabilities (e.g., customers' deposits) exceeds the value of its assets (e.g., loans, other securities, and cash on hand). Often, this happens when the bank's assets unexpectedly lose value (loans turn bad, stocks crash). In some circumstances, the government may offer a rescue or **bailout** to banks in such a damaged state, as it may be unwilling to see the bank fail (for political or even for economic reasons, if banks provide valuable intermediation services to the economy). This may happen in an incremental way, if the banks at first obtain a loan from the central bank, and then find their loans rolled over for a very long time, or even forgiven with some or all interest and principal unpaid. Suppose the central bank balance sheet was originally 500 reserves and 500 domestic credit, with base money supply of 1,000. The cash from a bailout (say, 100) goes to the private bank and domestic credit rises (by 100) to 600 on the central bank's balance sheet. Because there has been no increase in base money demand, as more cash has gone into circulation, reserves must fall (by 100) to 400, as in Figure 9-9, panel (a). It is like (and indeed is equivalent to) the central bank buying bonds worth 100 directly from the government (clearly, a sterilization, as we saw previously) and the government then bailing out the private bank with the proceeds. Bottom line: Bailouts are very risky for the central bank because they cause reserves to drain, endangering the peg.

---

[12] This argument (which applies also to sterilized interventions under floating rates, which do not alter the level of the money supply) supposes that the central bank trades a large enough amount of the country's government debt that it can affect the default premium. If that were true, then an expansion of domestic credit would lower the amount of government debt that the private sector would have to hold and might convince private investors to tolerate a lower-risk premium. This might then filter through into long- and short-term interest rates in the home economy, with beneficial effects. However, while this line of argument is true in theory, the evidence is often weak and inconsistent and a source of ongoing controversy. See Maurice Obstfeld, 1982, "Can We Sterilize? Theory and Evidence," *American Economic Review*, 72(2), 45–50; Lucio Sarno and Mark P. Taylor, 2001, "Official Intervention in the Foreign Exchange Market: Is It Effective and, If So, How Does It Work?" *Journal of Economic Literature*, 39(3), 839–868.

FIGURE 9-9

The Central Bank and the Financial Sector In panel (a), a bailout occurs when the central bank prints money and buys domestic assets—the bad assets of insolvent private banks. There is no change in demand for base money (cash), so the expansion of domestic credit leads to a decrease of reserves. In panel (b), private bank depositors want to shift from holding deposits to holding cash. If the central bank acts as a lender of last resort and temporarily lends the needed cash to illiquid private banks, both the demand and supply of base money (cash) rise, so the level of reserves is unchanged.

- *Illiquidity and bank runs.* A private bank may be solvent, but it can still be **illiquid:** It holds some cash, but its loans cannot be sold (liquidated) quickly at a high price and depositors can withdraw at any time. If too many depositors attempt to withdraw at once, the bank is in trouble if it has insufficient cash on hand: This is known as a **bank run.** In this situation, the central bank may lend money to commercial banks that are running out of cash. What is going on? Suppose the monetary base is M0 and equals 1,000 as in the last example, but broad money is M2 (including bank deposits) and equals 2,000. The difference of 1,000 is the value of bank checking and saving deposits. Now let there be a run at a bank. Customers rush in and demand 100 in cash, and the bank has to borrow 100 from the central bank to satisfy them. We suppose the bank is at zero cash or at the lowest level permitted by regulation—so it is constrained. Because every other bank is likewise constrained, fearful of lending to the troubled bank, or also in a run, the problem cannot be solved by interbank lending. The central bank is then the **lender of last resort.** Crucially, as well as the central bank expanding domestic credit (by 100) to 600, we also have base money demand (demand for cash) rising (by 100) to 1,100. This means we have a combination of the two types of shocks we have studied: an increase in domestic credit *and* an increase in (base) money demand, as shown in Figure 9-9, panel (b). Now reserves do not change; they stay at 500. Why? The central bank is satisfying a demand for more cash, which absorbs the expansion of domestic credit. The situation will just revert to normal when the run ends and the private bank pays back its loan to the central bank. Bottom line: Providing liquidity to solvent banks is not risky for the central bank because there is no reserve drain to threaten the peg.

This simple classification is useful but the reality is more complex. The difference between insolvency and illiquidity is unclear. If depositors fear that banks have either problem, and that the central bank may bail them out slowly or partially, they will seek to withdraw their deposits and put them in a safe place. If the problem is big, the fear may affect all depositors and all banks, and due to uncertainty, nobody knows which banks are safe, which illiquid, and which insolvent. In many emerging markets and developing countries, this kind of panic often leads to a flight from deposits not into local currency but into foreign bank deposits, since the extent of any bailout may be unclear, and so the survival of the peg may be in doubt, too. The beliefs can also be self-fulfilling. A bank that faces a run may have to sell illiquid assets in a hurry at a low price, damaging itself and magnifying the problem. As depositors demand foreign currency, they drain reserves and make it more likely that devaluation will happen. A country at risk of devaluation faces a higher-risk premium, worsening economic conditions and encouraging a flight from the currency. If a depreciation did happen, then banks and firms that have foreign currency liabilities will be in even worse shape, so running looks even better. And so the vicious circle continues.

The Old Lady doth protest too much: In September 2007 the Bank of England assured Northern Rock depositors that the bank would not fail. The bank's balance sheet was widely believed to be healthy (solvency), but the bank had run short of cash to fund mortgages (illiquidity). Despite official assurances, depositors ran all the same, preferring cash in hand to government promises.

To get a sense of the challenges faced by a central bank when confronted with difficulties in the banking sector under a fixed exchange rate, let us return to the case of Argentina after the Mexican Tequila Crisis.

APPLICATION

The Argentine Convertibility Plan after the Tequila Crisis

When we left Argentina at the end of the last application, the Mexican Tequila Crisis had just hit in December 1994, and base money supply had fallen by a billion pesos. This change was shown in Figure 9-7 by the move from point 2 to point 3. With domestic credit steady, this meant that reserves also fell by a billion pesos to a level of 10 billion in January/February 1995.

Banking Crisis, 1995 Higher interest rates were reducing output as the private sector struggled with the high cost of credit. The government's budget deficit grew as tax revenues fell. Commercial bank balance sheets were damaged by bad loans and depressed asset prices. The country now faced the threat of a banking crisis.[13]

The central bank began extending loans, even to banks of questionable solvency. The loans became more abundant and for a much longer duration. Concerns grew that the central bank had stepped up to, or over, the line between acting as a lender of last resort and bailing out.

People feared that banks would fail, but they could not easily tell the difference between a strong bank and a weak one. People withdrew checking and saving deposits, but the run made it only more likely that banks would fail. Contagion and uncertainty meant that the panic hit all banks, weak and strong alike. Dollar deposits caused an additional problem. If people wanted to withdraw pesos, the central bank's peso loans helped, but if they wanted to withdraw dollars, the peso loans would head right back to the central bank as the commercial banks demanded dollar reserves to satisfy the dollar claims.

Even as people started to run from bank deposits to cash, higher interest rates and lower output depressed the demand for cash. Reserves drained, casting more doubt on the viability of the fixed exchange rate, raising the currency premium, and draining more reserves. Given the fears of a banking crisis *and* exchange rate crisis, cash and bank deposits were switched into dollars and moved to banks in Montevideo, Miami, or other offshore locations. People were now starting to run from the currency, too.

The consequences for the central bank balance sheet were dramatic. Domestic credit expanded from 4 billion pesos to 9 billion pesos in the first half of 1995, as seen in Figure 9-7 at point 4 in panel (a), even as base money supply remained more or less steady near 14 billion pesos. Cash demand held up, but people were moving bank deposits into pesos and then offshore—and the central bank was providing the peso liquidity (to banks) and then the dollar liquidity (to people) to allow this capital flight to happen. As a result of this sterilization, reserves fell to a low of just 5 billion pesos, with the backing ratio collapsing to a low of about 36% (5/14). In the central bank balance sheet diagram in Figure 9-7, panel (b), the country was now moving vertically up to point 4 and getting perilously close to the floating line, the dangerous place where reserves run out.

Help from the IMF and Recovery In late 1994 Argentina was at the point of being cut off from further official lending by the International Monetary Fund as a result of its failure to reduce its fiscal deficit and pursue other reforms. With private credit mar-

---

[13] See Laura D'Amato, Elena Grubisic, and Andrew Powell, 1997, "Contagion, Bank Fundamentals or Macroeconomic Shock? An Empirical Analysis of the Argentine 1995 Banking Problems," Working Paper No. 2, Central Bank of Argentina, Buenos Aires; Charles W. Calomiris and Andrew Powell, 2001, "Can Emerging Market Bank Regulators Establish Credible Discipline? The Case of Argentina, 1992–1999," in *Prudential Supervision: What Works and What Doesn't*, Frederic S. Mishkin, ed. (Chicago: University of Chicago Press).

kets screeching toward a sudden stop after the Tequila Crisis, and the government running a large deficit, the situation looked bleak.

However, after the Tequila Crisis, the United States advanced a large assistance package to Mexico, and the IMF took a more lenient view of the Argentine situation, fearing the possibility of a global financial crisis if Argentina crashed, too. IMF lending resumed. This was seen as "catalytic" in putting an end to the sudden stop, and a "Patriotic Bond" was issued in private capital markets. The loans provided desperately needed dollars. Some of the dollars could then be poured into the central bank. This replenished reserves, but it also revealed the scale of the bailing out. A substantial fund was set up to salvage insolvent commercial banks, a move that finally erased the stain of the bailouts from the central bank's balance sheet (bad commercial bank debt to the central bank was socialized and then turned into a government debt to foreigners).[14]

The Argentine authorities squeaked through a crisis, the economy recovered, capital flows resumed, and eventually the central bank's emergency loans were paid back. By 1996 economic growth had picked up, interest rate spreads eased, and confidence returned. The central bank reversed its earlier sterilization policies and replenished reserves by contracting domestic credit. By November 1996 domestic credit was back down to 4 billion pesos (its precrisis level), and by May 1997 the central bank had gone further and reduced domestic credit to zero. These steps are shown in the central bank balance sheet diagram in Figure 9-7, panel (b), by the moves from point 4 to point 5 to point 6.

Postscript Argentina's central bank ended up with a 100% backing ratio and was in a position to act as a strict currency board. However, it did not do so and in subsequent turbulent times continued to exercise discretion in its use of sterilization policies. The Convertibility Plan came to an end in 2001, however, when its room for maneuver finally ran out: The economy was in recession, the government was deeper in debt, the IMF and private creditors had reached their lending limits, and the government was reduced to raiding the banks and the central bank for resources. The details of that story, which are tied up with the Argentine 2001 default, are taken up in the last chapter. ■

The Central Bank Balance Sheet and the Financial System

We can see from the experiences of Argentina and many other countries that the existence of a financial system affects the operations and balance sheet of the central bank. In particular, whether as a result of its own policy choices, formal laws and regulations, or political pressure, the typical central bank takes on the responsibility for monitoring, regulating, and—in an emergency—protecting a country's commercial banking system.

A More General Balance Sheet As a result of its interactions with banks, the central bank's balance sheet is in reality more complicated than we have assumed in our simplified model. Typically, it looks something like this, with some hypothetical values inserted:[15]

---

[14] For a detailed account of Argentina's travails, see Paul Blustein, 2005, *And the Money Kept Rolling In (and Out): Wall Street, the IMF, and the Bankrupting of Argentina* (New York: Public Affairs).
[15] For simplicity, we assume that the bank has zero net worth, so total assets equal total liabilities. In general, this will not be true from day to day as the central bank can make gains and losses on its assets and liabilities, and it may also have operating profits and losses. However, net worth is typically not very large and, over the longer run, any gains and losses are typically absorbed by the government treasury.

GENERAL CENTRAL BANK BALANCE (MILLIONS OF PESOS)			
Assets		**Liabilities**	
Foreign assets	950	**Foreign liabilities**	50
of which:		of which:	
Foreign reserves (all currencies)	950	Foreign currency debt issued by the central bank	50
Gold	0		
Domestic assets	500	**Domestic liabilities**	400
of which:		of which:	
Domestic government bonds bought	300	Domestic currency debt issued by the central bank	400
Loans to commercial banks	200		
		Money supply M	1,000
		of which:	
		Currency in circulation	900
		Reserve liabilities to commercial banks	100

In the first row, the central bank's *net foreign assets* are worth 900, given by 950 minus 50. We see that foreign assets can include other currencies besides the anchor currency (the dollar) and may also include gold. There may also be offsetting foreign liabilities if the central bank chooses to borrow. In this example, gold happens to be 0, foreign reserves are 950, and foreign liabilities are 50.

In the second row, *net domestic assets* are worth 100, 500 minus 400. We see that domestic assets may be broken down into government bonds (here, 300) and loans to commercial banks (here, 200). All of these assets can be offset by domestic liabilities, such as debt issued in home currency by the central bank. In this example, the central bank has issued 400 in domestic debt, which we shall assume was used to finance the purchase of foreign reserves.

Finally, the money supply is a liability for the central bank worth 1,000, as before. However, not all of that currency is "in circulation" (i.e., outside the central bank, in the hands of the public or in commercial bank vaults). Typically, central banks place *reserve requirements* on commercial banks and force them to place some cash on deposit at the central bank. This is considered a prudent regulatory device. In this case, currency in circulation is 900, and 100 is in the central bank as part of reserve requirements.

Despite all these refinements, the lessons of our simple model carry over. For example, in the simple approach, money supply (M) equaled foreign assets (R) plus domestic assets (B). We now see that, in general, money supply is equal to *net foreign assets* plus *net domestic assets*. The only real difference is the ability of the central bank to borrow by issuing nonmonetary liabilities, whether domestic or foreign.

Sterilization Bonds Why do central banks expand their balance sheets by issuing such liabilities? To see what the central bank can achieve by borrowing, consider what the preceding balance sheet would look like if the central bank had not borrowed to fund the purchase of reserves.

Without issuing domestic liabilities of 400 and foreign liabilities of 50, reserves would be lower by 450. In other words, they would fall from 950 to their original level of 500 seen in the example at the start of this chapter. Domestic credit would then be 500, as it was in that earlier example, with money supply of 1,000. Thus, what borrowing to buy reserves achieves is not a change in monetary policy (money supply and interest rates are unchanged, given the peg) but an increase in the backing ratio. Instead of a 50% backing ratio (500/1,000), the borrowing takes the central bank up to a 95% backing ratio (950/1,000).

But why stop there? What if the central bank borrowed, say, another 300 by issuing domestic debt and used the proceeds to purchase more reserves? Its domestic liabilities would rise from 400 to 700 (net domestic assets would fall from +100 to −200), and on the other side of the balance sheet, reserves (foreign assets) would rise from 950 to 1,250. Money supply would still be 1,000, but the backing ratio would be 125%. This could go on and on. Borrow another 250, and the backing ratio would be 150%.

As we have seen, these hypothetical operations are all examples of changes in the *composition* of the money supply—in terms of net foreign assets and net domestic assets—holding fixed the *level* of money supply. In other words, this is just a more general form of sterilization. And *sterilization is just a way to change the backing ratio, all else equal.*

What is new here is that the central bank's *net* domestic assets (assets minus liabilities) can be less than zero because the central bank is now allowed to borrow. Many central banks do just this, by issuing bonds—or **sterilization bonds** as they are fittingly described. This allows the backing ratio to potentially exceed 100%.

Looking back at Figure 9-8, we could depict this by allowing reserves R to represent *net* foreign assets, credit B to represent *net* domestic assets, and B to be less than zero. The key equation $M = R + B$ still holds, and the fixed and floating lines work as before, as long as we interpret zero *net* foreign assets as the trigger for a switch from fixed to floating.[16] So we can imagine that the fixed line in Figure 9-8 can extend down below the horizontal axis.

Going below the horizontal axis means that net domestic credit is negative, and the backing ratio is more than 100%. Why might countries want backing that high? As we saw, Argentina had high backing of more than 70% on the eve of the Tequila Crisis, but this would not have been enough for the peg to survive a major run from the financial system to dollars. In Figure 9-8, the zone below the horizontal axis would be an ultrasafe place, even farther from the floating line. Many countries have recently sought refuge in that direction (see **Side Bar: The Great Reserve Accumulation in Emerging Markets**).

Summary

In this section, we examined the constraints on the operations of the central bank when a fixed exchange rate is in operation. We focused on the central bank balance sheet, which in its simplest form describes how the narrow money supply (monetary base) is backed by foreign assets (reserves) and domestic assets (domestic credit). We have seen how, in response to money demand shocks, the central bank buys or sells reserves, to defend the peg. The central bank can also change the composition of the money supply through sterilization operations, which keep the money supply constant.

Two Types of Exchange Rate Crises When reserves go to zero, the country is floating, changes in domestic credit cause changes in the money supply, and the peg breaks.

---

[16] As we have argued, the precise level of that trigger may be arbitrary without affecting the insights from this analysis.

SIDE BAR

The Great Reserve Accumulation in Emerging Markets

An illustration of reserve buildup via sterilization is provided by the activities of the People's Bank of China, whose central bank balance sheet diagram is shown in Figure 9-10 in yuan (¥) units. The vertical distance to the 45-degree line represents net foreign assets R, which were essentially the same as foreign reserves because the bank had close to zero foreign liabilities.*

From 1995 to 2003 net domestic credit in China grew very slowly, from ¥1,409 billion to ¥2,218 billion, but rapid economic growth and financial development caused base money demand to grow rapidly. It more than doubled, from ¥2,076 billion to ¥5,284 billion. Thus, most of the base money supply growth of ¥3,208 billion was absorbed by ¥2,399 billion of reserve accumulation. In this period, the backing ratio rose from 32% to 58%.

From 2003 to 2009 net domestic credit fell by ¥6,202 billion and eventually turned negative as the central bank sold large amounts of sterilization bonds. Money supply growth continued, rising from ¥5,284 billion to ¥14,399 billion, an increase of ¥9,115 billion. But the sterilization caused reserves to rise by almost twice as much, by ¥15,317 billion. The backing ratio rose from 58% to 128%.

Given the country's economic (and political) importance, the Chinese case attracts a lot of attention—but it isn't the only example of this type of central bank behavior. Figure 9-11 shows the massive increase in reserves at central banks around the world in recent years: It started in about 1999, it mostly happened in Asia in countries pegging (more or less) to the dollar, and much of it was driven by large-scale sterilization. What was going on?

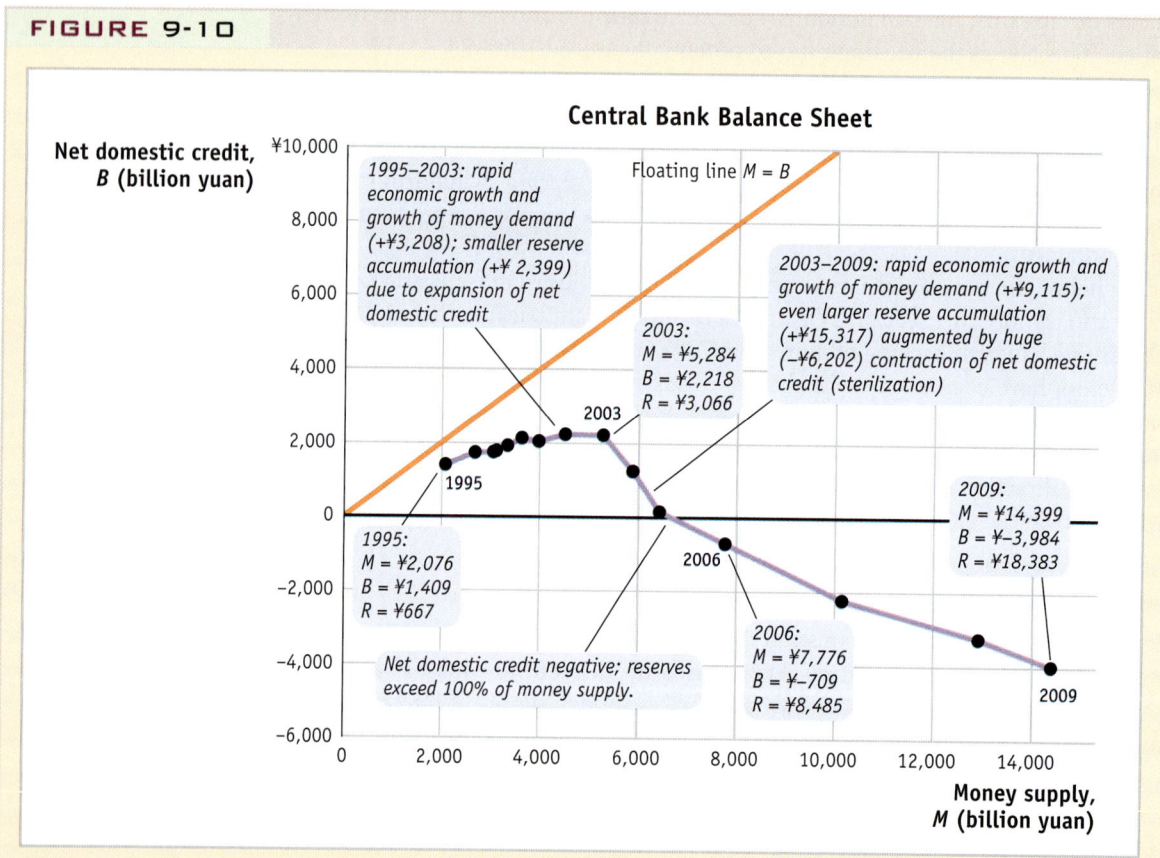

FIGURE 9-10

Sterilization in China By issuing "sterilization bonds," central banks can borrow from domestic residents to buy more reserves. With sufficient borrowing of this kind, the central bank can end up with negative net domestic credit and reserves in excess of 100% of the money supply. The chart shows how this has happened in China in recent years: from 1995 to 2003 net domestic credit in China was steady, and so reserve growth was almost entirely driven by money demand growth (large movement to the right). From 2003 to 2009 extensive sterilization (large movement down) sent net domestic credit below zero, and, despite still-strong money demand growth, sterilization accounts for about 40% of the reserve growth in the later period. China's reserves even grew during the 2008–2009 global financial crisis period, a time when other countries ran down their reserves somewhat (see Figure 9-11). *Source: People's Bank of China.*

Causes of the Reserve Accumulation

Why are these countries, most of them poor emerging markets, accumulating massive hoards of reserves? There are various possible motivations for these reserve hoards, in addition to simply wanting greater backing ratios to absorb larger shocks to money demand.** For example, the countries may fear a sudden stop, when access to foreign capital markets dries up. Foreign creditors may cease to roll over short-term debt for a while, but if reserves are on hand, the central bank can temporarily cover the shortfall. This precautionary motive leads to policy guidelines or rules suggesting that an adequate and prudent level of reserves should be some multiple either of foreign trade or of short-term debt. In practice, such ratios usually imply reserve levels less than 100% of M0, the narrow money supply.

An alternative view, illustrated by the case of Argentina that we studied, would tend to focus on a different risk, the fragility of the financial sector. If there is a major banking crisis with a flight from local deposits to foreign banks, then a central bank may need a far greater level of reserves, adequate to cover some or all of M2, the broader measure of money that includes deposits and other liquid commercial bank liabilities. Because M2 can be several times M0, the reserve levels adequate for these purposes could be much larger and well over 100% of M0. Because reserves now far exceed traditional guidelines based on trade or debt levels, fears of financial fragility might be an important part of the explanation for the scale of the reserve buildup, with reserve backing in excess of 100% of M0. As economist Martin Feldstein pointed out after the Asian crisis, it is unrealistic to expect safe and crisis-free banking sector operations in emerging markets (in 2007 and 2008 we even saw bank runs in "developed countries" like the United Kingdom and the United States). But if countries are pegged, they then need to watch out for the peg: ". . . Sufficient liquidity, either through foreign currency reserves or access to foreign credit, would let a government restructure and recapitalize its banks without experiencing a currency crisis. The more international liquidity a government has, the less depositors will feel that they must rush to convert their currency before the reserves are depleted. And preventing a currency decline can be the best way to protect bank solvency."†

Thus, current reserve levels can be seen as a reaction, in part, to the financial crises of the recent past: policy makers have taken a "never again" stance, with a large war chest of reserves piled up to guard against any risk of exchange rate crises. Is this wise? The benefits may seem clear, but many economists think this "insurance policy" carries too heavy an economic cost as countries invest in low-interest reserves and forsake investments with higher returns.

---

* In this period, foreign liabilities were just 1% of foreign assets.
** For a survey of the various possible explanations of the reserve buildup, see Joshua Aizenman, 2008, "Large Hoarding of International Reserves and the Emerging Global Economic Architecture," *Manchester School*, 76(5): 487–503; Olivier Jeanne, 2007, "International Reserves in Emerging Market Countries: Too Much of a Good Thing?" *Brookings Papers on Economic Activity*, 38(1): 1–80.
† See Martin S. Feldstein, 1999, "A Self-Help Guide for Emerging Markets," *Foreign Affairs* 78(2), 93–109.

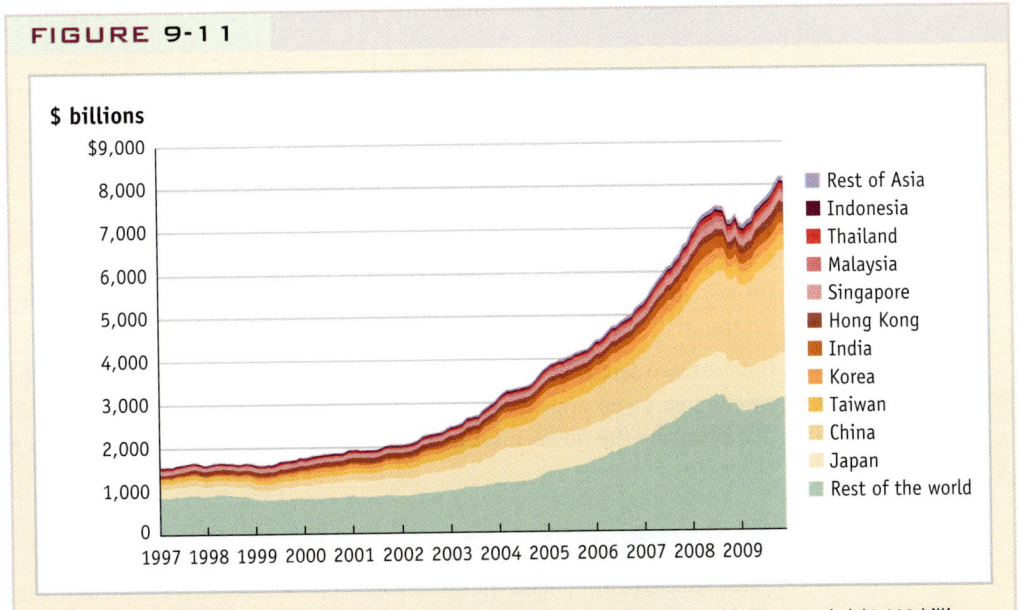

FIGURE 9-11

Reserve Accumulation, 1997–2009 By the end of 2009, reserve holdings worldwide exceeded $8,000 billion, more than five times their level in 1997. Most of the growth occurred in emerging markets, especially Asia. Much of these additional reserves were acquired through sterilization and have caused several countries' holdings of foreign exchange reserves to exceed 100% of the monetary base. *Source: IMF, International Financial Statistics.*

FIGURE 9-12

Two Types of Exchange Rate Crisis The central bank balance sheet diagram gives us a way to think about what actions will cause the peg to break. Two types of crisis are highlighted here. In panel (a), a permanent and ongoing expansion of domestic credit is incompatible with a fixed exchange rate regime because, sooner or later, reserves will be reduced to zero, and then the money supply starts to expand. In panel (b), a temporary expansion of domestic credit and the money supply will lower interest rates and depreciate the exchange rate, even if a reversal of this policy is expected in the future. Both policies take the country off the *fixed line* and onto the *floating line*.

The central bank balance sheet diagrams in Figure 9-12 show two ways in which pegs can break:

- In panel (a), in the first type of crisis, domestic credit is constantly expanding, so the central bank is pushed up the fixed line until reserves run out. At this point, the currency floats, the money supply then grows without limit, and, in the long run, the exchange rate depreciates.

- In panel (b), in the second type of crisis, no long-run tendency exists for the money supply to grow, but there is a short-run temptation to expand the money supply temporarily, leading to a temporarily lower interest rate and a temporarily depreciated exchange rate.

In the next two sections, we develop models of these two types of crisis. Although the descriptions just given appear simple, a deeper examination reveals some peculiar features that illustrate the powerful role played by market expectations in triggering crises.

3 How Pegs Break I: Inconsistent Fiscal Policies

We begin with a so-called **first-generation crisis model** of inconsistent fiscal policies in a country with a fixed exchange rate, a model proposed by the economist Paul Krugman.[17] This kind of crisis model has been successfully applied to many historical cases, including a series of Latin American crises in the 1980s.

---

[17] Paul Krugman, 1979, "A Model of Balance-of-Payments Crises," *Journal of Money, Credit and Banking*, 11(3), 311–325.

The Basic Problem: Fiscal Dominance

In this model, the level of output plays no role, so we assume output is fixed at some level Y. However, the price level P plays an important role, and we allow the price level to be flexible and determined by purchasing power parity (PPP), as in the chapter on the long-run monetary model. For now we keep all our earlier assumptions from this chapter.

In this model, the government is running a persistent deficit DEF because of insufficient tax revenue, and the government's situation is so dire, it is unable to borrow from any creditor. It therefore turns to the central bank for financing. In this type of environment, economists speak of a situation of **fiscal dominance** in which the monetary authorities ultimately have no independence. The treasury hands over bonds in the amount DEF to the central bank, and receives cash in the amount DEF in return, and uses the cash to fund the government deficit. As a result, domestic credit B increases by an amount $\Delta B = DEF$ every period. For simplicity, we assume that domestic credit B is growing at a constant positive rate, $\Delta B/B = \mu$. For example, if $\mu = 0.1$, then domestic credit B is growing at 10% per period.

Given our previous graphical analysis of the central bank balance sheet, we can see that the fixed exchange rate is doomed. As in Figure 9-12, panel (a), every change in the level of domestic credit leads to an equal and opposite change in the level of reserves. This process can't go on forever. Reserves must eventually run out. At that point, the peg breaks and the central bank shifts from a fixed exchange rate regime to a floating regime, in which the money supply equals domestic credit, $M = B$. We note a key point:

Once reserves run out, the money supply M, which was previously fixed, grows at the same rate as domestic credit, $\Delta M/M = \Delta B/B = \mu$.

The reason the peg breaks in this situation is simple. There is an inconsistency between the authorities' commitment to a monetary policy of a fixed exchange rate and a fiscal policy of continuously monetizing deficits through a limitless expansion of domestic credit. On the face of it, crisis results from elementary incompetence on the part of the authorities; to be more generous, we might say that the crisis happens because authorities are willing to let it happen because of overriding fiscal priorities.

A Simple Model

In many ways, this situation is familiar. We have already seen the implications of long-run money growth. In the chapter on exchange rates in the long run, we learned what happens in response to an *unexpected* increase in the rate of money supply growth: If prices can adjust flexibly, then, after the change, the economy ends up with all nominal values growing at the rate μ, the rate of growth of domestic credit. There will be inflation as prices P rise at a rate μ, and depreciation as the exchange rate E rises at a rate μ.

The Myopic Case Figure 3-14 described a case in which the rate of growth of the money supply unexpectedly increased by a fixed amount. We apply the same analysis here and assume that investors are *myopic* and do not see the crisis coming. (To be more realistic, we relax this assumption in a moment, but the myopic case provides useful insights.)

Drawing on what we know, Figure 9-13 uses an example to describe this kind of crisis scenario, assuming that prices are stable in the foreign country, that the foreign interest rate is $i^* = 5\%$, and that all variables evolve continuously through time. For simplicity, we start with $M = P = E = 1$, and at all times we assume the foreign price level is 1, $P^* = 1$.

Starting at time 1, in the fixed regime, domestic credit is less than the money supply, $B < M$, and reserves are positive, $R > 0$. But because of the monetization of deficits, B is gradually rising, and, as a result, R is steadily falling. Eventually, reserves run out,

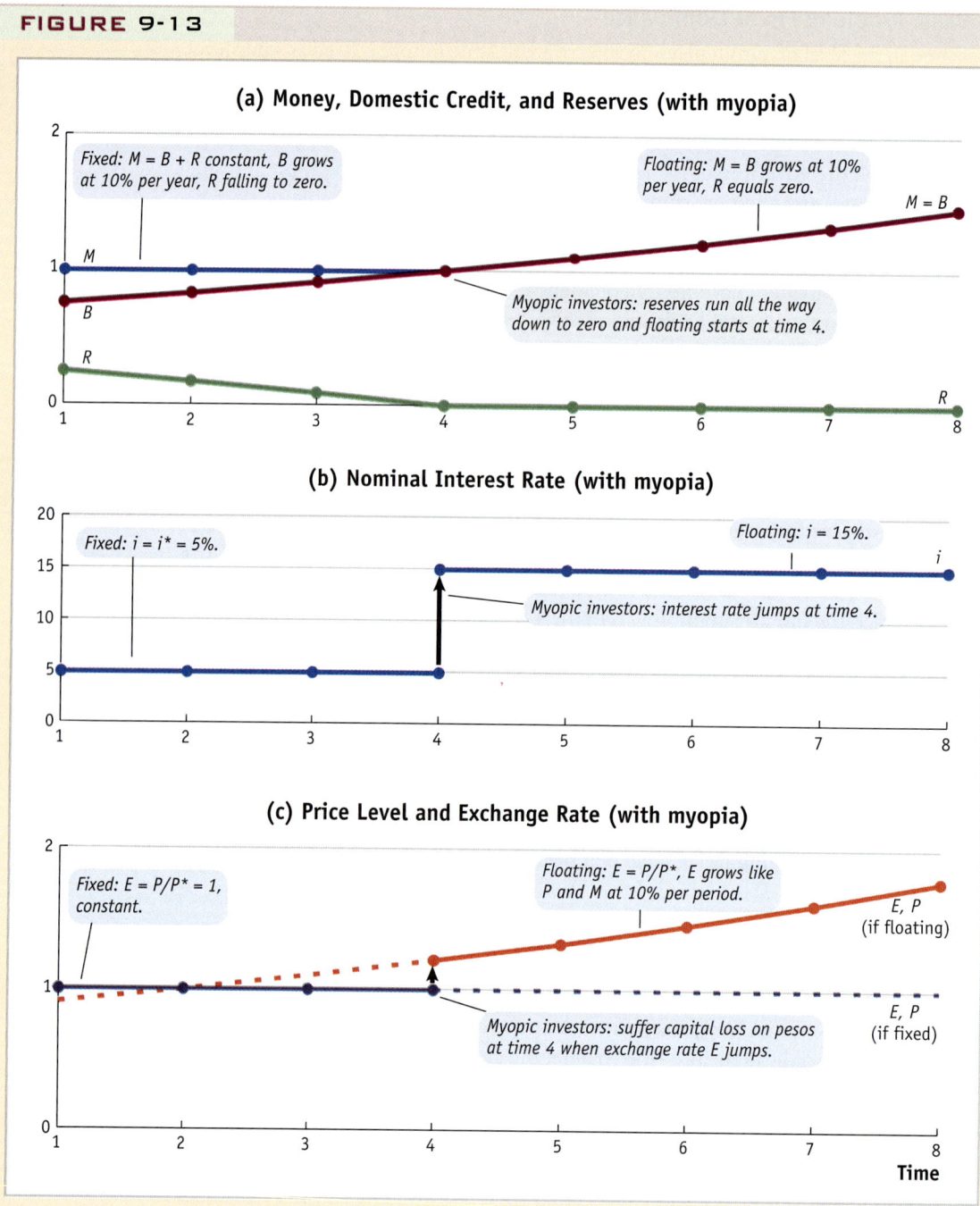

FIGURE 9-13

An Exchange Rate Crisis due to Inconsistent Fiscal Policies: Myopic Case In the fixed regime, money supply M is fixed, but expansion of domestic credit B implies that reserves R are falling to zero. Suppose the switch to floating occurs when reserves run out at time 4. Thereafter, the monetary model tells us that M, P, and E will all grow at a constant rate (here, 10% per period). The expected rates of inflation and depreciation are now positive, and the Fisher effect tells us that the interest rate must jump up at period 4 (by 10 percentage points). The interest rate increase means that real money demand $M/P = L(i)Y$ falls instantly at time 4. The money supply does not adjust immediately, so this jump in M/P must be accommodated by a jump in prices P. To maintain purchasing power parity, E must also jump at the same time. Hence, myopic investors face a capital loss on pesos at time 4.

and thereafter $B = M$ and $R = 0$. We assume for now that the regime change occurs at time 4. In the fixed regime, up to that point, money supply M is fixed, but when floating starts, M grows at a rate μ. This is shown in panel (a).

Because prices are flexible, the monetary model of exchange rates in the long run tells us that P will be fixed until time 4 and then it will grow at a rate μ. Thus, inflation rises by an amount μ at time 4. The Fisher effect tells us that an increase in the home inflation rate causes a one-for-one increase in the home interest rate. So the home interest rate i must rise by an amount μ as we move from the fixed to the floating regime. This is shown in panel (b).

An increase in the home interest rate i at time 4 lowers the demand for real money balances, $M/P = L(i)Y$, because in the money demand function, L is a decreasing function of i. Thus, M/P falls discontinuously (jumps) as we change from fixed to floating. Because the money supply M does not change at time 4, the discontinuous drop in M/P can be accommodated only by a jump in the flexible price level P at time 4. Because PPP holds continuously (and because $P^* = 1$), $E = P/P^* = P$, the discontinuous rise in P also means a discontinuous rise in E at time 4, and a depreciation of the home currency. Both E and P jump up and start to grow at rate at μ time 4, as shown in panel (c).

To sum up, in Figure 9-13, the exchange rate crisis is at time 4, but the exchange rate doesn't merely drift continuously away from its previous fixed level. It *jumps* away discontinuously. The new floating path of the exchange rate is a rising trend, with growth rate μ, which is above the old fixed rate at time 4.

For example, if the money growth rate is 10% after the crisis, as assumed, then there is a 10 percentage point increase in the interest rate from 5 to 15%. Now suppose this reduces real money demand by 20%, from 1.00 to 0.80. Because the nominal money supply M equals 1 just before and just after the crisis, it does not jump at time 4, so to get M/P to fall from 1.00 to 0.80, P must jump up, from 1.0 to $(1/0.80) = 1.25$, implying an instantaneous 25% increase in P. To maintain purchasing power parity, there must also be a 25% increase in the exchange rate E, to 1.25, followed by growth at 10%.

One significant implication of the jump in nominal values is that anyone holding a peso that was worth 1 dollar will suddenly be left holding a peso that is worth only $1/1.25 = 0.8$ dollars. Investors holding pesos at the moment of crisis will suffer a capital loss (in dollar terms) if this model accurately describes their behavior.

The Forward-Looking Case There is good reason to believe that investors will not be as shortsighted as we have assumed. It is usually well known when a government has a deficit that is being monetized, even if the authorities try to conceal the problem.

Let us move to the other extreme, *forward-looking* behavior, which for now we take to mean *perfect foresight*. We refer to Figure 9-14, which explains how this scenario departs from the myopic version we just saw in Figure 9-13. Suppose peso holders see that domestic credit is rising and reserves are falling. Knowledgeable people will speculate that the fixed rate is going to break in the near future. They will foresee that pesos will experience a sudden loss of dollar value if they hold them until the bitter end at time 4 when reserves would run out under myopia. They will therefore decide to dump pesos sooner. But when? And how?

All investors will want to dump pesos at the same time (in this model, all investors are identical). When investors sell all their holdings of a particular currency, it is known as a **speculative attack.** When such an attack occurs, the economy must *immediately* switch to the floating regime we have already studied, since once it has zero reserves, the money supply M will forever be equal to domestic credit B—which has been and

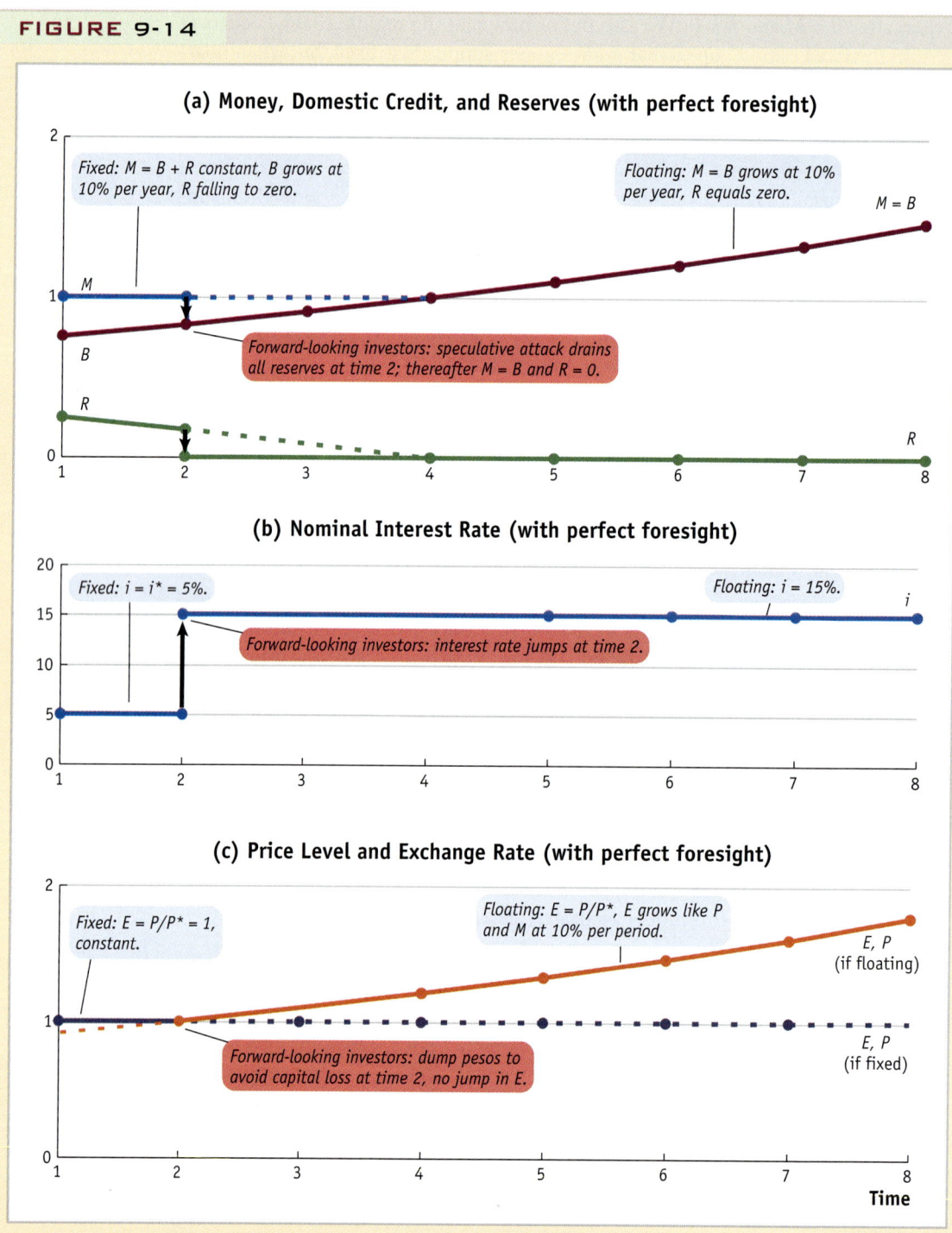

FIGURE 9-14

An Exchange Rate Crisis due to Inconsistent Fiscal Policies: Perfect-Foresight Case Compare with Figure 9-13. If investors anticipate a crisis, they will seek to avoid losses by converting the pesos they are holding to dollars before period 4. The rational moment to attack is at time 2, the point at which the switch from fixed to floating is achieved without any jumps in E or P. Why? At time 2, the drop in money demand (due to the rise in the interest rate) exactly equals the decline in the money supply (the reserve loss), and money market equilibrium is maintained without the price level having to change.

will be growing at the constant rate μ. At that same moment in time, the nominal interest rate will also jump up, as the Fisher effect kicks in as before, and there will be a jump down in both money demand (as the interest rise hits) and in money supply (as the attack drains all remaining reserves).

In our example, the key lesson is that once an attack occurs, the economy completely switches over to the floating regime. Under myopia the switch occurred at time 4. But now, the switch happens well before time 4, and at the time of the attack the economy's inflation, exchange rates, prices, and interest rates all flip over to their new trajectories. This leaves one question: When does the speculative attack occur? From Figure 9-14, the answer must be: at time 2. In this case, the path of the price level P and the exchange rate E are continuous as we switch from fixed to floating. Only then can the switch occur without any expected dollar gains or losses on holding pesos.

How does this pin down the attack at time 2? Suppose the attack were at any time later than 2, such as time 3. As we can see from the diagram, this requires a jump up in the exchange rate, a *discontinuous depreciation*. If they wait to attack until time 3, peso holders suffer a capital loss and they have waited too long. What if the attack is before time 2, say, at time 1? An attack at time 1 implies a *discontinuous appreciation* of the peso. But if that were so, any individual peso holder would enjoy capital gains (in dollars) from holding on to pesos rather than exchanging them for reserves at the central bank at the prior fixed rate. They would then desire to wait and let everyone else attack and pocket the gains. But if one person thinks like that, all do, and the attack cannot materialize.

The speculative attack model teaches an important lesson. One moment, a central bank may have a pile of reserves on hand, draining away fairly slowly, giving the illusion that there is no imminent danger. The next moment, the reserves are all gone. The model can therefore explain why fixed exchange rates sometimes witness a sudden collapse rather than a long, lingering death.

APPLICATION

The Peruvian Crisis of 1986

An example of a crisis driven by inconsistent fiscal policies and excessive expansion of domestic credit is provided by the events in Peru from 1985 to 1986, illustrated in Figure 9-15.

In the early 1980s Peru's political and economic conditions were highly unfavorable. The country had endured a period of social unrest and military rule in the 1970s, and the government had an enormous external debt burden. World commodity prices fell, exports and economic growth slowed, and government deficits grew. At the same time, world interest rates sharply increased.

The Peruvian government defaulted on its debt obligations and began negotiations with the IMF and other creditors. Denied fresh loans from world capital markets, and with low tax receipts that could not cover rising spending, government financing came to rely on money printing by the central bank—that is, the inflation tax. Domestic credit grew by 65% in 1982, 165% in 1983, and 93% in 1984—a rough doubling every year, on average. The dollar value of Peru's currency, the sol, rapidly sank.

As economic conditions deteriorated further and political violence by guerilla groups intensified, President Alan García Pérez was elected to office in 1985. One important economic measure he instituted immediately was a fixed exchange rate. This stopped the depreciation and was intended to give Peru a firm nominal anchor. But, as we now know, its durability would depend on whether García's administration

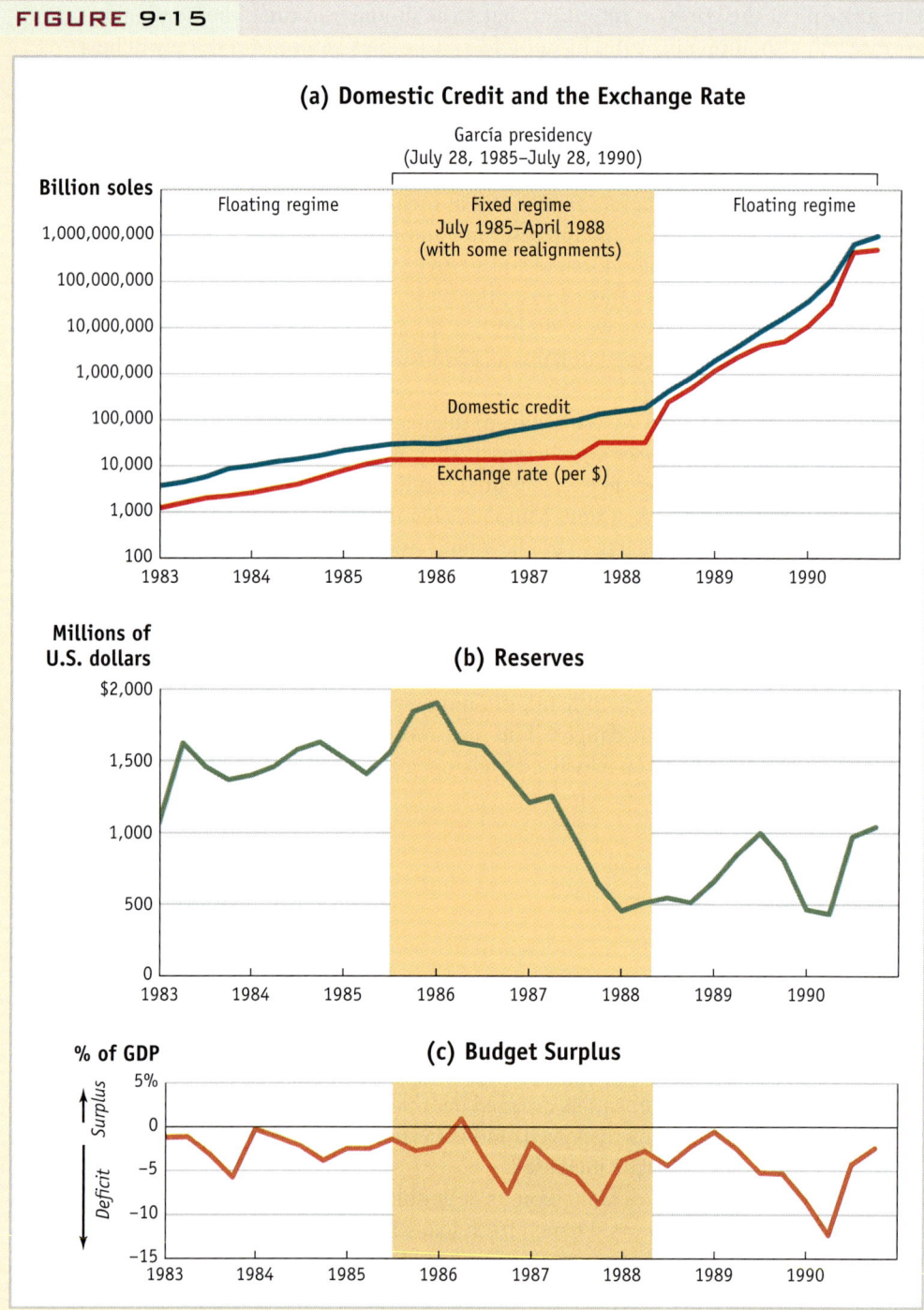

FIGURE 9-15

A Crisis in Peru: The Inconsistent Policies of the García Administration From 1985 to 1986 the Peruvian government implemented a fixed exchange rate regime, but government budget problems required significant monetization of budget deficits. Monetary and fiscal policies were inconsistent: A peg was in place, but domestic credit grew exponentially (note that the exchange rate and domestic credit are shown on logarithmic scales). The central bank lost three-quarters of its reserves in two years, and the peg had to be abandoned.

Source: IMF, International Financial Statistics.

could solve its fiscal problems and put an end to the monetization of government deficits.

Some fiscal reform was attempted, and the economy recovered slightly: The government budget improved at first. But the administration could not get the government budget out of the red for long. The deficit fell from 2% to 3% of GDP to near zero in early 1986, but by mid-1986 it was growing again, averaging over 5% and peaking at 8% to 9% of GDP in late 1986 and 1987. The printing presses of the central bank kept running, and domestic credit grew 84% in 1985, 77% in 1986, and 146% in 1987—still, on average, a rough doubling every year.

Only now, under a fixed exchange rate, something had to give. With domestic credit exploding, the central bank was continually selling reserves to defend the peg.[18] Reserves fell from a peak of $2,000 million in early 1986 to $500 million in early 1988. The authorities finally threw in the towel in April 1988 before the attack was complete and so avoided losing all their dollar reserves. The sol began to float and depreciation was rapid: The sol hit 250,000 sol/$ in September, 500,000 in November, and 1,200,000 by March 1989, and Peru was heading into a hyperinflation.[19]

The data closely match the predictions of the model. Under the peg, reserves drain as domestic credit grows, and the exchange rate is stable. Under the float, reserves are stable, and the exchange rate grows hand in hand with the expansion of domestic credit.

By the time García left office, Peru was in economic shambles. García's popularity sank. The 1990 presidential election was won by a political newcomer, Alberto Fujimori, who would struggle with the problems created by his predecessor (and problems of his own). Yet, remarkably, in 2006 Alan García Pérez was elected president of Peru for a second time. Twenty years is a long time in politics. ■

Expectations and the Critical Level of Reserves What determines the *critical level of reserves* R_c at which the crisis occurs? In the speculative attack model, the size of the sudden reserve loss, and hence the timing of the crisis, depend critically on market expectations about the future growth rate of domestic credit. The reserves R_c lost at the moment of crisis will depend on how much money investors want to convert into reserves when they attack. This, in turn, depends on how much money demand shrinks as we move from fixed to floating, and that is driven by the change in the interest rate.

Let's assume that each percentage point increase in the interest rate causes a ϕ% fall in real money balances.[20] At the moment of attack, the interest rate rises by an amount $\Delta i = \mu$, so the proportional fall in money demand is given by ϕ times that change. Thus, the change in money demand is given by $-\Delta M / M = \phi \times \mu$.

But we also know that the change in the money supply at the moment of attack $-\Delta M$ has to correspond exactly to the size of the reserve drain at the moment of attack, which equals the critical level of reserves R_c that are lost at that instant. Thus,

$$\underbrace{\frac{R_c}{M}}_{\text{Critical backing ratio when attack occurs}} = \frac{-\Delta M}{M} = \underbrace{\phi}_{\substack{\text{Responsiveness} \\ \text{of money demand} \\ \text{to interest rate changes}}} \times \underbrace{\mu}_{\substack{\text{Future} \\ \text{rate of growth of} \\ \text{domestic credit}}}$$

---

[18] The peg spent most of its time close to 17,300 sol/$. Various realignments to 20,000 and then 33,000 sol/$ in late 1987 bought a little time at the end.
[19] A common currency unit is used throughout this case study for consistency and commensurability. In reality, there were two currency reforms in Peru as a result of inflationary finance. The inti replaced the sol on February 1, 1985, at 1 inti per 1,000 soles, and on July 1, 1991, the nuevo sol replaced the inti at a rate of 1,000,000 nuevos soles per inti.
[20] This ϕ is called the interest semi-elasticity of money demand.

This expression tells us the ratio of the critical level of reserves R_c to the money supply M. It depends on the sensitivity of money demand to the interest rate and on the *expected future rate of growth* of domestic credit μ (remember, investors are *forward-looking*).

To illustrate, and continue our previous example, if the growth rate of domestic credit is expected to be $\mu = 10\%$, and if ϕ is 1.5, then the fall in money demand and money supply at the moment of attack is 10% times 1.5, or 15%. Thus, when reserves have drained so far that the backing ratio falls to the critical level $R_c = 15\%$, the peg will break. But if μ rises to 20%, the critical level R_c would be twice as large, 30%.

We can now see that if people *expect* a fiscal problem to worsen (expect the deficit to increase, and thus domestic credit to grow faster to finance it), then reserves drain away faster, and the crisis hits sooner, at a higher critical level of reserves R_c. Thus, an increase in the *expected* rate of deficit monetization shortens the length of time that the peg will survive.

This result emphasizes the importance of market beliefs. Suppose a country has reserves well above the critical level. There is no imminent crisis. Then market beliefs change, perhaps because news or rumors emerge about a budget problem. Investors now expect a higher growth rate of domestic credit. Suppose that, as a result of this change in expectations, the critical level of reserves rises so much as to equal the current level of reserves. With the change in expectations, the time for a speculative attack is now. A crisis will happen immediately, *even though there has been no change in the economic situation as of today!*

Summary

The first-generation crisis model tells us that inconsistent fiscal policies can destroy a fixed exchange rate. Yet it is not actual fiscal policy that matters, but *beliefs* and *expectations* about future fiscal policy. But beliefs about future deficits may or may not be justified, so the model opens up the possibility that countries will be punished for crimes they do not intend to commit.

For example, some economists have argued that expected future deficits were a factor in the Asian currency crisis of 1997: The countries were affected by "crony capitalism" and the banking sectors were insolvent because of bad loans to insiders. Once the scale of these problems became known, investors believed that the monetary authorities would bail out the banks. Fears of a rapid future expansion of domestic credit thus undermined the pegs.[21]

4 How Pegs Break II: Contingent Monetary Policies

In the previous section, we found that inconsistent fiscal policies under a fixed exchange rate regime eventually cause an exchange rate crisis. However, the crises of the 1990s often did not conform to a model based on deficit monetization because budget problems were absent in many cases. In particular, the ERM crisis of 1992 affected developed countries in Europe, most of which were unlikely to monetize deficits. In

---

[21] See, for example, the discussion of Korea's precrisis weaknesses in the operation and regulation of the banking sector, and the central bank's willingness to furtively channel dollar reserves to bail out the banks, in Frederic Mishkin, 2006, *The Next Great Globalization: How Disadvantaged Nations Can Harness Their Financial Systems to Get Rich* (Princeton, N.J.: Princeton University Press). See also Craig Burnside, Martin Eichenbaum, and Sergio Rebelo, 2001, "Prospective Deficits and the Asian Currency Crisis," *Journal of Political Economy* 109(6), 1155–1197.

countries with apparently sound economic policies, foreign currency speculators went for the attack and pegs broke.[22]

Economists therefore developed alternative models of crises, with the pioneering work on the **second-generation crisis model** being done by Maurice Obstfeld. These types of models can explain how, even when policy making is rational and purposeful—rather than incompetent and inconsistent—there may still be situations in which pegs break for no apparent reason.[23]

The Basic Problem: Contingent Commitment

The essence of the model is that policy makers are not committed to the peg under all circumstances. Defending the peg is therefore a **contingent commitment** (a slight oxymoron): if things get "bad enough," the government will let the exchange rate float rather than put the country through serious economic pain. The problem is that everyone—notably, investors in the forex market—knows it and they will adjust their expectations accordingly.

To develop some intuition, we return to Britain and Germany in 1992, the example we saw at the start of Chapter 8 when we studied fixed and floating regimes. Let's recap the basic story: The German central bank raised interest rates to deal with a domestic shock, the fiscal expansion arising from German unification after 1989. This left Britain with a higher interest rate and a lower output level than was desired. What would Britain do in response?

If German interest rates are fairly low, so too are British interest rates, output costs in Britain are low, and nobody expects Britain to leave the peg. The peg is *credible*. But if German interest rates rise to high levels, output in Britain falls to an intolerably low level, and nobody expects Britain to stay on the peg for long. Instead, everyone thinks Britain will float and use expansionary monetary policy to boost output and depreciate the pound. The peg is *not credible*, and the market now expects a depreciation in the future.

The problem for Britain is that an expected depreciation will introduce a *currency premium*, as we saw earlier in this chapter. Investors will demand even higher interest rates in Britain to compensate for the imminent depreciation—and this will mean even lower output and even higher pain for Britain!

This creates a gray area. How? It is quite possible that the German interest rate can be at some "intermediate" level at which pegging is tolerable with no expected depreciation: People would expect the peg to hold and the peg would hold. But if there is an expected depreciation and a currency premium, pegging might be intolerable: People would expect the peg to fail and the peg would fail. Crucially, in both scenarios, ex ante market expectations are validated ex post, and hence would be considered "rational."

Based on these insights from the Britain-Germany example, we now develop an economic model with such *self-fulfilling expectations*. In this model we may not always find a single, unique equilibrium but rather **multiple equilibria.** Whether there is a crisis or not depends entirely on market sentiment, and not simply economic fundamentals.

---

[22] A helpful survey is provided by Sweta C. Saxena, 2004, "The Changing Nature of Currency Crises," *Journal of Economic Surveys* 18(3), 321–350.
[23] Maurice Obstfeld, 1986, "Rational and Self-Fulfilling Balance-of-Payments Crises," *American Economic Review* 76(1), 72–81.

FIGURE 9-16

A Simple Model

In this type of model, we need a measure of the cost of maintaining the peg. The simplest cost measure is the deviation of output Y in the short run below its full employment level. To allow output to vary, we need to use the IS-LM-FX model introduced in the chapter on macroeconomic policy, which means that we reverse some of the assumptions we made before. From now on, output Y will be variable rather than fixed, and it will be determined by the model. And from now on, prices will be sticky, not flexible, and treated as given.[24]

For simplicity, we assume there are *some* benefits from pegging, say, the gains from increased trade. Let these benefits be $b > 0$ and constant. Against the benefits of

---

[24] The reason for this change in assumptions is that at the heart of this model the crisis is not driven by a set of policies that will ultimately break the nominal anchor—inflation plays no role here, so prices can be assumed steady; instead, the key mechanism in this model is the desire *in certain circumstances* to stabilize output by using temporary shifts in monetary policy, which means that the exchange rate must be allowed to float.

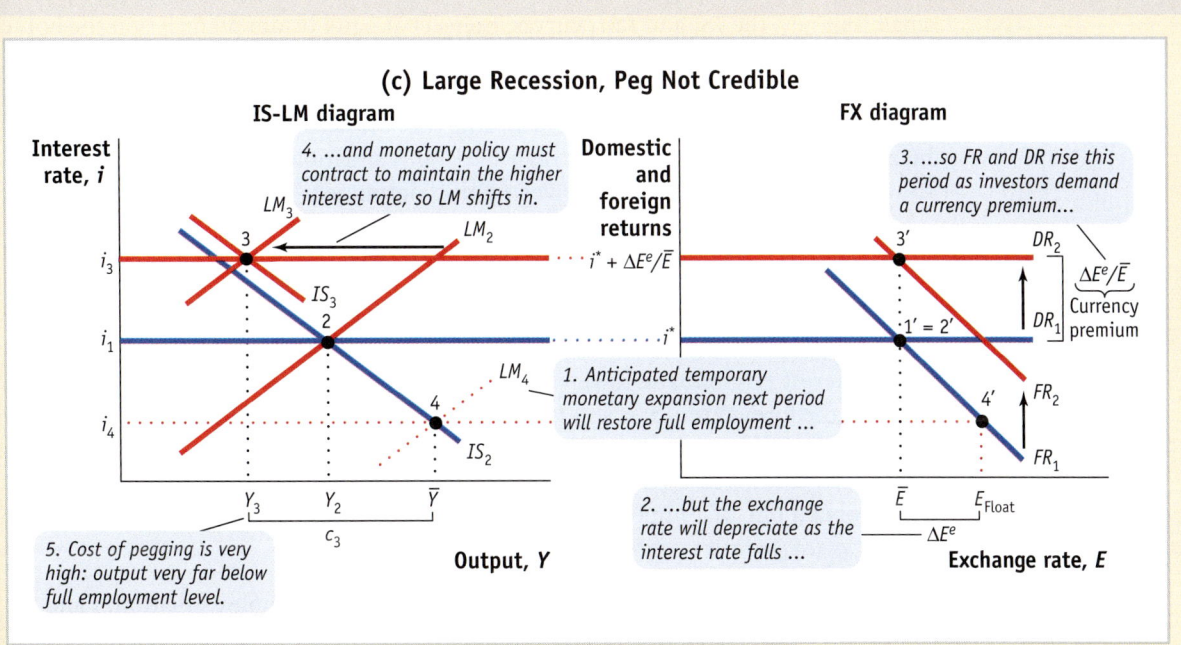

Contingent Commitments and the Cost of Maintaining a Peg This figure describes how the IS-LM-FX equilibrium changes as demand shocks occur and as the credibility of the peg weakens. The economy is pegging at a fixed exchange rate $\bar{E}$. In panel (a), the economy is at IS-LM equilibrium at point 1, with the FX market at point 1'. Output is a little below desired output, so the cost of pegging c_1 is small. In panel (b), there is an adverse shock to domestic demand, and the IS curve shifts in. LM shifts in, too, to maintain the peg. The new IS-LM equilibrium occurs at point 2, with FX market equilibrium at point 2' (same as 1'). The cost of pegging c_2 is higher. Panel (c) shows that if the country wants to attain full employment output next period, it must move to point 4, shifting the LM curve out and allowing the FX market to settle at point 4' with the exchange rate depreciating to E_{float}. The peg would still be in operation today, but, by definition, it would no longer be credible if such a policy change were anticipated. Because of the lack of credibility, investors would insist on receiving a positive currency premium *today*, and the home interest rate would rise to i_3, squeezing demand even more and moving the IS-LM equilibrium to point 3 and the FX market to point 3'. Now the cost of pegging c_3 is even higher: having a noncredible peg is more costly than having a credible peg.

pegging, the government weighs costs c that equal the "output gap": full-employment $\bar{Y}$ output minus current output Y. If costs exceed benefits, we assume that the government will elect to float next period and use monetary policy to restore full employment output. For simplicity, we assume each period lasts one year. (Restricting attention to this type of rule keep things simple while illustrating the key trade-offs.)

In Figure 9-16, we use the home IS-LM-FX diagram to look at how outcomes under the peg can depend on both economic fundamentals and market expectations. We assume foreign output is fixed at Y^*, and we also assume there is no fiscal policy change, so we can focus only on home monetary policy choices. Most important, we assume that investors are aware of the contingent commitment to the peg.

In this setup, it does not matter where adverse output shocks originate. They could result from increases in the foreign interest rate (as in the ERM example). Or they could be caused by a decline in the demand for home goods overseas. All that matters is that the home economy is in some kind of pain with output below the desired level.

Small Recession, Peg Credible Panel (a) shows a situation in which the pain is small. Initially, the IS_1 and LM_1 curves intersect at equilibrium point 1, and the home interest rate is $i_1 = i^*$ to maintain the peg. In the FX diagram, the domestic return is DR_1 and the foreign return FR_1. They intersect at point 1′ and the exchange rate is fixed at $E_1 = \overline{E}$. Home output is at Y_1, but we assume that the desired full employment level of home output is $\overline{Y}$, slightly higher than Y_1. In this situation, when the peg is credible, the economy suffers a small cost given by the "output gap": $c_1 = \overline{Y} - Y_1$.

Large Recession, Peg Credible Panel (b) shows a situation in which the adverse shock to output is large. The IS_2 and LM_2 curves now intersect at equilibrium point 2. The IS curve has moved left by assumption: it is the source of the adverse shock. The LM curve has moved in to maintain the peg and preserve interest parity, so that the home interest rate remains at $i_1 = i^*$. In the FX diagram, the domestic return is still DR_1 and the foreign return is still FR_1, and they intersect at point 2′, the same as point 1′, with $E_1 = \overline{E}$. Home output is now much lower at Y_2. Here, the economy suffers an even larger cost given by the "output gap": $c_2 = \overline{Y} - Y_2$.

We obtain our first important result: *If the market believes that the peg is credible, the output gap (cost) increases as the size of the adverse shock increases.*

Large Recession, Peg Not Credible This is the most complex situation. Panel (c) assumes a large recession as in panel (b), but shows what happens if investors believe that the authorities will choose to depreciate next year to achieve desired output. We suppose exchange rate expectations are unchanged next year at the pegged rate. The IS curve will still be at IS_2, and the required monetary expansion next year will shift the LM curve to LM_4 so that the new equilibrium will be at point 4 with output at the desired level $\overline{Y}$, and a low interest rate of i_4. This will lead to a (temporary) depreciation next year, the peg will break, and the exchange rate will rise from $\overline{E}$ to E_{float}. We can also see that to achieve full employment output, the lower that Y_2 is, the larger the required shift in the LM curve will be next year and the larger the resulting depreciation.

However, the government's response *next year* will be anticipated by investors. If they know that output is low enough to prompt a depreciation, they will expect a depreciation over the coming year of a size given by $\Delta E^e/\overline{E} = (E_{\text{float}} - \overline{E})/\overline{E} > 0$. This expected depreciation will appear as a currency premium *today* in the FX market of panel (c). The current period's (risk-adjusted) foreign return curve is shifted up by an amount equal to the currency premium as far as FR_2.

If the central bank wants to maintain the peg, despite it not being credible, it has to ensure forex market equilibrium at point 3′, so it must raise the home interest rate to i_3. At today's pegged rate $\overline{E}$, uncovered interest parity now requires a higher home interest rate $i_3 = i^* + \Delta E^e/\overline{E}$. Graphically, this means the domestic return curve must also shift up by an amount equal to the currency premium, as far as DR_2.

As we know from the earlier chapters on policy and regimes, this shift will depress home demand and lead to even lower home output today, which is shown at Y_3.

In more detail, today the IS curve moves out slightly to IS_3 due to expected depreciation, but the LM curve moves in a long way to LM_3 to defend the peg. The latter effect dominates, because we know that demand and output have to be lower today given the combination of the same exchange rate (no change in the trade balance) and a higher interest rate (lower investment demand). So the new IS-LM equilibrium is at point 3, to the *left* of point 2.

We also note that to achieve this monetary contraction, the central bank must sell reserves—and the drain can take the form of a speculative attack if the currency premium appears suddenly as a result of a switch in beliefs.

The loss of credibility makes a bad recession even worse. If the peg is not credible, a higher interest rate causes the costs of pegging rise to $c_3 = \overline{Y} - Y_3$. Finally, we note that this cost will be higher when the output gap is higher, because a larger output gap implies a larger depreciation to restore full employment.

Our second important result: *If the forex market switches to believing that the peg is not credible, then reserves drain, the interest rate rises, and the output gap (cost) increases; also, the cost increases more if the output gap is larger to begin with.*

The Costs and Benefits of Pegging Our IS-LM-FX analysis is now complete, and all we need to do is consider the implications.

Figure 9-17 sums up the cost–benefit analysis. The horizontal axis measures the output gap, or the cost of pegging, *when the peg is credible*. We denote these costs $c(\overline{E})$. This notation indicates that this is the cost c when the exchange rate is expected to be at $\overline{E}$ next period. The first of our results showed that this cost rises, and we move right along the horizontal axis, whenever the country suffers an adverse shock under the peg.

The vertical axis measures and compares the costs and benefits of pegging. Benefits are constant at b. The costs when the peg is credible are equal to $c(\overline{E})$ so these will fall on the 45-degree line, since $c(\overline{E})$ is measured on the horizontal axis.

Finally, the cost of pegging when the peg is not credible is denoted $c(E_{\text{float}})$. This notation indicates that this is the cost c when the exchange rate is expected to be at E_{float} next period.

The second of our results showed that the costs of pegging when the peg is not credible are always greater than the costs when the peg is credible, due to the rise in the currency premium associated with an expected depreciation. In other words, the $c(E_{\text{float}})$ line is above the $c(\overline{E})$ line, as shown. We also saw that the difference gets larger as the costs grow larger. In Figure 9-17, this means that the $c(E_{\text{float}})$ curve diverges from the $c(\overline{E})$ curve, as shown.

Corresponding to the previous analysis in Figure 9-16, point 1 (cost c_1) represents a small recession with a credible peg; point 2 (cost c_2) represents a large recession with a credible peg; point 3 (cost c_3) represents the same large recession with a noncredible peg.

With this basic apparatus, we can now analyze the "game" between the authorities and investors. To keep it simple, we suppose investors can choose from two beliefs about what the government will do: {peg, depreciate}. And we suppose the authorities then choose from two actions: {peg, depreciate}. Faced with this type of problem, economists search for what might be considered a rational outcome of the game. We look for a **self-confirming equilibrium,** that is, combinations of investor beliefs and government actions for which the ex post outcome validates the ex ante beliefs.

We can identify several such equilibria using Figure 9-17:

- In Zone I, $b > c(E_{\text{float}}) > c(\overline{E})$, so the benefits b of pegging always outweigh both kinds of costs, no matter what the market believes. The authorities will always choose to "peg." Anticipating this, the market belief will also be peg, and this is the only ex ante belief that will be validated ex post. Benefits are always given by b, and costs are always those of a credible peg $c(\overline{E})$. There is a unique self-confirming equilibrium: peg, with costs corresponding to the solid portion of the line $c(\overline{E})$. (Example: point 1.)

FIGURE 9-17

Contingent Policies and Multiple Equilibria Building on Figure 9-16, this figure shows how the costs of pegging depend on whether the peg is credible, and how that affects the game between the authorities and investors. The costs of pegging *when the peg is credible* are shown on the horizontal axis. To measure these costs on the vertical axis, we can read off from the 45-degree line (the orange line, dotted or solid). We know that the costs of pegging when the peg is not credible will be even higher (the red line, dotted or solid), because costs rise when investors do not believe in the peg. We assume the government believes the benefits of pegging (e.g., lower trade costs) are fixed and equal to b. Equilibria in this world correspond to points on the *solid segments* of the red and orange cost lines. The peg is always credible in Zone I, where benefits always exceed costs: the government never wants to depreciate and investors know it. The peg is always noncredible in Zone III, where costs always exceed benefits: the government always wants to depreciate and investors know it. Zone II is the gray area: if investors believe the peg is credible, costs are low and the peg will hold; if investors believe the peg is noncredible, costs are higher and the peg will break.

- In Zone III, $c(E_{\text{float}}) > c(\overline{E}) > b$, so both kinds of costs of pegging always outweigh the benefits b, no matter what the market believes. The authorities will always choose to "depreciate." Anticipating this, the market belief will also be depreciate, and this is the only ex ante belief that will be validated ex post. Benefits are then always given by b, and the costs are always those of a noncredible peg $c(E_{\text{float}})$. There is a unique self-confirming equilibrium: depreciate, with costs corresponding to the solid portion of the line $c(E_{\text{float}})$. (Example: point 5.)

- In Zone II, $c(E_{\text{float}}) > b > c(\overline{E})$. If the market belief is "depreciate," then the benefits b of pegging are less than the costs of the noncredible peg $c(E_{\text{float}})$; authorities will then choose depreciate, and market beliefs are validated for this case. Conversely, if the market belief is peg, then the benefits b of pegging are greater than the costs of a credible peg $c(\overline{E})$; authorities will then choose peg, and the market beliefs are also validated for this case. There are two self-confirming equilibria in this zone. Zone II is shown as a gray area in the diagram. And appropriately so! In this range, there is no unique equilibrium, and depending on market beliefs, costs may correspond to the solid portions of either line $c(\overline{E})$ or line $c(E_{\text{float}})$. (Examples: points 2 and 3.)

APPLICATION

The Man Who Broke the Bank of England

Our analysis of contingent policies is highly simplified but advances our understanding of the potential for capricious outcomes driven by shifts in market sentiment. Changes in market sentiment, often called "animal spirits," emerge here from a model based on rational actors.

In some circumstances, the instability problem is much worse than we have suggested, for a couple of reasons. First, we have assumed that the government does not exit the peg immediately when it suffers pain, so expectations of depreciation are slow. If a 10% devaluation is feared in one year, this causes a 10% currency premium. But if it is expected to happen in three months (next quarter), then the expected rate of depreciation on an *annualized* basis is much higher and is given by a fourfold compounding of a 10% increase: this is 46% (because 1.10 to the power 4 equals 1.46). So the currency premium would be approximately 46%, a heavy penalty. If the 10% devaluation were expected in one month, the premium would be more than 200% on an annualized basis.[25] As the time frame shrinks, the currency premium explodes!

For example, in 1992 Swedish interest rates climbed astronomically as investors speculated on the imminent demise of the krona's peg to the German mark. The annualized short-term (overnight) lending rate climbed to 75% on September 8 and 500% on September 19. Such an interest rate was not politically tenable for very long. Investors knew this, and they were proved right.

A second issue is how beliefs form in the first place. Suppose we are in Zone II at the "no crisis" self-confirming equilibrium, with beliefs and actions corresponding to "peg." A mass switch in beliefs to "depreciate" would also be a self-confirming equilibrium. How does the market end up in one equilibrium or the other?

If traders are a group of many individuals, spread diffusely throughout the market, then it is unclear how they could all suddenly coordinate a switch to a new set of beliefs. And if each trader can place only a small bet, then it would be irrational for any trader to switch beliefs—unless all traders switch, and without coordination the switch is not going to happen and the peg stands a chance of holding.

But what if there are only a few traders? Or even just one very large trader who can make very big bets? If that single trader changes beliefs, the entire market goes from believing "peg" (no bets) to believing "depreciate" (making as big a bet against the home currency as possible). The coordination problem is solved. This is illustrated by the British ERM crisis of 1992. The large trader was the Quantum Fund, owned by the famous (to some, infamous) investor George Soros, who likes to use the term "reflexivity" to describe how markets shape events, as well as vice versa.

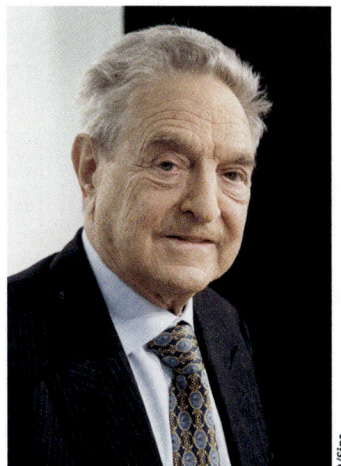

George Soros: "Reflexivity is, in effect, a two-way feedback mechanism in which reality helps shape the participants' thinking and the participants' thinking helps shape reality."

---

[25] In these cases, the rate of depreciation is not small, so the UIP approximation formula is not appropriate. For precision, the exact UIP formula should be used: $1 + i = (1 + i^*)E^e/E$. For example, to use this formula, if the foreign interest rate is 2%, but a 10% devaluation is expected after one quarter, then the formula says that on an annual basis the home interest rate will be given by $1 + i = (1.02) \times (1 + 0.10)^4 = 1.4934$. So the home interest rate is about 49.3%, and subtracting the foreign rate of 2%, we find a currency premium of 47.3%, still close to the 46% given by the approximation formula. In the case of a 10% depreciation expected after 1 week, with 52 weeks per year, the home interest rate will be given by $1 + i = (1.02) \times (1 + 0.10)^{12} = 3.2012$, so the home interest rate is 220% and the currency premium is 218%.

Soros's firm placed one big bet after another, until he had borrowed billions of pounds and parked all the money in German mark deposits. "It was an obvious bet, a one-way bet," he later recalled.[26] If the pound held, he could convert his marks back to pounds. having paid a small interest cost (the difference between pound and mark interest rates for a few days); if the peg broke, he made billions as the pound fell. And who sold him the marks in exchange for pounds? The Bank of England, under orders from the U.K. Treasury, was intervening furiously, selling marks to prop up the pound at the limits of the ERM band.

The sudden increase in the currency premium was inducing a massive reserve drain. On the morning of September 16, 1992, the pressure on the pound became intense. The government made a feeble defense, raising the Bank's interest rates too little, too late, from 10% to 12% and, at the last gasp, to 15%. The bears were unimpressed. With market sentiment so strong, reserve outflow was unlikely to halt without stronger measures, such as the Swedes had taken the week before. But with the British economy performing weakly, the government had little stomach for triple-digit interest rates—something investors well knew.

It was all over by lunchtime, with the bulk of the reserves lost, and an estimated £4 billion spent in a futile defense. The event has gone down in history as one more legendary British exchange rate fiasco. ■

Summary

Our results are striking. If government policies are contingent, then they will depend on market sentiment. But market sentiment, in turn, depends on what the market believes the government will do. If costs of pegging are "low," then pegs hold when they "should"—when the government has no desire to exit. If costs of pegging are "high," then crises happen when they "should"—when the government clearly wants to exit. But in between these extremes, an ambiguity arises in the form of multiple equilibria because for some "medium" range of costs, a crisis occurs if and only if the market expects a crisis.

5 Conclusions

Fixed exchange rates exhibit no signs of disappearing. Despite all their potential benefits, however, history shows another persistent feature—the recurrent crises that mark the collapse of fixed regimes.

In this chapter, we studied two kinds of crises. Adverse fiscal conditions can send the money supply out of control. And changes in the real economy can weaken the commitment to a peg. Expectations matter in each case—shifts in investor sentiment can make the crises occur "sooner" (i.e., when economic fundamentals are better), leading to worries that some crises are an unnecessary and undeserved punishment.

Can We Prevent Crises?

With these insights, we can now confront the major policy problem: How can these crises be prevented? A number of solutions have been proposed that merit mention:

---

[26] Ashley Seager, "Black Wednesday Still Haunts Britain," Reuters, September 16, 2002.

- *The case for capital controls.* Crises occur in the forex market. Shut down that market, and the risk of crisis should be lower. However, experience shows that capital controls are hard to implement and never watertight. Empirically, there seems to be no consistent evidence that controls work (in terms of various measures such as crisis frequency, growth, monetary autonomy). In addition, countries tend to want to maintain financial openness as a way to obtain some of the gains described in the chapter on financial globalization. Controls could be slapped on as a temporary device, but, given the speed with which crises can unfold, the door often ends up being shut after the reserves have bolted. For some examples (Malaysia after 1997, Spain after 1992), a case can be made that controls resulted in a positive difference in a time of crisis, but in large samples, the effects are weak or negative.[27]

- *The case against intermediate regimes.* One lesson of the models presented in this chapter is that a change in market expectations can trigger "unnecessary" crises, with no deterioration in fundamentals today. After the experience of the 1990s, many leading economists came around to the view that intermediate regimes, the so-called dirty floats and soft pegs, were very risky in this regard. Under such regimes, the extent of the authorities' commitment to the exchange rate target would be seen as questionable, meaning that departures from the target to monetize deficits or pursue monetary autonomy might be suspected, leading to self-fulfilling crises. Solution: In the trilemma diagram, countries should get out of the middle and move to the corners. This view came to be known as the **corners hypothesis** or the *missing middle*. Given the prevailing view that controls were not a viable option, this reduced the trilemma to a dilemma: In this "bipolar" view, only the two extremes of a hard peg or a true float were recommended (an idea dating back to Milton Friedman, quoted at the start of this chapter). Evidence has mounted that intermediate regimes have been more crisis-prone in the past (up to five times as likely to have a crisis as a hard peg, according to one study), but the move away from such regimes appears to be very slow.[28]

- *The case for floating.* In a crisis, a peg breaks. If there isn't a peg, there is nothing to break. It might be desirable for all countries to float from that perspective. However, in the chapter on fixed and floating regimes, we saw that there can

---

[27] See, for example, Sebastian Edwards and Jeffrey A. Frankel, eds., 2002, *Preventing Currency Crises in Emerging Markets* (Chicago: University of Chicago Press); Sebastian Edwards, ed., 2007, *Capital Controls and Capital Flows in Emerging Economies: Policies, Practices, and Consequences* (Chicago: University of Chicago Press); Reuven Glick, Xueyan Guo, and Michael Hutchison, 2006, "Currency Crises, Capital-Account Liberalization, and Selection Bias," *Review of Economics and Statistics*, 88(4), 698–714; Rawi Abdelal and Laura Alfaro, 2003, "Capital and Control: Lessons from Malaysia, *Challenge*, 46(4), 36–53.

[28] After Friedman, the corners hypothesis gained new life in the 1990s and became influential in the minds of leading international economists and policy makers, such as Andrew Crockett, Barry Eichengreen, Stanley Fischer, and Lawrence Summers. For surveys of the intellectual history and arguments for and against the bipolar views, see Morris Goldstein, 2002, *Managed Floating Plus*, Policy Analyses in International Economics, no. 66 (Washington, D.C.: Peterson Institute for International Economics); Thomas D. Willett, 2007, "Why the Middle Is Unstable: The Political Economy of Exchange Rate Regimes and Currency Crises," *World Economy*, 30(5), 709–732. On crisis frequency and evidence for a trend away from the middle, see Andrea Bubula and Inci Otker-Robe, 2004, *The Continuing Bipolar Conundrum, IMF Finance and Development*. Evidence of no such trend is given by Kenneth Rogoff, Ashoka Mody, Nienke Oomes, Robin Brooks, and Aasim M. Husain, 2004, "Evolution and Performance of Exchange Rate Regimes," IMF Occasional Paper no. 229.

be powerful reasons to peg, especially in emerging market and developing countries with *fear of floating*. And empirically, there is no overwhelming trend toward floating regimes in recent years. Thus, the floating corner has not attracted all that many countries in practice.

- *The case for hard pegs.* If floating is out, then the "bipolar view" suggests that (short of dollarizing) countries should go the other way and adopt a really hard peg like a currency board. According to the IMF classification, only a few countries have taken this route, such as Estonia, Hong Kong, and—until its 2001–2002 crisis—Argentina. Not all of these regimes were *strict* currency boards, but they could all be considered hard pegs, with high reserve ratios and some rules to try to limit domestic credit. Did they work? Some worked very well. It may seem pedantic to point out that the Hong Kong Monetary Authority wasn't following the strict rules; the system has worked, and the massive reserves kept the peg alive even in times of financial market turmoil. But hard pegs can also break like any other kind of government commitment, if the authorities deem it necessary, as in Argentina. Lesson: All fixed exchange rates can end up being cheap talk, no matter how much armor they appear to have.[29]

- *The case for improving the institutions of macroeconomic policy and financial markets.* If hard pegs are not a panacea, then risks to pegged regimes might be minimized if the rest of the macroeconomic and financial structure in a country could be endowed with greater strength, increased stability, and enhanced transparency. Admittedly, these goals are always desirable no matter what the exchange rate regime, but they take on added importance when a country is pegging because fiscal and banking problems have emerged as the root cause of so many crises. The steps involved may be slow, incremental, bureaucratic, and unglamorous. But their defenders would claim that, although they lack the magic-bullet quality of currency boards and other schemes tried by mercurial finance ministers, these improvements are the foundations on which any successful fixed exchange rate regime must be built.

- *The case for an international lender of last resort.* We have seen that the adequate level of reserves to avert a crisis can depend on market sentiment. Why not borrow more reserves? This solution is not possible if lenders worry about an imminent crisis and you face a sudden stop. This is where the **International Monetary Fund (IMF)** can help. The IMF may lend to countries in difficulty if it thinks they can restore stability in a timely fashion with the help of a loan. But making the right judgments is far from easy. The IMF may impose unwelcome loan conditions that require policy change, including, for example, stricter control of budget deficits. These conditions are sometimes ignored (possibly leading to a suspension of the loan program). The IMF has also been criticized on occasion for being too hard (Korea in

---

[29] With the exception of Bosnia and Estonia, most modern "currency boards" have violated the strict rule against using domestic credit and have not kept the backing ratio close to 100%. See "Measures of Activism in Monetary Policy for Currency Board-Like Systems," by Kurt Schuler, June 2005 (http://www.dollarization.org/), based on data from the IMF, International Financial Statistics.

1997) or too soft (Argentina in 2001). Moreover, its capacity to lend is limited and is increasingly dwarfed by private capital flows, causing concerns that future attacks may be too large for any IMF program to contain. Not that larger rescue capacity is necessarily good—at a basic level, many worry that the prospect of IMF bailouts, like any kind of insurance, may encourage lax behavior (*moral hazard*), which could worsen the crisis problem. Not surprisingly, the role of the IMF has been constantly questioned in the current era of globalization.[30]

- *The case for self-insurance*. What if a country wants to peg, but none of the above ideas offers much comfort? What if controls are unattractive, floating too risky, and currency boards too much of a straightjacket? What if a country knows that its domestic macroeconomic and financial architecture is still in a state of remodeling? What if the country looks back at the 1990s and worries that IMF programs will be too small, too late, too full of conditions, or not available at crunch time? In some ways, this describes many of the Asian countries, and other emerging markets, in the 2000s. The vast reserve buildup of recent years may be seen as a giant exercise in saving for a rainy day to protect these countries against the vicissitudes of global finance.

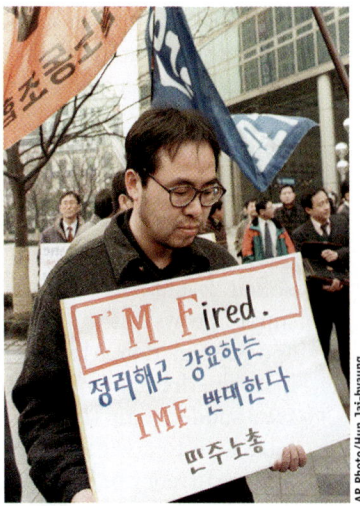

After what happened in 1997, some Asian countries may not turn to the IMF again—and with their reserve accumulation, they may not need to.

KEY POINTS

1. An exchange rate crisis is a large and sudden depreciation that brings to an end a fixed exchange rate regime.

2. Such crises are common. The typical fixed exchange rate lasts only a few years. History shows that crises can affect all types of countries—advanced, emerging, and developing.

3. Crises have economic costs that tend to be very large in emerging markets and developing countries. Political costs are also large.

4. To avoid a crisis, the central bank in a country with a fixed exchange rate regime must have the ability to peg the exchange rate. In practice, this means the central bank needs foreign currency reserves, which can be bought or sold in the forex market at the fixed rate.

5. In a simple model of a central bank, the money supply consists of domestic credit and foreign reserves. Money demand is exogenous and is determined by interest rates and output levels that we assume are beyond the control of the authorities when the exchange rate is pegged. In this model, reserves are simply money demand minus domestic credit.

6. If money demand rises (falls), holding domestic credit fixed, reserves rise (fall) by the same amount.

7. If domestic credit rises (falls), holding money demand fixed, reserves fall (rise) by the same amount and the money supply is unchanged. The combined result is called sterilization.

---

[30] For a critical and nontechnical appraisal of IMF actions from 1994 to 2002, see Paul Blustein, 2001, *The Chastening: Inside the Crisis That Rocked the Global Financial System and Humbled the IMF* (New York: Public Affairs); and Paul Blustein, 2005, *And the Money Kept Rolling In (and Out): Wall Street, the IMF, and the Bankrupting of Argentina* (New York: Public Affairs).

8. When the central bank gives assistance to the financial sector, it expands domestic credit. If it is a bailout, money demand is unchanged, and reserves drain. If it is a loan to satisfy depositors' demand for cash, then reserves stay constant.

9. A first-generation crisis occurs when domestic credit grows at a constant rate forever, usually due to the monetization of a chronic fiscal deficit. Eventually, reserves drain and the money supply grows at the same rate, causing inflation and depreciation. Myopic investors do not anticipate the drain, and when reserves run out, they see a sudden jump (depreciation) in the exchange rate. Investors with foresight will try to sell domestic currency before that jump happens and by doing so will cause a speculative attack and a sudden drain of reserves.

10. A second-generation attack occurs when the authorities' commitment to the peg is contingent. If the domestic economy is suffering too high a cost from pegging, the authorities will consider floating and using expansionary monetary policy to boost output by allowing the currency to depreciate, thus breaking the peg. If investors anticipate that the government will break the peg, they will demand a currency premium, making interest even higher under the peg and raising the costs of pegging still further. In this setup, at some intermediate costs, the authorities will maintain the peg as long as investors find the peg credible, but they will allow their currency to depreciate if investors find the peg not credible. This creates multiple equilibria and self-fulfilling crises.

KEY TERMS

exchange rate crisis, p. 346
banking crisis, p. 348
default crisis, p. 348
twin crises, p. 350
triple crises, p. 350
domestic credit, p. 352
reserves, p. 353
central bank balance sheet, p. 353
assets, p. 353
liabilities, p. 353
floating line, p. 356
fixed line, p. 356
currency board, p. 356
backing ratio, p. 357
risk premium, p. 359
interest rate spread, p. 360
currency premium, p. 360
country premium, p. 360
credibility, p. 362
contagion, p. 362
sterilization, p. 365
insolvent, p. 367
bailout, p. 367
illiquid, p. 369
bank run, p. 369
lender of last resort, p. 369
sterilization bonds, p. 373
first-generation crisis model, p. 376
fiscal dominance, p. 377
speculative attack, p. 379
second-generation crisis model, p. 385
contingent commitment, p. 385
multiple equilibria, p. 385
self-confirming equilibrium, p. 389
corners hypothesis, p. 393
International Monetary Fund (IMF), p. 394

PROBLEMS

1. The economic costs of currency crises appear to be larger in emerging markets and developing countries, than they are in advanced countries. Discuss why this is the case, citing the interaction between the currency crisis and the financial sector. In what ways do currency crises lead to banking crises in these countries? In what ways do banking crises spark currency crises?

2. Using the central bank balance sheet diagrams, evaluate how each of the following shocks affects a country's ability to defend a fixed exchange rate.
   a. The central bank buys government bonds.
   b. Currency traders expect an appreciation in the home currency in the future.
   c. An economic expansion leads to a change in home money demand.
   d. The foreign interest rate increases.

3. Consider the central bank balance sheet for the country of Riqueza. Riqueza currently has $1,800 million escudos in its money supply, $1,100 million of which is backed by domestic government bonds; the rest is backed by foreign exchange reserves. Assume that Riqueza maintains a fixed exchange rate of one escudo per dollar, the foreign interest rate remains unchanged, and money demand takes the usual form, $M/P = L(i)Y$. Assume prices are sticky.
   a. Show Riqueza's central bank balance sheet, assuming there are no private banks. What is the backing ratio?
   b. Suppose that Riqueza's central bank sells $200 million in government bonds. Show how this affects the central bank balance sheet. Does this change affect Riqueza's money supply? Explain why or why not. What is the backing ratio now?
   c. Now, starting from this new position, suppose that there is an economic downturn in Riqueza, so that real income contracts by 10%. How will this affect money demand in Riqueza? How will forex traders respond to this change? Explain the responses in the money market and the forex market.
   d. Using a new balance sheet, show how the change described in part (c) affects Riqueza's central bank. What happens to domestic credit? What happens to Riqueza's foreign exchange reserves? Explain the responses in the money market and the forex market.
   e. How will the change above affect the central bank's ability to defend the fixed exchange rate? What is the backing ratio now? Describe how this situation differs from one in which the central bank buys government bonds, as in part (b).

4. What is a currency board? Describe the strict rules about the composition of reserves and domestic credit that apply to this type of monetary arrangement.

5. What is a lender of last resort and what does it do? If a central bank acts as a lender of last resort under a fixed exchange rate regime, why are reserves at risk?

6. Suppose that a country's money supply is $1,200 million and its domestic credit is equal to $800 million in the year 2005. The country maintains a fixed exchange rate, the central bank monetizes any government budget deficit, and prices are sticky.
   a. Compute total reserves for the year 2005. Illustrate this situation on a central bank balance sheet diagram.
   b. Now, suppose the government unexpectedly runs a $100 million deficit in the year 2006 and the money supply is unchanged. Illustrate this change on your diagram. What is the new level of reserves?
   c. If the deficit is unexpected, will the central bank be able to defend the fixed exchange rate?
   d. Suppose the government runs a deficit of $100 million each year from this point forward. What will eventually happen to the central bank's reserves?
   e. In what year will the central bank be forced to abandon its exchange rate peg and why?
   f. What if the future deficits are anticipated? How does your answer to part (e) change? Explain briefly.

7. Consider two countries with fixed exchange rate regimes. In one country, government authorities exert fiscal dominance. In the other, they do not. Describe how this affects the central bank's ability to defend the exchange rate peg. How might this difference in fiscal dominance affect the central bank's credibility?

8. The government of the Republic of Andea is currently pegging the Andean peso to the dollar at $E = 1$ peso per dollar. Assume the following:

   In year 1 the money supply M is 2,250 pesos, reserves R are 1,250 pesos, and domestic credit B is 1,000 pesos. To finance spending, B is growing at 50% per year. Inflation is currently zero, prices are flexible, PPP holds at all times, and initially, $P = 1$. Assume also that the foreign price level is $P^* = 1$, so PPP holds. The government will float the peso if and only if it runs out of reserves. The U.S. nominal interest rate is 5%. Real output is fixed at $Y = 2,250$ at all times. Real money balances are $M/P = 2,250 = L(i) Y$, and L is initially equal to 1.

   a. Assume that Andean investors are myopic and do not foresee the reserves running out. Compute domestic credit in years 1, 2, 3, 4, and 5. At each date, also compute reserves, money supply, and the growth rate of money supply since the previous period (in percent).
   b. Continue to assume myopia. When do reserves run out? Call this time T. Assume inflation is constant after time T. What will that new inflation rate be? What will the rate of depreciation be? What will the new domestic interest rate be? (*Hint:* Use PPP and the Fisher effect.)
   c. Continue to assume myopia. Suppose that at time T, when the home interest rate i increases, then $L(i)$ drops from 1 to 2/3. Recall that Y remains fixed. What is M/P before time T? What will be the new level of M/P after time T, once reserves have run out and inflation has started?
   d. Continue to assume myopia. At time T, what is the price level going to be right before reserves run out? Right after? What is the percentage increase in the price level? In the exchange rate? (*Hint:* Use the answer to part (c) and PPP.)
   e. Suppose investors know the rate at which domestic credit is growing. Is the path described above consistent with rational behavior? What would rational investors want to do instead?
   f. Given the above data, when do you think a speculative attack would occur? At what level of reserves will such an attack occur? Explain your answer.

9. A peg is not credible when investors fear depreciation in the future, despite official announcements. Why is the home interest rate always higher under a noncredible peg than under a credible peg? Why does that make it more costly to maintain a noncredible peg than a credible peg? Explain why nothing more than a shift in investor beliefs can cause a peg to break.

10. You are the economic advisor to Sir Bufton Tufton, the prime minister of Perfidia. The Bank of Perfidia is pegging the exchange rate of the local currency, the Perfidian albion. The albion is pegged to the wotan, which is the currency of the neighboring country of Wagneria. Until this week both countries have been at full employment. This morning, new data showed that Perfidia was in a mild recession, 1% below desired output. Tufton believes a downturn of 1% or less is economically and politically acceptable but a larger downturn is not. He must face the press in 15 minutes and is considering making one of three statements:

    a. "We will abandon the peg to the wotan immediately."
    b. "Our policies will not change unless economic conditions deteriorate further."
    c. "We shall never surrender our peg to the wotan."

    What would you say to Tufton concerning the merits of each statement?

11. What steps have been proposed to prevent exchange rate crises? Discuss their pros and cons.

The Euro

10

1. The Economics of the Euro
2. The History and Politics of the Euro
3. Eurozone Tensions in Tranquil Times, 1999–2007
4. The Eurozone in Crisis, 2008–2010
5. Conclusions: Assessing the Euro

There is no future for the people of Europe other than in union.
Jean Monnet, a "founding father" of the European Union

This Treaty marks a new stage in the process of creating an ever closer union among the peoples of Europe, in which decisions are taken as closely as possible to the citizen.
Maastricht Treaty (Treaty on European Union), 1992, Title 1, Article A

Political unity can pave the way for monetary unity. Monetary unity imposed under unfavorable conditions will prove a barrier to the achievement of political unity.
Milton Friedman, Nobel laureate, 1997

In 1961 the economist Robert Mundell wrote a paper discussing the idea of a *currency area*, also known as a **currency union** or *monetary union*, in which states or nations replace their national monies with a single, common currency.

At the time, almost every country was a separate currency area, so Mundell wondered whether his research would have any practical relevance: "What is the appropriate domain of a currency area? It might seem at first that the question is purely academic since it hardly appears within the realm of political feasibility that national currencies would ever be abandoned in favor of any other arrangement."[1]

Almost forty years later, in 1999, 11 nations in Europe elected to form such a currency area, now known as the *Euro area*, or **Eurozone.** Later that year, Mundell found himself the recipient of a Nobel Prize.

The Eurozone has since expanded and continues to expand. By 2011 there will be 17 member countries. They will all use the new notes and coins bearing the name **euro** and the symbol € that have taken the place of former national currencies (francs, marks, liras, and others).

---

[1] Robert Mundell, 1961, "A Theory of Optimum Currency Areas," *American Economic Review*, 51, 657–665.

Euro notes and coins.

The euro remains one of the boldest experiments in the history of the international monetary system, a new currency that is used by more than 300 million people in one of the world's most prosperous economic regions. The euro is having enormous economic impacts that will be felt for many years to come and is an essential object of study for those interested in today's global macroeconomy.

The goal of this chapter is to understand as fully as possible the logic of the euro project. We first examine the euro's economic logic by exploring and applying theories, developed by Mundell and others, that seek to explain when it makes economic sense for different economic units (nations, regions, states) to adopt a common currency and when it makes economic sense for them to have distinct monies. To spoil the surprise: based on the current evidence, most economists judge that the Eurozone may not make sense from a purely economic standpoint, at least for now.

We then turn to the historical and political logic of the euro and discuss its distant origins and recent evolution within the larger political project of the European Union. Looking at the euro from these perspectives, we can see how the euro project unfolded as part of a larger enterprise. In this context, the success of the euro depends on assumptions that the EU functions smoothly as a political union and adequately as an economic union—assumptions that are constantly under question.

The Ins and Outs of the Eurozone Before we begin our discussion of the euro, we need to familiarize ourselves with the EU and the Eurozone. Way back at the start of the euro project policy makers imagined that the euro would end up as the currency of the **European Union (EU).** The EU is a mainly economic, but increasingly political, union of countries that is in the process of extending across—and some might argue beyond—the geographical boundaries of Europe. The main impetus for the euro project came in 1992 with the signing of the Treaty on European Union, at Maastricht, in the Netherlands. Under the **Maastricht Treaty,** the EU initiated a grand project of *Economic and Monetary Union* (EMU). A major goal of EMU was the establishment of a currency union in the EU whose monetary affairs would be managed cooperatively by members through a new European Central Bank (ECB).[2]

The map in Figure 10-1 shows the state of play at the time of this writing in January 2011. The map depicts some of the EU's main political and monetary alignments. The two are not the same: different countries choose to participate in different aspects of economic and monetary integration, a curious feature of the EU project known as *variable geometry.*

- As of 2010, the EU comprised 27 countries (EU-27). Ten of these had joined as recently as 2004, and Romania and Bulgaria joined in 2007. Four more official

---

[2] Some very small non-EU, non-Eurozone states also use the euro: Monaco, San Marino, Vatican City, and Andorra have legal agreements allowing them to use the euro as their de jure currency (they had previously used the national currencies of their neighbors). All these countries except Andorra can mint their own euro coins. Some other economies also use the euro as their de facto currency, notably Montenegro and Kosovo, who are keen to assert their autonomy from Serbia and its currency, the Serbian dinar.

candidate countries were formally seeking to join—Croatia, Iceland, Macedonia, and Turkey.[3]

- A country can be in the EU but not in the Eurozone. It is important to remember who's "in" and who's "out." In 1999 just 3 out of 15 EU members opted to stay out of the Eurozone and keep their national currencies: these "out" countries were Denmark, Sweden, and the United Kingdom. The other 12 all went "in" by 2001. Since then 12 new entrants have joined the EU, with all of them initially "out" of the euro. Then, on January 1, 2007, the first of these countries, Slovenia, became a member of the Eurozone, followed by Cyprus and Malta (2008), Slovakia (2009), and Estonia (2011). The other 7 new entrants still remain "out" of the Eurozone.

- Most of the "outs" want to be "in." The official accession procedure requires that those who wish to get "in" must first peg their exchange rates to the euro in a system known as the *Exchange Rate Mechanism* (ERM) for at least two years and must also satisfy certain other qualification criteria. Three countries were part of the ERM as of 2011: Denmark, Latvia, and Lithuania. For all but Denmark, participation in the ERM was taken as an indication of the intent to adopt the euro shortly. We discuss the ERM, the qualification criteria, and other peculiar rules later in this chapter.

FIGURE 10-1

EU à la Carte This map shows the state of Europe as of 2011, indicating members in the EU, the Eurozone, and the ERM and potential future members.

Notes:
EU-Eurozone (17): Austria, Belgium, Cyprus, Estonia, Finland, France, Germany, Greece, Ireland, Italy, Luxembourg, Malta, Netherlands, Portugal, Slovakia, Slovenia, Spain.
EU-ERM (3): Denmark, Lithuania, Latvia.
EU-Other (7): Bulgaria, Czech Republic, Hungary, Poland, Romania, Sweden, United Kingdom
Candidates (4): Croatia, Iceland, Macedonia, Turkey.

---

[3] Until a naming dispute with Greece is resolved, Macedonia is often referred to in official communications as "the Former Yugoslav Republic of Macedonia" or, if you prefer acronyms, FYROM.

1 The Economics of the Euro

In the nineteenth century economist John Stuart Mill thought it a "barbarism" that all countries insisted on "having, to their inconvenience and that of their neighbors, a peculiar currency of their own." Barbaric or not, it has long appeared that national currencies are the norm, while currency unions are rare.[4] Economists presume that such outcomes reflect a deeper logic. A common currency may be more convenient and provide other benefits, but it also has some costs. For the "barbarism" of national currencies to persist, the costs must outweigh the benefits.

The Theory of Optimum Currency Areas

How does a country decide whether to join a currency union? To answer this question, let's see if one country, Home, should join a currency union with another country, Foreign. (Our analysis can be generalized to a case in which Foreign consists of multiple members of a larger currency union.)

If countries make a decision that best serves their self-interest—that is, an optimizing decision—when they form a currency union, then economists use the term **optimum currency area (OCA)** to refer to the resulting monetary union. How can such a decision be made?

To decide whether joining the currency union serves its economic interests, Home must evaluate whether the benefits outweigh the costs. This decision is similar to the decision to select a fixed or floating exchange rate, which we discussed in an earlier chapter. Two familiar ideas from that previous discussion can be applied and extended to the currency union decision.

Market Integration and Efficiency Benefits Adopting a common currency implies that the two regions will have an exchange rate fixed at 1. Hence, the same market integration criterion we used to discriminate between fixed and floating regimes can be applied to the case of an OCA:

If there is a greater degree of economic integration between the home region (A) and the other parts of the common currency zone (B), the volume of transactions between the two and the economic benefits of adopting a common currency due to lowered transaction costs and reduced uncertainty will both be larger.

Economic Symmetry and Stability Costs When two regions adopt a common currency, each region will lose its monetary autonomy, and the monetary authorities who have control of the common currency will decide on a common monetary policy and set a common interest rate for all members. Hence, the similarity criterion we used to discriminate between fixed and floating regimes can be applied to the case of an OCA:

If a home country and its potential currency union partners are more economically similar or "symmetric" (they face more symmetric shocks and fewer asymmetric shocks), then it is less costly for the home country to join the currency union.

---

[4] Many currency unions involve the unilateral adoption of a foreign currency by a country that plays no role in managing the common currency (e.g., Panama's use of the U.S. dollar). Even when a foreign country adopts a currency other than the dollar, this situation is often called *dollarization*. In only a few cases are currency unions multilateral in which all member countries participate in the monetary affairs of the union. The Eurozone is the most notable example of a multilateral currency union.

Simple Optimum Currency Area Criteria

We are now in a position to set out a theory of an optimum currency area by considering the *net benefits* of adopting a common currency. The net benefits equal the benefits minus the costs. The two main lessons we have just encountered suggest the following:

- *As market integration rises, the efficiency benefits of a common currency increase.*
- *As symmetry rises, the stability costs of a common currency decrease.*

Summing up, the OCA theory says that if either market integration or symmetry increases, the net benefits of a common currency will rise. If the net benefits are negative, the home country would stay out based on its economic interests. If the net benefits turn positive, the home country would join based on its economic interests.

Figure 10-2 illustrates the OCA theory graphically, using the same symmetry-integration diagrams used in the previous chapter on fixed and floating exchange rates. The horizontal axis measures market integration for the Home-Foreign pair. The vertical axis measures the symmetry of the shocks experienced by the Home-Foreign pair. If the Home-Foreign pair moves up and to the right in the diagram, then the benefits increase, the costs fall, and so the net benefit of a currency union rises. At some point, the pair crosses a threshold, the OCA line, and enters a region in which it will be optimal for them to form a currency union based on their economic interests.

The figure looks familiar. The derivation of the OCA line here is identical to the derivation of the FIX line in Chapter 8, which raises an important question.

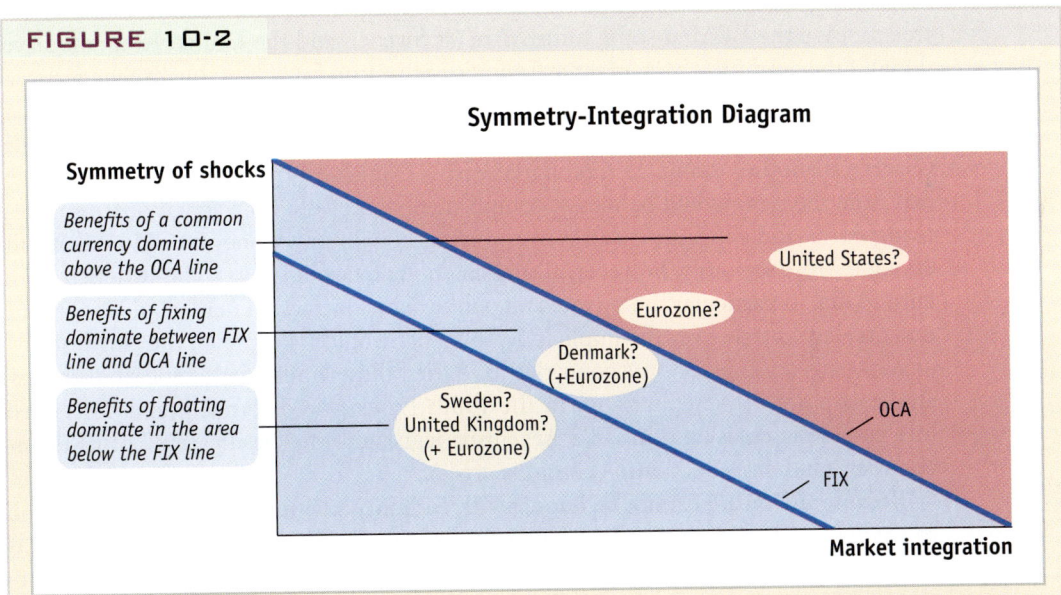

FIGURE 10-2

Stylized OCA Criteria Two regions are considering a currency union. If markets become more integrated (a move right on the horizontal axis), the net economic benefits of a currency union increase. If the economic shocks they experience become more symmetric (a move up the vertical axis), the net economic benefits of a currency union also increase. If the parts of the region move far enough up or to the right, benefits exceed costs, net benefits are positive, and they cross the OCA threshold. In the shaded region above the line, it is optimal for the parts of the region to form a currency union. In practice, the OCA line is likely to be above and to the right of the FIX line.

What's the Difference between a Fix and a Currency Union?

If choosing to fix and choosing to form a currency union were identical decisions, then the FIX and OCA lines would be one and the same. In reality, we think they are likely to differ—and that the OCA line is likely to be above the FIX line, as drawn in Figure 10-2. Thus, when countries consider forming a currency union, the economic tests (based on symmetry and integration) set a higher bar than they set for judging whether it is optimal to fix.

Why might this be so? To give a concrete example, let's consider the case of Denmark, which we studied in an earlier chapter on exchange rates, as an example of the trilemma in Europe. The Danes are in the ERM, so the krone is pegged to the euro. But Denmark has spent a long time in the ERM and shows no signs of taking the next step into the Eurozone. This preference has been democratically expressed—proposals to join the Eurozone have been defeated by referendum. The Danish position looks slightly odd at first glance. Denmark appears to have ceded monetary autonomy to the ECB because its interest rate tracks the euro interest rate closely. Yet the Danes do not gain the full benefits of a currency union because transactions between Denmark and the Eurozone still require a change of currency.

Still, one can make a logical case for Denmark to keep its own currency. By doing so, it better preserves the *option* to exercise monetary autonomy at some future date, even if the option is not being used currently. For one thing, even under the ERM, although the krone is pegged very tightly to the euro within ±2% by choice, the Danes could employ the full ±15% band allowed by ERM and give themselves much more exchange rate flexibility. (A ±15% band isn't a very hard peg—recall that the standard de facto threshold for a peg is no more than ±2% variation in one year.) And because they have only gone as far as pegging to—and not joining—the euro, the Danes are always free to leave the ERM at some future date (as Sweden and the United Kingdom have done) if they want the even greater flexibility of a more freely floating exchange rate.

Now, contrast the position of Denmark with that of Italy, one of several countries in which rumors of departure from the Eurozone have surfaced from time to time (Greece is another example). Compared with a Danish exit from the ERM, an Italian exit from the euro would be messy, complicated, and costly. The actual process of retiring euros and reprinting and reintroducing new lira as money would be difficult enough. More seriously, however, all Italian contracts would have to be switched from euro to lira, in particular the private and public debt contracts. There would be a monumental legal battle over the implicit defaults that would follow from the "lirification" of such euro contracts. Some countries have tried these kinds of strategies, but the examples are not too encouraging. In the 1980s Liberia de-dollarized (and descended into economic crisis) and in 2002 Argentina legislated the "pesification" of its dollar contracts (and descended into economic crisis).

Because the future cannot be known with certainty, countries may value the option to change their monetary and exchange rate regime in the future. Exit from a peg is easy—some might say too easy—and happens all the time. Exit from a common currency is much more difficult (the Eurozone has *no* exit procedure) and is expected to be costly. We conclude that because a country's options are more limited after joining a common currency than after joining a peg, the country will set tougher conditions for the former; thus, the optimal OCA region will be smaller than the optimal fixing region, as shown in Figure 10-2.

Other Optimum Currency Area Criteria

Our simple model in Figure 10-2 illustrated two basic motives for joining a currency union, but there could be many other forces at work. These other considerations can still be examined using the same framework, which allows us to consider several additional arguments for joining a currency union.

Labor Market Integration In the analysis so far, the home and foreign countries trade goods and services, but labor is immobile between the two countries. But what if we suppose instead that Home and Foreign have an integrated labor market, so that labor is free to move between them: What effect will this have on the decision to form an optimum currency area?

Labor market integration allows for an alternative adjustment mechanism in the event of asymmetric shocks. For example, suppose Home and Foreign initially have equal output and unemployment. Suppose further that a negative shock hits Home, but not Foreign. If output falls and unemployment rises in Home, then labor will start to migrate to Foreign, where unemployment is lower. If this migration can occur with ease, the impact of the negative shock on Home will be less painful. Furthermore, there will be less need for Home to implement an independent monetary policy response for stabilization purposes. With an excess supply of labor in one region, adjustment can occur through migration.

This reasoning suggests that the cost to Home of forming a currency union with Foreign, due to the loss of monetary policy autonomy, will be lower when the labor market integration between Home and Foreign is higher, because labor mobility provides an alternative mechanism through which Home can adjust to the shock. All else equal, the possibility of gains of this sort would lower the OCA threshold, as reflected in the shift down of the OCA line from OCA_1 to OCA_2 in Figure 10-3. This shift expands the shaded zone in which currency union is preferred: countries are more likely to want to form a currency union when their labor markets are more integrated.

Fiscal Transfers We have now examined two possible mechanisms through which countries in an OCA can cope with asymmetric shocks: monetary policy and labor markets. We have ignored fiscal policy. All else equal, one might argue that a country's fiscal policy is autonomous and largely independent of whether a country is inside or outside a currency union. But there is one important exception: fiscal policy will not be independent when a currency union is built on top of a federal political structure with fiscal mechanisms that permit interstate transfers—a system known as *fiscal federalism*.

If a region also has fiscal federalism, then a third adjustment channel is available: when Home suffers a negative shock, the effects of the shock can be cushioned by fiscal transfers from Foreign, allowing more expansionary fiscal policy in Home than might otherwise be the case. For this argument to be compelling, however, the fiscal transfers must be large enough to make a difference. They must also help overcome some limit on the exercise of Home's fiscal policy; that is, the transfers must finance policies that Home could not finance in some other way (e.g., by government borrowing).

If these conditions are satisfied, then the presence of fiscal transfers will lower the costs of joining a currency union. We show the possibility of gains of this sort in Figure 10-3, where, all else equal, enhanced fiscal transfers mean a lower OCA threshold,

FIGURE 10-3

Changes in Other OCA Criteria Several other criteria can make a currency union more attractive, even for given levels of market integration. Factors that lower costs or raise benefits will shift the OCA line down and to the left, expanding the OCA zone.

and a shift down from OCA_1 to OCA_2. This shift expands the shaded zone in which currency union is preferred: the better the fiscal transfer mechanisms, the more countries are likely to want to join the currency union.

Monetary Policy and Nominal Anchoring One important aspect of Home joining a currency union is that Home's central bank ceases to manage monetary policy (or ceases to exist altogether). Monetary policy is then carried out by a common central bank, whose policies and actions may be subject to different designs, objectives, and political oversight. This may or may not be a good thing, depending on whether the overall monetary policy performance of Home's central bank is (or is expected to be) as good as that of the common central bank.

For example, suppose that Home suffers from chronic high inflation that results from an **inflation bias** of Home policy makers—the inability to resist the political pressure to use expansionary monetary policy for short-term gains. In the long run, on average, inflation bias leads to a higher level of expected inflation and actual inflation. But average levels of unemployment and output are unchanged because higher inflation is expected and inflation has no real effects in the long run.

Suppose that the common central bank of the currency union would be a more politically independent central bank that could resist political pressures to use expansionary monetary policy for short-term gains. It performs better by delivering low inflation on average, and no worse levels of unemployment or output. In this case, joining the currency union improves economic performance for Home by giving it a better nominal anchor: in this scenario, loss of monetary autonomy can be a good thing.

There is a possibility that this criterion was important for several Eurozone member states that historically have been subject to high inflation—for example, Italy, Greece, and Portugal. We can represent the possibility of monetary policy gains of this sort in Figure 10-3, where, all else equal, a worsening in the home nominal anchor (or an improvement in the currency union's nominal anchor) shifts the OCA line down. For countries with a record of high and variable inflation, the OCA threshold will fall, so again the OCA line moves down from OCA_1 to OCA_2. This shift also expands the shaded zone in which currency union is preferred: given levels of market integration and symmetry, high-inflation countries are more likely to want to join the currency union and the larger are the monetary policy gains of this sort. (Later on we consider the concerns of the low-inflation countries in this scenario.)

Political Objectives Finally, we turn to noneconomic gains and the possibility that countries will join a currency union even if it makes no pure economic sense for them to do so. For instance, one can imagine that Home's "political welfare" may go up, even if pure economic welfare goes down. How?

Suppose a state or group of states is in a situation in which forming a currency union has value for political, security, strategic, or other reasons. For example, when the United States expanded westward in the nineteenth century, it was accepted, without question, that new territories and states would adopt the U.S. dollar. In recent times, eastward expansion of the EU comes with an assumption that, in the end, accession to the union will culminate in monetary union. These beliefs, assumptions, and accords did not rest very much, if at all, on any of the OCA criteria we have discussed so far. Instead, they were an act of political faith, of a belief in the states' common political future, a statement about destiny.

Political benefits can also be represented in Figure 10-3 by the OCA line shifting down from OCA_1 to OCA_2. In this scenario, for countries between OCA_1 and OCA_2, there are *economic costs* to forming a currency union, but these are outweighed by the *political benefits*. The political dimension of the European Union has played a significant role in EU and Eurozone history, a topic we discuss later in the chapter.

APPLICATION

Optimum Currency Areas: Europe versus the United States

At first glance, the theory of optimum currency areas helpfully sets out the important criteria by which we can judge whether it is in a country's interest to join a currency union. But while the OCA criteria work well in theory, in reality, the costs and benefits of a currency union cannot be measured with any great accuracy.

Recognizing this, we can try an alternative approach and use comparative analysis to shed some light on the issue by answering a slightly different question: How does Europe compare with the United States on each of the OCA criteria? Clearly, if one took the view that the United States works well as a common currency zone, and if we find that Europe performs as well as or better than the United States on the OCA criteria, then these findings would lend indirect support to the economic logic of the euro.

Goods Market Integration within the EU European countries trade a lot with each other. But as far as we can tell (the available data are not entirely comparable), the individual states within the United States trade even more with one another. For the large census regions of the United States shown in Figure 10-4, panel (a), manufacturing trade ranges from 30% to 70% of gross state product. The figure for EU countries is typically much smaller, especially in the larger EU countries that are comparable in size with the census regions. At best, it might be argued that the creation of a "single market" in the EU is still a work in progress (as we see in the next section), and so it might well be that these intra-EU trade flows will rise further as the EU's internal market becomes more integrated. On this test, Europe is probably behind the United States for now.

Symmetry of Shocks within the EU A direct way to look at the symmetry of shocks is to compare the correlation of a state's GDP annual growth rate with the annual GDP growth of the entire zone. These data are shown in Figure 10-4, panel (b), and most EU countries compare quite favorably with the U.S. states on this test: in both cases, the average correlation with the entire zone's GDP growth rate is close to 0.5. (Although there are some distinct outliers in the EU case, they are small countries and we would find some outliers at the state level in the U.S. data as well.) This result is not too surprising: there is no strong consensus that EU countries are more exposed to local shocks than the regions of the United States. However, as we see in a moment, one potential problem for the EU is what happens in the future: one effect of deeper EU goods market integration could be that EU countries start to specialize more. In that case, the risk of asymmetric shocks will increase and the EU will be less likely to satisfy the OCA criteria.

Labor Mobility within the EU The data in Figure 10-4, panel (c), show what is well known: labor in Europe is much less mobile between states than it is in the United States. More than 30% of U.S. residents were born in a different U.S. state than the one in which they live. In the EU, only 1.5% of people were born in a different EU country than the one in which they live. The same is true, as one would expect, of the year-to-year flow of people between regions: it is also an order of magnitude larger in the United States than in the EU. There are obvious explanations for this: differences in culture and language present obstacles to intra-EU migration that are largely absent in the United States. In addition, although the EU is working to ease such frictions, the local regulatory environment and red tape make it burdensome for Europeans to live and work in another EU country, even if they have a legal right to do so. Finally, labor markets in Europe are generally less flexible, making it harder to hire and fire workers, something that may dissuade workers from moving from one place to another in search of better opportunities. Economists have found that differences in unemployment across EU regions tend to be larger and more persistent than they are across the individual states of the United States. In short, the labor market adjustment mechanism is weaker in Europe. On this test, Europe is far behind the United States.

Fiscal Transfers A survey of the literature suggests that when a U.S. state goes into a recession, for every $1 drop in that state's government revenue, the federal government compensates with an offsetting transfer of about 15 cents.[5] Stabilizing transfers of this kind are possible only when states agree to engage in fiscal federalism, whereby substantial taxing and spending authority are given to the central authority. The United States has such stabilizing transfers, but the EU does not. Although individual states in the EU achieve similar results within their own borders, at the level of the EU as a whole, the fiscal transfer mechanism is nonexistent: the EU budget is little more than 1% of EU GDP and is devoted to other purposes, notably agricultural subsidies.

---

[5] HM Treasury, 2003, *The United States as a Monetary Union* (London: HMSO).

FIGURE 10-4

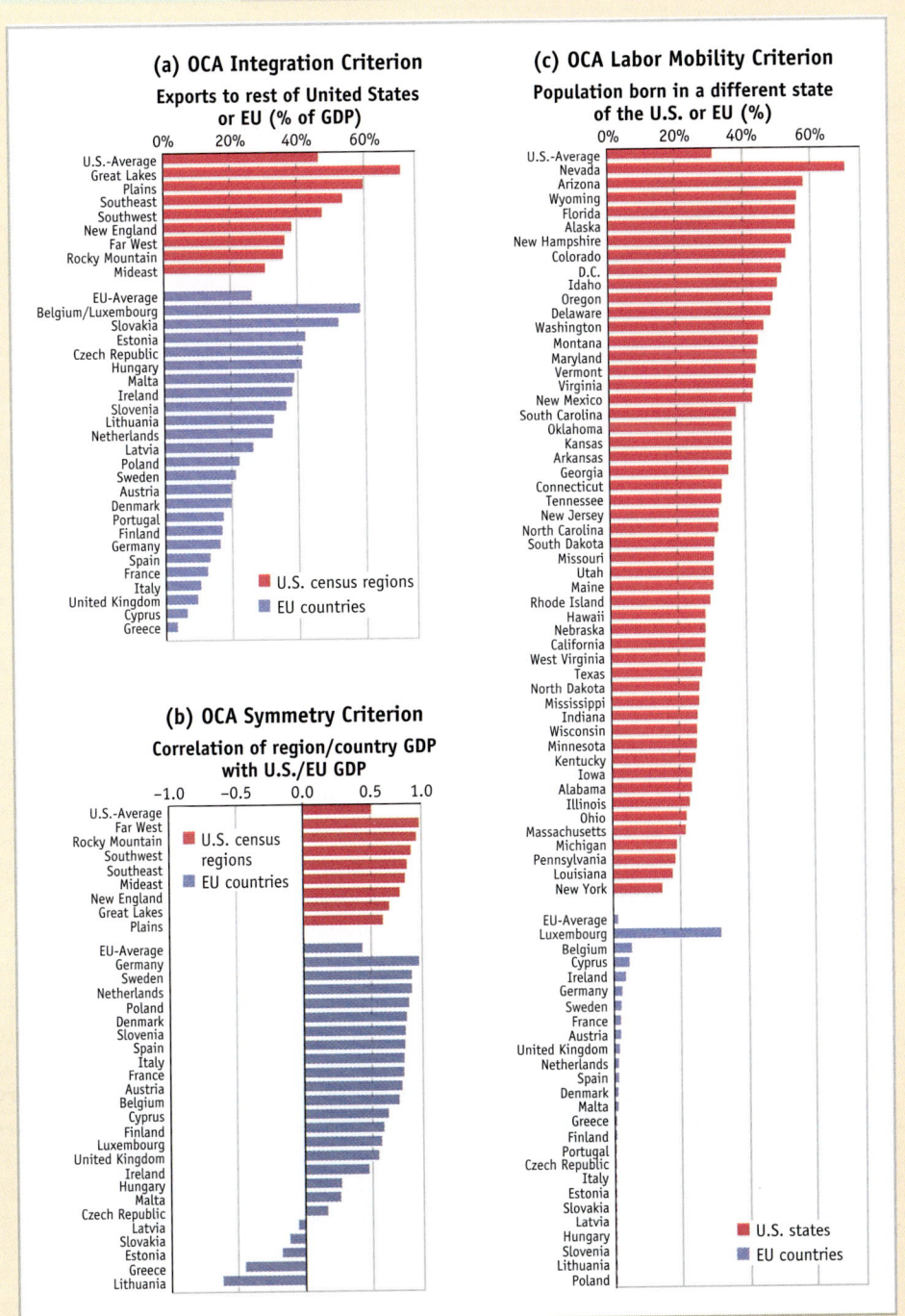

OCA Criteria for Europe and the United States Most economists believe that the United States is much more likely to satisfy the OCA criteria than the EU is. Why? Data in panel (a) show that interregional trade in the United States rises to levels much higher than those seen among EU countries. Data in panel (b) show that U.S. and EU shocks are comparably symmetric. Data in panel (c) show that U.S. labor markets are very integrated compared with those of the EU.

Sources: HM Treasury, 2003, The United States as a Monetary Union (London: HMSO); Paul de Grauwe, 2003, Economics of Monetary Union, 6th ed. (Oxford: Oxford University Press); Eurostat; bea.gov.

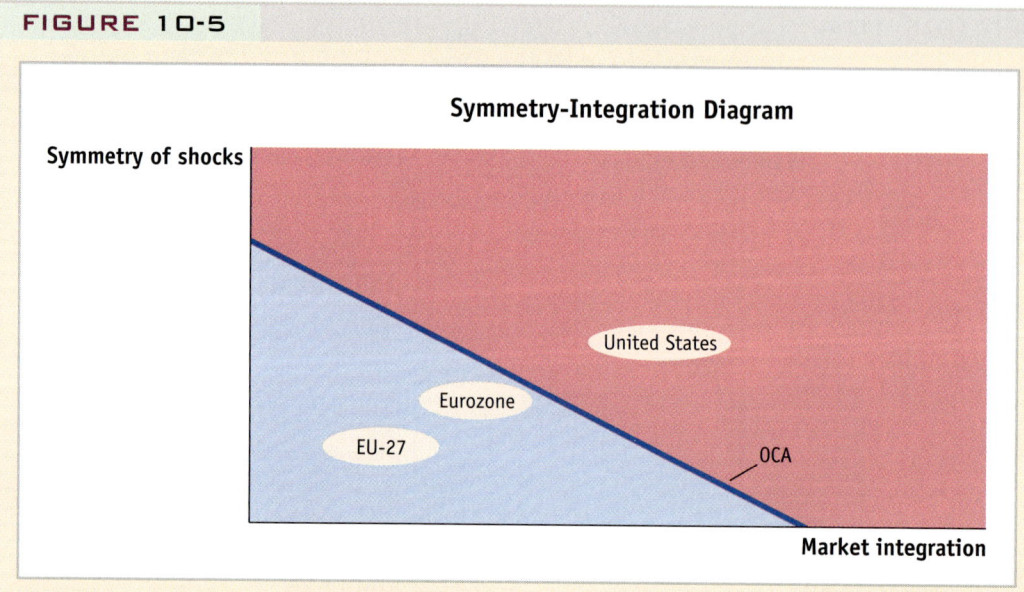

FIGURE 10-5

Stylized OCA View of the EU and the United States Most economists consider that the Eurozone and EU countries do not satisfy the OCA criteria—they have too little market integration and their shocks are too asymmetric. The Eurozone may be closer to the OCA line since integration runs deeper there, but it is still far behind the United States on the OCA criteria. If we expand to the EU of 27, it is likely that this larger zone fails to meet OCA criteria by an even larger margin, with lower integration and higher asymmetry than the current Eurozone.

Summary On the simple OCA criteria, the EU falls short of the United States as a successful optimum currency area, as shown in Figure 10-5. Goods market integration is a little bit weaker, fiscal transfers are negligible, and labor mobility is very low. At best, one can note that economic shocks in the EU are fairly symmetric, but this fact alone gives only limited support for a currency union given the shortcomings in other areas.

Some economists argue that the economic stability costs are exaggerated: they have doubts about stabilization policy in theory (e.g., the Keynesian view that prices are sticky in the short run) or in practice (e.g., the caveats about policy activism noted in the chapter on short-run macroeconomic policies). But most economists think there are still costs involved when a country sacrifices monetary autonomy. They worry that some or all Eurozone countries now have an inappropriate one-size-fits-all monetary policy, and that there are additional risks such as the absence of a well-defined lender of last resort mechanism in the Eurozone.

On balance, economists tend to believe that the EU, and the current Eurozone within it, were not an optimum currency area in the 1990s when the EMU project took shape and that nothing much has happened yet to alter that judgment. ∎

Are the OCA Criteria Self-Fulfilling?

Our discussion so far has taken a fairly static view of the OCA criteria. Countries treat all of the conditions just discussed as given, and, assuming they have adequate information, they can then judge whether the costs of forming a currency union outweigh the benefits. However, another school of thought argues that some of the OCA criteria are not given (i.e., exogenous) and fixed in stone, but rather they are economic outcomes (i.e., endogenous) determined by, among other things, the creation of the currency union itself. In other words, even if the Eurozone isn't an OCA now, by adopting a common currency, it might become an OCA in the future.

Consider goods market integration, for example. The very act of joining a currency union might be expected to promote more trade, by lowering transaction costs. Indeed, that is one of the main supposed benefits. In that case, if the OCA criteria were applied *ex ante* (before the currency union forms), then many countries might exhibit low trade volumes. Their low integration might mean that the OCA criteria are not met, and the currency union might not be formed based on those characteristics. However, if the currency union went ahead anyway, then it might be the case that *ex post* (after the currency union is up and running) countries would trade so much more that in the end the OCA criteria would indeed be satisfied.

This kind of argument is favored by euro-optimists, who see the EU single-market project as an ongoing process and the single currency as one of its crucial elements. This logic suggests that the OCA criteria can be self-fulfilling, at least for a group of countries that are ex ante close to—but not quite—fulfilling the OCA requirements. For example, suppose the EU started out at point 1 in Figure 10-6, just below the OCA line. If the EU countries would only "just do it" and form a monetary union, then they would wake up and discover that they had jumped to point 2 once the common currency had boosted trade among them, and, hey, presto: while monetary union didn't

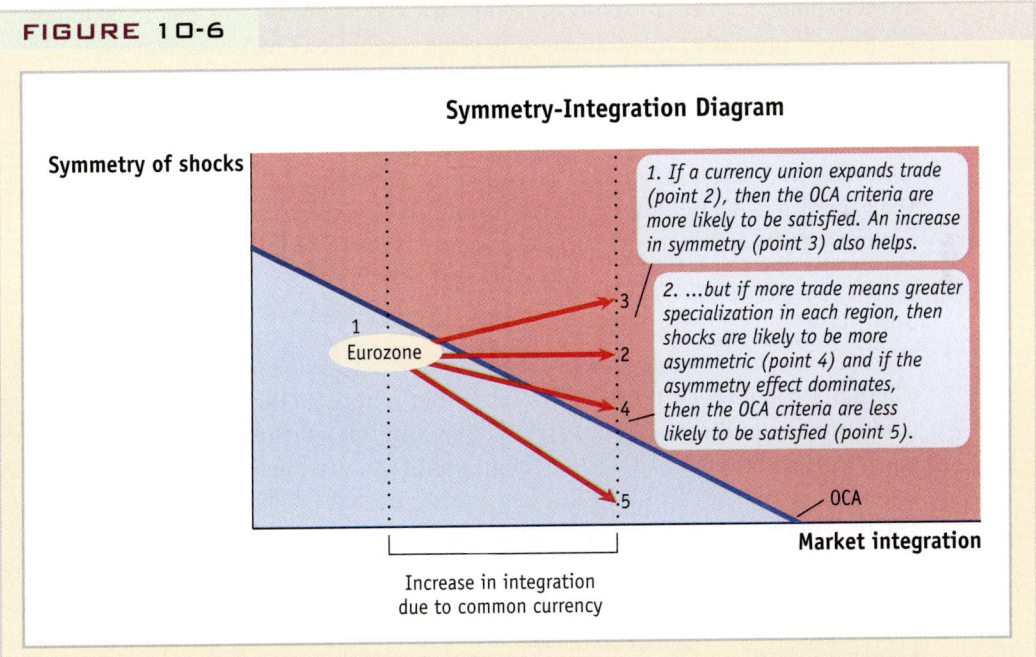

FIGURE 10-6

Symmetry-Integration Diagram

1. If a currency union expands trade (point 2), then the OCA criteria are more likely to be satisfied. An increase in symmetry (point 3) also helps.

2. …but if more trade means greater specialization in each region, then shocks are likely to be more asymmetric (point 4) and if the asymmetry effect dominates, then the OCA criteria are less likely to be satisfied (point 5).

Self-Fulfilling OCA Criteria Euro-optimists believe that the OCA criteria can be self-fulfilling. Suppose the Eurozone is initially at point 1, but then the effects of EMU start to be felt. Eventually, there will be an increase in market integration (more trade, capital flows, migration), moving the zone to point 2. There may also be a greater synchronization of shocks in the Eurozone, moving the zone to point 3. However, euro-pessimists note that market integration and more trade might also lead to more specialization by each country in the EU. In that case, the shocks to each country are likely to become more *asymmetric*, implying a move toward point 4 or point 5. In the case of point 5, the case for an OCA grows weaker, not stronger, after the long-run effects of the currency union have been worked out.

make sense beforehand, it does after the fact. Thus, even if the EU or the Eurozone does not look like an OCA now, it might turn out to be an OCA once it is fully operational. However, Euro-pessimists doubt that this self-fulfilling effect will amount to much. Evidence is mixed, and the exact magnitude of this effect is subject to considerable dispute (see **Headlines: Currency Unions and Trade**).[6]

A further argument made by optimists is that greater integration under the EU project might also enhance other OCA criteria. For example, if goods markets are better connected, a case can be made that shocks will be more rapidly transmitted within the EU and will be felt more symmetrically. Thus, creating the Eurozone will not only boost trade but also increase the symmetry of shocks, corresponding to a shift from point 1 to point 3 in Figure 10-6. Such a process would strengthen the OCA argument even more.

Set against this optimistic view is the worrying prospect that further goods market integration might also lead to more specialization in production. According to this argument, once individual firms can easily serve the whole EU market, and not just their national market, they will exploit economies of scale and concentrate production. Some sectors in the EU might end up becoming concentrated in a few locations. Whereas in the past trade barriers and other frictions allowed every EU country to produce a wide range of goods, in the future we might see more clustering (the United States provides many examples, such as the auto industry in Detroit or high technology in Silicon Valley). If specialization increases, each country will be less diversified and will face more asymmetric shocks. In Figure 10-6, this might correspond to a move from point 1 to point 4, where the case for OCA would strengthen, though not by much; or even a move to point 5, where the costs of asymmetric shocks are so large that they dominate the gains from market integration, so that the case for an OCA is weakened.

Some speculate that certain other OCA criteria could be affected by the adoption of the euro: maybe the common currency will encourage greater labor and capital mobility? Maybe it will encourage more fiscal federalism? As with the arguments about the effects on trade creation and specialization, evidence for these claims is quite sketchy. We cannot make a definitive judgment until the Eurozone experiment has run for a few more years and there are sufficient data to make reliable statistical inferences.

Summary

We have seen how a calculation of economic costs and benefits can help us decide whether a common currency makes sense. But it appears that the EU is almost certainly not an optimum currency area. Admittedly, this conclusion does not apply with equal force to the entire EU. Some subgroups of countries may have satisfied the OCA criteria. For decades Luxembourg has, in fact, used the Belgian franc as a currency; and the Dutch guilder has been closely tied to the German mark. The BeNeLux countries, and maybe Austria too, were always well integrated with Germany and therefore stronger candidates for a currency union. Other countries also had some very strong criteria for joining: for Italy, perhaps, where monetary policy was often more erratic, a better nominal anchor might have outweighed other negatives.

So if the EU is not an OCA, then why does the euro exist? The euro project was seen as something bigger. This was a currency designed to unify a whole continent of

---

[6] Some believe a common currency will have other effects, perhaps also encouraging labor and capital mobility within the Eurozone. These might also change the OCA calculus, but significant evidence on these effects has not been found as yet.

HEADLINES

Currency Unions and Trade

Will Eurozone trade rise as a result of the adoption of the euro? The effects seen so far do not appear to be very large.

In the continuing controversies about Europe's bold experiment in monetary union, there has at least been some agreement about where the costs and benefits lie. The costs are macroeconomic, caused by forgoing the right to set interest rates to suit the specific economic conditions of a member state. The benefits are microeconomic, consisting of potential gains in trade and growth as the costs of changing currencies and exchange-rate uncertainty are removed.

A recent study[*] by Richard Baldwin, a trade economist at the Graduate Institute of International Studies in Geneva, scythes through previous estimates. He works out that the boost to trade within the euro area from the single currency is much smaller: between 5% and 15%, with a best estimate of 9%. Furthermore, the gain does not build up over time but has already occurred. And the three European Union countries that stayed out—Britain, Sweden and Denmark—have gained almost as much as founder members, since the single currency has raised their exports to the euro zone by 7%.

Interest in the potential trade gains from the euro was primed . . . by a startling result from research into previous currency unions. In 2000 Andrew Rose, an economist at the University of California, Berkeley, reported that sharing a currency boosts trade by 235%.[**] Such a number looked too big to be true. It clashed with earlier research that found exchange-rate volatility reduced trade only marginally. . . .

Despite such worries, researchers continued to find large trade effects from currency unions. Mr. Baldwin explains why these estimates are unreliable. The main problem is that most of the countries involved are an odd bunch of small, poor economies that are in unions because of former colonial arrangements. Such is their diversity that it is impossible to model the full range of possible influences on their trade. But if some of the omitted factors are correlated with membership of a monetary union, the estimate of its impact on trade is exaggerated. And causality is also likely to run the other way: small, open economies, which would in any case trade heavily, are especially likely to share a currency. . . .

The intractable difficulties in working out the trade effect from previous currency unions means that previous estimates are fatally flawed. But the euro has now been in existence since the start of 1999, with notes and coins circulating since January 2002, so there is an increasing body of evidence based on its experience. That has certainly highlighted the macroeconomic disadvantages for its 12 member states. The loss of monetary sovereignty has hobbled first Germany and, more recently, Italy.

Despite these drawbacks, some studies have pointed to a substantial increase in trade within the euro area arising from monetary union, for example, by 20–25% in the first four years. As with the previous currency unions, however, many other explanatory influences might have come into play. Fortunately, unlike those earlier unions, there is a "control" group: the three countries that stayed out. This is particularly useful because they have shared other relevant aspects of membership of the EU, such as trade policy. It is on the basis of this that Mr. Baldwin reaches his best estimate of a 9% increase in trade within the euro area because of monetary union.

As important, he establishes that the boost to trade did not occur, as expected, by lowering the transaction costs for trade within the euro area. Had it done so, the stimulus would have been a fall in the prices of goods traded between euro-zone members relative to those traded with countries outside the currency union. However, Mr. Baldwin fails to find either this expected relative decline or the trade diversion it would have generated from the three countries that stayed out. He argues that another mechanism was at work. The introduction of the euro has in effect brought down the fixed cost of trading in the euro area. This has made it possible for companies selling products to just a few of the 12 member states to expand their market across more or all of them. This explains why the boost to trade has essentially been a one-off adjustment; and why countries that stayed out have benefited almost as much as those that joined.

There is also an important lesson for the 12 members of the euro area. Even if their economies were insufficiently aligned to be best suited for a currency union, one hope has been that the euro would make them converge as they trade much more intensively with one another. The message from Mr. Baldwin's report is that this is too optimistic. Countries in the euro area will have to undertake more reforms, such as making their labour markets more flexible, if they are to make the best of life with a single monetary policy.

---

[*] Richard Baldwin, *In or Out: Does It Matter? An Evidence-Based Analysis of the Euro's Trade Effects* (London: Centre for Economic Policy Research, 2006).

[**] Andrew K. Rose, 2000, "One Money, One Market: The Effect of Common Currencies on Trade," *Economic Policy*, 30, 7–45.

Source: Excerpted from "Economics Focus: The Euro and Trade," Economist, June 22, 2006.

disparate economies, to include France and Germany, Italy and the United Kingdom, to run from west to east, from Scandinavia to the Mediterranean—and it developed with very little reference to the OCA criteria. To understand why the euro happened, we need to study political logic, the topic of the next section.

2 The History and Politics of the Euro

The political origins of the European Union and the euro project can be found in the past. As long ago as 1861, the eminent French writer and statesman Victor Hugo could imagine that "a day will come in which markets open to commerce and minds open to ideas will be the sole battlefields." The timeline in Table 10-1 provides a summary of some of the most important events that have shaped European economic history since 1870. The course of events reveals a European project guided by politics as well as economics.

A Brief History of Europe

The table shows major political and economic events since 1870 and highlights the most important developments affecting monetary policy over the same time period. The table is divided into two periods: panel (a) sketches the more distant history that shaped the creation of the EU and progress toward EMU, culminating in the Maastricht Treaty of 1991; panel (b) supplies more detail on important recent events affecting the EU and the EMU project.

The EU project emerged as a cooperative response to a history of noncooperation among nations on the continent, which twice in the twentieth century spilled over into violent military conflict, in World War I (1914–1919) and World War II (1939–1945). Even during the interwar years, political tensions ran high and economic cooperation suffered. The situation was not helped by the punishing economic burdens placed on Germany by the Allied powers after World War I.[7] Matters only became worse during the severe economic downturn that was the Great Depression of the 1930s: protectionism surged again and the gold standard collapsed amid beggar-thy-neighbor devaluations (as discussed in the chapter on fixed and floating regimes).

In 1945, as a weak Europe emerged from the devastation of World War II, many feared that peace would only bring about a return to dire economic conditions. More economic suffering might also sow the seeds of more conflict in the future. At an extreme, some feared it would undermine the legitimacy of European capitalism, with the neighboring Soviet bloc all too eager to spread its alternative Communist model.

What could be done? In a speech in Zurich, on September 19, 1946, Winston Churchill presented his vision:

> And what is the plight to which Europe has been reduced? . . . Over wide areas a vast quivering mass of tormented, hungry, care-worn and bewildered human beings gape at the ruins of their cities and their homes, and scan the dark horizons for the approach of some new peril, tyranny or terror. . . . That is all that Europeans, grouped in so many ancient states and nations . . . have got by tearing each other to pieces and spreading havoc far and wide. Yet all the while there

---
[7] John Maynard Keynes, 1919, *The Economic Consequences of the Peace* (London: Macmillan).

is a remedy.... It is to recreate the European family, or as much of it as we can, and to provide it with a structure under which it can dwell in peace, in safety and in freedom. We must build a kind of United States of Europe.

Back from the Brink: Marshall Plan to Maastricht, 1945–1991 Into this crisis stepped the United States, to offer what has gone down in history as the most generous and successful reconstruction plan ever undertaken, the **Marshall Plan**.[8] From 1947 to 1951 Americans poured billions of dollars worth of aid into the war-torn regions of Western Europe to rebuild economic infrastructure (the Soviet bloc refused to take part in the plan).

The Marshall Plan required that the funds be allocated and administered by a European High Authority, composed of representatives of all countries, which encouraged collective action to solve common problems. Many cooperative arrangements were soon established: to smooth international payments and help trade (European Payments Union, or EPU, in 1950); to encourage trade and diminish rivalries in key goods like coal and steel (European Coal and Steel Community, or ECSC, in 1954); and to promote atomic and nuclear science without military rivalry (Euratom, in 1957).

In 1957 the **Treaty of Rome** was signed by six countries—France, West Germany, Italy, Belgium, Netherlands, and Luxembourg. They agreed to create the *European Economic Community*, or EEC, with plans for deeper economic cooperation and integration. In 1967 they went further and merged the EEC, the ECSC, and Euratom to create a new organization referred to as the *European Communities*, or EC. Two supranational bodies were created: the Council of Ministers, a decision-making body formed of national ministers, and an administrative body, the European Commission.

A poster created by the Economic Cooperation Administration, an agency of the U.S. government, to promote the Marshall Plan in Europe.

The dropping of the word "economic" (in the move from EEC to EC) was significant. By the 1960s two future paths had emerged. Would the EC create just a zone of economic integration? Or would it go further and aspire to a political union or a federal system of states—and if so, how far? The question has been hotly debated ever since.

In the 1970s two major challenges to the EC project emerged: problems of expansion and problems of monetary affairs. The expansion problem involved deciding when and how to admit new members. By 1973 the first enlargement added Denmark, Ireland, and the United Kingdom. The EC (i.e., the Council of Ministers) viewed these states as the right type to gain entry—they had solid credentials in terms of economic development and stability, and all were established democracies. In contrast, the second and third enlargements included countries with weaker economic and political claims—but all the same, Greece (1981), Portugal (1986), and Spain (1986) were soon admitted to the growing club.

The problem of monetary affairs was precipitated by the collapse of the Bretton Woods system of fixed exchange rates in the early 1970s. As we saw in the fixed-floating chapter, the world had been operating since 1946 under a system of fixed dollar exchange rates with monetary autonomy, with the trilemma being resolved through the imposition of capital controls. In the 1970s this system broke down and

---

[8] George C. Marshall (1880–1959), American military leader during World War II and named U.S. Secretary of State in 1947, proposed the postwar reconstruction effort for Europe in a speech at Harvard University, Thursday, June 5, 1947.

TABLE 10-1

(a) European Integration through 1993 This table shows major political and economic events over the past century or more.

	Major Political and Economic Events	Monetary Developments
1870–1914	Largely peaceful era; economic growth and stability.	The **gold standard** system of fixed exchange rates prevails.
1914–1945	World Wars I and II; economic malaise, Great Depression.	Collapse of gold standard, floating exchange rates with instability; capital controls widespread.
1946	Period of postwar rapid growth begins, and will last until 1970s.	The **Bretton Woods system** of fixed exchange rates established.
1947–1951	**Marshall Plan** reconstruction financed by United States and overseen by the **European High Authority.**	**European Payments Union** (EPU) is created to free up the European payments system and facilitate trade.
1954–1965	In 1954, France, West Germany, Italy, Belgium, Netherlands, Luxembourg form **European Coal and Steel Community** (ECSC). In 1957 they sign **Treaty of Rome** to form **European Economic Community** (EEC). In 1967 the **European Communities** (EC) merges EEC, ECSC, and Euratom; **Council of Ministers** and **European Commission** established.	
1971–1973	**1st enlargement:** Denmark, Ireland, and United Kingdom join (1973) to form an EC of 9 countries.	The **Bretton Woods system** of fixed exchange rates collapses.
1973–1979	**European Parliament** directly elected (1979).	**European Monetary System** (EMS) of monetary cooperation creates a currency basket called the **ecu** (a precursor of the euro) and the **Exchange Rate Mechanism** (ERM), a system of quasi-fixed exchange rates (1979). Belgium, Luxembourg, Denmark, Germany, France, Ireland, Italy, and Netherlands join EMS/ERM; United Kingdom joins EMS only.
1981–1986	**2nd and 3rd enlargements:** Greece (1981), Portugal and Spain (1986) expand EC to 12 countries.	Greece, Portugal, and Spain join EMS but not ERM.
1987–1990	**Single European Act** (1987) has goal of EC "single market" by 1992.	Spain (1989) and United Kingdom (1990) join ERM.
1990	**German reunification** in 1990 creates new unified German state, adding former East Germany to the EC.	Capital controls abolished in EC.
1991	**Maastricht Treaty** transforms EC into **European Union** (EU); to take effect in 1993. EU citizenship and EU enlargement process established. Plan for **Economic and Monetary Union** (EMU) adopted.	Plan for EMU includes a common currency (Britain and Denmark retain right to opt out), with ERM seen as an entry route. Rules for membership and **convergence criteria** established.
1992		Portugal joins ERM. **ERM crisis:** Britain exits ERM; ERM bands eventually widened.
1993	EU sets out **Copenhagen Criteria,** the political and economic conditions that future EU applicants must satisfy.	Applicants are expected to enter ERM/EMS and achieve the requirements for monetary union within a given period of time.

floating exchange rates became the norm in the advanced economies. At that time, except for wars and crises, Europe had spent roughly a century under some form of a fixed exchange rate system, and European policy makers worried that exchange rate instability might compromise their goals for economic union. Indeed, as early as 1969, the EC's visionary Werner Report anticipated a path via a transitional fixed

(b) European Integration since 1995 This table shows major political and economic events in recent years.

	Major Political and Economic Events	Monetary Developments
1995	**4th enlargement:** Austria, Finland, and Sweden expand EU to 15 countries. **Treaty of Schengen** will create common border system and immigration policies and free travel zone (Ireland and United Kingdom opt out; non-EU countries Iceland, Norway, and Switzerland opt in.)	Austria, Finland, and Sweden join EMS. Austria (1995) and Finland (1996) join ERM.
1997	**Treaty of Amsterdam** addresses EU citizenship, rights, powers of European Parliament, employment, and common foreign and security policy.	**Stability and Growth Pact** (SGP) is adopted to further enforce the Maastricht budgetary rules.
1998	11 countries say they will adopt the euro: France, Germany, Italy, Belgium, Netherlands, Luxembourg, Ireland, Portugal, Spain, Austria, Finland	The **European Central Bank** (ECB) is created. The 11 euro countries freeze their bilateral exchange rates on December 31.
1999		The **euro** is introduced as a unit of account on January 1. Euro notes and coins will appear in 2002 and replace national currencies. Greece, Denmark join ERM.
2000		In Denmark voters reject euro adoption in a referendum.
2001	**Treaty of Nice** addresses EU expansion, amends and consolidates Rome and Maastricht treaties, and modifies voting procedures.	Greece becomes the 12th country to join the Eurozone.
2003		In Sweden voters reject euro adoption in a referendum.
2004	**5th enlargement:** Cyprus, the Czech Republic, Estonia, Hungary, Latvia, Lithuania, Malta, Poland, Slovakia, and Slovenia expand EU to 25 countries.	Estonia, Lithuania, and Slovenia join ERM.
2005	Ratification of EU **Constitutional Treaty** postponed indefinitely following rejection by voters in French and Dutch referenda. Controversial accession negotiations start for Turkey (an EU candidate since 1999 and an associate member of EEC/EC/EU since 1963).	Cyprus, Latvia, Malta, and Slovakia join ERM. 12 out of 25 Eurozone members are in violation of the Stability and Growth Pact rules.
2007	**6th enlargement:** Bulgaria and Romania expand EU to 27 countries. **Treaty of Lisbon** amends treaties, adds President, a single foreign affairs post, strengthens fundamental rights, allows exit, weakens unanimous voting, etc.	Slovenia becomes the 13th country to join the Eurozone.
2008–2011	**Global financial crisis** (2008); peripheral countries (Greece, Ireland, Portugal, Spain) in deep recession and at risk of default (2009–); **European Financial Stability Facility** and IMF programs created (2010).	Cyprus and Malta (2008), Slovakia (2009), and Estonia (2011) expand Eurozone to 17 countries; ECB (with the EU) takes extraordinary steps to support banks and governments.

exchange rate system toward a single currency within 10 years, although the process would take much longer than that. European leaders did take the first and fateful step down this road when they announced that they would create essentially a new mini-Bretton Woods of their own, the *European Monetary System*, or EMS, which began operation in 1979.

The centerpiece of the EMS was the **Exchange Rate Mechanism (ERM),** a fixed exchange rate regime based on bands. The ERM defined each currency's central parity against a basket of currencies, the so-called *ecu* (European currency unit), the precursor to the euro. In practice, the non-German currencies ended up being pegged to the German mark, the central reserve currency in the system (just as the U.S. dollar had been the central reserve currency in the Bretton Woods system).

The ERM permitted a range of fluctuation on either side of the central value or *parity*: a narrow band of ±2.25% for most currencies (the escudo, lira, peseta, and pound were at times permitted a wider band of ±6%). In 1979 all EC countries except the United Kingdom joined the ERM; later, Spain joined in 1989, the United Kingdom in 1990, and Portugal in 1992. In principle, it was a "fixed but adjustable" system and the central parities could be changed, giving potential encouragement to speculators (also like Bretton Woods).

Crises and Opportunities: EMU and Other Projects, 1991–1999

The EC entered the 1990s with the drive for further integration still going strong. Since 1979 a directly elected European parliament had been at work. In 1987 the Single European Act was passed with the goal of reducing further the barriers between countries through the creation of a "single market" by 1992.

If, within the EC, the political momentum was still strong, it was soon given another push by the end of the Cold War in 1989. The Soviet Union disintegrated and Communist rule in Eastern Europe came to an end, symbolized by the fall of the Berlin Wall. What was the EC going to do in response? The Germans had no doubts—East and West Germany would be reunited quickly, to form Germany again. German reunification was formally completed on October 3, 1990. For the EC as a whole, though, there was the question of how to react to the new states on their eastern flank.

Eastern Europe was keen to move quickly and decisively away from Communism and autocracy and toward capitalism and democracy, and they saw joining the EC as a natural means to that end. From a political and security standpoint, the EC could hardly say no to the former Communist countries, and so plans for further eastern enlargement had to be made rather quickly. Other countries also waited in the wings. In the early 1990s wars broke out in the Balkans, forcing the EC to confront the big hole in its map between Italy and Greece. Did the former Yugoslav states and Albania belong in "Europe," too? And discussion of the eastern frontier of the EC soon brought to the fore the question of Turkey, a country that has had EC associate member status since 1963 and yet had to wait until 2005 for formal admission talks to begin.

In the face of these political challenges, the EC needed to act with purpose, and the grandest treaty to date, the 1991 Treaty on European Union, or the Maastricht Treaty, was the response, reasserting more than ever the goal of creating an "ever closer union among the peoples of Europe." Adding more federal flavor, the treaty gave the EC a new name, the European Union, or EU, and created a notion of EU citizenship. The treaty also laid down the process for enlargement that would eventually take the EU, via three further enlargements to 15 in 1995, 25 in 2004, and 27 in 2007.

Later political developments in the 1990s built on Maastricht. The 1993 Copenhagen Criteria provided formal conditions for new members wanting admission, such as rule of law, human rights, democracy, and so on. The 1995 Schengen Treaty established a zone for the free movement of people (though Ireland and the United Kingdom opted out).

The 1997 Amsterdam Treaty forged ahead in EU foreign and security policy and strengthened the rights of EU citizenship and the powers of the European parliament.

The most ambitious part of the Maastricht Treaty was its economic element: the EU-wide goal of **Economic and Monetary Union (EMU).** The economic union would take the idea of a single market even further—to all goods and services, to capital markets, to labor markets—and would call on the European Commission to ensure that national laws and regulations did not stand in the way. But more than this, monetary union would propose a new currency (soon given the name "euro") for the entire EU. Under the plan for the euro, countries would transition from their pegged rates within the ERM into an *irrevocable peg* with the euro at an appointed date. But this plan almost immediately came into doubt.

The ERM proved to be a fragile fixed exchange rate system like any other. As we saw in the last chapter, its worst moment came in 1992. In the **ERM crisis,** several ERM countries suffered exchange rate crises and their pegs broke: the British pound, Italian lira, Portuguese escudo, and Spanish peseta. (Other non-ERM currencies such as the Swedish krona and the Finnish markka pegged to the mark also experienced crises and broken pegs.) Even the currencies that stayed within the ERM had to have their bands widened so much as to make their pegs look more like floats for a while. The whole system was reduced to a near shambles.

As we saw in the past two chapters, the fundamental cause of these crises was a tension between the macroeconomic objectives of the center country, Germany (tight monetary policy to prevent overheating after a large fiscal shock caused by reunification), and the objectives of the pegging countries (whose authorities wanted to use expansionary monetary policy to boost output during a period of global slowdown).

The ghosts of the 1992 crisis still roam today. Many countries rejoined the ERM, some at a new rate or with a wider band: Spain, Italy, and Portugal all regrouped, reentered ERM, and ultimately adopted the euro. But Britain permanently left the ERM and turned its back on the common currency. Sweden, officially committed to the euro, has never shown any interest in joining even the ERM. Today, in both Britain and Sweden, public opposition to the euro remains high. And there is always the fear that another ERM crisis could erupt in new EU members that are pegging to the euro as part of their preparation for joining the common currency.

Still, despite the exchange rate crisis in 1992, the ERM was patched up, and most countries remained committed to the plan to launch the euro. The ERM bands were widened in 1993 to a very slack ±15%, and most were happy to live within those limits and get ready for euro admission.

The Eurozone Is Launched: 1999 and Beyond The euro was launched in 11 countries on January 1, 1999, and administered by a newly created central bank, the **European Central Bank (ECB).**[9] The ECB took control of monetary policy in all Eurozone countries on that date from each national central bank.[10] The national central banks

---

[9] The European Central Bank was established on June 1, 1998. It succeeded a prototype monetary authority, the European Monetary Institute (EMI), which for four and a half years had undertaken much of the groundwork for the euro project.
[10] All EU central banks cooperate as a group in the European System of Central Banks (ESCB). Within that group, the central banks of Eurozone member states (known, confusingly, as the Eurosystem banks) have a much closer relationship with the ECB. Only Eurosystem banks have representation on the ECB's Council.

still have responsibilities. They represent their country on the ECB Council, and still supervise and regulate their own country's financial system. The euro immediately became the unit of account in the Eurozone, and a gradual transition took place as euros began to enter circulation and national currencies were withdrawn.

Table 10-2 shows the history and current state of play in the EU at the time of this writing in January 2011. The table shows the dates of membership in the EU, the ERM,

TABLE 10-2

The EU-27 and the Euro Project in 2011 This table shows the progress of each country through EU membership, ERM membership, and adoption of the euro, as of 2011. The euro parities of Eurozone members and ERM members are also shown, although the former have now abolished their national currencies. Dates for future euro adoption are in many cases uncertain or unknown (shown by a question mark).

		YEAR THAT COUNTRY JOINED				
		EU	ERM	Eurozone	Euro Parity (€1 =)	National Currency (current or former)
Countries in the Eurozone	Austria	1995	1995	1999	13.7603	schilling
	Belgium	1959	1979	1999	40.3399	frank
	Cyprus	2004	2005	2008	0.585274	pound
	Estonia	2004	2004	2011	15.6466	kroon
	Finland	1995	1996	1999	5.94573	markka
	France	1959	1979	1999	6.55957	franc
	Germany	1959	1979	1999	1.95583	mark
	Greece	1981	1999	2001	340.75	drachma
	Ireland	1973	1979	1999	0.787564	pound
	Italy	1959	1979	1999	1936.27	lira
	Luxembourg	1959	1979	1999	40.3399	franc
	Malta	2004	2005	2008	0.4293	lira
	Netherlands	1959	1979	1999	2.20371	guilder
	Portugal	1986	1992	1999	200.482	escudo
	Slovakia	2004	2005	2009	30.126	koruna
	Slovenia	2004	2004	2007	239.64	tolar
	Spain	1986	1989	1999	166.386	peseta
Countries in the ERM	Denmark*	1973	1999	?	7.46038	krone
	Latvia	2004	2005	?	0.702804	lat
	Lithuania	2004	2004	?	3.4528	litas
Other EU Countries	Bulgaria	2007	?	?	?	lev
	Czech Republic	2004	?	?	?	koruna
	Hungary	2004	?	?	?	forint
	Poland	2004	?	?	?	zloty
	Romania	2007	?	?	?	leu
	Sweden*	1995	?	?	?	krona
	United Kingdom*	1973	1990–92	?	?	pound

* The United Kingdom and Denmark can legally opt out of the euro. Sweden is opting out de facto by not joining the ERM. All other countries are expected to join at some point.

and the Eurozone. Also shown are the fixed exchange rate parities of all ERM and euro members—for the latter, these were frozen upon euro entry and became obsolete once the national currencies were retired.[11]

As of 2011, the Eurozone contains 17 "in" countries. Eleven made the switch to the euro in 1999, Greece entered in 2001, Slovenia in 2007, Cyprus and Malta in 2008, Slovakia in 2009, and Estonia in 2011. There are 10 "out" countries. In the ERM "waiting room," there are 3 countries, and one of them, Denmark, has been waiting a long time. There are 7 countries not in ERM, although all except the United Kingdom and Sweden are expected to join the ERM and the euro in the medium term of five to ten years. Of the "out" countries, only Denmark and the United Kingdom can legally opt out of the euro indefinitely, although Sweden is acting as if it can, too; all three countries have popular opposition to the euro and are not expected to adopt the euro anytime soon.

Summary

History shows that the countries of Europe have some deep tendency to prefer fixed exchange rates to floating rates. Apart from brief crisis episodes in times of turmoil (during wars, the Great Depression, and the early 1970s), most European countries have maintained pegged exchange rates against each other since the 1870s. They have now taken the additional step of adopting a common currency.

There have certainly been some economic changes in Europe that make it more likely to satisfy the OCA criteria now than at anytime in the past. The EU project has pushed forward a process of deep economic integration, with major steps such as EMU and the Treaty of Schengen bringing Europe closer to the ideal of a single market. But integration is still very much a work in progress, and the OCA criteria are unlikely to be met soon.

Instead, European history leads us to the conclusion that the common currency fits as part of a political project rather than as a purely economic choice. To consider some of the implications of this conclusion, in the remainder of this chapter we consider some of the operational issues and problems faced by the Eurozone during its first decade of existence.

3 Eurozone Tensions in Tranquil Times, 1999–2007

From its launch in 1999 until 2007 or so, the Eurozone was considered a success. Compared with what came next, this was a time of economic growth and stability for the Eurozone—a period with no recession and with the ECB untroubled by problems either with its explicit inflation target goal or its broader responsibility to support Eurozone economic and financial stability.

In this section we review this fortunate period, focusing on the way in which the ECB's monetary policy rules were devised, and the broader concerns about fiscal stability. This period will be remembered for a somewhat narrow and limited policy focus and a general complacency concerning some of the ultimately more dangerous macroeconomic trends that we discuss in the section that follows.

---

[11] Since 1999 the original ERM has been replaced with a modified ERM II, with the euro replacing its predecessor, the ecu, as the base currency for pegging. Notwithstanding the Maastricht Treaty, all ERM members now operate in a de jure ±15% band (although Denmark sticks to the old, narrow ±2.25% band).

The European Central Bank

Suppose some German economists from the 1950s or 1960s, after having traveled forward in time to the present day, pop up next to you on a Frankfurt street corner, and say, "Take me to the central bank." They are surprised when you lead them to the gleaming glass and steel Eurotower at Kaiserstrasse instead of the old Bundesbank building.

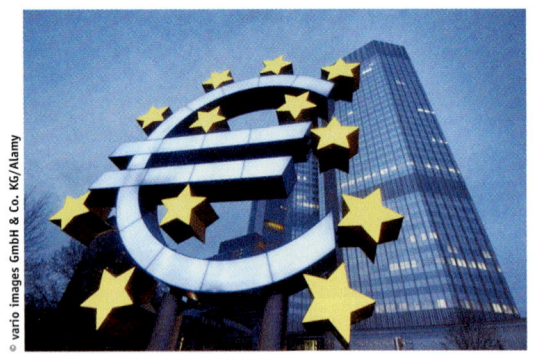

The ECB Tower and euro logo, Frankfurt.

That the European Central Bank is located in Frankfurt is no coincidence, however. It is a testament to the strong influence of German monetary policy makers and politicians in the design of the euro project, an influence they earned on account of the exemplary performance of the German economy, and especially its monetary policy, from the 1950s to the 1990s. To see how German influence has left its mark on the euro, we first examine how the ECB operates and then try to explain its peculiar goals and governance.

For economists, central banks have a few key features. To sum these up, we may ask: What policy instrument does the bank use? What is it supposed to do (goals) and not do (forbidden activities)? How are decisions on these policies made given the bank's governance structure? To whom is the bank accountable, and, subject to that, how much independence does the bank have? For the ECB, the brief answers are as follows:

- *Instrument and goals.* The instrument used by the ECB is the interest rate at which banks can borrow funds. According to its charter, the ECB's primary objective is to "maintain price stability" in the euro area. Its secondary goal is to "support the general economic policies in the Community with a view to contributing to the achievement of the objectives of the Community." (Many central banks have similar instruments and goals, but the ECB has a relatively strong focus on inflation.)

- *Forbidden activities.* To prevent the use of monetary policy for other goals, the ECB may not directly finance member states' fiscal deficits or provide bailouts to member governments or national public bodies. In addition, the ECB has no mandate to act as a lender of last resort by extending credit to financial institutions in the Eurozone in the event of a banking crisis. (Most central banks are not so constrained, and they typically can act as a lender of last resort.)

- *Governance and decision making.* Monetary policy decisions are made at meetings of the ECB's Governing Council, which consists of the central bank governors of the Eurozone national central banks and six members of the ECB's executive board. In practice, policy decisions are made by consensus rather than by majority voting. Meetings are usually held twice each month.

- *Accountability and independence.* No monetary policy powers are given to any other EU institution. No EU institution has any formal oversight of the ECB, and the ECB does not have to report to any political body, elected or otherwise. The ECB does not release the minutes of its meetings. The ECB has independence not only with respect to its instrument (it sets interest rates) but also with respect to its goal (it gets to define what "price stability" means). (A small but growing number of central banks around the world has achieved some independence, but the ECB has more than most.)

On all three points, the working of the ECB has been subject to strong criticisms.

Criticisms of the ECB There is controversy over the price stability goal. The ECB chooses to define price stability as a Eurozone consumer price inflation rate of less than but "close to" 2% per year over the medium term. This target is vague (the notions of "close to" and "medium term" are not defined). The target is also asymmetrical (there is no lower bound to guard against deflation), a characteristic that became a particular worry as inflation rates fell toward zero during the Great Recession following the global financial crisis of 2008.

There is controversy over having only price stability as a goal. On paper, the ECB technically has a secondary goal of supporting and stabilizing the Eurozone economy. But in practice, the ECB has acted as if it places little weight on economic performance, growth, and unemployment, and where the real economy is in the business cycle. In this area, the ECB's policy preferences are different from, say, those of the U.S. Federal Reserve, which has a mandate from Congress not only to ensure price stability but also to achieve full employment. The ECB also differs from the Bank of England, whose Governor Mervyn King once famously used the term "inflation nutter" to describe a policy maker with an excessive focus on price stability. The ECB's early obsessive focus on money and prices was thought to reflect a combination of its Germanic heritage and its relative lack of long-term reputation.

There is controversy over the ECB's way of conducting policy to achieve its goal. In addition to the "first pillar," which uses an economic analysis of expected price inflation to guide interest rate decisions, the bank has a "second pillar" in the form of a reference value for money supply growth (4.5% per annum). As we saw in the chapter on exchange rates in the long run, however, a fixed money growth rate can be consistent with an inflation target only by chance. For example, in the quantity theory model, which assumes a stable level of nominal interest rates in the long run, inflation equals the money growth rate minus the growth rate of real output. So the ECB's twin pillars will make sense only if real output just happens to grow at less than 2.5% per year, for only then will inflation be, at most, $4.5 - 2.5 = 2\%$ per year. Perhaps aware of the inconsistency of using two nominal anchors, the ECB has given the impression that most of the time it ignores the second pillar; nonetheless, concern about money supply growth is occasionally expressed.

There is controversy over the strict interpretation of the "forbidden activities" rules. What happens in the event of a large banking crisis in the Eurozone? When banking crises hit other nations, many central banks would choose to extend credit to specific troubled banks or to relax lending standards to the banking sector as a whole, and they could print money to do so. In the Eurozone, officially the ECB can print the money but it cannot implement either type of additional lending; the national central banks of countries in the Eurozone can do the lending but can't print the money. National central banks can devise limited, local credit facilities or arrange private consortia to manage a small crisis, or they can hope for fiscal help from their national treasuries. Big crises could therefore prove more difficult to prevent or contain.

There is controversy over the decision-making process. Consensus decisions may favor the status quo, causing policy to lag when it ought to move. Insistence on having all central bank governors on the Council leads to a very large body in which consensus is more difficult to achieve. This design will become even more cumbersome as more countries join the euro, but the structure of the Council is set in the Maastricht Treaty and would be impossible to change without revising the treaty.

There is controversy over the ECB's lack of accountability. Because it answers to no political masters, some fear that people in the Eurozone will conclude that the ECB lacks legitimacy. Although the EU is a collection of democratic states, many of its decisions are made in places that are far from the people in these states. Many EU bodies suffer a perceived "democratic deficit," including the work of the unelected Commission and the treaties pursued at the intragovernmental level with no popular ratification and little consultation. The ECB can appear to be even further removed at a supra-governmental level. There is nothing akin to the U.S. requirement that the Federal Reserve chairman regularly answer questions from Congress. Rather, the ECB has a more informal dialogue and consultations with the Council, Commission, and Parliament. In response, the finance ministers of the Eurozone have ganged up to form the *Eurogroup*, which meets and opines about what is happening in the Eurozone and what the ECB is (or should be) doing. Occasionally, national heads of governments weigh in to attack the ECB's policy choices or to defend them. Along with the EU's commissioner for economic and monetary affairs, heads of government can make pronouncements and lobby, but they can do little more unless a treaty revision places the ECB under more scrutiny.

The German Model

Some of these criticisms are valid and undisputed, but others are fiercely contested. Supporters of the ECB say that strong independence and freedom from political interference are exactly what is needed in a young institution that is still struggling to achieve credibility and that the dominant problem in the Eurozone in recent years has been inflation not deflation. For many of these supporters, the ECB is set up the right way—almost a copy of the Bundesbank, with a strong focus on low inflation to the exclusion of other criteria and a complete separation of monetary policy from politics. Here, German preferences and German economic performance had been very different from those for the rest of the Eurozone, yet they prevailed. How can this be understood?

German preferences for a low-inflation environment have been extremely strong ever since the costly and chaotic interwar hyperinflation (discussed in the chapter on exchange rates in the long run). It was clear that the hyperinflation had been driven by reckless fiscal policy, which had led politicians to take over monetary policy and run the printing presses. After that fiasco, strong anti-inflation preferences, translated from the people via the political process, were reflected in the conduct of monetary policy by the Bundesbank from 1958 until the arrival of the euro in 1999. To ensure that the Bundesbank could deliver a firm nominal anchor, it was carefully insulated from political interference.

Today, as we learned when studying exchange rates in the long run, a popular recipe for sound monetary policy is a combination of central bank independence and an inflation target. Sometimes, the inflation target is set by the government, the so-called *New Zealand model*. But the so-called *German model* went further and faster: the Bundesbank was not only the first central bank to be granted full independence, it was also given both *instrument independence* (freedom to use interest rate policy in the short run) and *goal independence* (the power to decide what the inflation target should be in the long run). This became the model for the ECB, when Germany set most of the conditions for entering a monetary union with other countries where the traditions of central bank independence were weaker or nonexistent.

Monetary Union with Inflation Bias

We can see where Germany's preferences came from. But how did it get its way? A deep problem in modern macroeconomics concerns the *time inconsistency* of policies.[12] According to this view, all countries have a problem with inflation bias under discretionary monetary policy. Policy makers would like to commit to low inflation, but without a credible commitment to low inflation, a politically controlled central bank has the temptation to use "surprise" monetary policy expansions to boost output. Eventually, this bias will be anticipated, built into inflation expectations, and hence, in the long run, real outcomes—such as output and unemployment—will be the same whatever the extent of the inflation bias. Long-run money neutrality means that printing money can't make an economy more productive or create jobs.

The inflation bias problem can be solved if we can separate the central bank from politics and install a "conservative central banker" who cares about inflation and nothing else. This separation was strong in Germany, but not elsewhere. Hence, a historically low-inflation country (e.g., Germany) might be worried that a monetary union with a high-inflation country (e.g., Italy) would lead to a monetary union with on average a tendency for middling levels of inflation—that is, looser monetary policies on average for Germany and tighter on average for Italy. In the long run, Germany and Italy would still get the same real outcomes (though in the short run, Germany might have a monetary-led boom and Italy a recession). But, while Italy might gain in the long run from lower inflation, Germany would lose from the shift to a high-inflation environment. Germany would need assurances that this would not happen, and because Germany was such a large and pivotal country in the EU, a Eurozone without Germany was unimaginable (based on simple OCA logic or on political logic). So Germany had a lot of bargaining power.

Essentially, the bargaining over the design of the ECB and the Eurozone boiled down to this: Other countries were content to accept that in the long run their real outcomes would not be any different even if they switched to a monetary policy run by the ECB under the German model, and thus had to settle for less political manipulation of monetary policy.

Or so they said at the time. But how could one be sure that these countries did in fact mean what they said? One could take countries' word for it—trust them. Or one could make them prove it—test them. In a world of inflation bias, trust in monetary authorities is weak, so the Maastricht Treaty established some tests; that is, some rules for admission.

The Rules of the Club

The Maastricht Treaty established five rules for admission to the euro zone, as shown in Table 10-3. All five of these **convergence criteria** need to be satisfied for entry. Two of the five rules also serve as ongoing requirements for membership. The rules can be divided into two parts: three rules requiring convergence in nominal measures closely related to inflation and two rules requiring fiscal discipline to clamp down on the deeper determinants of inflation.

Nominal Convergence
In the chapters on short- and long-run exchange rates, we explored some of the central implications of a fixed exchange rate, implications that

---

[12] Finn E. Kydland and Edward C. Prescott, 1977, "Rules Rather Than Discretion: The Inconsistency of Optimal Plans," *Journal of Political Economy*, 87, 473–492; Guillermo Calvo, 1978, "On the Time Consistency of Optimal Policy in a Monetary Economy," *Econometrica*, 46, 1411–1428; Robert J. Barro and David B. Gordon, 1983, "Rules, Discretion and Reputation in a Model of Monetary Policy," *Journal of Monetary Economics*, 12, 101–121.

TABLE 10-3

Rules of Euro Membership The Maastricht Treaty of 1991 established five conditions that aspiring members of the Eurozone must satisfy prior to entry. The last two fiscal rules are also supposed to be obeyed by members even after entry.

Rule (*prior to entry only)	Criterion
Exchange rate*	Two consecutive years in ERM band with no devaluation (no change in central parity)
Inflation rate*	No more than 1.5 percentage points above the level in the three member states with the lowest inflation in the previous year
Long-term nominal interest rate*	No more than 2 percentage points above the level in the three member states with the lowest inflation in the previous year
Government deficit	No more than 3% of GDP in previous financial year[1]
Government debt	No more than 60% of GDP in previous financial year[2]

Notes:
The ERM bands in effect at the time of the Maastricht Treaty were *narrow* (±2.25% or ±6%); since 1993 they have been *wide* (±15%). The first rule is now applied using the wide bands. Escape clauses are included in the last two fiscal rules, as follows:
[1] Or "the ratio must have declined substantially and continuously and reached a level close to 3% or, alternatively, must remain close to 3% while representing only an exceptional and temporary excess."
[2] Or "the ratio must have sufficiently diminished and must be approaching the reference value at a satisfactory pace."

---

also apply when two countries adopt a common currency (i.e., a fixed exchange rate of 1). Let's consider three implications:

- Under a peg, the exchange rate must be fixed or not vary beyond tight limits.
- Purchasing power parity (PPP) then implies that the two countries' inflation rates must be very close.
- Uncovered interest parity (UIP) then implies that the two countries' long-term nominal interest rates must be very close.

In fact, we may recall that the Fisher effect says that the inflation differential must equal the nominal interest rate differential—so if one is small, the other has to be small, too.

These three conditions all relate to the nominal anchoring provided by a peg, and they roughly correspond to the first three Maastricht criteria in Table 10-3.

The rules say that a country must stay in its ERM band (with no realignment) for two years to satisfy the peg rule.[13] It must have an inflation rate "close to" that of the three lowest-inflation countries in the zone to satisfy the inflation rule. And it must have a long-term interest rate "close to" that in the three low-inflation countries.[14] All three tests must be met for a country to satisfy the admission criteria.

---

[13] The two-year requirement for the ERM means a country can't cheat by stabilizing its currency at the last minute, possibly in an opportunistic way to get in at a favorable (depreciated) rate that boosts demand for the country's output. Still, as currently interpreted, the ERM rule means that a currency only has to stay within the wide (post-1993) ±15% ERM bands, so the constraint is not all that tight. Also, following the exchange rate crises of 1992 in the United Kingdom and Sweden that gave the ERM a bad name, the two-year ERM membership rule might be waived if either of these two countries wishes to adopt the euro.

[14] The interest rate rule relates to the long-term interest rate for government borrowing, not the short-term rate that is central to UIP. Over the long run, the two move together and on average are generally separated by a positive *term premium*. Under a peg, then, countries will share identical *long-term* interest rates if and only if (1) there is no risk premium difference between them and (2) there is no term premium difference either. In practice, risk premiums and term premiums are higher for riskier borrowers, so in some ways this rule is also related to fiscal discipline (discussed in the next section).

What is the economic sense for these rules? They appear, in some ways, superfluous because if a country credibly pegged to (or has adopted) the euro, theory says that these conditions would have to be satisfied in the long run anyway. For that reason they are also difficult to criticize—except to say that, if the rules are going to be met anyway, why not "just do it" and let countries join the euro without such conditions? The answer relates to our earlier discussion about inflation bias. If two countries with different inflation rates adopt a common currency, their inflation rates must converge—but to what level, high or low?

The way the rules were written forces countries to converge on the lowest inflation rates in the zone. We have argued that this outcome is needed for low-inflation countries to sign up, although it will require possibly painful policy change in the high-inflation countries. The Maastricht criteria ensure that high-inflation countries go through this pain and attain credibility by demonstrating their commitment to low inflation before they are allowed in. This process supposedly prevents governments with a preference for high inflation from entering the Eurozone and then trying to persuade the ECB to go soft on inflation. These three rules can thus be seen as addressing the credibility problem in a world of inflation bias. All current euro members successfully satisfied these rules to gain membership, and the end result was marked inflation convergence as shown in Figure 10-7. Current and future ERM members are required to go through the same test.

Fiscal Discipline The Maastricht Treaty wasn't just tough on inflation, it was tough on the causes of inflation, and it saw the fundamental and deep causes of inflation as being not monetary, but fiscal. The other two Maastricht rules are openly aimed at

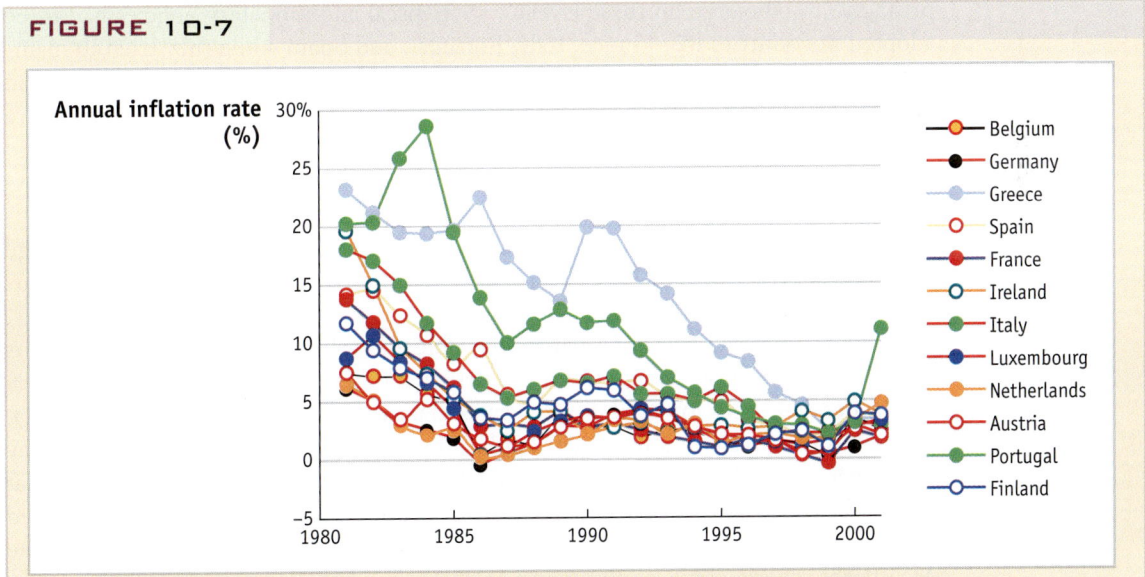

FIGURE 10-7

Inflation Convergence To meet the Maastricht Treaty's convergence criteria, the first 12 members of the Eurozone had to reduce their inflation level below a moving target. This target was equal to average inflation in the three lowest-inflation countries in the bloc plus 1.5 percentage points. This process ensured that the Eurozone began with a low inflation rate. The countries currently in the ERM must pass the same test before they can adopt the euro.

Source: European Economy, Statistical Annex, Autumn 2005.

constraining fiscal policy. They are applied not just as a condition for admission but also to all member states once they are in. The rules say that government debts and deficits cannot be above certain reference levels (although the treaty allows some exceptions). These levels were chosen somewhat arbitrarily: a deficit level of 3% of GDP and a debt level of 60% of GDP. However arbitrary these reference levels are, there still exist economic rationales for having some kinds of fiscal rules in a monetary union in which the member states maintain fiscal sovereignty.

Why might inflation ultimately be a fiscal problem? Consider two countries negotiating the treaty, one with low debt levels (e.g., Germany) and one with high debt levels (e.g., Italy). Germany has several possible fears in this case. One is that if Italy has high nominal debt (measured in lira, but soon to be measured in euros), Italy will lobby for high inflation once in the union (because inflation destroys the real value of the government's debt). Another fear is that Italy has a higher default risk, which might result in political pressure for the ECB to break its own rules and bail out Italy in a crisis, which the ECB can do only by printing euros and, again, generating more inflation.

The main arguments for the fiscal rules are that any deal to form a currency union will require fiscally weak countries to tighten their belts and meet criteria set by fiscally strong countries in order to further ensure against inflation.

Criticism of the Convergence Criteria
Because these rules constitute the main gatekeeping mechanism for the Eurozone, they have been carefully scrutinized and have generated much controversy.

First, these rules involve asymmetric adjustments that take a long time. In the 1980s and 1990s, they mostly involved German preferences on inflation and fiscal policy being imposed at great cost on other countries. Germany had lower inflation and larger surpluses than most countries, and the criteria were set close to the German levels, not surprisingly. To converge on these levels, tighter fiscal and monetary policies had to be adopted in countries like France, Italy, Portugal, and Spain while they tried to maintain the peg (to obey rule 1: staying in their ERM bands). As we saw in the chapter on output, exchange rates, and macroeconomic policy, fiscal contractions are even more contractionary under a peg than under a float. Such policies are politically costly, and hence the peg may not be fully credible. As we saw in the chapter on crises, foreign exchange traders often have doubts about the resolve of the authorities to stick with contractionary policies, and these doubts can increase the risk of self-fulfilling exchange rate crises, as happened in 1992. The same costs and risks now weigh on current Eurozone applicants seeking to pass these tests.

Second, the fiscal rules are seen as inflexible and arbitrary. The numerical targets have little justification: Why 3% for the deficit and not 4%? Why 60% and not 70% for the debt level? As for flexibility, the rules in particular pay no attention to the stage of the business cycle in a particular applicant country. A country in a recession may have a very large deficit even if on average the country has a government budget that is fairly balanced across the whole business cycle. In other words, the well-established arguments for the prudent use of countercyclical fiscal policy are totally ignored by the Maastricht criteria. This is an ongoing problem, as we shall see in a moment.

Third, whatever good might result from the painful convergence process, it might be only fleeting. For example, the Greek or French governments of the 1990s may have subjected themselves to budgetary discipline and monetary conservatism. Have their preferences really changed or did they just go along with the rules (or pretend to) merely as a way to get in? The same question applies to current Eurozone applicants. As Figure 10-8

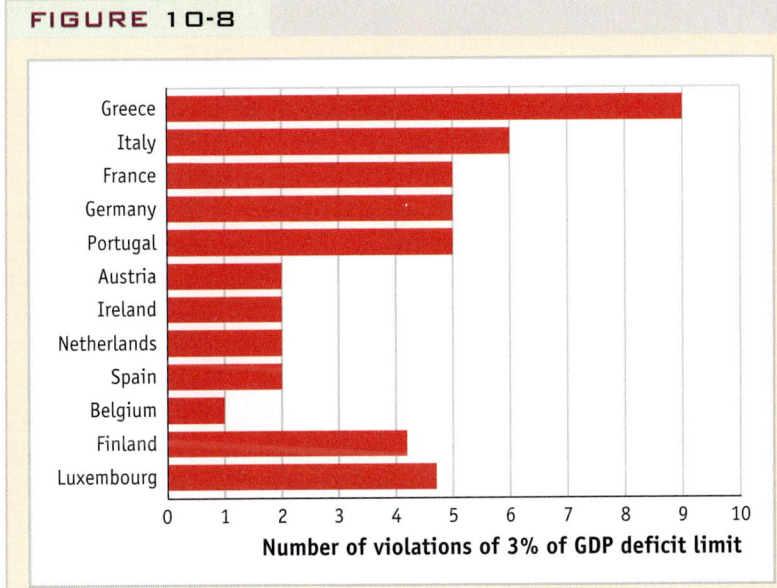

FIGURE 10-8

Breaking of Fiscal Rules The fiscal convergence criteria laid down by the Maastricht Treaty and affirmed by the Stability and Growth Pact have been widely ignored. This figure shows the number of times that each of the original 12 members of the Eurozone have violated the 3% of GDP government deficit limit since joining the Eurozone.

Source: Martin Wolf, "Implications of the Crisis for Stability and Growth in the Eurozone," World Bank Workshop on Inclusive Growth in Advanced Countries, New York University, October 8, 2010.

shows, once the original dozen members of the Eurozone were in the club, their commitment to fiscal discipline (as reflected in their fiscal deficits) started to weaken in the subsequent decade, in some cases dramatically so.

The problems just noted do not disappear once countries are in the Eurozone. Countries continue to have their own fiscal policies as members of the Eurozone, and they all gain a share of influence on ECB policy through the governance structure of the central bank. Countries' incentives are different once the carrot of EMU membership has been eaten.

Sticking to the Rules

If "in" countries desire more monetary and fiscal flexibility than the rules allow, and being "in" means they no longer risk the punishment of being excluded from the Eurozone, then a skeptic would have to expect more severe budgetary problems and more lobbying for loose monetary policy to appear once countries had entered the Eurozone.

On this point, as we see, the skeptics were to some extent proved right, but the problems they identified were not entirely ignored in the Eurozone's design. On the monetary side, success (low and stable Eurozone inflation) would rest on the design of the ECB as an institution that could withstand political pressure and act with independence to deliver low inflation while ignoring pleas from member governments. In that respect, we have already noted the formidable efforts to make the ECB as independent as possible. On the fiscal side, however, success (in the shape of adherence to the budgetary rules) would rest on the mechanisms established to enforce the Maastricht fiscal criteria. This did not turn out quite so well.

The Stability and Growth Pact Within a few years of the Maastricht Treaty, the EU suspected that greater powers of monitoring and enforcement would be needed. Thus, in 1997 at Amsterdam, the EU adopted the **Stability and Growth Pact (SGP),** which the EU website has described as "the concrete EU answer to concerns on the continuation of budgetary discipline in Economic and Monetary Union." In the end, this provided no answer whatsoever and even before the ink was dry, naysayers were unkind enough to term it the "stupidity pact."

Throwing another acronym into the mix, the SGP was aimed at enforcing the 3% deficit rule and proposed the following to keep states in line: a "budgetary surveillance" process that would check on what member states were doing; a requirement to submit economic data and policy statements as part of a periodic review of "stability and convergence programs"; an "early warning mechanism" to detect any "slippage"; a "political commitment" that "ensures that effective peer pressure is exerted on a Member State failing to live up to its commitments"; and an "excessive deficits procedure" with "dissuasive elements" in the event of failure to require "immediate corrective action and, if necessary, allow for the imposition of sanctions."[15]

The shortcomings of the SGP, which became clear over time, were as follows:

- Surveillance failed because member states concealed the truth about their fiscal problems. Some hired private-sector accounting firms to make their deficits look smaller via accounting tricks (a suspiciously common deficit figure was 2.9%). In the case of Greece, the government simply falsified deficit figures for the purpose of gaining admission to the euro in 2001 and owned up once it was in.

- Punishment was weak, so even when "excessive deficits" were detected, not much was done about it. Peer pressure was ineffective, perhaps because so many of the governments were guilty of breaking the pact that very few had a leg to stand on. Corrective action was rare and states "did their best," which was often not very much. Formal SGP disciplining processes often started but never resulted in actual sanctions because heads of government in Council proved very forgiving of each other and unwilling to dispense punishments.

- Deficit limits rule out the use of active stabilization policy, but they also shut down the "automatic stabilizer" functions of fiscal policy. Recessions automatically lower government revenues and raise spending, and the resulting deficits help boost aggregate demand and offset the recession. This makes deficit limits tough to swallow, even if monetary policy autonomy is kept as a stabilization tool. In a monetary union, where states have also relinquished monetary policy to the ECB, the pain of hard fiscal rules is likely to be intolerable.

- Once countries joined the euro, the main "carrot" enticing them to follow the SGP's budget rules (or to pretend to follow them) disappeared. Hence, surveillance, punishment, and commitment all quite predictably weakened once the euro was up and running.

These failures of the SGP came to light only gradually, but by 2003 the pact was in ruins, once it became clear that France and (ironically) Germany would be in breach of the pact and that no serious action would be taken against them. As we see next, fiscal problems in the Eurozone have only gotten worse, although whether the principles of the SGP can, or should, be reinstated is the subject of ongoing disagreement.

---

[15] European Commission, Directorate General for Economic and Financial Affairs, The Stability and Growth Pact. Published online. For a copy of this document, go to http://www.eubusiness.com/Finance/eu-stability-growth-pact/.

4 The Eurozone in Crisis, 2008–2010

For almost ten years, Eurozone policy making had focused on two main macroeconomic targets: the ECB's monetary policy credibility and inflation target, which was a broad success; and the Eurozone governments' commitment to fiscal integrity, which was basically a failure given the general disregard for the SGP rules. However, ECB policy makers (like policy makers all over the world) largely ignored many key macroeconomic and financial developments that were to plunge the Eurozone into crisis in 2008 and beyond.

With a fanatical devotion to inflation targeting, the ECB (and its constituent central banks) paid insufficient attention to one of the ancient responsibilities of central banks, namely, financial stability. Within some parts of the Eurozone (as elsewhere) debtors in the private sector were engaged in a credit-fueled boom. At the same time, in other parts of the Eurozone, creditors and their banks funneled ever more loans toward the borrowers. In the Eurozone, the creditors were core Northern European countries like Germany and the Netherlands; the debtors were fast-growing peripheral nations such as Greece, Ireland, Portugal, and Spain.

In Greece, much of the borrowing was by a fiscally irresponsible government that was later found to be fudging its accounts. In the other peripheral nations, however, the flow of loans funded rapid investment and consumption surges, including a residential construction boom that in places (e.g., the environs of Dublin and Barcelona) rivaled the property bubble in California and certain other parts of the United States. In Ireland and Spain, even as this boom took place, the governments had maintained a fiscal position close to balance, or even surplus.

However, trouble arose once the global boom turned to bust and dragged Europe down with it. Much of the construction, like all of the overconsumption, was revealed to have been unjustified and unsustainable. Along the way, however, the boom had bid up the prices of assets (notably houses) and of many nontraded services (and thus wages), and had left households in the peripheral nations saddled with high debts and uncompetitive, high wage levels that could not be sustained once the artificially high demand of the boom years was exhausted.

A vicious spiral began in the peripherals. Construction and nontraded sectors started to collapse, which lowered demand. House prices fell, as did the value of firms. Wealth collapsed, lowering demand further. Output fell in the short run, as did tax revenues. Households cut spending further, and the governments also tightened their belts. With everyone suffering lower incomes and wealth, banks tightened lending, which hurt demand still more. As the spiral continued, banks found that their loans were often turning bad, and many debts would be repaid only partially if at all.

Governments tried to limit their spending cuts, and also took the controversial step of trying to guarantee their private banks and prevent bank runs by bank debt holders that would cause even more economic pain. But this method of preventing bank failures merely socialized private losses, and transferred the financial sector's massive hole onto the government's books. For example, by late 2010 the Irish government had to admit a loss of about 20% of GDP just to cover the banks' bad debts. The overall fiscal deficit for Ireland that year was an unheard of 32% of GDP.

The other countries of the Eurozone made little effort to provide assistance to the peripherals beyond more lending. The belief was that every country was responsible for its own fiscal position. However, in a stance that was somewhat at odds with this view, the EU leadership desperately wanted to prevent any country from defaulting. The ECB was also dragged into the fray as the only Eurozone institution willing and capable of lending a hand. The ECB's official policy was to make loans to member states' banks if they offered "eligible" Eurozone government bonds as collateral. Thus, an unfortunate process developed: peripheral private banks would keep shaky loans on their books and resist taking losses by liquidating them; their own governments, in need of money, would ask these private banks for loans, and issue bonds to them that paid a high interest rate; the banks could then profit by using the bonds as collateral to obtain low-interest loans from the ECB. The governments kept borrowing from the private banks, the banks kept earning profits, and the ECB continued to lend to the private banks against the ever-weaker collateral of the peripheral governments' bonds.

For the ECB, this may have been a reasonable "collateralization" policy when governments and banks were solvent. But by 2009 and 2010 the bonds issued by some of the peripheral governments were being given near-junk credit ratings. Prior to the crisis, the ECB had supposedly said it would refuse to lend against such government bonds when their ratings fell, but when push came to shove, the ECB's lending criteria were relaxed time and again, because to do otherwise would have triggered a funding crisis for both the banks and their respective governments.

To the skeptical, this was a giant "extend and pretend" refinancing scheme that would fail unless all parties developed a plan to write down or restructure the underlying losses and get to the bottom of the peripherals' problems: by recapitalizing the banks and/or restoring fiscal health to the governments. But resolution was slow as the EU, ECB, and member governments struggled to agree on what to do. In early 2010 all of these concerns raised fears in financial markets that quickly snowballed and spread from the peripheral countries to the rest of the Eurozone. Government risk premiums on peripheral debt grew to alarming levels amid fears of an imminent default in Greece and perhaps other peripherals, as seen in Figure 10-9. Clearly, had these punitive costs of borrowing persisted for long, all the peripheral countries would have become insolvent sooner or later. And with the realization that these countries and their banks owed massive sums to core EU private banks (in France and Germany, especially), even risk premiums on some core Eurozone debt began to widen. As the value of the euro itself started to collapse in May 2010, EU leaders were finally forced into action.

Note that in principle the governments (and also the banks) of the peripherals could have been allowed to default (and may yet) and this would have solved their debt problems. Their debts could have then been partially or totally written off, and they could have been allowed to resume operation in a more creditworthy state. Instead, the EU decided on a "moral hazard" or "bailout" approach of trying to ensure that no bank or government creditors were hurt. This controversial step had several motivations, many of them understandable, including the desire to protect core EU banks, to protect the collateral of the ECB, to avoid further contagion and panic in financial markets, and perhaps to defend the reputation of the euro as a serious global currency. The EU's decision cast aside the prior notion that every Eurozone country was responsible unto itself and the idea that the ECB would not go along in any bailouts.

In 2010 debt problems in Greece and elsewhere were symptoms of deeper macroeconomic problems that put the Eurozone at risk.

FIGURE 10-9

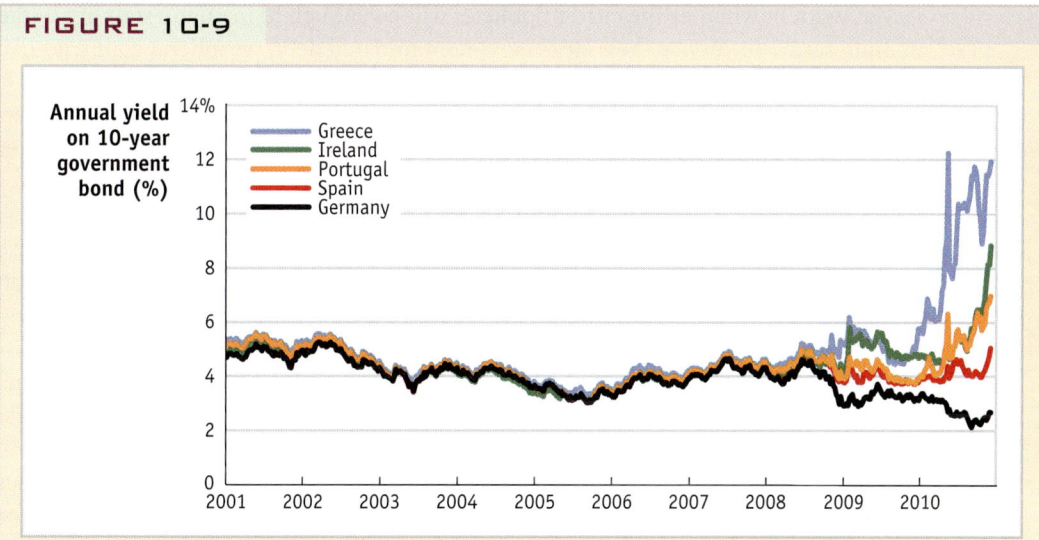

Country Risk Premiums Explode in the Peripheral Countries After the global financial crisis and recession, the so-called peripheral countries of the Eurozone (Greece, Portugal, Ireland, Spain) experienced severe downturns, financial stress, high deficits, and a rapid deterioration of government creditworthiness as the fear of default alarmed investors. They could only borrow, if at all, at very high interest rates relative to the benchmark German government bond. Shown here are data on the 10-year government bond yields. In contrast, prior to the crisis, such risks had been utterly ignored by markets and the countries had been able to borrow all too plentifully at rates virtually indistinguishable from the German rate.

Source: Martin Wolf, "Implications of the Crisis for Stability and Growth in the Eurozone," World Bank Workshop on Inclusive Growth in Advanced Countries, New York University, October 8, 2010.

On May 2, 2010, the EU and International Monetary Fund (IMF) jointly devised a plan to stave off disaster in Greece, the most troubled debtor country. Together, they would provide €110 billion of emergency financing that would provide Greece with two to three years of guaranteed funding. This help would only be provided under strict conditions that the Greek government radically cut its spending. Financial market panic continued, however, and further measures were announced on May 7. To help other troubled nations, all EU countries established a fund known as the *European Financial Stability Facility* (EFSF) to provide loans of up to €440 billion, founded on the good credit of the other EU members and a once unimaginable bond-buying commitment from the ECB. In addition, funds of up to €60 billion from the EU budget and €250 billion from the IMF provided a theoretical credit line of up to €750 billion. This was thought to be large enough to cope with financing problems in Ireland and Portugal, should the needs arise. If financing problems spread to larger countries like Spain (or, even worse, Italy and France), the EU and IMF would likely have to come up with more resources.

At the time of writing, in late 2010, the announcement of these measures had only served to keep panic at bay for a time. The risk premiums of the peripherals spiked again in November 2010, after EU leaders spoke of their desire to possibly impose losses on bondholders in similar circumstances at some unspecified future date. By mid-November, Ireland became the first country to ask the EFSF for help, and confidence in the peripherals and in the euro itself was shaken again.

Many doubt whether the current policies will be enough to maintain stability in the medium term. To service their large euro-denominated debt, peripheral countries like Greece, Ireland, Portugal, and Spain need to see their economies recover and their nominal GDP grow (as measured in euros). In the near term, however, growth forecasts for these economies are dismal. Their real economies continue to shrink, and neither private nor government consumption will provide any relief. Investment might rebound and bring about some economic growth, but only if net exports rise first. A boost to net exports would normally require a real depreciation in a nation's currency. Because peripherals have no currencies to depreciate (they use the euro), the only way they can restore competitiveness and output is by a large decline in wages and costs, a process being forced rapidly along by high unemployment. In addition to severe social and political pain, this harsh deflation may keep nominal GDP low and falling for a long time, causing the countries' debt burdens to grow ever larger as a fraction of income, despite their best efforts to cut government expenditures.

If these efforts fail and political will evaporates, one or more peripheral countries may default. Huge sacrifices will have been made by their populations, seemingly for naught. Core countries will have also taken large losses in their attempts to prop up the system, and may balk at a continuing "transfer union" based on payments to a group of peripherals purely to defend the honor of the single currency. Should a scenario like this unfold, the political tensions would only rise further and the Eurozone in its present form might be in peril (see **Headlines: Can the Euro Survive?**).

HEADLINES

Can the Euro Survive?

As the Eurozone crisis unfolded in late 2010, spreading beyond Greece, precipitating an IMF/EU rescue for Ireland, and threatening further damage, Martin Wolf of The Financial Times *picked over the wreckage and summarized the future prospects for the single currency.*

The fault lines in the currency union stand revealed. The promise was that the eurozone would deliver its members from currency crises. But, as I, and others, warned, be careful what you wish for: credit crises would replace currency crises—and these are likely to be even worse.

Why would a currency union lead to credit crises? One answer is that divergences in relative costs lead to structural trade imbalances—large external deficits when the less competitive economies are close to potential output. The private or public sectors must then spend more than their incomes to sustain full employment. Such excess spending must, in turn, be financed from abroad. In the end, such lending will vanish. If the lending goes via the banking sector, as in Ireland or Spain, there will first be a financial crisis. If the lending goes via the public sector, as in Greece, the crisis will first be in state finances.

A deeper answer is that the common interest rate will appear very low in some member countries. In the eurozone, the fact that global interest rates were low and demand in core economies weak, exacerbated this effect. These ultra-low interest rates triggered asset price bubbles and credit booms in peripheral economies. These, in turn, encouraged construction booms. In these circumstances, what the late John Kenneth Galbraith called the "bezzle"—the stock of financial crime—rises, to emerge in the crash. As the financial system implodes, the economy collapses and the public finances, seemingly strong in the boom, turn sharply for the worse.

The result is a huge credit crisis. Under a floating exchange rate, some of the pressure would be relieved by a rising exchange rate in the boom and a falling rate in the bust. With a pegged rate, the collapse in the currency would normally restore competitiveness and growth, as happened to the worst-hit

Asian countries in the late 1990s. In a currency union, these safety valves are lost. Instead, we have a joint credit and competitiveness crisis. The solution for the loss of competitiveness is a sharp fall in prices. But that worsens the credit crisis: this, then, is debt deflation, as Ireland knows.

That is one respect in which a currency crisis is less bad than a credit crisis. But a sovereign default also shakes confidence in the state, which is the foundation of the legal and political order. A banking crisis is almost as harmful. A currency crisis, on its own, simply is not.

This is the context in which the eurozone crisis must be understood. In the old days of the European Monetary System, there would have been currency crises in peripheral countries, whereupon the Greek, Irish, Portuguese, Spanish, Italian and, maybe, other currencies would have collapsed against the old D-Mark. That has already happened to the pound sterling. If Ireland were still in the sterling area, the punt would have fallen with it.

Now the eurozone must tackle its credit crises, instead. It is not doing well. Despite heroic improvisations, indicators of risk on the sovereign debt of the less credible countries have reached exalted levels. Markets ignored risks in the boom and turned savagely against the weaker credits in the bust.

The underlying dynamic is, again, similar to those of currency crises. In the latter, governments feel forced to offer such high interest rates that they undermine credibility, rather than increase it. In credit crises, markets again impose unbearable rates. A credible country enjoys low interest rates that strengthen trust. A country lacking in such credibility faces interest rates that undermine trust. Expectations are self-fulfilling. This is what is now emerging in peripheral eurozone credit: slow-growing countries with large fiscal deficits cannot promise sufficient tightening, given the high interest rates, to strengthen their credibility. Austerity may fail to deliver the credibility it promises.

So what, against this background, needs to be done by individual countries and the eurozone? Not what was done in Ireland, is one answer. The Irish banking system is worse than too big to fail; it is too big to save. The first duty of the state is to save itself, not to load its taxpayers with obligations to rescue careless lenders. If the eurozone is not a "transfer union", that has to work both ways: taxpayers of one state should not rescue those of others from having to save their banks from their follies.

The Irish state should have saved itself by drastic restructuring of bank liabilities. Bank debt simply cannot be public debt. If bank debt is to be such debt, bankers should be viewed as civil servants and banks as government departments. Surely, creditors must take the hit, instead.

That leaves the sovereigns. What is needed here, as eurozone leaders recognise, is a combination of generous funding with restructuring: the former is to reverse self-fulfilling panics; the latter is to recognise the realities of insolvency. Managing this combination would be very tricky.

Moreover, however helpful such expedients might be, membership of the currency union has transformed the financial position of members, which are deprived of a tame central bank and currency flexibility. As a result, they are far more likely to be driven to outright default than they used to be, as markets realise. The only ways out would be for the European Central Bank to buy the public debt or a fiscal union, with the capacity to bail out members in difficulty. Both are inconceivable. Germany would surely exit first.

So the big question now is not whether the eurozone can avoid a wave of fiscal cum financial crises. The question is whether the union will survive....

This is a political more than an economic issue. It is possible for a currency union to survive sovereign defaults. The question is, rather, whether members believe the arrangement remains beneficial. The difficulty for surplus countries is that they must finance those in deficit, accept external adjustment or push the eurozone into external surplus. The difficulty for deficit countries is that the cost of leaving the eurozone is to face debt crises. If those have happened already, the costs will seem smaller. If they think they have replaced currency crises with credit crises, which do not even restore competitiveness and growth, they may see the union as a bad deal. Political glue could melt. Such calamities do happen. It is now up to the members to see that they do not.

Source: Martin Wolf, "Why the Irish Crisis Is Such a Huge Test for the Eurozone," Financial Times, December 1, 2010.

5 Conclusions: Assessing the Euro

The euro project must be understood at least as much in political terms as in economic terms. We have seen how the OCA criteria can be used to examine the logic of currency unions, but in the case of the EU these are not the whole story: Europe does not appear to satisfy the narrow definition of an optimum currency area. In contrast, some of the most important criteria for the survival of the euro may relate to the non-OCA criteria that were included in the Maastricht Treaty. How well can the euro hold up in the future? Even after the crisis, both optimistic and pessimistic views persist. At the risk of caricature, we will contrast the views at the extremes of the debate.

Euro-Optimists For true optimists, the euro is already something of a success: it has functioned in a perfectly adequate way (apart from a crisis that has troubled many other countries, too) and can be expected to become only more successful as time goes by. More countries are lining up to join the Eurozone. Even if there are costs in the short run, the argument goes, in the long run the benefits will become clear.

Optimists tend to stress that the OCA criteria might be self-fulfilling. In the long run, they believe the euro will create more trade in the Eurozone. It may also create more labor and capital mobility. They downplay the risk that shocks will become more asymmetric, or at least think this will be outweighed by greater market integration. This will enhance the Eurozone's claim to be an OCA. Since the euro is only a few years old, data are scarce, and these claims can be neither proved nor refuted decisively at present. However, the little evidence we have suggests that although labor mobility has not changed much, goods and services trade in the Eurozone is rising (even if no faster than outside) and that capital market integration has perhaps improved even more dramatically, as measured by the increase in cross-border asset trade and FDI flows in the Eurozone.[16]

Optimists also tend to believe that the ECB will prove to be a strong, credible, independent central bank that can resist political interference or the temptation to print money for the sake of expediency. On paper, the ECB certainly has such characteristics, with a very high degree of independence compared with other central banks. Again, the costs of a common currency may be large in the short run, but as long as the ECB can deliver on its low-inflation target, the optimists reckon it will, in the end, command the respect of the peoples and politicians of the Eurozone.

At a global level, optimists note that the euro is increasingly becoming a reserve currency for foreign central banks, a vehicle currency for trade, and is now the dominant currency used in international bond markets. These developments show the market's confidence in the currency and also augur well for the future, since trade and financing costs may be expected to fall as the euro becomes more widely used around the globe.

Finally, like a "father" of the European Union, Jean Monnet, the optimists believe that the adoption of the euro, like entry to the EU itself, means "no going back": there is simply no imaginable political future for Europe apart from union. Neither the euro nor the EU has exit mechanisms. Perhaps such an idea was inconceivable to the institutional designers. For true believers, the EU project ultimately rests on a deep belief in the political logic of the process and in a presumed common destiny for the peoples of Europe.

Euro-Pessimists For true pessimists, the preceding arguments are not convincing. Market integration will not radically change because the impact of the euro on (already high) intra-EU trade levels will be small. Because cultural and linguistic barriers will persist, labor migration will be limited and held back even more by inflexible labor market institutions in most countries. In all markets, regulatory and other frictions will remain.

Moreover, there is resistance to further economic integration. In 2005 an EU directive to liberalize services proved unpopular in many countries and contributed to the failure of referenda on the proposed EU Constitutional Treaty in France and the Netherlands. In many countries, the implications of a single market in all dimensions

---

[16] For an excellent survey, see Philip R. Lane, 2006, "The Real Effects of European Monetary Union," *Journal of Economic Perspectives*, 20(4), 47–66.

(goods, services, labor, capital) are only now being dimly understood. Governments and the Commission disagree about how far the process should go.

If integration stops for lack of political support, a key economic rationale for the euro unravels. If political support for the EU stalls, then the political logic is weakened. If some countries press ahead with deeper federalism while others stand aside, the variable geometry of the EU may be stretched so much as to undermine any sense of a common destiny among all EU nations.

On the other key OCA criterion, pessimists note that there is often wide divergence in the countries of the Eurozone. Low-growth, low-inflation countries tend to want looser monetary policy. High-growth, high-inflation countries tend to want tighter monetary policy. If different countries desire very different policies from the ECB, tensions may rise and governments may lose respect for the ECB's independence.

The euro could also be threatened by fiscal problems. The rules say governments cannot lobby the ECB for low interest rates or high inflation to make their debt payments lower, or to reduce the real value of their debts. But as history has typically shown, governments tend to trump central banks and will push them around if times get tough. Pessimists note that the Maastricht fiscal rules have evaporated and the Stability and Growth Pact has been emptied of meaning. If some states lobby for loose money, more fiscally prudent nations will object, and the resulting fight will cause uncertainty and undermine the credibility of the euro.

The ECB was continually voicing its concerns in this area prior to the crisis, but with seemingly little effect on member states' behavior. For example, in November 2005 the ECB asserted its power to deny Eurozone banks the right to use government bonds as collateral if those bonds' credit rating fell too low; but as soon as this vow was put to the test after the 2008 crisis, the ECB caved in and continued to lend against peripheral country government debt of declining quality. The ECB then joined in the fiscal rescue of May 2010 by pledging to fund part of the EFSF program, taking its departure from the "no bailout" position even further.

As the crisis drags on, pessimists see no end to the monetary and fiscal policy tensions born of trying to impose a monetary union on a region with too many economic and political differences. At best, even if the euro survives, pessimists believe the region will suffer slow growth and ongoing internal conflicts. At worst, the tensions could be so great as to cause the breakup of the Eurozone into blocs or the reintroduction of the former national currencies.

Summary On the upside, the political dimension of the EU might yet carry the day in the long run, despite current setbacks; in the medium run, the OCA criteria might turn out better than one might think; and even if they don't in the short run, the Eurozone can still survive and function, a workable albeit economically costly currency union.

On the downside, EU enlargement undercuts the OCA logic in the short run and could make the ECB's governance more cumbersome and make resolution of conflicts more difficult; as the member states of the Eurozone cope with severe fiscal problems, there is a significant risk of a clash between the fiscal goals of the governments and monetary goals of the ECB; and should the current crisis intensify (e.g., should any member country default or desire to leave the euro) the project would be in uncharted waters.

What do the people think? The results of successive Eurobarometer polls indicate that only about 50% to 60% of the citizens of the Eurozone think that the euro has been beneficial. In some countries that figure is higher, in some lower. The euro remains an experiment—its arrival did not mark the end point of European monetary history, and its long-run fate is not entirely certain.

KEY POINTS

1. A currency union occurs when two or more sovereign nations share a common currency. Sometimes these arrangements are unilateral, such as when a country like Ecuador adopts the U.S. dollar. But some are multilateral, the most prominent example being the Eurozone.

2. The euro is (as of 2011) the currency of 17 European Union (EU) countries, and they manage it collectively by a common monetary authority, the European Central Bank (ECB). Most of the EU's 27 countries are expected to join the euro eventually.

3. According to the theory of optimum currency areas (OCAs), regions should employ a common currency only if they are well integrated and face fairly similar (symmetric) economic shocks. If these criteria are met, efficiency gains from trade should be large, and the costs of forgone monetary autonomy small.

4. A currency union is usually a more irreversible and costly step than simply fixing the exchange rate. The OCA threshold is therefore higher than the threshold for a fixed exchange rate.

5. Additional economic factors can strengthen the case for an OCA. If regions have high labor mobility or large fiscal transfers, these mechanisms may make the costs of a currency union smaller for any given asymmetric shock. In addition, countries with a poor nominal anchor may be eager to join a currency union with a country with a better reputation for inflation performance.

6. Political considerations can drive monetary unions, as when countries feel they have a common destiny and wish to treat monetary union as part of a broader goal of political union.

7. The Eurozone has fairly high trade integration, although not quite as high as that of the United States. The Eurozone might or might not pass this OCA test.

8. The Eurozone has fairly symmetric shocks for most countries. The Eurozone probably does pass this OCA test.

9. The Eurozone has very low labor mobility between countries. The Eurozone almost certainly fails this OCA test.

10. The OCA criteria may fail ex ante, but they may be self-fulfilling: thanks to the common currency, after some years, trade and labor mobility may increase, tipping the balance in favor of an OCA ex post. But increasing specialization because of trade may cause more asymmetric shocks, which would push in the opposite direction.

11. The lack of compelling economic arguments for the euro leads us to study its historical and political origins. The EU must be understood as a political project, and the euro is an important part of the conception of the EU. Although many EU citizens have trust in this project, polls show that such a view is held by only a bare majority.

12. The European Central Bank plays the pivotal role in securing the future of the euro. If it can deliver low inflation and economic stability comparable to the German central bank, after which it was designed, the euro is more likely to succeed as a currency in the EU and as a global currency.

13. Attempts to exert political influence on the ECB continue and the Council of Ministers have often proved weak at punishing countries that break the rules of the Eurozone (the Maastricht criteria and the Stability and Growth Pact).

14. The global financial crisis of 2008 and Great Recession were the first real test of the euro, and a stern test at that. Like other economies, the Eurozone suffered from excessive lending, financial bubbles, fiscal indiscipline, bailouts of banks, and (as a result) pressure on the central bank to deviate from established policies to support the real economy, banks, and governments. These problems were difficult to handle because they affected Eurozone countries in an asymmetric fashion. As a result, ECB and EU authorities struggled to devise effective policy responses based on broad cooperation except in the direst moments. The economic and political situation remains fragile, especially in the hard-hit peripheral economies of Greece, Ireland, Portugal, and Spain.

KEY TERMS

currency union, p. 399
Eurozone, p. 399
euro, p. 399
European Union (EU), p. 400
Maastricht Treaty, p. 400
optimum currency area (OCA), p. 402
inflation bias, p. 406
Marshall Plan, p. 415
Treaty of Rome, p. 415
Exchange Rate Mechanism (ERM), p. 418
Economic and Monetary Union (EMU), p. 419
ERM crisis, p. 419
European Central Bank (ECB), p. 419
convergence criteria, p. 425
Stability and Growth Pact (SGP), p. 429

PROBLEMS

1. One could view the United States as a currency union of 50 states. Compare and contrast the Eurozone and the United States in terms of the optimum currency area (OCA) criteria.

2. After German reunification and the disintegration of Communist rule in Eastern Europe, several countries sought to join the European Union (EU) and later the Economic and Monetary Union (EMU). Why do you believe these countries were eager to integrate with Western Europe? Do you think policy makers in these countries believe that OCA criteria are self-fulfilling? Explain.

3. The Maastricht Treaty places strict requirements on government budgets and national debt. Why do you think the Maastricht Treaty called for fiscal discipline? If it is the central bank that is responsible for maintaining the fixed exchange rate, then why does fiscal discipline matter? How might this affect the gains/losses for joining a currency union?

4. The following figure shows some hypothetical OCA criteria with the Eurozone for selected countries. *Assume that these are based solely on economic criteria*—that is, without reference to other political considerations. Refer to the diagram in responding to the questions that follow.

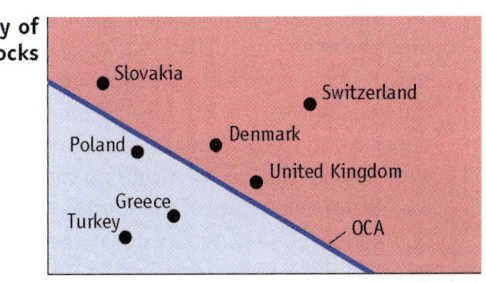

   a. Which of the countries satisfy the OCA criteria for joining a monetary union?
   b. Compare Poland and the United Kingdom in terms of the OCA criteria regarding *market integration* with the Eurozone. Discuss one possible source of differences in integration (with the EU) in the two countries.
   c. Compare Poland and the United Kingdom in terms of the OCA criteria regarding *symmetric versus asymmetric shocks* (relative to the Eurozone). Discuss one possible source of differences in symmetry (with the EU) in the two countries.
   d. Suppose that policy makers in both Poland and the United Kingdom care only about being able to use policy in response to shocks. Which is more likely to seek membership in the EMU and why?

e. What did the ERM crises reveal about the preferences of the United Kingdom? Why has the United Kingdom sought membership only in the EU without seeking membership in the Eurozone? Consider other costs and benefits not in the diagram, both economic and political.

f. What did membership of the Eurozone reveal about the preferences of Greece? Consider other costs and benefits not in the diagram, both economic and political.

5. Congress established the Federal Reserve System in 1914. Up to this point, the United States did not have a national currency; Federal Reserve notes are still the paper currency in circulation today. Earlier attempts at establishing a central bank were opposed on the grounds that a central bank would give the federal government monopoly over money. This was a reflection of the historic debate between maintaining states' rights versus establishing a strong centralized authority in the United States. That is, the creation of the Fed and a national currency would mean that states would no longer have the authority to control the money supply on a regional level. Discuss the debate between states' rights versus centralized authority in the context of the Economic and Monetary Union and the European Central Bank.

6. In recent years there have been reports that a group of six Gulf countries (Bahrain, Kuwait, Oman, Qatar, Saudi Arabia, and the United Arab Emirates) were considering the introduction of a single currency. Currently, these countries use currencies that are effectively pegged to the U.S. dollar. These countries rely heavily on oil exports to the rest of the world, and political leaders in these countries are concerned about diversifying trade. Based on this information, discuss the OCA criteria for this group of countries. What are the greatest potential benefits? What are the potential costs?

7. Before taking office as the new Federal Reserve chairman, Ben Bernanke advocated for the adoption of an inflation target to promote price stability in the United States. Compare and contrast the Fed and European Central Bank in terms of their commitment to price stability and economic stability. Which central bank has more independence to pursue price stability as a primary objective? Explain.

8. Why do countries with less independent central banks tend to have higher inflation rates? Is it possible for the central bank to increase output and reduce unemployment in the long run? In the long run, is the German model a good one? Explain why or why not.

9. Compare the Maastricht Treaty convergence criteria with the OCA criteria. How are these convergence criteria related to the potential benefits and costs associated with joining a currency union? If you were a policy maker in a country seeking to join the EMU, which criterion would you eliminate and why?

NETWORK

Do some research on the Internet to construct an updated version of the map in Figure 10-1. You can find membership information on the websites of the European Union (http://europe.eu) and the European Central Bank (www.ecb.int). Since this book was written, have any new countries joined the EU, or applied to join? Have any countries entered the ERM, or exited from it? Have any new countries adopted the euro?

Topics in International Macroeconomics

Economics is a science of thinking in terms of models joined to the art of choosing models which are relevant to the contemporary world.

John Maynard Keynes, 1938

Like other fields of economics, international macroeconomics is evolving continually. New empirical analyses are constantly appearing, deepening our understanding, and bringing attention to new phenomena. New theoretical models are always being developed, to better explain long-standing puzzles or to confront new ones. The fast-changing global economic environment of recent years has pushed forward research faster than ever.

In the four stand-alone sections of this final chapter, we examine several important topics that have occupied researchers for many years and that remain at the cutting edge. In these "mini-chapters" we explore new issues as well as important extensions to the core models presented earlier in the book:

- We ask whether purchasing power parity really works as a long-run theory of exchange rates. Evidence shows that a better theory has to explain why price levels are higher in richer countries. We develop such a theory and show how it can be applied to improve exchange rate forecasts.

- We ask whether uncovered interest parity really works as a short-run theory of exchange rates. We show that forex traders often make massive profits (and also losses) and that such profits may even have a predictable component. If arbitrage operates to support uncovered interest parity in an efficient market, such profits ought to be eliminated. One explanation might be that there are limits to arbitrage, such as an aversion to the extreme riskiness of profits in the forex market.

1 Exchange Rates in the Long Run: Deviations from Purchasing Power Parity

2 Exchange Rates in the Short Run: Deviations from Uncovered Interest Parity

3 Debt and Default

4 The Global Macroeconomy and the 2007–2009 Crisis

- We study the problem of defaults by governments on their debt. Some of the facts to be explained are why any lenders lend given the risk of default, why borrowers choose to default when they do, and what price they pay for defaulting. We develop a model in which adverse economic shocks (low output) make countries more likely to default. The bigger such shocks are, the more the countries default, and the less willing lenders are to lend, unless they receive a higher interest rate. The model fits various facts: Poorer countries have more volatile output, are charged higher interest rates, default more often even at lower levels of debt, and lenders don't make much profit.
- We look at the performance of the global macroeconomy before, during, and after the 2007–2009 global financial crisis and subsequent Great Recession. We look to understand some of the causes and consequences of this event using the tools we have developed throughout the book, even as the repercussions of this event continue to unfold.

1 Exchange Rates in the Long Run: Deviations from Purchasing Power Parity

According to the most recent data from the World Bank, in 2009 gross national income per capita in the United States was $47,240, but by converting incomes using the exchange rate, it was found that gross national income per capita in China was only $3,590, about 7.5% of the U.S. level. Were the Chinese really that poor in terms of material living standards? No.

When the calculations were repeated by comparing dollar incomes with the dollar prices of baskets of consumer goods, Chinese gross national income per capita was found to be about $6,770 in terms of U.S. consumer goods, so that nation's living standards were now seen to be almost twice as high, at 14% of the U.S. level. The reason: In dollar terms, most goods cost a lot less in China than in the United States. The dollar price level in China was lower than in the United States. The implication: PPP does not hold, and the real exchange rate is a long way from 1.

These adjustments have many implications: For example, they affect calculations of living standards, poverty, allocations of aid, and projections of growth, consumption, demographics, pollution, and so on. So we need to understand these deviations from PPP for many reasons, including the need to refine our theory of exchange rates. When we learned about long-run exchange rates, we showed that the expected future exchange rate could be predicted using the monetary approach to exchange rates, *if* purchasing power parity holds; that is, if baskets of goods sell for the same price in all locations. This theory provided a workable model of real exchange rates, but it was far from perfect. In this section, we address a major deficiency in PPP theory: Its assumption that all goods are costlessly tradable.

Limits to Arbitrage

One way to set up a more realistic economic model would be to introduce costs of trading, which is now an important area of research in international economics.

To gain familiarity with trade costs and to see how they matter, let's assume that the cost of trading the good is equal to some fraction of the unit cost of the good at its source. For example, suppose there is one good, and it sells for $P = \$100$ in Home. It costs $10 to ship the good from Home to another country, Foreign. The **trade cost** is $c = 0.1 = 10\%$. The cost of the good on arrival in Foreign, including the trade cost, would be $P \times (1 + c) = \$110$.

How do trade costs affect arbitrage? If you were considering trying to make an arbitrage profit by shipping a $100 widget from Home to Foreign, then you wouldn't even think of doing it unless the Foreign price converted into dollars EP^* was at least $110 (where E is Home's exchange rate, and P^* is the Foreign price in Foreign currency). Otherwise, you make a loss once the trading costs are taken into account. Similarly, going from Foreign to Home, you wouldn't ship goods unless the Home price P was at least 10% above the foreign price EP^*.

More formally, the ratio of the prices in the two locations can be written in proportional terms as $q = EP^*/P$. As we learned in our study of long-run exchange rates, for any basket of goods, q is also known as the *real exchange rate* of the home country. Thus, if $P = \$100$ and $EP^* = \$110$, then this relative price ratio would be $(110/100) = 1.1$.

As we have just seen, arbitrage from Home to Foreign is profitable only if the Foreign price is higher than the Home price adjusted for the trade cost, which requires $q = EP^*/P > 1 + c$. Conversely, arbitrage the other way is profitable only if the Home price is sufficiently higher than the Foreign price, with $1/q = P/(EP^*) > 1 + c$.

Thus, if q is below $1 + c$, there will be no arbitrage from Home to Foreign. And if q is above $1/(1 + c)$, there will be no arbitrage from Foreign to Home. So we have shown that, taking trade costs into account, the *no arbitrage condition* for market equilibrium is

$$\frac{1}{1+c} \leq \underbrace{\frac{EP^*}{P}}_{\text{Real exchange rate } q} \leq 1 + c$$

Let's look at what this condition implies for various levels of trading costs.

- *Zero costs.* With $c = 0$, the no arbitrage equilibrium condition reduces to an equality because both left- and right-hand sides equal 1, implying that $q = 1$. This equality is the condition for the law of one price (LOOP), which we expect to hold when arbitrage is costless. An illustration is shown in Figure 11-1, panel (a), which plots the hypothetical relative price q over time for Home and Foreign.

- *Low costs.* Suppose c is low, say, 10%, as in our example. If the price difference between source and destination is less than 10%, then there is no arbitrage. Hence, q is free to wander in what is called a **no-arbitrage band** between $1/(1 + c) = (100/110)$ and $1 + c = (110/100)$. For values of q between 0.91 and 1.1, then, the market is considered to be in equilibrium. This is shown in Figure 11-1, panel (b). Small deviations from LOOP are possible, but LOOP is still approximately true.

- *High costs.* Suppose c is high, say, 50%. If the price difference is less than 50%, there will be no arbitrage. There is a wider no-arbitrage band between $1/(1 + c) = (100/150)$ and $1 + c = (150/100)$ in which the market is in equilibrium and no arbitrage is possible. This is shown in Figure 11-1, panel (c). Deviations from LOOP are possible in the range 0.67 to 1.5, and LOOP no longer applies.

This analysis shows that when trade costs or *costs of arbitrage* are higher, arbitrage will not happen for small price deviations, and the possible deviations from LOOP become

FIGURE 11-1

No Arbitrage Bands The hypothetical relative price ratio q is shown in three cases. In panel (a), trade costs are zero, so the law of one price (LOOP) holds and q has to equal 1. In panel (b), trade costs are small, say, 10%, so the prices in the two locations can differ. The high price can exceed the low price by up to 10%, so q can range between 100/110 (0.91) and 110/100 (1.1). In panel (c), trade costs are high, say, 50%, so the high price may exceed the low price by up to 50%, so q can range between 150/100 and 100/150. Thus, as costs of arbitrage increase, deviations from simple LOOP and PPP become larger, and these "laws" become less useful.

greater. If the prices of many goods deviated from LOOP, this would imply deviations from PPP. If costs are huge, then arbitrage is practically impossible and the prices of the same good in two locations need not bear any relation to one another and can be very far apart. Under such conditions, goods are almost always nontraded, and LOOP and PPP will not apply.

Trade Costs in Practice These results show that when evaluating LOOP for one good or PPP for a basket of goods, we must take into account trade costs and consider how they affect deviations from price equality. Empirical research suggests that trade costs are affected by economic policies, as well as by characteristics of goods and their markets.[1]

An important part of trade costs is costs of transportation. For U.S. imports, for example, estimated freight rates vary from 1% of the good's price (for transport equipment) to 27% (for fertilizer). In many countries with worse transport infrastructure, these costs can be much higher: one estimate suggests that the average landlocked country has transport costs 55% higher than the average coastal country.

---

[1] Charles Engel and John H. Rogers, 1996, "How Wide Is the Border?" *American Economic Review*, 86(5), 1112–1125; Maurice Obstfeld and Alan M. Taylor, 1997, "Nonlinear Aspects of Goods-Market Arbitrage and Adjustment: Heckscher's Commodity Points Revisited," *Journal of the Japanese and International Economies*, 11(4), 441–479; David C. Parsley and Shang-Jin Wei, 2001, "Explaining the Border Effect: The Role of Exchange Rate Variability, Shipping Costs, and Geography," *Journal of International Economics*, 55(1), 87–105; James E. Anderson and Eric van Wincoop, 2004, "Trade Costs," *Journal of Economic Literature*, 42(3), 691–751.

A major factor that influences trade costs is a country's trade policy. Average tariffs of 5% (rich countries) or more than 10% (developing countries) constitute an additional cost, and such tariffs vary widely by type of good. Quotas (limits to import quantities) and regulatory barriers (such as health and environmental regulations) also add to trade costs, but the costs they add are difficult to compute. In addition to transport and policy costs, economists have found statistical evidence of other causes of price gaps between markets, including distance between markets, crossing international borders, having different currencies, having floating exchange rates, and so on.

Following is a summary of international trade costs for advanced countries.[2] Like the variable c above, these costs are expressed as a percentage markup over the pre-shipment price of the goods. The data are averaged over all types of goods and based on direct measurements and econometric estimates:[3]

Total international trade costs, 74%
- Transport costs, 21%
  - Freight costs, 11%
  - Transit costs (time), 9%
- Costs at the border, 44%
  - Tariffs and nontariff barriers, 8%
  - Language barrier, 7%
  - Different currencies, 14%
  - Security and other costs, 9%

(Note that the subcosts are aggregated by compounding: e.g., a 21% markup on top of a 44% markup on a $1 good in the middle column results in a 74% markup in the left column, because $1.21 \times 1.44 \times \$1 = \$1.74$.)

These data show that trade costs are large—and typically, they are even larger outside the advanced countries and create a very wide no-arbitrage band.

Trade costs matter.

APPLICATION

It's Not Just the Burgers That Are Cheap

If real exchange rates can deviate from the PPP-implied value of 1, the next question to ask is, how do they vary, and why? One place to find a clue is in the pattern of deviations from PPP. For example, look at the *Economist* newspaper's Big Mac index by Googling "economist big mac index." If deviations from PPP were random, the deviations might easily be dismissed as an approximation error. However, deviations from PPP in the Big Mac index are not entirely random: Burgers tend to be cheaper in poorer countries. In 2010, for example, the *Economist* found that, expressed in U.S. dollars, a Big Mac cost 30% less in Mexico and 39% less in Malaysia than it did in the United States.

---

[2] From Prabir De, 2006, "Why Trade Costs Matter?" Working Papers 706, Asia-Pacific Research and Training Network on Trade (ARTNeT), an initiative of UNESCAP and IDRC, Canada. Based on James E. Anderson and Eric van Wincoop, 2004, "Trade Costs," *Journal of Economic Literature*, 42(3), 691–751.
[3] Another important trade cost element is the *intranational* distribution and retail costs that are incurred as a good moves within a country from the sellers/importers to buyers/exporters. Intranational distribution costs may be around 35 to 50% of a good's cost in developed countries, but there is wide variation. In the United States, for example, distribution costs can be as low as 14% (electronic equipment) or as high as 216% (ladies' clothing).

FIGURE 11-2

(a) Wages and Big Mac Prices

(b) GDP per Person and Price Levels

Price Levels in Rich and Poor Countries Panel (a) shows that richer countries (measured by higher wages) tend to have higher Big Mac prices (measured in a common currency). Panel (b) shows that richer countries (measured by higher GDP per person) tend to have higher overall price levels (measured in a common currency).

Source: Michael R. Pakko and Patricia S. Pollard, November 2003, "Burgernomics: A Big Mac™ Guide to Purchasing Power Parity," Review, Federal Reserve Bank of St. Louis, 9–28.

It isn't too difficult to think of a reason for this finding—the presence of nontraded goods. A Big Mac is a combination of some traded goods (such as flour, beef, and special sauce) and some nontraded goods (such as cooks and cleaners). The nontraded goods contain a strong element of local labor input, so they tend to cost less in a poor country. The evidence in Figure 11-2, panel (a), supports this logic. This scatterplot shows that the dollar price of the Big Mac is strongly correlated with the local hourly wage in dollars.

Why stop here? The argument shouldn't apply only to burgers, and indeed in 2004 the *Economist* did a parallel experiment and compared the prices of another globally uniform and omnipresent consumer product: the Starbucks tall latte. Similar patterns emerged: in dollar terms, the latte cost 15% less in Mexico and 25% less in Malaysia than the corresponding frothy beverage in the United States.

The argument applies to most goods that are included in calculations of national price levels. Almost all goods have some local, nontraded component—some local value added or some local retail and distribution costs. Thus, the general price level might be expected to vary systematically in the same way, and it does. Figure 11-2, panel (b), shows that a country's price level is strongly correlated with the level of GDP per person. Rich countries have higher price levels; their baskets cost more. In other words, the real exchange rate $q = EP^*/P$ is *not* equal to 1 for all countries—PPP does not hold, even in the long run. The remainder of this section explores this pattern using economic theory and considers what effect the lack of PPP has on the exchange rate models and predictions we derived earlier in the book. ■

Latte disparity: Starbucks in the Forbidden City, Beijing.

Nontraded Goods and the Balassa-Samuelson Model

Trade costs have major implications for international macroeconomics. In fact, by expanding our analysis from one good that is traded to two goods—one traded and one not traded—we can explain price level differences and deviations from PPP.

We assume there are two countries: Home and Foreign (values for Foreign are denoted by an asterisk). Thus, w denotes the Home wage and w^* denotes the Foreign wage, each measured in the respective currencies. The Home exchange rate is E (units of Home currency per unit of Foreign currency). There are two goods. Each good is produced competitively and labor is the only input needed. One is a nontraded, service good (say, a haircut), denoted N, and its trade costs are effectively infinite. The other is a costlessly tradable good (say, a DVD player), denoted T, that has no trade costs at all. Prices of goods will be denoted p and p^*, each measured in the respective currencies, with subscripts T and N to denote traded and nontraded goods.

A Simple Model The model can be solved in three steps, with assumptions as follows:

1. *The traded good has the same price in both countries.* This is true because trade costs are zero. For simplicity, we assume that the traded good has a price of 1 when measured in Home currency (say, dollars). This is its price in Home and Foreign, so

$$p_T = 1 \qquad Ep_T^* = 1$$

   In our example, the DVD player sells for $1 everywhere.

2. *Productivity in traded goods determines wages.* Suppose that one Home worker can make A units of the traded good (the DVD player) per hour. Then the worker's hourly wage w will be equal to A because each unit of the good sells for $1 and competition means that the wage will equal the value of the output produced by each hour of labor input. Similarly, if Foreign workers can make A^* units of the traded good per hour, their dollar wage Ew^* will be equal to A^*. Thus, wage levels in each country are equal to productivity levels:

$$w = A \qquad Ew^* = A^*$$

   In our example, if Home workers make ten $1 DVD players per hour, their hourly wage is $10 per hour. If Foreign workers make only five per hour, their hourly wage is $5.

3. *Wages determine the prices of nontraded goods.* Crucially, we assume that the level of productivity in nontraded goods is stagnant and the same everywhere and equal to 1. In our example, it always takes one hour to get a haircut in Home and Foreign, but with the wages given previously, this means the cost of a haircut will be equal to exactly one hour of labor. In general, the dollar price of the nontraded good in each country equals the wage, so $p_N = w$ and $Ep_N^* = Ew^*$. Because these wages are given by productivity (as we saw in the second step),

$$p_N = A \qquad Ep_N^* = A^*$$

To continue our example, if the productivities are 10 and 5 in Home and Foreign, we showed that the hourly wages must be $10 and $5, respectively, and so we now see that Home haircuts will cost $10 and Foreign haircuts $5.

The conclusion from these three assumptions? Countries with higher traded goods productivity will have relatively high wages and hence relatively high prices of nontraded goods. This means they will also have relatively higher overall price levels, depending on how large the share of nontraded goods in the consumption basket is. To see this, suppose the nontraded goods share of consumption is n (so the traded share is $1-n$).

Changes in Productivity Now suppose Home productivity A increases, with the proportional change given by $\Delta A/A$. What happens to the Home price level? The price of traded goods is unchanged and stays at 1, but the price of nontraded goods is equal to A and it rises. Taking the weighted average, we can compute the (percentage) change in the Home price level as

$$\underbrace{\frac{\Delta P}{P}}_{\text{Change in Home price level}} = \underbrace{(1-n)}_{\text{Share of traded goods}} \times \underbrace{\left(\frac{\Delta P_T}{P_T}\right)}_{\substack{\text{Change in Home traded goods price} \\ = \text{zero}}} + \underbrace{n}_{\text{Share of nontraded goods}} \times \underbrace{\left(\frac{\Delta P_N}{P_N}\right)}_{\substack{\text{Change in Home nontraded goods price} \\ = \Delta A/A}} = n\frac{\Delta A}{A}$$

By the same logic, the same is true for Foreign: a change in its dollar price level will result from a change in foreign productivity:

$$\underbrace{\frac{\Delta(EP^*)}{(EP^*)}}_{\text{Change in Foreign price level}} = \underbrace{(1-n)}_{\text{Share of traded goods}} \times \underbrace{\left(\frac{\Delta(EP_T^*)}{(EP_T^*)}\right)}_{\substack{\text{Change in Foreign traded goods price} \\ = \text{zero}}} + \underbrace{n}_{\text{Share of nontraded goods}} \times \underbrace{\frac{\Delta(EP_N^*)}{(EP_N^*)}}_{\substack{\text{Change in Foreign nontraded goods price} \\ = \Delta A^*/A^*}} = n\frac{\Delta A^*}{A^*}$$

The last two equations are intuitive. For our example, a 1% rise in Home DVD player productivity A will raise Home wages w by 1%; therefore, Home haircut prices rise 1% and, because these haircuts have a weight $n < 1$ in the overall basket, the overall price index rises by $n\%$.

By putting together these last two results, we can solve for the change in the real exchange rate q. Recall that q is equal to EP^*/P, so the percentage change in q is given by the percentage change in the numerator EP^* minus the percentage change in the denominator P. But we have just computed those changes in the last two equations. Hence, subtracting the first equation above from the second, the change in the real exchange rate is given by

$$\underbrace{\frac{\Delta q}{q}}_{\substack{\text{Change in real exchange rate} \\ \text{(Foreign price level } EP^* \\ \text{relative to Home } P\text{)}}} = \underbrace{n}_{\text{Share of nontraded goods}} \times \underbrace{\left(\frac{\Delta A^*}{A^*} - \frac{\Delta A}{A}\right)}_{\substack{\text{Change in Foreign traded productivity level relative to Home}}} \qquad (11\text{-}1)$$

Thus, relative productivities in the traded goods sector drive relative prices, through their effects on wages in and prices in the nontraded sector.

Generalizing The choice of DVD players and haircuts was for illustration. The model generalizes, and it embodies the logic of the cheap Big Mac story told earlier. A country has relatively low wages because it has relatively low labor productivity in traded goods. Low productivity and wages hold down the prices of nontraded goods and the nontraded part of the overall price level.

This equation describes an important relationship between productivity and the real exchange rate known as the **Balassa-Samuelson effect,** named for the economists Bela Balassa and Paul Samuelson:

When compared with other countries, a country experiencing an increase in productivity will see wages and incomes rise and will see its real exchange rate appreciate, meaning that its price level will rise.[4]

Overvaluations, Undervaluations, and Productivity Growth: Forecasting Implications for Real and Nominal Exchange Rates

The Balassa-Samuelson model makes a firm prediction that is supported strongly by evidence: Price levels are higher in rich countries. The scatterplot in Figure 11-2, panel (b), showed this fact, and we zoom in to examine a part of it in Figure 11-3.

In such a figure, a point on the line of best fit is the predicted **equilibrium real exchange rate** $\tilde{q}$ of the Balassa-Samuelson model. Figure 11-3 plots the U.S. real exchange rate against each foreign country—it shows foreign dollar prices EP^* relative to U.S. prices P. So an increase on the vertical axis is a rise in the relative price of foreign goods: it is a U.S. real depreciation, or a foreign real appreciation. The actual data do not sit precisely on the line of best fit. That is, the observed real exchange rate q may differ from its equilibrium value $\tilde{q}$.

FIGURE 11-3

Predicted Real Exchange Rate Adjustments in Emerging Markets The scatterplot shows national price levels and GDP per person relative to the United States for the year 2000, as in Figure 11-2(b). The Balassa-Samuelson model would predict convergence to equilibrium in all cases (arrows 1, 3, 4). In relatively fast-growing countries, this would be augmented by trend real appreciation (arrows 2 and 5). Thus, real appreciations were expected for the Chinese yuan and the Slovak koruna, and a real depreciation for the Argentine peso.

---

[4] Note that the traded goods sector is the *only* sector in which productivity can vary, so the only way for a country to get richer is by raising the productivity level in that sector, leading to higher wages and output. Also, in this model, GDP is equal to wages times the supply of labor. Thus, high wages are also synonymous with high output per person.

As we saw in the long-run exchange rates chapter, the typical real exchange rate q can from time to time experience an overvaluation or undervaluation relative to its equilibrium value $\tilde{q}$. But there we assumed that the equilibrium value was 1, as predicted by PPP theory. Here, the equilibrium $\tilde{q}$ isn't necessarily 1, and is given the Balassa-Samuelson theory.

Here, we judge deviations from equilibrium by looking at the distance from the equilibrium, that is, from the line of best fit. For example, if actual q is 10% above predicted $\tilde{q}$, then foreign prices are "too high": We would say that the U.S. real exchange rate is *undervalued* and the foreign real exchange rate *overvalued* relative to the equilibrium level.

We can now begin to see how the Balassa-Samuelson theory can improve our theory of exchange rates in the long run and the forecasts that depend on such a theory.

Forecasting the Real Exchange Rate By comparing actual exchange rates with their predicted equilibrium values, forecasting the real exchange rate can be broken down into two problems: (1) how quickly q will return toward its equilibrium value $\tilde{q}$ and (2) how quickly the equilibrium value $\tilde{q}$ will change over time as a result of productivity changes. In other words, q may be heading toward a target level $\tilde{q}$, but our model tells us that it might be a moving target that is moving along a trend. This means that real exchange rate prediction must be broken down into two parts.

For example, suppose q is currently 0.5 but the Balassa-Samuelson model says the equilibrium value of $\tilde{q}$ is 0.6. Clearly, q is predicted to rise by 0.1, or by 20%, to return to equilibrium (0.1/0.5 = 20%). How long will this take?

Convergence The first step is to figure out the speed of convergence to equilibrium. Empirical estimates indicate that real exchange rate deviations from equilibrium might decay slowly: *the consensus "half life" of deviations from PPP has been reported to be five years*. For illustration, we adopt this *rule of thumb* estimate in the rest of this section. Thus, in our example, if half of the 20% gap is likely to be closed over five years, then over five years, q would rise by approximately 10% from 0.5 to 0.55, an increase of about 2% per year.

Trend The second step is to figure out whether $\tilde{q}$ is a moving target and forecast what its trend rate of growth will be. The Balassa-Samuelson theory shows how. In our example, suppose that the home country is expected to grow rapidly, with GDP per capita and wages rising; then $\tilde{q}$ could be much higher than 0.6 in five years' time. For example, if the nontraded share is 0.4, then Equation (11-1) says that a country's $\tilde{q}$ will rise 0.4% for every 1% of real GDP per capita growth in excess of the U.S. growth rate. So if a country is growing at, say, 8% per year faster than the United States, then $\tilde{q}$ should be rising by 0.4 × 8%, or 3.2% per year.

Convergence + Trend For this numerical example, we would conclude that the observed real exchange rate q is likely to increase at 2% per year toward its equilibrium and to increase at a further 3.2% a year due to the upward drift of that equilibrium, resulting in a predicted real appreciation for the foreign country at a rate of about 2 + 3.2 = 5.2% per year. (Note that adding growth rates in this way is only an approximation.)

Forecasting the Nominal Exchange Rate This kind of real exchange rate forecast can then help us predict nominal exchange rates, an essential component in the asset approach to exchange rates. How?

By definition, the real exchange rate is $q = EP^*/P$; by rearranging, we find $E = qP/P^*$, and we have an expression for the nominal exchange rate. When PPP holds, this equation becomes $E = P/P^*$: Under PPP, the real exchange rate q equals 1, and the exchange rate is equal to the ratio of national price levels.

When PPP *doesn't hold*, however, we have to worry about possible changes in q. Since $E = qP/P^*$, then taking rates of change, we find

$$\underbrace{\frac{\Delta E}{E}}_{\text{Rate of nominal depreciation}} = \underbrace{\frac{\Delta q}{q}}_{\text{Rate of real depreciation}} + \underbrace{\left(\frac{\Delta P}{P} - \frac{\Delta P^*}{P^*}\right)}_{\text{Inflation differential (home minus foreign)}} \qquad (11\text{-}2)$$

In the long-run exchange rates chapter, we saw a simpler version of this expression: PPP forced q to be constant and equal to 1, and the first term on the right vanished. We were left with a result, known as *relative PPP*, which said that changes in nominal exchange rates depended on inflation differentials alone. Taken literally, forecasters could then focus just on inflation forecasts.

When the Balassa-Samuelson effect is present, PPP fails, but we can still forecast future exchange rate changes using Equation (11-2). In using this equation, however, we not only have to forecast inflation, we have to forecast changes in the real exchange rate, too. Thus, in real-world financial markets, foreign exchange traders have to pay attention to many macroeconomic forecasts before forming an expectation about how E is likely to evolve over time.

Adjustment to Equilibrium Finally, we note that the Balassa-Samuelson model does not tell us how the real exchange rate will adjust. Suppose we have forecast a 1% real appreciation (−1% change in q). In Equation (11-2), this could imply either a 1% nominal appreciation (−1% on the left) or an extra 1% of home inflation over and above foreign inflation (+1% on the right), or some combination of the two.

Thus:

- If the model says there is currently a real undervaluation, either relative home goods prices have to rise or the value of the home currency has to rise—there is no other way to make home goods more expensive.

- If the model says there is currently a real overvaluation, either relative home goods prices have to fall or the value of the home currency has to fall—there is no other way to make home goods less expensive.

APPLICATION

Real Exchange Rates in Emerging Markets

To see how these ideas can be put to work to make forecasts of real and nominal exchange rates, we examine three cases in Figure 11-3 that were in the news a few years ago. The data are for the year 2000, which allows us to look back and see how well the predictions of the model turned out in subsequent years.

China: Yuan Undervaluation?
The Balassa-Samuelson model predictions: In 2000 the real exchange rate with China was $q = 0.231$, well below (0.088 below) the predicted equilibrium level of $\tilde{q} = 0.319$. The yuan was undervalued according to the model and would have to experience a 38% real appreciation (0.088/0.231) against the U.S. dollar to close the gap. Using our old rule of thumb, half of this gap, or 19%,

would be eliminated in five years, implying an approximate 3.5% annual increase in q due to convergence.

However, in addition, China was a fast-growing economy at this time and its GDP per capita was growing about 6% per annum faster than U.S. GDP per capita. So the real exchange rate would have to appreciate *even more* due to Balassa-Samuelson effects. Figure 11-3 suggests that every 1% gain in GDP per capita is associated with an approximate 0.4% real appreciation (as expected if the nontraded share were 0.4). So a 6% differential growth rate per year (China minus United States) would imply a further $0.4 \times 6 = 2.4\%$ per year real appreciation in the yuan due to the trend of the moving target.[5]

What actually happened: Adding up both effects, the model predicts a real yuan appreciation of $3.5 + 2.4 = 5.9\%$ per year. As noted previously, this would imply either a nominal appreciation of the yuan against the dollar, or higher inflation in China. Inflation did start to rise in China, up to as much as 4.1% in 2004, although the data are not considered terribly accurate. This was not that much higher than U.S. inflation. Until mid-2005 China pegged the yuan to the dollar but then decided to switch to an unofficial crawling peg, allowing the yuan to appreciate gradually against the dollar, but very slowly. Many commentators saw this as a response to protectionist pressure in the United States, where cheap Chinese imports were raising hackles. But the Chinese had reasons of their own to let the yuan rise: to keep domestic inflation at a reasonable level.

Argentina: Was the Peso Overvalued?

The Balassa-Samuelson model predictions: Figure 11-3 clearly shows that Argentina's currency was overvalued in 2000: Argentina's price level was 0.656, but the predicted equilibrium level of $\tilde{q}$ was 0.512. For a country at that level of GDP per capita, Argentina's dollar prices would have had to fall by 22% to reach that equilibrium. Argentina's growth had slowed after 1998, so, unlike in the China case, very little rise in the equilibrium $\tilde{q}$ could have been expected (which would have mitigated the need for a fall in actual q).

What actually happened: Argentina was pegging the peso to the dollar at 1:1, so adjustment had to come through a fall in Argentine prices relative to U.S. prices. With U.S. inflation at only 2%, this would happen slowly unless Argentine prices actually dropped. Unfortunately, this deflation process was slow and politically painful, involving wage and price cuts in an economy that was far from liberalized and competitive. The overvalued exchange rate was also hurting the demand for Argentine goods. Although the peg held for a long time, the country was driven into crisis by fiscal and financial sector problems. In the crisis of 2001–2002, the peso depreciated to three per dollar: the overvaluation was eliminated, and then some.

Slovakia: Obeying the Rules?

The Balassa-Samuelson model predictions: Figure 11-3 also shows Slovakia. Like China, Slovakia was a fast-growing country, part of a group of countries in Eastern Europe lined up to join the EU and ultimately the Eurozone. Slovakia's real exchange rate was $q = 0.282$ in 2000 and undervalued relative to the predicted equilibrium $\tilde{q} = 0.534$. Here, q needed to rise by 89% to reach

---

[5] Jeffrey A. Frankel, "The Balassa-Samuelson Relationship and the Renminbi," Harvard University, December 2006.

equilibrium. Using our rule of thumb, half of this gap, or 45%, would be closed in five years, implying a real appreciation of about 7.5% per year. In addition, fast GDP per capita growth relative to the EU probably added another 1 to 2% on top of that, as in the China case, as a result of the moving target. Thus, the expected real appreciation would have been 8 to 10% per year.

What actually happened: Slovakia notched up high rates of real appreciation of between 5 and 10% per annum from 1992 to 2004, as did many other countries in Eastern Europe.[6] The situation was like that in China: it required some combination of nominal appreciation and inflation. But Slovakia (and many of its neighbors) also wanted to join the euro. As we saw in the chapter on the euro, the Maastricht criteria would require Slovakia to peg to the euro (no appreciation) and keep its inflation within limits (within 2% of the "best" in the EU). Our model suggests this would be impossible: the koruna would have to appreciate or Slovakia's inflation would have to accelerate! As an exercise, you may wish to explore in more detail what actually happened. (See **Net Work** problem (2) at the end of the chapter and **Headlines: Eastern Europe and the Euro.**) ■

Conclusion

In general, PPP does not hold. Goods prices are not the same in all countries. Arbitrage fails, most likely because of trade costs. The Balassa-Samuelson theory can explain how prices vary when goods are not traded and why rich countries have higher price levels. As countries get richer, their wages rise, driving up the prices of their nontraded goods (which use local labor as an input). This will drive up the overall price index and will cause the real exchange rate to fall—that is, a real appreciation. The theory finds strong empirical support and can be used to make better models of real and (hence) nominal exchange rates, with improved predictions, in situations in which an assumption of PPP is inappropriate.

2 Exchange Rates in the Short Run: Deviations from Uncovered Interest Parity

When we studied exchange rates in the short run, we examined interest arbitrage in the forex market and introduced uncovered interest parity (UIP), the fundamental condition for forex market equilibrium. Recall that UIP states the expected return on foreign deposits should equal the return on domestic deposits when both are expressed in domestic currency.

For such an important foundation of exchange rate theory, however, UIP remains subject to considerable debate among international macroeconomists. The topic is important because any failure of UIP would affect our theories about exchange rates and the wider economy. For that reason, in this section we further explore the UIP debate to better understand the mechanism of arbitrage in the forex market.

---

[6] Balázs Égert, Kirsten Lommatzsch, and Amina Lahrèche-Révil, 2006, "Real Exchange Rates in Small Open OECD and Transition Economies: Comparing Apples with Oranges?" *Journal of Banking and Finance*, 30(12), 3393–3406.

HEADLINES

Eastern Europe and the Euro

The ERM rules were originally devised for a group of mostly rich Western European countries, where similarities in GDP per capita meant that Balassa-Samuelson effects were weak. Nobody adjusted the rules when a very different group of poorer countries arrived on the threshold of the Eurozone.

Estonia, Lithuania, Slovenia, Latvia and Slovakia have joined the exchange rate mechanism of the European monetary union and are candidates for near-term eurozone membership. . . . [Note: Slovenia joined the euro in 2007, Slovakia in 2008, and Estonia in 2011. Lithuania and Latvia remained in the ERM and, like future entrants, were subject to the issues raised below.]

All candidate countries easily meet most of the Maastricht criteria for eurozone membership. They satisfy the exchange rate and interest rate criteria and only Slovakia narrowly misses one of the two fiscal criteria. This is in contrast to Belgium, Germany, France, Italy and Greece, which, if they were not already eurozone members, would not be able to join today, as they do not meet the fiscal criteria. However, according to the European Central Bank and the European Commission, only Slovenia satisfies the inflation criterion, which specifies that annual inflation cannot exceed the average of "the three best performing EU member countries in terms of price stability" by more than 1.5 percentage points in the year prior to the examination.

Forcing candidate countries to meet both an exchange rate criterion and an inflation criterion makes no economic sense. Neither the ECB nor the Bank of England attempts the impossible: to control both inflation and their exchange rate. Opting for stable exchange rates, the Baltic candidate countries have seen their inflation rates rise with energy price increases and impressive productivity gains in their traded sectors. The latter factor, which occurs as the candidate countries rapidly catch up with the eurozone, means that the relative price of non-traded goods rises faster than in the eurozone and is known as the Balassa-Samuelson effect. A conservative estimate of its contribution to the candidate countries' inflation is 1.5 per cent per year. . . .

The ECB's egregious misinterpretation of the term "best performing" further compounds the injustice. In March 2006 (the most recent month for which we have data), the three lowest inflation rates belonged to Sweden, Finland and either Poland or the Netherlands. These countries, two of which are not eurozone members, had an average inflation of 1.2 per cent. Adding 1.5 points to this rate yields an inflation criterion of 2.7 per cent. Slovenia meets this benchmark and Lithuania, with inflation of 2.7 per cent, scrapes by. Estonia, Slovakia and Latvia do not.

Defining "best performing" as having the lowest (positive) inflation rate contradicts the ECB's own formulation of price stability for the eurozone. The ECB defines price stability as inflation below, but close to, 2 per cent. By its own definition, inflation in Sweden, Finland, Poland and the Netherlands is far too low. The ECB itself has not managed to maintain inflation in the eurozone as a whole below 2 per cent. If we accept the ECB's own definition of what price stability means, then the target, achieved by several EU countries, should be about 1.8 per cent, putting the benchmark at 3.3 per cent. Slovenia, Lithuania and Slovakia satisfy this criterion but Estonia and Latvia do not. We maintain that sound economics would increase the benchmark by 1.5 points to allow for the Balassa-Samuelson effect, allowing Estonia to pass the test.

All that stands between Estonia, Lithuania and Slovakia and near-term eurozone membership is a rigid application of an inconsistent interpretation of a flawed inflation criterion. What should be done when "the law is an ass"? Failure to enforce a law weakens the rule of law and respect for rule-bound behaviour, but so does enforcing a harmful and senseless rule.

Source: Extract from Willem Buiter and Anne Sibert, "Europe Must Relax Its Inflation Test for Euro Entrants," *Financial Times, May 3, 2006*.

APPLICATION

The Carry Trade

UIP implies that the home interest rate should equal the foreign interest rate plus the rate of depreciation of the home currency. If UIP holds, it would seem to rule out the naive strategy of borrowing in a low interest rate currency and investing in a high interest rate currency, an investment referred to as a **carry trade**. In other words, UIP implies that the expected profit from such a trade is zero:

$$\text{Expected profit} = \underbrace{i_F}_{\substack{\text{Interest rate} \\ \text{on foreign currency}}} + \underbrace{\frac{\Delta E^e_{H/F}}{E_{H/F}}}_{\substack{\text{Expected rate of depreciation} \\ \text{of the home currency}}} - \underbrace{i_H}_{\substack{\text{Interest rate} \\ \text{on home currency}}} \quad (11\text{-}3)$$

The first two terms bracketed as: Expected home currency rate of return on foreign deposits. The last two terms bracketed as: Cost of carry.

From the home perspective, the return to an investment in the foreign currency (the foreign return) consists of the first two terms on the right-hand side of the preceding equation. Let's suppose the foreign currency (that of Australia, say) has a high interest rate of 6%. Now suppose the home country (Japan, say) has a low interest rate of 1%. The final term in the preceding equation is the cost of borrowing funds in local currency (Japanese yen) or, in financial jargon, the *cost of carry*. The interest rate differential, 5%, would be the profit on the carry trade *if the exchange rate remained unchanged*. If UIP is true, however, it would be pointless to engage in such arbitrage because the low-yield currency (the yen) would be expected to appreciate by 5% against the high-yield currency (the Australian dollar). The exchange rate term would be –5%, leaving zero expected profit.

The Long and Short of It In the past decade or two, the predominant low interest rate currencies in the world economy have been the Japanese yen and the Swiss franc, and carry traders have often borrowed ("gone short") in these currencies and made an investment ("gone long") in higher interest rate major currencies such as the U.S. dollar, pound sterling, euro, Canadian dollar, Australian dollar, and New Zealand dollar. The profits from these trades have been very handsome. Has UIP failed?

To grasp how a carry trade functions, Figure 11-4, panel (a), shows actual monthly profits (in percent per month) from a carry trade based on borrowing low-interest yen in the Japanese money market and investing the proceeds in a high-interest Australian dollar money market account for one month. Also shown are the cumulative profits (in yen) that would have accrued from a ¥100 carry trade initiated on January 1, 1992. Panel (b) shows the underlying data used to calculate these returns. We see that over this entire period, the annual Australian dollar interest rate exceeded the Japanese yen interest rate, often by five or six percentage points. Thus, returns would be positive for this strategy if the yen depreciated or even appreciated only slightly against the Australian dollar. But if the yen appreciated more than slightly in any month, returns would be negative, and losses would result.

Panel (a) shows that in many months the high interest being paid on the Australian dollar was not offset by yen appreciation, and the carry trade resulted in a profit; this pattern was seen frequently in the period from 1995 to 1996, for example. There were other periods, however, when a sharp yen appreciation far exceeded the interest differential, and the carry trade resulted in a loss; this pattern occurred quite a bit in late 1998 and again during the global financial crisis of 2008. In 1998, for example, in each of three months, in fact—August, October, and December 1998—the Australian dollar lost about 10% in value, wiping out the profits from *two years' worth of interest differentials* in all three cases. Overall, we see that the periods of positive and negative returns were driven not by the fairly stable interest differential seen in panel (b), but by the long and volatile swings in the exchange rate.

FIGURE 11-4

Carry Trades In the 1990s and 2000s, the yen had a lower interest rate than many other currencies. Carry trades borrow in low-yield yen to invest in higher-yield currencies like the Australian dollar. Such trades can be profitable for long periods, but dramatic reversals, though rare, can quickly undermine profits.

Sources: oanda.com and econstats.com.

To sum up, the carry trade strategy was subject to a good deal of volatility, and over the decade from the start of 1992 to the end of 2001, the highs and lows canceled each other out in the long run. On November 1, 2001, for example, the average return on this carry trade was virtually zero. Cumulative interest since 1992 on the two currencies expressed in yen was virtually the same, about 13%. Over that period, 100 yen placed in either currency at the start would have been worth 113 yen by the end.

What happened after that date? Subsequent trends again caused the value of Australian investment to pull ahead, as can be seen in panel (a) by the mostly positive returns registered month after month from 2002 to 2006. By June 2007 cumulative profits were well over ¥100. The reason? As panel (b) shows, the yen persistently weakened against the Australian dollar over this 5-year period (by about 6% to 7% per year), reinforcing the interest differential (about 6% to 7% also) rather than offsetting it. Adding up, from 2002 to 2006 the cumulative return on the carry trade was about 15% per year! Would that trend continue or was there to be another sudden swing resulting from yen appreciation? As we can see, another wipeout came along in 2008. This question brings us to a consideration of the role of risk in the forex market.

Investors face very real risks in this market. Suppose you put up $1,000 of your own capital and borrow $19,000 in yen from a bank. You now have 20 times your capital, a ratio, or *leverage*, of 20 (not uncommon). Then you play the carry trade, investing the $20,000 in the Australian dollar. It takes only a 5% loss on this trade to wipe you out: 5% of $20,000 eats all your capital. And without that *margin* to back you up, the bank bids you goodbye. As we have seen, losing 5% in a month is quite possible, as is losing 10% or even 15%.

For policy makers and market participants, the broader fear is that while big losses for households would be bad enough, big losses at large, high-leverage financial institutions could have damaging spillover effects in the global macroeconomy. For example, in June 2007, Jim O'Neill, Goldman Sachs chief global economist, said investment firms had been caught on the wrong side of huge bets against the Japanese yen: "There has been an amazing amount of leverage on currency markets that has nothing to do with real economic activity. I think there are going to be dead bodies around when this is over. The yen carry trade has reached 5% of Japan's GDP. This is enormous and highly risky, as we are now seeing."[7] Days later Steven Pearson, chief currency strategist at HBOS bank, said, "A sizeable reversal at some point is highly likely, but the problem with that statement is the 'at some point' bit, because carry trades make money steadily over long periods of time."[8]

In the carry trade, as history shows, a big reversal can always happen as everyone rushes to exit the carry trades and they all "unwind" their positions at the same time. The answer to the dangling question above is yes, a big reversal did come along for the trade in question: after rising another 10% against the yen from January to July 2007, the Australian dollar then fell by 15% in the space of a month, eating up about three years' worth of interest differential for anyone unlucky enough to buy in at the peak. Many hedge funds and individual investors who made ill-timed or excessively leveraged bets lost a bundle (see **Headlines: Mrs. Watanabe's Hedge Fund**).

Still, given the persistence of profits, anyone predicting such reversals may appear to be crying wolf. Money managers often face incentives to follow the herd and the market's momentum keeps the profits flowing—until they stop. All this ensures high

---

[7] Ambrose Evans-Pritchard, "Goldman Sachs Warns of 'Dead Bodies' after Market Turmoil," telegraph.co.uk, June 3, 2007.
[8] Veronica Brown, "Carry Trade Devotees Keep Faith in Testing Times," Reuters, June 12, 2007.

HEADLINES

Mrs. Watanabe's Hedge Fund

The OECD estimated the total yen carry trade at $4 trillion in 2006. This trade involves not just large financial institutions but increasing numbers of Japanese individual investors, who place money in high-yielding foreign currency deposits or uridashi bonds.

TOKYO—Since the credit crisis started shaking the world financial markets this summer, many professional traders have taken big losses. Another, less likely group of investors has, too: middle-class Japanese homemakers who moonlight as amateur currency speculators.

Ms. Itoh is one of them. Ms. Itoh, a homemaker in the central city of Nagoya, did not want her full name used because her husband still does not know. After cleaning the dinner dishes, she would spend her evenings buying and selling British pounds and Australian dollars.

When the turmoil struck the currency markets last month, Ms. Itoh spent a sleepless week as market losses wiped out her holdings. She lost nearly all her family's $100,000 in savings.

"I wanted to add to our savings, but instead I got in over my head," Ms. Itoh, 36, said.

Tens of thousands of married Japanese women ventured into online currency trading in the last year and a half, playing the markets between household chores or after tucking the children into bed. While the overwhelmingly male world of traders and investors here mocked them as kimono-clad "Mrs. Watanabes," these women collectively emerged as a powerful force, using Japan's vast wealth to sway prices and confound economists. . . .

Now Japan's homemaker-traders may become yet another casualty of the shakeout hitting the debt, credit and stock markets worldwide. . . . Most analysts estimate that Japanese online investors lost $2.5 billion trading currency last month. . . .

Some of the women used their own money, some used their husband's, and some used a combination of both. But by trading, they challenged deeply held social prohibitions in Japan against money, which is often seen here as dirty, especially when earned through market speculation.

"There are strict taboos against money that isn't earned with sweat from the brow," said Mayumi Torii, a 41-year-old mother of one who said she earned $150,000 since she started margin trading in currencies early last year.

Ms. Torii is one of Japan's most famous housewife-traders. She has written a book on her investing strategies and founded a support group for home traders, the FX Beauties Club, which now has 40 members. (FX is financial shorthand for "foreign exchange."). . .

One reason Japan's homemakers can move markets is that they hold the purse strings of the nation's $12.5 trillion in household savings. For more than a decade, that money languished in banks here at low interest rates. But as the rapid aging of Japan's population has brought anxiety about the future, households are starting to move more of it overseas in search of higher returns.

A tiny fraction of this has flowed into risky investments like online currency accounts. Most of these accounts involve margin trading, in which investors place a cash deposit with a brokerage that allows them to borrow up to 20 or even 100 times their holdings for trading.

The practice has been popular not only because it vastly raises the level of potential profits, but also because it allowed wives to trade at home, said Hiroshi Takao, chief operating officer of TokyoForex, an online trading firm.

"FX Beauties" founder Mayumi Torii

The housewife-traders were so secretive that many market analysts did not realize how widespread the trend had become until this summer, when the police arrested a Tokyo housewife accused of failing to pay $1.1 million in taxes on her foreign exchange earnings. . . .

For a time, margin trading seemed like a surefire way to make money, as the yen moved only downward against the dollar and other currencies. But last month, in the midst of the credit turmoil, the yen soared as hedge funds and traders panicked.

Ms. Itoh recalled that she had wanted to cry as she watched the yen jump as much as 5 percent in value in a single day, Aug. 16.

"But I had to keep a poker face, because my husband was sitting behind me," Ms. Itoh said.

She did not sell her position, thinking the yen would fall again. But by the next morning, only $1,000 remained in her account, she said. . . .

[M]ost of the half dozen homemaker-traders interviewed for this article said they were already trading again, and the rest said they soon would be—including Ms. Itoh, who said she would probably invest her remaining $1,000 in savings.

"There's no other way to make money so quickly," she said.

Source: Excerpted from Martin Fackler, "Japanese Housewives Sweat in Secret as Markets Reel," New York Times, September 16, 2007.

levels of stress and uncertainty for anyone in the forex trading world and for some of the households engaged in this kind of risky arbitrage.

Carry Trade Summary Our study of the carry trade focuses our attention on several facts. First, even if expected returns from arbitrage are zero, actual realized returns are often not zero. Second, such returns appear to be persistent. Third, the returns are also very volatile, or risky. All of these issues need to be addressed as we judge the success or failure of UIP. ∎

APPLICATION

Peso Problems

The example of carry trades between the Japanese yen and the Australian dollar shows how actual returns from interest arbitrage may be nonzero (but risky) for a pair of currencies that are floating. But the same can be true for two currencies that are fixed. To illustrate this case, we turn to recent data involving the U.S. dollar pegs of two emerging market countries, Hong Kong and Argentina.

As we saw in the chapter on fixed and floating regimes, in the case of a credibly fixed peg with no risk of a depreciation or any other risks (no currency premium and no default risk premium), the UIP condition states that the home interest rate should equal the foreign interest rate because investors treat domestic and foreign currency as perfect substitutes that always have been and always will be interchangeable at a fixed rate. Thus, the interest differential between the two currencies should be zero. Again, if true, this outcome would seem to rule out any desire on the part of investors to engage in arbitrage (e.g., via the carry trade). But there is an important exception: when pegs are not credible, risk premiums can cause large interest differentials—and cause investors to smell a profit.

Figure 11-5, panel (a), shows data for Hong Kong from 1990 to 2000, including the crucial period in 1997 when many Asian countries were in crisis and their exchange rate pegs were breaking. Most of the time, the interest differential between the Hong Kong dollar and the U.S. dollar was zero, as one would expect for what was perceived to be a credible peg. Hong Kong was operating a quasi-currency board with reserves of approximately 300% of the (base) money supply. Short of dollarization, this was considered about the most bulletproof peg around.

Nonetheless, in late 1997 investors started to fear that Hong Kong might suffer the same fate as other Asian economies. Expecting a future depreciation of the Hong Kong dollar, they started to demand a currency premium. At its peak, the Hong Kong interest rate rose almost 20% per year above the U.S. interest rate. However, *the expected depreciation never happened.* The Hong Kong dollar's peg to the U.S. dollar survived. Investors may have been reasonable to fear a crisis and demand a premium beforehand (ex ante), but after the fact (ex post), these unrealized expectations became realized profits. As a result, there was handsome money to be made from the carry trade for those willing to park their money in Hong Kong dollars during all the fuss.

Should you always bet on a peg to hold in a crisis? No. Figure 11-5, panel (b), shows data for Argentina from 1991 to 2001. This includes the period of looming crisis for the Argentine economy in 2001, as the likelihood of default and depreciation grew. The country was in fiscal trouble with an ailing banking sector. It no longer had the ability to borrow in world capital markets and was about to be cut off

FIGURE 11-5

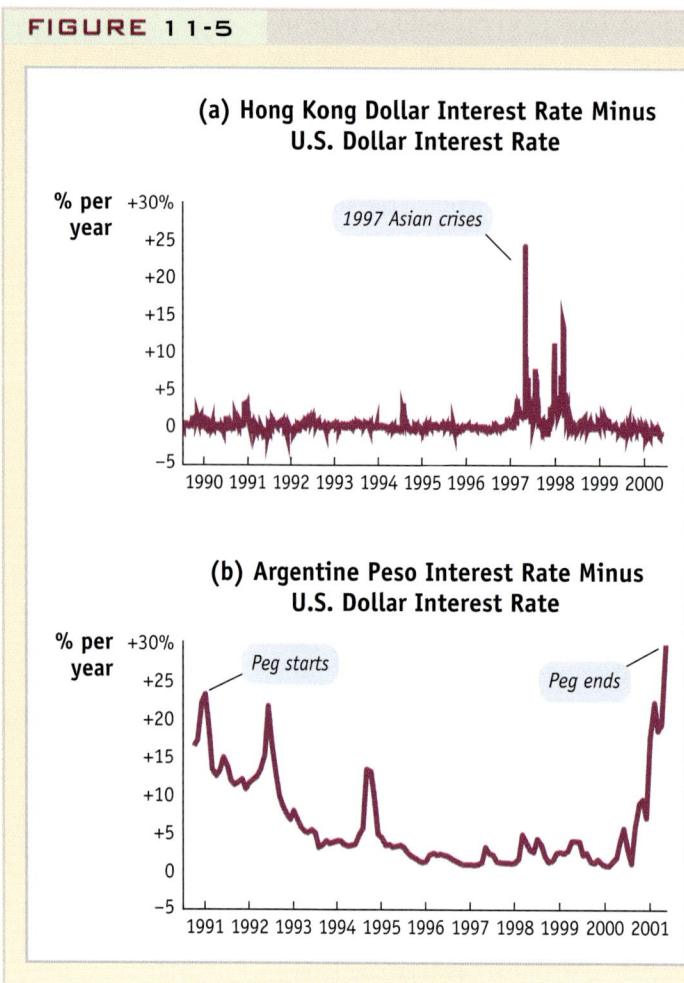

Peso Problems If exchange rates are fixed (and credible), then the interest rate on the home currency and the base currency should be the same. As seen here, however, the Hong Kong dollar and Argentina peso often had large currency premiums. Hong Kong's peg held, and carry trade profits were made. Argentina's peg broke, and losses were massive.

Sources: Global Financial Data and econstats.com.

from International Monetary Fund (IMF) assistance. A recession was deepening. All of this was raising the pressure on the government to use monetary policy for purposes other than maintaining the peg. Investors began to demand a huge currency-plus-default premium on Argentine peso deposits to compensate them for the risk of a possible depreciation and/or banking crisis. Peso interest rates at one point were more than 25% above the U.S. interest rate. But in this case, investors' fears were justified: In December to January 2001 the Argentine government froze bank deposits, imposed capital controls, and the peg broke. The peso's value plummeted, and soon the exchange rate exceeded three pesos to the dollar, erasing more than two-thirds of the U.S. dollar value of peso deposits. In retrospect, the precrisis interest differentials had been too small: The carry traders who gambled and left their money in peso deposits eventually lost their shirts.

We can now see how expectations may not be realized, even when exchange rates are fixed. Fixed exchange rates often break, and investors may reasonably demand currency premiums at certain times. However, after the fact, such premiums may lead to returns from interest arbitrage that are positive (when pegs hold, as in the Hong Kong case) or negative (when pegs break, as in the Argentine case).

International economists refer to this phenomenon as the **peso problem** (given its common occurrence in a certain region of the world). But again, it is far from clear that the profits seen are a sign that UIP fails or that investors are acting irrationally. The collapse of a peg can be seen as a rare event, an extreme occurrence that is hard to predict but that will lead to large changes in the values of assets. This situation is not unlike, say, fire or earthquake insurance: Every year that you pay the premium and nothing happens, you make a "loss" on the insurance arrangement, a pattern that could go on for years (hopefully, for your entire life), but you know that the insurance will pay off to your advantage in a big way if disaster strikes. ∎

Peso problems: a man hammers on the door of a bank in a protest over frozen accounts, Buenos Aires, June 2002.

The Efficient Markets Hypothesis

Do carry trade profits disprove UIP? To explore this question further, let us rewrite Equation (11-3), which calculates expected profits, by replacing *expected* or *ex ante* values of the exchange rate with *actual* or *ex post* realized values.

$$\text{Actual profit} = \underbrace{i_F}_{\substack{\text{Interest rate} \\ \text{on foreign currency}}} + \underbrace{\frac{\Delta E_{H/F}}{E_{H/F}}}_{\substack{\text{Actual rate of depreciation} \\ \text{of the home currency}}} - \underbrace{i_H}_{\substack{\text{Interest rate} \\ \text{on home currency}}} \quad (11\text{-}4)$$

$$\underbrace{\hspace{5cm}}_{\text{Actual home currency rate of return on foreign deposits}} \qquad \underbrace{\hspace{2cm}}_{\text{Cost of carry}}$$

Note the one subtle difference: The disappearance of the superscript "*e*," which denoted expectations of future exchange rate depreciation. This expression can be computed only after the fact: Although interest rates are known in advance, the future exchange rate is not. We know actual profits only after the investment strategy has run its course.

Thus, the sole difference between actual and expected profits is a **forecast error** that corresponds to the difference between actual depreciation and expected depreciation. (Again, the importance of exchange rate forecasts is revealed!) This forecast error is the difference between Equation (11-3) and Equation (11-4), that is,

$$\text{Forecast error} = \binom{\text{Actual}}{\text{profit}} - \binom{\text{Expected}}{\text{profit}} = \frac{\Delta E_{H/F}}{E_{H/F}} - \frac{\Delta E^e_{H/F}}{E_{H/F}} \quad (11\text{-}5)$$

Armed with this way of understanding *unexpected* profits, we can now confront an important and controversial puzzle in international macroeconomics: What can the behavior of this forecast error tell us about UIP and the workings of the forex market? One way to attack that question is to study expected and actual profits side by side to see the size of the forecast error and its pattern of behavior.

Expected Profits On the one hand, strictly speaking, UIP itself says nothing about the forecast error. It says only that before that fact, or *ex ante*, expected profits should be zero. Expectations are not directly observable in markets, but we can recall the evidence presented in the chapter on exchange rates in the short run based on surveys of traders' expectations for major currencies from 1988 to 1993. As a recap, Figure 11-6, panel (a), presents this evidence again. The figure plots the expected depreciation against the interest differential for several major currencies.[9]

On the 45-degree line, these two terms are equal, and expected profits will be zero, according to Equation (11-3). As in several studies of this sort, on average, the data line is close to, but not exactly on, the 45-degree line, so they are not wildly inconsistent with UIP. The slope is close to 1. But the survey data are probably prone to error and cover only some (but not all) of the traders in the market. Even using formal statistical tests, it is difficult to reject UIP based on shaky evidence of this sort. The hypothesis that UIP holds can typically survive this kind of test.

Actual Profits On the other hand, we know that actual profits are made. It is enlightening to see exactly how they are made by replacing the expected depreciation in panel (a) with actual depreciation, after the fact, or *ex post*. This change is made in panel (b), which, to be consistent, shows actual profits for the same currencies over the same period.

The change is dramatic. There are plenty of observations not on the 45-degree line, indicating that profits and losses were made in some periods. Even more striking, the line of best fit has a slope of about 0.2. This means that for every 1% of interest differential in favor of the foreign currency, we would expect only a 0.2% appreciation of the home currency, on average, leaving a profit of 0.8%. At larger interest differentials, the line of best fit means even larger profits. (Some studies find zero, or even negative slopes, implying even bigger profits!)

The UIP Puzzle A finding that profits can be made needs careful handling. On its own, this need not imply a violation of UIP: Random profits could arise due to variation about a zero mean. However, looking at actual profits, the pattern of the deviations from the 45-degree line is systematic. The slope of the best-fit line is well below 1, indicating, for example, that when the interest differential is high, actual depreciation is typically less than expected and less than the interest differential. In other words, *on average*, the carry trade (borrowing in the low-yield currency to invest in the high-yield currency) is profitable. Actual profits are risky, but they appear to be forecastable. Forecastable profits are like a grail to economists: mythical, sought after, and a cause of division in the court.

This finding is widely considered to be a puzzle or anomaly. If such profits are forecastable, then the forex market would be violating some of the fundamental tenets of the modern theory of finance. The **rational expectations hypothesis** argues that, on average, all investors should make forecasts about the future that are without *bias*: On average, actual and expected values should correspond. But, as we just saw, the difference between actual and expected exchange rates reveals a clear bias.

In addition, the **efficient markets hypothesis,** developed by economist Eugene Fama, asserts that financial markets are "informationally efficient" in that all prices reflect all known information at any given time. Hence, such information should not be useful in forecasting future profits; that is, one should not be able to systematically beat the market.

Ultimately then, the UIP puzzle isn't just about UIP. The expectations data (the best that we have) suggest that UIP does hold. The real UIP puzzle is why *UIP combined with the rational expectations and efficient markets hypotheses* fails to hold. Yet these hypotheses seemingly do fail. This appears to be an **inefficient market** instead. Why are those big forecastable profits lying around?

---

[9] Recall that given *covered* interest parity, which does hold, the interest differential also equals the forward premium.

FIGURE 11-6

(a) Test of UIP Using Survey Data on Expectations

Expected rate of depreciation (home/foreign, % per annum)

Line of best fit: slope = 1.27

Interest differential (home minus foreign, % per annum)

(b) Test of the Efficient Markets Hypothesis

Actual rate of depreciation (home/foreign, % per annum)

Line of best fit: slope = 0.23

Interest differential (home minus foreign, % per annum)

UIP and the Efficient Markets Hypothesis Each dot represents an actual 12-month period for a given currency versus the U.S. dollar. According to trader surveys, expected depreciations were, *on average,* more or less in line with UIP, as seen in panel (a), where the slope is not far from 1. But panel (b) shows that, after the fact, these forecasts were not very good, and systematically wrong, in this sample. Actual depreciations were far out of line with expectations: the slope is only 0.23. On average, high-yield currencies systematically depreciated only 23% as much as the interest differential would have forecast under UIP.

Notes: Line of best fit is through the origin. Data shown are monthly for the German mark, Swiss franc, Japanese yen, British pound, and Canadian dollar against the U.S. dollar from February 1988 to October 1993.

Source: From Menzie Chinn and Jeffrey A. Frankel, "Survey Data on Exchange Rate Expectations: More Currencies, More Horizons, More Tests," in W. Allen and D. Dickinson, eds., 2002, Monetary Policy, Capital Flows and Financial Market Developments in the Era of Financial Globalisation: Essays in Honour of Max Fry *(London: Routledge), pp. 145–167.*

Limits to Arbitrage

Economists have proposed a number of ways to resolve these puzzles, and at some level all of these can be described as explanations based on a **limits to arbitrage** argument. What does this mean? In the first section of this chapter, we argued that there were limits to arbitrage, in the form of trade costs, that can help explain the PPP puzzle: Purchasing power parity will not hold if there are frictions such as transport costs, tariffs, and so on that hamper arbitrage in goods markets.

Limits to arbitrage arguments can also be applied in the world of finance. But how? And can they help explain the UIP puzzle?

Trade Costs Are Small It is tempting but ultimately not fruitful to look for the same kinds of frictions that we saw in goods markets. Conventional trade costs in financial markets are simply too small to have an effect that is large enough to explain the puzzle. There are bid-ask spreads between currencies, and there may be other technical trading costs, for example, associated with when a forex trade is placed during the day and which financial markets are open. But none of these frictions provides a sufficient explanation for the forecastable profits and the market's inefficiency.

There is also the problem that if one wishes to make a very large transaction, especially in a less liquid currency, the act of trading itself may have an adverse impact on the exchange rate and curtail profitable trades. For example, an order for $1 billion of more liquid yen is more easily digested by the market than an order for $1 billion of less liquid New Zealand dollars. But again, this possibility is not likely to explain the UIP puzzle because investors can avert such a situation by breaking their trades up into small pieces and spreading them out over time. So even though these trading costs are real, they may not be large enough to offset the very substantial profits we have seen.

If trading costs are the sole limit to arbitrage, there is still a puzzle. We must look elsewhere.

Risk versus Reward A promising approach to the puzzle examines traders' alternative investment strategies, draws on other puzzles in finance, is based less on introspection and more on observations of actual trading strategies, and connects with the frontiers of the emerging field of behavioral economics.

To approach this research and to make the investment problem facing the trader a little clearer, we can reconsider the data shown in Figure 11-6. In panel (b) we saw that the slope was only 0.23, meaning that for every 1% of interest differential, we would predict only 0.23% of offsetting depreciation, leaving a seemingly predictable profit of 0.77%. Suppose we followed a carry trade strategy of borrowing in the low interest rate currency and investing in the high-interest currency. If the interest differential were 1%, then we would expect to net a profit of 0.77%; if the interest differential were 2%, we would expect to double that profit to 1.54%; a differential of 3% would yield 2.31% profit, and so on, if we simply extrapolate that straight line.

This strategy would have delivered profits. However, there are two problems with it. First, profits do not, in fact, grow linearly with the interest differential. The straight-line model is a poor fit. At high-interest differentials there are times when profits are very good, and other times when the carry trade suffers a reversal, and large losses accrue, as we have seen. The second problem is a related one. At all levels of the interest differential, Figure 11-6 clearly shows the extreme volatility or riskiness of these returns due to the extreme and unpredictable volatility of the exchange rate. Actual rates of depreciation can easily range between plus or minus 10% per year, and up to plus or minus 30% in some cases.

One measure of the volatility of returns used by economists is the standard deviation, which we can now put to use to explore why these positive but risky profits are left unexploited.

The Sharpe Ratio and Puzzles in Finance Carry trade profits are the difference between a risky foreign return and a safe domestic interest rate. This kind of return difference is called an **excess return,** and to analyze it further, we can draw on one of the standard tools of financial economics.

The **Sharpe ratio** is the ratio of an asset's average annualized excess return to the annualized standard deviation of its return:

$$\text{Sharpe ratio} = \frac{\text{Mean (annual excess return)}}{\text{Standard deviation (annual excess return)}}$$

The ratio was invented by William Forsyth Sharpe, a Nobel laureate in economics. As a ratio of "rewards to variability," the Sharpe ratio tells us how much the returns on an asset compensate investors for the risks they take when investing in it.

Figure 11-7 displays data on returns to the simple carry trade strategy for several major currencies against the British pound for the period 1976 to 2005. For each pair of currencies, it is assumed that each month a trader would have borrowed in the low

FIGURE 11-7

Risk versus Reward in the Carry Trade This chart shows details of returns for carry trades between the British pound and selected foreign currencies (and an equally weighted portfolio of all such trades). The strategy supposes that each month an investor borrowed in the low interest rate currency and invested in the high interest rate currency, and transaction costs are assumed to be negligible. Panel (a) shows that there have been predictable excess returns to the carry trade based on data from 1976 to 2005, on average, about 4% per year. However, the standard deviation of these returns has been substantial, at about 10% per year. Thus, the average Sharpe ratio for this strategy has been about 0.4, as shown in panel (b). The diversified portfolio does a little better with a Sharpe ratio of 0.6.

Note: Returns and Sharpe ratios are annualized.

Source: Craig Burnside et al., 2006, "The Returns to Currency Speculation," NBER Working Papers 12489. Monthly means, standard deviations, and Sharpe ratios have been annualized.

interest rate currency and invested in the high interest rate currency. Details on the returns to a portfolio of all such trades (equally weighted) are also shown.

In panel (a) we see that the returns to these strategies were positive for all currencies (they were also statistically significant), and, on average, they were about 4% per year. However, the volatility of the returns was even larger in all cases, as measured by the standard deviation. On average, this was about 10% on an annual basis, although falling to 6% for the portfolio (due to gains from diversification). In panel (b) the corresponding Sharpe ratios are shown, and we can see that they fall below 1 in all cases. The average for all currencies is 0.4 and, thanks to a reduction in volatility due to diversification, the equally weighted portfolio has a modestly higher Sharpe ratio of 0.6.

We now must ask: Should Sharpe ratios of around 0.5 be considered "big" or "small"? Do they signal that investors are missing a profit opportunity? Should people be rushing to take profits in investments that offer this mix of risk and reward? If this can be judged to be a "big" Sharpe ratio, then we have a puzzle as the market would seem to be failing in terms of efficiency.

It turns out that many investors in the forex market would consider that 0.5 is a fairly small Sharpe ratio. To see why, and to understand how this approach may "solve" the UIP puzzle, we note that historically, as shown in panel (b), the annual Sharpe ratio for the U.S. stock market has been about 0.48, based on the excess returns of the broad S&P 500 index over and above risk-free U.S. Treasury bonds. This reference level of 0.48 might be thought of as a hurdle that competing investment strategies must beat if they are to attract additional investment. But we can see from panel (b) that forex carry trades either fall below this bar, or just barely surmount it.

There are indeed excess returns in the stock market, but investors are not rushing to borrow money to buy stocks to push that Sharpe ratio any lower. Admittedly, many economists consider the stock market finding to be a puzzle (called the *equity premium puzzle*) because under various standard theories and assumptions about risk aversion, it is hard to understand why investors sit back and leave such excess returns on the table. And yet they do, a fact that leads other economists to postulate that some very nonstandard assumptions, some drawn from psychology, may now need to be included in models to properly explain investor behavior. Research in *behavioral finance*, a branch of behavioral economics, attempts to explain such seemingly irrational market outcomes using various principles such as rational action under different preferences (e.g., strong aversion to loss) or more limited forms of rationality (e.g., models with slow or costly learning).

To sum up, there are now theories that might explain why nobody arbitrages the stock market when its Sharpe ratio is 0.48. That just isn't a high enough reward-risk ratio to attract investors. But in our forex market data, the Sharpe ratio is about the same, and most other studies find carry trade Sharpe ratios that are little larger than the stock market's 0.48.[10] So we may have an answer to the question why arbitrage does not erase all excess returns. The ratio of rewards to risk is so very small that investors in the market are simply uninterested. Indeed, surveys of trader behavior in major firms by economist Richard Lyons suggest that, in the forex market, if the predicted Sharpe ratio of a strategy falls below even 1, then this is enough to discourage investor interest.[11]

---

[10] Furthermore, in illiquid markets, traders may be concerned that the act of trading itself will cause adverse price movements, eliminating profits. In that case, observed Sharpe ratios may overstate the size of unexploited profits.

[11] Richard K. Lyons, 2001, *The Microstructure Approach to Exchange Rates* (Cambridge, Mass.: MIT Press). Lyons also found carry trade Sharpe ratios of about 0.4 using a historical sample of currencies.

Predictability and Nonlinearity Can we do better than a straight-line or linear predictions of returns and crude carry trade strategies? More complex and diversified forex trading strategies may be able to jack up the Sharpe ratio a little, but not too much. As an alternative way of describing the data, for example, we can use nonlinear models that fit the data quite well.[12]

Nonlinear models show that at low interest differentials (say, 0% to 2%), profits are inherently low, and nobody has been much interested in arbitrage given the risks; conversely, at high differentials (say, 5% or more), the rewards have often vanished as investors have rushed in, bid up the high-yield currency to its maximum value, causing a reversal that wipes out carry trade profits. At the extremes, arbitrage has tended to work when it should (or shouldn't). Only in the middle do moderate, positive Sharpe ratios emerge, it seems, for investors willing to take some risks. Thus, our "small" average Sharpe ratios are a mix of these low and high returns, suggesting more sophisticated strategies should ensure that the investment decision depends on the size of the expected return. But the rewards relative to risk are still quite meager and Sharpe ratios are still fairly low even when arbitrage looks most promising.

Conclusion

The main lesson here is that risky arbitrage is fundamentally different from riskless arbitrage. Based on this sort of standard financial analysis, many economists conclude that although there may be excess returns, even *predictable* excess returns, in the forex market, the risk-reward ratio is typically too low to attract additional investors.[13] In that sense, there is no puzzle left and arbitrage has not failed—it has just gone as far as might be reasonably expected, at least given investor behavior in equity markets and elsewhere. In forex market research, nobody has yet proved that there are large amounts of low-risk money lying on the table (though if they did, they might not publish the result).

What are the implications? Here, there is common ground between the UIP and PPP puzzles. In the case of the PPP puzzle studied earlier in the chapter, limits to arbitrage in the goods market (mainly due to transaction costs) may create a band of inaction allowing for deviations from parity in purchasing prices. In the case of the UIP puzzle, limits to arbitrage in the forex market (mainly due to risk) may allow for deviations from interest parity in some situations.

3 Debt and Default

In the chapter on the gains from financial globalization, when global capital markets work well, they can deliver gains in the form of consumption smoothing and investment efficiency. Yet international financial relations are often disrupted by

---

[12] Jerry Coakley and Ana-Maria Fuertes, 2001, "A Non-Linear Analysis of Excess Foreign Exchange Returns," *Manchester School*, 69(6), 623–642; Lucio Sarno, Giorgio Valente, and Hyginus Leon, 2006, "Nonlinearity in Deviations from Uncovered Interest Parity: An Explanation of the Forward Bias Puzzle," *Review of Finance*, 10(3), 443–482.
[13] There may be a few exceptions to this general statement, and indeed, some currency hedge funds and other large firms with deep pockets and an appetite for risk may be able to eke out worthwhile profits through complex trading strategies, but only time will tell whether these players will whittle down the Sharpe ratio any further.

sovereign default, which occurs when a sovereign government (i.e., one that is autonomous or independent) fails to meet its legal obligations to make payments on debt held by foreigners.

Sovereign default has a long history. Perhaps the first recorded default was in the fourth century BC, when Greek municipalities defaulted on loans from the Delos Temple.[14] Many of today's advanced countries have defaulted in the past. In 1343 a warweary Edward III of England defaulted on short-term loans consigning the major merchant banks of Florence to ruin. In 1557 Phillip II of Spain defaulted on short-term loans principally from South German bankers.[15] Spain defaulted six more times before 1800 and another seven times in the nineteenth century. France defaulted eight times between 1558 and the Revolution in 1789. A group of German states, Portugal, Austria, and Greece defaulted at least four times each in the 1800s, and across Europe as a whole, there were at least 46 sovereign defaults between 1501 and 1900.[16] The United States has maintained a clean sheet during its brief existence, although several U.S. states defaulted when they were emerging markets in the 1800s.[17]

The advanced countries of today tend not to default, although the large debts they have incurred during the global financial crisis may put some of them at greater risk (as of late 2010, countries such as Greece, Ireland, Portugal, and Spain have been under grave strain). In contrast, default has been, and remains, a recurring problem in emerging markets and developing countries. One count shows that countries such as Argentina, Brazil, Mexico, Turkey, and Venezuela have defaulted between five and nine times since 1824 (and at least once since 1980) and have spent 30% of the time failing to meet their financial obligations. Another count lists 48 sovereign defaults in the period from 1976 to 1989, many in Latin America but others dotted throughout the world, and 16 more in the period from 1998 to 2002, including headline crises in Russia (1998) and Argentina (2002).[18]

One of the most puzzling aspects of the default problem is that emerging markets and developing countries often get into default trouble at much lower levels of debt than advanced countries. Yet default is a serious macroeconomic and financial problem for these countries. Because they attract so few financial flows of other kinds, government debt constitutes a large share (more than 30%) of these nations' external liabilities.[19]

To understand the workings of sovereign debt and defaults, we must first look at some of the peculiar characteristics of this form of borrowing.

---

[14] Federico Sturzenegger and Jeromin Zettelmeyer, 2007, *Debt Defaults and Lessons from a Decade of Crises* (Cambridge, Mass.: MIT Press), Chapter 1.
[15] Meir G. Kohn, "Merchant Banking in the Medieval and Early Modern Economy," February 1999, Dartmouth College, Department of Economics Working Paper No. 99-05.
[16] Carmen M. Reinhart, Kenneth S. Rogoff, and Miguel A. Savastano, 2003, "Debt Intolerance," *Brookings Papers on Economic Activity*, 1, 1–74.
[17] For example, see Section 258 of the Mississippi state constitution. The American colonies did default, for example, on the paper bills known as *continentals*, issued from 1775 to 1779 to finance the Revolutionary War. However, in an attempt to make good, the colonies' bad debts were assumed by the United States in 1790 on the urging of the first U.S. Secretary of the Treasury, Alexander Hamilton, a statesman with an acute understanding of the importance of good credit.
[18] Carmen M. Reinhart, Kenneth S. Rogoff, and Miguel A. Savastano, 2003, "Debt Intolerance," *Brookings Papers on Economic Activity*, 1, 1–74; Federico Sturzenegger and Jeromin Zettelmeyer, 2007, *Debt Defaults and Lessons from a Decade of Crises* (Cambridge, MA: MIT Press), Chapter 1.
[19] About 50% of the external liabilities of these countries consist of debt, and of that, approximately 75% is government debt. Data for 2004 from the World Bank; Global Development Finance database; and Gian Maria Milesi-Ferretti and Philip R. Lane, 2006, "The External Wealth of Nations Mark II: Revised and Extended Estimates of Foreign Assets and Liabilities, 1970–2004," IMF Working Paper No. 06/69.

A Few Peculiar Facts about Sovereign Debt

The first important fact about sovereign debt is that debtors are almost never forced to pay. Military responses, always costly, are certainly out of fashion. Legal responses are also largely futile: When developing country debt is issued in a foreign jurisdiction (e.g., in London or New York), there is practically no legal way to enforce a claim against a sovereign nation, and the recent increase in sovereign default litigation has done very little to change this state of affairs.[20]

The repayment of a sovereign debt is thus a matter of choice for the borrowing government. It is really about *willingness* to pay, not *ability* to pay. Economists are therefore inclined to look for a rational explanation in which default is triggered by economic conditions. A key question is, then, how painful does repayment have to become before default occurs?

To answer this question, we must evaluate the costs and benefits of default. The benefits are clear: No repayment means the country gets to keep all that money. Are there costs? While not as apparent as the benefits, there must be costs to default—if there were no costs, countries would never pay their debt, and, as a result, no lending would happen in the first place! Thus economists, discounting more sentimental motives for repayment such as honor and honesty, have focused on two types of costs that act as a "punishment" for defaulters and provide the incentive for nations to repay their debts.[21]

Old-style punishment: In response to a default, the French invaded and occupied Mexico in 1862, suffering only one major defeat at the battle of Puebla (now commemorated by the Mexican holiday Cinco de Mayo).

- *Financial market penalties.* Empirical evidence shows that debtors are usually excluded from credit markets for some period of time after a default. This could expose them to greater consumption risk and other disadvantages. However, economic theory casts doubt on whether these costs alone are sufficient to ensure the possibility of repayment if the exclusion period is short or when borrowers have other ways to smooth consumption (such as investing previously borrowed wealth, purchasing insurance, or going to a different set of financial intermediaries).

- *Broader macroeconomic costs.* These could include lost investment, lost trade, or lost output arising from adverse financial conditions in the wake of a default. These adverse conditions include higher-risk premiums, credit contractions, exchange rate crises, and banking crises. If these costs are high enough, they can encourage nations to repay, even if financial market costs are insufficient.

Summary Sovereign debt is a **contingent claim** on a nation's assets: Governments will repay depending on whether it is more beneficial to repay than to default. With a simple model of how a country makes the decision to default, we can better understand why borrowers default some of the time and repay some of the time; what ultimately causes

---

[20] On litigation, see Federico Sturzenegger and Jeromin Zettelmeyer, "Has the Legal Threat to Sovereign Debt Restructuring Become Real?" CIF Working Paper, Universidad Torcuato Di Tella, April 2006. In theory, foreign assets of defaulters can be legally seized, but defaulting nations naturally avoid this by repatriating such assets shortly before going into default. In contrast, advanced country debt is usually issued at home, in the country's own jurisdiction, where creditors (domestic and foreign) have stronger legal claims against the sovereign.

[21] Jonathan Eaton and Mark Gersovitz, April 1981, "Debt with Potential Repudiation: Theoretical and Empirical Analysis," *Review of Economic Studies*, 48(2), 289–309; Jeremy Bulow and Kenneth Rogoff, February 1989, "A Constant Recontracting Model of Sovereign Debt," *Journal of Political Economy*, 97(1), 155–178; Kenneth M. Kletzer and Brian D. Wright, June 2000, "Sovereign Debt as Intertemporal Barter," *American Economic Review*, 90(3), 621–639; Laura Alfaro and Fabio Kanczuk, March 2005, "Sovereign Debt as a Contingent Claim: A Quantitative Approach," *Journal of International Economics*, 65(2), 297–314.

these contingent outcomes; why some borrowers get into default trouble even at low levels of debt, while others do not; and how lenders respond to this state of affairs and why they continue to lend to defaulting countries. The model we develop is simple, but it provides useful insights on all of these questions.[22]

A Model of Default, Part One: The Probability of Default

In this section, we present a static, one-period model of sovereign debt and default. The first part of the model focuses on default as a contingent claim that will be paid only under certain conditions.

Assumptions The model focuses on the desire of borrowers to default in hard times, when output is relatively low, so that they may smooth their consumption. Thus, for now we ignore any investment motives for borrowing and concentrate on the consumption-smoothing or "insurance" benefits that a country derives from having the option to default on its debt and consume more than it otherwise would.

If repayment is to be contingent in our model, on what will it be contingent? To introduce some exogenous fluctuations, we assume, realistically, that a borrowing country has a fluctuating level of output Y. Specifically, Y is equally likely to take any value between a minimum $\overline{Y} - V$ and a maximum $\overline{Y}$. The difference between the minimum and maximum is a measure of the volatility of output, V. Although the level of output Y is not known in advance, we assume that everyone understands the level of V and the probability of different output levels Y. We suppose the government is the sole borrower and it takes out a one-period loan in the previous period, before the level of output is known. The debt will be denoted L for loan (or liability, which it is) and carries an interest rate r_L, which we call the *lending rate*. We suppose this loan is supplied by one or more competitive foreign creditors who have access to funds from the world capital market at a risk-free interest rate r, which we assume is a constant.

We suppose the loan is due to be paid off after the country finds out what output Y is in the current period. The problem we have is as follows: to figure out the lending terms (the debt level and lending rate) and to understand what the country chooses to do when the loan comes due (default versus repayment). As in many problems in economics, we must "solve backward" to allow for expectations.

The Borrower Chooses Default versus Repayment We assume the sovereign borrower faces some "punishment" or cost for defaulting. There are debates about what forms these costs could take, and we discuss this later in this section. For now we do not take a stand on exactly what these costs are but assume that if the government defaults, then it faces a cost equivalent to a fraction c of its output: that is, cY is lost, leaving only $(1 - c)Y$ for national consumption. Note that these costs are unlike debt payments: they are just losses for the debtor with no corresponding gains for the creditors.

Now that we have established some costs of defaulting, the choice facing the country becomes clearer. For simplicity, we assume two possible courses of action: repay or default.[23] If the government repays the debt, the country will be able to consume only output Y minus the principal and interest on the loan $(1 + r_L)L$. If the government de-

---

[22] The model is based on Luis Catão and Sandeep Kapur, 2006, "Volatility and the Debt-Intolerance Paradox," *IMF Staff Papers*, 53(2), 195–218.
[23] Intermediate cases of partial default are possible in theory and in reality, as is renegotiation, but we focus on a binary default versus repayment choice for simplicity.

faults, the country can consume output Y minus the punishment cY. Thus, the government will act as follows:

$$\text{Repay if} \quad \underbrace{Y - (1 + r_L)L}_{\text{Consumption after repayment (line RR)}} > \underbrace{Y - cY}_{\substack{\text{Consumption after nonrepayment} \\ \text{and default (line NN)}}}$$

Figure 11-8 plots both sides of this inequality against Y for the case in which both repayment and default will occur within the range of possible output levels between maximum output $\overline{Y}$ and minimum output $\overline{Y} - V$. At some critical level of output, called the **repayment threshold,** the government will switch from repayment to default. At this critical level, the two sides of the preceding inequality have to be equal; that is, the debt payoff amount $(1 + r_L)L$ must equal the punishment cost cY. By rearranging the preceding inequality, we can find the level of Y at the repayment threshold Y_T and can restate the government's choice as

$$\text{Repay if} \quad Y \geq \underbrace{\frac{(1 + r_L)L}{c}}_{\substack{\text{Repayment threshold} \\ = Y_T}}$$

FIGURE 11-8

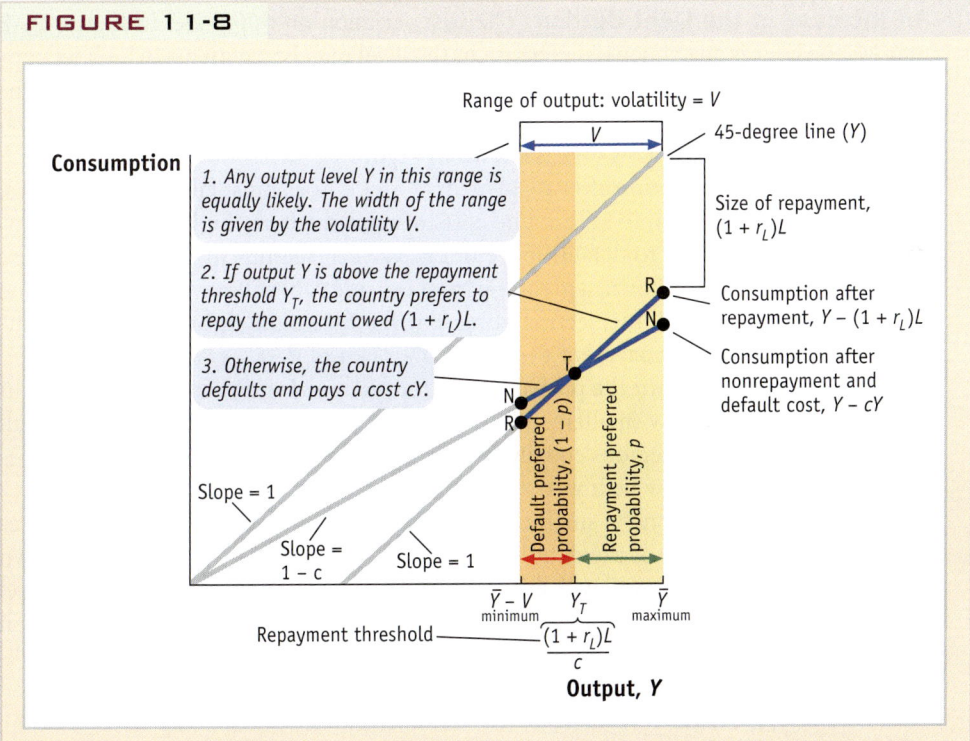

Repayment versus Default When output is high, the country repays its debt with probability p (yellow region) because the cost of defaulting is greater than the cost of repayment. In this region, consumption after repayment (shown by line RR) is greater than consumption after defaulting (line NN). When output is low, the country defaults with probability $1 - p$ (orange region). In this region, the cost of defaulting is less than the cost of repayment because line NN is above line RR. The switch from default to repayment occurs at point T, where the critical level of output reaches the repayment threshold Y_T.

For the case shown in Figure 11-8, we assume that this repayment threshold, $Y_T = (1 + r_L)L/c$, is within the range of possible outputs between the minimum $\overline{Y} - V$ and the maximum $\overline{Y}$.

The value of consumption after repayment, $Y - (1 + r_L)L$, is shown by the repayment line RR, which has a slope of 1: every extra \$1 of output goes toward consumption, net of debt repayments. The value of consumption after nonrepayment and default, $Y - cY$, is shown by the nonrepayment line NN, which has a slope of $(1 - c)$, which is less than 1: when a country has decided to default, from every extra \$1 of output gained by not repaying the country's debts, only \$$(1 - c)$ goes toward consumption, allowing for the net punishment cost.

The lines RR and NN intersect at the critical point T, and the corresponding level of output Y_T is the repayment threshold. Given that the slope of NN is less than the slope of RR, we can see that the country will choose to repay when output is above the repayment threshold Y_T (i.e., to the right of T) and to default when output is below the repayment threshold Y_T (i.e., to the left of T).

Note that the size of the repayment region relative to the default region tells us how likely repayment is to occur relative to default. Let the probability of repayment be p. The key piece of the puzzle is to figure out what determines p. We now show how it depends on two factors: how volatile output is and how burdensome the debt repayment is.

An Increase in the Debt Burden

The first variation on the model in Figure 11-8 that we consider is an exogenous increase in the level of debt payments, which we suppose increase from the original level $(1 + r_L)L$ to a new higher level $(1 + r'_L)L'$. This increase could be due to a change in the debt level, a change in the lending rate, or some combination of the two. This case is shown in Figure 11-9.

The value of consumption after repayment, $Y - (1 + r_L)L$, must fall as $(1 + r_L)L$ rises, so line RR will shift down to R'R'. The costs of repayment are higher, and the country will find it beneficial to default more often. We can see this in the figure because after the RR curve shifts down, a greater part of the line NN will now sit above the line R'R', and the new critical intersection point T will move to the right at T', corresponding to the new higher repayment threshold, $Y'_T = (1 + r'_L)L'/c$.

What does this mean for the probability of repayment? It must fall. The repayment region on the right is now smaller, and the default region on the left is larger. With all output levels in the two regions equally likely, the probability p that output is in the repayment region must now be lower.

We have considered only a small change in the debt burden, so the repayment region hasn't vanished. But if the debt burden increases sufficiently, RR will shift down so far that the critical point T will shift all the way to the right, to the maximum level of output, the repayment region will disappear, and the probability of repayment will be zero (or 0%). If the debt burden is high enough, the country is always better off taking the punishment.

Conversely, if the debt burden *decreases* sufficiently, RR will shift up so far that the critical point T will shift all the way to the left, to the minimum level of output, the default region will disappear, and the probability of repayment will be 1 (or 100%). If the debt burden is low enough, the country will always repay.

Thus, the outcome shown in Figure 11-8 applies only when the debt burden is at some intermediate level such that the repayment threshold is between the minimum and maximum levels of output.

FIGURE 11-9

An Increase in the Debt Burden An increase in the level of debt or the lending rate raises the repayment sum and so reduces consumption after repayment at all levels of Y, causing RR to shift down. This shift makes repayment less likely (the yellow region gets smaller) and default more likely (the orange region gets larger). The probability of repayment p falls. The switch from default to repayment occurs at a higher critical level of output at T', the new repayment threshold Y'_T.

An Increase in Volatility of Output The second variation on the model in Figure 11-8 that we consider is an increase in the volatility of output, which we suppose increases from its original level V to a new higher level V'. This case is shown in Figure 11-10. There could be many reasons why a country is subject to higher output volatility: weather shocks to agricultural output, political instability, fluctuations in the prices of its exports, and so on.

In this case, the consumption levels after repayment on line RR and after default on line NN are unchanged because the debt burden is unchanged. What has changed is that there is now a much wider range of possible output levels. Higher volatility V means that output can now fall to an even lower minimum level, $\overline{Y} - V'$, but can only attain the same maximum $\overline{Y}$.

Thus, an increase in V makes default more likely. In Figure 11-8, the country wanted to default whenever output fell below the critical level T, so it will certainly want to default in the wider range of low outputs brought into play by higher volatility. The default region gets larger and now includes all these new possible levels of output to the left of T. Conversely, the range of outputs to the right of T where repayment occurs is unchanged because the repayment threshold, $Y_T = (1 + r_L)L/c$, is unaffected by a change in V. Hence, the probability p that output is in the repayment region must fall because the repayment region is now smaller relative to the default region.

FIGURE 11-10

An Increase in Volatility An increase in volatility expands the range of low output possibilities. The repayment threshold Y_T stays the same because it is unrelated to V and depends only on the cost of defaulting and the size of the repayment burden. Even though the repayment region (yellow) remains the same size, the increased volatility makes default more likely because the default region (orange) is now relatively larger. The probability of repayment p falls.

To sum up, a rise in volatility lowers the level of debt L at which default becomes a possibility and after that point makes default more likely at any given level of L, up to the point at which default occurs with probability 100%.

The Lender Chooses the Lending Rate All of the preceding results assume a given interest rate on the loan. But now that we know how the likely probability of repayment p is determined, we can calculate the interest rate that a competitive lender must charge. Competition will mean that lenders can only just break even and make zero expected profit. Thus, the lender will set its lending rate so that the expected revenues from each dollar lent, given by the probability of repayment p times the amount repaid $(1 + r_L)$, equal the lender's cost for each dollar lent, which is given by $(1 + r)$, the principal plus the risk-free interest rate at which the lender can obtain funds.

$$\text{Break-even condition for lender:} \quad \underbrace{\underbrace{p}_{\substack{\text{Probability} \\ \text{of repayment}}} \times \underbrace{(1 + r_L)}_{\substack{\text{Lender's revenue} \\ \text{if repaid}}}}_{\text{Lender's expected revenue}} = \underbrace{(1 + r)}_{\text{Lender's costs}}$$

What do we learn from this expression? The right-hand side is a constant, determined by the world risk-free rate of interest r. Thus, the left-hand side must be constant, too. If p were 1 (100% probability of repayment), the solution would be straightforward: With no risk of default and competitive lenders, the borrower will rightly obtain a lending rate equal to the risk-free rate r. But as the probability of repayment p falls, to keep the left-hand side constant, the lenders must raise the lending rate r_L. That is, to compensate for the default risk, the lenders charge a risk premium so that they still just break even.

APPLICATION

Is There Profit in Lending to Developing Countries?

Our break-even assumption may seem a little odd. A popular belief is that rich country creditors, like loan sharks, are making huge profits from lending to developing countries. But the long-run empirical evidence suggests otherwise.

Economists Christoph Klingen, Beatrice Weder, and Jeromin Zettelmeyer looked at how lenders fared in emerging markets from the 1970s to the 2000s by computing the returns on government debt in 22 borrower countries.[24] They did not look at the *ex ante returns* that consisted of the promised repayments in the original loan contracts. Instead, they looked at the *ex post returns*, the realized rates of interest actually paid on the loans, allowing for any defaults, suspensions of payments, reschedulings, or other deviations from the contractual terms.

The results were striking, as shown by Figure 11-11. The average returns on emerging market bonds in this period were 9.1% per year. This was barely above the three-year U.S. government bond returns of 8.6% over the same period and below returns on ten-year U.S. government bonds (9.2%) and U.S. corporate bonds (10.5%). This is not because the borrowers were charged low interest rates beforehand. They were charged typical risk premiums. But if the loans had been paid off *according to those terms*, we would have expected that lenders would have reaped much larger returns ex post. For example, based on the typical risk premiums seen in emerging markets in the period 1998 to 2007,

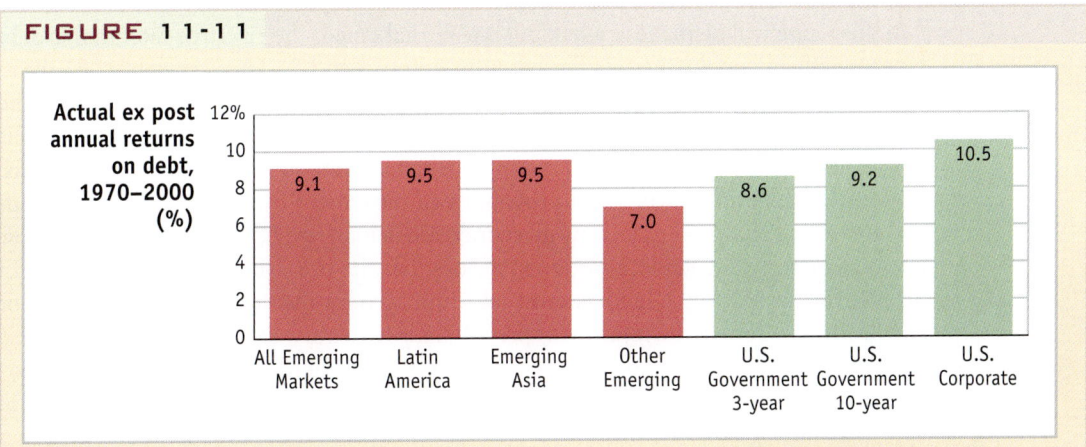

FIGURE 11-11

Returns on Emerging Market Debt, 1970s–2000s The ex post realized returns on emerging market debt have been 9.1% on average, as high as 9.5% in Latin America and Asia, but as low as 7% elsewhere (columns 1–4). Given their riskiness, these returns compare unfavorably with returns on safe U.S. government debt and U.S. corporate debt (columns 5–7). Whatever ex ante risk premiums were charged to emerging markets, defaults ate them all up and lenders only just broke even.

Source: Ex post returns from Christoph Klingen, Jeromin Zettelmeyer, and Beatrice Weder, 2004, "How Private Creditors Fared in Emerging Debt Markets, 1970–2000," IMF Working Paper No. 04/13.

---

[24] Christoph Klingen, Jeromin Zettelmeyer, and Beatrice Weder, 2004, "How Private Creditors Fared in Emerging Debt Markets, 1970–2000," IMF Working Paper No. 04/13.

an extra 2.8% return would have been demanded as a risk premium ex ante, pushing ex post returns up to around 12 to 13%. But such high ex post returns were not seen, as Figure 11-11 shows: defaults ate up the risk premiums and the lenders barely broke even.

Considering the highly risky nature of emerging market debt, as compared with U.S. corporate debt, this finding is remarkable and it suggests that the break-even assumption of our simple model is not far wrong. Admittedly, there were periods when emerging market bonds paid off handsomely. In the early 1990s there were few defaults and lenders were repaid at high interest rates. But there were also periods with massive defaults, like the early 1980s, in which repeated postponements and restructurings meant that creditors got back only pennies on each dollar they had lent to the defaulting countries. Defaults are rare but cataclysmic events for creditors, so only a long-run sample can be informative. But judging from the data in Figure 11-11, lenders to emerging markets have only just broken even, if that. ■

A Model of Default, Part Two: Loan Supply and Demand

The first steps we took in constructing the model were to understand the problem from the lender's standpoint. Knowing the probability p that borrowers will default when output is low, lenders adjust the lending rate r_L they charge depending on the volatility of output V and the level of debt L. Knowing the lending rate and the debt amount determines the loan supply curve for a country, which, combined with an understanding of loan demand, will allow us to determine equilibrium in the loan market.

Loan Supply Suppose output volatility is at some low level V. The probability of repayment is shown in Figure 11-12, panel (a). The loan supply curve $LS(V)$ is shown in panel (b).

At low levels of debt, as we saw, the probability of repayment is 100%, so a loan of size L in this range will be made at a lending rate r_L that equals the risk-free rate. In this debt range, the loan supply curve is flat between points 1 and 2. Then, as debt rises above some loan size L_V that depends on the volatility of the borrowing country's output, the probability of repayment starts to fall below 1 (100%), and the break-even condition tells us that lenders will have to start increasing the lending rate so they don't lose their shirts. At point 2 (the point at which the probability of repayment falls below 100%), the supply curve starts to slope up. For any given increase in loan size L, lenders must decide how much to increase the lending rate r_L to ensure that the break-even condition is met. In making this decision, the lenders must take into account that any increases in L and/or r_L will adversely affect the repayment probability p (as we saw earlier). Finally, as the loan size approaches its maximum L_{MAX}, the rising repayment burden (higher L and higher r_L) will cause the probability of repayment to approach zero. The lending rate will have to approach infinity to ensure that the loan will break even, so the loan supply curve becomes vertical as the debt limit L_{MAX} is reached. No loans are supplied above this level of debt.

Loan Demand The equilibrium market outcome must be somewhere on the lender's loan supply curve. But it must also be on the borrower's loan demand curve. How is that determined? The formal derivation of borrowing demand depends on the country's consumption preferences, including its aversion to risk; this is mathematically complex, but we can sum up the results intuitively by drawing a loan demand curve $LD(V)$ that depends on two factors: the lending rate charged, r_L, and the volatility of output, V. We restrict our attention to the normal case in which the demand curve slopes down

FIGURE 11-12

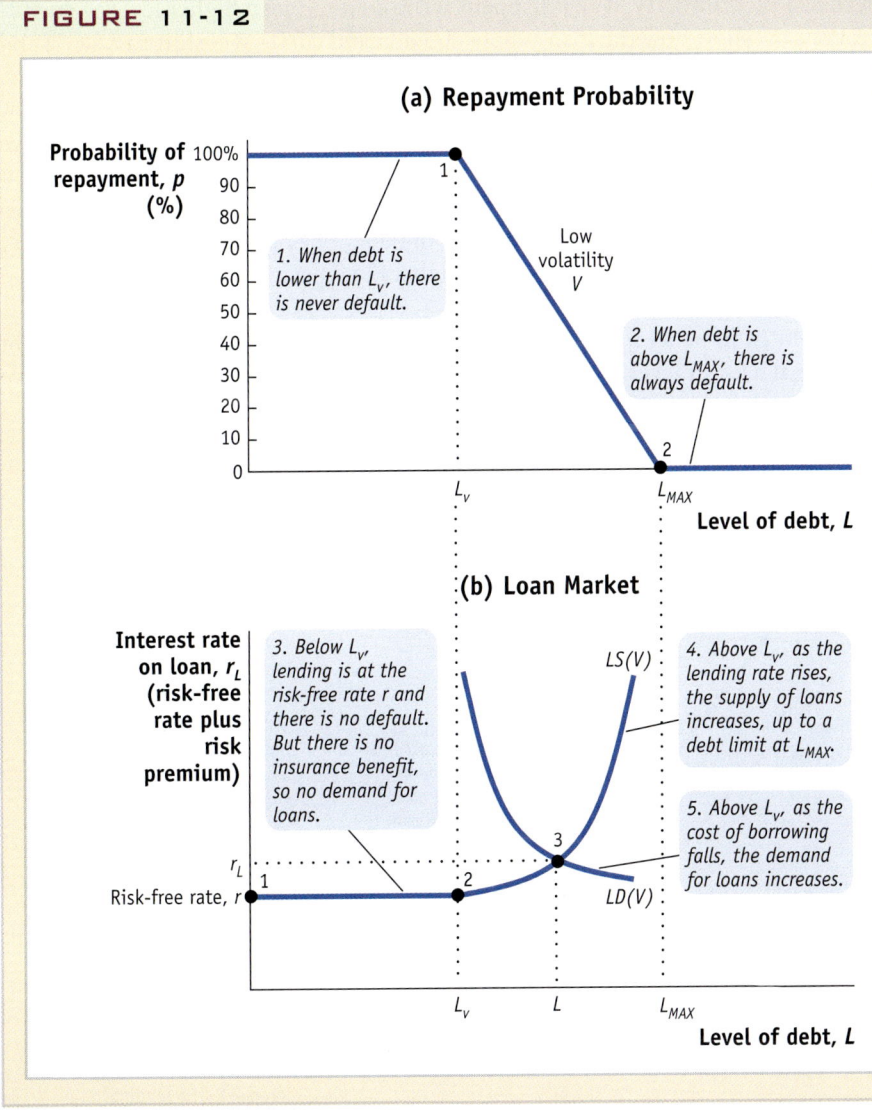

Loan Market Equilibrium When Volatility Is Low A higher level of debt means the probability of repayment falls (and the probability of default increases) between points 1 and 2 in panel (a), starting at the debt level L_V. As the probability of repayment falls, lenders increase the lending rate as the quantity of debt increases, so the loan supply curve LS slopes up in panel (b). As the lending rate falls, more debt is demanded by the country as insurance against consumption risk, so the loan demand curve LD slopes down. The equilibrium is at point 3 where demand and supply intersect.

so that an increase in the interest cost of the loan (a rise in r_L) causes a decrease in the size of loan demanded (a fall in L).

We can now finish our graphical representation of the loan market equilibrium, and in Figure 11-12, panel (b), equilibrium is at point 3, where loan supply LS and loan demand LD intersect. Note that this intersection will be, as shown, between L_V and L_{MAX}. Why? Below debt level L_V, the country never defaults and so debt provides no consumption-smoothing insurance in this range, and the country will want to borrow more and move up and to the right along the loan supply curve. As the cost of borrowing rises, however, the country must consider the trade-off between the amount of insurance it obtains from the debt and the rising cost of that insurance. At some point, this trade-off evens out and we reach the loan quantity the country desires. In Figure 11-12 the quantity of loans supplied and demanded will be equal at equilibrium point 3 with debt level L and lending rate r_L.

An Increase in Volatility What happens if the country has a higher level of volatility V'? We now show how the loan supply and demand curves will shift to $LS(V')$ and $LD(V')$, as shown in Figure 11-13.

In panel (a), higher volatility means that default starts to become a possibility at a low level of debt compared with the low volatility case, as we saw previously. Once above that level of debt, repayment is less likely than when volatility is low. This means that the lending rate rises more quickly to ensure the lenders break even, and the probability of repayment reaches zero at a lower level of debt. The debt ceiling falls to a lower level L'_{MAX}, because higher interest rates mean that the repayment burden will rise more quickly in this case as debt increases.

Consequently, in panel (b), the interest rate is higher at every debt level, and debt hits a ceiling at a lower level of debt. That is, we have shown that the loan supply curve

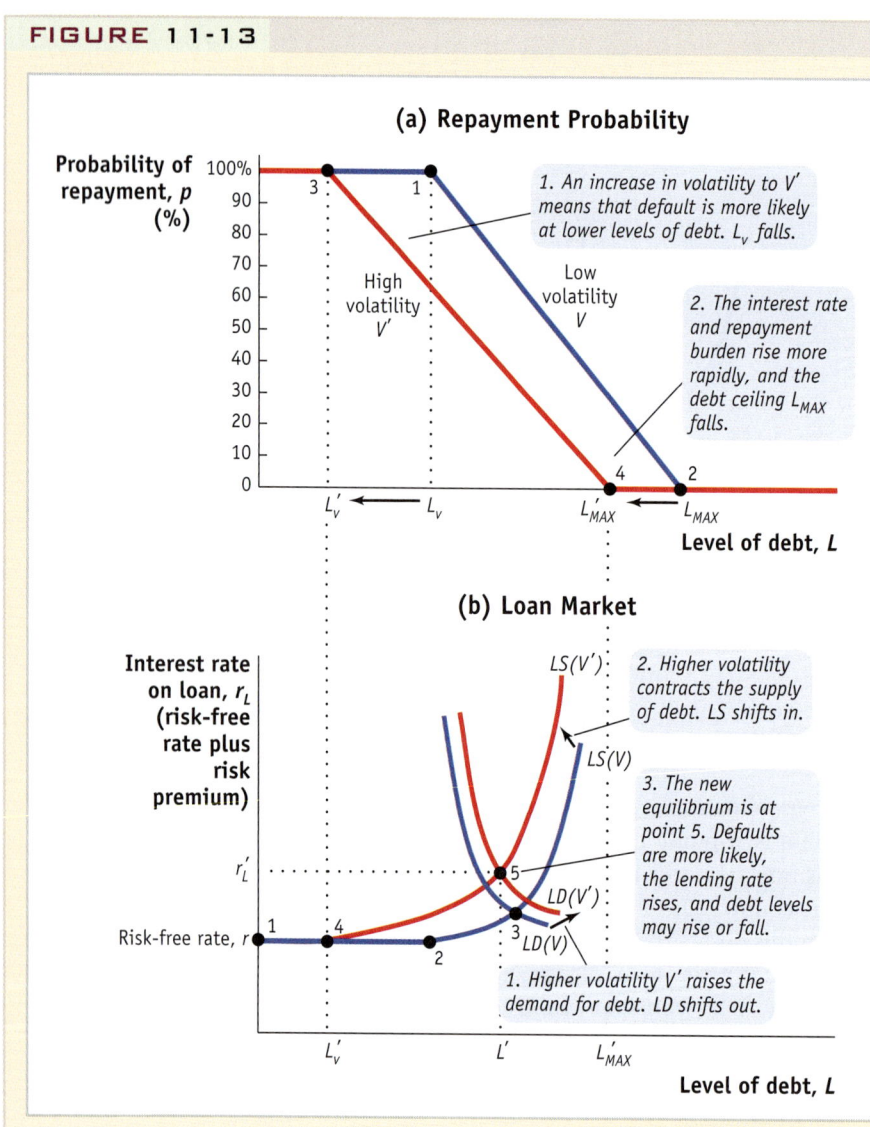

FIGURE 11-13

Loan Market Equilibrium When Volatility Is High More debt means a higher probability of default between points 3 and 4 in panel (a), so repayment probabilities now decline more rapidly starting at the debt level L'_V. In panel (b), therefore, to the right of point 4, default is now possible, and the loan supply curve LS shifts up and to the left in that zone. At the same time, at any given lending rate, higher volatility causes demand for debt to expand so as to give the country better insurance, so the loan demand curve LD shifts right. The new equilibrium is now at point 5 where demand and supply intersect. The lending rate rises; defaults are more likely; debt levels may rise or fall.

shifts left and up. The lending rate starts to rise at point 4, at a lower debt level L'_V, because higher volatility can lead to the possibility of defaults at lower levels of debt. Second, at higher debt levels, higher volatility always means a higher probability of default, so higher interest rates are imposed by lenders, all the way up to the ceiling at L'_{MAX}.

What about loan demand? When volatility rises, the loan demand curve also shifts. With typical preferences (which include risk aversion), higher volatility means that the country will want more insurance, or more consumption smoothing, all else equal. In this model, defaultable debt is the only form of insurance a country can get, so, at any given lending rate, it will want to have more debt. The loan demand curve shifts right to $LD(V')$.

The net result of the shifts in loan supply and demand is a new equilibrium at point 5. If loan supply moves left/up and loan demand moves right, the lending rate will definitely increase. The net effect on the amount of debt is ambiguous, however, and depends on whether the demand shift is larger than the supply shift. If the supply effect dominates, the country will end up with less debt, higher-risk premiums, and more frequent defaults—the very characteristics we see in emerging markets as compared with advanced countries.

APPLICATION

The Costs of Default

Our model of default, like many others, relies on punishment costs to give debtors an incentive to repay. Is this realistic? How big are the costs? Defaulters do not get away scot-free, and to see why, we consider evidence from a Bank of England study and other research.[25]

Financial Market Penalties First, defaulters are excluded from further borrowing until the default is resolved though negotiations with the creditors. These exclusion periods may vary. The Bank of England study found that in the 1980s defaulters were denied market access for an average of four and a half years; however, in the easy credit atmosphere of the 1990s and 2000s, that figure dropped to an average of three and a half months. Exclusion from credit markets can create future consumption costs when the cushion of borrowing is no longer there to smooth consumption. Exclusion may impair investment, too.

Second, default is associated with a significant downgrade in credit ratings and corresponding increases in risk premiums.[26] The Bank of England study found that 7 out of 8 nondefaulters had credit ratings of BBB+ or better (the exception was India), but 12 out of 13 past defaulters were ranked BB+ or worse (the one exception was Chile). These results applied to countries with a variety of income per capita and debt-to-GDP levels. This kind of penalty has a long history: In the first wave of globalization before 1914, defaulters on average paid an extra 1% per year in interest rate risk premiums, controlling for other factors.[27]

Finally, defaulters may face another major inconvenience when borrowing: an inability to borrow in their own currency. The Bank of England study found that nondefaulting countries, including India, China, Korea, Czech Republic, Malaysia, and Hungary, were able to issue between 70 and 100% of their debt in domestic currency;

---

[25] This application is based on Bianca De Paoli, Glenn Hoggarth, and Victoria Saporta, 2006, "Costs of Sovereign Default," *Bank of England Quarterly Bulletin*, Fall.
[26] Carmen M. Reinhart, Kenneth S. Rogoff, and Miguel A. Savastano, 2003, "Debt Intolerance," *Brookings Papers on Economic Activity* (1), 1–74.
[27] Maurice Obstfeld and Alan M. Taylor, 2003, "Sovereign Risk, Credibility and the Gold Standard: 1870–1913 versus 1925–31," *Economic Journal*, 113(487), 241–275.

in contrast, a group of past defaulters, including Brazil, Mexico, Philippines, Chile, and Venezuela, only issued between 40 and 70% of their debt in their own currency. In studying fixed and floating regimes, we learned that the disadvantage of liability dollarization is that depreciations increase the costs of debt principal and interest in domestic currency terms. These changes can lead to destabilizing wealth effects because these impacts amplify debt burdens on the balance sheets of households, firms, and governments.

Broader Macroeconomic Costs and the Risk of Banking and Exchange Rate Crises

The financial penalties are not the only cost that would-be defaulters must weigh. Default may trigger additional output costs, including the serious threats of twin or triple crises.

A default can do extensive damage to the domestic financial system because domestic banks typically hold a great deal of government debt—and they may have been coerced to hold even more such debt in the period right before a default.[28] The banks will likely call for help, putting further fiscal strain on the government. But the government usually has no resources to bail out the banks at a time like this (often, it has been trying to persuade the banks to help out the government). A default crisis can then easily spawn a banking crisis. At best, if the banks survive, prudent management requires the banks to contract domestic lending to rebuild their capital and reduce their risk exposure. At worst, the banks fail. The disappearance of their financial intermediation services will then impair investment activity, and negative wealth effects will squeeze the consumption demand of depositors who lose their access to their money, temporarily or permanently, in a bank that is closed or restructured. The result is lower demand and lower output in the short run and hence more risk for banks because debtors find it harder to pay back their bank loans in recessions. Financial disruption to the real economy also disrupts a nation's international trade. Default can disrupt the short-term credit (provided by domestic and foreign lenders) that is used to finance international trade, and there is some evidence that large and persistent trade contractions follow a default.[29]

In addition to a banking crisis, a default can trigger an exchange rate crisis if the country (like many emerging markets) is trying to preserve a fixed exchange rate. An increase in risk premiums on long-term loans to the government may be matched by a similar increase in risk premiums on bank deposits, especially if a banking crisis is feared. A risk premium shock of this sort, as we learned when we studied exchange rate crises, contracts money demand and causes a drain of foreign exchange reserves at the central bank as the peg is defended. At the same time, if the pleading of banks for fiscal help is ignored, the central bank will be under pressure to do a sterilized sale of reserves to allow it to act as a lender of last resort and expand domestic credit. But such activity will cause reserve levels to fall even further. The reserve drain may be large enough to break the peg, or at least damage the peg's credibility. Expected depreciation will then enlarge the risk premium further, compounding the reserve drain. In the meantime, interest rate increases further dampen investment in the home economy,

---

[28] Although some governments, notably Argentina in 2002, have shown great cunning in trying to honor debt held by domestic creditors while defaulting on foreigners, this kind of discrimination strategy may be difficult to execute legally and technically. Anna Gelpern and Brad Setser, Summer 2004, "Domestic and External Debt: The Doomed Quest for Equal Treatment," *Georgetown Journal of International Law*, 35, 795.

[29] Andrew K. Rose, June 2005, "One Reason Countries Pay Their Debts: Renegotiation and International Trade," *Journal of Development Economics*, 77(1), 189–206.

lowering output and making it harder for debts to be serviced, which hurts the banks again, lowers output again, and compounds all of the problems just outlined.

Lower output and higher-risk premiums can be expected during a default crisis, but they can also trigger banking and exchange rate crises. Low output and high interest rates can break a contingent commitment to a peg; as we have seen in this chapter, they can generate a greater incentive to default; and we also know they can only worsen domestic financial conditions by making it harder for everyone to service their debt to banks and by damaging bank balance sheets.

From all these circuitous descriptions, presented schematically in Figure 11-14, the potential for a "vicious circle" of interactions should now be clear, explaining why so often the three types of crisis are observed together.

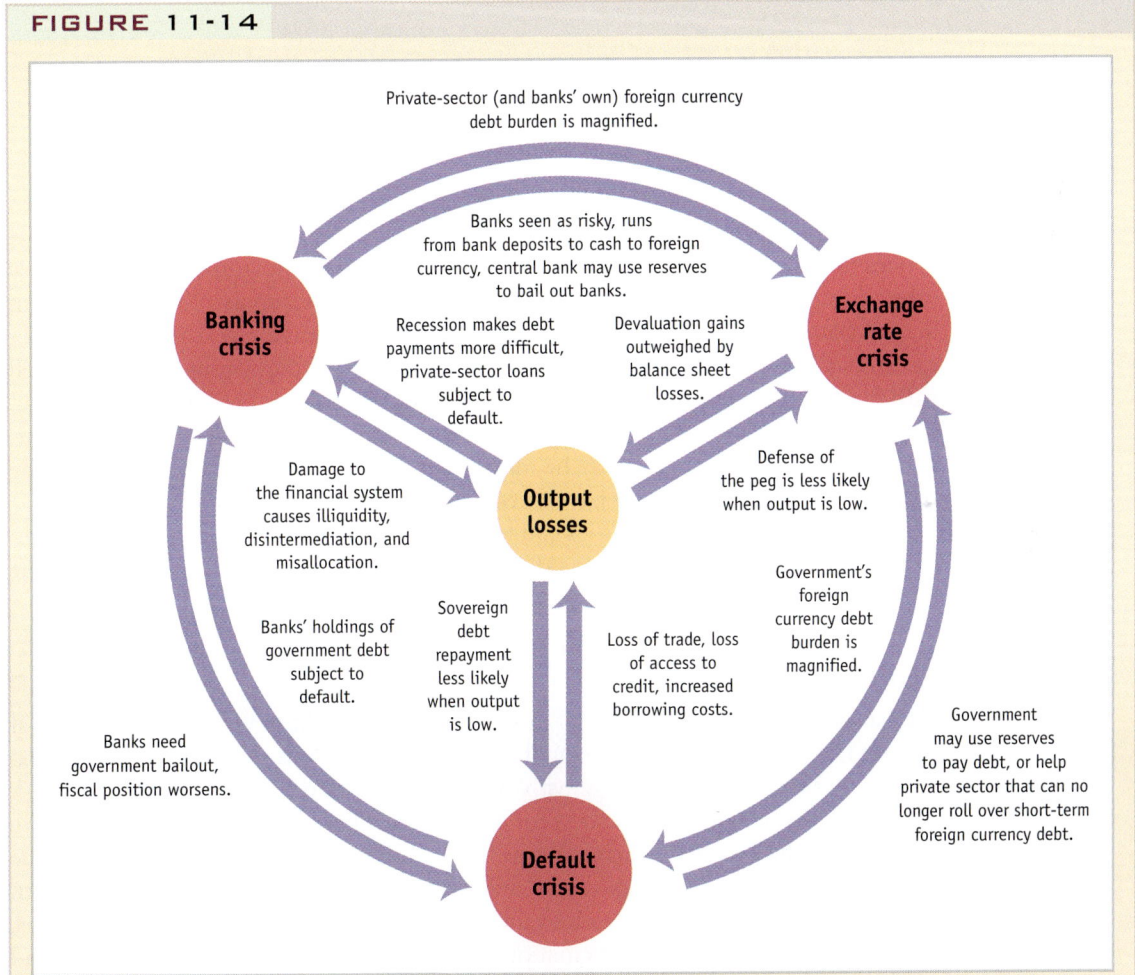

FIGURE 11-14

Vicious Circles in Twin and Triple Crises The chart shows that in developing countries and emerging markets there are complex feedback linkages between banking crises, default crises, and exchange rate crises. A depreciation magnifies foreign currency debt burdens, weakening the financial position of the government, private sector, and banks. A default weakens banks and cuts off foreign credit, leaving reserves as the only remaining buffer. A banking crisis can lead to costly bailouts, undermining either the government's fiscal position or the central bank's reserve. All three types of crisis can have serious output costs, which exacerbate the problem.

Source: Based on Bianca De Paoli, Glenn Hoggarth, and Victoria Saporta, 2006, "Costs of Sovereign Default," *Bank of England Quarterly Bulletin*, Fall.

TABLE 11-1

Costs of Sovereign Defaults, 1970–2000 Output losses can be very large after a default, as measured by deviation from trends. While a default-only crisis may be short and not costly, the more common twin and triple crises last much longer and have very high costs.

Type of Crisis	Number of Crises	Average Length (years)	Mean Cost per Year (% of GDP)
Default only	4	3	−1.0
Default and exchange rate crisis	13	5	10.3
Default and banking crisis	7	8	13.2
Triple crisis	21	10	21.7
All crises	45	8	15.1

Source: Bianca De Paoli, Glenn Hoggarth, and Victoria Saporta, "Costs of Sovereign Default," *Bank of England Quarterly Bulletin, Fall 2006.*

The consequences of default are therefore not pleasant. As Table 11-1 shows, when default crises occur *on their own*, there appear to be no costs; unfortunately, that applies in only 4 out of 45 cases, less than 10% of all defaults in the sample. In every other case, there is either a twin default/exchange rate crisis (13 cases), a twin default/banking crisis (7 cases), or a triple default/exchange rate/banking crisis (21 cases). In all these other cases (more than 90% of defaults), the output losses associated with the crisis are significant, measured by deviation from trend output growth: on average, around 15% of GDP per year for eight years. That is a large cost, even if comparisons with normal trends may be misleading, because it is difficult to estimate the costs that the countries would have faced had they not defaulted.[30]

To sum up, if financial penalties and legal action provide insufficient motives for repayment, there is reason to believe that many other costs of default exist that provide enough incentive for contingent debt repayment. ■

Conclusion

We have developed a simple model in which sovereign debt is a contingent claim that will not be paid in hard times. In equilibrium borrowers obtain consumption-smoothing via debt (a form of insurance against volatile consumption levels) at a price—the risk premium—that compensates lenders for default risk. The model is too simple to capture all aspects of the default problem, such as the tendency of borrowing to move in volatile cycles, and the scope for contagion and "animal spirits" in this asset market as in any other.

Nonetheless, the model provides valuable insights and leads us to deeper questions. For example, the model assumes that output volatility is the root cause of default, and we know that output volatility is high in poorer countries. But what is behind that? In

---

[30] That is to say, output may have fallen anyway because of the economic shocks that preceded the observed default. Obtaining more precise estimates of default costs remains a goal of ongoing research. See Eduardo Levy-Yeyati and Ugo Panizza, "The Elusive Costs of Sovereign Defaults," Research Department Working Paper 581, Inter-American Development Bank, November 2006.

some developing countries, it could be a result of commodity specialization, terms-of-trade shocks, climate, and other economic disturbances. Yet an alternative explanation might be the poor institutional framework in these countries, which is correlated with both low incomes and high volatility. Thus, the default problem may be, deep down, a reflection of poor institutions. Poor institutions may also be generating default at lower debt levels through nonvolatility channels: they may obscure financial transparency, generate weak property rights, prevent credit monitoring, encourage corruption and bribery, allow for the misuse of loans, lead politicians to focus on the short term (with risky overborrowing), and so on—all of which add to the risk premium, all else equal.

How did advanced countries eventually find a way to avoid these outcomes? Our model suggests that all countries want to default at some debt level, but for advanced countries, that level might be very high. Why? The model says it must be that the costs of default in such countries are much higher. There may be truth to this on two dimensions: economic and political. Economically, a sovereign default in an advanced country would wreck a highly developed financial system, whereas in poorer countries the very lack of financial sophistication probably keeps such costs lower. In addition, the political costs bite harder in advanced countries, in that a large, democratically empowered, and wealth-holding middle class is likely to punish governments that take such actions; in poorer countries, the political costs may be smaller if the losers are fewer or political accountability is weaker.

Every few years, in a tranquil time, some expert predicts that there will not be any more sovereign defaults. They can't be taken very seriously. History does suggest that many of the deep and intertwined underlying political-economy problems can be solved, but it may take an awfully long time for countries to overcome these impediments and emerge from the serial default club.[31]

APPLICATION

The Argentina Crisis of 2001–2002

In this section we focused on the problem of default. But we also emphasized (as in Figure 11-14) the feedback mechanisms at work in twin and triple crisis situations in which default crises, exchange rate crises, and banking crises may simultaneously occur. Just as in the case of self-fulfilling exchange rate crises (explained in the chapter on crises), these "vicious circles" may lead to self-fulfilling twin and triple crises where, as the economist Guillermo Calvo puts it, "If investors deem you unworthy, no funds will be forthcoming and, thus, unworthy you will be." In general, theory and empirical work suggest that bad fundamentals only make the problem of self-fulfilling crises worse, and disentangling the two causes can be difficult, leading to ongoing controversy over who or what is to blame for any given crisis. The Argentina crisis of 2001–2002 dramatically illustrates these problems.[32]

---

[31] Philip T. Hoffman, Gilles Postel-Vinay, and Jean-Laurent Rosenthal, 2007, *Surviving Large Losses: Financial Crises, the Middle Class, and the Development of Capital Markets* (Cambridge, MA: Harvard University Press).
[32] For further reading about the Argentine crisis, see Michael Mussa, 2002, *Argentina and the Fund: From Triumph to Tragedy* (Washington, D.C.: Institute for International Economics); Gerardo della Paolera and Alan Taylor, 2003, "Gaucho Banking Redux," *Economía*, 3(2), 1–42; Andrew Powell, 2003, "Argentina's Avoidable Crisis: Bad Luck, Bad Economics, Bad Politics, Bad Advice," in Susan M. Collins and Dani Rodrik eds., *Brookings Trade Forum 2002* (Washington, D.C.: The Brookings Institution), pp. 1–58; Paul Blustein, 2005, *And the Money Kept Rolling In (and Out): Wall Street, the IMF, and the Bankrupting of Argentina* (New York: Public Affairs).

Background Argentina successfully ended a hyperinflation in 1991 with the adoption of a rigidly fixed exchange rate system called the Convertibility Plan, and a 1-to-1 peg of the peso to the U.S. dollar. As we noted in Chapter 9, this system operated with high reserve backing ratios and (in theory) strict limits on central bank use of sterilization policy. The Convertibility Plan was a quasi currency board.

With a firm nominal anchor, Argentina's economy grew rapidly up to 1998, apart from a brief slowdown after the Mexican (Tequila) Crisis in 1994. The country was able to borrow large amounts at low-interest rates in the global capital market. The only troubling sign at this point was that despite boom conditions the government ran persistent deficits every year, increasing the public debt to GDP ratio. Most of this debt was held by foreigners, which increased Argentina's net external debt relative to GDP. Given the long-run budget constraints (for the government, and for the country) these deficits were unsustainable.

In 1997 crises in Asia were followed by increases in emerging market risk premiums, and these shocks were magnified by crises in 1998 in Russia and Brazil. The Brazil crisis also led to a slowdown and depreciation in one of Argentina's major trading partners. At the same time, the U.S. dollar started to appreciate, dragging the Argentina peso into a stronger position against all currencies. Higher interest rates, lower demand abroad, and an appreciated exchange rate put the Argentine economy into a recession.

Dive With these changes in external conditions, Argentina's macroeconomic regime started to unravel. The recession worsened an already bad fiscal situation. Because no surpluses had been run in the good times, there was no cushion in the government accounts, and the red ink grew. Public debt, which had been 41% of GDP in 1998, grew to 64% of GDP in 2001. Foreign creditors began to view these debt dynamics as possibly explosive and inconsistent with the long-run budget constraint, implying a risk of default. The creditors demanded higher interest rates for new loans and refinancings, which only increased the rate of debt explosion. Risk premiums on long-term government debt blew up, from 3%–4% in late 1997 to 7%–8% in late 2000.

The fiscal situation thus damaged the economy and the banking sector, as higher interest rates depressed aggregate demand in the short run, and caused a deterioration of banks' balance sheets (as loans went bad and other assets declined in value). This deterioration, in turn, made the fiscal situation worse, because in a recession tax revenues tend to fall and government social expenditures tend to rise. The government needed to borrow more, even as the lenders started to withdraw.

In addition, the situation posed a threat to the monetary regime and the Convertibility Plan. People were worried that if the government accounts worsened further, then all public credit would be turned off, and if the government were then unwilling to impose the austerity of spending cuts in midrecession, it would have had to finance the deficit using the inflation tax. Finally, even if the government did not use inflationary finance, it still might want to use temporary monetary policy autonomy to relieve the recession through a devaluation and lower interest rates, both of which would make the peg not credible. Either or both of these threats would expose the peg to the risk of a speculative attack.

In addition, people knew that if the banks got into trouble, they would need to call on the central bank to act as a lender of last resort, as they had in 1994 (when reserves had plummeted and a crisis was averted only by a last-minute lifeline from the IMF).

If people felt that their deposits would be safer in Miami or Montevideo, there would be a massive run from deposits to peso cash to dollars, overwhelming even the substantial foreign exchange reserves at the central bank.

Crash In 2001 all of these forces gathered in a perfect storm. Politically, fiscal compromise proved impossible between the two main political forces (the weak President Fernando de la Rúa of the Radical Party and the powerful Peronist provincial governors). The provinces collected and spent large amounts of national tax revenue and were not willing to make sacrifices to help de la Rúa, a political opponent. They gambled, correctly, that a crisis would bring them to power (even at the cost of destroying the country).

By mid-2001 private creditors had almost walked away from Argentina and the last-gasp effort involved a swap of short-term high interest rate debt for long-term *very high* interest rate debt, with an annual yield near 15%. Markets were unimpressed—this scheme bought a few months of breathing space on principal payments, but left Argentina with an even worse debt service problem down the road. Private lending dried up and despite a (noncredible) announcement of a zero deficit rule in July, the risk premium on government debt exploded, from 10% in June to 15% in August, and approached 20% in October. As the debt burden grew and the economy sank, we know from this chapter that default would be increasingly likely.

There was only one lender left now, the IMF. But they were increasingly as unimpressed with Argentina's policy shenanigans as everyone else. In a move that it doubted at the time and regretted soon thereafter, the IMF made one last big loan to Argentina in August 2001. The money was poured into the government's coffers and into the Central Bank's dwindling pot of reserves, but it didn't last very long.

The banks were in a parlous state. Economic conditions were raising the number of nonperforming loans anyway. But banks had also been coerced or persuaded that it would be a good idea for them to buy large amounts of the government's debt in 2001. This dollar debt carried a high interest rate, but was also risky, because of the possibility of default and/or exchange rate depreciation after a crisis. Depositors knew this and they also knew that banks would probably fail if the central bank and the government could not protect them.

The End The three crises were all now shaping up to happen, encouraged by output contractions, consistent with the "vicious circle" dynamics shown in Figure 11-14. The final act came in November. The IMF concluded that the economy was not being turned around by any of the policies in place and that further loans were therefore a waste of time unless Argentina made radical adjustments, including considering the possibilities of devaluing, defaulting, and even dollarizing. The government would have none of it, and when the IMF announced no more credit, the public knew the game was up, and seeking to put their assets in a safe haven, they started a massive run on the banks. To stem the flow, the government imposed capital controls (*corralito*) to stop such activity, and also froze the majority of bank deposits.

This triggered a political explosion, violence and unrest, and within days de la Rúa was history, airlifted from the Casa Rosada by helicopter. His numerous successors over the following weeks initiated a default on the public debt (the world's biggest-ever default at the time) and allowed the exchange rate to float (it fell to 4 pesos to the dollar very quickly). The private sector was awash with unserviceable dollar liabilities, so the government "pesified" them, causing utter chaos in the courts and grave economic uncertainty. The banks were barely functional for several months, and the savings of many Argentines vanished. Taxes were raised and government spending cut. The economy went from a bad recession to total meltdown, amid scenes of previously unimaginable poverty and deprivation.

Argentina's policies were inconsistent. When the government chose a fixed exchange rate, it had to accept its pros and cons, including the risk of larger recessions when external conditions were unfavorable. But they also had to accept that a fixed exchange rate ruled out the inflation tax and placed limits on the lender of last resort capacity of a central bank faced with capital flight. Such concerns would not have been as important if the country had kept its fiscal policy in check and maintained access to credit, but in 2001 the country simply had no more room for maneuver. ■

Postscript As of 2007, there had been no major crisis since 2001, world economic conditions had been fairly benign, and many countries had built up large exchange reserves. This led many observers to call into question the need for the IMF, given its perceived failings in the 1997–2001 crises, and the small size of its lending capabilities in the face of growing private sector financial flows. On the other hand, international economic crises have been around for a very long time, so to more seasoned observers, it seemed a little premature for some to be calling for dismantling the only emergency service we have (see **Headlines: Is the IMF "Pathetic"?**). They were proved right when during and after the global financial crisis in 2008, the IMF was called to the scene of many macroeconomic accidents, including in several so-called advanced countries, to provide rescue funding.

4 The Global Macroeconomy and the 2007–2009 Crisis

The **Global Financial Crisis** of 2007–2009 and the associated **Great Recession** constitute one of the most significant global macroeconomic events of modern history. Even now, when the full implications are as yet unclear, we may anticipate that when these times are assessed by economic historians in the distant future, they will probably rank in the memory not far behind such momentous events as the 1930s Great Depression. And already, looking only to the very near future, in terms of the economic damage created, the current recessions will not be forgotten quickly by our generation of households, firms, banks, or governments, all of whom have been affected by the downturn, and many of whom have endured serious suffering.

In this section of the chapter, we look at the crisis using the tools of international macroeconomics developed throughout this book. We begin by looking at the origins of the crisis not only in events of the previous decade, but also as part of longer-term trends in the U.S. and global economies. We then look at the Great Recession itself, how events unfolded, and what we can learn about the economic shocks and policy responses. Next, we look at how the global economy can recover from this shock, a process that was under way, but still fragile and with a long way to go as this chapter was written in late 2010.

Macroeconomists have much to learn from the crisis. Some key macro-financial and policy issues have been known about since the early 1800s, but they had been ignored or forgotten by many economists, and more future research is likely to focus on these important issues.

HEADLINES

Is the IMF "Pathetic"?

The IMF is the closest thing to a global lender of last resort. When times are calm, it may be tempting to think of abolishing the institution. As this precrisis column pointed out, to have done so would have been a remarkably complacent idea.

Meral Karasulu did what any seasoned International Monetary Fund staffer would do: She grinned and, for the umpteenth time, listened to suggestions that the institution was to blame for the 1997 Asian financial crisis.

"Thank you for your question," she replied to an audience member at a May 14 EuroMoney conference in Seoul. Then, she launched into a defense of the IMF's actions.

As the IMF's representative in South Korea, Karasulu is used to the drill. After all, many Koreans routinely refer to the "IMF crisis." It's a reminder that a decade after Asia's turmoil, the IMF is still explaining itself wherever it goes.

Three weeks after the Seoul conference, there was similar griping at an event I attended in Buenos Aires. The mood had barely changed since March 2005, when President Nestor Kirchner scored points with many of Argentina's 40 million people by calling the IMF "pathetic." He has been demanding that the institution stop criticizing the Latin American country.

Korea and Argentina have little in common. Yet Korea is among the nations stockpiling currency reserves to avoid having to go to the IMF for a bailout ever again. Argentina, meanwhile, continues to tout the end of its IMF-backed program last year as an economic victory.

This column isn't a defense of the IMF's actions during the Asian crisis or Argentina's in the early 2000s. The Washington-based fund has a small army of well-compensated people to do that. And the IMF has had its fair share of blunders, including telling Asian countries to tighten fiscal policy during a crisis.

Yet all this talk of IMF irrelevance is overdone. What's more, the chatter suggests the creation of a new bubble called complacency.

"It's ironic to my mind that people say the fund isn't needed anymore because nothing in the global financial system is broken at the moment," John Lipsky, the IMF's first deputy managing director, said in an interview last month in Tokyo. "It strikes me we are trying to anticipate and prepare for when things may go wrong again.". . .

Sure, Asia has insulated itself from markets with trillions of dollars of currency reserves. The IMF's phones may be ringing off the hook if China's economy hits a wall, the U.S. dollar plunges, the so-called yen-carry trade blows up, a major terrorist attack occurs, oil prices approach $100 a barrel or some unexpected event roils world markets.

The thing is, the IMF and its Bretton Woods sister institution, the World Bank, have scarcely been more necessary. How efficient and cost-effective they are is debatable; what's not is that today's global economy needs the buffering role that both of them play. . . .

The IMF was never set up to play the role it did during crises in Mexico, Asia and Russia in the 1990s and turmoil in Latin America since then. Even so, it will be called upon the instant a crisis in one country spreads to another. As imperfect as the IMF is, the world needs the economic equivalent of a fire brigade when markets plunge.

There's much chatter about how global prosperity is reducing the need for billion-dollar IMF bailouts. As of March, IMF lending had shriveled to $11.8 billion from a peak of $81 billion in 2004. A single nation, Turkey, accounted for about 75 percent of the IMF's portfolio.

Isn't that a good thing? The IMF is like a paramedic: You hope you won't need one, but it's great that one is just a phone call away. Plenty of things could still go awry and necessitate a call to the IMF. . . .

Complacency looms large in today's world. All too many investors think the good times are here to stay and all too many governments are ignoring their imbalances for similar reasons. . . .

All this means that, far from being irrelevant, the IMF may be in for a very busy couple of years.

Source: Extract from William Pesek, "Is IMF 'Pathetic' or Just Awaiting Next Crisis?" bloomberg.net, June 12, 2007.

Backdrop to the Crisis

Several features of the precrisis global economy can help us understand some of the calamitous events that were to follow. Keep in mind, however, that the benefits of hindsight should not cause us to underestimate the difficulties observers had in understanding these developments as they were unfolding at the time. Although a number of these trends were recognized by some observers as problematic, opinions were split as to whether any one of these issues was serious enough to justify any corrective action prior to the crisis.

Preconditions for the Crisis The global financial crisis was primarily a story of investments turned bad; that is, of savings unwisely allocated. To get a sense of what fueled the boom and bust cycle, it is worth asking where those savings materialized at a global and macroeconomic level and where they ended up.

As we saw in the chapter on crises, a large source of global saving in the ten years prior to the crisis was the group of *emerging market* (EM) countries that consistently ran surpluses on their current accounts, as their investment rates (quite high) were consistently exceeded by their saving rates (even higher). Because the world as a whole has to have a current account equal to zero, these EM surpluses had to be offset by equal and opposite *developed market* (DM) current account deficits, as shown in Figure 11-15, panel (a). Given their sheer size, the largest surplus and deficit countries—China and the United States, respectively—often came to dominate the discussion, but when we adjust for country size, the trends were much broader than that. Most EMs ran significant current account surpluses (along with some DMs like Japan and Germany) and many DMs ran current account deficits of a size comparable to or exceeding those in the United States (e.g., the United Kingdom, Spain, Ireland, Portugal, and Greece).

This unusual situation soon drew the attention of economists and policy makers, and began to generate its own vocabulary. The unidirectional flow from EM to DM was referred to as the problem of **global imbalances;** the high level of savings in the EMs that was a part of it was referred to as the **savings glut.** Because real interest rates had fallen in this era, analysts recognized that even if the global level of savings supply and investment demand had risen in parallel, the fall in interest rates suggested that, on net, it was an increase in the supply of savings (relative to investment demand) that had upset the global equilibrium. What were the causes and consequences of this shift? To understand the causes, we need to assess policies in the EM economies where the flows originated; to grasp the consequences, we need to focus on the DM economies where the funds were put to use.

On the EM side, at the broadest level, economists understand the dramatic increase in savings after 1997 as a conscious act of self-insurance. Many of these countries (especially those in Asia) had been very high saving societies for many, many years, and much of this was private saving. However, the new twist was the rapid increase in public (government) saving. As we saw in the balance of payments chapter, holding fixed private saving and investment, an increase in government saving necessarily sends the current account toward more surplus. Why did governments want to save? As we saw in the chapter on crises, and even in the introduction to macroeconomics, EM countries pay a high economic and political cost for crises. This outcome became painfully clear in the 1990s, starting with the Mexican crisis of 1994, but the lesson was rammed home by the chaos in Asian economies unleashed by the 1997 crisis, when currencies collapsed, deep recessions took hold, and governments were overturned when access to external financing dried up.

Looking back on those bleak times and on the inability of private capital markets or multilateral agencies such as the IMF to offer financial help that was both constructive and sufficient, many EM policy makers reached two key conclusions. First, they knew that they did not want to be the next Suharto, the Indonesian president humiliated by having to do the bidding of the IMF in exchange for funding; and they knew that to

FIGURE 11-15

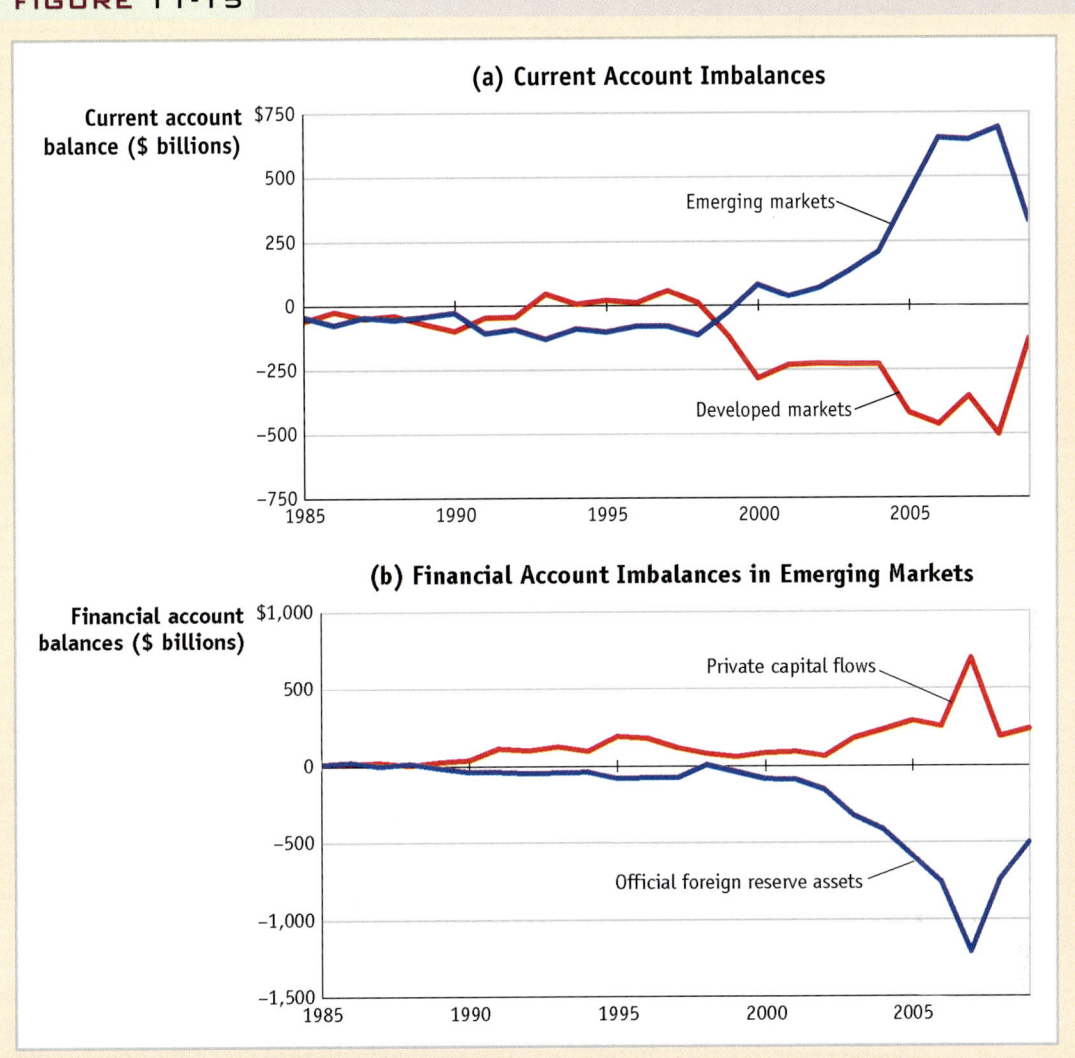

Global Imbalances and Their Composition Panel (a) shows that the chronic current account deficits of developed markets were offset by chronic surpluses in emerging markets. Looking just at the emerging markets, panel (b) shows that the emerging markets' financial accounts were in deficit because of massive official foreign reserve accumulation, offset somewhat by private capital flows.

Sources: IMF and Haver.

avoid being put in that position, they would have to take responsibility for their own financial security and, instead of relying on access to borrowed funds, would instead have to build up a war chest of liquid savings that could be drawn down in the event of a crisis.

The private sectors in EM countries also learned and made some changes to their behavior after the 1990s crises: For example, there was typically a shift toward less borrowing in foreign currency to reduce the liability dollarization problem that we noted in the chapter on global financialization as one of the peculiar risks for EM countries. However, the first-order change was the step taken by EM policy makers to begin a large, concerted accumulation of public external assets in their central bank or treasury accounts. That is, there was an increase in the purchase of official foreign assets as recorded in the Official Settlements Balance of the balance of payments (described in the BOP chapter). In balance of payments terms, these large-scale imports of official assets by EMs was their Financial Account counterpart to their large Current Account (CA) surpluses, as seen in Figure 11-15, panel (b).

Thus, official capital was flowing from EM to DM economies. Indeed, the official savings were so large as to dwarf the private sector capital flows that were generally moving in the opposite direction, from DM and into EM. On net, as some described it, capital was flowing *uphill* from poor to rich countries, an outcome viewed as perverse by some observers because once might generally expect capital to flow *downhill* from rich to poor countries, given the need for poor countries to invest to finance growth and economic development. As we saw in the chapter on the gains from financial globalization, economists had identified many reasons (summed up in the catch-all term "productivity") to explain why capital might not flow from rich to poor countries. But there was a new development in the first decade of the new century: the flows had not simply stopped, they had reversed! As we have argued, however, this change might have been for good reason.

What impact did these flows have on the rich DM countries? First let us note that although the EM economies were largely engaged in the purchase of official assets like U.S. Treasuries, the effect of the massive purchase programs was felt in all credit markets. Buying a large amount of U.S. government debt bids down the yield on that debt (as the prices of the bonds are bid up). A result is that other holders of Treasuries now decide, on the margin, that they don't find the asset so attractive anymore, and they seek higher returns from other assets. This change in portfolio balance lowers yields on other forms of debt such as corporate debt, loans, mortgages, and so on. This large flow of EM savings thus created a large wave of liquid funds in global capital markets seeking profitable investment opportunities, and allowing borrowers access to capital on some of the most generous terms that had been seen in a very long time.

This "quest for yield" could, in principle, have been benign. That is, on the face of it, access to a large flow of credit on extremely favorable terms sounds like a fantastically beneficial opportunity for the DM economies: What's not to like? However, behind that view is the assumption that given such an increase in economic opportunities, DM economies would use the funds wisely, with due regard to the risk and return on each project. In theory, good investments would be supported and the benefits realized from those investments (the marginal product of capital) would be positive and high enough to exceed the real costs of borrowing. In other words, if the financial systems of the world, and particularly those in the DM economies, had been efficient in their allocation of such capital flows, and if all projects by private or public borrowers had been a wise use of funds, then all would have been well.

Unfortunately, such an outcome, often assumed in theory, is not guaranteed in practice. Many observers of emerging economies, and of the deeper history of the developed countries, were acutely aware of this possibility because they had seen repeated episodes of credit booms and busts that ended in tears for developing economies. These busts usually led to some combination of banking/currency/default crises, as we saw in the earlier chapters on crises. These observers saw that the DM countries now risked a similar fate, as the decade of the 2000s witnessed the expansion of credit in developed economies rise to a level not seen before in the entire recorded history of financial capitalism, as revealed by the trends shown in Figure 11-16.

FIGURE 11-16

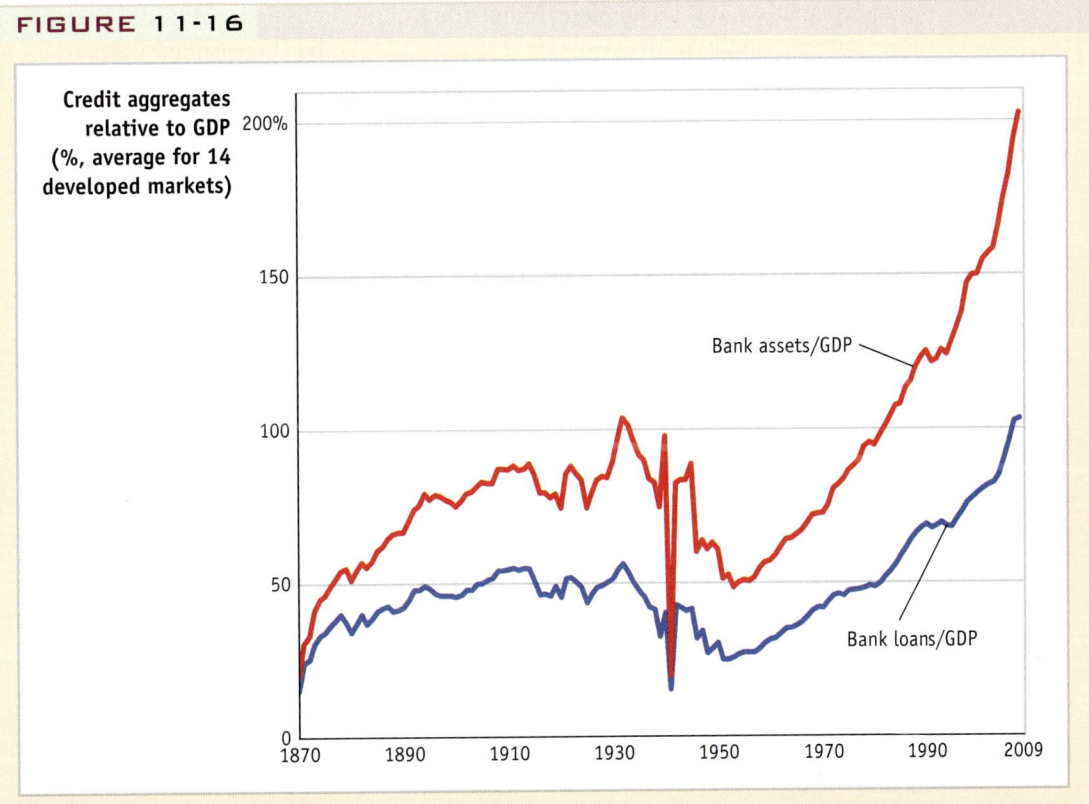

Developed Market Credit Trends over 140 Years This chart shows average data for fourteen developed markets since 1870. The ratio of bank loans and total bank assets to GDP was stable in the early twentieth century and fell during the 1930s following the Great Depression. In the postwar period these ratios surpassed their previous peaks around 1980 and kept on growing as modern economies built their economic model around more and more debt.

Source: Moritz Schularick and Alan M. Taylor, 2009. "Credit Booms Gone Bust: Monetary Policy, Leverage Cycles and Financial Crises, 1870–2008," NBER Working Papers 15512.

The view that the DM world could absorb these savings and put them to good use, and do so at ever higher levels of debt, depended on a particularly presumptive, some might say arrogant, view that despite the lessons from emerging economies, somehow the developed economies were "different." The DM optimists' argument could be summed up along the following lines: "Sure, those rather backward emerging countries with all their political problems and unsophisticated financial systems are inevitably going to have banking crises now and then and all the resulting problems, but we'll never see that sort of thing here, because we are developed, and that sort of thing doesn't happen to us anymore." A period of relatively stable economic performance in the 1990s and early 2000s lent support to the claim that even if occasional financial shocks hit the economy, policy makers had developed the tools needed to contain such problems and ensure that this "Great Moderation" of the business cycle could continue. However, for a few skeptical observers (including, notably, the economists at the Bank for International Settlements), this attitude appeared overconfident, and it was soon exposed as such in a rather spectacular way.

Exacerbating Policies and Distortions The discussion of the longer-run forces behind capital flows from DM to EM countries provides a backdrop to the crisis, but as an explanation, it is incomplete. Many other questions remain. Why did these flows accelerate so rapidly in the years 2004 to 2007? Why did these capital flows result in such poor economic outcomes in places as diverse as the United States, Ireland, Latvia, or Greece? Was the problem generated by failures in economic policy making and regulation, or was it primarily a result of mistakes by market participants themselves? At the time of writing, these remain contested issues, but we can summarize some of the more influential and persuasive viewpoints.

- Some observers believe that monetary policies in the EM economies, particularly China and other Asian economies, made the problem worse by pursuing a policy of deliberately **undervalued exchange rates.** This policy promoted an overly rapid, export-led growth strategy highly dependent on the Western (mainly U.S.) consumer being willing to go deeper into debt to purchase a growing supply of manufactured goods. However, it is hard to find robust evidence that, given their stage of development, these economies' exchange rates were drastically out of line with normal historical or cross-country levels. These countries might just have been saving more for the precautionary reasons noted above.

- Some argue that much of the blame for the crisis resides with monetary policy makers in the DM economies, and especially the **too-easy monetary policy** of the U.S. Federal Reserve. These critics feel that under former Chairman Alan Greenspan, the Fed kept interest rates too low for too long in the period after the 9/11 terrorist attacks. These low interest rates encouraged lending across all credit markets at a time when the wave of savings from EMs hit the system, and facilitated bubbles at least in some places (e.g., the California and Florida housing markets). A similar argument can be leveled at the European Central Bank, which also pursued rates that were "too low" for some euro member countries where similar bubbles were ignited (e.g., Ireland and Spain). However, it can be argued that the Fed was following its legal dual mandate of low inflation and high employment, with no sign of failure on either target. It can also be argued that a low interest rate policy should not necessarily compromise a good financial system's ability to do proper credit risk evaluation.

- Others would argue that the problem was a **failure of regulation and supervision** in that the Fed, the ECB, the Bank of England, and countless other central banks, as well as national regulatory bodies and lawmakers, simply allowed the financial systems to run out of control. This process had much deeper roots, going back to the trend toward financial deregulation seen around the world since the 1970s. This view is supported by the telling observation that under the more stringent regulatory regimes created after the 1930s disaster (e.g., legislation such as the U.S. Glass-Steagall Act, and more proactive regulators employing stricter standards), no developed country witnessed any banking crises whatsoever from 1945 to 1970. A slightly different take would argue that regulations did not shift, so much as they were simply outpaced by the scale of financial innovation, which both allowed the system to take on greater risks through new products (e.g., the securitization of credit with a reliance on rating agencies and the use of unregulated derivatives) and to expand so much as to create large, complex, "too big to fail" (or in some countries "too big to save") banks. Either way, regulators share some of the blame either for relaxing rules too much or not keeping up with the times.

- Some analysts believe that **government failure** is to blame because governments distorted private incentives in various ways, over and above any impact of easy monetary policies noted above. For example, in the United States, the government gave implicit backing to quasi-official organizations like Fannie Mae and Freddie Mac, which purchased or guaranteed large shares of the mortgage market, and ended up effectively bankrupt. The government was also seen as offering implicit backstops to many "too big to fail" banks. When this happens, the implicit insurance incentivizes people to take too much risk, knowing that they will be bailed out of some or all losses, a problem known as *moral hazard*. Similar concerns arose about European banks, which in some countries were larger than those in the United States, and even more leveraged when the crisis struck. In addition, the central banks stood accused of offering some kind of similar downside protection, by seeming to declare, when asked, that their doctrine concerning asset price bubbles was not to pop them or lean against them, but rather to wait for them to collapse and then step in to fix any problems. Yet against these points, it could be noted that large swathes of credit market excess—indeed, the majority—flowed through channels quite distant from the government's reach, and that ex post, whatever the perceived bailouts the bankers thought they might get, in practice most of those exposed found themselves with a lot of "skin in the game," of which they lost a great deal (or, in the case of Lehman Brothers and many other entities around the world, almost all of it).

- Many other observers see widespread evidence of **market failure,** in which irrational investors, herding, imperfect information, and asymmetric information all created serious inefficiencies in financial systems. According to this view, which is hundreds of years old, the financial markets are capable of sustained bouts of euphoria followed by revulsion, a kind of mood swing where investors switch from being willing to take on lots of risk, only to then switch quickly to avoid the same risks, an oscillation between greed and fear that has no real connection to market fundamentals and that creates unnecessary and unwelcome volatility in the economy. Yet even if this view often looks persuasive after the fact, spotting the bubble or the imminent crisis beforehand is a very different matter: even if we can now agree that there was a U.S. housing bubble, as it unfolded, it took an awfully long time for more than just a few observers to voice their concerns.

Summary History shows that economies based on financial capitalism have experienced banking crises throughout the modern era. This is true whether one is speaking of developed markets or emerging markets, with the possible exception of a brief interlude of calm during the financially repressed post-1945 era, as shown in Figure 11-17. However, as the financial sector was deregulated in the last three or four decades, it regrouped and expanded, and we have once again found ourselves in what is, to the economic historian, if not the economist, a very familiar place characterized by periodic episodes of financial instability. With some success, policy makers mitigated some of these shocks, but after credit and leverage grew to unprecedented levels, there came a shock so large that it defied control and sent the world economy into the most severe slump since the 1930s Great Depression.

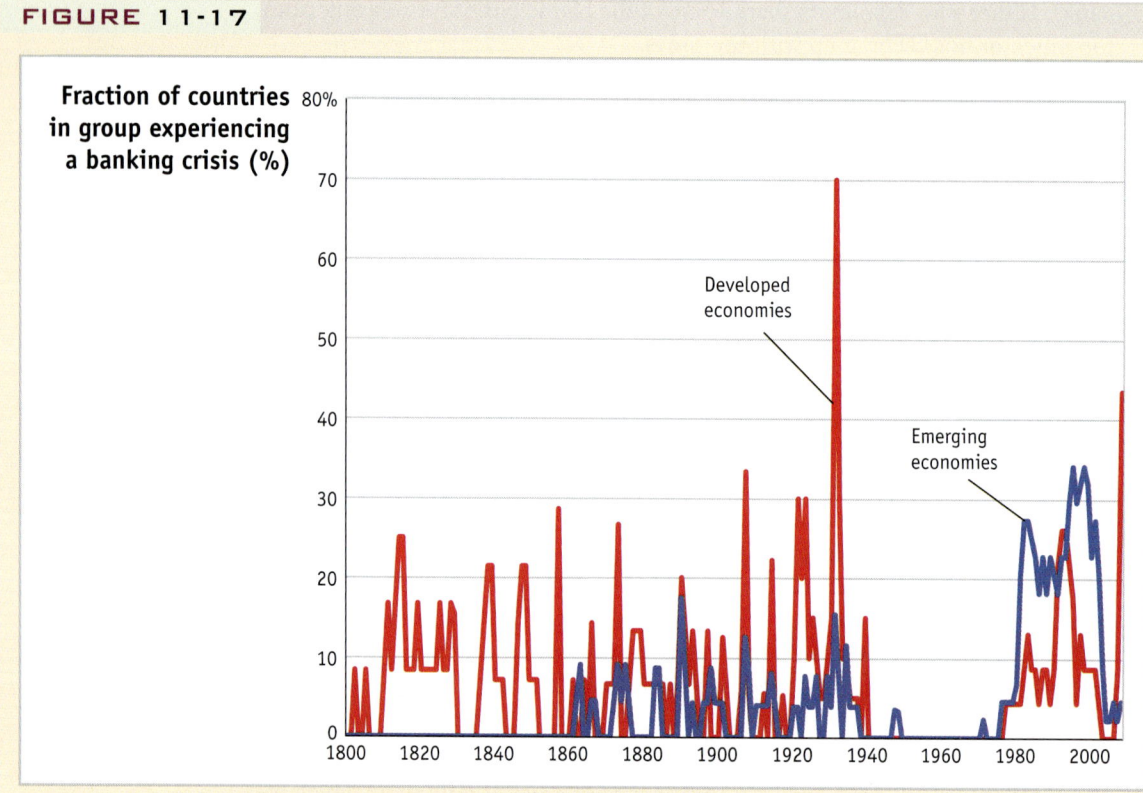

Banking Crises in History This chart tracks the frequency of banking crises each year in both developed (high-income) and emerging (middle- to low-income) economies.

Source: Rong Qian, Carmen M. Reinhart, and Kenneth S. Rogoff, 2011. "On Graduation from Default, Inflation and Banking Crises: Elusive or Illusion?" NBER Macroconomics Annual 2010. Forthcoming.

Panic and the Great Recession

In 2007 the Global Financial Crisis started to unfold quickly from a latent set of risks into a massive catastrophe that would wreak havoc on the global economy for the next several years (see the timeline in Table 11-2).

Like almost all financial crashes seen over the course of modern economic history, some particular event triggered a flight from risk to safety in capital markets. In this case, the trigger was a deterioration in the perceived quality of U.S. residential mortgages. As house price appreciation stalled and delinquencies rose in 2006 and 2007, problems quickly became evident in the newly expanded and risky subprime sector. Similar stresses also erupted in the financial and housing markets in other countries such as the United Kingdom and Ireland.

The losses were centered on major financial institutions in the United States and overseas including commercial banks (some of the very largest like Citibank or Bank of America in the United States, and RBS in the United Kingdom), investment banks (which held some of the mortgage risk), and insurance companies (like AIG, which had provided lucrative but ultimately underpriced default insurance policies on many mortgage products that it was ill-equipped to honor).

TABLE 11-2

Timeline for the Global Financial Crisis This table highlights key events in the 2007–2010 period.

Date	U.S. events	Rest of world events
2007	Housing price declines becoming evident in the United States, distress in subprime mortgages as losses revealed (failure of New Century Financial, April; losses at Bear Stearns, June/July, etc.), economy slows and enters recession; credit spreads widen; stock market falls; by the year's end the Fed is easing and has started its first special programs (Term Auction Facility; swap lines with some foreign central banks).	Weakness in other housing markets (e.g. Ireland) and slowing of economic growth; run on the bank at Northern Rock (U.K.) and government guarantees all deposits; BNP Paribas suffers losses (August); stocks start to fall everywhere.
Early 2008	Failure of Bear Stearns investment bank (taken over by J.P. Morgan with Fed support); more Fed facilities and expanded swap lines.	Recession spreads to Europe.
Summer 2008	FannieMae and FreddieMac (U.S. government housing agencies) get Treasury credit lines; IndyMac bank fails; widespread mortgage distress evident; creditworthiness of banks and other financial entities decline since much of mortgage risk is dispersed via securitization.	Distress in several European banks exposed to same mortgage risk is dispersed via securitization.
September–December 2008	Full financial panic starts; FannieMae and FreddieMac go into government conservatorship; Failure of Lehman Brothers investment bank (bankruptcy) and takeover of Merrill Lynch (by Bank of America); failure of AIG insurance company, supported by Fed; Reserve Primary money market fund shares "break the buck"; Washington Mutual and Wachovia banks taken over in distress; start of extraordinary financial sector support by Fed and US Treasury (TARP plan changed from toxic asset purchases to capital injections; money market fund guarantees; Fed buys mortgage-backed securities); extra support for megabanks Bank of America and Citigroup; stock market collapses further.	Bank failures in several countries (RBS, Lloyds TSB and some UK building societies; Fortis, Dexia, ING, German regional banks, etc.). Government of Ireland guarantees all of its bank debt. Global stock market collapse and general financial panic everywhere, flight to safe assets and to the U.S. dollar until March 2010.
2009	Large fiscal stimulus program ($700 billion over 3 years). Stock market bottoms in March, at less than half its previous peak; credit crisis continues; unemployment rises to 10%. Fed starts QE program. Massive government support to auto industry. Banks subject to stress tests and begin recapitalization.	Europe and Japan in recession. Recession in developed markets turns out to be largest since 1930s. Variety of fiscal stimulus measures, longer term monetary easing. But emerging markets suffer no banking/currency/default crises and quickly recover, notably China and India, but also Brazil.
2010	U.S. recovery remains sluggish, especially in midyear. Unemployment remains near 10% and inflation falls to near 1%. Fed begins QE2 program in the fall, with no prospect for any further fiscal stimulus.	Core Europe recovering, strongly in Germany; UK pursuing strong austerity; European peripherals in grip of debt deflation, unemployment, budget deficits and exploding debt. Both Greece and Ireland take EU-IMF rescue packages. Midyear bank stress tests not so rigorous (no sovereign stress) and bank recapitalization slow. Intra-EU tensions over who should absorb losses in current and future crises.

A Very Modern Bank Run Once the problems of bad mortgages had spread, and given the very thin (some would later say, too thin) capitalization of the financial system in general, it became very difficult not only for outsiders to borrow from banks, but also for banks to borrow from outsiders and from each other. People feared that banks might end up unable to repay their loans. With one or two exceptions, deposit runs were mostly avoided thanks to deposit insurance. But in today's economy banks also fund themselves by short-term loans, and it was these funding facilities that shrank in size, or became prohibitively expensive, when the creditworthiness of banks came into question.

This inability to borrow had the same effect as a run on deposits: banks had to shrink their balance sheets and scramble for liquid funds to fill the funding gap left by their inability to borrow. To free up and conserve cash, they had to stop making new loans and/or allow old loans to "roll off" their books. They also had to sell their securities starting with the most liquid, but as the crisis took its toll, they then had to sell more illiquid assets (such as hard-to-value mortgages and derivatives) into collapsing markets at what would later turn out to have been "fire sale" prices precipitated by the usual lack of buyers in a panic. Because the banks were taking steep losses not only on their loan books but also now on securities, their capital was soon depleted. As their share values fell, many banks were on the edge of bankruptcy. Several huge banks, including the investment banks Bear Stearns and Lehman Brothers and retail banks such as Washington Mutual, either failed outright or were bought in a takeover for pennies. In September 2008 it would be fair to say that the financial systems in the United States and all over the world were plagued with a banking panic of a magnitude not seen since the early 1930s.

Financial Decelerators As always, the financial crisis had the effect of depressing real economic activity, through the so-called financial accelerator mechanism (or in this case, decelerator). Much of business depends on a reliable financial system to fund day-to-day activities and the massive problems in the financial system added a real friction to the economy. Also, when wealth is destroyed by a panic, the impaired households and firms tend to rebuild their wealth by saving to pay off liabilities or accumulate assets, thus dampening the demand for goods and services. Lost wealth also impedes access to credit, making recovery slower than it otherwise would be. In 2008 and 2009 there was also policy uncertainty as authorities in the United States and throughout the world tried to devise a sequence of monetary, financial, and fiscal policies to stem the crisis.

A curious side effect of the crisis was the effect on the dollar and the unusually high spread between U.S. government interest rates and private sector interest rates: At the height of panic, investors sought out U.S. dollar assets as a safe haven (a typical experience for a reserve currency). This caused the dollar to appreciate markedly and the yields on U.S. government bills to approach zero. That is to say, risk premiums became endemic in all currency and asset markets, not just in emerging countries, and these forces rather than, say, policy interest rates became for a while the major drivers of market rates and currency values.

The End of the World Was Nigh It took until March 2009 for the collapse of U.S. stock markets to end (the S&P 500 Index hit a low point of 666). By this time three of the big five U.S. specialist investment banks had failed or been taken over and a $700 billion bank recapitalization scheme had been created by the U.S. Treasury in fits and starts during the last days of the Bush administration and the first days of the Obama administration. Confidence in the ability of the economic and financial situation to recover was low, to put it mildly. Bank recapitalization projects took shape in other countries, too (the United Kingdom took the lead on this front), and a greater sense of calm was restored by the April 2009 G-20 summit in London, at which a united front of global leaders pledged greater support and cooperation. Fiscal policy makers had by then stepped in with large-scale stimulus plans in most countries (see Table 11-3) and monetary policy had been eased everywhere, in many countries all the way down to zero interest rates. Credit was still tight, but for those who could get it, costs had fallen. Despite fears of a return to 1930s-style protectionism, world trade policies stayed open, thanks in part to countries' commitments to and oversight by the WTO, and trade volumes started to pick up.

As these efforts took hold, the freefall of the world economy halted, and trends in GDP and trade, which had been diving along trajectories eerily similar to those seen after 1929, hit bottom. But by now the economic costs of the financial meltdown had reached unfathomable heights (see Figure 11-18 for U.S. evidence).

TABLE 11-3

Discretionary Fiscal Policies in the Great Recession After the crisis, as output growth slowed or turned negative, many countries increased government spending or cut taxes to try to provide additional macroeconomic stimulus. The table shows data on discretionary fiscal stimulus measures for the G-20 taken in 2008–2010 relative to a 2007 baseline, as a percent of GDP.

	2008	2009	2010
Argentina	0.0	1.5	—
Australia	0.7	2.1	1.7
Brazil	0.0	0.6	0.8
Canada	0.0	1.9	1.7
China	0.4	3.1	2.7
France	0.0	0.7	0.8
Germany	0.0	1.6	2.0
India	0.6	0.6	0.6
Indonesia	0.0	1.3	0.6
Italy	0.0	0.2	0.1
Japan	0.3	2.4	1.8
Korea	1.1	3.9	1.2
Mexico	0.0	1.5	—
Russia	0.0	4.1	1.3
Saudi Arabia	2.4	3.3	3.5
South Africa	1.7	1.8	−0.6
Turkey	0.0	0.8	0.3
United Kingdom	0.2	1.4	−0.1
United States	1.1	2.0	1.8
G-20 PPP-GDP weighted average	0.5	2.0	1.5
G-20 discretionary impulse	0.5	1.5	−0.5

Source: IMF, "Update on Fiscal Stimulus and Financial Sector Measures," April 26, 2009.

FIGURE 11-18

FIGURE 11-18 Continued

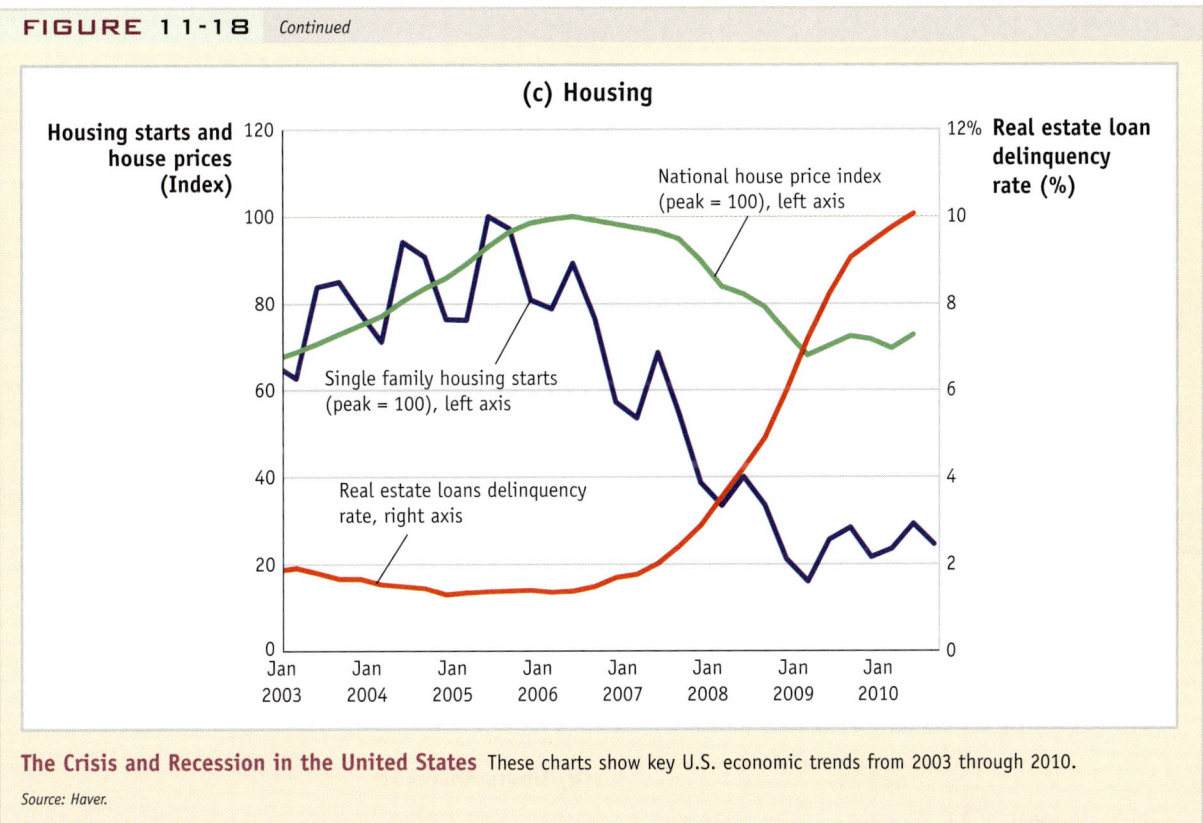

The Crisis and Recession in the United States These charts show key U.S. economic trends from 2003 through 2010.

Source: Haver.

Despite initial concerns, it was not the actual direct costs of financial bailouts that were the main problem. In the United States, the terms obtained in the depths of the crisis were so favorable that taxpayers made a small profit; in other countries, such as the United Kingdom, and especially Ireland, the costs to the public purse of bailing out the banks were huge. Instead, the main problem would be that in the United States and elsewhere output was 5% or more below capacity and unemployment near to or above 10%, conditions that were likely to persist for years. In terms of lost output and employment, this was to be the worst U.S. and global slump in 80 years. In terms of the massive lost tax revenues for governments, along with some much smaller increases in spending, this event had blown a large hole in the fiscal stability of many developed countries that is likely to last for decades. In some cases the economic crisis brought to question the very solvency of the government itself. Thus, as history has shown time and again, a banking crisis can quickly mutate into a sovereign debt crisis as governments, to try to prop up the system, socialize the losses of the financial system at significant fiscal cost.

Europe As the crisis wore on, and recovery started, the full extent of the shock and the policy responses varied in different countries. One of the most striking examples of divergence was the experience of the Eurozone during this episode. The traditional core countries of the Eurozone, especially Germany, managed to escape quite lightly, even though their banking systems had been infected by U.S. toxic assets. Deep trouble was brewing on the periphery of Europe, however (see Figure 11-19).

FIGURE 11-19

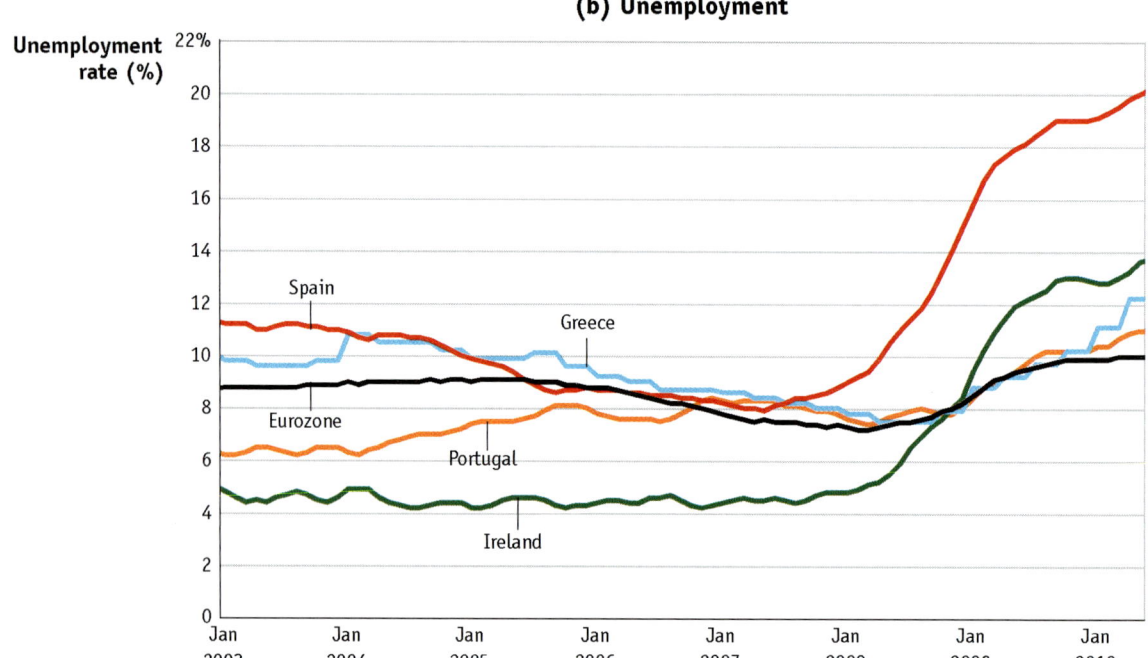

The Crisis and Recession in the Eurozone These charts show key Eurozone economic trends from 2003 through 2010, with an emphasis on the four peripheral countries: Portugal, Ireland, Greece, and Spain.

Source: Haver.

In Ireland a large property boom went bust and the banking system was at risk of collapse. All these potential losses were rather hastily absorbed by the government in September 2008, but their eventual size grew to about half of GDP in late 2010 (still unclear and growing at the time of writing), and the necessary fiscal adjustment, already austere, had to be tightened even further. Despite these efforts, Ireland was seen by markets to be at an elevated risk of default. The use of monetary policy to boost the economy was not an option: the Irish had joined the euro and could pull no policy lever but the one marked "fiscal," which was hard in reverse. Output fell by 8% in 2009 and unemployment rose dramatically.

Similar forces were at work in places as far afield as the Baltic states (Estonia, Latvia, and Lithuania), Greece, and Spain and Portugal. Although the Baltics still had their own currencies, they chose not to break their peg to the euro and suffered greatly as a result. Spain had a housing boom and bust, but fortunately, it was less extreme than Ireland's. Less exposed to a housing meltdown and domestic banking crisis, the less-developed economies of Portugal and Greece faced the more traditional problem of a chronically large budget deficit that blew out to a massive gap in 2009 and 2010 once recessions caused tax revenues to evaporate. Greece faced an additional and long-standing credibility problem as a result of reporting falsified economic data that disguised its true problems.

Even though the cause of their fiscal disasters was different, however, Portugal and Greece were lumped together with Ireland and Spain in the uncharitably named "PIGS" group, and given low (near-junk) credit ratings. By 2010 this group had access to financial markets, if at all, only at very high interest rates. They skirted very close to insolvency and, at the time of writing in November 2010, had avoided default only through funds advanced by the ECB, the EU, and the IMF.

In March 2010, for example, Greece needed a special EU-IMF loan rescue package. But this only staved off the problems for a while. By October 2010 the peripherals were facing punitive market interest rates, and in November and the Irish government was persuaded to follow Greece into a very contentious EU-IMF loan rescue package to allow it to pay off (at taxpayer expense) the vast losses of its banks. The chances were by then rising that Portugal (and worryingly, maybe some "core" EU countries) would end up needing similar help.

Needless to say, this debacle exposed the deep problems of how to regulate cross-border banking and finance within Europe, and, most serious of all, raised many profound questions about the long-term viability of the euro project (as we saw in the chapter on the euro). For example: What, if anything, should be done about Eurozone fiscal policy rules after the spectacular failure of previous efforts? Is it possible for such disparate economies to be safely put into a common currency given the asymmetric shocks they face? Can a way be found for European cross-border banks to operate safely? How can the "global imbalance" problem within the Eurozone microcosm be resolved to temper the flow of capital from sober and restrained high-savers in Germany and elsewhere to persistent-deficit, credit-bubble, and crisis-prone low-saving peripheral countries? Can the Eurozone tolerate a default by either a state or a banking system, or will moral hazard prevail? Will it be the ECB who will be left to pick up the bill? Or will it be the the taxpayers, and if so, which ones?

The Rest of the World What about the rest of the world? Outside of the United States and the Eurozone, the impacts were less catastrophic. Japan escaped lightly for the rather depressing reason that its economy had already been in a quasi-slump for over 15 years, had already seen its banking system delever and collapse, and had vital economic signs already in a flatline state (very slow growth and near-zero rates of inflation and interest).

The most remarkable outcome was, however, in the emerging market world where rapid growth quickly resumed. These countries had experienced strong precrisis economic growth, were not exposed so much to financial sector risk at home (or to problems in the developed market's financial world), carried less debt in their economies, and had also amassed war chests of reserves. In many cases, these nations spent their reserves to support fiscal policy expansions that buffered their economies from the global shock, without necessitating new borrowing (when credit markets were impaired) or placing their exchange rate regimes at risk. These nations had saved for a rainy day, and now it was pouring.

The main locus of this rapid EM recovery was in Asia (except for Japan), which was buttressed by strong support measures in China, including a large-scale public spending program. Latin America also turned around very quickly, led by boom conditions in Brazil and deft deployment of reserves in Chile. Only Mexico, more closely tied to the economic disaster in the neighboring country to its North, had to contend with macroeconomic difficulties. The luck of Brazil, as a commodity exporter, was also shared by a few DM countries, like Australia, Canada, and Norway, whose valuable natural resources were quickly in demand again after the resumption of growth in China and other EM countries.

In this way, a remarkable "two-track" economic recovery started to take shape in 2009 and continued into 2010 (see Figure 11-20). It was something never witnessed before: the DM countries were unable to kick start a true recovery, but the EM countries powered ahead regardless, largely under their own steam. The "decoupling" of the EM fate from the DM trend was, to say the least, unusual. From a historical point of view, however, it was even more striking that the world had gone through its greatest synchronized global financial crisis ever and not a single EM country had experienced a banking, currency, or sovereign default crisis. Had anyone suggested this outcome before the fact, they would surely have been greeted with incredulity.

The Road to Recovery The question going forward is how long this state of affairs can persist. When, if ever, will the DM countries, and especially the United States, return to "normal" (whatever that means)? As of late 2010, the global recovery was by no means guaranteed to continue in a sustained and uninterrupted fashion. Several risks, albeit remote in some cases, still lurked in the background:

- In the United States, as in most DM countries, fiscal policies were due to be tightened in 2010 and later years as part of "austerity" programs. Some countries may have had to do this to prevent increases in public debt levels (peripheral Europe), but for others the case was less clear-cut (the United Kingdom and United States). Critics argued that this austerity might tip economies back into recession before recovery was complete, in which case public debts would get worse still.

- Monetary policy had hit the zero interest rate lower bound at the Fed and other central banks. This left no further room for easing using conventional tools when such easing was badly needed (especially when fiscal stimulus started to be withdrawn in conditions of still-high unemployment and below target inflation).

- The conventional transmission mechanisms of monetary policy remained impaired as many banks continued to struggle with damaged balance sheets, and many households held zero or negative equity in their homes and were unable to borrow or refinance at low rates.

FIGURE 11-20

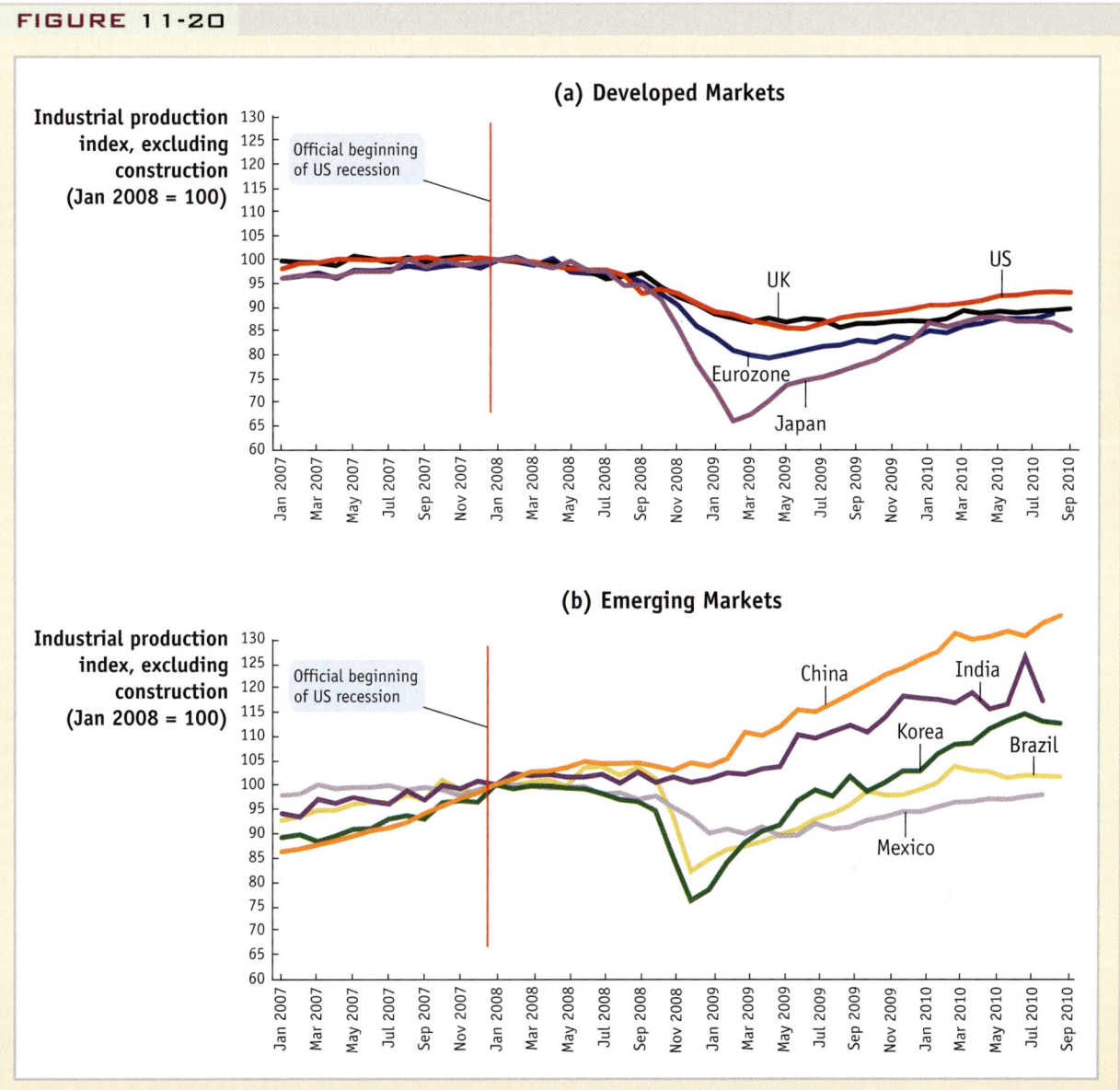

The "Two-Track" Global Recovery Using data on industrial production, these two charts contrast the sluggish recovery in developed markets (panel a) with the rapid resumption of growth in emerging markets (panel b).

Source: Morgan Stanley Research.

- The Fed had instituted unconventional measures such as quantitative easing (QE) used in the crisis and QE2, another round undertaken in 2010, causing the Fed's balance sheet to expand. These (unsterilized) *large-scale asset purchases* could provide stimulus through a variety of channels to lower interest rates throughout the market, support asset prices and wealth, and also weaken the U.S. dollar. The latter effect was not broadly welcomed by trading partners in 2010 and sparked concerns of a global "currency war" that could then mutate into a protectionist battle or trade war. And supporting asset markets in such an open and sustained way marked a controversial new step for the Fed.

- How the Fed or Bank of England or Bank of Japan would exit from QE-type measures and how the ECB would pull back its special liquidity support and (sterilized) bond purchase programs were future problems still to be resolved. Can these steps be taken without igniting inflation if liquidity isn't contracted sharply enough? Can they be done without sparking bankruptcies or defaults if interest rates rise too quickly and hurt those on floating interest rates? It is hard to find precedents for these unusual monetary experiments.

- As of late 2010, the Eurozone remained in a fragile state: the peripheral countries still had weak banks and fiscal positions, and there was no well-established procedure to deal with those issues beyond the steady liquidity provided by the ECB, the Greek rescue, and the new IMF-EU program open to Ireland and potentially others. Officially, Europe's new European Financial Stability Facility (EFSF) runs only through 2013 and its initial size would be unable to cope with crises in multiple countries all at once. Beyond this scheme no larger or more permanent arrangements to handle Eurozone financial instability and sovereign crises had yet been determined.

- It remains unclear whether the global economic engine can continue to function satisfactorily when three out of four main cylinders are not working properly (the United States, Japan, and Eurozone), and only the EM part of the world is experiencing robust growth. Here again, we are in uncharted waters.

At a deeper level, and perhaps in the more medium term, the world will discover how, if at all, some of the conditions that helped shape the crisis might be ameliorated in the future. Can better financial regulation prevent damaging credit booms? Can suitable bankruptcy regimes help resolve failing banks quickly and with less damage to the economy or the taxpayer? Can more EM economies find alternative insurance mechanisms, or else achieve an adequate level of reserves? Will global imbalances persist at the levels seen in the last decade, or will they moderate either through smooth adjustments, or in response to more brute-force policy activism?

Conclusion: Lessons for Macroeconomics

The above description of the global financial crisis and its aftermath is necessarily incomplete. The event itself is far from over, and it represents a massive shock to the world economy, both economically and politically. Its full repercussions may unfold over many years and are impossible to predict with certainty.

What is more certain is that the crisis is already causing serious intellectual repercussions and is profoundly changing our thinking with respect to the way that macroeconomists do their research and teaching. It is now clear that many defects of existing, standard macroeconomic models need to be remedied. It is not enough to model the real side of the economy and ignore the financial sector. Deeper thinking will be needed to integrate finance and macroeconomics and to modernize the rather neglected area of money and banking, which had once been a core subject of macroeconomics. In this respect, economists will need to think carefully about what drives the demand for money and other safe assets when markets fail, and how to understand and incorporate rival views of crises, such as irrational herding, limits to arbitrage, imperfect information, moral hazard, and so forth.

The scope of policy objectives will have to be carefully scrutinized to determine whether and how the authorities can develop sufficient (and sufficiently sharp) instruments to meet their targets of not just price stability and, possibly, maximal employment, but also financial stability (that most ancient and original, but somewhat forgotten, responsibility of central banks). Here, a narrow focus on interest rate policy will be joined by a broader investigation of what a sensible *macroprudential policy* for the financial sector might look like.

Lastly, the challenges will require new evidence to guide theory and refute or confirm hypotheses. Financial shocks of the kind we have just witnessed are rare events. For the purposes of empirical study, a sample of comparable episodes can be found, but only if one looks back into the deeper recesses of economic history. Our recent quiescent economy, the so-called Great Moderation, lulled many into thinking that we had entered a new era, where "this time is different"; it turned out to be an illusion. Greater attention to the lessons of economic history might well have negated some of that complacent and naïve thinking. In the end, economists and policy makers face the task of better linking aggregate economic outcomes to financial conditions, a task that will surely take economic research down some new and interesting paths. There is much work to do.

KEY POINTS

1. Purchasing power parity does not hold between rich and poor countries, in either relative or absolute form. Prices of goods are systematically higher in rich countries. As countries become relatively richer, we can therefore expect their price levels to rise and, hence, their real exchange rates to appreciate. Exchange rate forecasts (real and nominal) need to be adjusted accordingly, as do judgments as to whether a country's exchange rate is under- or overvalued.

2. The Balassa-Samuelson theory explains price differences across countries as a result of differences in the wage (labor) costs embodied in nontraded goods. It assumes that nontraded goods have zero (or small) productivity differences. Under those assumptions, large differences in traded goods productivity are associated with large differences in income per capita, wages, and the prices of nontraded goods.

3. Uncovered interest parity appears to hold when market expectations are measured directly using data from surveys of traders. But the joint hypothesis of UIP and rational expectations (the efficient markets hypothesis) appears to be invalid because exchange rate forecasts seem to be systematically and predictably wrong.

4. On average, exchange rate movements have been smaller than predicted by UIP, so a carry trade strategy of borrowing in the low-yield currency and investing in the high-yield currency delivers profits or excess returns. However, these excess returns are risky, with a Sharpe ratio well below 1, and typically close to 0.4 to 0.5. As with the stock market, few investors are willing to devote speculative capital to such risky investments.

5. Default is as old as capital markets. Sovereign defaults on international lending have been widely documented for several centuries. In the modern era, defaults are associated with economic downturns, and a good deal of this pain seems to be a result of default. This "punishment" for the defaulter creates one important benefit—it makes lending possible in the first place, since sovereigns otherwise face no incentive to repay.

6. A simple model of default can explain why countries default in bad times. They need to insure against really painful outcomes and default allows them to do this. The price of such insurance is the risk premium they must pay on top of the risk-free rate when they borrow, so that the lender breaks even. This kind of model explains

the existence of default as an equilibrium outcome. Nonetheless, many other factors can precipitate default crises, including complex feedback between default, banking crises, and exchange rate crises.

7. Before 2008, large capital flows from EM to DM created global imbalances, and some similar imbalances could be found within the DM world. Some of these flows ended up financing unsustainable private or public consumption or failed housing investments in certain DM economies (United States, Britain, Ireland, Spain, etc.) and as the malinvestments contaminated balance sheets of banks globally, the stage was set for the Global Financial Crisis.

8. The subsequent Great Recession saw contractions in aggregate demand and credit, and ballooning government debts and deficits in many DM countries. The financial crisis now created a fiscal problem and in some cases brought governments to a near-insolvent position, and in other cases necessitated rescue packages (the euro periphery). EM economies bounced back quickly, but the DM economies had a deep slump, making the global recovery weak and doubtful.

KEY TERMS

trade cost, p. 443
no-arbitrage band, p. 443
Balassa-Samuelson effect, p. 449
equilibrium real exchange rate, p. 449
carry trade, p. 455
peso problem, p. 461
forecast error, p. 461
rational expectations hypothesis, p. 462
efficient markets hypothesis, p. 462
inefficient market, p. 462
limits to arbitrage, p. 464
excess return, p. 465
Sharpe ratio, p. 465
sovereign default, p. 468
contingent claim, p. 469
repayment threshold, p. 471
Global Financial Crisis, p. 486
Great Recession, p. 486
global imbalances, p. 488
savings glut, p. 488
undervalued exchange rates, p. 492
too-easy monetary policy, p. 492
failure of regulation and supervision. p. 492
government failure, p. 493
market failure, p. 493

PROBLEMS

1. (PPP) Richland and Poorland each have two industries: traded TVs and nontraded house maintenance. The world price of TVs is R$100 (R$ = Richland dollar). Assume for now that the exchange rate is R$1 = 1 PP (PP = Poorland peso) and that prices are flexible. It takes 1 day for a worker in each country to visit and maintain 1 house. It takes 1 day for a Richland worker to make a TV, and 4 days for a Poorland worker.

   a. What is the Richland wage in R$ per day? What is the Poorland wage in PP per day? In R$ per day? What is the ratio of Poorland to Richland wages in a common currency?

   b. What is the price of a house maintenance visit in each country?

   c. Assume people in each country spend half their income on TVs and half on house maintenance. Compute the CPI (consumer price index) for each country given by the square root of (TV price) times (house maintenance prices).

   d. Compute the standard of living in each country by dividing local currency wages by the CPI from part (c)? Is Poorland really as poor as suggested by the last answer in part (a)?

   e. Productivity now doubles in the Poorland TV industry, all else equal. How many days

does it now take for Poorland workers to make a TV? What happens to the wage in Poorland? The price of house maintenance? The CPI?

f. If the central bank of Poorland wants to avoid inflation in this situation, how would it like to adjust the exchange rate?

2. (PPP) "Some fast-growing poorer countries face a conflict between wanting to maintain a fixed exchange rate with a rich country and wanting to keep inflation low." Explain the logic behind this statement. Use the examples of Slovakia and China to illustrate your argument.

3. (UIP) What is a peso problem? In the case of fixed exchange rates, explain how peso problems can account for persistent interest rate differentials. Study the U.S.–Britain short-term (end-of-month) nominal interest rate differentials shown below for the year 1896 (from NBER series 13034). Both countries were on the gold standard at a fixed exchange rate of $4.86 throughout this year. Did the United States have a peso problem? When did it become really big? When did it go away? (*Extra Credit:* Do some research on the Web and discover the political reasons for the timing of this peso problem.)

Jan 1896	3.84%
Feb 1896	2.94%
Mar 1896	2.76%
Apr 1896	2.40%
May 1896	1.63%
Jun 1896	1.20%
Jul 1896	1.43%
Aug 1896	3.77%
Sep 1896	3.70%
Oct 1896	8.51%
Nov 1896	2.60%
Dec 1896	−1.39%

4. (UIP) You are in discussion with a forex trader.

   a. She reveals that she made a 10% annual rate of return last year. Based on these data, can we say that the forex market in question violates the efficient markets hypothesis (EMH)?

   b. The trader reveals that she can make predictable 10% annual rates of return on forex trades for a pair of currencies, with a standard deviation of 25%, and has been doing so for a long time. Calculate the Sharpe ratio for these trades. Based on these data, does the forex market in question satisfy EMH?

   c. Can the trader's predictable profits be explained by trading frictions? By risk aversion?

5. (Default) "Poor countries are exploited when they borrow in global capital markets, because they are charged an extortionate rate of interest." Explain how empirical evidence and theoretical arguments might counter this assertion.

6. (Default) The Republic of Delinquia has a nondisaster output level of $100 each year. With 10% probability each year, output falls to a disaster level of $80, and the country will feel so much pain that it will default and pay neither principal nor interest on its debts. The country decides to borrow $20 at the start of the year, and keep the money under the mattress. It will default and keep the money in the event that output is low, but this will entail sacrificing $4 in punishment costs. Otherwise, it pays back principal and interest due. Lenders are competitive and understand these risks fully.

   a. What is the probability of default in Delinquia?

   b. The interest rate on safe loans is 8% per annum, so a safe loan has to pay off 1.08 times $20. What is the lending rate charged by competitive lenders on the risky loan to Delinquia?

   c. What does Delinquia consume in disaster years? In nondisaster years?

   d. Repeat part (c) for the case where Delinquia cannot borrow. Is Delinquia better off with or without borrowing?

7. (Global Crisis) When emerging markets elected to accumulate vast sums of reserves in the 2000s decade, did this create a problem in developed markets? How might this problem be resolved, or resolve itself, going forward? Does the EM decision to accumulate the reserves look like a wise one, after the fact?

8. (Global Crisis) In 2010 there was a risk that the state of Ireland was at risk of going broke because it had poured too much money into its insolvent banks to try to keep them alive, but already incomes had fallen massively and public services were being cut harshly, too. Describe the tradeoffs involved in the various options: (a) increasing austerity (raising taxes and cutting spending) even more to keep the banks alive; (b) letting the State default on its external debt to keep the banks alive and limit austerity; (c) allow the banks to fail to save the State's creditworthiness and limit austerity. Consider the problem from a purely Irish national interest perspective first. Now think of an EU level perspective: how is your analysis of who should foot the bill affected by the fact that many of the Irish bank creditors were foreign (many in the EU), and that many of the risks of financial damage were due to contagion to other (principally EU) foreign countries.

N E T W O R K

1. (PPP) Find the price of some of your favorite books or CDs on Amazon.com in the United States. Now find the price of the same items at Amazon.co.uk in the United Kingdom. Are there arbitrage opportunities? What if you ordered 100 or 1,000 items? What are the shipping costs as a fraction of the cost of your order? How would you determine the tariffs and duties you would need to pay? Are there any other barriers to trade?

2. (PPP) In the mid-2000s, the EU accession countries faced appreciation and/or inflation pressure. In March 2007 a step was taken to resolve these problems in the case of the Slovak koruna. The EU gave permission for Slovakia to "bend the rules" a bit. Which one of the Maastricht criteria was relaxed? Use the Internet to find out (*Hint:* Google "Slovak koruna"). What does this say about the importance that EU authorities attach to low inflation? Suppose Slovakia was still relatively poor but in the Eurozone. The Balassa-Samuelson effect would still be present even with a common currency, so how would inflation rates differ in the rich and poor parts of Europe? Why could that be a problem for ECB policy makers?

3. (UIP) Imagine you are a carry trader. Go to the ft.com site and locate the "Market data" part of the site. Find one-month LIBOR interest rates for some major currencies: U.S. dollar, pound, euro, Japanese yen, Swiss franc, Canadian dollar, and Australian dollar (*Hint:* Google "ft.com money rates"). Find the lowest-yield currency, and call it X. How much interest would you pay in X units after borrowing 100X for one month? (*Hint:* The raw data are annualized rates.) Compute the exchange rate between X and every other higher-yield currency Y (*Hint:* Google "ft.com cross rates"). For each Y, compute how much 100X would be worth in Y units today, and then in a month's time with Y-currency interest added. Revisit this question in a month's time, find the spot rates at that moment, and compute the resulting profit from each carry trade. Did all your imaginary trades pay off? Any of them?

Index

Note: Page numbers followed by f indicate figures; page numbers followed by n indicate notes; page numbers followed by t indicate tables; key terms are in **boldface** type.

A

Abdelal, Rawi, 393n
Absolute PPP, 66–68, 70
   nominal exchange rate and, 68, 68f
   real exchange rate and, 67
Abu Dhabi, sovereign wealth funds of, 220
Account, money as unit of, 76
Acemoglu, Daron, 20n
Adimark GfK, 221
Advanced countries
   financial openness of, 14–15, 15f
   sovereign rating and public debt level of, 210, 211f
   sudden stops in, 212, 212f
Afghanistan, U.S. war in, 217
Africa. *See also specific countries*
   Live Aid concert and, 235
Aizenman, Joshua, 220n, 375
Albania
   currency crisis of 1997 in, 6f
   in EC, 418
Alfaro, Laura, 233n, 393n, 469n
Algeria, sovereign wealth funds of, 220
America(s). *See specific countries*
American Recovery and Reinvestment Act (ARRA), 293–294, 295n
American terms, 28
Amsterdam Treaty, 419
Anderson, James E., 72n, 444n, 445n
Andorra, currency of, 400n
Appreciation, 28–30
   adjustment to FX market equilibrium and, 116
   discontinuous, 381
   real, 67
Arbitrage, 26, 43–57, 57f
   adjustment to FX market equilibrium and, 115–116
   covered interest parity and, 47–51, 49f, 50f

cross rates and vehicle currencies and, 46–47
interest rates and, 47–57
limits to, 442–445, 444f, 464–467
riskless, 47–51, 49f, 50f
risky. *See* Risky arbitrage
with three currencies, 45, 46f
triangular, 45
with two currencies, 44f, 44–45
uncovered interest parity and, 51–55, 53f, 55f
Argentina
   banking crisis of 1995 in, 370
   Big Mac index and, 75t
   bond rating of, 13
   capital flow to, 232t
   Convertibility Plan in, 362, 363f, 364, 370–371, 484
   currency crisis of 2001–2002 in, 5, 6f, 7–8, 483–486
   currency of, 404
   defaults by, 12, 468
   discretionary fiscal stimulus measures in, 497t
   dollar peg and, 459–460
   economic crisis of 1980–1982 in, 351t
   exchange rate crisis in, 347f, 349
   exchange rate of, 36, 36f
   external wealth of, 11–12, 12f
   hard peg of, 394
   hyperinflation in, 90
   IMF and, 370–371, 395, 487
   manipulation of statistics by, 191
   real exchange rate with, 452
   risk premiums in, 360–362, 361f
   sovereign rating and public debt level of, 211f
ARRA. *See* American Recovery and Reinvestment Act (ARRA)
Asda, 260
Asia. *See also specific countries*
   economic crisis of 1997 in, 287–289, 288f, 289f
   exchange rates of, 492

Great Recession in, 501–502, 503f
risk premiums in, 362
Asian Tigers, 235. *See also specific countries*
   foreign aid to, 236
Asplund, Marcus, 315n
Asset(s), 348
   exports of, flow of payments and, 162
   home and foreign, balance of payments and, 179–180
   imports of, flow of payments and, 162
   liquidity of, 51
   rate of return of, 51
   risk of, 51
Asset approach to exchange rates, 111–153
   economic policy and, 127–131
   equilibrium in FX market and, 114t, 114–118, 115f
   fixed exchange rates and, 141–148
   fundamental equation of, 113, 113f
   graphical solution for, 125–127, 126f
   long-run policy analysis and, 132–138
   monetary approach unified with, 131–140, 133f
   overshooting and, 138–140, 139f, 140f
   risky arbitrage and, 112–113, 113f
   short-run money market equilibrium and, 118–125
   trilemma and, 145–148, 146f, 147f
   uncovered interest parity and, 113, 113f
Asymmetric shocks, 311
Australia
   Asian crisis of 1997 and, 287–289, 288f, 289f
   Big Mac index and, 75t
   budget deficit of, 10f
   discretionary fiscal stimulus measures in, 497t
   dollarization of trade and, 263t

exchange rate of, 340
expenditure switching and dollar devaluation and, 259
foreign aid from, 169
FX trade in, 39
Great Recession in, 502
sovereign rating and public debt level of, 211f
sovereign wealth funds of, 220
Austria
   in Eurozone, 420t
   Eurozone convergence criteria and, 429f
   exchange rate of, 148, 337
   sovereign default of, 468
   sovereign rating and public debt level of, 211f

B

Bachelet, Michelle, 221
Backing ratio, 357–359
Bahamas, sovereign rating and public debt level of, 211f
Bahrain, sovereign rating and public debt level of, 211f
Bailouts, 367
Balanced budget, 257
Balance of payments, 8–11, 9t, 10f, 178–186. *See also* Financial globalization
   accounting for home and foreign assets and, 179–180
   capital account and, 178–179
   data for, 182–186, 183t
   double-entry principle in, 182
   information provided by, 186
   macroeconomic view of, 180
   microeconomic view of, 180–182
   statistical discrepancy and, 185, 185f
Balance of payments (BOP) accounts, 158
   flow of payments and, 160, 161f, 162
Balassa, Bela, 447
Balassa-Samuelson effect, 447–453, 454
   in emerging markets, 451–453
Baldwin, Richard, 413
Ball, Laurence M., 78n
Bands, 34

I-1

Bank(s)
    central. *See* Bank of England; Central bank(s); European Central Bank (ECB); Federal Reserve System (Fed)
    commercial, in foreign exchange market, 42
Banking, risk of, 480–482, 481f, 482t
Banking crises, 348. *See also* ERM crisis; Great Recession; Tequila Crisis (Mexico)
    countries experiencing, 493, 494f
Bank of England, 423
    control of interest rates by, 123–124
    ERM and, 308–310
    ERM crisis and, 391–392
    sovereign default and, 479
Bank runs, 369
Banrel, Alberto, 7
Barbados, sovereign rating and public debt level of, 211f
Barro, Robert J., 99n, 425n
Barton, Frederick, 169
Base currency, 33, 306
Beggar-thy-neighbor policy, 333
Belgium
    in Eurozone, 420t
    Eurozone convergence criteria and, 429f
    sovereign rating and public debt level of, 211f
    Treaty of Rome and, 415
Belize, sovereign rating and public debt level of, 211f
Benin
    economic crisis of 1988–1990 in, 351t
    sovereign rating and public debt level of, 211f
Bernanke, Ben S., 221
Bias
    home, 242–244, 243f, 244f
    inflation. *See* Inflation bias
Big Mac index, 74, 75t, 445–446, 446f
Bilateral exchange rates, 30–31, 31f
Black markets, 43
"Black Wednesday," 349
Blanchard, Oliver, 104
Blustein, Paul, 371n, 395n, 485n
BMW, 291

Bolivia, sovereign rating and public debt level of, 211f
Bond(s), sterilization, 372–373
Bond ratings, 13
Boot, Max, 235
BOP accounts. *See* Balance of payments (BOP) accounts
BOP credits, 181
BOP debits, 181
BOP identity, 180
Borrowers, net, 184
Bosnia & Herzegovina, gross national disposable income in, 168f
Bosworth, Barry, 208n
Botswana
    foreign aid to, 236
    sovereign rating and public debt level of, 211f
Boys, Sebastian, 221
Brazil
    Big Mac index and, 74, 75t
    capital flow to, 232t
    currency crisis of 1999 in, 5, 6f
    currency mismatch and, 326
    default by, 468, 480
    discretionary fiscal stimulus measures in, 497t
    exchange rate crisis in, 347f
    Great Recession in, 502
    hyperinflation in, 88
    risk premiums in, 362
    sovereign rating and public debt level of, 211f
Bretton Woods system, 328, 338–339, 339f, 340, 415–417
Britain. *See also* United Kingdom
    Big Mac index and, 74, 75t
    borrowing to finance wars and, 217
    currency of, 419
    ERM and, 308–310
    exchange rate crisis in, 347f, 349
    exchange rate of, 337
    foreign aid from, 169
    sovereign default of, 468
    switch to floating exchange rate, 305
Brooks, Robin, 317n, 320t, 393n
Brown, Gordon, 349
Brown, Veronica, 457n
Bruno, Michael, 99n
Bryant, William Jennings, 336
Bubula, Andrea, 393n
Budget, balanced, 257

Budget deficits, 175, 257
    of United States, 9f, 9–10, 10f
Budget surpluses, 175, 257
Bulgaria
    in EU, 400, 420t
    sovereign rating and public debt level of, 211f
Bulow, Jeremy, 469n
Bundesbank, 424
    ERM and, 306, 330
Bundy, Nikki, 260
Burger, John D., 326n
Burnside, Craig, 384n
Burundi, gross national disposable income in, 168f
Bush, George W., 236

C

CA. *See* Current account (CA)
Cagan, Phillip, 87f, 88f
Cai, Fang, 244n
Calls, options and, 41
Calomiris, Charles W., 370n
Calvo, Guillermo A., 212, 212f, 425n, 485
Cameron, David, 349
Canada
    basket of consumer goods in, 63–64
    Big Mac index and, 75t
    discretionary fiscal stimulus measures in, 497t
    exchange rate of, 27t, 34, 35f, 340
    Great Recession in, 502
    price level in, 111
    sovereign rating and public debt level of, 211f
Canjels, Eugene, 334n
Cape Verde, gross national disposable income in, 168f
Capital
    marginal product of, 225
    movement between countries. *See* Foreign direct investment (FDI)
Capital account (KA), 162, 178–186
Capital controls, 42–43
    to prevent exchange rate crises, 393
Capital flow, to rich and poor countries, 230–234, 232t
Capital gains, 11
Capital mobility, asset approach to exchange rates and, 127
Caribbean. *See specific countries*
Carry trade, 454–459, 456f

Sharpe ratio and, 465f, 465–466
Cassel, Gustav, 63
Catão, Luis, 470n
Cavallo, Domingo, 349
Cavallo, Michele, 324f, 324n
Celtic Tiger, 165–167, 166f
Center currency, 306
Central America. *See specific countries*
Central bank(s), 77–78. *See also* Bank of England; European Central Bank (ECB); Federal Reserve System (Fed)
    control of interest rate by, 123–124
    foreign exchange market and, 43
    independence of, 103, 424
    inflation targets and, 424
    as lender of last resort, 369
    reserve buildup in emerging markets and, 374f, 374–375, 375f
Central bank balance sheet, 352–353, 371–373
    graphical analysis of, 355f, 355–356
CFA Franc zone, 37
CFP Franc zone, 37
Cheung, Yin-Wong, 134
Chile
    Big Mac index and, 75t
    capital flow to, 232t
    default by, 12, 480
    economic crisis of 1981–1986 in, 351t
    Great Recession in, 502
    sovereign rating and public debt level of, 211f
    sovereign wealth fund of, 221
China
    Big Mac index and, 75t
    budget surplus of, 10f
    capital flow to, 232t
    discretionary fiscal stimulus measures in, 497t
    economic crisis of 1990s in, 351t
    exchange rate of, 4, 492
    foreign aid to, 236
    Great Recession in, 502
    gross national income per capita in, 442
    manipulation of statistics by, 191
    real exchange rate with, 451–452

sovereign rating and public debt level of, 211f
sovereign wealth funds of, 220
Chinn, Menzie D., 15f, 55f, 134, 176n, 463f
Churchill, Winston, 414–415
CIP. *See* Covered interest parity (CIP)
Cline, William R., 208n
Closed economy, flow of payments in, 158–160, 159f
CLS system. *See* Continuously linked settlement (CLS) system
Coakley, Jerry, 467n
Codelco, 221
Cohn, Laura, 4n
Collins, Susan M., 208n
Colombia
  Big Mac index and, 75t
  bond rating of, 13
  currency mismatch and, 326
  economic crisis of 1982–1987 in, 351t
  exchange rate of, 36, 36f
  sovereign rating and public debt level of, 211f
Commercial banks, in foreign exchange market, 42
Common currency, 16
  comparing prices in using exchange rates, 31t, 31–33
Common shocks, idiosyncratic shocks versus, 251–252
Comoros, gross national disposable income in, 168f
Competition. *See* Imperfect competition
Congo, Democratic Republic of
  capital flow to, 232t
  currency crisis of 2009 in, 6f
Connally, John, 340
Consumption
  demand in an open economy and, 255f, 255–256
  exogenous change in, 262
  government, 256
  marginal propensity to consume and, 256
Consumption function, 255f, 255–256
Consumption smoothing, 212–220
  financial openness and, 218f, 218–219
  numerical example and generalization of, 213–217
  precautionary saving and, 219–220

wars and the current account and, 217
Contagion, 362
Contingent claims, 469–470
Contingent commitment, 385
Continuously linked settlement (CLS) system, 39n
Convergence, 230
  speed of, 71–72
Convergence criteria, 425–430
  compliance with, 429–430
  criticism of, 428–429, 429f
  fiscal discipline and, 427–428
  nominal, 425–427, 427f
Convertibility Plan (Argentina), 362, 363f, 364, 370–371, 484
Cooperative arrangements, 328
Copenhagen Criteria, 418
Corners hypothesis, 393
Corporations, in foreign exchange market, 42
Cost(s)
  of asymmetric shocks, 311
  of exchange rate crises, 346–350, 348f, 351t
  menu, 119
  of pegging, 389–390
  trade. *See* Trade costs
  transaction. *See* Transaction costs
Costa Rica
  Big Mac index and, 74, 75t
  foreign aid to, 236
  sovereign rating and public debt level of, 211f
Côte d'Ivoire, economic crisis of 1988–1991 in, 351t
Country premium, 360
Country risk, 13
Covered interest parity (CIP), 47–51, 49f, 50f
Crawl, 36–37
Crawling bands, 37
Crawling pegs, 37
Credibility, 362
  of peg, 385, 388–389
Credit, domestic. *See* Domestic credit
Creditors, net, 187
Credit ratings, for countries, 13, 210, 211f
Croatia
  EU and, 400
  sovereign rating and public debt level of, 211f
Crockett, Andrew, 393n

Cross rates, 45–47
  vehicle currencies and, 46–47
Crowding out, 283–284
Cullen, Joe, 167n
Currencies
  appreciation of. *See* Appreciation
  base, 33, 306
  center, 306
  common, 16
  depreciation of. *See* Depreciation
  overvalued, 67
  redenomination of, 90
  undervalued, 67
  vehicle, cross rates and, 46–47
Currency areas. *See* Currency unions; Eurozone; Optimum currency areas (OCAs)
Currency boards, 38, 38f, 356, 359
Currency mismatches, 322
Currency premium, 360, 385
Currency unions, 37, 399. *See also* Eurozone; Optimum currency areas (OCAs)
  trade and, 413
Current account (CA), 9, 9f, 162, 169
  global imbalances and, 173–177, 174f, 175f, 177f
  information provided by, 172–173
  wars and, 217
Current account identity, 173
Cyprus
  currency of, 401
  euro coins of, 16
  in Eurozone, 420t, 421
  sovereign rating and public debt level of, 211f
Czech Republic
  Big Mac index and, 74, 75t
  dollarization of trade and, 263t
  economic crisis of 1991 in, 351t
  in EU, 420t
  sovereign rating and public debt level of, 211f

D

D'Amato, Laura, 370n
De, Prabir, 445n
Debt, government, monetizing of, 318
Debtors, net, 187

Default(s), 5
  sovereign. *See* Sovereign default; *specific countries*
Default crises, 348
Default risk, 39
Deficits, 9. *See also* Budget deficits; Trade deficits
Deflation, 104
De Gregorio, Jose, 221
de la Rúa, Fernando, 349, 485
della Paolera, Gerardo, 485n
Dell'Ariccia, Giovanni, 104n
Demand
  in an open economy, 254–266
  consumption and, in an open economy, 255f, 255–256
  determinants of, 266–268, 267f
  disposable income and, in an open economy, 255
  exogenous changes in, 262, 265f, 265–266
  goods market equilibrium and, 266
  government and, in an open economy, 256–257
  investment and, in an open economy, 256, 257f
  for money. *See* Money demand
  trade balance and, in an open economy, 257–264, 261f
Demand curve, factors shifting, 268–269
Denmark
  Big Mac index and, 75t
  currency of, 401, 404, 421
  in EC, 415
  in ERM, 401, 420t
  exchange rate of, 27t, 146
  foreign aid from, 169
  risk premiums in, 360, 361f
  sovereign rating and public debt level of, 211f
  trilemma and, 147f, 147–148
De Paoli, Bianca, 479n, 481f, 482f
Depreciation, 28–30
  adjustment to FX market equilibrium and, 116
  contractionary, fixed exchange rates and, 321–326, 323f, 324f, 325t
  discontinuous, 381
  expected rate of, 54
  money growth and inflation and, 81–82
  real, 67
Derivatives, 40f, 40–41
Devaluation, 331

Developed countries. *See also specific regions and countries*
  exchange rate regimes in, 34, 35f
  global financial crisis and, 488
Developing countries. *See also specific regions and countries*
  capital flow to, 232t
  exchange rate regimes in, 34–37, 36f
  financial openness of, 14–15, 15f
  governance in, 18–19
  lending to, 475f, 475–476
  sovereign rating and public debt level of, 210, 211f
di Giovanni, Julian, 317, 318f
Dirty float, 35
Disposable income
  demand in an open economy and, 255
  gross national, 160, 161f, 162
Divergence, 231
Diversification, 237–245
  common versus idiosyncratic shocks and, 251–252
  home bias and, 242–244, 243f, 244f
  numerical example and generalization of, 237–238, 238t
Dollar, exchange rate of, 4
Dollarization, 16, 37, 402n
  of trade, 263t, 263–264
Domestic credit, 352–353
  shocks to, 365–366, 366f
Dominican Republic, defaults by, 12
Dornbusch, Rudiger, 140
Double-entry principle, in balance of payments, 182
Dugger, Celia W., 89
Durdu, Ceyhun Bora, 220n

E

Easterly, William, 99n, 236
Eastern Caribbean Currency Union, 37
Eastern Europe. *See also specific countries*
  euro and, 454
Eaton, Jonathan, 469n
EC. *See* European Community (EC)
ECB. *See* European Central Bank (ECB)
Economic activity
  expenditure approach to measuring, 163–164
  income approach to measuring, 163, 167–168, 168f
  product approach to measuring, 163, 164–167, 166f
Economic and Monetary Union (EMU), 400, 419
Economic efficiency
  integration and, 310–311
  symmetry-integration diagram and, 312f, 312–313
Economic fundamentals, forecasting exchange rates using, 134
Economic integration
  exchange rate regimes and, 310–311
  symmetry-integration diagram and, 312f, 312–313, 327, 327f
Economic shocks. *See also* Monetary policy shocks
  asymmetric, 311
  common versus idiosyncratic, 251–252
  consumption smoothing and, 213–220
  to domestic credit, 365–366, 366f
  hurricanes and, 200, 200f
  money demand, fixed exchange rates and, 364
  to money demand, fixed exchange rates and, 356–359, 358f
  OPEC and, 225
  symmetric, 311
  symmetry of, in EU, 408
Economic similarity, exchange rate regimes and, 310, 311
Economic symmetry, optimum currency areas and, 402
ECSC. *See* European Coal and Steel Community (ECSC)
Ecuador
  default by, 12
  dollarization in, 16
  economic crisis of 1988 in, 351t
  exchange rate of, 36f, 37
  sovereign rating and public debt level of, 211f
Edwards, Sebastian, 218f, 221
EEC. *See* European Economic Community (EEC)
Effective exchange rates, 30–31, 31f
Efficiency
  economic. *See* Economic efficiency
  social, 232–233
  technical, 231
Efficient investment, 220, 222–236
  basic model for, 222
  delinking saving from investment and, 225–227, 226f
  numerical example and generalization for, 222–225, 223t
  poor countries and, 227–236
Efficient markets hypothesis, 461–462, 463f
EFSF. *See* European Financial Stability Facility (EFSF)
Egeland, Jan, 169
Égert, Balázs, 453n
Egypt
  Big Mac index and, 75t
  currency crisis of 2003 in, 6f
  sovereign rating and public debt level of, 211f
Eichenbaum, Martin, 384n
Eichengreen, Barry, 325, 325t, 326n, 335n, 337n, 346n, 393n
Elasticities, 302
El Salvador
  dollarization in, 16
  gross national disposable income in, 168f
  sovereign rating and public debt level of, 211f
Emerging markets
  capital flow to, 232t
  financial openness of, 14–15, 15f
  global financial crisis and, 488, 492
  long-run budget constraint and, 210, 211f, 212, 212f
  real exchange rate in, 451–453
  reserve accumulation in, 374f, 374–375, 375f
  sovereign rating and public debt level of, 210, 211f
  sudden stops in, 212, 212f
EMS. *See* European Monetary System (EMS)
EMU. *See* Economic and Monetary Union (EMU)
Engel, Charles, 444n
Engerman, Stanley L., 20n
England. *See* Britain; United Kingdom
EPU. *See* European Payments Union (EPU)
Equilibrium(a), 43
  in foreign exchange market. *See* Foreign exchange market equilibrium
  in FX market. *See* Foreign exchange market equilibrium
  general, 270
  in goods market. *See* Goods market equilibrium condition
  long-run. *See* Long-run equilibrium
  in money market. *See* Money market equilibrium; Short-run money market equilibrium
  multiple, 385
  self-confirming, 389–390
  short-run. *See* Short-run money market equilibrium
Equilibrium real exchange rate, 447
Equity premium puzzle, 466
Eritrea, gross national disposable income in, 168f
ERM. *See* Exchange Rate Mechanism (ERM)
ERM crisis, 391–392, 419
ESCB. *See* European System of Central Banks (ESCB)
Estevadeordal, Antoni, 313n, 336n
Estonia
  Big Mac index and, 75t
  currency of, 401
  euro and, 16, 454
  in Eurozone, 420t, 421
  Great Recession in, 501
  hard peg of, 394
  sovereign rating and public debt level of, 211f
EU. *See* European Union (EU)
Euratom, 415
Euro, 399–438
  adherence to rules and, 429–430
  assessment of, 435–437
  coin designs for, 16
  convergence criteria for, 425–429, 426f
  crisis of 2008–2010 and, 431–435, 433f
  Eastern Europe and, 454
  European Central Bank and, 422–425
  exchange rate for, 4, 27t
  expenditure switching and dollar devaluation and, 259
  future prospects for, 434–435

history of Europe and, 414–421
optimum currency areas and. *See* Optimum currency areas (OCAs)
Euro area. *See* Eurozone
Eurogroup, 424
Europe. *See also specific countries*
history of, 414–421, 416t–417t
Marshall Plan and, 415
optimum currency area of U.S. compared with, 407–410
trilemma in, 147f, 147–148
European Central Bank (ECB), 400, 419–420, 422–425
control of interest rates by, 123–124
criticisms of, 423–424
exchange rates and, 492
German model and, 424
inflation bias and, 424–425
nominal anchoring by, 130–131, 131f
European Coal and Steel Community (ECSC), 415
European Community (EC), 415
ERM and, 418
European Economic Community (EEC), 415
European Financial Stability Facility (EFSF), 433, 504
European Monetary System (EMS), establishment of, 417
European Payments Union (EPU), 415
European System of Central Banks (ESCB), 419n
European terms, 28
European Union (EU), 400. *See also* Eurozone; *specific countries*
composition of, 400
Eurozone and, 401
foreign aid from, 169
origins of, 414
Stability and Growth Pact and, 429–430
variable geometry feature of, 400
Eurosystem banks, 419n
Eurozone, 16, 37, 399–401, 401f, 421–430. *See also* European Central Bank (ECB)
Big Mac index and, 75t

convergence criteria and, 425–430
countries maintaining their own currencies and, 404
European Union and, 401
exchange rates and, 4–5
Great Depression and, 504
Great Recession in, 499, 500f, 501
launch of, 419–421, 420t
during 1999–2007, 421–430
during 2008–2010, 431–435, 433f
Evans-Pritchard, Ambrose, 457n
Ewing, Jack, 4n
Excess returns, 465
Exchange, money as medium of, 76
Exchange rate(s), 25–39. *See also* Foreign exchange *entries*
appreciations and depreciations and, 28–30
arbitrage and, 43–45
asset approach to. *See* Asset approach to exchange rates
behavior of, 3f, 3–4
bilateral, 30
Bretton Woods system and, 415–417
changes in, effects on economies, 4–5
comparing prices in a common currency using, 31–33, 32t
currency unions and, 37
defining, 26–28, 27t
depreciation of, relative PPP and inflation and, 69
dollarization and, 37
effective, 30
expected. *See* Expected exchange rate
fixed (pegged). *See* Fixed exchange rates; Fixed exchange rate systems
floating (flexible). *See* Floating exchange rates
forecasting. *See* Forecasting exchange rates
limits to arbitrage and, 442–446, 445f, 446f
in long run, 442–453
monetary approach to. *See* Monetary approach to exchange rates; Purchasing power parity (PPP)
multilateral, 30–31, 31f

nontraded goods and Balassa-Samuelson model and, 447–453, 454
over- and undervaluations and productivity growth and, 449f, 449–451
real. *See* Real exchange rates
recent experiences with, 34–39
risk of, 480–482, 481f, 482f
shifts in demand curve and, 269
shifts in IS curve and, 273
in short run, 453–467
spot, 39, 52–53
spreads and, 27n, 40
trilemma and, 144–148, 146f, 147f
undervalued, 492
Exchange rate crises, 5–6, 6f, 35, 345–396
contingent monetary policies and, 384–392
costs of, 346–350, 348f, 351t
definition of, 346, 347f
first-generation crisis model of, 376–384
fixed exchange rate operation and, 351–376
inconsistent fiscal policies and, 376–384
preventing, 392–395
second-generation crisis model of, 384–392
triple, 350
twin, 350
types of, 373, 376, 376f
Exchange Rate Mechanism (ERM), 146, 147f, 147–148, 305–310, 328, 330, 346, 401, 418
ERM crisis and, 391–392
ERM II and, 421n
Exchange rate regimes, 33–39
choice of, 16f, 16–17, 305–318
economic similarity and, 310, 311
fixed versus floating, 33–34. *See also* Fixed exchange rates; Floating exchange rates
integration and similarity and, 310
intermediate, 34, 146, 393
monetary regimes and, 99–104
nominal anchors and, 101–102, 102t
recent experiences with, 34–39

Exchange rate targets, 100
Expectations, 26
Expected dollar return, 52
Expected exchange rate, 52, 113
change in, FX market equilibrium and, 117f, 118
Expected rate of depreciation, 54
Expected rate of return, 51
Expected real interest rate, 256
Expenditure, 9
Expenditure approach to measuring economic activity, 163–164
Expenditure switching, 258
barriers to, 263t, 263–264, 264f
dollar devaluation and, 259
Export(s)
factor service, 160
flow of payments and, 160
net, 164
External assets, balance of payments and, 179–180
External liabilities, balance of payments and, 179–180
External wealth, 11–12, 12f, 186–190
change in, calculating, 203
changes in, 187–188
data on, 188–190, 189t
future, calculating, 203
information provided by, 190
level of, 187
precautionary saving and, 219–220
recent trends in, 190
total wealth and, 197–198

F

FA. *See* Financial account (FA)
Fackler, Martin, 458
Factor income from abroad, net, 160, 161f
Factor service exports, 160
Factor service imports, 160
Failure of regulation and supervision, 492–493
Fannie Mae, 493
FDI. *See* Foreign direct investment (FDI)
Fear of floating, 327
Federal Reserve System (Fed)
failure of regulation and supervision and, 492–493
policy rate of, 123
quantitative easing and, 123

Feldstein, Martin, 226, 295n, 375
Financial account (FA), 162, 178
Financial crises. *See* ERM crisis; Global Financial Crisis; Tequila Crisis (Mexico)
Financial flows, changes in wealth due to, 187
Financial globalization, 8–13, 199–246
 balance of payments and, 8–11, 9t, 10f
 defaults and credit ratings and, 12–13
 diversification of risk and. *See* Diversification
 economic shocks and, 200, 200f
 efficient investment and, 220–227, 223t, 226f
 external wealth and, 11–12, 12f
 long-run budget constraint and. *See* Long-run budget constraint (LRBC)
 poor countries and, 227–236
Financial markets, improving to prevent exchange rate crises, 394
Financial openness, 14–15, 15f
 consumption volatility and, 218f, 218–219
Finland
 economic crisis of 1991–1994 in, 351t
 in Eurozone, 420t
 Eurozone convergence criteria and, 429f
 exchange rate crisis in, 347f
 sovereign rating and public debt level of, 211f
First-generation crisis model, 376–384
Fiscal dominance, 377
Fiscal federalism, 405
Fiscal policy, 280
 under fixed exchange rates, short-run IS-LM-FX model and, 284–287, 285f
 under floating exchange rates, short-run IS-LM-FX model and, 283–284, 284f
Fiscal transfers, in optimum currency areas, 405–406, 408
Fischer, Stanley, 99n, 393n
Fisher, Irving, 94, 104
Fisher effect, 93–96
 evidence on, 95f, 95–96, 96f

Fixed exchange rates, 4, 33–34, 38f, 141–148
 Argentine Convertibility Plan and, 362, 363f, 364, 370–371, 484
 central bank balance sheet and, 352–353, 355f, 355–356, 371–373
 changes in composition of money supply and, 364–369
 changes in level of money demand and, 356–359, 358f
 contingent monetary policies and, 384–392
 costs and benefits of pegging and, 389–390
 criteria for, 312f, 312–313
 ERM and, 305–310
 exchange rate crises and. *See* Exchange rate crises
 fiscal discipline, seigniorage, and inflation and, 318–321, 320t
 fiscal policy under, short-run IS-LM-FX model and, 284–287, 285f
 floating rates versus, 141
 hard pegs and, 394
 inconsistent fiscal policies and, 376–384
 liability dollarization, national wealth, and contractionary depreciations and, 321–326
 mechanics of, 351–376
 monetary autonomy and stability and, 315–318
 monetary policy autonomy and, 141–144, 143f
 monetary policy under, short-run IS-LM-FX model and, 282f, 282–283
 pegged currency blocs and, 291
 recent experiences with, 34–39
 reserves and, 353, 354–355
 risk premiums in advanced and emerging markets and, 351f, 359–362
 trade promotion and, 313–315
 trilemma and, 144–148, 146f, 147f
Fixed exchange rate systems, 328–335
 Bretton Woods system, 328, 338–339, 339f, 340

 cooperative and noncooperative adjustments to exchange rates and, 331–333, 332f
 cooperative and noncooperative adjustments to interest rates and, 328–330, 329f
 gold standard and, 333–335
Fixed line, 356
Flandreau, Marc, 313n
Flexible exchange rates, 4. *See also* Floating exchange rates
Floating exchange rates, 4, 33–34, 38f
 fiscal policy under, short-run IS-LM-FX model and, 283–284, 284f
 monetary policy under, short-run IS-LM-FX model and, 281f, 281–282
 recent experiences with, 34–39
 reserves and, 354–355
Floating line, 356
Flow of payments
 circular, 158
 in closed economy, 158–160, 159f
 in open economy, 160, 161f, 162
Ford, Alec, 253
Forecast error, 461
Forecasting exchange rates
 methodologies for, 134
 monetary approach to exchange rates and, 82–85, 84f
 using general model, 97–99, 98f
 when real exchange rate is under- or overvalued, 73
Foreign aid, 234
Foreign direct investment (FDI), 164
Foreign exchange, 2–8, 25. *See also* Exchange rate(s)
 market for, 25
Foreign exchange (forex or FX) market, 39–43
 asset approach to exchange rates and, 126–127
 derivatives and, 40f, 40–41
 equilibrium in. *See* Foreign exchange market equilibrium
 government actions and, 42–43
 private actors in, 42
 spot contracts and, 39–40

 transaction costs and, 40
 in wartime, 148–152
 Foreign exchange market equilibrium, 114t, 114–118, 115f
 adjustment to, 115–116
 changes in domestic and foreign returns and, 116–118, 117f
 IS curve derivation and, 269–275
Foreign reserves, 220
Forex market. *See* Foreign exchange (forex or FX) market
Forward(s), 40, 41
Forward cover, 48
Forward exchange rate, 47–49
 determinants of, 48–49
Forward premium, 54
France
 borrowing to finance wars and, 217
 discretionary fiscal stimulus measures in, 497t
 dollarization of trade and, 263t
 in Eurozone, 420t
 Eurozone convergence criteria and, 428, 429f
 foreign aid from, 169
 FX trade in, 39
 sovereign rating and public debt level of, 211f
 Treaty of Rome and, 415
 U.S. "exorbitant privilege" and, 208
Frankel, Jeffrey A., 55f, 264, 346n, 349, 349f, 452n, 463f
Frantz, Brian, 313n, 336n
Freddie Mac, 493
Free float, 34
Friberg, Richard, 315n
Friedman, Milton, 303, 305, 345, 393, 399
Fuertes, Ana-Maria, 467n
Fujimori, Alberto, 383
Fundamental equation of the asset approach to exchange rates, 113, 113f
Fundamental equation of the monetary approach to exchange rates, 80–81, 96
Fundamental equation of the monetary model of the price level, 79, 96
Futures, 40, 41
FX Beauties Club, 458

FX market. *See* Foreign exchange (forex or FX) market
FX market diagram, 114–115, 115f

G

Galbraith, John Kenneth, 434
Gambia, gross national disposable income in, 168f
García Pérez, Alan, 381, 383
Gargan, Edward A., 42n
GDP. *See* Gross domestic product (GDP)
G-8 economies, 235
Geldof, Bob, 235
Gelpern, Anna, 480n
General equilibrium, 270
German model, 424
Germany. *See also* West Germany
   covered interest parity for United Kingdom and, 49–50, 50f
   discretionary fiscal stimulus measures in, 497t
   dollarization of trade and, 263t
   ERM and, 306–310
   in Eurozone, 420t
   Eurozone convergence criteria and, 428, 429f
   exchange rate of, 148, 337
   expenditure switching and dollar devaluation and, 259
   foreign aid from, 169
   Great Recession in, 499
   hyperinflation in, 88
   monetary policy of, 330
   reparations to, 217
   reunification of, 418
   sovereign rating and public debt level of, 211f
Gersovitz, Mark, 469n
Ghana
   economic crisis of 1982–1989 in, 351t
   gross national disposable income in, 168f
   sovereign rating and public debt level of, 211f
Ghosh, Atish R., 316n
Glass-Steagall Act, 492
Glick, Reuven, 336n, 393n
Global Financial Crisis, 486–505, 494f
   backdrop to, 487–494
   exacerbating policies and distortions and, 491–493

   Great Recession and, 486, 494, 495t, 496–504
   preconditions for, 488–491, 489f, 491f
Global imbalances, 488
Globalization, of finance, Financial globalization
GNDI. *See* Gross national disposable income (GNDI)
GNE. *See* Gross national expenditure (GNE)
GNI. *See* Gross national income (GNI)
GNP. *See* Gross national product (GNP)
Goal independence, 424
Goldberg, Linda, 263t
Goldberg, Pinelopi Koujianou, 315n
Gold standard, 303–304, 333–338
   rise and fall of, 335–338, 338f
Gold Standard Act of 1900, 336
Goldstein, Maurice, 393n
Gollin, Douglas, 227n
Gono, Gideon, 89
Goodenough, Simon, 260
Goods, nontraded, deviations from purchasing power parity and, 72
Goods market equilibrium condition, 266–275
   determinants of demand and, 266–268, 267f
   factors shifting the demand curve and, 268–269
   IS curve derivation and, 269–275
Goods market integration, in EU, 407–408
Gordon, David B., 425n
Gourinchas, Pierre-Olivier, 208n
Governance. *See also* Institutions
   in developing countries, 18–19
Government
   demand in an open economy and, 256–257
   foreign exchange market and, 42–43
Government consumption, 256
Government debt, monetizing of, 318
Government failure, 493
Government saving, 175f, 175–176

Government spending
   shifts in demand curve and, 268
   shifts in IS curve and, 273
Granada, sovereign rating and public debt level of, 211f
Great Britain. *See* Britain; United Kingdom
Great Depression, gold standard and, 337
Great Recession, 486, 494–504, 497t, 498f–499f
   Europe and, 499, 500f, 501
   financial decelerators and, 496
   recovery from, 502–504
   rest of world and, 501–502, 503f
   timeline for, 495t
Greece
   dollarization of trade and, 263t
   in EC, 415, 418
   economic crisis in, 124
   EU/IMF emergency funding for, 432–433
   in Eurozone, 420t, 421
   Eurozone convergence criteria and, 429f
   Great Recession in, 501
   manipulation of statistics by, 191
   sovereign default of, 468
Greenspan, Alan, 253, 492
Gros, Daniel, 210
Gross domestic product (GDP)
   flow of payments in a closed economy and, 158–160, 159f
   flow of payments in an open economy and, 160, 161f, 162
   gross national expenditure and, 163–164
   gross national income and, 164–165
   Irish Miracle and, 165–167, 166f
   long-run budget constraint and, 206–210
Gross national disposable income (GNDI), 9, 160, 161f, 162
   gross national income and, 167–168, 168f
Gross national expenditure (GNE), 9
   flow of payments in a closed economy and, 158, 159f, 160

   flow of payments in an open economy and, 160, 161f, 162
   gross domestic product and, 163–164
   long-run budget constraint and, 206–210
Gross national income (GNI)
   flow of payments in a closed economy and, 159, 159f, 160
   flow of payments in an open economy and, 160, 161f, 162
   gross domestic product and, 164–165
   gross national disposable income and, 167–168, 168f
Gross national product (GNP), 165n
Grubisic, Elena, 370n
Guidotti, Pablo E., 212n
Guinea-Bissau, gross national disposable income in, 168f
Guinnane, Timothy W., 150n
Gulde, Anne-Marie, 316n
Gumbel, Peter, 4n
Guo, Xueyan, 393n
Guyana, gross national disposable income in, 168f

H

Half-life, 72
Hall, Robert E., 229n
Hamilton, Alexander, 468n
Hausmann, Ricardo, 209n, 325, 325t, 326n
Hedging, 41
Hickman, Leo, 260
High-grade bonds, 13
Hoffman, Philip T., 485n
Hoggarth, Glenn, 479n, 481f, 482f
Home bias, 242–244, 243f, 244f
Home goods, marginal propensity to consume, 261
Honduras, gross national disposable income in, 168f
Hong Kong
   Big Mac index and, 75t
   budget surplus of, 10f
   dollar peg and, 459
   FX trade in, 39
   hard peg of, 394
Horioka, Charles, 226
Hugo, Victor, 414

Hungary
  Big Mac index and, 74, 75t
  dollarization of trade and, 263t
  economic crisis of 1991–1995 in, 351t
  in EU, 420t
  hyperinflation in, 88, 90
  sovereign rating and public debt level of, 211f
Hupfeld, Herman, 63
Hurricanes, economic shocks and, 200, 200f
Husain, Aasim M., 317n, 320t, 393n
Hussein, Saddam, 150, 151f, 152
Hutchison, Michael M., 212n, 393n
Hyperinflation, 86
  money demand in, 88, 88f, 90
  purchasing power parity and, 86–88, 87f
  redenomination and, 90
  in Zimbabwe, 89, 90

I

IBRD. *See* International Bank for Reconstruction and Development (IBRD)
Iceland
  Big Mac index and, 75t
  currency crisis of 2008 in, 5, 6f
  EU and, 400
  sovereign rating and public debt level of, 211f
Idiosyncratic shocks, common shocks versus, 251–252
Illiquidity, 369
Imbs, Jean, 315n
IMF. *See* International Monetary Fund (IMF)
Imperfect competition, deviations from purchasing power parity and, 72–73
Import(s)
  factor service, 160
  flow of payments and, 160
  marginal propensity to consume, 260–261
Income, 9
  gross national, 159, 159f, 160
  trade balance and, 258, 259f, 260
Income account, 183
Income approach to measuring economic activity, 163, 167–168, 168f
Income per capita, 19
Income volatility, 19

India
  capital flow to, 232t
  discretionary fiscal stimulus measures in, 497t
  exchange rate of, 35, 36f
  foreign aid to, 235
  sovereign rating and public debt level of, 211f
Indonesia
  Big Mac index and, 75t
  budget surplus of, 10f
  capital flow to, 232t
  currency crisis of 1997 in, 5, 6f
  default by, 12
  discretionary fiscal stimulus measures in, 497t
  economic crisis of 1997 in, 287–289, 288f, 289f, 351t
  exchange rate crisis in, 347f, 349
  sovereign rating and public debt level of, 211f
Inefficient markets, 462
Inflation, 68. *See also* Hyperinflation
  interest rates and, in long run, 92–93
  money growth and depreciation and, 81–82
  nominal anchors and, 99, 100–102
  relative PPP and exchange rate depreciation and, 68–69
Inflation bias, 406
  monetary union and, 424–425
Inflation target(s), 424
Inflation target plus interest rate policy, 101
Inflation tax, 318–321, 320t
Inside lag, 290
Insolvency, 367
Institutions, 14
  economic performance and, 17f, 17–20
Instrument independence, 424
Interbank trading, 42
Interest rates
  arbitrage and, 47–57, 57f
  central bank control of, 123–124
  changes in level of, fixed exchange rates and, 356–359, 358f
  cooperative and noncooperative adjustments to, fixed exchange rate systems and, 328–330, 329f

  domestic, FX market equilibrium and, 116, 117f
  exchange rates in short run and. *See* Asset approach to exchange rates
  fall in, IS curve derivation and, 272–273
  foreign, FX market equilibrium and, 117f, 118
  inflation and, in long run, 92–93
  market, 123
  nominal. *See* Nominal interest rate
  policy fate of Federal Reserve, 123
  real. *See* Real interest rate
  shifts in demand curve and, 268
  shifts in IS curve and, 273
  short-run money market equilibrium and. *See* Short-run money market equilibrium
  transmission mechanism and, 123
Interest rate spread, 360
International Bank for Reconstruction and Development (IBRD), 235
International finance
  financial openness and, 14–15, 15f
  regulation of, 14–15, 15f
International Monetary Fund (IMF), 5, 394–395
  evaluation of, 487
  exchange rates and, 37n
  loans to Argentina from, 370–371, 395
International trade
  fixed exchange rates and, 313–315
  free. *See* Free trade *entries*
  levels of, fixed exchange rates and, 313–314, 314f
International transactions of account (ITA), 182n
Intertemporal approach, 201
Intervention, 43
Investment
  delinking saving from, 225–227, 226f
  demand in an open economy and, 256, 257f
  efficient. *See* Efficient investment
  exogenous change in, 265
  foreign. *See* Foreign direct investment (FDI)

Investment-grade bonds, 13
Iraq, U.S. war in, 217
Iraq War, foreign exchange market and, 150, 151f, 152
Ireland
  in EC, 415
  in Eurozone, 420t
  Eurozone convergence criteria and, 429f
  foreign aid to, 236
  Great Recession in, 501
  growth in economic activity of, 165–167, 166f
  sovereign rating and public debt level of, 211f
Irish Miracle, 165–167, 166f
Irrevocable peg, 419
IS curve, 269–275
  derivation of, 272–273
  factors shifting, 273–275, 274
  IS-LM-FX model, short-run, 279f, 279–287
  fiscal policy under fixed exchange rates and, 284–287, 285f
  fiscal policy under floating exchange rates and, 283–284, 284f
  macroeconomic policies in short run and, 280
  monetary policy under fixed exchange rates and, 282f, 282–283
  monetary policy under floating exchange rates and, 281f, 281–282
  IS-LM model, adjustments to exchange rates and, 331–332, 332f
Israel
  Big Mac index and, 75t
  economic crisis of 1977–1983 in, 351t
  foreign aid to, 236
  sovereign rating and public debt level of, 211f
ITA. *See* International transactions of account (ITA)
Italy
  budget deficit of, 10f
  currency of, 404
  discretionary fiscal stimulus measures in, 497t
  dollarization of trade and, 263t
  in EC, 418
  in ERM, 419
  in Eurozone, 420t
  Eurozone convergence criteria and, 428, 429f

exchange rate crisis in, 347f
manipulation of statistics by, 191
sovereign rating and public debt level of, 211f
Treaty of Rome and, 415
Ito, Hiro, 15f, 176n
Itoh, Ms., 458
Izquierdo, Alejandro, 212f

J

Jamaica
  economic crisis of 1995–2000 in, 351t
  sovereign rating and public debt level of, 211f
Japan
  Big Mac index and, 74, 75t
  budget surplus of, 10f
  discretionary fiscal stimulus measures in, 497t
  dollarization of trade and, 263t
  economic crisis of 1991 in, 351t
  exchange rate of, 27t, 34, 35f, 340
  FX trade in, 39
  Great Recession in, 501–502, 503f
  online currency trading in, 458
  sovereign rating and public debt level of, 211f
J curve, 264, 264f
Jeanne, Olivier, 220n
Jefferson, Thomas, 1, 2
Johnson, Simon, 20n
Jones, Charles I., 229n, 232n
Jordan
  gross national disposable income in, 168f
  sovereign rating and public debt level of, 211f
Junk bonds, 13

K

KA. *See* Capital account (KA)
Kalemli-Ozcan, Sebnem, 233n
Kaminsky, Graciela L., 350n
Kanczuk, Fabio, 469n
Kapur, Sandeep, 470n
Karasulu, Meral, 487
Kaufmann, Daniel, 17f
Kazakhstan
  currency crisis of 1999 in, 6f
  sovereign rating and public debt level of, 211f

Kenya, capital flow to, 232t
Keynes, John Maynard, 111, 303, 304, 338, 441
Keynesian consumption function, 255f, 255–256
Keynesian cross, 267f, 267–268
King, Mervyn, 150n, 151f, 423
Kisselev, Kate, 324f, 324n
Kitchen, John, 208n
Klein, Michael W., 314, 314f, 354n
Kletzer, Kenneth M., 469n
Klingen, Christoph, 475
Kohm, Meir G., 468n
Korea. *See also* South Korea
  dollarization of trade and, 263t
  economic crisis of 1997 in, 287–289, 288f, 289f
Kose, M. Ayhan, 15f, 219n, 245n
Kosovo, currency of, 400n
Krugman, Paul, 295n, 376
Kuwait, sovereign wealth funds of, 220
Kydland, Finn E., 425n
Kyrgyz Republic, gross national disposable income in, 168f

L

Labor market integration, in optimum currency areas, 405, 407f
Labor mobility, in EU, 408, 409f
Lahrèche-Révil, Amina, 453n
La Maison Removals, 260
Lamont, Norman, 349
Lamy, Pascal, 259
Lane, Philip R., 12f, 15f, 326n, 436n, 468n
La Porta, Rafael, 20n
Latin America. *See also specific countries*
  exchange rates in, 36, 36f
Latvia
  Big Mac index and, 75t
  dollarization of trade and, 263t
  in ERM, 401, 420t
  euro and, 16, 454
  Great Recession in, 501
  sovereign rating and public debt level of, 211f
Law of one price (LOOP), 64–66, 443–444
Lee, Jaewoo, 220n

Legal obstacles, deviations from purchasing power parity and, 72–73
Lehman Brothers, 493
Lehman Brothers Holdings Inc., 221
Lender(s), net, 184
Lender of last resort, 369
  international, case for, 394–395
Lending rate, 470
  lender choice of, 474–475
Leon, Hyginus, 467n
Lesotho, gross national disposable income in, 168f
Levy-Yeyati, Eduardo, 12n, 317n, 482n
Lewis, Karen K., 242, 243f
Liabilities, 353
  dollarization of, fixed exchange rates and, 321–326, 323f, 324f, 325t
Liberia
  currency crisis of 1998 in, 5, 6f
  currency of, 404
  gross national disposable income in, 168f
Libya, sovereign wealth funds of, 220
Limited flexibility policy, 35
Limits to arbitrage, 464–467
Lincoln, Abraham, 150
Lipsky, John, 487
Liquidity, 51
  of money, 76
Liquidity trap, 291–295, 292f, 294f
Lithuania
  Big Mac index and, 75t
  in ERM, 401, 420t
  euro and, 16, 454
  Great Recession in, 501
  sovereign rating and public debt level of, 211f
Live Aid, 235
Live 8, 235
LM curve, 275–279
  derivation of, 277
  factors shifting, 277–278, 278f
Loans
  from IMF, 370–371, 395
  perpetual, 205–206
  sovereign default and. *See* Sovereign default; *specific countries*
  supply and demand for, 476–479, 477f
  war, from United States, 217

Lommatzsch, Kirsten, 453n
Long run
  exchange rates and. *See* Monetary approach to exchange rates
  monetary policy autonomy in, fixed exchange rates and, 143–144
Long-run budget constraint (LRBC), 201–220
  consumption smoothing and, 212–220
  determination of, 202–203
  emerging markets and, 210, 211f, 212, 212f
  implications for gross national expenditure and gross domestic product, 206–210
  perpetual loan and, 205–206
  in two-period example, 203–205
Long-run equilibrium, in money market, 92
Loonies, 34
LOOP. *See* Law of one price (LOOP)
López Córdova, J. Ernesto, 313n
Lopez-de-Silanes, Florencio, 20n
Lothian, James R., 233n
LRBC. *See* Long-run budget constraint (LRBC)
Lucas, Robert E., Jr., 230, 232t
Luxembourg
  in Eurozone, 420t
  Eurozone convergence criteria and, 429f
  sovereign rating and public debt level of, 211f
  Treaty of Rome and, 415
Lyons, Richard K., 466

M

Maastricht Treaty, 399, 400, 414, 416, 418, 423
Macedonia
  economic crisis of 1993–1994 in, 351t
  EU and, 400
  gross national disposable income in, 168f
  name of, 400n
Macroeconomic policy. *See also* Exchange rate(s); Fiscal policy; Foreign exchange *entries*; Monetary policy
  beggar-thy-neighbor, 333
  constraints on, 290

Macroeconomic policy (*continued*)
  improving to prevent exchange rate crises, 394
  incomplete information and inside lag and, 290
  in liquidity trap, 291–295, 292f, 294f
  long-horizon plans and, 290
  pegged currency blocs and, 291
  policy response and outside lag and, 290
  problems in design and implementation of, 290–291
  in short run, 280
  weak links from nominal to real exchange rate and, 290–291
  weak links from real exchange rate to trade balance and, 291
Madagascar, currency crisis of 2004 in, 6f
Major, John, 349
Malaysia
  Big Mac index and, 75t
  budget surplus of, 10f
  currency crisis of 1997 in, 5, 6f
  dollarization of trade and, 263t
  economic crisis of 1985–1988 in, 351t
  exchange rate crisis of 1997 in, 393
  prices in, 446
  sovereign rating and public debt level of, 211f
  sovereign wealth funds of, 220
Malta
  currency of, 401
  euro coins of, 16
  in Eurozone, 420t, 421
  sovereign rating and public debt level of, 211f
Managed float, 35
Mankiw, N. Gregory, 99n
Marginal product of capital (MPK), 225
  financial globalization and, 227–234
Marginal propensity to consume (MPC), 256
  foreign imports and, 260–261
  home goods and, 261
Marginal propensity to save (*MPS*), 256
Market failure, 493
Market for foreign exchange, 25

Market frictions, 40
Market integration
  in optimum currency areas, 405, 407f, 407–408
  optimum currency areas and, 402
Market power, deviations from purchasing power parity and, 72–73
Market rates of interest, 123
Marks and Spencer, 260
Marsh, Ian W., 134
Marshall, George C., 415n
Marshall-Lerner condition, 300–301
Marshall Plan, 415
Mastruzzi, Massimo, 17f
Maturity, of forward contracts, 41
Maurel, Mathilde, 313n
Mauritania, economic crisis of 1984–1993 in, 351t
Mauro, Paolo, 104n
McCandless, George T., Jr., 149f, 150n
McKinley, William, Jr., 336
McKinnon, Ronald, 303, 305
Medium of exchange, money as, 76
Meissner, Christopher M., 209n, 304f, 313n, 326n, 336n
Mejia, Luis-Fernando, 212f
Mendoza, Enrique G., 220n
Menu costs, 119
Mexico
  Big Mac index and, 75t
  bond rating of, 13
  capital flow to, 232t
  currency mismatch and, 326
  default by, 12, 468, 480
  discretionary fiscal stimulus measures in, 497t
  economic crisis of 1994–1997 in, 351t, 488
  exchange rate crisis in, 347f
  Great Recession in, 502
  marginal product of capital of, 229–230
  prices in, 446
  risk premiums in, 362
  sovereign rating and public debt level of, 211f
  Tequila Crisis in, 364, 369–371
Middle East. *See specific countries*
Milesi-Ferretti, Gian Maria, 12f, 15f, 468n
Mill, John Stuart, 1–2, 157, 402
Millennium Challenge Account, 236

Mishkin, Frederic, 384n
Missing middle, 393
Mitchell, Wesley, 150n
Mladenovic, Zorica, 87f
M0 money measure, 76–77
M1 money measure, 77
M2 money measure, 77
M3 money measure, 77n
M4 money measure, 77n
Mobutu Sese Soko, 235
Mody, Ashoka, 317n, 320t, 393n
Mohamad, Mahathir, 42
Moldova
  currency crisis of 1998 in, 6f
  gross national disposable income in, 168f
Monaco, currency of, 400n
Monetary approach to exchange rates, 63–105
  asset approach unified with, 131–140, 133f
  evidence for, 85f, 85–86, 86f
  exchange rate depreciation and, 68–69
  exchange rate forecasts and, 82–85
  fundamental equation of, 80–81, 96
  general model for, 90–99
  hyperinflation and, 86–90
  law of one price and, 64–66
  long-run policy analysis and, 132–138
  monetary regimes and exchange rate regimes and, 99–104
  money market equilibrium and, 76–82
  nominal exchange rate and, 68, 68f
  overshooting and, 138–140, 139f, 140f
  purchasing power parity and. *See* Purchasing power parity (PPP)
  real exchange rate and, 67, 73
Monetary autonomy, fixed exchange rates and, 315–318
Monetary model of the price level, fundamental equation of, 79, 96
Monetary policy, 280
  autonomy of, fixed exchange rates and, 141–144, 143f
  contingent, fixed exchange rates and, 384–392

  exchange rate regime choice and, 16f, 16–17, 305–318
  under fixed exchange rates, short-run IS-LM-FX model and, 282f, 282–283
  under floating exchange rates, short-run IS-LM-FX model and, 281f, 281–282
  optimum currency areas and, 406–407
  time inconsistency of, 425
  too-easy, 492
Monetary policy shocks
  permanent, domestic, asset approach to exchange rates and, 134–135, 136f
  permanent, asset approach to exchange rates and, 132–138
  permanent, overshooting and, 138–140, 139f, 140f
  temporary, domestic, asset approach to exchange rates and, 127–129, 128f
  temporary, foreign, asset approach to exchange rates and, 129f, 129–130
Monetary regimes, 100
  exchange rate regimes and, 99–104
Monetary unions, 37
Monetizing, of government debt, 318
Money, 76
  definition of, 76
  functions of, 76
  liquidity of, 76
  measurement of, 76–77, 77f
  quantity theory of, 78
Money demand, 78–79
  changes in level of, fixed exchange rates and, 356–359, 358f
  general model of, 91, 92f
  in hyperinflations, 88, 88f, 90
Money market, asset approach to exchange rates and, 125–127, 126f
Money market equilibrium, 79
  LM curve and, 275–279
  long-run, 92
  short-run. *See* Short-run money market equilibrium
Money of zero maturity (MZM), 77n
Money supply, 77–78
  change in, money market equilibrium and, 121–122, 122f

change in composition of, fixed exchange rates and, 364–369
foreign, shock to, asset approach to exchange rates and, 129f, 129–130
home, shock to, asset approach to exchange rates and, 127–129, 128f
inflation and depreciation and, 81–82
Money supply targets, 100–101
Mongolia, sovereign rating and public debt level of, 211f
Monnet, Jean, 399, 436
Montenegro, currency of, 400n
Moore, J. S., 313
Moral hazard, 326, 395, 493
Morgenthau, Henry, 339
Morocco, sovereign rating and public debt level of, 211f
Mozambique, foreign aid to, 236
MPC. *See* Marginal propensity to consume *(MPC)*
MPK. *See* Marginal product of capital (MPK)
MPS. *See* Marginal propensity to save *(MPS)*
Mugabe, Robert, 89
Multilateral exchange rates, 30–31, 31f
Multiple equilibria, 385
Mumtaz, Haroon, 315n
Mundell, Robert, 253, 399
Mussa, Michael, 485n
MZM. *See* Money of zero maturity (MZM)

N

National economic aggregates
current account and, 169, 172–173
data for, 170t, 170–172, 171f, 172f
global imbalances and, 173–177, 174f, 175f, 177f
information provided by, 168–170
measurement of. *See* Economic activity
National income and product accounts (NIPA), 158, 182n
National income identity, 172
National saving, 173
National wealth, fixed exchange rates and, 321–326, 323f, 324f, 325f

Nepal, gross national disposable income in, 168f
Net borrowers, 184
Net creditors, 187
Net debtors, 187
Net exports, 164
Net factor income from abroad (NFIA), 160, 161f, 165
Netherlands
in Eurozone, 420t
Eurozone convergence criteria and, 429f
exchange rate of, 148
sovereign rating and public debt level of, 211f
Treaty of Rome and, 415
Net lenders, 184
Moral hazard, 326, 395, 493
Net unilateral transfers (NUT), 160, 161f
Network externalities, 336
Net worth. *See* External wealth; Wealth
New Zealand
Asian crisis of 1997 and, 287–289, 288f, 289f
Big Mac index and, 75t
Pitcairn Islands' use of currency of, 37
sovereign rating and public debt level of, 211f
New Zealand model, 424
NFIA. *See* Net factor income from abroad (NFIA)
Nicaragua, gross national disposable income in, 168f
Nigeria
capital flow to, 232t
currency crisis of 1999 in, 6f
default by, 12
NIPA. *See* National income and product accounts (NIPA)
No-arbitrage band, 443
No-arbitrage condition, 43
Nominal anchors, 99, 100–102
asset approach to exchange rates and, 130–131, 131f
choice of, 101–102, 102t
exchange rate regimes and, 101–102, 102t
in theory and practice, 102–104, 103t
Nominal concepts, 67
Nominal exchange rate
absolute PPP and, 68, 68f
forecasting, 450–451
weak links to real exchange rate, 290–291
Nominal interest rate

change in, money market equilibrium and, 121–124, 122f
determination of, 118–120
Nominal rigidity, 119
Nonbank financial institutions, in foreign exchange market, 42
Nontraded goods, deviations from purchasing power parity and, 72
North America. *See specific countries*
Norway
Big Mac index and, 75t
economic crisis of 1987–1993 in, 351t
exchange rate of, 27t
foreign aid from, 169
Great Recession in, 502
oil boom in, 225–227, 226f
sovereign rating and public debt level of, 211f
sovereign wealth funds of, 220
Noy, Ilan, 212n
Nth currency problem, 328
NUT. *See* Net unilateral transfers (NUT)

O

Obama, Barack, 295n
Obstfeld, Maurice, 50f, 96f, 315n, 335n, 338n, 354n, 367n, 385, 444n, 479n
OCAs. *See* Optimum currency areas (OCAs)
ODA. *See* Official development assistance (ODA)
OECD countries. *See* Organization for Economic Cooperation and Development (OECD) countries
Officer, Lawrence, 335n
Official development assistance (ODA), 167
Official markets, 43
Oganes, Luis, 221
Oman, sovereign rating and public debt level of, 211f
O'Neill, Jim, 457
O'Neill, Paul, 25, 26
Online currency trading, 458
Oomes, Nienke, 304f, 317n, 320t, 326n, 393n
OPEC. *See* Organization of Petroleum Exporting Countries (OPEC)

Open economies
demand in, 254–266
flow of payments in, 160, 161f, 162
short-run IS-LM-FX model of. *See* IS-LM-FX model, short-run
Optimum currency areas (OCAs), 402–414. *See also* Currency unions
criteria for, 403, 403f, 405–412, 410f, 411f
economic stability and, 402
efficiency benefits of, 402
in Europe versus United States, 407–410, 410f
fixed versus currency unions and, 404
market integration and, 402
stability costs of, 402
Options, 40, 41
Organization for Economic Cooperation and Development (OECD) countries, 169
Organization of Petroleum Exporting Countries (OPEC), 225
Orresta, Beatriz, 7, 8
Orresta, Jonatan, 8
Orresta, Santiago, 7, 8
Ostrey, Jonathan D., 316n
Otker-Robe, Inci, 393n
Output
changes in level of, fixed exchange rates and, 356–359, 358f
increase in output of, sovereign debt and, 473–474, 474f
Output volatility, fixed exchange rates and, 316–318, 318f
Outside lag, 290
Overshooting, 138–140, 139f, 140f
Overvalued currencies, 67

P

Pakistan
Big Mac index and, 75t
capital flow to, 232t
default by, 12
foreign aid to, 235
sovereign rating and public debt level of, 211f
Pakko, Michael R., 446f
Panama, sovereign rating and public debt level of, 211f

Panizza, Ugo G., 12n, 325, 325t, 326n, 482n
Papua New Guinea, sovereign rating and public debt level of, 211f
Paraguay
  economic crisis of 1995–1999 in, 351t
  sovereign rating and public debt level of, 211f
Parallel markets, 43
Parity conditions
  covered interest parity and, 47–51, 49f, 50f
  uncovered interest parity and, 51–55, 53f, 55f
Parsley, David C., 264, 444n
Pass-through, 263
Payments. *See* Balance of payments; Balance of payments (BOP) accounts; Flow of payments
Pearson, Steven, 457
Pegged exchange rates, 33–34. *See also* Fixed exchange rates
People's Bank of China, 374
Perpetual loans, 205–206
Perri, Fabrizio, 324f, 324n
Peru
  Big Mac index and, 75t
  defaults by, 12
  economic crisis of 1986 in, 381, 382f, 383–384
  sovereign rating and public debt level of, 211f
Pesek, William, 487
Peso problem, 459–461
Petrovic, Pavle, 87f
Philippines
  Big Mac index and, 75t
  currency crisis of 1997 in, 5, 6f
  default by, 12, 480
  economic crisis of 1998 in, 351t
  sovereign rating and public debt level of, 211f
Pitcairn Islands, dollarization in, 37
Poland
  Big Mac index and, 75t
  bond rating of, 13
  sovereign rating and public debt level of, 211f
Policies, 14–21
  macroeconomic. *See* Fiscal policy; Macroeconomic policy; Monetary policy
Political costs, of exchange rate crises, 349, 349f

Political objectives, of optimum currency areas, 407
Politics, forecasting exchange rates and, 134
Pollard, Patricia S., 446f
Polonius, 1, 2
Ponzi, Charles, 202n
Ponzi games, 202
Portugal
  in EC, 415
  economic crisis in, 124
  in ERM, 418, 419
  in Eurozone, 420t
  Eurozone convergence criteria and, 428, 429f
  Great Recession in, 501
  sovereign default of, 468
  sovereign rating and public debt level of, 211f
Postel-Vinay, Gilles, 485n
Powell, Andrew, 370n, 485n
PPP. *See* Purchasing power parity (PPP)
Prakash-Canjels, Gauri, 334n
Prasad, Eswar S., 15f, 219n, 245n
Precautionary saving, 219–220
Premiums, forward, 54
Prescott, Edward C., 425n
Present value, 204
Price(s)
  comparing in a common currency using exchange rates, 31t, 31–33
  inflation and. *See* Inflation
  law of one price and, 64–66
  purchasing power parity and. *See* Purchasing power parity (PPP)
  simple monetary model of, 79–80, 80f
  stickiness of, deviations from purchasing power parity and, 73–74
Price convergence, fixed exchange rates and, 315
Price level. *See also* Hyperinflation; Inflation
  Canada-U.S. comparison of, 111
  fundamental equation of monetary model of, 79, 96
  monetary model of, fundamental equation of, 79, 96
  shifts in demand curve and, 269
  shifts in IS curve and, 274
Private saving, 174–176, 175f

Product approach to measuring economic activity, 163, 164–167, 166f
Production function, 227–228, 228f
Productivity, 227
  changes in, prices and, 448
Purchasing power, 64
Purchasing power parity (PPP), 66–74, 112, 442–453
  absolute, 66–68, 70
  Big Mac index and, 74, 75t
  deviations from, explanations for, 72–74
  evidence for, 70f, 70–71, 71f
  exchange rates in long run and, 442–453
  fiscal dominance and, 377
  hyperinflation and, 86–88, 87f
  nominal exchange rate and, 68, 68f
  real exchange rate and, 67
  relative, 68–70
  speed of convergence to, 71–72
Puts, options and, 41

Q

Qatar
  sovereign rating and public debt level of, 211f
  sovereign wealth funds of, 220
Quantitative easing (QE), 123, 503
Quantity theory of money, 78, 90
Quantum Fund, 391–392

R

Rajan, Raghuram G., 234, 236
Ranciere, Romain, 220n
Rapach, David E., 86n
Rate of return, 51
  expected, 51
Rational expectations hypothesis, 462
Ravn, Morten O., 315n
Real appreciation, 67
Real concepts, 67
Real depreciation, 67
Real exchange rates
  absolute PPP and, 67
  arbitrage and, 443
  in emerging markets, 451–453

  equilibrium, 447
  forecasting, 450
  Marshall-Lerner condition and, 300–301
  multilateral, 302
  over- and undervaluations and productivity growth and, 449f, 449–451
  trade balance and, 257–258, 261f, 261–262
  weak links to nominal exchange rate, 290–291
  weak links to trade balance from, 291
Real interest parity, 94–95
Real interest rate, 94–95
  expected, 256
  world, 94–95, 202
Real money demand function, 91
Rebelo, Sergio, 384n
Recessions. *See also* Great Recession
  credibility of peg and, 388–389
Redenomination of currencies, 90
Regimes, 14
  exchange rate. *See* Exchange rate regimes
  monetary. *See* Monetary regimes
Reich, Gabriel Chodorow, 208n
Reinhart, Carmen M., 37n, 212, 350n, 468n, 479n
Relative PPP, 69
  inflation and exchange rate depreciation and, 69
  inflation and interest rates in long run and, 93
Repayment threshold, 471
Reserve(s), 353, 354–355
  accumulation in emerging markets, 374f, 374–375, 375f
  adjustment to maintain peg, 354–355
  critical level of, 383–384
  fixed versus floating exchange rates and, 354
  foreign, 220
Reserve currency systems, 328
Revaluation, 331
Rey, Hélène, 208n, 315n
Ricardian equivalence, 176, 294
Rigidity, nominal, 119
Risk, 51
  of banking and exchange rate, 480–482, 481f, 482t

country, 13
diversifiable, 251
diversification of. *See*
  Diversification
undiversifiable, 251
Risk-adjusted foreign returns, 360
Riskless arbitrage, 47–51, 49f, 50f
Risk premiums, 359
  in advanced and emerging markets, 351f, 359–362
Risky arbitrage, 47, 51–55, 53f, 55f
  asset approach to exchange rates and, 112–113, 113f
Robinson, James A, 20n
Rogers, John H., 444n
Rogoff, Kenneth S., 15f, 37n, 103t, 245n, 317n, 320t, 354n, 393n, 468n, 469n, 479n
Romania, in EU, 400, 420t
Roodman, David, 169
Rose, Andrew K., 139n, 346n, 413, 480n
Rosen, Harvey S., 150n
Rosenthal, Jean-Laurent, 485n
Roubini, Nouriel, 324f, 324n
Russia
  Big Mac index and, 75t
  budget surplus of, 10f
  currency crisis of 1998 in, 5, 6f
  default by, 468
  defaults by, 12
  discretionary fiscal stimulus measures in, 497t
  economic crisis of 1998–1999 in, 351t
  exchange rate crisis in, 347f
  risk premiums in, 362
  sovereign rating and public debt level of, 211f
  sovereign wealth funds of, 220

S

Sachs, Jeffrey D., 89
Sainsbury's, 260
Samoa, gross national disposable income in, 168f
Samuelson, Paul, 447
San Marino, currency of, 400n
Saporta, Victoria, 479n, 481f, 482f
Sarno, Lucio, 367n, 467n
Saudi Arabia
  Big Mac index and, 75t
  discretionary fiscal stimulus measures in, 497t
  sovereign rating and public debt level of, 211f
  sovereign wealth funds of, 220
Savastano, Miguel A., 468n, 479n
Saving
  delinking from investment, 225–227, 226f
  government, 175f, 175–176
  marginal propensity to save and, 256
  national, 173
  precautionary, 219–220
  private, 174–176, 175f
Savings glut, 488
Schengen Treaty, 418
Schuler, Kurt, 356n, 394n
SD. *See* Statistical discrepancy (SD)
Seager, Ashley, 392n
Second-generation crisis model, 384–392
Seigniorage, 318–321, 320t
Self-confirming equilibrium, 389–390
Self-fulfilling expectations, 385
Self-insurance, to prevent exchange rate crises, 395
Senegal
  economic crisis of 1988–1991 in, 351t
  sovereign rating and public debt level of, 211f
Serbia
  currency of, 400n
  gross national disposable income in, 168f
  hyperinflation in, 88
Setser, Brad, 480n
Settlement date, for forward contracts, 41
Settlement risk, 39
Seychelles, currency crisis of 2007 in, 6f
SGP. *See* Stability and Growth Pact (SGP)
Shambaugh, Jay C., 37n, 314, 314f, 317, 318f, 326n, 354n
Sharpe, William Forsythe, 465
Sharpe ratio, 465f, 465–466
Shleifer, Andrei, 20n
Short run
  exchange rates and. *See* Asset approach to exchange rates
  monetary policy autonomy in, fixed exchange rates and, 141–142, 143f
Short-run equilibrium, in money market. *See* Short-run money market equilibrium
Short-run IS-LM-FX model. *See* IS-LM-FX model, short-run
Short-run money market equilibrium, 118–125, 121f
  adjustment to, 120–121
  changes in money supply and nominal interest rate and, 121–124, 122f
  changes in real income and nominal interest rate and, 122f, 124
  graphical solution for, 120, 120f
  nominal interest rate determination and, 118–120
Singapore
  Big Mac index and, 75t
  budget surplus of, 10f
  FX trade in, 39
  sovereign wealth funds of, 220
Slovakia
  currency of, 401
  dollarization of trade and, 263t
  euro and, 16, 454
  in Eurozone, 420t
  exchange rate of, 146
  real exchange rate with, 452–453
  sovereign rating and public debt level of, 211f
Slovenia
  currency of, 401
  euro and, 454
  in Eurozone, 420t, 421
  sovereign rating and public debt level of, 211f
Small open economies, 202
Smith, Adam, 18
Social efficiency, 232–233
Sokoloff, Kenneth L., 20n
Soros, George, 42n, 391–392
South Africa
  Big Mac index and, 75t
  capital flow to, 232t
  defaults by, 12
  discretionary fiscal stimulus measures in, 497t
  sovereign rating and public debt level of, 211f
South America. *See specific countries*
South Korea. *See also* Korea
  Big Mac index and, 75t
  budget surplus of, 10f
  currency crises of 1997 in, 5, 6f
  discretionary fiscal stimulus measures in, 497t
  economic crisis of 1997 in, 351t
  exchange rate crisis in, 347f
  exchange rate of, 35, 36f
  foreign aid to, 236
  IMF and, 487
  loan from IMF to, 394–395
  poverty overcome by, 235
  sovereign rating and public debt level of, 211f
Sovereign debt, 467–486
  as contingent claim, 469–470
  creditors and, 475f, 475–476
  default on. *See* Sovereign default
  increase in debt burden and, 472, 473f
Sovereign default, 468. *See also specific countries*
  costs of, 479–482
  probability of, 470–475
Sovereign wealth funds, 220, 221
Soviet Union. *See also* Russia
  disintegration of, 418
Spain
  budget deficit of, 10f
  dollarization of trade and, 263t
  in EC, 415
  economic crisis of 1977–1985 in, 351t
  in ERM, 418, 419
  in Eurozone, 420t
  Eurozone convergence criteria and, 428, 429f
  exchange rate crisis in, 347f, 393
  Great Recession in, 501
  sovereign default of, 468
  sovereign rating and public debt level of, 211f
Speculation, 41
Speculative attack, 379, 381
Spending. *See* Expenditure entries; Government spending
Spot contracts, 39–40
Spot exchange rate, 39
  determinants of, 52–53
Spread, 27n, 40
Sri Lanka
  Big Mac index and, 75t
  economic crisis of 1989–1993 in, 351t
Stability and Growth Pact (SGP), 429–430

Stabilization policy, 287–289, 288f, 289f
Starbucks, 446
Statistical discrepancy (SD), 185, 185f
Statistics, manipulation of, 191
Stein, Ernesto, 326n
Sterilization, 365–366
  in emerging markets, 374f, 374–375, 375f
Sterilization bonds, 372–373
Sterling Shopping, 260
Sterne, Gabriel, 103n
Steventon, John, 260
Sticky prices, deviations from purchasing power parity and, 73–74
"Stimulus" bill, 293–294
Store of value, money as, 76
Sturzenegger, Federico, 37n, 209n, 212n, 317n, 468n, 469n
Subramanian, Arvind, 234, 236
Sudden stops, 212, 212f
Summers, Lawrence, 345, 393n
Supply
  goods market equilibrium and, 266
  of money. *See* Money supply
Suriname, currency crisis of 1999 in, 6f
Surpluses, 9. *See also* Budget surpluses; Trade surpluses
Swaps, 40, 41
Sweden
  Big Mac index and, 75t
  currency of, 401, 419, 421
  in EU, 420t
  exchange rate crisis in, 347f
  exchange rate of, 27t
  interest rate in, 391
  sovereign rating and public debt level of, 211f
Switzerland
  Big Mac index and, 75t
  exchange rate of, 27t
  FX trade in, 39
  sovereign rating and public debt level of, 211f
Symmetric shocks, 311
Symmetry-integration diagrams, 312f, 312–313, 327, 327f

T

Taiwan
  Big Mac index and, 75t
  budget surplus of, 10f
  economic crisis of 1997–1998 in, 351t
  foreign aid to, 236
  poverty overcome by, 235
  sovereign wealth funds of, 220
Tajikistan, gross national disposable income in, 168f
Tanzania, economic crisis of 1980s and 1990s in, 351t
Taxes, 256
  inflation, 318–321, 320t
  shifts in demand curve and, 268
  shifts in IS curve and, 273
Taylor, Alan M., 50f, 74n, 96f, 209n, 226f, 313n, 315n, 334n, 335n, 336n, 338n, 444n, 479n, 485n
Taylor, Mark P., 74n, 367n
TB. *See* Trade balance (TB)
Technical efficiency, 231
Tequila Crisis (Mexico), 364, 369–371
Terrones, Marco E., 219n, 220n
Thailand
  Big Mac index and, 75t
  currency crisis of 1997 in, 6f
  dollarization of trade and, 263t
  economic crisis of 1997 in, 287–289, 288f, 289f, 351t
  exchange rate crisis in, 347f
  exchange rate of, 35, 36f, 37n
  sovereign rating and public debt level of, 211f
Tille, Cedric, 190n, 263n
Timor-Leste, gross national disposable income in, 168f
Tonga, gross national disposable income in, 168f
Too-easy monetary policy, 492
Torii, Mayumi, 458
Total wealth, external wealth and, 197–198
Trade
  currency unions and, 413
  dollarization of, 263t, 263–264
Trade balance (TB), 160
  demand in an open economy and, 257–264, 261f
  exogenous change in, 265–266
  Marshall-Lerner condition and, 300–301
  real exchange rate and, 257–258, 261f, 261–262
  weak links from real exchange rate to, 291
Trade costs, 443–446, 443–449, 445f, 446f, 464
  nontraded goods and the Balassa-Samuelson model and, 447–453, 454
  in practice, 444–445
Trade deficits, 164
Trade surpluses, 164
Trade weights, 30
Transaction costs
  deviations from purchasing power parity and, 72
  in FX market, 40
Transfer programs, 256–257
Transmission mechanism, 123
Treaty of Rome, 415
Treaty on European Union. *See* Maastricht Treaty
Triangular arbitrage, 45
Trichet, Jean-Claude, 253, 259
Trilemma, 144–148, 146f, 147f, 316, 317f
Trinidad and Tobago, sovereign rating and public debt level of, 211f
Triple crises, 350
Tunisia, sovereign rating and public debt level of, 211f
Turkey
  Big Mac index and, 74, 75t
  default by, 468
  discretionary fiscal stimulus measures in, 497t
  in EC, 418
  economic crisis of 2000 in, 351t
  EU and, 400
  foreign aid to, 236
  IMF and, 487
  sovereign rating and public debt level of, 211f
Twin crises, 350
Two-period budget constraint, 203–204

U

UAE, Big Mac index and, 75t
Uganda, foreign aid to, 236
UIP. *See* Uncovered interest parity (UIP)
Ukraine
  Big Mac index and, 75t
  currency crisis of 1998 in, 6f
  default by, 12
  sovereign rating and public debt level of, 211f
Uncovered interest parity (UIP), 51–55, 53f, 55f
  asset approach to exchange rates and, 113, 113f
  efficient markets hypothesis and, 461–462, 463f
  inflation and interest rates in long run and, 93
  risk premiums in advanced and emerging markets and, 359
Undervalued currencies, 67
Undervalued exchange rates, 492
Unilateral transfers, net, 160, 161f
United Kingdom. *See also* Britain; Ireland
  budget deficit of, 10f
  covered interest parity for Germany and, 49–50, 50f
  currency of, 401, 421
  discretionary fiscal stimulus measures in, 497t
  dollarization of trade and, 263t
  in EC, 415
  in ERM, 418
  in EU, 420t
  exchange rate of, 27t, 34, 35f, 340
  FX trade in, 39
  money measure in, 77n
  sovereign rating and public debt level of, 211f
  trilemma and, 147f, 147–148
United States
  balance of payments of, 184, 185f, 185–186
  basket of consumer goods in, 63–64
  Big Mac index and, 74, 75t
  budget deficits of, 9f, 9–10, 10f
  Civil War in, foreign exchange market and, 149f, 149–150
  discretionary fiscal stimulus measures in, 497t
  dollar devaluation and, 259
  dollarization of trade and, 263t
  ECB interest rate and, 130–131, 131f
  exchange rate of, 27t, 30–31, 31f, 34, 35f, 340
  external wealth of, 11, 12f, 188–190, 189t

foreign aggregate demand/inflation curve from, 169
foreign aid from, 236
FX trade in, 39
government failure in, 493
Great Recession in, 498f–499f
long-run budget constraint and, 207–210
marginal product of capital of, 229–230
Marshall Plan and, 415
money market in, asset approach to exchange rates and, 125–127, 126f
optimum currency area of Europe compared with, 407–410
price level in, 111
real exchange rate and trade balance of, 261f, 261–262
sovereign rating and public debt level of, 211f
war loans from, 217
United States Millennium Challenge Corporation, 234
Unit of account, money as, 76
Uruguay
Big Mac index and, 75t
currency crisis of 2002 in, 6f
currency mismatch and, 326
defaults by, 12
economic crisis of 1981–1985 in, 351t
sovereign rating and public debt level of, 211f

V

Valente, Giorgio, 467n
Valuation, changes in wealth due to, 187–188
Value, money as store of, 76
Value-added, 159
van Wincoop, Eric, 72n, 444n, 445n
Vatican City, currency of, 400n
Veblen, Thorsten, 20
Vehicle currencies, cross rates and, 46–47
Velasco, Andres, 221
Venezuela
currency crisis of 2002 in, 6f
default by, 468, 480
economic crisis of 1994–1995 in, 351t
sovereign rating and public debt level of, 211f
Verboven, Frank, 315n
Vietnam War, foreign exchange market and, 340

Villar, Agustin, 212n
Vishny, Robert, 20n
Volkswagen, 4
Volosovych, Vadym, 233n

W

Waitrose, 260
War(s)
current account and, 217
foreign exchange market and, 148–152, 340
gold standard and, 336
Warnock, Francis E., 244n, 326n
Wealth, 11
external. *See* External wealth
total, external wealth and, 197–198
The Wealth of Nations (Smith), 18
Weder, Beatrice, 475
Wei, Shang-Jin, 15f, 245n, 264, 444n
Werner Report, 416–417
West Germany. *See also* Germany
Treaty of Rome and, 415
White, Harry Dexter, 338
Wilde, Oscar, 25, 26
Willard, Kristen L., 150n
Willett, Thomas D., 393n
Wohar, Mark E., 86n
Wolf, Holger C., 316n
Wolf, Martin, 19, 244f, 351t, 433f, 434, 435
World Bank, 12, 234, 235, 487. *See also* International Monetary Fund (IMF)
World real interest rates, 94–95, 202
World War I, gold standard and, 336
Wright, Brian D., 469n
Wyplosz, Charles, 346n

Y

Yacyreta Dam, 235
Yeyati, Eduardo Levy, 37n
Yugoslav states, in EC, 418

Z

Zero lower bound (ZLB), 123, 293
Zettelmeyer, Jeromin, 468n, 469n, 475
Zimbabwe
capital controls in, 15
currency crisis of 1997 in, 6f
hyperinflation in, 89, 90
ZLB. *See* Zero lower bound (ZLB)

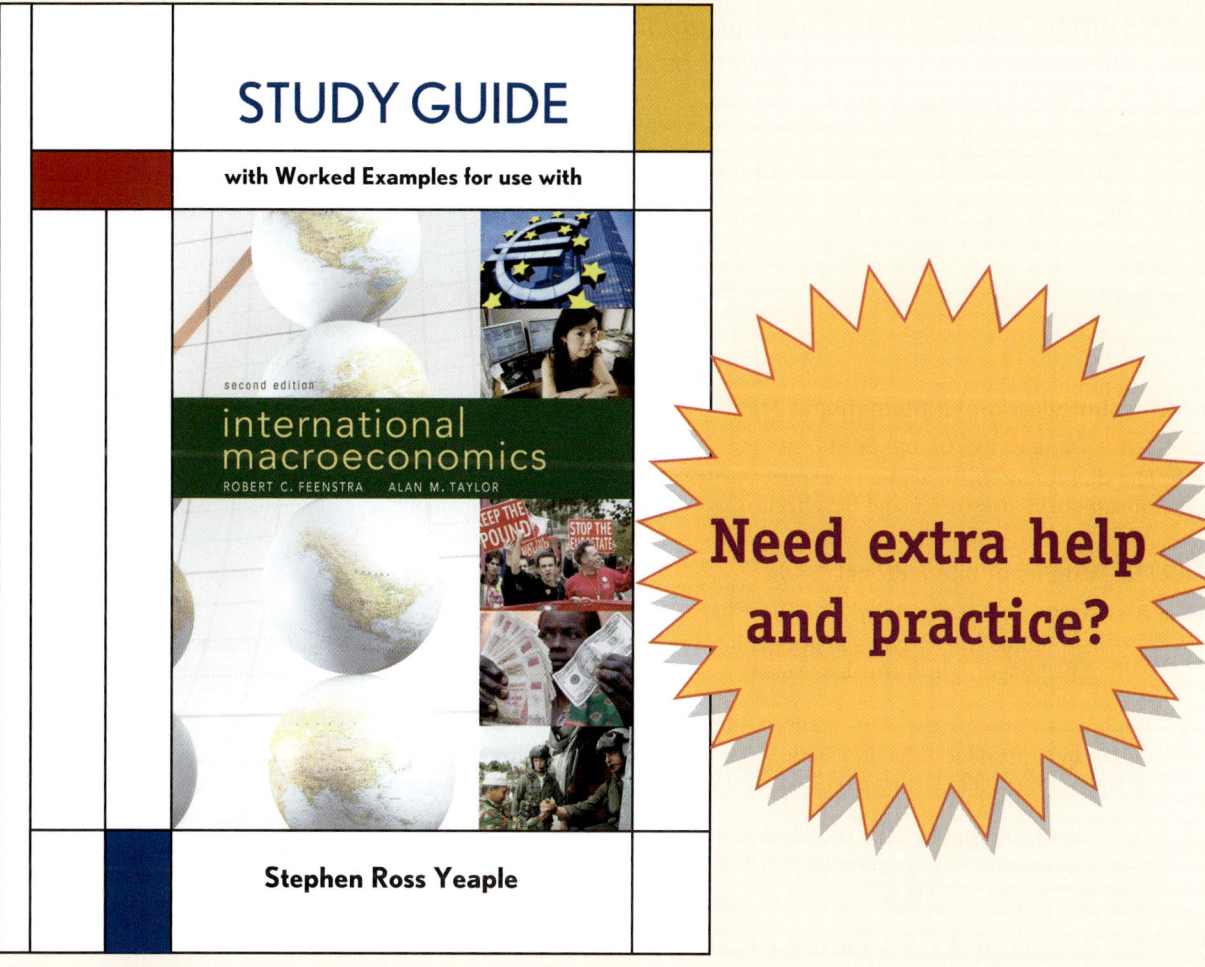

Purchase the **STUDY GUIDE** directly from Worth Publishers at a discount by visiting **worthpublishers.com/feenstrataylor_intlmacropreview**

For each key section of each chapter, the Study Guide with Worked Examples provides:

- *Key themes:* detailed discussions of key concepts.

- *Key terms:* a summary of important vocabulary within each chapter, including space for students to record their own notes.

- *Review questions with tips:* detailed, thorough problems for students to test their comprehension, along with tips to help students work through the problems. To identify common mistakes and to demonstrate common features of different types of economic problems, tips are provided immediately following questions that delve into particularly important or difficult topics.

- *Worked-out solutions:* includes solutions to all Study Guide review questions.

International Economics is available in four versions: a two-semester, twenty-two chapter hardcover edition, paperback split editions of *International Trade* and *International Macroeconomics*, and a shorter one-semester *Essentials of International Economics* edition. See inside front cover for a chapter correlation guide.

The following annotated table of contents for the full two-semester version of the text describes the main goal for each chapter and notes what makes each chapter unique.

PART 1: Introduction to International Trade

CHAPTER 1 Trade in the Global Economy
The study of international trade examines patterns of trade in goods and services, the processes of immigration and foreign direct investment, and the effects of government policies on these flows.

PART 2: Patterns of International Trade

CHAPTER 2 Trade and Technology: The Ricardian Model
The first of three core chapters in international trade theory presents the Ricardian model and includes a full treatment of real wages, which rise due to trade.

CHAPTER 3 Gains and Losses from Trade in the Specific-Factors Model
This chapter introduces the distributional conflict that can arise from trade. In contrast to the Ricardian model, in the short-run specific-factors model, labor does not necessarily gain, but one specific factor gains and the other loses.

CHAPTER 4 Trade and Resources: The Heckscher-Ohlin Model
This long-run model poses a different distributional conflict from trade in which the abundant factor gains and the scarce factor loses. The factor content of trade and the Leontief Paradox are discussed and resolved.

CHAPTER 5 Movement of Labor and Capital between Countries
Both the short-run and long-run models are used to analyze the effects of immigration and foreign direct investment on the earnings of labor and capital.

PART 3: New Explanations for International Trade

CHAPTER 6 Increasing Returns to Scale and Monopolistic Competition
A graphical treatment of the monopolistic competition model is developed and used to analyze NAFTA's effects on productivity and real wages in Mexico, Canada, and the United States. The gravity equation is discussed.

CHAPTER 7 Offshoring of Goods and Services
This relatively new form of international trade can have many positive effects such as increasing the relative wages of skilled workers in both countries. We discuss concerns about the gains from offshoring that have been raised by some economists (e.g. Samuelson, 2004).

PART 4: International Trade Policies

CHAPTER 8 Import Tariffs and Quotas under Perfect Competition
Our comprehensive treatment of trade policy begins with perfect competition and looks at U.S. steel and tire tariffs as specific cases.

CHAPTER 9 Import Tariffs and Quotas under Imperfect Competition
Trade policies have different effects on a country's welfare under imperfect competition. We look at home and foreign monopolies and also the infant-industry argument for protection.